canadian political philosophy

canadian political philosophy

contemporary reflections

edited by
ronald beiner & wayne norman

70 Wynford Drive, Don Mills, Ontario M3C 1J9
www.oupcan.com

Oxford University Press is a department of the University of Oxford.
It furthers the University's objective of excellence in research, scholarship,
and education by publishing worldwide in

Oxford New York

Athens Auckland Bangkok Bogotá Buenos Aires Calcutta Cape Town Chennai Dar es Salaam Delhi Florence Hong Kong Istanbul Karachi Kuala Lumpur Madrid Melbourne Mexico City Mumbai Nairobi Paris São Paulo Singapore Taipei Tokyo Toronto Warsaw

with associated companies in Berlin Ibadan

Oxford is a trade mark of Oxford University Press
in the UK and in certain other countries

Published in Canada
by Oxford University Press

First published 2001

Canadian Cataloguing in Publication Data
Main entry under title:
Canadian political philosophy : contemporary reflections
Includes bibliographical references.
ISBN 0-19-541608-2 (bound) ISBN 0-19-541448-9 (pbk.)
1. Multiculturalism – Canada. 2. Nationalism – Canada. 3. Citizenship – Canada. 4. Canada – Politics and government. 5. Political science – Philosophy. I. Beiner, Ronald, 1953- . II. Norman, Wayne, Dr.
JC253.C36 2000 320.971 C00-932291-4

Cover design: Joan Dempsey

2 3 4 - 04 03 02 01
This book is printed on permanent (acid-free) paper ∞.
Printed in Canada

Contents

Introduction / 1

PART ONE: RETHINKING LIBERALISM AND CITIZENSHIP

JOSEPH H. CARENS
Cosmopolitanism, Nationalism, and Immigration: False Dichotomies and Shifting Presuppositions / 17

JAMES TULLY
Democracy and Globalization: A Defeasible Sketch / 36

SIMONE CHAMBERS
New Constitutionalism: Democracy, Habermas, and Canadian Exceptionalism / 63

DANIEL M. WEINSTOCK
Saving Democracy from Deliberation / 78

EAMONN CALLAN
Self-Defeating Political Education / 92

PART TWO: EQUALITY, JUSTICE, AND GENDER

G.A. COHEN
History, Ethics, and Marxism / 107

CHRISTINE SYPNOWICH
Egalitarianism Renewed / 118

JENNIFER NEDELSKY
Citizenship and Relational Feminism / 131

INGRID MAKUS
Birth, Maternity, Citizenship: Some Reflections / 147

PART THREE: MINORITY RIGHTS, MULTICULTURALISM, AND IDENTITY

WILL KYMLICKA
The New Debate over Minority Rights / 159

MARGARET MOORE
Liberal Nationalism and Multiculturalism / 177

DENISE G. RÉAUME
Legal Multiculturalism From the Bottom Up / 194

Stephen L. Newman
What Not to Do About Hate Speech: An Argument Against Censorship / 207

Melissa S. Williams
Toleration, Canadian-Style: Reflections of a Yankee-Canadian / 216

Clifford Orwin
Charles Taylor's Pedagogy of Recognition / 232

PART FOUR: NATIONALISM AND SELF-DETERMINATION

Dominique Leydet
Lifeboat / 249

W. James Booth
Communities of Memory / 263

Philip Resnick
Civic and Ethnic Nationalism: Lessons from the Canadian Case / 282

Guy Laforest
The True Nature of Sovereignty: Reply to my Critics Concerning *Trudeau and the End of a Canadian Dream* / 298

Stéphane Dion
The Supreme Court's Reference on Unilateral Secession: A Turning Point in Canadian History / 311

Dale Turner
Vision: Towards an Understanding of Aboriginal Sovereignty / 318

PART FIVE: IN DIALOGUE WITH THE HISTORY OF POLITICAL PHILOSOPHY

Thomas L. Pangle
The Platonic Challenge to the Modern Idea of the Public Intellectual / 335

Arthur Ripstein
Coercion and Disagreement / 349

Edward Andrew
Liberalism and Moral Subjectivism / 363

Barry Cooper
Weaving a Work / 374

Charles Taylor
The Immanent Counter-Enlightenment / 386

Notes on Contributors / 401

Introduction

Less than a decade ago, Robertson Davies delivered a speech in which he remarked that the 'wine of Canadian political thought is a watery tipple at present [whereas] the brandy of Canadian literature is well overproof!'[1] Although Davies' challenge was likely aimed more at politicians than at political philosophers, he nevertheless drew at least one sharp retort from the academic community. Leah Bradshaw, a political theorist at Brock University, responded to Davies in a letter to the editor of the *Globe and Mail*: 'It may well be that a country on the periphery of imperial ambition produces a superior reflective consciousness.'[2] It suffices to consider a few of the leading theorists of the eighteenth century—the Swiss Rousseau, the Scot Hume, and the Irishman Burke, not to mention the plucky intellectual founders of the American republic—to realize how well-founded Bradshaw's claim was. In any case, if there is one thing one can hope for from this volume, it is a definitive refutation of the notion that Canadian political thought is a watery tipple.

To document in detail the impact that Canadian theorists are having upon contemporary intellectual and political life around the world is obviously beyond the scope of this introduction. Let us merely relate a few recent anecdotes. Just before starting to write the introduction, one of the co-editors received a communication from a colleague at Jawaharlal Nehru University in New Delhi. In it Niraja Jayal expressed interest in coming to Canada to get first-hand experience of the political philosophy scene here because, in her words, 'the most lively debates on citizenship are in fact Canadian debates.' Ross Poole, an Australian political philosopher, has written: 'Perhaps not surprisingly, some of the most important contributions to the debates about multiculturalism (and also indigenous rights, secession, and citizenship) have come from Canada.'[3] These observations from India and Australia echo comments we have heard regularly in recent years from leading political thinkers across Europe, some of whom even refer to a 'Canadian School' of political philosophy. The same is increasingly true even in the United States, where Canadian political philosophers used to 'pass' as American. At a recent roundtable reviewing a major conference on citizenship and cosmopolitanism at the University of Wisconsin, Michael Walzer, one of the leading American political theorists, bemoaned what he considered to be the abstract and apolitical character of most of the contributions. He exempted from this judgment, however, the Canadian participants at the conference. Surely there was nothing abstract or apolitical about *their* efforts to address problems of nationality and citizenship: for the Canadians, Walzer observed, there was something real at stake—namely, the continued survival of their political community—and the stakes were large ones. These days one can find essays and books by such leading Canadian political philosophers as Charles Taylor, Will Kymlicka, James Tully, and G.A. Cohen in several languages in bookstores around the world. In Catalonia, for instance, interest in Kymlicka's work is so intense that a Catalan translation of one of his books has recently appeared, even though all Catalonian intellectuals could just as easily read the book in the Spanish translation that was already available. We could tell many more such anecdotes; clearly, Canadian theorists and philosophers are now recognized internationally for their unique contributions to normative debates about citizenship, multiculturalism, and nationalism (as well as much else).

Indeed, the fact that some of our political thinkers are better known abroad than at home was one of our reasons for undertaking this project. As far as we are aware, this is the first time a single volume has brought together new essays by most of the leading Canadian political thinkers. Of course, such a project raises the question, 'Who is a Canadian?' To ask this question is actually to engage some of the philosophical issues wrestled with by our contributors. Yet we needed to answer the question in order to select our contributors. We opted for an expansive definition: native-born citizens who continue to reside here; expatriate Canadians who now write and teach abroad; and immigrants to Canada who currently teach at Canadian universities and who may still be in the process of weighing (both in their theorizing and in their civic lives) their Canadianness with their residual non-Canadian identity—and whether or not to apply for Canadian citizenship. This approach to defining a Canadian political philosopher is perhaps contestable, but if this volume teaches anything, it is that no significant aspect of the problem of civic identity can fail to be contestable, theoretically or practically.

We have tried to aim at genuine intellectual diversity, though no doubt we have fallen well short of the desideratum. There is certainly great diversity both in the topics raised and in the conclusions argued for. If one considers, for instance, the sharp contrast between attitudes towards multiculturalism in the political thinking of Will Kymlicka and Melissa Williams, on the one hand, and Christine Sypnowich and Clifford Orwin, on the other, one will at least see that the collection makes no pretense of suggesting a homogeneity of views among Canadian theorists. We have tried to represent work in political philosophy across various academic disciplines (though the volume is probably somewhat tilted towards political philosophers working in political science departments). We have tried to represent the work of people at different stages of their careers, though we have favoured younger scholars to some degree. We have tried, imperfectly, to represent regional and cultural diversity across Canada (although some might see the collection as more Torontocentric than it ought to be). We make no claim to have succeeded fully in any of these aims. In particular, doing justice to the full range of lively intellectual currents in Quebec would require a separate volume of its own. But the very fact that our selection of contributors involved such hard choices that we were obliged to leave out some very talented theorists, and that space constraints, if not modesty, led us to nix the idea of contributing to the volume ourselves, reconfirms our point that political philosophy in Canada today is a thriving discipline.

Why is this so? Part of the answer might well reside in the fact that Canada has long been in a state of more or less permanent constitutional crisis. To grow up within the Canadian polity is to come to political consciousness amid profound tensions between opposing visions of political membership. To think through these alternatives at the level of root-and-branch philosophical reflection may be one existential response to this predicament. Of course other societies have experienced comparable political–existential cleavages. Nonetheless, Canada's particular circumstances may help to explain, for instance, the extraordinary fact that two successive holders of the Chichele Chair in Social and Political Theory at Oxford (both of whom are represented in this volume) have been *Montréalais*. It's true that Canada is in many ways a highly privileged society, compared with other nations; but in its greater openness to the contemporary realities of cultural diversity, polyethnicity, and multi-ethnicity, the Canadian community is required to think through what these realities mean for its civic life more ambitiously than societies that pretend to be exempt from these challenges. Moreover, given the political realities in this country, it can neglect issues of nationality and citizenship only at great peril to its own continued existence.

If Canadian political thinkers are now finding a wider international audience, it is partly because the cultural diversity of most modern states means that they more closely resemble Canada than they do the states whose political philosophers have until recently hogged most of the limelight. It has always been possible for American, British, French, and German political thinkers to write unapologetically about their own current events or political history and to draw general normative theories and speculations therefrom. But in their (often presumed, not actual) cultural homogeneity, these four classic 'nation-states' are in fact quite atypical in the world, and much of the political philosophy based on their agendas has largely ignored the intercultural challenges that occupy so much of political life in 'multination states' like Canada. In fact, more than 90 per cent of states are shared by more than one major ethnocultural group, and most wealthy democracies are now also home to large populations of immigrants. It used to be that when Canadian political philosophers wrote on peculiarly Canadian issues (such as multiculturalism, or collective rights for the Québécois and Aboriginal peoples) they wrote for a domestic audience; but now these kinds of issues are all the rage on the international scene, and Canadians can philosophize about their own constitutional conundrums in ways that people around the world can find relevant to their own situations. In turn, many Canadian theorists have worked to learn more about the history and problems of other multination states, in order to ensure that the general insights derived in part from their Canadian experience are not unnecessarily parochial. And perhaps this helps explain why, at a time when Canadian political philosophers have become more identifiably Canadian to their international readership, they have also become less prone to a certain kind of intellectual navel-gazing than they were a generation ago. For example, although we invited the authors in this volume to reflect (if they were so inclined) upon the meaning and significance of their Canadian cultural context, such reflections in fact make up a relatively small portion of the book. This strikes us as a healthy sign.

Part One: Rethinking Liberalism and Citizenship

Joseph Carens has probably done more than any other contemporary theorist to show that reflection on normative problems of immigration—that is, on how to justify enforcement of boundaries between insiders and outsiders, citizens and aliens—opens up profound questions concerning citizenship and the nature of political membership. His chapter for this volume nicely exemplifies the kind of radical questions yielded by his mode of utopian theorizing. Theory as such is utopian, insofar as it involves interrogating actually existing political life in the light of normative standards that are invariably yet to be realized. But Carens, in his other published work and again in this chapter, argues that most theorists have not been bold enough in probing the limits of a world where states have the political discretion to enforce their own boundaries of membership. Using philosophy to enlarge our political imagination can have significant implications for current state practices such as the discretionary deportation of non-citizens. Greater awareness of citizenship and immigration as a problem for political philosophy at the same time means that these practices are exposed to a tough challenge, namely, to justify themselves in the face of ambitiously cosmopolitan moral standards.

In what is perhaps the most intellectually demanding chapter in this book, James Tully discusses another of the great challenges that arise when we stop assuming that the frontiers of political philosophy are the frontiers of the nation-state: the ongoing struggles between democracy and globalization. Over the past two decades Tully has become one of the most influential political thinkers in Canada, first as a colleague of Charles Taylor's at McGill University, and more recently at the University of Victoria. In this chapter he combines his scholarly talents in two fields, the history of ideas and contemporary political theory, to reflect on what he sees as a 'trend towards the dispersion of practices of government and democracy'. Examples of this trend include the dispersion of certain practices of representative government that are no longer located exclusively within nation-states, and the dispersion of 'non-representative' democratic practices in collectivities such as the Green movement within and across states with representative governments. There is, according to Tully, a globalization of politics that goes along with the more familiar economic globalization, and in many ways this trend towards 'global politics and global governance can be compared to the messy overlapping of practices of government in the late-medieval period prior to the early-modern consolidation of centralized European states'. He argues that fashionable clichés about the 'end of sovereignty' underestimate 'the resilience of practices of modern politics'. Readers interested in some of the forms this 'modern politics' takes in a Canadian context can turn to a discussion of Tully's work in our next chapter, by Simone Chambers.

Chambers sets out to explore what she considers to be a new strand in the evolution of liberal democratic theory. She calls this development 'new constitutionalism', and to illustrate its rationale and implications she draws on two quite different sources: the recent political philosophy of the German philosopher Jürgen Habermas, and an interpretation of Canadian constitutional history. Social contract theory offers a grounding for liberal democracy that was revived by John Rawls in the 1960s and 1970s, and, according to Chambers, Habermas must be credited with a decisive transformation of Rawlsian contractarianism. For Rawls, just arrangements are ones that would be agreed to by parties in an 'original position', choosing and bargaining behind a 'veil of ignorance' that keeps them from knowing about their own identity and place within their society. Habermas tries to remove some of the static, hypothetical elements from this model by thinking about the social contract in terms of the requirements for an ideal discourse or democratic dialogue. Chambers sees Canadian constitutional history, particularly over the last fifteen years or so, as exemplifying, in a rough-and-tumble way, this Habermasian ideal. As she puts it, 'constitutionalism in an age of democratic diversity is more about keeping a conversation going than about getting all the parties to sign on the dotted line at one time and place.'

Daniel Weinstock's chapter is also concerned with the idea of 'deliberative democracy', which has been very much in vogue among political philosophers in recent years. Weinstock starts by suggesting that theories of liberal democracy operating under the gravitational force of American thinkers like John Rawls and Ronald Dworkin privilege the liberal moment over the democratic moment. The promise of the literature on deliberative democracy is that it would redress the balance, giving added weight to the *democratic* dimension of liberal democracy. But does the theory of deliberative democracy fulfill this promise? Weinstock argues persuasively that theorists of deliberative democracy impute their own norms of public reason to democratic citizens in a way that sells short the genuine pluralism characteristic of a democratic culture. What captivates those theorists is the notion of rational consensus across the whole of liberal society; thus the hypothetical deliberators that they postulate are assumed to be more ready to disconnect their political engagements from their broader moral-cultural commitments than real democratic deliberators would be. In consequence, the acknowledgment of 'deep pluralism' is short-circuited.

Eamonn Callan too is a liberal critic of Rawlsian liberalism. The particular focus of Callan's critique is the problem of political education. According to Rawls, liberals should embrace a form of political education that avoids appeals to comprehensive moral, religious, or philosophical commitments; but as Callan shows, Rawls's account of 'the burdens of judgment' (that is, the reasons why reasonable individuals arrive at legitimately different moral conclusions), and the doctrine of toleration it implies, exceeds the limits of Rawls's own 'minimalist' doctrine of political education. Rejecting Rawlsian minimalism, Callan offers a lucid and incisive demonstration that liberalism entails a robust vision of mutual respect and reciprocity that liberal citizens must internalize, and to which they must be socialized through moral education. Like

Weinstock, Callan is interested in investigating whether liberal political philosophy developed along Rawlsian lines can be faithful to the deep commitment to moral pluralism that defines liberalism, and whether it can supply the philosophical framework required to properly uphold that commitment.

Part Two: Equality, Justice, and Gender

In the English-speaking world through the 1970s and 1980s, equality, justice, and gender constituted the core of academic political philosophy for two reasons: on the one hand, the influence of Rawls, and on the other, the steadily rising influence of women in the academy. During this period there were many notable Canadian political thinkers who—like many internationally known actors and news anchors—were undoubtedly assumed on both sides of the Atlantic to be either American or British. The absence of any identifiably Canadian element in their work had something to do with the abstract nature of analyses of justice and the universality of gender inequalities, to be sure. Since the late 1980s, however, a younger generation of Canadian political thinkers, themselves schooled in the debates about justice and gender, have expanded these discussions to address issues of identity, multiculturalism, and nationalism. And on these topics their Canadianness has been impossible to conceal. We will turn to a sample of these writers and topics in Parts Three and Four. It is worth remembering, though, that the core conceptual issues of justice and equality (including equality and inequality across genders) long predate Rawls—Aristotle comes to mind—and they remain worthy topics of academic research, even as studies involving the politics of cultural identity have come to predominate.

Part Two begins with two chapters by philosophers trying to reconceptualize the ideals of the left in the wake of the collapse of communism and their own misgivings about Marxist theory. Jerry Cohen gives us an exquisite piece of intellectual autobiography, tracing the underpinnings of his political philosophy from his teenage years as a young communist in Montreal to the end of the 'second third' of his career, as the current Chichele Professor of Social and Political Theory at Oxford. It is not the proletariat that will rebel against capitalism, according to the mature Cohen, but the Earth itself. Marx's vision of an egalitarian future rested on the faith that the increasing technological sophistication of the capitalist production process would eventually produce an abundance that would render the capitalists themselves unnecessary. But it is now clear that the planet cannot sustain that level of abundance for all its people. So modern socialists cannot share 'Marx's optimism about material possibility'; but they also must not share his pessimism about the impossibility of an egalitarian society in the absence of abundance. 'We cannot rely on technology to fix things for us,' Cohen now argues; 'if they can be fixed, then we have to fix them through hard theoretical and political labour.'

Christine Sypnowich, a philosopher at Queen's University, also takes up the challenge of reformulating a commitment to equality and redefining the left at the beginning of the twenty-first century. But she starts from within the broad liberal-democratic tradition. More specifically, she is trying to reinvigorate some of the philosophical debates about justice and equality typical of the 1970s by incorporating in them some of the insights into identity and culture that emerged from liberal political philosophy in the 1990s. In her words, this approach to political philosophy 'aspires to be mindful of the past century and hopeful for the next'. It is committed to a duty to promote equality and autonomy through social and economic policy, as well as a 'nuanced sense of nationality'. These ideals are also tempered with 'a sense of finitude and the limitations of the human condition, invoking the politics of civility inherent in the rule of law'.

Jennifer Nedelsky, one of the notable feminist legal and political theorists in Canada today, is engaged in a project to rethink central liberal categories, such as autonomy, rights, and citizenship, in the light of the best contemporary feminist theorizing. Nedelsky, like many other authors in this volume, is particularly concerned with the idea of citizenship. She wants to balance the moral universalism that defines the liberal tradition with a greater sensitivity to the more close-at-hand relationships (such as that between parent and child) that compose the texture of our moral selves. Nedelsky gives eloquent expression to an insight she draws from a certain strand of feminist theory (but that perhaps could also be drawn from some communitarian writers): that although we cannot forgo the universalism associated with liberal egalitarianism, neither can a full theory of politics do without a theory of the self and of its constitutive relationships.

Most of the chapters in the first four sections of this volume reflect the 'ahistorical', analytic, or post-analytic tradition exemplified by Rawls. Yet there is also a strong tradition among both English- and French-speaking political theorists in Canada that draws on the arguments and world views of the Great Thinkers of past centuries. This tradition is the particular focus of Part Five, but Ingrid Makus's chapter in Part Two is another case in point. While her aim is to anticipate the philosophical and political challenges that the idea of citizenship will face in the new century, her inspiration comes from the writings of Hobbes, Rousseau, and Simone de Beauvoir. Noting that 'birthright' will likely remain a fundamental ground for citizenship in the new millennium, notwithstanding the proliferation of new reproductive technologies, Makus favourably contrasts Hobbes's ideas on 'birth' with Beauvoir's. By properly distinguishing between 'giving birth' and 'giving life', she argues, Hobbes can be seen as having provided a justification for a right to access to abortion as an extension of what both Hobbes and Makus see as one of the fundamental rights of citizenship: the right to govern one's own body.

PART THREE: MINORITY RIGHTS, MULTICULTURALISM, AND IDENTITY

Few political philosophers of *any* nationality have enjoyed as much discussion and citation of their work over the past decade—and around the world—as Will Kymlicka. He was raised in London, Ontario, and educated first at Queen's University (where he has now returned to teach) and then at Oxford (where he was supervised by Jerry Cohen). Astonishingly, Kymlicka published two important books in the United Kingdom well before his thirtieth birthday. In the decade following his first book, he added a string of other influential books, including one specifically on the 'Canadian question' (or questions), *Finding Our Way: Rethinking Ethnocultural Relations in Canada* (Oxford University Press, 1998). Kymlicka is widely credited with having forced liberal thinkers to come to grips with the problems of culture, identity, and ethnicity that had been almost completely ignored in the mainstream Anglo-American tradition after the Second World War. In recent years, almost everyone writing on these topics (including many of the authors in this volume) has had to begin by explaining where they stand in relation to Kymlicka's work. For this reason, he has been invited to lecture in virtually every multi-ethnic state in Europe (and beyond), and his books have been translated into at least eighteen languages. Therefore it is a bit staggering that he is virtually unknown outside the corridors of academia and government (where he has worked and consulted frequently)—despite the fact that his writing style is accessible almost to a fault. *Finding Our Way*, one of the most rigorous and compelling analyses of Canadian public philosophy in a generation, received only a short-form review, a few centimetres long, in the *Globe and Mail.* In his chapter here, Kymlicka gives an explanatory survey of the evolution of debates about minority rights over the past decade or two. He is, as always, overly modest about his own role in driving this evolution; but several of the other authors in this volume give credit where it is due.

Margaret Moore, for example, takes up a familiar Kymlickian theme in her chapter: that there has been an unhelpful and artificial separation of debates about, on the one hand, the need to develop a stronger sense of common citizenship in liberal societies and, on the other, the need to grant recognition and special rights and accommodations to marginalized minority groups. It is often assumed that promoting common citizenship and diversity at the same time is not possible. After considering a number of brief case studies, however, Moore, like Kymlicka, casts doubt on this assumption.

In her chapter Denise Réaume takes up a similar challenge by looking closely at attempts to accommodate diversity within one of the most fundamental political institutions: the law. She argues that almost any area of law can 'contribute to or fail to foster cultural autonomy', and that the 'only legal test that can be formulated is that cultural autonomy should be respected unless its exercise in a particular case is repugnant to justice.' Réaume explains, for example, how the courts in Canada used a similar principle in the famous *Hofer* case, refusing to overturn the scheme of communal property ownership within the Hutterite community even in an instance where it might have seemed unfair for individuals leaving the community not to be given any share of the assets they helped to build. The point of the principle is that it 'encourages judges to take seriously the normative life of the cultural community in question and temper the tendency to fall back on mainstream perspectives'.

Like Réaume, Stephen Newman looks at the impact of specific legislation, and the judicial interpretation of legislation, on cultural communities and their members. He focuses on the question of when hate-speech legislation may be an appropriate response to threats to minority groups and to social stability in general. As the title of his chapter makes clear, Newman is inclined to oppose censorship of hate speech—but not because he thinks we should be indifferent to it. Democracy is founded on trust, he argues, and 'deep and abiding hatred makes trust impossible.' But so too 'does fear of those who hate'. After careful deliberation on the nature of democracy and the pros and cons of censorship, Newman concludes that 'We should not allow our fear of those who hate to endanger our trust in democracy by subverting our faith in the practical intelligence and good will of our fellow citizens.'

Melissa Williams, like Stephen Newman, is concerned with offering an adequate theory of toleration. Her mixed Canadian–American identity, she tells us, has enlarged her sense of the possible ways of thinking about how a political–legal order can accommodate cultural difference. In particular, the uniquely Canadian device of the notwithstanding clause, included in the 1982 Constitution, highlights the fact that traditions of practice can lead to solutions that mere theory could never devise. ('What's the notwithstanding clause?' asked Nathan Glazer, a noted American sociologist, with bewilderment when political debate began to rage among the Canadian scholars and journalists in attendance following a recent talk of his; perhaps Canadians shouldn't congratulate themselves *too* much on the international impact of their constitutional innovations.) Williams argues that the characteristically Canadian concern with peace and social order can provide grounds not only for *limits* to our society's toleration of culturally threatening minority practices but also for *expansion* of practices of cultural accommodation.

The next chapter offers the most direct engagement by one contributor with the work of another. Here Clifford Orwin probes Charles Taylor's argument on behalf of the politics of recognition in the latter's famous essay of that title, and uncovers what he believes are some interesting tensions in Taylor's account. For instance, one of Taylor's aims is to endorse the multiculturalist challenge to Western cultural imperialism—but in order to do so he appeals to palpably Western notions, such as the presumption of the equal worth of all cultures. Orwin identifies two main problems with Taylor's argument: first, that it requires a reification of cultures, when in fact the most interesting opinions about the human condition cannot be reduced to the cultures they supposedly express; and second, that Taylor anticipates a convergence of cultural horizons that, insofar as it is even thinkable, would more likely than not lead to precisely the kind of banal Westernization of the world that Taylor wants to avoid. 'It may well be,' Orwin writes, 'that in the course of time the fundamental human alternatives have already been articulated, and that what defines the human situation is not ultimate synthesis but only hard choices.' He concludes that only a redoubled exertion of philosophizing about the most interesting alternatives can keep intercultural dialogue properly vital.

Part Four: Nationalism and Self-Determination

Just as Canadian theorists have been unmistakably prominent in theoretical debates concerning multiculturalism and group rights, so they have also been at the forefront in normative debates on issues related to nationalism and the challenges it poses to citizenship. Canadians were prominent, for instance, among the contributors to two recent anthologies bringing together notable theoretical treatments of citizenship and nationalism, produced with an American publisher by one of the editors of this volume: of the twelve contributors to the citizenship book, five were Canadian, and Canadians contributed fully half of the sixteen chapters in the volume on nationalism.

What is a political community? Is it a fortuitous conjoining of individuals who happen to find themselves sharing the same territory and are therefore obliged to fabricate mutually advantageous principles of coexistence? Or is it something more like a natural belonging-together of people who share not just a physical space but also a history, an identity, and in some sense a joint destiny? Nationalists, and liberals who sympathize with nationalism, will certainly favour the latter image of political community over the former. Dominique Leydet, in a forceful and elegant reflection on the nature of political community, concedes that the contractualist view indeed fails to do justice to the role played by a shared history in developing a sense of political membership. On the other hand, she sees serious perils in the more nationalist rendering of political community: for example, the danger that historiography will deviate into myth-making for the sake of inventing an official national history, or that cultural minorities will be enlisted in a 'national' project with which they do not truly identify. That there is more contingency inscribed in modern political communities than nationalists like to acknowledge helps us to see the virtues of a liberal contractualist conception of political community.

James Booth, like Dominique Leydet, is concerned with defining political community in a way that gives history and memory their due. Booth is sensitive to the attractions of Jürgen Habermas's idea of constitutional patriotism, but he also sees important tensions in that idea. Habermas's efforts to establish a safe distance between the definition of citizenship and ideas of national belonging are difficult to square with his emphasis on the civic obligation to accept responsibility for Germany's culpable political past. The 'presence of the past' requires a culturally 'thicker' conception of civic identity than Habermas (with his acute awareness of the perils of nationalism) wishes to allow. These themes have clear relevance to the Canadian experience.

One important pivot of recent philosophical debates about nationalism has been the idea that various nationalisms in the contemporary world can be sorted into two categories, civic and ethnic, with the civic given normative advantage over the ethnic. Philip Resnick argues that this is not a helpful way of tackling the moral challenges posed by modern nationalism. In fact, ostensibly civic nations are typically underpinned by ethnocultural bonds of identity; and conversely, forms of nationalism that their critics denounce as ethnic proclaim their civic bona fides. In a more directly political vein, Resnick makes the case that Canadian critics of Québécois nationalism are more likely to achieve a constructive dialogue with their nationalist adversaries if they take the latter at their word when they insist that their nationalism is civic, and if critics of nationalism drop their strident rhetoric directed against ethnic nationalism.

Resnick's argument here is one that would certainly be welcomed by our next contributor, Guy Laforest. Laforest is one of the leading nationalist intellectuals in Quebec, and perhaps the most forceful exponent of the view that the constitutional changes of 1982 were a betrayal of the binational character of the Canadian federation. In his chapter, he cites Stéphane Dion's view 'that the genius of Canada resides in its promotion of "plural identities".' Laforest joins Dion in embracing the notion of plural identities, acknowledging, in a spirit of moderation, that it not only complicates the secessionist aims of the more uncompromising nationalists but also has implications for how the more general nationalist project relates to minorities in Quebec. Nevertheless, in the face of critics of his well-known work on the legacy of Pierre Trudeau, Laforest continues to insist that without substantial revisions to the constitutional regime introduced by Trudeau, the federalist ideal of Canada as (among other things) a binational partnership cannot be sustained.

Stéphane Dion, a former political science professor, became an important political actor in the Canadian constitutional drama. In the years following the 1995 referendum in Quebec he has shouldered a major share of the responsibility for formulating the federal government's anti-secessionist strategy, and in this role he has engaged in some notable and highly publicized debates with leading political figures in Quebec through the medium of open letters.[4] More recently, Dion and Daniel Turp of the Bloc Québécois (another academic-turned-politician) have crossed swords over the meaning of the 1998 Supreme Court reference on the legality of Quebec secession.[5] Dion's contribution to this volume is a continuation of those debates; it is both a political text and an attempt to reflect on the normative philosophical issues raised by nationalist secessionism in democratic states.

Of course, Quebec nationalism is not the only challenge posed to Canadian civic commonality; Aboriginal claims based on sentiments of distinct nationhood (or, more precisely, nationhoods) pose a very serious challenge as well. How well does the (modern European) concept of sovereignty function in capturing Aboriginal conceptions of shared political identity, or in clarifying the place of Aboriginal communities within the political structures of the majority culture? And how can Aboriginal intellectuals ensure that Aboriginal philosophical traditions and ways of understanding the world receive serious consideration in contemporary academic, legal, and political debates about political community? These are the important questions that Dale Turner raises in his chapter on the cultural and political resources arising from Aboriginal experience. There can certainly be no denying that Aboriginal claims to nationhood (whether articulated in the language of sovereignty or in some other language), no less than Québécois claims to nationhood, offer a profound impetus to normative reflection on citizenship on the part of political philosophers nourished by Canadian political experience.

Part Five: In Dialogue with the History of Political Philosophy

As we noted earlier, not all of what is best in Canadian political philosophy comes from the analytic or post-analytic tradition, in which the main object is to propose and justify political institutions and systems. Canadians are also well represented in the scholarly circles concerned with continuing the Great Debates that draw on the Great Books in the history of philosophy. Political philosophy as an intellectual discipline is of course a Platonic tradition, rooted in the radicalism of Socratic–Platonic questioning of opinions about justice, virtue, and the nature of the good for human beings. Thomas Pangle is right to remind us of the Platonic roots of this intellectual tradition. He argues that the modern post-Enlightenment conception of the political philosopher as public intellectual has obscured the insights offered by ancient thought into the tension-ridden relationship between the presuppositions of civic life and the epic demands and aspirations of the life of theory. In so doing, Pangle offers a forceful and eloquent picture of the political philosopher's vocation in the light of that vocation's Platonic origins.

Arthur Ripstein's chapter explores an interesting caesura in the liberal tradition, a tradition that has roots in the writings of both the seventeenth-century English philosopher John Locke and the eighteenth-century German Immanuel Kant. Ripstein distinguishes between two versions of liberalism, a Lockean version and a rival Kantian version. According to Ripstein, Lockean liberalism offers an account of equal respect for persons based on individuals' *consent* to public arrangements regulating the interaction between citizens. Kantian liberalism, by contrast, is based on a notion of *reciprocity* yielding what is at its limit a coercive public order that does not necessarily depend on grants of consent. Ripstein sides with Kant against Locke here, for the requirement of consent would accord a veto power to each individual, including those who reject the legal norms of a liberal order, which in turn would violate the principle of reciprocity. The appeal to consent clearly cannot exhaust the moral foundations of the liberal state, for the fundamental normative problem is how to justify coercion on the part of public authority (for instance, with respect to the requirements of private law), and coercion, by definition, refers to cases where consent is lacking. This acute distinction (between respect as requiring consent and respect as enforcing reciprocity) not only illuminates an important tension in the liberal tradition but sheds significant light on contemporary debates about liberalism.

Edward Andrew's chapter summarizes his ambitious trilogy on what, at the beginning of his chapter, he calls (and one of us has elsewhere called) 'the moral vocabulary of liberalism'. According to Andrew, three central pillars of this moral vocabulary are rights, values, and conscience; and the privileging of these particular idioms of moral discourse by modern liberalism goes a long way towards explaining the distinctive shape of the political world in which we happen to live. Greater reflectiveness about the relationship between the words we speak and the shaping of political possibilities is sure to be a major dividend of the mode of political philosophy that Andrew exemplifies; as he nicely puts it in his book *Shylock's Rights*: 'The specific care of the political philosopher is political words. . . . Thus the unique charge of political theorists is . . . to safeguard political language.'[6] Above all, Andrew shows how canonical debates in the history of political philosophy (between Plato and Nietzsche, between Locke and Marx, and so on) continue to inform and illuminate contemporary social experience.

Barry Cooper, in his chapter, offers an interesting narrative of his intellectual odyssey as a theorist and as a student of leading theorists of the twentieth century. In part, his essay is a reflection on his continuing dialogue with such towering thinkers as Eric Voegelin, Alexandre Kojève, Hannah Arendt, and Leo Strauss. But Cooper is no less concerned to understand why notions of Canada typical of Ontario intellectuals fail to square with those of their counterparts in western Canada. The result is a radical contestation over political identity, and Cooper's intention is to draw insights from political philosophy that might help us to deal with the problem (as he sees it) of regional symbolizations that pretend to be pan-Canadian. Cooper's essay, no less than Guy Laforest's in the preceding section, gives expression to the deep cleavages in what is very far from being a unified Canadian identity. Cooper says he puzzles over the 'quite distinct visions' of Canada that define its complexity, and his narrative encourages us to puzzle over them as well.

Towards the end of the twentieth century, many intellectuals came to the view that we have now moved beyond the boundaries of modernity, just as modernity itself surpassed premodern intellectual horizons. What does the transition to a postmodern era mean for our relationship to the Western philosophic tradition as a whole? It is easy to interpret postmodernism as a radicalization of the Enlightenment's challenge to a world shaped by traditional beliefs; but Charles Taylor urges a more complex appreciation of the relations between tradition, Enlightenment, and postmodernity. In his view, postmodernists have failed to understand themselves fully, for their Nietzschean-inspired reactions against secular humanism express a longing to connect with something higher than 'mere life'—a kind of unconscious desire for the transcendent corresponding to the longings previously articulated by traditional religions. As Clifford Orwin notes at the beginning of his chapter, Taylor has had an astonishing influence on a wide range of contemporary political debates (for instance, debates about multiculturalism in the United States and elsewhere) and of course he has been very active in political efforts to heal the radical cleavages in Canadian identity highlighted in the chapters by Laforest and Cooper. But in this provocative chapter we see Taylor in his proper role as a philosopher of the human condition, scaling the heights of philosophical reflection.

Not surprisingly, the start of a new millennium has been accompanied by a lot of hype. One should try to avoid getting carried away by this millennial hype (and after all, as political philosophers, our commitment to critical reflection should help to insulate us from it). Nonetheless, it may perhaps be appropriate, as we enter the new century, for us to accept congratulations on the current vitality of our intellectual discipline and to look forward to its continuing vitality as we move into the twenty-first century.

Notes

The editors would like to thank Bryn Williams-Jones for his tireless efforts at all stages of this project, and acknowledge with gratitude very helpful funding from the Centre in Applied Ethics at the University of British Columbia. We also owe a deep debt to our copy editor, Sally Livingston, for her work on the manuscript.

1. *Globe and Mail*, 25 Sept. 1992.
2. Ibid., 5 Oct. 1992.
3. Ross Poole, *Nation and Identity* (London: Routledge, 1999), 200.
4. See, for instance, Dion's texts addressed to Quebec Premier Lucien Bouchard (*Globe and Mail*, 12 Aug. 1997 and 26 Aug. 1998); to Quebec Deputy Premier Bernard Landry (ibid., 28 Aug. 1997); and to former Quebec Liberal Party leader Claude Ryan (ibid., 7 Feb. 1998), as well as Landry's reply to Dion's first letter to Bouchard (ibid., 14 Aug. 1997).
5. *Globe and Mail*, 9 Aug. 1999 and 20 Aug. 1999.
6. Edward Andrew, *Shylock's Rights: A Grammar of Lockian Claims* (Toronto: University of Toronto Press, 1988), 196.

PART ONE

RETHINKING LIBERALISM AND CITIZENSHIP

Cosmopolitanism, Nationalism, and Immigration: False Dichotomies and Shifting Presuppositions

Joseph H. Carens

In recent years, familiar debates between universalism and particularism, or between liberalism and communitarianism, have re-emerged under the headings of cosmopolitanism and nationalism. Like those other categories, cosmopolitanism and nationalism have many different guises, but most ways of thinking about them entail some tension between the two. I propose to look at cosmopolitanism and nationalism through the lens provided by the issue of immigration, because this lens can both clarify the moral claims of the two positions and reveal some of their ambiguities.

Looking through the lens of immigration, we might see the tension between cosmopolitanism and nationalism as the potential conflict between outsiders and insiders. The outsiders are immigrants, actual or potential. The insiders are current citizens or the political community taken collectively. In this light, we can say that the cosmopolitan perspective articulates the moral claims of immigrants, the nationalist perspective the moral claims of citizens.[1] The strongest version of cosmopolitanism might insist that any favouring of the interests of citizens over the interests of immigrants is morally problematic, while the strongest version of nationalism might insist that any constraint on pursuing the interests of citizens for the sake of pursuing the interests of immigrants is morally problematic. I think both of these extreme versions are implausible. My task in this chapter will be to consider some of the ways in which the interests or moral claims of immigrants can conflict with the interests or moral claims of citizens (or of the political community) and to indicate how I think these conflicts should be resolved. However, this way of contrasting cosmopolitanism and nationalism can be misleading as well as helpful, and I will comment in places on this danger.

In looking at the tensions between cosmopolitanism and nationalism with regard to immigration, we may find that our arguments and conclusions are shaped in crucial ways by what we presuppose about the context of our inquiry. All inquiries have presuppositions. In order to investigate some issues we must take other things as given: the meanings of words, moral norms, facts about the world, and so on. I do not mean to suggest that anything is entirely beyond investigation. We may start with a presupposition that we choose to challenge in another context or even later in the course of the same inquiry. Nevertheless, we cannot challenge everything at once. In any particular inquiry, we have to start with presuppositions.

Let me mark out two extreme presuppositions on a continuum of possible presuppositions that could frame an inquiry into the justice of cosmopolitan and nationalist claims. First, we might want to ask what justice requires in some sort of absolute sense. Here we situate our inquiry in a context where we set to one side obstacles to justice that might be posed by the existing order of things: particular histories, established institutions, the distribution of power, conventional (but problematic) moral norms, the unwillingness of agents to act justly, and so on. Of course, this kind of inquiry cannot be *entirely* detached from reality: it is still constrained by the principle that *ought* implies *can*. But it views the constraints of 'can', of what is possible, in a minimalist light. What justice requires must be humanly possible, even if only under ideal circumstances. It need not be immediately feasible. This is a familiar sort of presupposition for philosophers. It is rather like the sort of inquiry Rawls seems to undertake in *A Theory of Justice* when he discusses ideal theory, or Aristotle in the *Politics* when he writes about the best regime, a regime without presuppositions under circumstances that one would pray to the gods for. But both Rawls and Aristotle take a single regime as their focus, presupposing a division of the world into regimes and saying little about what justice entails for the claims of outsiders (individual or collective) on those within the regime. By contrast, an exploration of cosmopolitanism and nationalism may want to take the whole world order into account. In other words, in thinking about the tensions between cosmopolitanism and nationalism with regard to immigration (or human rights, or international distribution), we may want to ask what justice requires in a context in which everyone acts justly, all institutions are just, there is no need to worry about overcoming past injustices, and so on. Presupposing this sort of context enables us to focus more sharply on fundamental principles and allows us to gain a critical perspective on unjust arrangements, even if they are deeply entrenched and not likely to change. For example, this presupposition would give us space to criticize the modern state system as unjust (from either a nationalist or a cosmopolitan perspective), even if we conceded that it was here to stay for the foreseeable future. I am not arguing here that the state system is unjust, but rather that it is sometimes important to have the space to reflect on that issue. Let's call this end of the continuum, where we assess the implications of cosmopolitanism and nationalism for various issues in the context of a just world, the just-world presupposition.

At the other end of the continuum, we might want to ask what justice requires of us in the here and now, all things considered. This situates our inquiry in a context where we must take into account all of the factors that we excluded with the just-world presupposition, because we want to know how we should act in the world as it is. For that reason the idea that *ought* implies *can* acts as a much more serious constraint on our inquiry. We have to assess the feasibility of various courses of action. We want to be realistic. So we have to take much of the world as given because it is not subject to our control or easily changed. For example, we have to take as part of this presupposition the division of the world into states with vastly different amounts of power and wealth because, whatever one thinks of this fact from an ideal perspective (under a just-world presupposition), it is a feature of our world that is not likely to change in the immediate future. As well, we have to take into account not only the likelihood that we can persuade others in our own community to adopt a given policy (assuming that we are talking about some sort of collective action), but also how we think other relevant actors will behave given their own interests, beliefs, and circumstances. This way of thinking about normative issues is also familiar, though more frequently the kind of approach adopted by policy-makers than philosophers. It is the sort of presupposition we assume when, for instance, we ask (from a moral perspective) what our policy ought to be with regard to Kosovo. In thinking about that question, we cannot simply assume the willingness of others to act justly—if we did, Milosevic and the question itself would disappear from our view. Similarly, we cannot assume that domestic support will be available for whatever course of action we would want to pursue. That, too, is one of the constraints we must take into account. Let's call this end of the continuum, where we explore the implications of cosmopolitanism and nationalism for various issues in the context of the world as we find it, the real-world presupposition. I would add that the real-world presupposition does not preclude criticism, even sharp criticism, of the status quo. I will show how that is possible later in the paper.

In contrasting the just-world and real-world presuppositions, I do not mean to imply that the meaning of either is self-evident or uncontested. On the contrary, people disagree deeply about both. Indeed, if what we care about in the real world (for these purposes) is the set of feasible options for various issues (and the relative feasibility of those options), it is probably fair to say that people sometimes disagree about what the real world is as much as (if not more than) they disagree about what a just world would look like. Nevertheless, I hope that it is already intuitively clear that adopting one presupposition rather than the other can have a considerable effect on the kinds of questions we ask, the evidence we consider, and the arguments we advance. How great that effect is depends on how wide we think the gap is between the real world and a just world. The wider the gap, the greater the effect of adopting one presupposition rather than another. And this may vary from one issue area to another, as I will show below.

As I said at the outset, the just-world and real-world presuppositions mark out two extremes on a continuum. There are many points in between. For purposes of moral inquiry, we may want to abstract from some of the constraints of the real world but not others. It may be useful, for example, to ask what we think justice requires of us with regard to Kosovo without paying attention (right away) to the question of whether it is feasible. Even so, that sort of inquiry will presuppose (implicitly or explicitly) many features of the real world. Or we might want to ask what a just refugee regime would look like. That question requires even more abstraction from the real world than the question of what we should do about

Kosovo, but it does not fully assume the just-world presupposition. After all, in a world in which everyone was acting justly there would be no refugees. This illustrates, by the way, why we should not assume that the just-world presupposition always offers a superior perspective on moral questions. Some of the most urgent moral questions simply disappear from view in a just world.

What presuppositions should we adopt in thinking about the implications of cosmopolitanism and nationalism for immigration? I do not think there is one right answer to this question. It depends in part on the purposes of our inquiry. There are advantages and disadvantages to any given presupposition, and it is often helpful to move from one point in the continuum to another in order to see how that affects the arguments we have constructed. But I do think it is important that we be as conscious of and as explicit about our presuppositions as possible. I will try to show concretely later in this paper how changing the presuppositions can have a big impact (in some cases) on both the questions we ask and the conclusions we reach.

In what follows I have selected two issues somewhat arbitrarily from among the many that one might explore with regard to the implications of cosmopolitanism and nationalism for immigration. The first concerns the legal distinctions that may be drawn between citizens and non-citizens, with specific attention to the issue of deportation; the second concerns the criteria that may be used for the admission and exclusion of immigrants.

I will explore the first issue—the question of how the rights of non-citizens should resemble or differ from those of citizens—as it actually emerges in the world. (Following this discussion, I will comment on the way my analysis strays—just a bit—from the real-world presupposition.) Thus, for example, I assume as a general background the division of the world into sovereign states with (at least) considerable discretion over whom they admit or exclude. To simplify matters, I will focus only on non-citizens who have been legally admitted and who have the status of permanent residents.

One of the most striking developments in relation to citizenship over the past century, especially since the Second World War, has been the erosion of the legal significance of the distinction between citizens and non-citizen permanent residents in the liberal democratic states of Europe and North America. In one area after another, rights and privileges that had previously been enjoyed only by citizens have been extended to non-citizen permanent residents, and restrictions that had been imposed on non-citizens have been abolished[2] (Schuck 1984; Soysal 1994). Some people suggest that we view this development as the triumph of cosmopolitan norms over nationalist ones, or of human rights over the rights of citizenship (Soysal 1994). In other words, what matters most is personhood, not citizenship. The obligation of equal treatment, non-discrimination, and so on is owed to people in virtue of their humanity, not their political membership.

I think that this way of describing the development can be quite misleading, however. There are indeed some rights—mainly civil rights—that people enjoy simply because they are human beings, physically present within the territory of a given state. Among the rights that we would regard as fundamental in any liberal democratic regime are security of the person and of property, freedom of conscience and of religious practice, the right to a fair trial if accused of a crime. Different liberal democratic states interpret and implement these rights in somewhat different ways, but in doing so they do not distinguish between citizens and others. For example, the police are supposed to protect *people*, not just citizens or even residents, from assault and theft, from religious persecution, and so on. Even people present without authorization (i.e., 'illegal immigrants' or 'undocumented workers') are, in principle, entitled to these protections. (In practice, of course, their desire to avoid contact with the authorities renders them more vulnerable.) Let's call rights of this kind 'general human rights' because they are enjoyed by everyone. Within the context of liberal democracy, no one, not even the most fervent chauvinist, argues that basic civil rights of this sort should be denied to non-citizens.

On the other hand, there are many civil and social rights that are not enjoyed by everyone within a given territory but only by those who live there. Rights to get a job, to join a local union, to receive unemployment benefits or health care are the sorts of rights normally enjoyed only by citizens and residents. These rights, or at least some of them, can also reasonably be described as human rights in the sense that they appeal to standards of justice that we think ought to constrain all regimes. For example, we may say that it is a violation of human rights when a regime makes it impossible for a member of society to find employment. But to call the right to work a human right is to use the term in a somewhat different sense from the way it was used in the previous paragraph. These sorts of rights are derived not from one's general humanity but from one's social location, that is, from the kinds of ties one has to the society. It is not a violation of human rights to deny a tourist the right to work. Rights of this second sort mark off both citizens and residents on the one hand from those who are present only on a temporary basis (or without authorization).[3] If we call these rights human rights, we should call them something like 'membership-specific human rights'. Perhaps it would be simpler just to call them rights of membership. Still, the extension of these social and economic rights to non-citizen permanent residents does represent a constraint upon the nationalist tendency to favour citizens over non-citizens, so it is reasonable to describe this practice as a kind of cosmopolitanism, so long as one keeps the caveats regarding its restrictiveness in mind.

I think that, for the most part, the great reduction in the distinctions between the rights of citizens and the rights of non-citizens is something that is morally required as a matter of justice (though I am not suggesting that that is the reason it has come about). Nevertheless, I don't want to defend that view here.[4] Instead I want to focus critically on one area where the rights of citizens and the rights of residents still diverge sharply: the right to be secure against deportation.

In most liberal democratic states non-citizens who have been admitted for an indefinite period enjoy considerable security of residence. Nevertheless, they are normally subject to deportation if convicted of a serious criminal offence or a series of offences. From a nationalist perspective, this exception makes a lot of sense, at least if it is not applied in too draconian a fashion.[5] It is not in the interest of the national community (however defined) to keep non-citizen drug dealers, murderers, and rapists in our midst. Citizen criminals we are simply stuck with. Citizens may not be deported, even if there is someplace willing to take them. At one time exile was used as a punishment for citizens, but now it is considered morally unacceptable, a violation of basic human rights, to force even heinous criminals to live outside their own societies. But we are able to get rid of non-citizen criminals, and often we do, not only in the United States but also in Canada and in most European countries. Indeed the deportation of non-citizens convicted of crimes is usually presented not as a punishment but simply as a routine exercise of a state's power to exclude unwanted immigrants, that is, of a state acting in its own national interest. (Of course, from the perspective of the non-citizen, deportation is often a much harsher sanction than the penalty imposed by the criminal justice system.) In what follows then, I want to take it as a given that it is desirable from a nationalist perspective for the state to have the option to deport convicted criminals.

In most cases, the amount of time the non-citizen has been present is treated as legally irrelevant, or at most, as something that authorities have the discretion to take into account when deciding whether or not to seek deportation. It is not uncommon for people who have spent most or even all of their lives in a country to be deported to a place where they know no one and sometimes where they do not even speak the local language. I regard this practice as a scandal, a blatant and severe injustice against non-citizens.

I will now offer three interrelated reasons why the deportation of long-term residents convicted of serious criminal offences is morally wrong: membership, fairness to other societies, and the rights of family members.

The first and most important reason is that long-term residents are members of society, and, for that reason, ought to be entitled to stay regardless of their conduct. Of course, by definition, the residents in question are not citizens, not formal members of the political community. But they are members of civil society. They participate in labour and housing markets, they pay taxes, they have families that connect them to others in society in myriad ways, they send children to school, they participate in neighbourhood and other associations, they are involved in cultural and recreational activities. In short, they belong. And that belonging matters morally.

To elaborate this argument I will begin with the easiest case and then show why the principles for that sort of case should be extended to less obvious ones. So, consider first non-citizens who come to the society at a very young age, perhaps even are born there if the country has no *ius soli* rule (a rule that grants citizenship automatically to anyone born on the territory). They grow up speaking the local language, using their parents' native tongue only at home, if at all. Their schooling, their friendships, their cultural experiences (television, music, etc.), their formal and informal socialization are very similar to those of the children of citizens in the land where they live and very different from those of the children in the land from which their parents came. To suggest that such children are not integrated into society would be ludicrous. To classify them as aliens would be to deny reality.

On what grounds might someone say that such children are not members of the society in which they have always lived, that is, members in the fullest sense of people entitled to live there all their lives whatever their conduct and behaviour? Two possible answers occur to me. First, that they are not entitled to stay because they possess citizenship in another country. Secondly, that their failure to naturalize when they had the opportunity to do so implies a tacit consent to the conditions that distinguish permanent residents from citizens. Neither is persuasive.

Their right to remain in the land where they live is not lessened if their parents' country of origin happens to grant them citizenship because that citizenship does not secure their place in the society to which they most clearly belong. If they are members of any society, they are members of the society where they have lived their entire lives, the society whose language they speak and whose culture they share. Surely they are much more members of that society than of the one from which their parents came—a land where they have never lived and have no friends, whose culture and customs are unfamiliar at best. Perhaps they have some claim to membership in both societies. But to refuse them the right to stay in the land where they live, and thus formal legal recognition and protection of their status as members of society, is to treat them unjustly.

What about their failure to naturalize? Even for adults, consent counts as a justification only when it reflects a genuine choice or at least a free affirmation. In many cases, children do not become citizens because of their parents' choices (or inaction), and by the time they are old enough to choose for themselves, they have already become embroiled in the legal system in ways that preclude naturalization. Even when these obstacles do not exist, it is unreasonable to infer from inaction the deliberate forfeiture of such a vital interest as the right to stay in one's home, the place where one has grown up. If people are to give up that sort of fundamental right, it must be done as a deliberate and conscious choice in circumstances that are not coercive. Finally, even those who do choose freely and consciously not to naturalize are entitled to protection against deportation, because the right to remain in a society of which one is a member, even if not a citizen, is a fundamental human interest that ought to be respected.

So far I have focused on people who have spent virtually their whole lives in the country. What about those who come at a later age? The general principle is that the longer the presence, the stronger the claims to membership; the shorter the presence, the weaker the claims. A child who comes to a country as an infant is virtually indistinguishable, in moral terms, from one who was born there. People who spend all or most of their formative years as children in a country have powerful ties and a powerful moral claim to remain there. (On the other hand, those who spend only a year or two have little moral claim per se, even if they were born there and have an indisputable legal claim because a state happens to have a *ius soli* rule.) How long must children spend in a country before they have become members with a moral claim to remain? I can't answer that question precisely, but I would think that several years (especially ones spent between the ages of six and eighteen) should be enough.

If we turn now to the question of what claims to remain are possessed by people who come as adults, we find that the same sorts of principles apply. The longer one stays, the more one becomes a member. The shorter the stay, the weaker the claim. If someone arrives as an immigrant and commits a serious crime within six months or a year, I do not think it would be wrong to deport him, given the background presupposition that I am not challenging here, that is, the basic principle of the state's right to control immigration. He will not have built up the kinds of social ties that make expulsion so inhuman. But if he has been there for ten years, then the case is entirely different.[6]

How long must adults spend in a society before they have the kind of claim to membership that should bar deportation? Again, I won't try to answer this question precisely. But it is important to recognize that in assessing the claims that come from living in a society, there is a threshold after which the length of time does not matter because the claim should be regarded as absolute. Five years seems to me a reasonable length of time for such a threshold, though I don't pretend that the question can be precisely settled on the basis of a theoretical principle. After a while, the terms of admission become irrelevant. Regardless of the original conditions of entry, once people have established themselves firmly as members of society, they have a moral claim to stay.

'But these are criminals,' someone will object. 'They cause social problems. They are destructive to the rest of society. Isn't it in our interest to send them away?' Let us assume that this is true.[7] Why is it fair to dump such people on another society, a place where they have a legal membership but no real social connection? Are they any less likely to engage in criminal behaviour there? Every society has people who are involved in criminal activity and who create social problems. It seems only fair that a society should deal with its own problems, not try to foist them off on someplace else. Again, the argument is especially powerful with regard to people who have grown up in the society that seeks to expel them. It is that society, not the one of their nominal citizenship, that is most responsible for their social formation, for successes and failures in the inculcation of social norms and values, and for the creation of opportunities and obstacles in social life. In short, one important response to the objection above is to say, 'These people may be problems, but they are *our* problems, not someone else's, and we should be the ones to cope with them as we do with criminals who are citizens.' I might add that political spokespeople from some poor countries have complained that deportees from Canada and the United States sometimes bring with them sophisticated criminal arms, technologies, and networks that overwhelm the capacities of their law enforcement agencies.

The final argument against deportation of non-citizens concerns the effect of such deportations upon family members who may themselves be citizens or who, in any event, have done no wrong themselves. I regard this argument as somewhat weaker than the preceding two, because the same objection can be posed against any sanction (i.e., that it affects not only the person against whom it is directed but also those to whom he or she is closely connected). Nevertheless, it appropriately draws attention to the particular nature of deportation as a harm, and a harm additional to what citizen criminals have to suffer. Ironically, it is this sort of argument, constructed on the basis of guarantees to family life, that has proven most effective in a number of European court cases in providing a barrier to deportation.

In the way I have proposed to use the terms 'nationalist' and 'cosmopolitan', all of these arguments are cosmopolitan in the sense that they assert that the claims of non-citizens should prevail over the collective interests and claims of the citizenry. But it may be worth commenting a bit further on other ways in which the first two arguments might or might not be viewed as cosmopolitan.

The first argument may be described as cosmopolitan in that it constructs the right not to be deported as an individual human right that limits the ways in which political communities may pursue their interests. At the same time, it is not a right that everyone in the world possesses against every political community. It is a right of membership, a right that derives from one's social location and circumstances, from the fact of long-term residence in a particular place. In that sense it is quite different from, say, a right not to be tortured.

The second argument can also be seen as cosmopolitan in that it invokes a norm of fairness between nations as a reason for limiting the pursuit of national self-interest. On the other hand, it might be possible to argue that a norm of fairness between nations is something that emerges naturally from a certain kind of nationalist perspective (which requires us to respect the claims of other nations so that ours will be respected in turn), and from this perspective a barrier to deportation could be internal to nationalism.

I draw attention to these different ways of characterizing the arguments as a reminder that it is too easy to construct cosmopolitanism and nationalism as dichotomous categories and then spend time debating whether a given argument fits in one category or the other. It is more valuable, I think, simply to explore the issues and say what we think is right and wrong.

The issue I have just been discussing—the rights of resident non-citizens, especially with regard to deportation—is one that can fruitfully be discussed in the context of what I have called the real-world presupposition. I stray a bit from that presupposition in arguing for the restriction of states' rights to deport non-citizens, because the conventional view that states are entitled to deport non-citizen criminals is very deeply rooted in practice, in existing institutions, and in public opinion. This situation is unlikely to change in the near future. Convicted criminals are unpopular and courts tend to be highly deferential to political authorities on this issue. For that reason, I am not optimistic that my views will become policy in the near future, and those working on behalf of immigrants are probably better advised to focus on the excesses and inhumanity of an overly rigid deportation policy than to challenge the right to deport altogether.

As we have seen, however, the kinds of arguments I am advancing are not at odds with the development of conventional moral and legal norms regarding the rights of non-citizens in other areas. Viewed in that light, the deportation of non-citizens is something of an anomaly. Thus, changing this practice so that states would no longer be able to deport non-citizens who were long-term residents would pose no serious threat to most other existing institutional arrangements and practices. It could even be done by judicial fiat.[8] For example, some judicial decisions in Europe have restricted the rights of states to deport convicted criminals in the name of European human rights guarantees. So, while my argument is unrealistic, it is not wildly so. Acceptance of the argument would not require any profound transformation—only a marginal change—in the world as it currently is.

Adopting the real-world presupposition does not have much impact on this issue. My analysis would not change much if I moved along the continuum towards the just-world presupposition. However one constructs a just world, it would not be morally permissible to expel people from places where they have long been settled. As I have presented the argument above, the right to remain in a society where one has lived a long time should be regarded as a basic human right. Ipso facto, it will be a feature of any just world order.

I want to turn now to consider an issue where the background presupposition we adopt does have a major impact on the kinds of arguments we make and the conclusions we reach. That issue is the criteria that states may use for the admission and exclusion of immigrants. I begin as before with the real-world presupposition. From a nationalist perspective, as I defined it earlier, it would seem desirable for states to have complete discretion with regard to the criteria of admission and exclusion. Some would argue that states do in fact have this sort of discretion, but I think that overstates the case, both morally and empirically. It is true, of course, that as part of the international state system, states have considerable discretion over the admission and exclusion of immigrants, and that most people take it for granted that this sort of control is morally justifiable. But it is also true that all liberal democratic states recognize certain moral constraints upon the exercise of their sovereignty in this area, even if the constraints are self-imposed. (Self-imposed constraints may be formal, as is the case when states sign human rights treaties, refugee conventions, and so on, or informal, as is the case when states treat certain policy options as morally unacceptable even if legally permissible under international law.)

Let me cite a few examples. All liberal democratic states recognize a right of family reunification (i.e., the right of a non-resident with intimate family ties to a citizen or to a non-citizen permanent resident to enter and reside in the country where her family member lives) and a right of *non-refoulement* (that is, the right of a non-citizen who has arrived in the country and claimed refugee status not to be sent back to the dangerous situation from which she fled). *Non-refoulement* is more commonly, if less precisely, called the right of asylum. These examples show that some non-resident outsiders have moral claims to admission that the state is obliged to respect. These can be seen as cosmopolitan constraints upon the nationalist principle that states can control immigration however they want, although, as with the right not to be deported and other rights of membership, these rights are generated by specific kinds of connections to the country (family ties in the one case, physical presence in the other) and are not rights enjoyed by those without such ties. For example, a refugee has to arrive in the country to claim the right of asylum. She cannot make the same demand to be admitted while still abroad.

Family reunification and refugee asylum are cases where specific individuals have moral claims to admission, but even when that is not the case the criteria used in the selection and exclusion of immigrants are morally constrained. For example, it is now widely considered to be morally unacceptable to use race or religion as criteria of selection or exclusion, although such criteria were commonly used in the relatively recent past in Canada, the United States, and elsewhere.[9] These constraints upon states' immigration policies are even more clearly cosmopolitan in the sense that they are universal constraints, prohibiting the use of these criteria with regard to all potential immigrants. On the other hand, they do not secure admission for anyone. A state may choose to admit no immigrants at all without violating these constraints.

To the extent that questions about justice play any role in debates about immigration policy, they tend to come in the form of questions about how these sorts of constraints should be interpreted and applied, whether they should be extended or restricted, and whether other comparable constraints should be added. For example, there is a debate about how family should be defined for purposes of family reunification. No one doubts that family includes one's spouse and minor children, but should it be extended to include adult children, parents and grandparents, brothers and sisters, and so on? Some states have extended their principles of family reunification to include same-sex relationships. Is that something we should regard as morally permissible (i.e., within the moral discretion of states to adopt or not as they see fit) or, as I personally think, something that is morally required (i.e., something that should be regarded as a basic human right that it is wrong for states not to respect)?

We might also ask whether additional constraints besides race and religion should be placed on the criteria used by states for admission and exclusion. For example, is it acceptable for states to take ethnicity and/or culture into account in selecting immigrants? Various states do so in different ways. Canada selects people on a points system, and knowledge of French or English gives applicants a modest number of points. Germany and Ireland give preference to those with ethnic ties to the country, even if there are no longer any immediate family ties. Are these sorts of policies properly treated as within the discretion of states to adopt or not according to their own conceptions of their national interest, or should they be regarded as morally problematic in the way that racial and religious criteria are? What about the use of educational, occupational, and other economic criteria as factors in selection (or exclusion)? Countries that admit immigrants often take such factors into account. Is that morally acceptable or should we see it as a form of unjust discrimination? Most states that admit immigrants require them to pass some sort of physical exam. They exclude people with certain kinds of medical conditions (e.g., tuberculosis, AIDS). More generally, Canada will not admit people whom the immigration department judges likely to put an excessive burden on the health-care system. Are those sorts of policies morally permissible?

These are all interesting and important questions (though I won't try to pursue them further here) and all have two things in common. First, they are all concerned with the imposition of cosmopolitan constraints on the discretion of states to adopt whatever immigration policies they judge to be in their national interest. Second, however one answers these sorts of questions, they do not challenge the basic nationalist norm that, within wide limits, it is normally legitimate for states to adopt whatever immigration policy they choose. In that respect, cosmopolitanism remains marginal to the immigration debate in the real world.

Most contemporary political debates about immigration are not primarily concerned with what justice requires, permits, or prohibits, but with conflicting conceptions of what is good for the political community. People disagree about the social, economic, political, cultural, demographic, and environmental consequences of immigration and about whether any given set of consequences will be good or bad for the political community. What both sides in these debates normally share is the view that the policy should be determined, for the most part, by what is good for the existing political community (or some segment of it) and not by what is good for the immigrants. To challenge that view, to adopt a stronger cosmopolitan perspective, we have to move further away from the real-world assumption.

One way to do that would be to take as a presupposition the widely shared view that we are obliged to regard individuals as being of equal moral worth (a cosmopolitan assumption with deep roots in the liberal tradition) and to ask what that commitment would entail for the right of states to admit or exclude whomever they want. Note that this way of posing the question leaves much of the existing background in place: the division of the world into states with vast differences of power and wealth between them, the absence of adequate human rights protections in some states, and so on. But it deliberately abstracts from any questions about the practicality of the conclusions in order to focus on moral principles.

I have pursued this line of analysis on a number of occasions (e.g., Carens 1987, 1992). My basic conclusion is that if one took the commitment to equal moral worth seriously, then it would be impossible to justify the existing pattern whereby borders are generally closed and immigrants are admitted, for the most part, only when the political community judges that to be in its interest. I will summarize the main points.

First, a commitment to equal moral worth may not require us to treat people identically in every way, but it does require us to respect basic human freedoms. People should be free to pursue their own projects and to make their own choices about how they live their lives so long as this does not interfere with the legitimate claims of other individuals to do likewise. To enjoy this general sort of freedom, people have to be free to move where they want (subject to the same restraints as others with regard to respect for private property, the use of public property, etc.). The right to go where you want is itself an important human freedom. It is precisely this freedom, and all that this freedom makes possible, that is taken away by imprisonment. Thus conventional immigration controls improperly limit the freedom of noncitizens who are not threatening the basic rights and freedoms of citizens.

Second, a commitment to equal moral worth requires some sort of basic commitment to equal opportunity. Access to social positions should be determined by an individual's actual talents and capacities, not limited on the basis of arbitrary native characteristics (such as class, race, or sex). And freedom of movement is essential for equality of opportunity. You have to be able to move to where the opportunities are in order to take advantage of them. Again, the conventional pattern of border controls greatly restricts opportunities for potential immigrants.

A third, closely related point is that a commitment to equal moral worth entails some commitment to the reduction of existing economic, social, and political inequalities, partly as a means of realizing equal freedom and equal opportunity and partly as a desirable end in itself. Freedom of movement would contribute to a reduction of political, social, and economic inequalities. There are millions of people in the developing world today who long for the freedom and economic opportunity they could find in affluent developed countries. Many of them take great risks to come: Haitians setting off in leaky boats; Guatemalans being smuggled across the border in hot, airless trucks; Tamils paying to be set adrift off the coast of Newfoundland. If the borders were open, millions more would move. The exclusion of so many poor and desperate people seems hard to justify from a perspective that takes seriously the claims of all individuals as free and equal moral persons.

Consider the case for freedom of movement in light of the liberal critique of feudal practices that determined a person's life chances on the basis of his or her birth. Citizenship in the modern world is a lot like feudal status in the medieval world. It is assigned at birth; for the most part it is not subject to change through the individual's will and efforts; and it has a major impact upon one's life chances. To be born a citizen of an affluent country like Canada is like being born into the nobility (even though many belong to the lesser nobility). To be born a citizen of a poor country like Bangladesh is (for most) like being born into the peasantry in the Middle Ages. In this context, limiting entry to countries like Canada is a way of protecting a birthright privilege. Liberals objected to the way feudalism restricted freedom, including the freedom of individuals to move from one place to another in search of a better life. Yet modern practices of citizenship and state control over borders tie people to the land of their birth almost as effectively. If the feudal practices were wrong, what justifies the modern ones?

Finally, compare freedom of movement *within* the state to freedom of movement across state borders. Like every freedom involving human action, freedom of movement is not unlimited, but because it is an important liberty, limitations have to be justified in a way that gives equal weight to the claims of all. Some restrictions on movement are easy to justify, such as traffic regulations or a right to exclude others from one's home (assuming everyone has a home or a reasonable opportunity to obtain one). But imagine an attempt by officials in one city or province to keep out people from another. That sort of restriction is seen as fundamentally incompatible with a commitment to free and equal citizenship. Cities and provinces have borders but not to keep people in or out against their will. Indeed freedom of movement *within* the nation state is widely acknowledged as a basic human right, and states are criticized for restricting internal movement even by those who accept the conventional view of state sovereignty. People *are* generally free to change their membership in sub-national political communities at will, even though these sub-national communities often have important jurisdictional responsibilities (e.g., raising taxes and providing services) that can be affected by the movement of people into their territory.

If it is so important for people to have the right to move freely within a state, isn't it equally important for them to have the right to move across state borders? Every reason why one might want to move within a state may also be a reason for moving between states: one might want a job; one might fall in love with someone from another country; one might belong to a religion that has few adherents in one's native state and many in another; one might wish to pursue cultural opportunities that are only available in another land. Virtually every objection to freedom of movement across state borders can also be applied to freedom of movement across federal jurisdictional boundaries within states. The radical disjuncture that treats freedom of movement within the state as a moral imperative and freedom of movement across state borders as merely a matter of political discretion makes no sense from a perspective that takes seriously the freedom and equality of all individuals. It attaches a special kind of magic to the boundaries of the state and presupposes something that needs to be defended.

Even if we took the principle of equal moral worth seriously, it might still be possible to justify some limits on immigration. For example, all rights must be compatible with the ability to maintain public order, and there might be some levels of migration flows that would threaten this. On the other hand, it would be important to specify whether the breakdown in public order resulted from sheer numbers or from morally unjust behaviour by current citizens objecting to the new arrivals. The latter is the sort of constraint one must take into account in the real world, but is precisely the sort of thing one wants to abstract from in thinking about what justice requires as a matter of principle.

There might be other justifiable reasons for restricting free movement that would be compatible with a commitment to equal moral worth. After all, people have a variety of fundamental interests and sometimes they conflict with one another. The right to move freely across state borders is an important human freedom, but that does not make it absolute. Nevertheless, it seems clear that if we took the principle seriously, it would dramatically constrain the sorts of considerations that now drive immigration policy and would make borders much more open.

One might object that there is something odd about adopting a presupposition that abstracts so sharply from the real world but does not go all the way to the just-world presupposition. Isn't this an incoherent halfway house? After all, many of the factors impelling people to migrate (the denial of basic human rights, the absence of opportunities at home) are themselves manifestations of deep injustices in their home country and/or in the international order. Opening the borders won't do much to address these deeper injustices and won't help most people (since most wouldn't or couldn't move even if the borders were more open). Moreover, these deeper injustices are what make the right of free movement seem such an urgent and important freedom, so if they were actually addressed (i.e., if we did live in a just world), perhaps the right of free movement would not seem so fundamental after all.

This is an important challenge. I will return to the question of immigration in a just world in a moment. First I want to say why I think the halfway-house presupposition I have adopted is useful.

One of the common ways of defending the conventional view that states may (largely) choose whom to admit and whom to exclude among non-citizens is to say that control over immigration is inherent in the idea of political sovereignty or that it is inextricably tied up with the very idea of a self-determining political community. By adopting the halfway-house presupposition, we can critically examine this sort of claim. The idea that states must be unitary and sovereign and must have control over their borders is a myth that does not correspond to actual political arrangements in the real world. To sharpen the point I made above about intra-state mobility, federal systems often have complex separate and shared sovereignty arrangements (which may also extend to issues like immigration). It is sheer dogma to insist that the sovereignty of the component parts of a federal system is not real sovereignty. Like property, sovereignty is a bundle of rights that can be divided up in many different ways. Yet this sovereignty coexists with open borders among the various units. Of course, it is true that such openness has dynamic effects and that the various units may have to take migration incentives into effect in planning public policies, but in an interdependent world, political units have to take into account many factors that are outside the jurisdiction they control.

The policy of free movement within the European Union reveals even more starkly the ideological character of the claim that control over immigration is inherent in sovereignty or essential for a political community to retain its collective character. No one can seriously doubt that the European states are still real states today, with most of the trappings of state sovereignty, and that these states have more effective power of collective self-determination than many states elsewhere in the world. Nevertheless, they do not have the power to control immigration from other EU states. And it is a purely formal point to say that they could reacquire that power by withdrawing from the EU.

Someone may point out that the EU did not adopt its (internal) open borders policy out of a commitment to human rights but out of a concern for economic efficiency and that it waited to implement the policy until the economies of poorer states, like Spain, Portugal, and Italy, had improved sufficiently that the abolition of immigration restrictions within the EU would not lead to massive population movements from the poorer countries to the more affluent ones. I accept these claims entirely. From my perspective, they simply confirm the most fundamental point, namely that control over borders is essential to protect a community only when that community is so economically privileged relative to others that many people would consider moving there. Restrictions on migration basically serve as a protection for economic and political privilege. That becomes sharply visible from my halfway-house presupposition. I freely acknowledge that pointing this out will not change it. I do not imagine that moral criticism moves the world, at least not often. But one function this sort of criticism can perform is to unmask (for a moment) the pretensions to moral legitimacy that are supplied by the conventional view that every state has an inherent right to control its own borders.

A second advantage of the halfway-house presupposition is that it provides a space within which it is possible to challenge the common view of cosmopolitanism as requiring a degree of altruism that it is unreasonable to expect of human beings, individually and collectively. Cosmopolitanism comes in many forms and there may be some versions that are rightly subject to this charge. But the argument for open borders that I have advanced does not require individuals or communities to ignore their attachments. It is not a matter of caring for everyone to the same degree but of respecting basic individual rights. No one imagines that Tony Blair is or should be as concerned with the well-being of the Germans in Germany as he is (or should be) concerned with the well-being of people who live in the UK, even though Germans have the right to bring themselves within his circle of concern by moving to the UK. If Massachusetts sets up a particular social program, it does not have to provide the benefits of that program to everyone in Georgia. However, it cannot prevent people from moving to Massachusetts from Georgia, whether or not their motive for moving is to participate in the program (though studies suggest such motivations rarely drive international immigration). Not using force to prevent people from exercising a basic human freedom is not what we normally classify as altruism.

Finally, I want to say a few words about how the immigration issue is transformed when we adopt the just-world presupposition. Would a just world include the right to move freely into any political community or would some restrictions on mobility be morally legitimate? I use the word 'political community' but the questions we would have to ask about a just world include the following: should the world have more than one political community, and if so, should it be divided into relatively autonomous political communities like modern states, and, if so, what should be the basis for the dividing lines of these communities and what sorts of powers should these communities have? It would be hard to address the migration issue without taking such considerations into account, and this reveals both the advantages and the disadvantages of the just-world presupposition.

On the one hand, the just-world presupposition provides a context that allows for the most independent and critical perspective on the status quo. That is highly desirable, because even if our chances of bringing about a fundamental transformation of our social arrangements (or of ourselves) are slim, we should still assess current reality in the light of our highest ideals. If we are forced to choose between the lesser of two evils, it is essential not to delude ourselves into thinking that the lesser evil is really a good. Approaching moral questions with the just-world presupposition avoids legitimizing policies and practices that are morally wrong and gives the fullest scope to our critical capacities. Thus this approach avoids some of the problems inherent in the real-world presupposition.

On the other hand, the just-world presupposition detaches us from so many familiar landmarks that it is easy to lose our bearings and easier still to lose sight of the issue of immigration. Many considerations would have to come into play in any fundamental exploration of what a just world order would require—all of them highly contestable. For example, what sorts of differences in language, culture, and identity would we find in a just world and how would these differences matter in social and political institutions? We know that some of these differences make justice impossible to achieve, and others make it difficult. But would we assume them away altogether in a just world? Or should we treat such differences as given in a just world, as if they were natural facts like climates and soils (which are themselves no longer simply natural facts in the real world). What sort of history is required by a just world? These sorts of questions only scratch the surface of the just world, and many of these contestable considerations would be relevant to the question of migration in a just world. In an inquiry into the nature of a just world, questions about migration are bound to play a subordinate role. One has to worry whether one would ever reach them at all. In ordering dinner, it seems wiser to start with a menu than with the Cartesian *cogito*.

Still, I don't want to overstate the difficulties posed by a just-world presupposition (or forget the earlier point about why it is crucial to adopt this sort of presupposition as a way of getting a critical perspective on the status quo). There are a number of simplifying strategies one can adopt in trying to address what migration would look like in a just world. For example, one could assume a just world would be composed of different political communities with roughly the same level of economic development and with basic freedoms protected in each. Then one could consider the question of how fundamental the right to migrate would seem. I would argue that the analysis presented above suggests that it would still be an important right under these sorts of conditions, and also a less threatening right for the reasons indicated in my discussion of the EU.

Finally, even if we could determine what a just world order would look like, including just arrangements regarding migration, that would still leave open the question of how to get there from here. The best way to move in the direction of the overall ideal is not necessarily to try to reform some subordinate policy or practice to make it more closely approximate what it would be in an ideal world. For example, suppose that a just world would include free movement of people as one element in its arrangements. It does not necessarily follow that we should push to open borders as much as possible now. There are too many other factors and intervening variables. Even if the best arrangement is one of open borders, the second best may be one involving considerable closure so that other features required to create a just world may be developed within a protected space. I do not mean to endorse this particular argument, merely to show that the path from an understanding of what is required with respect to migration in a just world to an understanding of how we ought to act in the world today is not straight and smooth. The best approach, as I suggested at the beginning of this chapter, is to adopt a series of different presuppositions, using the analysis developed within each to shed critical light on the conclusions reached within the others.

Notes

This article was originally presented at a conference on Cosmopolitanism and Nationalism at Stanford University, 15–17 April 1999.

1. The second way of putting it assumes that there is a symmetry between nation and state so that every citizen is by definition a member of the nation. That is not always the case, as recent debates over the rights of national minorities illustrate, and it is an open and important question whether immigrants should be expected to join a nation (majority or minority), in some thick cultural sense, as a condition of admission to legal citizenship or social membership. Nevertheless, for the issues that I am going to discuss in detail, the distinction is not crucial and the contrast provides a useful simplification.
2. I do not mean to suggest that the trend is invariable or irreversible. For example, recent legislation passed in the United States that restricts the access of legal immigrants to various social welfare benefits clearly goes against this trend. (For a discussion of the moral legitimacy of such legislation, see Carens 2000.)
3. Indeed, even citizens who reside abroad may not be entitled to some of these rights (e.g., access to social programs) if they have returned only on a temporary basis and are not establishing residence.
4. For such a defence see Carens 2000. My critique of deportation draws upon the same article.
5. A recent US law requires the deportation of anyone convicted of a felony or of a drug-related crime, and this has led to a series of highly publicized cases in which people convicted of minor drug offences many years ago are now being deported, US Army combat veterans are being deported, and so on. One might argue—as critics of the law do—that this is undesirable even from a nationalist perspective.
6. I use the masculine pronoun advisedly in these sentences because the overwhelming majority of criminals, citizen or non-citizen, are male.
7. In fact, it is not always true. Some of those deported are not hardened criminals. Others may not be guilty at all. I want to assume here, as a way of taking up the harder challenge, that the convicted non-citizens are in fact guilty. But, at least in North America, it is not uncommon for accused people, especially racial minorities, to be held without bail for several months and then offered an official plea bargain under which they will be sentenced only to the time already served if they plead guilty. If they insist on their innocence but are subsequently convicted by a criminal justice system (which has already indicated

its doubts by keeping them in jail for an extended period), they will face years of additional incarceration. They receive legal counsel from greatly overworked lawyers who have their own incentives for settling quickly. In addition, the clients, and sometimes even the lawyers, do not always understand that a guilty plea will make them liable for deportation. Nevertheless, I set this sort of problem aside, because there is no doubt that many of those convicted are in fact guilty, and my aim is to show that even they should not be deported.

8. One might ask whether such judicial decisions would be sustainable in the face of deeply felt popular opposition, but, in many ways, this would be just one more example of the extension of the rights of criminal defendants and convicted criminals. There is not much popular support for those sorts of rights (regardless of whether the criminals are citizens), but they have been considerably extended over the past several decades.
9. The obvious exception here is Israel's Law of Return. In most cases the status of being a Jew, for purposes of the Law of Return, is acquired by birth not by religious commitment and so is more akin to ethnic preferences, which are morally contestable but practised by other countries as well and not universally regarded as morally problematic. However, for purposes of the Law of Return one can become a Jew by conversion, and in such cases being Jewish is clearly a religious status. This is an interesting and controversial case that requires a more detailed contextual exploration than I can provide here. I should also acknowledge that some people in Europe and North America advocate a return to the use of racial criteria, but, at least in its most blatant form, this view has not yet succeeded in gaining anything close to majority support.

References

Carens, Joseph H. 1987. 'Aliens and Citizens: The Case for Open Borders'. *Review of Politics* 49, 2 (Spring): 251–73.

———. 1992. 'Migration and Morality: A Liberal Egalitarian Perspective'. In *Free Movement*, ed. Brian Barry and Robert Goodin. London: Harvester-Wheatsheaf, 25–47.

———. 2000. 'The Rights of Residents'. In *Reinventing Citizenship: Dual Citizenship, Social Rights and Federal Citizenship in Europe and the US*, edited by Randall Hanson and Patrick Weil. Oxford: Berghahn Books, forthcoming.

Schuck, Peter. 1984. 'The Transformation of Immigration Law'. *Columbia Law Review* 34 (January): 1–90.

Soysal, Yasemin Nuhoglu. 1994. *Limits of Citizenship: Migrants and Postnational Membership in Europe*. Chicago: University of Chicago Press.

Democracy and Globalization: A Defeasible Sketch

James Tully

> When philosophy paints its grey in grey, then has a shape of life grown old. By philosophy's grey in grey it cannot be rejuvenated but only understood. The owl of Minerva spreads its wings only with the falling of the dusk.[1]

Introduction: A Political Philosophy of the Present

Recall that in this famous conclusion to the Preface of the *Philosophy of Right* Hegel advances two closely related claims about the relation between political philosophy and political practice. First, only when an organized form of political life has come to maturity and grown old can it be given adequate expression by means of philosophical reflection. Philosophy 'appears only when actuality is already there cut and dried after its process of formation has been completed'.[2] Second, at the same time, this philosophical reflection is provoked by a new and different form of political life coming into being out of the old. While the philosopher cannot help noticing this dawning activity, for it renders the present problematic and gives rise to critical reflection, she or he cannot grasp it adequately because it is different from, and often disruptive of, the shape of life in its twilight, which he or she paints so perspicuously in shades of grey. To use Hegel's example, while Plato adequately articulated the mature Greek political and ethical life in the *Republic*, he noticed but failed to understand adequately an emerging style of politics that 'was breaking into that life in his own time' and that would change the old ways forever.[3] This was 'a deeper principle', the 'free infinite personality': that is, the new form of political and ethical life based on *parrhesia*—modes of questioning oneself and other citizens, as exemplified by Socrates.[4] Plato failed to understand adequately the new way of being political not only because it was new and inchoate, but also because he tried to 'master' or comprehend it in the concepts appropriate to the old, and thus 'did fatal injury to the deeper impulse which underlay it'.[5] He could see what Socrates had introduced only 'as a longing still unsatisfied'—not as a principled mode of being open to philosophical comprehension.[6]

We are in an analogous situation today with respect to the puzzling kinds of democratic activity that are emerging in the context of globalization. We can see that they embody 'a longing still unsatisfied', but when we try to reflect critically upon them we misunderstand because we tend to characterize and seek to 'master' them in the concepts, theories, and traditions that are appropriate to democratic practices and institutions, which have come to maturity and grown old over the last two hundred years and in which we ourselves think and act. Alternatively, as Hegel explains, if we try to grasp and anticipate what is happening here and now in some new normative vocabulary, this too is bound to fail since we cannot 'jump over Rhodes': that is, transcend our contemporary world.[7] The result is groundless and idle speculation about the future, 'the erection of a beyond, supposed to exist, God knows where', and 'where anything you please may, in fancy, be built'.[8]

Certainly these two genres of contemporary political thought—reinscription of the new in terms of the old and idle speculation about the future—are common enough, especially at the beginning of a new millennium. Nevertheless, since the time of the young Hegelians a third school of political philosophy has developed in response to Hegel's conservative pessimism about understanding what is happening right now and it has established itself on the rough ground between Hegel's two extremes. From Kant in his 1784 essay 'What is Enlightenment?', Marx, Nietzsche, and Weber to Arendt, Wittgenstein, Foucault, Taylor, Giddens, Connolly, and Skinner, among others, this form of critical reflection on the present seeks to understand a new and problematic way of acting or language game (class struggle in the workplace, post-Christian ethics, the ascetics of capitalist behaviour, an enigmatic aspect of freedom). It does so not in terms of the dominant, cut and dried political institutions and traditions, nor of some new and fanciful vocabulary, but rather in terms of a relation of difference, of dissimilarity, relative to the dominant institutions and their traditions of thought. 'What difference does today introduce with respect to yesterday?' is Foucault's succinct summary of this whole orientation.[9] This careful, back-and-forth, reciprocal elucidation of an unsettling political activity of the present in terms of its difference from, as well as its similarity to, the prevailing forms of political thought and practice not only discloses the anomalous activity in a distinctive light; it also shows up these old forms, not as the taken-for-granted horizons in which we must understand the new, but as partial limits that the new activity may enable us, cautiously, to modify and venture beyond.[10]

Although this intermediate tradition has learned from and adapted Hegel's historical approach while taking his advice to remain as close as possible to contemporary experience (abjuring the temptation to jump over Rhodes), it nevertheless rotates his orientation 180 degrees around the fixed axis of our real need. Rather than comprehending and reconciling the new and problematic activity from the twilight of the old, this approach uses the dawning light of the novel activity to free ourselves from the sedimented conventions of the old ('se déprendre de soi-même'), to some limited and relative extent, in order to think differently ('penser autrement').[11] Through this form of philosophical investigation (*askesis*), one is able to 'test', in 'what is given to us as universal, necessary, obligatory' (the dominant institutions and their traditions), 'what place is occupied by whatever is singular, contingent, and the product of arbitrary constraints', and to what extent it is possible 'to go beyond them' ('de leur franchissement possible'): 'to grasp the points where change is possible and desirable, and to determine the precise form this change should take'.[12]

Such an approach is difficult, precarious, and uncertain. It has neither the security and comfort of reaffirming and legitimizing our most familiar and mature institutions and traditions of political thought nor the excitement and media fame of hurling bold conjectures at the world at large. Any reciprocal elucidation is relative, contextual, partial, and defeasible, and, therefore, open to continual reworking—a 'sketch' in Wittgenstein's sense rather than a 'theory'. We are thus always in the position of beginning again. Yet, in compensation, it is the orientation that has some chance of rendering aspects of the present world, to which we belong, a little less unclear, enabling us to find ourselves within it and perhaps even to go on. While Hegel is right to say that the owl of Minerva spreads its wings only with the falling of dusk, Bill Reid, the great Haida artist, reminds us that the raven of Haida Gwaii—the indigenous symbol of our ability to modify our ways of being human relative to our past and become other than we are—takes flight at dawn; indeed brings the dawn into being and so sets the scene.[13] In sum, then, the defining temperament of this enlightenment orientation, suspended between the owl's respect for and deep attachment to what our great teachers and predecessors have achieved and the raven's curiosity and always unsatisfied longing for what lies on our horizons, is perhaps expressed well by Nietzsche in the last paragraph of *Daybreak*, written in Genoa in 1880–81:

> All those brave birds which fly out into the distance, into the farthest distance—it is certain! Somewhere or other they will be unable to go on and will perch on a mast or a bare cliff-face—and they will even be thankful for this miserable accommodation! But who would venture to infer from that, that there was *not* an immense open space before them, that they had flown as far as one *could* fly! All our great teachers and predecessors have at last come to a stop and it is not with the noblest or most graceful of gestures that weariness comes to a stop: it will be the same with you and me! But what does that matter to you and me! *Other birds will fly farther!* . . . Whither does this mighty longing draw us, this longing that is worth more to us than any pleasure? Why just in this direction, thither where all the suns of humanity have hitherto *gone down*?[14]

This approach can be applied to some aspects of the puzzling forms of political activity that have emerged in the context of contemporary globalization. Section 1 distinguishes two kinds of practices of government and democracy (and two corresponding uses of the terms 'government' and 'democracy') woven historically into our ways of ruling and being ruled (thus not 'the erection of a beyond, supposed to exist, God knows where'). One, the 'restrictive' sense of 'government' and 'democracy', refers to the mature and predominant practices of government and democracy typical of *representative* democratic nation-states, their institutions, and the traditions of understanding in which they operate and are described and evaluated. The other, the 'nonrestrictive' sense of 'government' and 'democracy', refers to the less prominent practices of government and democracy that do not conform to the typical practices of representative government and democracy and so cannot be understood adequately in terms of theories and traditions of representative government. Yet, by reciprocal elucidation, these nonrestrictive practices have the capacity to throw light on a range of political activity under contemporary globalization. I will refer to the former as, interchangeably, 'restrictive' or 'representative', to the latter as 'nonrestrictive' or 'extensive' practices of government and democracy, and categorize both types as simply practices of government and democracy.

Section 2 summarizes how the practices of representative government and democracy came to predominate and appear universal, necessary, and obligatory, but now occlude understanding of anomalous forms of government and democracy, doing 'fatal injury' to the principles underlying them. Section 3 sets out a number of dimensions of contemporary political globalization that have rendered the present problematic and given rise to critical reflection. Section 4 surveys the extent to which these changes can be understood in terms of the owlish language of representative government and democracy, in its unmodified and modified forms. Section 5 suggests how other aspects of global politics can be best characterized and analyzed only in comparison to extensive practices of government and democracy.

1. Two Types of Practices of Government and Democracy: Restrictive and Extensive

> The forms and the specific situations of the government of men [and women] by one another in any given society are multiple; they are superimposed, they cross, impose their own limits, sometimes cancel one another out, sometimes reinforce one another. It is certain that in contemporary societies the state is not simply one of the forms or specific situations of the exercise of power—even if it is the most important—but that in a certain way all other forms of power relation must refer to it. But this is not because they are derived from it; it is rather because power relations have come more and more under state control (although this state control has not taken the same form in pedagogical, judicial, economic, or family systems [of governance]). In referring here to the restricted sense of the word 'government', one could say that power relations have been progressively governmentalized, that is to say, elaborated, rationalised and centralised in the form of, or under the auspices of, state institutions.[15]

In this quotation from a short, synoptic text written two years before his death (1982), Foucault looks back over twenty-five years of studying the history of practices of government in which Europeans have constituted themselves as subjects engaged in co-ordinated interaction and summarizes two major findings of his research. First, 'the forms and the specific situations of the government of men [and women] by one another in any given society are multiple': that is, the 'practices of government' and the 'forms of subjects' of each practice come in a multiplicity of forms. The ways in which men and women are governed, govern themselves, and respond to and modify forms of governance in families, schools, churches, militaries, corporations, markets, bureaucracies, unions, voluntary organizations, municipalities, indigenous nations, provinces, states, federations, international regimes and organizations, the United Nations, and global systems criss-cross and overlap in complicated but nonetheless analyzable ways. Second, while the multiple practices of government have proliferated since the Reformation—from the consolidation of absolutist states in the early modern period to the formation of representative democratic nation-states in the modern period—they have tended to be elaborated, rationalized, and centralized, either directly in the form of, or indirectly under the control of, the institutions characteristic of representative nation-states. The process of progressive governmentalization, then, is the historical process by which the restrictive practices of government—representative government—have come to maturity and predominance, tending to bring most forms of government under their auspices both in practice and in theory (what might be called the owl of Minerva effect).

Using David Held's classification of historical forms of globalization into early modern (fourteenth–eighteenth century), modern (nineteenth–twentieth century) and contemporary (1945–twenty-first century), my thesis is that one feature of contemporary political globalization is a new trend towards the dispersion of practices of government and democracy.[16] This trend has two major aspects. The first and more familiar is the dispersion of standard practices of representative government so that they are no longer centralized in nation-states and a Westphalian system of sovereign nation-states. It is this aspect Held refers to when he speaks of 'political globalization', 'multilayered governance and the diffusion of political authority', and 'cosmopolitan democracy'.[17] The dispersion of political authority in these ways does not displace the long-term trend of governmentalization across all three periods, but coexists with it. It can be seen as a *modification* of governmentalization in the restrictive sense, since many of the characteristics of representative government remain, while others, such as centralization, sovereignty, and uniformity, are amended and qualified by the dispersion. For example, the global human rights regime qualifies rather than displaces the regime of sovereign nation-states and has itself developed out of the juridical practices of representative nation-states. The modification of sovereignty in the contemporary period has also enabled us to see that the actual history of representative governments has been much less centralized and uniform than the prevailing political theories presume.[18] Accordingly, this aspect of dispersion can be understood by modifying the mature and dominant traditions of representative government from within, as long as one takes a 'critical' (raven-like) rather than 'regulative' (owl-like) attitude to some characteristics of these traditions while holding the others firm. Call this the modified owlish or Hegelian aspect of contemporary political globalization (Section 4).

The second aspect of this trend is the dispersion of *extensive* practices of government within and across representative nation-states. This is not a separate trend, but one that criss-crosses with the former, often forming two aspects of the same institutions: to recollect, 'they are superimposed, they cross, impose their own limits, sometimes cancel one another out, sometimes reinforce one another'. Moreover, this global process of *nonrestrictive* governmentalization also can be seen as a *modification* of an early-modern and modern set of processes: namely, the persistence and proliferation of non-representative practices of government since the Reformation and the Dutch army reforms. Recall that the contributions to the understanding of modernity offered by Marx, Nietzsche, Weber, Merleau-Ponty, Heidegger, Dreyfus, Bourdieu, Giddens, Foucault, Wittgenstein, Connolly, and Taylor have elucidated a multiplicity of practices of government that shape our identities and modes of interaction in ways that cannot be understood in the predominant traditions of political thought because they are different from and obscured by the more prominent practices of representative government (or by the more prominent features of these practices).[19] Accordingly, the second aspect of contemporary political globalization can be elucidated by comparing it with this body of work, and by contrasting it with the great theories of representative governments and their prominent institutions. Call this the modified raven aspect of contemporary political globalization (Section 5).

Most of the dispersed practices of government are not democratic. Many are bureaucratic, authoritarian, or systemic. They co-ordinate the interaction of the participants predominantly 'behind their backs', without their say, through the market, bureaucracy, or the functional intermeshing of the unintended consequences of their actions. They are on the face of it 'systems' rather than 'practices' insofar as the participants are more 'patients' or 'subjects' than 'agents' or 'citizens'.[20] Furthermore, despite the evidence for an uneven and forward-and-backward trend to 'democratization' (formal representative democracy), the spread of institutions of representative democracy to many decolonizing peoples after 1960 and 1989; the development of supranational regimes such as NAFTA and the EU; the increase in power of transnational corporations; the weakening of representative governments and social democratic practices under neo-liberalism; and the underfunding and bypassing of the democratic institutions of the United Nations have been accompanied by the distribution of decision-making and implementation powers to non-democratic institutions at the local and global levels. These trends have led to the strengthening of 'indirect infrastructural' rule and the emergence of a system of 'nodes in a global network'. The result appears to be a net global democratic deficit.[21]

Nevertheless, the dispersion of practices of government has been met by popular struggles that seek to alter those practices. The second half of my thesis is that these struggles are of two types, corresponding to the two types of practices of government. The first are struggles of and for democracy in the restrictive, representative sense: to make non-representative practices of government democratic in the representative sense (or make practices of representative government more representative) or to bring them under the control of dispersed, representative democratic government institutions (local, regional, national, global, and the UN) in traditional ways. The second type are struggles of and for democracy in the extensive sense:

to bring extensive practices of government under some new form of democratic control by the participants or to link them up in novel ways with representative institutions. These struggles are 'democratic' in the extensive sense just insofar as the participants in any practice of government struggle to be heard and to negotiate to some extent the relations of power that govern their conduct. The forms of this second type of democratic struggle in non-representative practices are closely related to the specific and diverse character of the practices of government in which the struggles occur and so do not conform to the dominant models of representative democratic activity.

To illustrate with an example taken up in Section 5, citizens struggle to bring global forest companies under the democratic control of representatives in provincial and federal parliaments, as well as in the democratic institutions of their customers in Europe, Asia, and the UN. At the same time, local and global concerned citizens and NGOs confront these multinationals on specific logging sites, negotiating face-to-face and challenging their immediate forest practices, hiring practices, and ecological claims; the way gender is governed in their company; their responsibility to local and global communities and to value-added industries; their stance towards indigenous peoples and to their shareholders; and the like. The example also illustrates the point that these two distinct types of democratic activity are not separate but often occur in the same nexus of dispersed practices of government.

These two types of democratic struggle are internally related to the multiplication and dispersion of practices of government definitive of contemporary political globalization. The struggles over how employees are governed in dispersed practices, how they relate to the environment broadly defined, and the effects of their activities on local and global communities are internal to the logic of the organization and dispersion of these practices of government. They cannot be understood or analyzed without taking into account the *agonism* between the attempts to govern the participants in a specific way and the responses to that mode of governance. Just as the development of capitalism and representative democracy are not autonomous historical processes, but involve and are shaped by the extensive struggles of workers and consumers over the practices of production and the restrictive struggles of citizens and representatives over the practices of government, so too contemporary political globalization is not composed of processes over which humans are powerless. The processes are partly constituted by the two types of democratic contestation. Therefore, the dispersion of practices of government and the democratic struggles over them have to be understood together. Foucault summarizes the general methodological point in the following way:

> This leads to the study of what could be called 'practical systems' [practices of government and struggles of democratic freedom]. Here we are taking as a homogeneous domain of reference . . . what they [participants] do and how they do it. That is, the forms of rationality that organize their ways of doing things (this might be called the technological aspect) and the freedom with which they act within these practical

systems, reacting to what others do, modifying the rules of the game, up to a certain point (this might be called the strategic side of these practices).[22]

These two types of struggle can also be seen as modifications of early-modern and modern forms of struggle. The first forms are a continuation of struggles for representative democracy, suitably modified to fit the dispersed character of practices of government in political globalization. They are struggles for 'democratization' as it is standardly defined in the literature. These in turn can be understood in the suitably modified owlish terms of comparison with the dominant theories of representative democracy over the last two hundred years, as Held has shown.[23] The second forms are a continuation and modification of the more specific contests for democratic control in extensive practices of government since the early-modern period. These struggles are heterogeneous because they are tailored to the specifics of the practice they challenge and seek to modify. Light can be shed on the dawning non-representative democratic activities involved in contemporary globalization by means of raven-inspired analogies and disanalogies with accounts of modern non-representative democratic struggles.[24]

Although this two-path approach to political globalization from the perspectives of both the owl and the raven may seem obvious, Hegel's Preface forewarns us that it is seldom followed. First, processes of globalization are often analyzed systemically, as if they unfolded independently of contingent human action. Second, even when the exercise of democratic freedom *vis-à-vis* dispersed practices of government is taken into account, it tends to be construed in the categories of representative democracy and its traditions of interpretation, or as 'movements' that are on their way to becoming familiar forms of representative democratic politics (parties, interest groups, labour organizations, struggles for rights, and so on). This modified Hegelian mode of understanding is accurate for one aspect of contemporary political globalization, but it tends to overreach its limits and claims to comprehend both aspects of political globalization, thus doing 'fatal injury' to the other. When the limitation is noticed, the auspices of restrictive governmentalization remain so hegemonic that the response is either to ignore what the dominant representative theories fail to explain or to treat the extensive practices of government and democracy as not really democratic at all, and to treat their traditions of interpretation as illegitimate or incoherent (as the response to Foucault's research amply illustrates), as if there could be nothing new under the sun. To see how this limited understanding of our present has come to seem the bounds of political reason itself—as if this resting place were as far as we could fly—we need to review how the concepts and practices of government and democracy have come to be restricted to representative government and democracy.

2. Practices of Representative Government and Democracy

The prevailing practices of representative government and democracy in capitalist societies developed in the early-modern and modern periods. They include some combination of the following: institutions of formal legislators or representatives elected by citizens in a multi-party competition; the rule of law and public procedures; a system of administrative bureaucracies to execute the laws uniformly; a judicial system to interpret, review, and apply them; a distinction between public and private; a public sphere of free speech, assembly, and dissent; a military accountable to the representative institutions; and a constitution that lays down the division of powers among institutions and federal units and the political, civil, and social rights and duties of citizens and groups.[25]

In turn, representative government is seen as the system of government appropriate to a modern nation-state, and democracy as its most legitimate form. The process of governmentalization in the restrictive sense refers to the gradual colonization of early-modern absolutist states by the practices of representative government and democracy. The modern nation-state is defined in terms of a national democratic community of citizens and a geographical and bounded territory. The community of citizens has the capacity to elect and hold accountable their representatives and the representatives have the capacity to make law and policy to govern their constituents' major affairs within their geographically bounded territory. Each nation-state is in turn sovereign. The political world consists of a system of sovereign representative nation-states—the Westphalian system, named after the Treaty of Westphalia in 1648, even though several of its features did not come into widespread practice until the modern period.[26]

Prior to the eighteenth century, 'democracy' was used *extensively* as a term of abuse to refer to the 'people' assembling together and demanding a direct voice in the specific manner in which they were governed in any practice of government. Athenian democracy and early-modern local 'revolts' stood as exemplars of this disruptive form of popular activity. Most of the canonical political theorists of the early-modern period, as Bernard Manin reminds us, saw representative government as directly opposed to democracy. They condemned democracy as popular, contentious, headless, licentious, and ill-suited to large modern states. By the early nineteenth century, the struggles between defenders of democracy and representative government were over and 'democracy' as a term of approval came to be routinely predicated of 'representative' government as the modern form of government appropriate to large commercial societies, thereby concealing the earlier struggles.[27]

'Democracy', as Kant puts it in his distinctive manner—presenting his side of an argument as the universal and necessary truth—'in the proper sense of the term, is necessarily a *despotism*,' and every 'form of government that is not *representative* is properly speaking *without form*'.[28] The restriction of 'democracy' to 'representative democracy' and the view of representative democracy as the only legitimate form of government are perhaps best codified by Thomas Paine. In his influential *Rights of Man* he states:

> Simple democracy was society governing itself without the aid of secondary means. By ingrafting representation upon democracy, we arrive at a system of government capa-

ble of embracing and confederating all the various interests and every extent of territory and population.[29]

With Benjamin Constant's famous speech of 1819, 'The Liberty of the Ancients as Compared with that of the Moderns', the semantic restriction was completed. Not only is representative democracy presented as the sole legitimate form of government appropriate to the sociological conditions of large capitalist states, but any unsatisfied longing for other, extensive forms of democracy is depicted as either romantic nostalgia for Athenian democracy or utopian speculation, and said to lead in practice to the Terror.[30]

A complementary restriction of the term 'government' occurred during the processes of governmentalization of the early-modern and modern periods. In the sixteenth century, 'government' was widely used to characterize any relation of power and authority in which the conduct or action of one person or group was guided by the conduct or action of another, whether the relation involved caring for children, educating pupils, mastering servants and apprentices, governing wives, caring for souls or the poor, or governing subjects and representatives at parochial, royal, county, regional, or national practices of government. That is, government in the extensive sense refers to any form of guidance with respect to the conduct of others and the range of possible actions those others may take in response:

> Basically power is less a confrontation between two adversaries [the strategic model] or the linking of one to the other [the contractual model] than a question of government. This word must be allowed the very broad meaning which it had in the sixteenth century. 'Government' did not refer only to political structures or to the management of states; rather it designated the way in which the conduct of individuals or of groups might be directed: the government of children, of souls, of communities, of families, of the sick. It did not only cover the legitimately constituted forms of political or economic subjection, but also modes of action more or less considered and calculated, which were destined to act upon the possibilities of action of other people. To govern, in this sense, is to structure the possible field of action of others. [31]

Consequently, a central concern of political writers was to sort out the various practices of government; not to confuse them or to purposefully collapse them into one canonical form, as Locke typically reminds his readers in 1689:

> That the power of a Magistrate over a Subject, may be distinguished from that of a Father over his Children, a Master over his Servant, a Husband over his Wife, and a Lord over his Slave. All which distinct Powers happening sometimes altogether in the same Man, if he be considered under these different Relations, it may help us to distinguish these Powers from one another, and shew the difference betwixt a Ruler of a Commonwealth, a Father of a Family, and a Captain of a Galley.[32]

Although the equipment employed in practices of government, the purposes for which human activity is co-ordinated in diverse associations, and the modes of comportment or identities the governed and governors bear in the multiplicity of overlapping games of government are various, as Locke illustrates, what they have in common is that the conduct of the governed is not determined but 'free'. As Foucault puts it, by 'this we mean individual or collective subjects who are faced with a field of possibilities in which several ways of behaving, several reactions and diverse comportments may be realized'.[33] The range of possible action, between 'domination' at one extreme (where movement is determined) and direct 'confrontation' between adversaries at the other (where a relation of governance gives way to a relation of revolt), is what Foucault referred to earlier as the strategic 'freedom' with which participants act within any practice of government. This freedom is 'democracy' in the extensive sense: the exercise of the abilities of the governed to negotiate the way their conduct is guided.

Throughout the modern period, 'government' gradually came to be restricted to the formal institutions of representative government in the so-called 'public' sector, and the broader use of 'government' fell into disuse. The modern disciplines of political science and political philosophy, with their restrictive focus on the public institutions of representative government and democracy, augmented this trend. Moreover, as Weber and Foucault have shown, the range of democratic free play in the multiplicity of practices of government came to be restricted as forms of control and reflexive monitoring of thought and behaviour were introduced to train, co-ordinate, and predict activity in detail.[34] These techniques of control changed the character of practices of government, as Hubert Dreyfus explains:

> Once machine tools took over . . . the dominant Western style changed from governing to controlling. No one governs a car. People control their cars, or they are in trouble. People control electric saws, power plants, chemical reactions, and so on. Rather than govern their sexual desires, people now control birth and the transmission of disease. Controlling manifests a different stance towards things and people and amounts to a different way of seeing them. It is a different style. We can see this in the difference between managers who try to govern their employees by having them join in the process of determining how goals will be met, and those who try to control them by simply setting work schedules and output requirements.[35]

Practices of control became integrated into larger systems of markets and bureaucracies. For reasons of efficiency and time constraints, attempts to negotiate their organization were seen to be inappropriate, not only in the form of unsuccessful efforts at large-scale planning in socialist countries but even in the more moderate form of social democracy and welfare liberalism, at least among neo-liberals. Finally, when moderns challenged the ways their conduct was regulated in extensive practices, they too expressed their demands in the language of control, speaking of participants' 'self-management' and 'self-control' more than 'self-government' and 'democracy'. To paraphrase Hegel, with this final semantic shift the process of formation of government and democracy exclusively as *representative* government and democracy has been completed.

The singular and contingent historical assemblage of modern representative government and democracy is the political world painted by the owl of Minerva in grey in grey as universal and necessary from the *Philosophy of Right* to the latest modern political theory. It is now being challenged and modified in the course of contemporary political globalization in two distinct ways.

3. Contemporary Political Globalization and Global Governance

Following Held, globalization can be thought of as

> a process (or set of processes) which embodies a transformation in the spatial organization of social relations and transactions—assessed in terms of their extensity, intensity, velocity and impact—generating transcontinental or interregional flows and networks of activity, interaction, and the exercise of power. . . . [F]lows refer to the movement of physical artefacts, people, symbols, tokens and information across space and time, while networks refer to regularized or patterned interactions between independent agents, nodes of activity, or sites of power.[36]

This means, first, that globalization is not a singular condition or a process of global integration but a cluster of uneven, hierarchical, and unpredictable processes of interregional networks and systems of interaction and exchange. Second, global interconnectedness weaves networks of relations between communities, states, international institutions, NGOs, and multinational corporations. The networks form processes of 'structuration'—the product of both individual and group actions and the cumulative interactions among agencies and institutions. Third, globalization occurs across all domains of social life. Fourth, global processes deterritorialize and reterritorialize socio-economic and political space so that it is no longer co-terminous with established legal and territorial boundaries. The twentieth century has experienced a shift from the direct, territorial forms of control characteristic of the long age of European and American imperialism to new forms of non-territorial imperialism based on control of peoples and markets by indirect, infrastructural control. Fifth, the organization and reach of power is expanded so the concentrated sites and exercise of power are increasingly at a distance from the subjects and locales that experience the consequences. The major domains of social life enmeshed in contemporary globalization are politics; organized violence; global trade and markets; global finance; corporations and global production networks; the movement of peoples, cultures, and nations; and the environment.[37]

Contemporary globalization is altering modern representative politics by the globalization of politics, or, as Held terms it, 'global politics'. These are forms of politics that do not fit neatly into the modern categories of either national or international politics:

> Global politics is a term which usefully captures the stretching of political relations across space and time; the extension of political power and political activity across the boundaries of the modern nation-state. Political decisions and actions in one part of the world can rapidly acquire worldwide ramifications. . . . [S]ites of political action and/or decision making can become linked through rapid communications into complex networks of decision-making and interaction. [Furthermore] 'action at a distance' permeates with greater intensity the social conditions and cognitive worlds of specific places or policy communities. . . . [D]evelopments at the global level frequently acquire almost instantaneous local consequences and vice versa.[38]

Global politics disaggregates the central features of modern representative government: that the national representative government governs the affairs of a territorially bounded community of fate and that this community holds its representatives accountable for the power exercised over them. Peoples are dispersed in overlapping communities of fate, and political power is shared, dispersed, contested, and battered by a range of forces and agencies.

Global politics has given rise to 'global governance'. Global governance does not consist in the institutions of modern representative governments or the international system of nation-states but is nonetheless a modification and expansion of these, with an aim to governing global politics. The United Nations, the World Trade Organization, non-governmental organizations, the political power of multinational corporations, social movements, governments (local, regional, federal, and supranational), international regimes, the global human rights regime, and global legal regimes—all are well-known examples of the exercise of global governance. They embody the shift from the 'territorially based politics' of the modern era to the 'emerging era of global politics and multilayered global and regional governance'.[39] In several respects, global politics and global governance can be compared to the messy overlapping of practices of government in the late-medieval period prior to the early-modern consolidation of centralized European states.

4. Unmodified and Modified Representative Practices of Government and Democracy

I will now sketch how the problematization of the present by global politics can be understood in the light of the two approaches laid out in Sections 1 and 2: unmodified and modified representative government and democracy, and unmodified and modified extensive government and democracy. First, as Held stresses, modern representative government and democracy persist into the contemporary era despite their decentring by global politics and the uneven emergence of multilayered global governance. The clichés of the 'end of sovereignty' and the impotence of representative national government in an era of globalization, fashionable among many neo-liberals and postmoderns, underestimate the resilience of practices of modern politics.[40]

For example, it is true that countries such as Canada lost considerable control over macroeconomic policy because they became publicly indebted to and dependent on global capital during the period of welfare liberalism. Nonetheless, the irony of neo-liberal deficit and debt reduction is that North Atlantic countries are now less dependent on global capital and thus more able to exercise the democratic powers over economic policy that neo-liberals and hyper-globalizers claim they no longer hold. There is little in global economic processes today to impede the development of, say, job creation policies. Such policies are impeded only by traditional constraints on representative will formation, and the rise of social democratic governments in Europe has shown that these can be overcome.[41]

Second, processes of globalization in the various domains affect different regions, sectors, and peoples differently. The increased ability of capital to move in response to economic policy, for example, holds only for certain areas of the economy. It is difficult to see how services, agriculture, education, fisheries, tourism, health care, retirement industries, and the like can move. Moreover, these uneven processes do not determine public policy. They are, or can be, mediated through representative democratic discussion and debate, and this explains many of the differences in policy across OECD countries. Even the uncontrolled flow of global financial capital could be governed by traditional co-ordination of nation states to, for instance, implement a Tobin tax.

Moreover, as Castells in particular underscores, cultural and migratory processes of globalization involve the multiplication of identities and loyalties, and these engender demands for policies of multiculturalism and multinationalism throughout the multilayered governments. It 'appears that our [contemporary] societies are constituted by the interaction between the "net" and the "self", between the network society and the power of identity'.[42] Nevertheless, the globalization of individual and collective identities has not diminished loyalty to the (multicultural and multinational) representative nation-state except in cases of outright secession (which are also cases of unmodified modern politics). In Canada, 80 per cent of Quebecers continue to value and care about their Canadian identity alongside their Quebec identity. The proliferation of supranational political associations such as the European Union and the North American Free Trade Agreement has not generated supranational political 'communities of fate' that replace or even seriously challenge the traditional national communities within. In most cases, citizens see whatever representation they have in these larger associations as the representation of their national community. Canadians do not see themselves as part of a larger North American 'community of fate', but rather as members of the federal community of Canada, which in turn is part of this larger non-communal association.[43]

The widespread dissatisfaction with and cynicism towards the potency of representative government do not seem to be the effects of globalization. Rather, they appear to be caused by the traditional faults in the practices of modern representative government themselves. The high cost of running for office; the failure to represent women adequately and to represent the growing cultural diversity of the electorate; the inequities of the first-past-the-post system of elections; the lack of proportional representation and the representation of territorial (riding) identity to the exclusion of all other identities; the impotence of backbenchers and parliamentary committees as decision-making power becomes concentrated in tiny elites; the abuse of party discipline and Orders-in-Council; and the absence of open democratic deliberation in parliaments are faults that have been well documented by countless studies and royal commissions. Such faults render representative government unresponsive to democratic will-formation and hence open to manipulation by the elites, who serve to gain by disempowering representative institutions under the rhetoric of globalization as a process that does not allow for democratic negotiation. Whether modern representative governments remain effective and retain the allegiance of their citizens will depend more on the successes of traditional reform movements in correcting these imperfections than on contemporary globalization.

If we turn to the institutions of global governance that are emerging in response to global politics, many of them can be seen either as modified versions of the practices of modern representative government (global human and environmental rights movements, the EU, and the proposed peoples' chamber of the UN) or as non-democratic concentrations of power that are sites of struggle for democratization in the representative sense (multinational corporations and NGOs). These are instances of the aspect of contemporary political globalization described in Section 1 as 'the dispersion of standard practices of representative government so that they are no longer centralized in nation-states and a Westphalian system of sovereign nation-states'. Held's global project of cosmopolitan democracy is perhaps the best-known and most promising example of this modified owlish orientation towards contemporary political globalization. In addition, he mentions two other approaches that are extensions and modifications of the traditions of interpretation of modern politics: 'liberal internationalism' and 'radical republicanism'.[44]

The projection of three traditions of modern political thought onto global politics and governance does bring to light aspects of them and the struggles to democratise them. Nevertheless, it is important not to treat these traditions as if they constituted a *comprehensive* way of understanding global politics, for this would be to misunderstand and do fatal injury to other forms of global governance and democratic activity. There are two distinct types of limitation in these three schools of modern political thought.

The first limitation is that they do not modify their own traditions enough in reflecting on global representative politics. They tend to project contingent features of modern representative government and democracy onto contemporary global politics and so misunderstand what is new in global practices of representative government. Recall that two equal principles underlie all the mature practices of modern representative government and democracy and give them their legitimacy: representative popular sovereignty and the rule of law. The tension distinctive of modern politics is the permanent difficulty of preserving the equality of these two principles: of ensuring that the people rule themselves through their representatives and so subject themselves to laws of their own authorship, and, at the same time, that these practices of representative democracy are carried out in accord with the rule of law.[45] As a result, there is always a reciprocal, back-and-forth movement between a provisional rule of law and a continuous process of its democratic discussion and reform.

Cosmopolitan democracy does not treat both principles equally, but gives priority to the rule of law. It 'attempts to specify the principles and the institutional arrangements for making accountable those sites and forms of power which presently operate beyond the scope of democratic control'.[46] Cosmopolitan theorists work out, by a process of solitary reflection on the European history of representative government and democracy, and then project globally—prior to any exercise of representative popular sovereignty in fora of democratic dialogue—a cosmopolitan public law that lays down the preconditions of global practices of democracy. This overrides the equality of the principle of representative popular sovereignty, which requires that any cosmopolitan public law be democratically discussed and agreed to by those subject to it, or their representatives, if it is to be legitimate.[47]

If the two principles are treated equally, then the extension of the rule of law and representative democracy to global politics will necessarily involve democratic discussion of the forms that each principle should take in the multiplicity of practices of governance, not once and for all, but over all time. In virtue of cultural diversity, a host of contextual factors, and the overlapping of communities and governments and identities, the legitimate processes of contemporary global constitutionalism and democratization are not predictable and cannot be specified or comprehended beforehand. There is always a range of possible free actions available to the participants. Thus, even in the attempts to understand political globalization in the modified terms of representative government and democracy, only the underlying principles, and not the more specific institutional forms these principles have taken in the early-modern and modern periods in the West, should be projected onto global politics if what is really going on is to be understood.[48]

The second limitation of the modified owlish approach is that it does not help us to understand the second aspect of contemporary political globalization described in Section 1: the dispersion of extensive practices of government within and across representative nation-states. This is the subject of the following section.

5. Unmodified and Modified Extensive Practices of Government and Democracy

Gathering together the features introduced in Sections 1 and 2, any co-ordinated form of human interaction is a practice of government because it involves reciprocal, multiple, and overlapping relations of power and authority in which the actions of some agents guide the actions of others. A relation of governance does not act directly on the agents, unmediated by their own thought and action (as a relation of force or violence does), but on their action. As a consequence, those over whom power is exercised are recognized and guided to the very end as agents who are free, that is, agents for whom a whole field of possible actions is available in the course of being guided,

At the two limits of this field of freedom in relations of governance are (1) sedimented structures of domination, in which freedom is reduced to a minimum by force or habituation (as in a prison system), and (2) the background possibility of confronting the relation of governance as a whole and seeking to overthrow it (as in a revolution). No one in a practice of government stands outside relations of governance: the mode of conduct by which one agent guides another is itself guided by others. For instance, the professor who guides a pupil in the practice of education is herself a professor in virtue of being educated by others and the ways in which she acted freely in those relationships, of interacting with the freedom of her pupils, and so on, across the many relational identities the participants bear.

Any practice of government, then, involves three complex elements: techniques of government, strategies of freedom, and modes of conduct. 'Government' in the extensive sense refers primarily to the first or technological side. It comprises, as Mitchell Dean outlines,

> any more or less calculated and rational activity, undertaken by a multiplicity of authorities and agencies, employing a variety of techniques and forms of knowledge, that seeks to shape conduct by working through our desires, aspirations, interests and beliefs, for definite but shifting ends and has a diverse set of relatively unpredictable consequences, effects and outcomes. An analysis of government, then, is concerned with the means of calculation, both quantitative and qualitative, the type of governing authority or agency, the forms of knowledge, technique and other means employed, the entity to be governed and how it is conceived, the ends sought and with the outcomes and consequences.[49]

The second element, strategies of freedom, or 'democracy' in the extensive sense, refers to the ways in which the participants question, negotiate, and modify *en passant* the specific techniques of government: that is, the forms of knowledge; systems of communication; organization of roles and tasks; and modes of production, distribution, and consumption of goods and services and their effects. The third element, modes of conduct, comprises the co-ordinated interaction that results from the interplay of the first two elements: what the participants do and the way they do it.[50]

Modern theorists of extensive practices have brought to light whole areas of government and democratic freedom in modern societies that the dominant traditions have bypassed. These practices of government and democracy take place outside the public boundaries of representative government and democracy, either in the private realm or beneath the features of representative practices that standardly figure in modern political theories. Marx's specific analysis of struggles over the length and organization of the working day in nineteenth-century British factories is a classic example of the former.[51] This type of struggle has commonly been understood in two generalized ways in the modern period: as struggles for socialism (direct confrontations over the relations of production by means of revolution) or struggles for social democracy (labour–management negotiations over unionization and working conditions, and the entrenchment of social and economic rights by means of strikes and the formation of social democratic parties). The social democratic understanding of such struggles has become predominant, especially with the decline of socialism after 1989 and the rise of social democratic parties in the 1990s. As a result, the rise of new social movements in the contemporary period, in response to both modern and global politics, has tended to be conceptualized and analyzed in terms of social democratic struggles and their tradition of interpretation.[52] While this unmodified form of general analysis does capture aspects of contemporary democratic struggles over extensive practices of government, it tends to construe them as all of one kind, as a social democratic variation on familiar struggles for representative government and democracy (unmodified or modified), and so overlooks and misunderstands their three distinctive features.

First, the terms 'conduct' and 'comportment' are meant to draw attention to a broad range of human action and interaction. Extensive democratic struggles are waged not only over the explicit rules, norms, exchange of public reasons, or deliberate means of gaining consent in a practice of government. At least as often they are waged over the pre-reflective yet non-mechanical modes of comportment—thought and action—that constitute the forms of subjectivity (identities and roles) of the participants in their circumspective coping, which make up the vast majority of the co-ordinated interaction of any practice of government, from a family to a multinational.[53] Similarly, the term 'techniques of government' refers just as much to the background 'processes of subjectivization' and infrastructural governance at a distance by which participants acquire the dispositions or abilities manifested in their specific modes of conduct. By focusing on abstract principles and deliberative reasoning, modern theories of representative government overlook these processes, which take place not only in market and bureaucratic practices, but also in public practices, beneath the threshold of the formal features of law and democracy. Here conduct is often governed by immanent norms of efficient interaction and reflexive monitoring rather than laws and representatives. For example, the pre-reflective orientation to nature, each other, and themselves that the participants are guided to acquire through participation is often one of 'resources to be enhanced, transformed and ordered simply for the sake of greater and greater efficiency', yet all this occurs beyond the reach of modern representative government and democracy.[54]

An illustration of this phenomenon is the widespread politics of identity and struggles over recognition. Struggles over recognition began in the modern period but they have become intensified and dispersed in the contemporary period through the globalization of cultures and migration.[55] These struggles concern legal, political, and constitutional recognition, either in institutions of representative governments or modified institutions of multilayered global governance. Notwithstanding, they are also struggles over racist, heterosexist, xenophobic, and other non-recognizing and mis-recognizing modes of comportment that hold enormous structures of social and economic inequality in place despite the formal workings of law and democracy. Such pre-reflective modes of interactive conduct can continue even after formal recognition of cultural, ethnic, gender, and other differences is achieved through group rights, federal structures, equity policies, and non-discrimination laws. The effective strategies of democratic freedom in such cases are counter-practices such as diversity training in the context of those practices of government in which racist and sexist conduct is first learned and internalized. Here, as David Owen argues, the specific 'politics of voice' of the participants, rather than the abstract politics of principles, is indispensable to calling into question, addressing, and altering unjust practices of social co-operation.[56]

Unless such practical activity is undertaken, the recourse to the remedies of representative government and democracy often further entrenches structures of domination as they regulate and alter them. As Taiaiake Alfred argues, a particularly tragic example is the struggle of indigenous peoples in Canada to free themselves by legal, political, and constitutional means from the practice of internal colonization. Instead of freeing indigenous peoples from this long-standing structure, the struggle for recognition has tended to reproduce it in an altered and ameliorated form without effectively challenging, negotiating, and modifying the deeply sedimented forms of colonial conduct on the part of both non-indigenous and indigenous peoples, which in fact sustain it. If indigenous peoples are to foster and manifest an indigenous way of being in the world, then formal self-government in itself is not enough: it must be accompanied by the appropriate strategy of freedom. It must also be the concrete counter-practice of 'self-conscious traditionalism' to modify and pass beyond the colonial modes of conduct in both representative and extensive practices of government.[57]

The second distinctive feature of extended practices of government and democracy consists in the specific strategies of democratic freedom—of questioning, negotiating, and modifying relations of governance. These disputation strategies take a multitude of forms. Some aim to move the dispute to courts and parliaments, in institutions of either modern or global governance, and others conform to the model of labour-management negotiations. However, as practices of government are dispersed in processes of political globalization and neo-liberal policies of downsizing and contracting-out, many disputes do not conform to these prototypes and are not brought under the control of representative governments in familiar ways.[58] Rather, they are taken up and resolved on site, in a manner that conforms to the specific practice in question. An entire field of activity devoted to resolving all these more or less autonomous disputes has come into being in the contemporary era and is now called 'dispute resolution'. In addition, a new discipline has arisen to study disputes and their resolutions and to educate specialists to facilitate, mediate, and arbitrate, or to teach those engaged in the negotiations to resolve it themselves. The rapidly expanding practices of dispute resolution and their accompanying academic discipline are separate from the practices of representative government and their accompanying disciplines of political science and political theory.

These activities of disputation and resolution are new forms of democracy in conditions of political globalization. They are unique in the following respects. First, the disputation concerns a practice-specific relation of governance. Consequently, the way the existing relation is called into question; the forms of participation and argumentation involved in negotiation and resolution; and the amendment agreed upon, implemented, and monitored are all grounded in and tied to the conditions of intelligibility of the practice of government in dispute. That is, the agents involved are embedded in the world of the relations of power and authority of the practice; in presenting their arguments, they exercise and appeal to the forms of practical reason and expertise of the very practice about which they speak; their very identities as participants in the practice are at risk; and the resolution is always defeasible (open to future challenge). In all four respects, Dreyfus points out, democratic disputation and resolution in extensive practices of government contrasts with the models of democratic deliberation in the public sphere in modern political theory. In these models, negotiation is supposed to be free of power, based on public reasons and abstract principles—disengaged argumentation over a generalizable norm—and resolved by an impartial consensus. The result is a 'disengaged discussion' of 'an array of principles' divorced from practice; whereas actual learning and resolution emerge from 'rootedness in particular problems' and 'the expertise acquired by risking action from a particular perspective and learning from one's successes and failures' in the context of 'power, partisanship and local issues.'[59]

The third and final distinctive feature of extensive practices of government and democracy is their location as nodes enmeshed in local and global networks. As we have seen in Section 3, contemporary practices of government are linked through the global politics of communications and information to complex networks:

> This is the new social structure of the Information Age, which I [Castells] call *the network society* because it is made up of networks of production, power, and experience, which construct a culture of virtuality in the global flows that transcend time and space. . . . The network society, as any other social structure, is not absent of contradictions, social conflicts, and challenges from alternative forms of social organization. But these challenges are induced by the characteristics of the network society, and thus, they are sharply distinct from those of the industrial era. The understanding of our world requires the simultaneous analysis of the network society, and of its conflictive challenges. [60]

Taking up this challenge for Canada, Steven Rosell argues that the 'methods of organizing and governing that were developed for a world of clearer boundaries and more limited flows of information' in the modern period are being transformed by the emergence of networks and the resulting 'restructuring of corporate and public bureaucracies; shifting boundaries between different sectors of society and levels of government; a growing interest in direct participation in decision-making; and new challenges to the legitimacy of many traditional institutions'.[61]

Just as extensive practices of government exist in global networks, so too do the strategies of democratic freedom that challenge them. The conduct of everyone in a network is affected, directly or indirectly, by the nodal practice of government—from the suppliers of capital, goods, services, and information, to the consumers and all those affected by the practice, its products, and 'externalities', who are thus, directly or indirectly, 'participants' in that practice. The ability to organize a disputation strategy across this governing network is essential to challenging the infrastructural practices of government at a distance that operate along the technological side of the network. Consequently, the organization of strategies of freedom in practices of government enmeshed in contemporary global networks is different from modern forms of representative and extensive democratic organizations. These three distinctive features of democratic freedom in contemporary political globalization—conduct, dispute resolution, and networking—can be illustrated by a brief sketch drawn from environmental politics.[62]

First, an environmental dispute often begins when a specific practice of co-ordinated interaction is called into question by some of the participants. What they challenge is the way in which their activity is organized to act on the environment, either directly, in production, distribution, and consumption, or indirectly, in the ways services obliquely affect the environment. For example, a multinational forestry company is confronted on one of its sites by employees or people affected by its practices. Their argument is that the way their action is governed leads them to relate to and act on the environment in a destructive manner, and thus needs to be changed. The initial response to such a challenge is to deny that the way private-sector corporations are organized to act on the environment is a legitimate topic of discussion. The time and efficiency constraints of the global market and the autonomous development of technology do not allow for a range of possible relations to the environment. These global processes determine the relation beyond negotiation. The practices of the company can be limited from the outside by the institutions of modern representative governments and international agreements, but not modified by the participants from the inside. To counter this response, the activists have to present plausible arguments that the challenge is itself a legitimate (extensive) democratic action, that the present relation to the environment is really destructive and could be otherwise, that local communities would not be adversely affected by the change, and that a host of other legitimate concerns must be considered. This involves networking with a wide range of persons: those with specific expertise in the company, local communities affected, academic communities, and global communities of concerned specialists. Moreover, they need to organize another local and global network of people capable of forcing the company to the negotiating table and keeping it there, from workers who want a clean environment for their children to consumers in distant countries who want environmentally benign products and investment portfolios.

The on-site negotiations are similarly complex and global, involving a range of stakeholders with a wide variety of concerns and modes of argumentation: non-unionized and unionized workers, the local indigenous peoples with their land claims, the local community, tourist industries, logging companies and their suppliers and investors, environmental activists, various academic specialists, local and national political representatives, and experts in dispute resolution and implementation. The negotiations are in turn connected almost instantaneously to other similar negotiations across the globe at other sites and in various legal and political institutions. These negotiations are not free of power or disengaged. They are complex, strategic-communicative dialogues involving a wide range of knowledge and forms of argumentation, enmeshed in the very relations of power and identity formation that are at issue, and are themselves subject to constraints of time, knowledge, partiality, inequality, and conflicting interests.[63]

One of the aims of such negotiations is to bring the forest practice under the control of representative institutions and international laws.[64] This strategy is necessary and laudable in the long term, but it is insufficient. The general laws and regulations do not change the environmentally destructive form of conduct and identity formation from the inside; only the participants themselves, engaging in the democratic activity of disputing and modifying their modes of conduct, can do this. Environmental legislation can be watered down in distant representative institutions and manipulated, ignored, and rolled back in practice by powerful economic interests. Finally, the contemporary trend towards global regulation of the environment appears to be ineffective and corresponds to the disempowerment of local participants and their practices of democratic disputation and monitoring of the implementation of specific resolutions.[65] For such strategies of freedom to be effective, therefore, the participants must not only develop unique forms of networking for the phases of initiation, negotiation, and resolution of disputes. They must also develop permanent networks to bind the particular company and infrastructural agents to the implementation and review process required of any resolution.

In conclusion, this chapter is a defeasible sketch of some forms of democracy in the context of contemporary globalization. Much of it will have to be revised as humans exercise their strategies of freedom in these circumstances over the twenty-first century. Other Canadian political philosophers 'will fly farther'. Still, it has been possible to go some distance in adumbrating several new and puzzling features of democratic practices that the owl and raven have in store for the twenty-first century. In deference to Hegel, the principle underlying them remains unclear, yet it appears to be an unsatisfied longing for a certain kind of democratic freedom of self-government. It seems to be a longing for concrete freedom within the diverse practices of government in which we find ourselves; that is, a freedom to question and modify them *en passant*. From my limited vantage point, the freedom of modern politics, defined in relation to representative popular sovereignty and the rule of law, appears in retrospect to be one particular form that this concrete democratic freedom of self-government can take, rather than the comprehensive understanding of human freedom that it has been assumed to represent throughout the modern period. If freedom is indeed an always unsatisfied longing, then we can reasonably expect democracy to be widely practised in more diverse forms in the contemporary period.

If there is to be a distinctive Canadian political philosophy in the twenty-first century, as there was in the twentieth, it may well be a philosophy in motion, a philosophy that plays a mediating role between citizens' cautious experiments with modifying our forms of conduct in practice and academics' constructive criticism of forms of knowledge and expertise. This would be a philosophy that combines the wisdom of the owl, who seeks to understand who we are and where we have come from, with the transformative ways of the raven, who is endlessly curious about where we are heading. And, if such political philosophers are exceptionally fortunate, they too may fly as far as those great Canadian teachers C.B. Macpherson and Charles Taylor.

Notes

I wish to thank David Laycock and David Owen for helpful comments on drafts of this chapter.

1. G.W.F. Hegel, *Philosophy of Right*, trans. T.M. Knox (Oxford: Clarendon Press, 1967), 13.
2. Ibid., 12–13.
3. Ibid., 10.
4. Ibid.
5. Ibid.
6. Ibid. Hegel argues that despite this lack of philosophical comprehension, Plato's peculiar 'genius' somehow enabled him to present a political theory that nevertheless 'turned' on the revolutionary principle that Socrates embodied (ibid., 10). This back-handed compliment seems to be a desperate attempt by Hegel to save his account of philosophical understanding. A simpler explanation is that there is another mode of philosophical understanding of the present, outlined later, which Plato exhibited in the to-and-fro movement of his dialogues.
7. Ibid., 11.
8. Ibid., 10, 11.
9. Michel Foucault, 'What is Enlightenment?', in *Michel Foucault: Ethics, Subjectivity and Truth*, ed. P. Rabinow (New York: New Press, 1994), 303–20, 305.
10. Although I draw on the later work of Foucault in the following paragraph to characterize this historical approach of reciprocal elucidation, it is shared in different ways by Ludwig Wittgenstein, *Philosophical Investigations*, trans. G.E.M. Anscombe (Oxford: Basil Blackwell, 1988), sect. 122, 130–3; Charles Taylor, 'Comparison, History, Truth', in *Philosophical Arguments* (Cambridge, Mass.: Harvard University Press, 1995), 146–65; William E. Connolly, *Why I Am Not a Secularist* (Minneapolis: University of Minnesota Press, 1999); and Quentin Skinner, *Liberty Before Liberalism* (Cambridge: Cambridge University Press, 1998). This school of political philosophy is examined in David Owen, 'Orientation and Enlightenment', in *Foucault Contra Habermas*, ed. Samantha Ashenden and David Owen (London: Sage, 1999), 21–44, and in Tully, 'To Think and Act Differently: Foucault's Four Reciprocal Objections to Habermas', ibid., 99–140.
11. Michel Foucault, 'Modifications', in *The Use of Pleasure*, trans. R. Hurley (New York: Pantheon Books, 1985), 3–13. For the importance of this short text, see Arpad

Szakolczai, *Max Weber and Michel Foucault: Parallel Life-works* (London: Routledge, 1998), 53–60.

12. Foucault, 'What is Enlightenment?', 315, 316, 319.
13. Bill Reid and Robert Bringhurst, *The Raven Steals the Light* (Vancouver: Douglas and MacIntyre, 1989).
14. Friedrich Nietzsche, *Daybreak*, trans. R.J. Hollingdale (Cambridge: Cambridge University Press, 1982), sect. 575, 228.
15. Foucault, 'The Subject and Power', in *Michel Foucault: Beyond Structuralism and Hermeneutics*, ed. Hubert Dreyfus and Paul Rabinow (Chicago: University of Chicago Press, 1982), 208–26, 224.
16. David Held, Anthony McGrew, David Goldblatt, and Jonathan Perraton, *Global Transformations* (Cambridge: Polity Press, 1999), 78–81. I am deeply indebted to the great work of David Held and his fellow researchers on historical forms of globalization and the trends towards cosmopolitan democracy.
17. Held et al., *Global Transformations*, 32–86. For 'cosmopolitan democracy', see David Held, *Democracy and the Global Order* (Stanford: Stanford University Press, 1995), and Daniele Archibugi, David Held, and Martin Kohler, eds, *Re-imagining Political Community* (Cambridge: Polity Press, 1998).
18. See Michael Keating, 'So Many Nations, So Few States', in *Struggles for Recognition in Multinational Societies: The Search for Justice and Stability in Belgium, Canada, Spain, the United Kingdom and the European Union*, ed. Alain-G. Gagnon and J. Tully (Cambridge: Cambridge University Press, 2000), chap. 1.
19. For an introduction to these philosophers of practices see Theodore R. Schatzki, *Social Practices: A Wittgensteinian Approach to Human Activity and the Social* (Cambridge: Cambridge University Press, 1996).
20. For Habermas's useful distinction between a practice and a system, or, rather, the practical and systemic *aspects* of an organized form of human co-operation, see Schatzki, *Social Practices*, 89–90.
21. David Potter, David Goldblatt, Margaret Kiloh, Paul Lewis, eds, *Democratization* (Cambridge: Polity Press, 1997). See Held et al., *Global Transformations*, 46–9, and 39–45, for a brief summary of the shift from direct imperial to indirect 'infrastructural' rule in the twentieth century. For the metaphor of 'nodes [of mostly non-democratic power and authority] in a global network', rather than representative nation-states in an international system, see Manuel Castells, *The Information Age: Economy, Society and Culture*, 4 vols. (Oxford: Basil Blackwell, 1998), especially vol. 3, *End of Millennium*, 335–60.
22. Foucault, 'What is Enlightenment?', 303–20, 317.
23. Held's work on 'cosmopolitan democracy' is the best example of this extension and modification of traditional representative democratic theory to understand and evaluate the first type of democratic struggles and the way in which they may be shaping dispersed practices of representative government. For a complementary analysis, see Andrew Linklater, *The Transformation of Political Community* (Cambridge: Polity Press, 1998).
24. Characteristics of non-representative democratic struggles are discussed by Foucault in 'The Subject and Power', 211–12, and 'What is Critique?' in *What is Enlightenment?* ed. James Schmidt (Berkeley: University of California Press, 1996), 382–99.

25. See David Held, *Models of Democracy*, 2nd ed. (Cambridge: Polity Press, 1996).
26. Held et al., *Global Transformations*, 35–9, 78–80. The development of the system of sovereign states and representative governments is treated in more historical detail in *Democracy and the Global Order.*
27. Bernard Manin, *The Principles of Representative Government* (Cambridge: Cambridge University Press, 1997).
28. Immanuel Kant, 'Perpetual Peace', in *Perpetual Peace and Other Essays* (Indianapolis: Hackett Publishing Co., 1983), 107–44, 113–14.
29. Thomas Paine, *Rights of Man* (Indianapolis: Hackett Publishing Co., 1992), 142. Compare Held, *Democracy and the Global Order*, 119.
30. Benjamin Constant, 'The Liberty of the Ancients as Compared to that of the Moderns', in *Political Writings*, ed. Biancamaria Fontana (Cambridge: Cambridge University Press, 1988), 308–28.
31. Foucault, 'The Subject and Power', 221.
32. John Locke, *Two Treatises of Government*, ed. Peter Laslett (Cambridge: Cambridge University Press, 1970), sect. 2, 286.
33. Foucault, 'The Subject and Power', 221.
34. The classic studies are Foucault, *Discipline and Punish*, trans. Alan Sheridan (New York: Pantheon Books, 1977), and Charles Taylor, *Sources of the Self* (Cambridge, Mass.: Harvard University Press, 1989), especially 159–76.
35. Hubert Dreyfus, Charles Spinosa, and Fernando Flores, *Disclosing New Worlds* (Cambridge: MIT Press, 1997), 26.
36. Held et al., *Global Transformations*, 16.
37. Ibid., 27–8, 430–1. A chapter is devoted to each of the domains of globalization. I have also drawn on the work of Ankie Hoogvelt, *Globalisation and the Postcolonial World* (London: Macmillan, 1997), and Gilbert Rist, *The History of Development* (London: Zed, 1997).
38. Held et al., *Global Transformations*, 49–50. Held's analysis draws on the groundbreaking work of R.B.J. Walker, *Inside/outside: International Relations as Political Theory* (Cambridge: Cambridge University Press, 1993).
39. Held et al., *Global Transformations*, 49–77, 80–1, 442–4. See also the Report of the Commission on Global Governance, in *Our Global Neighbourhood* (Oxford: Oxford University Press, 1995); Held, 'Democracy and Globalization', in *Re-imagining Political Community*, 11–27; and James Rosenau, 'Governance and Democracy in a Globalizing World', in *Re-imagining Political Community*, 28–57.
40. Held et al., *Global Transformations*, 444.
41. For these examples, see Will Kymlicka, 'Citizenship in an Era of Globalization: Commentary on Held', in *Democracy's Edges*, ed. Ian Shapiro and Casiano Hacker-Cordon (Cambridge: Cambridge University Press, 2000), 112–26.
42. Castells, *End of Millennium*, 352.
43. For Canadian and European examples, see Gagnon and Tully, eds, *Struggles for Recognition in Multinational Societies.*
44. Held et al., *Global Transformations*, 448.
45. These two equal principles are articulated and discussed by Jürgen Habermas, 'On the Internal Relation between the Rule of Law and Democracy', in *The Inclusion of the Other:*

Studies in Political Theory, ed. Ciaran Cronin and P. De Greiff (Cambridge: MIT Press, 1999), 265–90, and John Rawls, 'A Reply to Habermas', *Journal of Philosophy* XCII, 3 (March 1995), 109–78. They are accepted by Held, *Democracy and the Global Order*, 147.

46. Held, *Democracy and the Global Order*, 190–201. The justification for the unilateral imposition of a cosmopolitan public law is that its rights and duties are the preconditions of the exercise of popular sovereignty, of democratic deliberation. But, for a law to be a legitimate precondition of modern politics it must itself be subject to democratic deliberation, or else the principle of popular sovereignty is not given equal weight.
47. Held, *Democracy and the Global Order*, 159–218. Liberal internationalism and radical republicanism also project specific features of their traditions of representative government on to global governance.
48. I have discussed this approach to contemporary constitutionalism and democratization in *Strange Multiplicity: Constitutionalism in an Age of Diversity* (Cambridge: Cambridge University Press, 1995). For a brilliant analysis of European Union constitutionalism along similar lines, see Jo Shaw, 'Constitutionalism in the European Union', *Journal of European Public Policy* 6, 4 (1999), 579–97. Cosmopolitan democracy could accept this modification without losing its most important features.
49. Mitchell Dean, *Governmentality: Power and Rule in Modern Society* (Thousand Oaks, Cal.: Sage, 1999), 11. Dean provides an excellent analysis of the governmentality approach.
50. The analysis of practices in terms of these three complex elements and its critics are discussed in Tully, 'To Think and Act Differently', 94–100.
51. Karl Marx, *Capital, Volume One*, trans. B. Fowkes (New York: Vintage, 1977), chap. 10, 340–416.
52. For an excellent overview and defence, see Edward Broadbent, 'Social Democracy or Liberalism in the New Millennium?', in *The Future of Social Democracy*, ed. Peter Russell (Toronto: University of Toronto Press, 1999), 73–93. The rights that Held builds into the cosmopolitan democratic public law are an extension to global governance of the three classes of rights of the social democratic tradition (*Democracy and the Global Order*, 192–3).
53. See Hubert Dreyfus, *Being-in-the-World: A Commentary on Heidegger's Being and Time, Division 1* (Cambridge: MIT Press, 1992), 60–87; Schatzki, *Social Practices*, 133–67; and Connolly, *Why I Am Not a Secularist*, 19–47, 137–62, 163–88.
54. Dreyfus, *Being-in-the-World*, 338, and Dreyfus et al., *Disclosing New Worlds*, 1–15. For 'processes of subjectivization' see Tully, 'To Think and Act Differently', 126–9.
55. Held et al., *Global Transformations*, 283–375. See also Anthony H. Richmond, *Global Apartheid: Refugees, Racism and the New World Order* (Toronto: Oxford University Press, 1994).
56. David Owen, 'Cultural Diversity and the Conversation of Justice', *Political Theory* (October 1999), 579–96. See also Susan Bickford, *The Dissonance of Democracy: Listening, Conflict and Citizenship* (Ithaca: Cornell University Press, 1996), 141–75.
57. Taiaiake Alfred, *Peace, Power, Righteousness: An Indigenous Manifesto* (Toronto: Oxford University Press, 1999), 55–73, 80–8.
58. For example, the new 'partnerships' among public, volunteer, and private-sector institutions.
59. Dreyfus et al., *Disclosing New Worlds*, 77, 86–8.

60. Castells, *End of Millennium*, 350–1.

61. Steven A. Rosell, *Renewing Governance: Governing by Learning in the Information Age* (Toronto: Oxford University Press, 1999). The quotation is from the back cover.

62. I have discussed the following example in more detail in 'An Ecological Ethics for the Present', in *Government for the Environment*, ed. Brendan Gleeson and Nicholas Low (London: Macmillan, 2000), 147–64.

63. For the dilemmas of these complex forms of negotiation in contrast to the standard models, see Iris Marion Young, *Intersecting Voices: Dilemmas of Gender, Political Philosophy and Policy* (Princeton: Princeton University Press, 1997), 38–74, and Tully, 'To Think and Act Differently', 137–9.

64. Cosmopolitan democracy is a good example of this long-term strategy to entrench environmental regulation at the local, national, and global levels of governance.

65. See Ralph Nader and L. Wallach, 'GATT, NAFTA and the Subversion of the Democratic Process', in *The Case Against the Global Economy and for a Turn Towards the Local*, ed. Jerry Mander and E. Goldsmith (San Francisco: Sierra Books, 1996), 92–107, and Brendan Gleeson and Nicholas Low, *Justice, Society and Nature: An Exploration of Political Ecology* (London: Routledge 1998), 175–83.

New Constitutionalism: Democracy, Habermas, and Canadian Exceptionalism

Simone Chambers

1. New Constitutionalism

We are not at the end of history; the triumph of liberal democracy is not complete. Yet despite all the devastating challenges it has faced over the last hundred years, liberal democracy is entering the twenty-first century as the most persuasive political ideology available. One reason is its adaptability. Liberal democracy has come a long way since the contract theories of the seventeenth century, the liberal doctrines of the eighteenth century, and the democratic movements of the nineteenth century. There are many strands to this evolution. This paper discusses one such strand: new constitutionalism.

New constitutionalism finds theoretical expression in the democratization of contract theory. By democratization I mean a conceptual enfranchisement that pushes liberal contract theory to be ever more inclusive. When Hobbes thought about the social contract in the seventeenth century, for example, it did not occur to him that women must also populate the state of nature. Rawls in the twentieth century, by contrast, is very much aware of the 'fact of pluralism' and the fact that his description of the parties must embrace the interests of both men and women. Nevertheless, this is exactly the point upon which much criticism of Rawls rests. Many people feel that his contract model is not democratic enough. Too many voices and identities are excluded, marginalized, or left unrecognized by his approach. Women, religious identities, radical political ideologies, and ethnic solidarities are just a few of the perspectives that, in the opinion of many, do not have the franchise in a Rawlsian model.[1] In response, contemporary theory has sought to make liberalism more inclusive of difference.

In the real world of constitutionalism one finds a parallel trend. Constitutions have had to accommodate pluralism and diversity in a new way. Everyone wants a Bill of Rights, but not everyone understands rights in the same way. It is not just that constitutions should protect diversity through rights: it is that constitutions should *reflect* diversity in their rights statements. Most of the constitutions ratified (or almost ratified) in the last decade of the twentieth century (e.g., in Canada, South Africa, Chile, Australia, and numerous Central and Eastern European countries), while clearly influenced by the American model, went significantly beyond that model in their recognition of diversity. The American constitution could not have been ratified in many of these countries. It is not even clear that it would be ratified today by the American people or their representatives if it were put to the test. It is a constitution that protects (some forms of) diversity but does not reflect diversity. Despite long-standing constitutional controversies and shifting interpretations, the American constitution contains a unitary vision of political association.[2] The pursuit of life, liberty, and happiness, protected by individual rights and freedoms, stands at the centre of this vision. There is little or no room for the recognition of groups, asymmetrical federalism, or any other principles used to accommodate diversity. The controversial nature of the American vision became clear to many Canadians when, in the early 1980s, the federal government failed to get agreement on a constitution embodying a similar vision. The pronounced individualism of the American constitution does not fit a world in which we want Zulus, Chechens, French Canadians, and Chiapas Indians, as well as gays, women, and the disabled, to feel that they belong.

The theories that justify liberal democracy as well as the constitutions that structure such democracies have changed and must continue to change under democratic pressure for inclusion. I want to suggest that Jürgen Habermas and Canada can help us get a picture of some of the directions of that change. Habermas has taken contract theory in an innovative, democratic direction. For Habermas, the contract is now embodied in democratic discourse. At the heart of discourse theory still stands the Hobbesian insight that inaugurated a new era of political philosophy: 'the question of who is the better man, has no place in the condition of meer Nature; where, (as has been shewn before,) all men are equall. The inequallity that now is, has bin introduced by the Lawes civill.'[3] Pre-political equality means that the only justification for the inequality of power introduced by government is the consent of the governed. The push to accommodate diversity, including diversities that have yet to develop, turns the contract into an open-ended conversation into which new voices can enter at any time.

I begin with a discussion of the Canadian constitutional debate that highlights some of the main features of new constitutionalism. I then introduce some of the theoretical issues that underlie this view of constitution-making, by way of a discussion of Habermas's discourse theory.

2. CANADIAN EXCEPTIONALISM

Canada has been struggling with the creation of a constitution in a context of diversity. It has yet to resolve this struggle through popular ratification of a constitutional document. It is not clear that Canada will ever achieve this end. Perhaps the aspiration to resolve the constitutional question once and for all must be given up. But in giving up this hope, we need not give up the aspiration of having and living by a constitution. Canada's failure to ratify a constitution after almost twenty years of debate illustrates, like no other constitutional impasse, what is at the heart of the new constitutionalism. What is noteworthy in the Canadian case is not that Canadians have failed to ratify their constitution; it is that they have continued to try. Canadians have been talking for twenty years. One reason the conversation has continued is that it has been open to new voices and claims. It is the conversation, not the document, that embodies Canada's commitment to rights and recognition.

What apparently makes Canada the exception rather than the rule in constitution-making is not simply the lack of a clearly legitimized constitutional document; it is that Canada has yet to fall apart without such a document. But in this case, the exception does prove a rule. That Canada has not fallen apart despite being unable to agree on a document indicates that its continuity does not reside in a document. I want to suggest that what explains Canada's lasting power is the binding force of practised accountability. Furthermore, although the source of continuity is clearer in the Canadian case because there is no document, something similar is at work in most of the successful constitutional negotiations in the late twentieth century. For example, the success of the South African constitution has just as much to do with the way in which recognition and accountability were maintained throughout the process of constitutional negotiation as with the content of the final document.

Canadian citizens expect—and are often not disappointed in their expectation—that their claims will be heard and addressed. The darkest moments of Canadian unity have been when one group or another has felt that its claims were not being addressed in the conversation. As the country lurched from one constitutional crisis to the next in the past decade, Canada and its political theorists emerged at the forefront of what I call new constitutionalism. New constitutionalism is about rights that can accommodate diversity, identity, plurality, and difference. It is no accident that Canadians are producing some of the most interesting contemporary statements on these issues.[4] In what follows, I will briefly describe the challenges facing constitutionalism under conditions of diversity and then point to a Canadian response to these challenges.

It is generally agreed that Canadians today have embraced modern constitutionalism and the contract traditions that underpin it.[5] They now view a constitution as a document that is implicitly prefaced by 'We the people . . .' . A constitution that cannot carry this preface, that cannot be endorsed by the people, lacks the most important basis of legitimacy. In the American tradition, popular endorsement is thought of in terms of an original contract undertaken on behalf of citizens by their representatives. Societies like Canada, however, which find themselves making constitutions in the 1990s, have found it necessary to amend this contractual model. In 1787, a small American elite could begin a constitutional document with 'We the people' and (perhaps) believe that they spoke for the people, despite the fact that most citizens—not to mention women, Native Americans, and slaves—were neither consulted nor asked to endorse the document.[6] The pressures of egalitarian democracy combined with demands for the inclusion of different voices has made this type of constitution-making increasingly untenable. The failure of the 1987 Meech Lake Accord and the vocal accusations of elitism that followed the failure constitute evidence that Canadians expect to be consulted, and that previously excluded groups like Aboriginal people, women, and the disabled expect a hearing. The rising demands on the part of Canadians to participate in the constitutional debate and to be given the opportunity to vote on proposals illustrate the democratic bent of new constitutionalism.[7]

A number of other weaknesses emerge when the American constitutional model is applied to multicultural societies. Despite believing that constitutions must ultimately be endorsed by 'the people', Canadians do not deliberate as one people but as many peoples.[8] Under such conditions, a stage must be added to the process of constitution-making that did not occur to Locke, Paine, or the founding fathers of the US. Multicultural states characterized by deep diversity need to create a 'people' before they can hope to speak in terms of 'We the people'. The creation of a people, however, must be achieved without erasing difference. That is, given contemporary demands for recognition, assimilation, and homogenization are no longer morally or practically acceptable means of achieving 'agreement'. It has become increasingly difficult to maintain the position that only those people who think of themselves and their claims in liberal individualist terms may come to the negotiating table.

Constitution-making in culturally divided societies faces the following problem: on the one hand, we need a 'people' to be able to speak as one in order to fulfill the voluntarist aspiration of modern constitutionalism, while on the other hand, creating a people through assimilation (the American model) now appears to violate the very same democratic or voluntarist aspiration. Habermas's conversation model can perhaps point to a way out of this problem. The core idea here is that engaging in the democratic practice of deliberation can create bonds of solidarity between diverse actors without requiring immersion in a melting pot. Richard Bellamy and Dario Castiglione, who endorse a similar view of constitution-making, appeal to Bernard Crick's defence of the political in this context: 'Diverse groups hold together because they practice politics—not because they agree about "fundamentals". . . . The moral consensus of a free state is not something mysteriously above politics: it is the activity (the civilizing activity) of politics itself.'[9] What I would add to Crick's observation is that not all types of politics have a civilizing and binding effect. The type of practice that can hold together diversities and civilize our interactions has certain ground rules. In other words, engaging in a 'civilizing' politics does involve a commitment to fundamentals. But it represents acceptance of certain procedural rules regulating the practice rather than agreement about substantive political visions.

Canadian constitutional politics brings out this alternative view of the 'ties that bind'. Its failures are most evident when we try to force Canadian constitutional identity into a unitary mould, and its successes (of which there have been some) come to light when we look at the conversation rather than the outcome. The 'Canada clause' illustrates both of these points. The Canada clause in the 1992 Charlottetown Accord was intended to capture the complexity and diversity of

Canadian identities and conceptions of justice. To recall just how complex the identity statement was, I quote the clause in full:

> (1) The Constitution of Canada, including the *Canadian Charter of Rights and Freedoms*, shall be interpreted in a manner consistent with the following fundamental characteristics:
> (a) Canada is a democracy committed to a parliamentary and federal system of government and to the rule of law;
> (b) the Aboriginal peoples of Canada, being the first peoples to govern this land, have the right to promote their languages, cultures and traditions and to ensure the integrity of their societies, and their governments constitute one of the three orders of government in Canada;
> (c) Quebec constitutes within Canada a distinct society, which includes a French-speaking majority, a unique culture and a civil law tradition;
> (d) Canadians and their governments are committed to the vitality and development of official language minority communities throughout Canada;
> (e) Canadians are committed to racial and ethnic equality in a society that includes citizens from many lands who have contributed, and continue to contribute, to the building of a strong Canada that reflects its cultural and racial diversity;
> (f) Canadians are committed to a respect for individual and collective human rights and freedoms of all people;
> (g) Canadians are committed to the equality of female and male persons; and
> (h) Canadians confirm the principle of equality of the provinces at the same time as recognizing their diverse characteristics.

There is a lot going on in this clause and not all of it, at first sight, seems compatible. In fact, many thought it was a terrible mess that did more to confuse the meaning of Canada than to clarify it. One of the explanations for public rejection of the Charlottetown Accord was that it, and particularly the Canada clause, 'could appeal to no clear conception of justice'.[10] The document included many conceptions of justice, and they appeared to offset each other. For example, although the Accord recognized Quebec as a distinct society, from the point of view of Quebec nationalists this recognition was watered down not only by the principle of provincial equality, but by the inclusion of the distinct society clause in a clause alongside seven other distinct characteristics. Defenders of a strong Charter of Rights and Freedoms thought that the whole idea of the Canada clause was ludicrous.[11] The Canada clause jeopardized the idea of the priority of rights—what, after all, would this really mean for judicial review? How was the Supreme Court to remain 'consistent with (these) fundamental characteristics'? Defenders of the provincial equality principle could not understand how provinces could be considered equal while some of them were also described as 'distinct'. Finally, Native people were dissatisfied because the clause stopped short of recognizing an explicit right to self-government, a right that would have made many provincial governments very nervous. In trying to please everyone, the Canada clause pleased no one. It was viewed as a compromise that had something for everyone but did not constitute a coherent whole. Some even went so far as to imply that the Canada clause was evidence that Canada was not a nation in any normal sense, and that no unifying vision existed for a constitution to capture.

Not everyone, however, has taken such a dim view of the Canada clause. James Tully has attempted to shed a different light on the Charlottetown Accord. Of the Canada clause he asks:

> Could it not be that these are some, or even many, of the fundamental characteristics of Canada, giving it its distinctive character among the countries of the world? Maybe the characteristics are heterogeneous because Canada is heterogeneous. Perhaps it strikes us a mess because we are not accustomed to looking at Canada as the (negotiated) arrangement of all these diverse characteristics but rather, we are used to viewing Canada from the perspective of some subset of these characteristics, as if our customary subset constitutes the fundamental, or predominant, characteristic of Canada. I will call this customary, unilateral way of looking on Canada 'diversity blindness'.[12]

Tully argues that 'diversity blindness' was a major factor in the rejection of the Charlottetown Accord. Many individuals and groups evaluated the constitutional proposal from the point of view of their particular vision of Canada.[13] Because the constitutional proposal, particularly the Canada clause, contained many visions, it was rejected as being an inadequate expression of any one view. But, continues Tully, the predominant characteristic of Canada *is* its diversity. The Canada clause is a good articulation of what Canada is precisely because it does not contain one unitary vision of justice. The constitutional identity of Canadians was never fixed at some historical founding moment. Instead, the cultural history of Canada has been characterized by a series of customary and negotiated accommodations, adjustments, settlements, and compromises between various and diverse visions of federation and justice. Instead of condemning this history of accommodating diversity as the reason Canada is not really a nation, Tully argues that it should be embraced and indeed celebrated as the core of Canadian identity.

As long as the parties to the dispute suffer from diversity blindness, there will continue to be a serious impasse in the Canadian constitutional debate. If, on the one hand, a legitimate constitution must have wide popular support from all the major sectors of society but, on the other, each sector evaluates the constitution from its own perspective, then no solution will be possible. Either the constitution articulates one consistent view of justice and the nation, in which case it will alienate those who do not subscribe to that view, or it articulates the many views prevalent in the country, in which case it will be seen as confused, inconsistent, and a patchwork by all parties to the dispute.

Is there a solution to this impasse? If multicultural diversity is the predominant characteristic of Canada, as Tully and many others have suggested, then the first step in overcoming the impasse is to try to overcome diversity blindness. The cause of the impasse is not that Canadians cannot quite hit upon the right wording for their constitution, nor that the constitutional document needs a little more fine-tuning before it can be endorsed. The impasse is created by the way in which participants view the document in the first place: the expectation that it should present a unitary vision, as in the American tradition, coupled with the partisan notion that the unitary vision should be one's own. In giving up a unitary vision, however, we should not give up the goal of unity. Constitutional negotiation and dialogue is still about speaking as 'We the people'. This can be achieved in a conversation in which participants simply try to *understand* each other before they try to negotiate with each other or conclude a contract with each other. The sincere attempt to understand what one's interlocutor is saying, and why, can initiate a process that builds the bonds necessary to live together as a 'people' without requiring that we give up our differences and unique identities.

Although Tully and I disagree about the best way to articulate and describe these conversations (he uses the language of Wittgenstein; I, the language of Habermasian discourse theory), we agree that constitutionalism in an age of democratic diversity is more about keeping a conversation going than about getting all the parties to sign on the dotted line at one time and place.[14] In fact, Canada has been relatively good about keeping the conversation going. Consider, for example, the clear and significant difference between the 1987 Meech Lake round of negotiations and the 1992 Charlottetown round. In the five years between these two rounds of talks, complaints about exclusion, elitism, and inadequate democratic consultation were taken seriously. There were a number of well-intentioned, if not always successful, initiatives to include more voices in the constitutional debate. Good intentions are not irrelevant in this context. One reason Canada is still together and has suffered very little violence despite deep divisions is that it has, as Tully points out, a tradition in which grievances are listened to and not simply silenced. They are not always acted upon in the ways we might like, but they are heard. Take, for example, the status of Native Canadians. In the Meech Lake round they were excluded from the constitutional conversation. Their demands for inclusion and voice in the aftermath of Meech Lake have changed the face of Canadian constitutional politics forever. We still have no agreed-upon solution to the self-government question, but Aboriginal people are now permanent partners in constitutional negotiation. Such inclusion has become part of the Canadian 'constitution' in the sense that it reflects a deep and, I would argue, constitutive principle of recognition and reciprocity. Procedure and process are the components of the new constitutionalism.

The heart of diversity-friendly constitutional politics cannot be found in a document: it consists in sustaining a conversation over time. This conversation involves a commitment to talk to each other, respond to each other's claims and grievances, consider new options, and re-evaluate old ones. Rather than a means of arriving at a settled-once-and-for-all constitution, the commitment to ongoing conversation must be the essence of the constitution. It is when the conversation breaks down, not when we fail to ratify a document, that constitutional politics is in crisis; that is, when constitutional politics may degenerate into repression, secession, or war.

Jeremy Webber articulates this idea of a constitution as an ongoing conversation when he says that for him Canada is 'the people of this country, their rich diversity, and the way in which they have cooperated, disagreed, and in the end shaped each other. What matters most—what makes up the soul of our identity as Canadians—is the conversation we have had in this rich and magnificent land.'[15] I believe Alan Cairns is saying the same thing when he claims that 'constitutional politics is never-ending'.[16] For those who want the constitutional question to be settled once and for all, this is a depressing conclusion,[17] but I do not find it so. The legitimacy and stability of institutions depend on sustaining a balance of trust, recognition, and respect over time. The first principles of Canadian association are found in the *way* in which Canadians have dealt with diversity rather than a shared and unitary political philosophy. Charles Taylor echoes Webber's idea of conversational politics when he says that the bond between Canadians of different constitutional temperaments 'is precisely not based here on likeness, or (simply) on unity of purpose, but on the sense of a partnership formed over the decades by a common history. Or to put it another way, one common purpose for these people is maintaining this association—one might say, conversation—with people whom they recognize as different.'[18]

It was once thought to be Canada's great failing that it could not articulate a national identity in the form of an agreed-upon constitution. Failure after failure at the constitutional negotiating table was thought proof of the artificial nature of the federation. Once brought to light of day under the pressure of modern constitutionalism and the need, to use Paine's words, for a constitution in 'a visible form',[19] Canadian identity appeared to add up to a disjointed and discordant clamour of competing claims. However, the latest round of constitutional negotiation has spawned a new interpretation of the situation. This interpretation revolves around the idea of an ongoing open conversation between diversities rather than the idea of a unitary identity for a nation-state. On this view, it is Canada's great achievement and strength that it has built a political association without imposing a unitary identity on its diverse members. It has achieved this through a commitment to conversation rather than a unitary vision. This is the constitutional model of the future—a constitutional model that can accommodate multiculturalism and diversity.

3. DISCOURSE THEORY AND DEMOCRATIC LEGITIMACY

I now want to turn to some theoretical issues that underlie new constitutionalism. This may strike the reader as a case of 'it sounds good in practice, but will it work in theory?' But the elaboration of a theoretical framework is important for two reasons. First, such a framework can describe salient features of new constitutionalism; for example, the Habermasian approach focuses social scientific research on such things as the institutional conditions of public-opinion formation rather than on aggregative ratification procedures. Second, and more important, Habermasian discourse ethics is a critical/normative tool that can help us understand what goes wrong in constitutional deliberations and what goals we should be striving for in such discussions.

The two main characteristics of a new constitutionalism are increased recognition and respect for diversity and a growing demand for popular consultation and accountability. Two examples of these trends are the inclusion of Aboriginal representatives in constitutional negotiations and the growing use of town-hall meetings during constitutional debates. With regard to the first characteristic, Habermasian discourse theory can accommodate diversity while at the same time seeking commonality. Despite the fact that Habermas has not always been sensitive to diversity, the procedural essence of his discourse theory makes it amenable to difference politics. Thus many of Habermas's critics in the 'difference' camp use a similar notion of conversation or deliberation as the theoretical and institutional answer to diversity.[20]

Discourse theory sets out the basic rules under which we should talk and argue with each other. No limits are placed on who may enter debate, and no one may silence a participant. Furthermore, the theory does not stipulate what may be talked about or potentially agreed to. Indeed, participants may talk about the rules themselves. Real constitutional debate often has this self-referential character to it. Canadians are familiar with the problem of determining which rules should govern the conversation about the rules that will govern the constitutional debate, as well as the related problem of which decision rule shall be used to decide on a constitutional decision rule. The very open-ended nature of the topic of conversation may worry some, as it appears to open the door to the possibility of 'voting away' our freedoms. But, as I will argue below, we can do that without Habermasian discourse theory. The open-ended nature of the discourse model captures something very important about real constitutional debate: although it should not be a crap-shoot, such debate is—and ought to be—unpredictable. It ought to be unpredictable because we should not prejudge or even anticipate the claims, criticisms, and demands that citizens will make. We need a model of constitutional politics that allows for new voices and as yet unrecognized identities to enter the fray. Binding a diverse group, *whose diversity itself is shifting and changing*, into a shared political association that is perceived by all as legitimate requires a constant openness to claims, questions, and objections. Thus the procedural character of discourse theory makes it a valuable tool in theorizing a constitutional model that can accommodate difference and diversity.

Discourse theory can also help in understanding and structuring the second characteristic of new constitutionalism: popular consultation. Habermas has a rich theory of the public sphere that has developed into a theory of public opinion and will-formation. The normative core of this theory is the need to maintain freedom, equality, and mutual respect in the processes of deliberation. This ideal theory can give us a number of critical questions to ask in evaluating constitutional initiatives of consultation and ratification: What voices were excluded? How did power and money shape and perhaps distort constitutional negotiation? What idioms predominated and maybe disadvantaged some participants? How were levels of access maintained? Who controlled the agendas? These are some of the questions that come out of a Habermasian perspective and can inform our evaluation of the constitutional conversation.

I want to conclude by noting one more reason why a Habermasian model (or some version of discourse theory) is helpful in theorizing the significance of democratic demands for inclusion at the end of the twentieth century. Habermas offers a deep justification for a new constitutionalism. Habermas's theory has a sociological component that allows him to bridge a gap between concepts of stability and legitimacy. This in turn introduces a view of the relation between rights and democracy that makes sense of the exercise of popular sovereignty in the area of constitutionalism. Canada, South Africa, and Poland, to name only three countries, have been engaged in the process of democratically determining those rights that will limit their democracies. In this process, they have been limited by a respect for the very rights that they were (or are) in the process of establishing. I want to take a moment and look more closely at this circularity and what it means for legitimacy.

A discursive theory of political legitimacy has two components. First, there is the Weberian analysis of the real-world processes through which a citizen body generates the recognition of norms that are necessary to sustain a stable system of justice.[21] Culture and communication underpin this process. This analysis brings out the consensual foundation of all stable systems of rules and norms. Overlaid upon this social analysis is an ethical analysis, which identifies the optimal conditions under which this consensual process ought to take place if its outcomes are to represent the common interest. These ideal conditions are the conditions of authentic discourse: freedom, equality, and mutual respect. Like Kant's ethics of publicity, discourse ethics joins the requirements of stability (that people actually consider institutional arrangements to be in their interest) with the requirements of justice (that institutional arrangements actually are in everyone's interest). This is what Habermas means by bringing together the moment of facticity (*Faktizität*) with that of validity (*Geltung*), or fact with norm.[22]

Let me try to illustrate the relationship between facts and norms, or stability and legitimacy, using the controversy over English language signs in Quebec. In 1988, the Supreme Court of Canada ruled that the French-only signage law in Quebec was a violation of individual rights of expression. Much to the horror of American constitutional scholars, Quebec responded by introducing a 'notwithstanding' clause, which in effect exempted Quebec's Charter of French Language from the requirement to conform to the federal Charter of Rights. One interesting aspect of this story was that a Liberal government, not a Parti Québécois one, took these measures. It did so presumably because it felt that it could not sell a repeal of the language clause to the people of Quebec. This action appeared to represent a direct conflict between democracy and rights; furthermore, the American model would suggest that something has gone wrong when rights do not prevail over democracy. But such a conclusion is not necessarily warranted.

If the Quebec government had been 'forced' by a more powerful Supreme Court to repeal the language law, this would not have represented a legitimate solution in the eyes of Quebec francophones. As Claude Bariteau and his colleagues wrote at the time of the debate: 'It is in Quebec—among citizens of Quebec—that we must arrive at an equitable just agreement. Whatever its merits, a language policy, if imposed by the federal government or by the Supreme Court of Canada, cannot guarantee the true recognition of Quebec's linguistic communities and their rights.' [23] A lack of legitimacy at the grassroots level undermines stability. But perhaps we want to say that the issue here is right and wrong, not stability. If it was wrong for the Quebec National Assembly to ban the use of English signs, then that legislation should be overturned regardless of public opinion. Such a 'solution' would correspond to our intuitive understanding of the priority of justice. Justice means that there are certain rules (usually understood as rights) that we should not violate while pursuing our collective goals. Furthermore, these rules should not be affected by the vagaries of public opinion. But separating justice from public-opinion formation is a risky strategy in the long run. If we are interested in justice, then we should also be interested in maintaining justice over a long period of time, and it is not clear that maintaining justice can be accomplished by 'enforcing' just solutions to moral dilemmas in the public sphere.

The Supreme Court cannot, by itself, sustain a stable system of justice over time. If citizens are not in some way attached to that system, respect it, revere it, or believe in it, then no amount of court orders will sustain its viability. One need only think of the Weimar Republic to see the limits of a system of justice that is not mirrored in the political culture of its citizens. In the long run, what counts is how convincing rights are to citizens. Threats to rights come in the form of changing attitudes and beliefs. The main danger facing any system of rights arises when citizens no longer believe in the values that sustain and underpin that system. This was the fear of many English-speaking Quebecers when the Quebec National Assembly first passed the language legislation, for example. The widespread popularity of language legislation among French Quebecers—when, from the point of view of the English, it obviously infringed upon a right of free expression—inspired the fear that French Quebecers simply did not take rights seriously. What was called for in this situation was not the enforcement of rights so much as a public discourse that could remind French Canadians why it is important to safeguard rights while pursuing collective goals. In other words, Quebec needed a conversation that could re-establish public trust. Anglophones were not afraid that the Supreme Court would not uphold their rights, they were afraid that francophones would not find the Court's arguments persuasive.

Attitudes, beliefs, and shared understandings change over time. They erode, subtly shift, and mutate. Why would commitment to individual rights not erode as, for example, the commitment to religious intolerance did in the sixteenth century? The answer cannot simply be that respect for the autonomy of individuals is right and religious intolerance is wrong. The continuity of an understanding over time does not depend on there *being* good grounds for such an understanding, but on those good grounds and that understanding being *reproduced* within a culture. Assuming we reject any claims regarding the necessary course of history, then there is no reason why historically specific understandings must continue. That historically specific understandings can be justified on non-contingent, ahistorical grounds (natural rights theory, neo-Kantianism, and so on) is not a reason why they *will* continue; it is only a reason why they perhaps *ought* to continue. And if these understandings are to continue, the reasons why they ought to continue must be kept alive within the community.

But do we really want to appeal to the public on such important questions as rights? What about rights that individuals have *against* the public? What if public debates about rights turn into bargaining sessions? If the initial conditions of discourse are met, none of these fears is warranted. The conditions of discourse include individual freedom, equality, and mutual respect: all individuals must have the freedoms necessary to participate in discourse; all must be treated as equal partners in the process of will-formation; no one may be coerced, pressured, manipulated, or deceived into accepting an argument. If these conditions are respected, then we can be confident that agreements are not forced through against the will of some parties. It is unlikely that bigoted, racist, or intolerant arguments will sway those against whom they are directed. In addition, these conditions ensure that democratic deliberation about rights does not descend into a form of political bargaining.

But who enforces these rules? The answer is not comforting to those who want hard and fast guarantees for protections, yet I am convinced that it is the right answer. In the final analysis, we enforce these rules, as private persons and citizens. My argument contains an inevitable circularity: the values of liberty, equality, and mutual respect are maintained through the practice of liberty, equality, and mutual respect.

How does Habermas address this circularity? He discusses the relationship between democracy and rights by appealing to the interdependence of individual and public autonomy.[24] Individual autonomy corresponds to the liberal notion of individual freedom safeguarded, for the most part, through a system of rights. Public autonomy refers to notions of popular sovereignty. Popular sovereignty can be understood in foundational terms (as, for example, in liberal contract theory) or in day-to-day political terms (as, for example, in theories of deliberative democracy). Habermas argues that authentic public autonomy (in both the foundational and the day-to-day sense) is impossible without private autonomy, and private autonomy can be justified only through public autonomy. If we did not have strong guarantees of individual autonomy in the private sphere, our democratic outcomes would be suspect. No one was under the illusion that the votes taken in the Supreme Soviet of the USSR represented authentic democracy, for example. These votes were suspect because there was no corresponding system of rights and protections to give us confidence that individuals had been able to develop and express their true interests or opinions. Similarly, contract theories make sense only given the assumption that the parties are free and equal. Thus authentic and healthy democracy requires a wide system of rights guarantees. Undermining those guarantees undermines democracy. Without rights we would have no confidence that the opinions brought to the public (or the decisions made to remain silent) are authentic and autonomous.

Looked at from the reverse angle, the interdependence of public and private autonomy yields a different conclusion: because we can no longer rely on God, or Nature, or self-evident truth as a shared justification for rights, some version of public autonomy (Rawls's original position or Habermas's discursive democracy are two such versions) must be introduced to justify and legitimize the institutions of private rights. In answer to the liberal objection that discursive democracy privileges the people's will over rights, and to the democrat's objection that it privileges rights over the people's will, Habermas defends the 'co-originality' (*Gleichursprünglichkeit*) of rights and popular sovereignty; the chicken and the egg cannot be prioritized.[25] There is no people's will to speak of without rights, and there are no rights without the people's will endorsing them. Liberal democracy is what it says it is.

4. CONCLUSION

The project of creating a constitution in the early twenty-first century highlights the co-original nature of liberal democracy. Popular participation is necessary because it creates constitutional legitimacy and stability. But it is the extent to which the process itself embodies the ideals to be set out in the constitution that determines whether that constitution succeeds or fails. A 'good' or 'liberal' constitution that is rammed down the throats of citizens without consultation or concern for particular identities is likely to be unstable and cause resentment. A 'bad' or 'illiberal' constitution that is subject to an open, free, and critical popular debate is not likely to succeed either.

Perhaps C.H. McIlwain's distinction between ancient and modern constitutionalism might be helpful here.[26] New constitutionalism combines the centrality of rights found in modern constitutionalism with the role of practice in ancient constitutionalism. Modern constitutions, like the American one, are first and foremost written constitutions. As a written document, the modern constitution is a conscious and deliberate formulation of the fundamental law that defines and limits government. In the ancient conception, a constitution is not the product of a conscious deliberative act at one time and place but represents the accumulation of custom and practice of a political body over time. McIlwain describes the ancient constitution as 'the substantive principles to be deduced from a nation's actual institutions and their development'.[27]

The ancient constitution is the product of growth and maturation; the picture is of an organic whole in which natural development, selection, and adaptation produce the most harmonious result. The modern constitution is the product of human will and choice; here we have the Enlightenment aspiration that reason will design just and effective institutions. These two views of the constitution reflect two views of legitimacy. In the modern tradition, legitimacy is derived directly from the people. In the ancient tradition, legitimacy is derived only indirectly from the people. The legitimacy of the ancient constitution rests not on contract but on the test of time that is supposed to signal a deeper type of agreement on the part of citizens. The idea of an ongoing conversation stands between the voluntarism of the contract and the role of constitutive practice in the ancient tradition.

New constitutionalism, while not giving up the Enlightenment ideals of human rights and universalizable principles, shifts emphasis away from the discovery of abstract principles to be written up in a document and instead stresses the maintenance of a practice that presupposes rights. The idea here is that engaging in the democratic practices necessary to ratify a constitution in an age of diversity can create a constitution in the ancient sense.

NOTES

1. Susan Moller Okin, 'Review of John Rawls, *Political Liberalism*', *American Political Science Review* 87, 4 (December 1993), 1010–11; Samuel Scheffer, 'The Appeal of Political Liberalism', *Ethics* 105, 1 (October 1994), 16; and Seyla Benhabib, 'Deliberative Rationality and Models of Democratic Legitimacy', *Constellations* 1 (April 1994), 36.
2. For the unitary nature of the American Constitution see James Tully, *Strange Multiplicity: Constitutionalism in an Age of Diversity* (New York and Cambridge: Cambridge University Press, 1995).
3. Thomas Hobbes, *Leviathan* (Harmondsworth: Penguin Classics, 1968), 211.
4. For example, James Tully, Charles Taylor, Will Kymlicka, Ronald Beiner, Melissa Williams, David Kahane, and Daniel Weinstock.
5. See, for example, Peter H. Russell, *Constitutional Odyssey: Can Canada Become a Sovereign People?* (Toronto: University of Toronto Press, 1993), 7–11.
6. James Madison, Alexander Hamilton, and John Jay, *The Federalist Papers*, ed. Isaac Kramnick (New York: Penguin Books, 1987), no. II. For a critique of the claim to speak for the people, see Charles Beard, *An Economic Interpretation of the Constitution of the United States* (New York: Free Press, 1986); Jacques Derrida, 'Declaration and Independence', *New Political Science* 15 (1986), 7–15; and Tully, *Strange Multiplicity*, 93–5.
7. Similar trends towards popular consultation can be seen in South Africa and Australia.
8. Charles Taylor, *Reconciling the Solitudes: Essays on Canadian Federalism and Nationalism* (Montreal and Kingston: McGill-Queens University Press, 1993), 155–86; James Tully, 'Diversity's Gambit Declined', in *Constitutional Predicament: Canada after the Referendum of 1992*, ed. Curtis Cook (Montreal and Kingston: McGill-Queen's University Press, 1994), 157–61; Jeremy Webber, *Reimagining Canada: Language, Culture, and the Canadian Constitution* (Montreal and Kingston: McGill-Queen's University Press, 1994), 183–5.
9. Bernard Crick, *In Defense of Politics* (Harmondsworth: Penguin, 1962), 24, quoted in Richard Bellamy and Dario Castiglione, 'Review Article: Constitutionalism and Democracy—Political Theory and the American Constitution', *British Journal of Political Science* 26 (1996), 2032.
10. Alain Noël, 'Deliberating a Constitution: The Meaning of the Canadian Referendum of 1992', in *Constitutional Predicament*, 75.
11. Pierre Trudeau's response was to write a small pamphlet entitled *A Mess that Deserves a Big No* (Toronto: Robert Davis Publishing, 1992).
12. Tully, 'Diversity's Gambit Declined', 157.

13. For a similar diagnosis of the failure of the Charlottetown Accord see Taylor, *Reconciling the Solitudes*, 102, 191; and Webber, *Reimagining Canada*, 309–20.
14. Despite Tully's harsh criticism of Habermas (see *Strange Multiplicity*, 131, 173), his conversational norms of recognition, consent, and continuity are very similar to the norms of discourse.
15. Webber, *Reimagining Canada*, 319.
16. Alan C. Cairns, *Charter versus Federalism: Dilemmas of Constitutional Reform* (Montreal and Kingston: McGill-Queen's University Press, 1992), 98.
17. Peter Russell writes of the Canadian constitutional debate: 'if there are any among us who want to keep this soap opera going, they must be mad' (*Constitutional Odyssey*, 190).
18. Charles Taylor, 'Reply and Re-articulation', in *Philosophy in an Age of Pluralism: The Philosophy of Charles Taylor in Question*, ed. James Tully (Cambridge: Cambridge University Press, 1994), 255.
19. Thomas Paine, *Rights of Man* (Secaucus, NJ: Citadel Press, 1974), 82.
20. Iris Young, *Justice and the Politics of Difference* (Princeton: Princeton University Press, 1990).
21. Max Weber, *The Theory of Social and Economic Organization* (New York: Free Press, 1964), 324–8.
22. Jürgen Habermas, *Faktizität und Geltung: Beiträge zur Diskurstheorie des Rechts und des demokratischen Rechtsstaats* (Frankfurt: Suhrkamp, 1992), translated as *Between Facts and Norms: Contributions to a Discourse Theory of Law and Democracy*, trans. William Rheg (Cambridge, Mass.: MIT Press, 1996).
23. Claude Bariteau, Gary Caldwell, Yolande Cohen, Alain-G. Gagnon, Guy Laforest, Daniel Latouche, Alain Noel, Pierre-Paul Proulx, Francois Rocher, Daniel Salée, Daniel Turp, 'The Case of a New Language Accord in Quebec', *Inroads* 3 (Summer 1994), 9.
24. Habermas, *Between Facts and Norms*, 84–118.
25. Ibid., 104.
26. Charles Howard McIlwain, *Constitutionalism: Ancient and Modern* (Ithaca: Cornell University Press, 1947). James Tully also appeals to the ancient constitution as a diversity-friendly model of constitutionalism. He, however, rejects modern constitutionalism altogether while I wish to introduce flexibility into a rights-based model. See Tully, *Strange Multiplicity*.
27. McIlwain, *Constitutionalism*, 3.

Saving Democracy from Deliberation

Daniel M. Weinstock

There has in recent years been a veritable deluge of philosophical writing on the topic of 'deliberative democracy'.[1] Deliberative democrats believe that democratic practices (e.g., the debates that give rise to legislation in legislative assemblies) should consist in the exchange of *reasons* rather than the simple thrusting and counter-thrusting of rival interests. Those who participate in democratic debates should, on this view, take themselves to be considering different opinions and arguments about questions to do with the public good in a public-spirited manner, with a view to arriving at a truly general will. By contrast, 'proceduralist' or 'pluralist' conceptions of democracy view democratic practices in a more humble light as mere aggregation mechanisms. The idea here is that citizens and their representatives come to the public forum with rival preferences on a given debate determined in advance of any political debate or discussion. The role of democracy is first to reveal citizens' preferences (much as their consumer preferences are revealed when they walk into the music store rather than the shoe store), and then to tally up numbers so as to ensure that as many preferences as possible will be satisfied when it is impossible to satisfy all of them.

Morally, the deliberative conception of democracy is clearly more demanding than the proceduralist model it seeks to replace. The proceduralist model makes a virtue of citizens' selfishness. Only if they affirm their preferences sincerely and unabashedly will the aggregating mechanism of democratic majority rule be able to perform its function. The deliberative conception, on the other hand, requires that citizens and their representatives impose a certain discipline upon themselves. When entering a policy debate, they are to consider various positions on their independent merits, rather than simply on the basis of whether or not they conduce to the satisfaction of pre-politically formed policy preferences. They are to take up the point of view of 'public reason', a point of view that, as we shall see, is constituted by rules, both procedural and substantive, the function of which is to ensure that deliberators will actually prescind from considering policy debates from a narrowly partisan perspective.

Now the emergence of the deliberative democracy paradigm has at first glance had an altogether salutary effect on the landscape of contemporary liberal democratic theory. For years now, liberal democratic theorists, at least in the English-speaking world, have been liberals first and foremost, and democrats only grudgingly. They have devoted the bulk of their normative work to giving an account of the rights that citizens of liberal democracies ought to be able to enjoy. They have also sought to articulate the moral grounds of those rights, as well as to describe the institutions that must be put in place in order to protect them. But they have expended precious little intellectual energy on normative theorizing about the democratic practices and procedures that are to be housed within liberalism's normative confines.[2] It is almost as if they have assumed that the proceduralist democrat's account of democracy is the only one on offer. On this view, democracy is a 'morality-free' zone. The best that we can hope to achieve is to rein it in from without in order to avoid its degenerating into mob rule. This assumption is made abundantly clear, for example, in Ronald Dworkin's telling characterization of the institution of the court in liberal democracies as the only true 'forum of principle'.[3] The result has been a strangely lopsided liberal democratic theory, with the liberal side of the equation carrying all of the normative weight.

On closer examination, however, deliberative democracy begins to look like more of a mixed blessing. As we shall see, the rules of public reason that it imposes upon deliberators as a condition of their counting as truly 'deliberative' have not been defined with a view to realizing distinctively *democratic* goals and values. Rather, the discipline that deliberative democrats would impose upon deliberators seems dictated by theoretical preoccupations and values that are distinctive of liberalism but that liberalism has in recent years been deemed unable to address on the basis of its own theoretical resources. The result has been a strangely distorted picture of democratic practice—one that, if realized, would actually *hinder* democratic procedures from attaining distinctively democratic goals. Let me explain.

A traditional aspiration of liberal theory—one that runs from the natural-law arguments of a philosopher such as Locke, through the rationalism of Kant, to the constructivism of John Rawls—has been that of *rational justification*. Liberals have been loath to accept that the rights they endorse and the institutions they view as instrumentally required to secure those rights might simply be the result of tradition and convention. This would place liberal norms on foundations altogether too flimsy. Nor has it been possible for liberals to accept the idea that what rights we have are simply determined by our collective decisions, since the point of liberal norms is precisely to constrain the unruly and chaotic procedures of collective decision-making. So they have attempted to show that a liberal dispensation has an impeccably *rational* pedigree, one that all citizens could appreciate and recognize if only they could rid themselves of the individual and factional passions that tend to fetter the operations of their reason.

Consider, briefly, a central argument of Rawls's early theory.[4] Rawls believed that though citizens might very well differ on fundamental issues of political morality, these differences were symptoms of distortion and unreason rather than of some fundamental ambivalence written into reason itself. Adjust for those factors in everyday life that tend to breed distortion (lack of information, excessive emotion, the lure of self-interest, and the like), and you will, Rawls thought, arrive at a set of 'considered convictions' upon which all unfettered human intelligences would converge. The role of the philosopher is to quarry such convictions and to construct a theory of social justice on their basis. Such a theory would have the dual advantage of being rationally justified (the convictions are, after all, deliverances of practical judgment once it has been set free of all distortion) and of being acceptable to all (since once we are placed in the kind of 'laboratory conditions' for practical judgment that Rawls describes, we all share the same reason).

Note the heavy use made in this argument of what might be called a 'convergence assumption'. The governing idea is that reason unfettered speaks with one voice on moral and political issues. The task of the theorist is simply (or not so simply) to discover that voice through the din of unreason and prejudice.

Is the convergence assumption warranted? Many voices in the history of political philosophy have argued against it, Isaiah Berlin being perhaps its most well-known antagonist.[5] The conclusion that Rawls arrived at, in any case, is that regardless of our views concerning the deep, meta-ethical question of whether Reason speaks univocally on moral and political issues, we have no choice but to act as if the assumption was mistaken. This is because it seems clear that *reasonable* people can and do disagree on fundamental moral issues, even when their practical judgment is not clouded by unreason or other sources of distortion. As finite human beings, we exercise our reasoning capacities under certain unavoidable 'burdens of judgment': none of us possess exactly the same bundle of data, we rank relevant criteria differently, etc. This means that even in conditions in which our practical judgment is operating exactly as it should, we are likely to arrive at quite different conclusions on moral and political questions. Moral disagreement need not be a sign of unreason. The justification of political norms must therefore somehow be reconciled with the 'fact of pluralism'.[6]

Rawls's own way of trying to reconcile liberalism's justificatory promise with the fact of pluralism has been adjudged unsatisfactory by many.[7] First, he claims that while it is true that human reasoners labouring in conditions of intellectual freedom and subject to the burdens of judgment will inevitably come to form quite radically different views about the good life for human beings, these views may not be wholly determinate when it comes to matters of political justice. Second, on his view, while the theorist can no longer appeal to uniquely rational 'considered convictions' that all citizens can be taken to have once the effects of prejudice, emotion, and self-interest are corrected for, she can embark upon the project of constructing a theory of justice that will be rationally justifiable to all by quarrying the values already latent in the public political culture shared by all citizens of a given polity, irrespective of their broader philosophical differences. Thus, while the 'fact of pluralism' requires that the justification of liberal norms proceed somewhat differently, it does not pose insuperable obstacles. The moral and philosophical differences between citizens conveniently diminish where political matters arise, making it less likely that the 'fact of pluralism' will be an obstacle to the goal of rational justification. And the public political cultures of liberal democracies readily present us with coherent sets of principles on the basis of which a theory of justice acceptable to all can be constructed.

The somewhat self-serving nature of these moves is readily apparent. First, history simply gives us no reason to expect that people's comprehensive conceptions will not have implications for the political arena. And unless we question-beggingly relegate beyond the pale of the 'reasonable' all those whose conceptions of the good *do* incline them away from a liberal dispensation, it will turn out that the fact of pluralism poses a greater difficulty for the justification of political norms than Rawls is willing to acknowledge.[8] Second, it seems hopelessly optimistic to expect that the public political cultures of long-standing liberal democracies can satisfactorily be accounted for in terms of a set of principles sufficiently coherent to yield a determinate theory of justice. Such cultures are much messier than that, and can probably be interpreted in quite different ways. These differences in interpretation, moreover, will most likely mirror the society's ethical-political differences quite closely.

So Rawls correctly perceives that the fact of pluralism poses a problem for political justification, but he does not adequately gauge the severity of the problem. The emergence of deliberative democracy can in large measure be seen as an attempt by political philosophers to respond to the challenge posed by reasonable moral pluralism in a more thorough way. The core intuition of deliberative democrats is that, in conditions of pluralism, justification cannot take place against the backdrop provided either by uniquely rational norms or by norms conventionally adhered to by all citizens of a polity. Rather, citizens who cannot assume a shared set of basic norms but who nonetheless need to agree to laws around which to structure their common political life must arrive at such agreements through actual political dialogue and deliberation. In the absence of taken-for-granted norms, citizens must democratically 'make it up as they go' (to paraphrase the title of a recent book on public reason).[9] Thus the need for a more deliberative democratic politics has been linked in the arguments of its principal defenders to liberalism's justificatory predicament. For example, Gutmann and Thompson present their conception of deliberative democracy as the best solution available to the problem posed by the fact that, even though political disagreement in a society often points back to intractable moral differences, despite these differences 'citizens owe one another justifications for the laws they collectively impose on one another.'[10] Seyla Benhabib similarly finds the rationale for a deliberative politics in 'the assumption of value pluralism': 'agreements in societies living with value pluralism are to be sought for not at the level of substantive beliefs but at that of procedures, processes, and practices for attaining and revising beliefs. Proceduralism is a rational answer to persisting value conflicts at the substantive level.'[11] Examples such as these could be multiplied *ad nauseam*.

What does justification involve? Let us say that a policy is justified if it is supported by the balance of reasons. If justification is to be the goal of democratic exchanges, then it is clear that not just any old argumentative free-for-all can be expected to reach it. Deliberations must be structured so as to allow the strongest argument to prevail. So those aspects of real-world debates and conversations that tend to prevent reason from winning must be factored out. Participants in democratic fora who share the goal of arriving at mutually justifiable resolutions to their policy debates must accept what we might call the *discipline of public reason*. They must accept that deliberation will be governed by rules the function of which will be to prevent debates from reaching irrational conclusions as a result of say, threat, force, lack of time to consider all relevant alternatives, or the like.

What kinds of constraints will participants wanting to attain this goal accede to? First, they will undoubtedly define procedural rules aimed at blocking the effects of the kinds of factors just mentioned. These will include rules about turn-taking and agenda-setting, the illegitimacy of recourse to explicit or veiled threats, and so on. Theorists influenced by the work of Jürgen Habermas have probably done the most to define such procedural constraints. According to Habermas, they include requirements that all competent subjects be allowed to speak; that all be allowed to question or introduce any assertion and to express their attitudes, desires, and needs; and that no speaker be prevented from exercising these rights.[12]

Second, such rules will include what might be called *weak substantive constraints*. Principally what I have in mind here is the requirement that deliberators present one another with *reasons* as opposed to naked emotional appeals or unabashed expressions of individual or of group interest. To count as a reason, an utterance or assertion must have certain logical properties, such as generality. It must not make essential reference to particular persons or groups of persons (unless the context of deliberation makes it relevant that it do so), and it must allow for the drawing of inferences. It must also have certain semantic or pragmatic properties, most notably to do with relevance. A reason can be logically beyond reproach and still bear no obvious relevance to the issue at hand. I do not have the space to go into any detail here: what I want to make clear is that these kinds of substantive constraints are weak because they do not say anything about the permissible *content* of the reasons we advance. They merely require that our interventions *be* reasons.

Now it is clear that democratic procedures governed by such procedural and weak substantive constraints constitute moral progress when compared with the kind of name-calling, log-rolling, and pork-barrelling that might go on in purely procedural democratic assemblies. The question is whether they can deliver the justificatory goods. Is there any reason to think that citizens separated by substantial moral divides will be able to arrive at mutually justifiable resolutions of policy outcomes merely by conducting their deliberations within these fairly weak formal constraints?

They might, but there is no reason to think that they will do so reliably. The reason is that the moral pluralism that had motivated the move to deliberative democracy in the first place will still be present in deliberative assemblies. Pluralism implies that for many issues on the political agenda a plurality of conflicting reasons will be relevant, and that reasonable people might very well disagree on how to rank them. The weak constraints we have examined until now may filter out some sources of disagreement. For example, thinly veiled appeals to factional interests might be revealed for what they are. What's more, citizens holding radically different overall conceptions of the good life might, through deliberation, discover points of agreement on specific issues or on middle-level principles that might have been easily inferred from a mere examination of their broader philosophical commitments. Though deliberation may not close the gap between their general ethical conceptions, it may reveal points of overlap on more specific issues sufficient to break deadlocks in policy debates.[13] But in general there is no reason to think that the moral pluralism that threatens the traditional liberal justificatory project will be made any more tractable by being placed in the democratic arena.

It is undoubtedly for this reason that many deliberative democrats have insisted upon a further, stronger substantive constraint upon democratic deliberators. On this view, not only must they comply with certain procedural requirements and ensure that their interventions always take the form of reasons, but they must also observe a norm of what Gutmann and Thompson call 'reciprocity'. Reciprocity requires that in democratic deliberation one put forward reasons that could in principle be accepted by others who do not share one's broader moral and philosophical beliefs. According to Gutmann and Thompson, 'the reasons must be mutually acceptable in the sense that they can be acknowledged by each citizen in circumstances of equal advantage'.[14] This means that one must carefully prescind from making arguments that depend in some essential way upon one's deepest convictions and beliefs—unless, that is, it turns out that some 'aspects of those beliefs could be accepted as principles and policies by other citizens with whom they fundamentally disagree'.[15] Otherwise, one would be 'impos[ing] a requirement on other citizens to adopt one's sectarian way of life as a condition of gaining access to the moral understanding that is essential to judging the validity of one's moral claims'.[16]

By insisting upon the further, stronger substantive constraint of reciprocity, deliberative democrats make it more likely that democratic practices, as they imagine them, will be able to fulfill liberalism's justificatory promise. By limiting citizens and their representatives to reasons that could in principle be shared by others, they defuse the threat of moral pluralism. Those aspects of our moral and philosophical beliefs that are unlikely to be shared by others are left conveniently in the antechamber of democratic deliberation, and our debates are structured according to terms that make it more likely that consensus will arise.

I think it is quite clear that something has gone wrong with the deliberative democrat's argument at this point. In essence, the challenge of moral pluralism has been not so much addressed as circumvented by the requirement of reciprocity, in much the same way that Rawls skirts it by assuming that people's conceptions of the good will be either silent or indeterminate on political questions. Reciprocity assumes that any reasonable intervention one might want to make in a policy debate can be made in the terms of public reason, that citizens will always be able to 'translate' into the 'reciprocal' language of public reason the arguments they would have been inclined to make had they been permitted to appeal to their deepest convictions. But this is far from clear. Now it is true that, especially in these purportedly postmodern, disenchanted times, many citizens will have eclectic sets of moral, philosophical, and political views that will in no way form a system or a 'comprehensive conception of the good life'. For these people it will be easier to separate the reasons they have for favouring a given policy from the views they may have concerning more general and abstract moral and philosophical questions. Their beliefs will exhibit what philosophers of mind have called 'modularity', that is, strong independence from one another across domains. It will therefore be relatively easy for them to present arguments to their fellow citizens on issues of public policy that do not presuppose their broader views. Others, however, will have beliefs that are more of a piece with one another. They will perceive their political views as flowing organically from their more general conceptions of what a good human life is. Though they may be able to argue for their preferred policies in ostensibly public language, this will involve some distortion of their views and will put them at a disadvantage in deliberation with others, as the arguments that the requirement of publicity would have them make will seem somewhat foreign and distant to them, as if they had been made to take up a character not their own in a play. It is clear that the requirement of reciprocity weighs more heavily upon citizens whose views are more tightly structured, and unless we simply state, in a question-begging manner, that such people are unreasonable, we must recognize that application of the norm of reciprocity will involve some unfairness.

More important in the present context, I think we can see quite clearly that deliberative democrats who insist upon the norm of reciprocity commit an error analogous to the one we have already identified in Rawls's work. They conveniently assume that what I have above called modularity is true of all reasonable citizens. They suppose that people's moral, philosophical, and political views come in separable chunks, and that people can, without any violence or distortion to their views, address political questions in terms of a shared, neutral 'public reason', making no reference to the broader world views that may in fact be animating their political views. This is of course analogous to Rawls's assumption that citizens' 'comprehensive conceptions of the good' would conveniently exhibit indeterminacy and vagueness precisely in the area of political debate, and that moral pluralism need not pose too great an obstacle to citizens coming to share a conception of justice. Just like Rawls, deliberative democrats who emphasize a strong requirement of reciprocity do not take moral pluralism seriously enough.

Let us take stock. I have shown that deliberative democrats view democratic practices (duly constrained and regimented) as the proper response to the justificatory deficit to which liberalism is prey in circumstances of pluralism. Where norms cannot be taken for granted as the basis for the justification of policies, let citizens find such norms for themselves through democratic deliberation. Given pluralism, however, deliberation is unlikely to yield shared, mutually justifiable results unless deliberators accept strong substantive constraints designed to defuse the threat that pluralism poses to mutual justification. But such substantive constraints address the threat of pluralism in appearance only. It is not deliberation among citizens, but rather the theorists' external imposition of norms of public reason, that is doing the work in closing the gap between citizens' diverse moral conceptions. And there is no reason for citizens not already inclined towards such norms of public reason to view this kind of resolution as acceptable.

Deliberative democrats describe a democratic practice that would enable democracy to make good on liberalism's traditional longing for rational justification. We have seen that the project fails on its own terms. More problematic still, from the viewpoint of the future development of a distinctively *democratic* theory, is that it presents us with a picture of democracy that threatens the realization of certain distinctively democratic values. Or so I want to argue in the space I have left.

How should we characterize the moral distinctiveness of democracy and its institutions? There are undoubtedly many ways to do this. My strategy will be to identify two broad categories of goods that democratic institutions can plausibly be geared towards, and to show that in both cases the reciprocity requirement, upon which deliberative democrats insist, must be relaxed to allow citizens and their representatives (in certain contexts) to make plain the connection between their opinions concerning issues of public policy and their deeper moral and philosophical commitments.

Let me begin by giving a brief account of the collective goods with which democratic institutions have traditionally been associated. It is a truism of democratic institutions that they allow for collective self-rule. At a superficial level, in line with what we have above called a 'proceduralist' conception of democracy, this can be understood in a mechanistic manner as the tallying up of pre-politically formed preferences on policy issues and the determination of a policy that satisfies those preferences to as great a degree as possible. Now, the proceduralist story clearly contains part of the truth about democracy. Democratic institutions allow us to act collectively despite our differences and disagreements. When these disagreements are deep and unresolvable, voting and acting according to the will of the majority will be the only way to avoid deadlock.

But democracy also holds out the promise that, through discussion and debate, we can at least on some occasions and to some degree narrow our differences and fashion normative agreements. How might this be achieved? For the sake of illustration, and with no claim to exhaustiveness, I will focus on two kinds of discursive outcomes, which might be termed 'bridge-building' and 'compromise'.

Bridge-building occurs when, through the teasing out of the implications of their own views as well as of those of their interlocutors, holders of what might at first glance have seemed irreconcilable views about the good life and the good society discover unsuspected overlaps between their views, be it at the level of general principle or at that of specific policy debate. The assumption here is that world views that might 'on paper' appear mutually incompatible may begin to reveal unsuspected resonances with one another when their adherents work out their implications in a dynamic and dialogical way. Others with whom we are engaged in dialogue might be more adept at seeing logical implications of our views that we may have been brought up not to see. Conversation and debate may force us to uphold our views about the good life in more imaginative and creative ways.

The point I want to make in the present context is that bridge-building requires mutual intelligibility. In order for citizens' horizons to be fused, those horizons must at the outset be clearly in view. If, in the name of a strong norm of reciprocity, we all prescind from revealing those aspects of our most deeply held views that affect our opinions about policy matters, we actually cut off the possibility of bridge-building as I have described it. Citizens who reach too quickly for a ready-made moral Esperanto—the kind that theorists of public reason would provide us with—deny themselves the more demanding, but potentially richer, achievement of democratic community that mutual intelligibility makes possible.

I don't want to claim that bridge-building will always be possible. There will be times when moral differences will prove intractable. When conceptions of the good life really *are* incompatible, however, democratic citizens must stand prepared to compromise. Compromise is importantly different both from consensus and from bargaining.[17] Deliberation issues in consensus if all participants are convinced that they have arrived at an ideal resolution of their dispute or debate. In bargaining, at least one of the parties will have had to climb down from her optimal outcome, but where one ends up with respect to one's original position is the result of one's comparative 'bargaining power'—that is, one's ability, through the proffering both of credible threats and of equally credible rewards, to 'make' one's interlocutor move as far as possible towards one's own starting position. Compromise is something else altogether. It is like bargaining in that parties do not achieve their ideal outcomes; but it is like deliberation geared at consensus in that reasons rather than power differentials determine where one ends up.

In a society marked by the fact of deep pluralism, consensus will be a rare commodity indeed. But it is a mistake to view the inability of the members of a society to achieve consensus as a mark of their failure as a 'real' community. At the same time, however, participants in democratic politics should resort to bargaining as I have described it here only as a last resort, for bargaining is irreducibly adversarial, an occasion in which the power differentials and inequalities that permeate a society—and that really do threaten its ability to constitute a community—are laid bare and allowed to operate in an unimpeded manner. This means that in pluralist societies, compromise will often represent the best attainable outcome to policy disputes. Now compromise requires that, in deliberation with others, one come to an assessment of what in one's overall position is essential and what is peripheral, of what one can give up without thereby threatening one's integrity and identity, and so on. A compromise will be an outcome in which parties manage to preserve enough of their original position to make compromise preferable to bargaining, and in which they will have given up aspects of their original position deemed less essential. (Thus evaluative concepts are essential to understanding the nature of a compromise but are not essential where bargains are concerned).

As in the case of bridge-building, mutual intelligibility is a condition of the possibility of compromise. Compromise requires that each interlocutor, in deliberation as well as in solitary reflection, determine what aspects of his initial position are essential to the preservation of his integrity and what aspects can be abandoned without fear of losing identity or integrity. This requires that they each have a sense of the *point*, of the animating spirit of their initial policy preferences. They must have a clear grasp of the reasons that lie at the basis of these preferences, and of the compromises that these reasons both make possible and preclude; thus they must have a first-person relation to their positions and to the reasons that underpin them. For instance, imagine that, in the context of some experiment, two people at odds on a public policy debate were required to negotiate on the basis of the *other* party's position. They would presumably be hamstrung: the position would seem foreign to them and, in particular, they would have no way of determining the nature and degree of the compromises that the position allows. All aspects of it would seem unidimensional to the deliberator cast in this role. She would have no way of making the assessments of relevance and priority that would come naturally to the person genuinely 'at home' with a position.

In a sense, defenders of a strong norm of reciprocity would have citizens participate in this kind of experiment in perpetuity. That is, they would have them negotiate and deliberate with one another according to terms that for some might not permit the expression of the reasons they have for holding certain political positions. Faced with the need to compromise, such citizens would find themselves saddled with a normative vocabulary that, for reasons that should by now be clear, might paradoxically make it more rather than less difficult to compromise.

I've just spelled out some of the ways in which democratic practices and institutions allow citizens of a disparate polity to achieve collective self-rule. In particular, I have suggested, they permit what I have called bridge-building and compromise. But they only do so if deliberators are not constrained by a strong substantive constraint of reciprocity.

But there are also *individual* values that can be served by well-designed democratic institutions. Considerations of space prevent me from entering into this issue fully here.[18] I will simply point to one value that participation in democratic arenas fosters in individual lives. I would hold that democratic deliberation fosters individual *autonomy*. According to a standard picture, we lack autonomy when our desires and inclinations rule us, as it were, from without. When we are merely pulled in this direction and that by the force of the strongest occurrent desire, we are *wantons* in Harry Frankfurt's sense.[19] Autonomy requires that we endorse those desires upon which we act. But as Charles Taylor has pointed out, such endorsement requires that we articulate a grid of values on the basis of which to sort out our different desires.[20] Individual autonomy therefore depends upon our spelling out, at least to some degree, our conception of what matters, of what makes a human life good.

Clearly the level of articulacy required for autonomy, according to accounts like Taylor's, does not belong to human agents as a birthright. It can be realized to lesser and greater degrees, and social and political conditions will be among the determinants of the level of autonomy that individuals will be able to achieve.[21] I want to suggest here that democratic deliberation fosters individual autonomy. If we accept (as I think we should) that, though we should eschew a strong substantive requirement of reciprocity, we should nonetheless insist upon the weaker substantive requirement of reason-giving, then it follows that part of what democratic deliberation will involve is precisely the articulation of citizens' basic evaluative commitments, or at least of those aspects of their commitments that inform their political opinions. In order to make their positions intelligible to their fellow citizens, they will have to spell out, as explicit reasons, certain values and commitments at the outset that they may very well have held in an inchoate or tacit way. The requirements of democratic life will demand that they reflectively endorse values and beliefs that may have been handed down to them by tradition or convention. The process of articulation need not always result in endorsement. It can also lead to refinement, revision, and, in some cases, rejection. (The ability to revise and/or reject one's conception of the good is clearly part of what individual autonomy involves.)

Now, democratic practices can foster autonomy in this way only if participants are allowed to participate in democratic deliberation without having to abstract from their most deeply held convictions. Autonomy requires that one articulate and endorse those desires, preferences, beliefs, and so forth, that are actually effective in informing one's decisions. Framing one's reasons for holding a given policy preference in terms provided by a conception of public reason, therefore, does not contribute to individual autonomy unless, as is possible, there is some significant overlap between the content of that conception and one's own conception of the good life.

Thus, not only is the strong constraint of reciprocity upon which many deliberative democrats insist unlikely to contribute to the rational justification of political and legal norms, but that constraint would prevent us from realizing, through our democratic institutions, communal and individual values that can be seen as *distinctive* of democracy.

Let me end by making a number of remarks that I hope to develop in future work. First, it is no part of my intention to argue that democratic institutions should operate in the absence of any normative constraint. The procedural and weak substantive constraints described above strike me as entirely appropriate. Realization of the collective and individual goods towards which I have suggested that democratic institutions be geared probably requires that these constraints be in place.

What's more, I do not want to suggest that reciprocity as deliberativists describe it is never appropriate. First, there may be particular fora in which the kind of restraint that reciprocity enjoins is almost always appropriate. For example, John Rawls has limited the scope of application of his conception of public reason to the discourse of judges, government officials, and candidates for public office in the course of their campaigns,[22] and has maintained that 'the idea of public reason does not apply to the background culture with its many forms of nonpublic reason nor to media of any kind.'[23] Given that political actors such as these must represent or stand in for a plurality of constituents, who will most likely be quite divided among themselves on broader moral and philosophical issues, the requirement of reciprocity may very well be appropriate here. Insisting upon it becomes problematic only when its scope is extended to all manner of democratic decision-making bodies by theorists who, like the majority of deliberative democrats I have canvassed, believe that deliberation, with its accompanying norm of reciprocity, ought to permeate the political culture of a society from top to bottom.[24]

Nor do I deny that there may be occasions, even in democratic deliberations more mundane than those that take place in legislatures and courts, where the kind of restraint that reciprocity denotes is appropriate. Appeal to one's deepest convictions may at times foster discussion by clarifying a position that may have appeared incomprehensible to one's interlocutor when stated *in abstracto*. But it may also, depending on its timing or on the spirit in which it is made, act to inhibit conversation. In general, it is essential to see that there can be public-spirited uses of values and concepts that, according to advocates of a restrictive conception of public reason, would have to count as non-public. (For example, as Rawls acknowledges, abolitionists and civil-rights advocates used religious language to impeccably public ends in pointing to the incompatibility of Christian beliefs and slavery or segregation.[25]) And there can also be *non*-public-spirited uses of language that, again according to theorists of public reason, should count as unproblematically *public*. (Think, for example, of the strategic use made of public language by those who favour the non-public, religious/communal end of religious schools by invoking considerations of 'parental rights'.) As these two examples make clear, the independent variable here is the 'spirit' in which different conceptual resources are used, rather than the nature of those conceptual resources taken in abstraction. This suggests that what theorists of public reason should be looking for is on the order of a virtue rather than a set of rules.[26]

Normative democratic theory has in recent years been making a long overdue return. None of what I have argued should be read as suggesting that it should eclipse or supersede the continuing development of liberal theory. Democratic theorists should not, after all, make the same mistake as liberals in thinking that only one element of the liberal democratic compound can pull normative weight. What I do want to suggest is that democratic theorists should focus more than they have tended to on the distinctive virtues, goods, and values of democratic practices and institutions. Democratic theory is distorted if it simply inherits the traditional theoretical preoccupations of liberal theory.

Notes

1. The most important single work on the topic to date is undoubtedly Amy Gutmann and Dennis Thompson, *Democracy and Disagreement* (Cambridge, Mass.: Harvard University

Press, 1996). See also C.S. Nino, *The Constitution of Deliberative Democracy* (New Haven: Yale University Press, 1997); James Bohman, *Public Deliberation* (Cambridge: MIT Press, 1996); and Simone Chambers, *Reasonable Democracy* (Ithaca: Cornell University Press, 1997). See also the articles collected in the four following collections: Jon Elster, ed., *Deliberative Democracy* (Cambridge: Cambridge University Press, 1998); James Bohman and William Rehg, eds, *Deliberative Democracy* (Cambridge, Mass.: MIT Press, 1998); Seyla Benhabib, ed., *Democracy and Difference* (Princeton: Princeton University Press, 1996); and David Copp, Jean Hampton, and John Roemer, eds, *The Idea of Democracy* (Cambridge: Cambridge University Press, 1993). A valiant attempt at canvassing this literature sympathetically yet critically can be found in James Bohman, 'The Coming of Age of Deliberative Democracy', *Journal of Political Philosophy* 6 (1998), 400–25.

2. There have, of course, been exceptions. See, for example, Benjamin Barber, *Strong Democracy* (Berkeley: University of California Press, 1984); and Carole Pateman, *Participation and Democratic Theory* (Cambridge: Cambridge University Press, 1970).
3. Ronald Dworkin, 'The Forum of Principle', in Rawls, *A Matter of Principle* (Oxford: Oxford University Press, 1985), especially 57–71.
4. The central texts in this connection are John Rawls, 'Outline of a Decision Procedure for Ethics', originally published in 1951, reprinted in *Collected Papers*, ed. Samuel Freeman (Cambridge, Mass.: Harvard University Press, 1999); and Rawls, *A Theory of Justice* (Cambridge, Mass.: Harvard University Press, 1971), 48–51.
5. See, in particular, the essays collected in *Four Essays on Liberty* (Oxford: Oxford University Press, 1969). I have written about Berlin's pluralism in my 'The Graying of Berlin', *Critical Review* 11 (1997), 481–501.
6. John Rawls, *Political Liberalism* (New York: Columbia University Press, 1993), xxvii–xix.
7. Including the present author, whose views on this issue are developed at greater length in 'The Justification of Political Liberalism', *Pacific Philosophical Quarterly* 75, 3–4 (1995).
8. This point is also made in Jeremy Waldron, *Law and Disagreement* (Oxford: Oxford University Press, 1999), 151–3.
9. Fred D'Agostino, *Free Public Reason: Making It Up As We Go* (Oxford: Oxford University Press, 1996).
10. Amy Gutmann and Dennis Thompson, 'Why Deliberative Democracy Is Different', *Social Philosophy and Policy*, 17, 1 (2000), 61–2.
11. Seyla Benhabib, 'Toward a Deliberative Model of Democratic Legitimacy', in *Democracy and Difference*. Note that Benhabib's understanding of 'proceduralism' is, unlike Gutmann and Thompson's, fully compatible with deliberativist requirements.
12. Jürgen Habermas, 'Discourse Ethics: Notes on a Program of Philosophical Justification', in *Moral Consciousness and Communicative Action*, trans. Christian Lenhardt and Shierry Weber Nicholson (Cambridge: MIT Press, 1990), 89. Cf. Simone Chambers, 'Contract or Conversation? Theoretical Lessons from the Canadian Constitutional Crisis', *Politics and Society* 26 (1998), 156; Seyla Benhabib, 'Toward a Deliberative Model of Democratic Legitimacy', 70.
13. Cass Sunstein's idea of an 'incompletely theorized agreement' is relevant in this connection. See his *Legal Reasoning and Political Conflict* (Oxford: Oxford University Press, 1996), 37.
14. Gutmann and Thompson, *Democracy and Disagreement*, 54. Cf. James Bohman, *Public*

Deliberation, 25; and Joshua Cohen, 'Deliberation and Democratic Legitimacy', in *Deliberative Democracy*, 75.

15. Gutmann and Thompson, *Democracy and Disagreement*, 93.
16. Ibid., 57.
17. The only systematic treatment of compromise of which I am aware is Martin Benjamin, *Splitting the Difference: Compromise and Integrity in Ethics and Politics* (Lawrence: University of Kansas Press, 1990).
18. I develop these points at greater length in my forthcoming essay 'Democracy, Value and Truth'.
19. Harry Frankfurt, 'Freedom of the Will and the Concept of a Person', in *Free Will*, ed. Gary Watson (Oxford: Oxford University Press, 1983), 81–93.
20. Charles Taylor, 'What is Human Agency?', in *Philosophical Papers 1: Human Agency and Language* (Cambridge: Cambridge University Press, 1985).
21. I have developed this point at greater length in 'The Political Theory of Strong Evaluation', in *Philosophy in an Age of Pluralism: The Philosophy of Charles Taylor in Question*, ed. James Tully (Cambridge: Cambridge University Press, 1993).
22. John Rawls, 'The Idea of Public Reason Revisited', *University of Chicago Law Review* 64 (1997), 767.
23. Ibid., 768.
24. The following statement by Gutmann and Thompson is emblematic in this regard: '[T]he practice of deliberation should not be confined to the institutions of government. Unless citizens have the experience of reasoning together in other institutions in which they spend more of their time they are not likely to develop either the interest or the skill that would enable them to deliberate effectively in politics. That is why it is so important that the processes of decision-making that citizens encounter at work and at leisure should seek to cultivate the virtues of deliberation' (*Democracy and Disagreement*, 359).
25. John Rawls, *Political Liberalism*, 249–51.
26. I pursue this suggestion in my 'Vers une théorie kantienne de la vertu civique', in *Essais en hommage à Pierre Laberge*, ed. F. Duchesneau, G. Lafrance, and C. Piché (Paris: Vrin-Bellarmin, 2000).

Self-Defeating Political Education

Eamonn Callan

1.

Political education of some sort plays a role in sustaining any regime over time. But two facts about liberal democracy magnify the importance of this point. First, the ends of political education are more onerous for a free people than the thoughtless deference to authority that might suffice under undemocratic conditions. Democracy requires that we participate in a process of collective self-rule, and participation under the complex and conflict-ridden conditions of contemporary democracies will be dangerously incompetent unless it is informed by a fair degree of political understanding and commitment to democratic norms. Second, because the democracy we seek to perpetuate is liberal, it must keep faith with ideals of limited government and negative liberty that an illiberal republicanism could discount. Keeping faith must mean that we rely less on the coercive power of government and more on the understanding and virtue of citizens to safeguard our basic political practices against erosion. Therefore, educational processes that promote the relevant understanding and virtue become critical to the continuance of those practices.

Yet the same public ideals that underscore the importance of political education for us also motivate a certain wariness about state action undertaken in its name. An abiding theme of democratic thought is the freedom of each generation to revise its institutions in disregard of the dead hand of the past and to challenge traditions that so often protect the special interests of political and economic elites. New practices are commonly needed for new circumstances, and authentic self-rule is blocked by the irrational reverence for custom and entrenched patterns of dominance that persist in imperfectly democratic societies. But if the civic identity of each generation is shaped through state-mandated political education, then the dead hand of the past seems inescapable, and so far as it is, political education becomes anti-democratic. Parallel doubts about the state as educator are prompted by what is liberal in liberal democracy. One of our common-sense political distinctions is between an invasive politics of virtue, wedded to some partisan conception of the good and the right, and a liberal polity that leaves citizens free to discover or choose their own values within lax boundaries fixed by the basic rights of others. Reconciling that distinction with a substantial educational role for the liberal state poses an obvious question: How could a state whose distinctiveness lies in respecting the freedom of citizens to develop and express their own values claim the authority to mould their identity in its public aspects? A convincing answer may be especially elusive given that our identities do not neatly divide into discrete public and nonpublic components, and inculcating any particular set of civic virtues is liable to affect deeply the people we become outside politics as well. In a word, the education that presents itself as the necessary means of perpetuating liberal democracy is also liable to be renounced, once state power is exercised in its support, as a self-defeating process of civic homogenization, at odds with both democratic and liberal principles.

I want to draw the very rough outlines of a conception of political education that acknowledges and clarifies its pivotal role in the survival and flourishing of free political institutions. I also intend to show that the conception is not undermined by whatever prudent doubts we might have about the potentially self-defeating effects of public policy intended to implement the conception. Nevertheless, I think the hazards of self-defeat will always attend state action in the sphere of political education, even if they can be contained. Measures intended to dispel liberal worries about self-defeat will tend to exacerbate democratic concerns about the realization of genuine self-rule, and policies that answer to those concerns are liable to spur liberal worries about toleration.

2.

A political education for liberal democracy that is not self-defeating must satisfy at least a couple of conditions. The education we want must not bind the future of democracy through a pedagogy that would seal a political orthodoxy against all possibility of reflective assessment and revision in the future; it must also honour the values of limited government and individual liberty that are the hallmarks of liberal politics. These are strong considerations, and they might seem to support the demand for a political education that is *minimal* in scope. By forgoing all purposes beyond those necessary to ensure the continuity of our constitutive public practices across generations, the state's educational role is curtailed so as to protect liberal rights and leave the future of democracy open for the authentic self-rule of coming generations. On the other hand, educational measures that flout the minimal requirement will tend to defeat themselves by foreclosing the future of democracy and invading rights.

Described at this level of abstraction, the argument for minimal political education looks compelling. But almost everything depends on what we think lies inside or outside the particular array of public norms that gives substance to the minimal requirement. I claim we should interpret these in a manner that entails a morally substantial political education. If that education is minimal in a certain sense, it is certainly not negligible, and its implementation would likely have much more radical consequences than the contemporary adherents of minimalism would acknowledge.

The content of a minimal civic education derives from the core of political norms or practices that distinguish liberal democratic regimes from the alternatives.

Whatever these may be, their persistence across generations is necessary if liberal democracy is to endure, and so whatever skills, virtues, and the like are necessary to their persistence will be part of the civic minimum. What then are the relevant practices? Some obvious candidates are these: recognition of basic rights to privacy; freedom of conscience, expression, and association; equal consideration of all citizens under the rule of law; political rights that give each at least a formally equal voice in the process of collective self-rule. These are generic criteria of liberal democracy, and the formation of civic identity can hardly be confined to them when the stakes are the continuity and stability of specific liberal democratic regimes. Future citizens must understand and learn, at least provisionally, to endorse the specific content of the constitution under which they will live. So the civic minimum comprises common commitments and understandings that have to do with universal norms of liberal democratic government and their institutional embodiment in a particular political community. I want here to focus on the universalistic component of the civic minimum, since this raises the more basic philosophical questions.[1]

Think about shared commitment first. (I return to the issue of common understandings in Section 4.) On the least demanding reading, the civic minimum would not require that this have any moral source. So long as people adhere to the practices that make their society liberal and democratic, we should not worry about why they are committed, and therefore, we should not worry about why future citizens come to be committed. Compliance may draw on sheer self-interest, and so long as compliance is the result, we have no reason to favour one motivational source over another. Indifference to sources of compliance is nourished by several vague but influential ideas in post-Enlightenment thought: the loose association of public virtue with pre-liberal politics; the idea that free societies must in some way be 'neutral' regarding citizens' conceptions of their lives' meaning; and, perhaps most important of all, faith in the tendency of self-interest to minister to common ends under conditions of liberty. But there is no need to pursue any of these ideas far to see that indifference to sources of compliance is a bad mistake in the conduct of political education.

Part of what inclines people to make this mistake is the fact that marshalling many different motives to support the norms of liberal democracy is prudent statecraft. Racial discrimination in the workplace, say, is easier to combat when it comes to be seen as not merely an affront to human dignity but bad for business as well. Conversely, compliance is inevitably at risk if it is seen as requiring relentless and costly self-sacrifice. So learning to think of the society in which liberal democratic norms apply as an environment hospitable to the pursuit of one's own good is one important condition facilitating their internalization. Furthermore, the familiar postulate of universal self-interest, and its attendant skepticism about the self-proclaimed virtue of elites, have often served important ends by alerting the politically preyed-upon to the true intentions of their predators (Holmes 1995, 65). And because appreciating the dignity each of us must claim as a free and equal citizen involves an affirmation of *legitimate* self-interest, that affirmation is integral to the sense of entitlement that just societies will cultivate (Hampton 1997). But it does not follow that moral sources of compliance are unnecessary. The obvious possibilities of selective compliance and free-riding show that the accommodation to others' interests necessary for secure free institutions would be severely compromised if those institutions were widely valued only as means of advancing self-interest. The histories of self-styled liberal democracies offer many examples of groups excluded from the benefits of equal citizenship, and the persistence of exclusion can typically be explained, in part at least, by the advantages that exclusion creates for privileged groups (Smith 1997). To suggest that reasons of enlightened self-interest could always persuade the privileged to give up their unjust advantages is simply preposterous.

A deeper problem with the idea that the civic minimum has no necessary moral content is the assumption that moral attitudes are not intrinsic to our constitutive political practices. That assumption does not withstand scrutiny. For example, are we really to suppose that the avoidance of racial discrimination in the sense required by the equality of citizens does not entail any moral commitment on the part of those who avoid it? To say there is no such entailment implies that a society in which racial hatred continues to thrive behind a public pretense of racial harmony is just as consistent with liberal democratic norms as one in which genuine comity across racial divisions has taken hold. But that implication flies in the face of our ordinary understanding of what the basic equality of citizens signifies. Our constitutive political practices are not a bundle of rules to be followed for any reason at all; they are the public expression of shared moral attitudes.

What are these attitudes? The constitutional traditions of stable liberal democracies commonly attest to the fundamental role of mutual respect in public life. Consider the rationale that the Supreme Court of Canada gave for Section 15 of the Canadian Charter of Rights and Freedoms, which affirms a cluster of equality rights: 'The promotion of equality entails the promotion of a society in which all are secure in the knowledge that they are recognized at law as human beings equally deserving of concern, respect and consideration' (*Andrews v. Law Society of British Columbia*, 174). Thus the ultimate point of making non-discrimination a legal requirement is not merely to discourage forms of behaviour that can be described in a motivationally neutral way; it is to encourage the realization of a certain kind of political community in which the law expresses, and is publicly known to express, a recognition of the equal worth that inheres in each citizen's life. On this account, it is senseless to say that the norm of equality we share can endure without drawing upon distinctively moral sources. It is senseless because moral attitudes of reciprocal regard are internal to equality in the sense that matters politically.

A familiar objection is sure to be pressed at this point. The proposal that basic liberal democratic practices carry stringent moral demands is sure to be rejected by many who will see it as a way of advancing a particular, partisan ideology that some, but by no means all, citizens share. After all, the rationale for equality that the Supreme Court of Canada endorsed is a principle commonly adduced in arguments for affirmative action, minority rights, pay equity, and similar controversial measures. Those who reject the policies will be tempted to denounce the principle as well, and to regard it as a distortion of some more modest notion of impartial consideration that does belong within our defining public norms. But this response misses the point. Those who reject affirmative action, minority rights, pay equity, and the like characteristically do so on the grounds that these policies create arbitrary benefits for some at the cost of unjust burdens for others who are equally deserving. That is to say, the policies are rejected because they are thought to militate against 'a society in which all are secure in the knowledge that they are recognized at law as human beings equally deserving of concern, respect and consideration'. Of course, affirmative action might also be rejected because its intended beneficiaries are alleged to be inherently less worthy of consideration than others. But to make that argument is to opt out of serious public debate by declaring allegiance to some notion of ascriptive hierarchy that the government of a free people precludes. Serious debate about distributive justice is badly misrepresented as a choice between a morally onerous egalitarian norm and an undemanding alternative; the real debate is about how best to interpret the onerous norm when rival interpretations prescribe different burdens and benefits for different groups.

Any defensible civic education must include the cultivation of robust attitudes of mutual respect among future citizens. But even if that much is granted, nothing immediately follows about what is warranted in the way of state-mandated or -sponsored political education. At least one serious liberal argument suggests that we cannot countenance a substantial role for the state here, notwithstanding the foundational role of moral ideals to civic identity in liberal democracies. I want now to outline that argument, expose its inadequacy, and show how its animating ideas point to very different conclusions.

3.

At the root of liberal anxieties about self-defeating political education are the values of limited government and liberty. Given the argument of Section 2, a cogent interpretation of these values will surely regard them as moral commitments that flow from the mutual respect of citizens who seek to live together as free and equal citizens. But if that is so, it seems possible to accept the moral character of liberal democratic norms and the education that befits them and yet still insist that policies within the bounds of the civic minimum must ask very little of us because more ambitious conceptions are ruled out by considerations derived from those very norms.

That possibility is canvassed in the political liberalism that has recently moved to the centre of debate in liberal theory. Liberal theory since its very beginnings has sought to reconcile the wide range of lives that people freely choose under modern conditions with the socially unifying demands of justice and stability. According to John Rawls and other contemporary political liberals, this project of reconciliation has foundered because liberal philosophers have traditionally argued for principles of justice and stability on the basis of comprehensive metaphysical and moral doctrines. These traditional arguments, which are bundled together under the label of 'comprehensive liberalism', make liberalism into 'but another sectarian doctrine' by licensing the oppression of all who cannot in conscience accept them (Rawls 1993, 246). Political liberals take a different tack. In constructing their theories of justice, they appeal to common moral ideas in the civic culture, rather than controversial metaphysical and moral premises, and they emphasize that adherence to liberal justice may stem from many conflicting convictions and loyalties, both religious and secular. Thus so far as political liberalism extends respect to reasonable citizens whom comprehensive liberalism is said to exclude from full and equal participation in the public sphere, it constitutes a fuller realization of liberal justice. And to the extent that it elicits the support of those who would remain alienated from free institutions once these are wedded to comprehensive doctrines of any sort, the stability of the just state is also made more secure—or so the story goes.

Rawls claims that the superiority of political liberalism over its comprehensive rivals is evident in their divergent implications for political education. Since comprehensive liberals believe that the justice and stability of the state depend on our accepting the truth of some particular comprehensive doctrine, educational practices that aim at justice and stability must promote that politically privileged doctrine, even if its promotion triggers widespread dissent. But once the state embarks on that course, it abandons the restraints of limited government and violates the freedoms of those who conscientiously reject values that the state now forces on them and their children. Political education grounded in the tenets of comprehensive liberalism thus becomes self-defeating. Rawls assures us that political education in the spirit of political liberalism can avoid this impasse:

> The liberalisms of Kant and Mill may lead to requirements designed to foster the values of autonomy and individuality as ideals that govern much if not all of life. But political liberalism has a different source and requires far less. It will ask that children's education include such things as knowledge of their constitutional and civic rights so that, for example, they know that apostasy is not a legal crime, all this to ensure that their continued membership when they come of age is not based simply on ignorance of their basic rights or fear of punishment for offenses that do not exist. Moreover, their education . . . should also encourage the political virtues so that they want to honor the fair terms of social cooperation in their relations with the rest of society (Rawls 1993, 199).

The evident purpose of this passage is to stress how little the civic minimum demands once it is understood according to Rawls's political liberalism. The example of the child who might grow up thinking that apostasy is a legal crime underscores that purpose. (Imagine how intellectually impoverished and insular a child's upbringing would have to be for *that* thought to take root and endure in any constitutional democracy.) Yet Rawls's apparent endorsement of an austere educational minimalism makes no sense, given the logic of his own case for political liberalism.

His offhand allusion to virtues that support 'the fair terms of social cooperation' has to be understood in the light of his distinction between reasonable and unreasonable pluralism, as well as the so-called 'political conception of the person' he adduces to explain that distinction. I want now to elucidate the distinction and to show how it leads us back to the necessity of a morally exacting (and, in many cases, culturally subversive) political education.

I argued in Section 2 that the constitutive practices of liberal democracy revolve around an ideal of political community in which citizens' lives are tied together through bonds of mutual respect. If political liberalism gives us a better understanding of the justice and stability to which this kind of community can rightly aspire, that cannot be merely because it imposes fewer restrictions on the many ways of life that people happen to choose. Since people often freely choose to live in ways flatly opposed to norms of mutual respect, if we want mutual respect to prevail in public life we need a morally discriminating response to pluralism on the part of the state. The need for that discrimination is acknowledged in Rawls's claim that political liberalism seeks to accommodate reasonable but not unreasonable pluralism. But the bare concept of reasonable pluralism does not yield the necessary discrimination. Rawls needs a conception that can show how the discrimination is to be made in the ongoing civic life of a just society. That need is met through Rawls's political conception of the person.

The conception is offered as a gloss on the democratic truism that society is properly a scheme of fair co-operation between free and equal citizens: 'The basic idea is that in virtue of their two moral powers (a capacity for a sense of justice and a conception of the good) and the powers of reason (of judgment, thought and inference connected with these powers), persons are free. Their having these powers to the requisite minimum degree makes them equal' (Rawls 1993, 19). As citizens, we supposedly have highest-order interests in the realization of these powers, and our understanding of the just state and the just citizen must be developed accordingly. I am interested in what the conception says about the virtue of justice that citizens are enjoined to cultivate. That virtue is what enables them to distinguish the reasonable pluralism that deserves their respect from the unreasonable variety that does not.

Rawls employs a distinctive notion of 'the reasonable' to elucidate the content of the sense of justice. The application of the notion to persons has two aspects. First, a commitment to moral reciprocity is necessary. Reasonable persons want to establish fair terms of co-operation with others. They are ready to propose such terms to others and to discuss the counter-proposals that others might make in turn so that terms acceptable to all might be found. Once mutually acceptable terms are found, reasonable persons are ready to comply with the terms should others be willing to do likewise. The second aspect is 'the willingness to recognize the burdens of judgment and to accept their consequences for the use of public reason in directing the legitimate exercise of political power in a constitutional regime' (Rawls 1993, 54). Rawls introduces the idea of the burdens of judgment both to explain the possibility of irreconcilable moral disagreement among reasonable people and to justify the mutual accommodation that liberal politics will promote when that disagreement threatens to undermine co-operation. The 'burdens' are those particular sources of divergent judgment that persist among us when all factors that signify a remediable failure to reason competently and to exhibit reciprocity have been corrected. They are the contingent but inescapable imperfections of our capacity to reason together toward common judgments in public deliberation (Rawls 1993, 55).

Why should we assume that our capacity to reason together is inescapably burdened in such ways? To suppose that a shared reasonableness guarantees consensus is to overlook the general tendencies to disagreement that afflict even the most accomplished exercise of reason by different people, as well as the special difficulties we face when reason is harnessed to reciprocity in collective deliberation. In that setting, we face difficulties not only in weighing precisely our own interests against those of others, but also in balancing and understanding the interests of different others. These specific difficulties combine with the general frailties of reason to suggest that many sources of discordant judgment in our public life would survive the disappearance of the remediable vices of unreason—habitual logical bungling and the like. Rawls lists some of the unremediable sources of disagreement that constitute the burdens of judgment: all our ideas are to some degree subject to hard cases, but this is an especially prominent feature of our moral and political concepts; judgment is likely to be affected by contingencies of culture and experience whose pull towards partiality we cannot altogether escape, however reasonable we might be; the values we live by are chosen from a wide range of possibilities, those we choose have to be arranged in some order of priority, and both the choosing and the arranging can be done in many equally rational but incompatible ways.

Reciprocity as Rawls describes it is a virtue that almost everyone would commend. If some people reject it because they are indifferent to what fellow citizens of a different class or gender think is fair, or if they violate fair rules even when others are ready to comply, then the fact that Rawls would assign their views and conduct to the category of unreasonable pluralism does not go against the inclusive spirit of his political liberalism. As I noted earlier, it is the inclusion of reasonable pluralism that political liberals care about, and whenever the actions or judgments of some are clearly repugnant to the basic equality of citizens, these must be disregarded as instances of unreasonable pluralism. Conduct motivated by sheer inegalitarian prejudice might often warrant toleration, but liberals still have strong reasons to discourage it, by educational and other means. Thus the stipulation that learning to be a just citizen involves learning to evince reciprocity would appear to be uncontroversially valid, appealing as it does to well-established truisms about the equality of citizens. But acceptance of the burdens of judgment looks far more contestable. This is where Rawls's political conception of the person starts to look exigent and culturally subversive. Acceptance implies that just citizens will acknowledge the reasonableness of moral and other doctrines that may be sharply at odds with their own. Given that the acknowledgment is liable to weaken the psychological hold of traditional ways of life and encourage a propensity to individual autonomy, it will be viewed as a grave threat to the most basic convictions of many decent citizens.

At this point Rawls faces a dilemma. The alleged gap between comprehensive liberalism, with its agenda for a political education that would be pitted against the freedom of citizens to reject a broadly liberal reading of the good life, and a narrowly political liberalism, one that only lightly constrains the formation of public identity, is undermined by the requirement that future citizens should learn to accept the burdens of judgment. So Rawls must either abandon the distinction between political and comprehensive liberalism or else attenuate the political conception of the person by abandoning the idea of the burdens of judgment. The latter option will seem attractive if we think that reciprocity and acceptance of the burdens of judgment are independent conditions of reasonableness. If they were independent, the conception might be revised so that reciprocity alone gave the conception its moral content. Some political liberals have taken this option, dismissing the idea of the burdens of judgment as an unfortunate trace of comprehensive liberal theory that a more thoroughgoing political liberalism would erase (Wenar 1995; Strike 1996). But this is wrong. The idea of the burdens of judgment is one we are compelled to accept as part of our ideal of citizenship once we try to align social co-operation with the demands of reciprocity in conditions of diversity. To see why we are compelled, more needs to be said about reciprocity.

Reciprocity is a virtue designed to help us find mutually acceptable terms of co-operation in circumstances where we initially disagree about what fairness requires but agree in recognizing each other as moral equals. In exhibiting reciprocity, I begin by putting before you what I take to be fair. But I must also be ready to discuss the opposing proposals that you make in the hope of moving toward a common perspective that each of us could accept in good conscience. Your viewpoint is as important as mine to the fulfillment of that hope, and only through empathic identification with your viewpoint can I appreciate what moral reason there might be for what you say. If I am to weigh your claims as a matter of fairness, I must provisionally suspend the thought that you are wrong and instead enter imaginatively into the moral perspective you occupy. I must try to appreciate the interests you seek to protect in social co-operation, but I cannot succeed in that task without something akin to the insider's understanding of the way of life in which those interests arise. Empathic understanding does not mean that I am required unreflectively to endorse the perspective you take. Since you and I are reasoning about fairness, I cannot be uncritical about your view (or my own). If my counter-proposal were always simply to split the difference between us, I would be acting as if we were haggling over how to satisfy conflicting preferences rather than thinking together about justice. Empathic understanding must be combined with a willingness to bring the shared resources of reason to bear on the conflict at hand: for example, by assessing the comparative strength of the assumptions behind our pre-reflective judgments, or by exploring together the plausibility of the implications that flow from the rival moral principles we invoke in defence of our opposing views.

Within a diverse polity, the empathic identification that reciprocity-governed dialogue requires must mean that we come to understand, to some degree at least, the divergent doctrines and cultural identities that abound in the social background of public deliberation. Without that understanding, we cannot respect citizens whose creed or culture disposes them to see questions of social co-operation differently than we do, even though they may be no less reasonable than we are. This is the shared understanding that no morally credible interpretation of political education can preclude. But to say that reciprocity demands this of us is to say that it requires acceptance of the burdens of judgment.

If Rawls's dilemma cannot be solved by discarding the idea of the burdens of judgment, however, the problem of self-defeating political education has not been evaded. An education that teaches reciprocity will also encourage a form of mutual understanding with consequences that resonate far beyond the role of citizen, making it harder to sustain identification with traditional ways of life and nourishing an autonomy that cannot be safely confined to the public sphere. Citizens for whom these consequences are repugnant will condemn any role the state might take in furthering such education as a violation of the proper restraints of free government.

4.

I have argued that a political education in keeping with the moral demands of liberal democratic citizenship will tend to have a profound effect on the overall identity of citizens, not just the manner in which they perform one particular social role among others. But notice that this is an argument about the rightful ends of political education rather than the means of achieving them. Much liberal hand-wringing about self-defeating political education is misplaced because it rests on confusion between legitimate educational ends and appropriate or permissible means.

Nothing in what I have said about justice as a political virtue suggests that the state is fully justified in taking any coercive action that effectively diffuses that virtue. That view of justified coercion captures a distinctively pre-liberal way of thinking about the public significance of virtue. If virtue is identified with a particular religious creed, then conversions precipitated or heresies arrested at the point of a sword redound to the public good, and the end straightforwardly justifies the means. But part of the achievement of liberalism is that we can no longer think of justified coercion in this way. The liberal ideal of toleration requires forbearance towards those whose lives go against the grain of public virtue, and toleration is invoked in marking the proper limits of government and the boundaries of a right to freedom that is not contingent on either character or conviction. This is not the place to rehearse all the moral reasons that shape the practice of toleration. But prominent among them will be our need to minimize the suffering and humiliation we impose on people when we disrupt a cherished way of life, regardless of how far it falls short of the high demands of public virtue (Strike 1998, 358). However cogent my arguments about the ends of political education might be, to pursue these ends on the assumption that the triumph of public virtue will always justify the costs of coercion would be to engage in self-defeating political education by renouncing the toleration that lies at the core of liberal tradition.

Nevertheless, registering the importance of toleration in constraining the state's proper educational role is not a sufficient basis for understanding the full range of that role. Consider a couple of different things we should want from a normative theory of political education. It should tell us about the limits of what is politically *tolerable* in matters of children's teaching and learning. The relevant question here might be this: What forms of (mis)education are so grievous that they violate the basic rights of children or inculcate racial hatred or other attitudes inimical to the most elementary moral responsibilities of citizenship? The theory we want might also furnish at least a partial conception of the *best* education by prescribing a range of political virtues as ideal educational ends as well as practices conducive to their realization. The two desiderata must not be confused. One way of bringing out the contrast between them is to compare the different roles that appeals to individual autonomy might have in determining what is educationally tolerable and what is educationally best.

Arguments about what is tolerable will properly shape whatever policies the state enforces in the regulation of all schools, whether they are public or private, funded or unfunded by government. If autonomy is relevant here, it has to be a pretty modest conception that pertains to basic conditions of independent or non-servile agency. Otherwise we assume that ways of life inconsistent with some more or less sophisticated ideal of autonomous development are politically intolerable, and that surely does run counter to deep intuitions about the limits of legitimate government. On the other hand, a theory of what educational practices are best, as opposed to merely tolerable, might appeal to autonomy in a more ambitious way. If the argument of Section 3 is sound, then the best political education will conduce to the high degree of reflective autonomy that reasonable citizenship demands. Arguments about the best education are politically relevant to deliberation about the less invasive ways in which the state might intervene in the formation of future citizens—for example, debate about the terms on which state sponsorship might be extended to private schools rather than debate about the terms on which they are to be tolerated. Much more could and should be said about this. But the distinction between what is tolerable and what is best shows how an exacting conception of the ends of political education leaves room for state action that serves those ends without forfeiting scruples about liberty and the rightful limits of government.

5.

I noted at the beginning of this chapter that the problem of self-defeating political education comes in both liberal and democratic versions. In Section 4 I tried to address the liberal version. I shall conclude by saying a little about its democratic counterpart.

Democratic concerns have to do with the conditions of authentic collective self-rule, and the risk that a substantive educational role for the state will undermine these. Among the issues at stake here are obvious facts about the susceptibility of state power to corruption and the acute dangers that corruption poses in matters concerning the formation of identity. Genuine self-rule cannot exist when collective decisions are made under the pressure of grave external threats. But neither can it hold when powerful groups distort the process of collective deliberation to pre-empt options contrary to their interests, or when future citizens are constrained by some combination of ignorance, prejudice, and deference to authority that renders them incapable of participating rationally and justly in collective deliberation. To the extent that a role for the state in determining the content of education tends to undermine the conditions of genuine democratic rule, the state cannot be trusted to educate for democracy.

But if state power in education is susceptible to corruption, are we to assume that concentrations of power in other contexts are necessarily less susceptible? It would be the height of naïveté to suppose that once the state forgoes a substantive educational role, the other institutions that impinge on the formation of identity can be trusted to minister to authentic self-rule. Socialization in many families and associations of civil society also tends to produce a despotism over the mind because the inequalities of power they embody lend themselves to abuse. If the combination of ignorance, prejudice, and deference to authority that makes future citizens incapable of contributing to serious democratic deliberation is a consequence of what their parents taught or failed to teach them rather than the state, it is no less an erosion of authentic self-rule for that. The point here is not that states can be trusted not to abuse educational authority; the point is rather that nobody can. The best distribution of educational authority, given either democratic or liberal ends, is not a question to be settled a priori because any sensible answer will appeal to variable social contingencies (Raz 1986, 427–8). But in general there may be strong prima facie reasons to favour a sharing of authority among different institutions, including the state, in order that the partiality of one might counterbalance that of the others.

One final point. I suggested that authentic collective self-rule is achieved to the extent that citizens participate in public life rationally and justly. This ideal meshes with the liberal account I gave in Section 3 of political virtue. But notice that liberal concerns about self-defeating political education were assuaged by forswearing aggressive state action to promote virtue. The liberal state is committed to toleration, and though it might legitimately resort to coercion to arrest the cultivation of egregious political vice, it cannot force virtue on the citizenry without ceasing to be liberal. Yet this means that the liberal state, so far as it cleaves to toleration in its educational policies, acquiesces in the perpetuation of ways of life that impair the capacity of future citizens to participate rationally and justly in public life. That being so, the ideal of authentic self-rule must always elude us to some degree, because its single-minded pursuit would destroy what is liberal in liberal democracy.

Notes

The argument of this chapter draws on Callan 1997, especially in Section 3.

1. The particularistic aspects of political education are addressed in Callan (1997, 87–131). For a different perspective, see Nussbaum (1996).

References

Andrews v. Law Society of British Columbia (1989), 56 D.L.R. (4th) 1.

Callan, Eamonn. 1997. *Creating Citizens: Political Education and Liberal Democracy*. Oxford: Clarendon Press.

Hampton, Jean. 1997. 'The Wisdom of the Egoist'. *Social Philosophy and Policy* 14, 1: 21–51.

Holmes, Stephen. 1995. *Passions and Constraint: On the Theory of Liberal Democracy*. Chicago: University of Chicago Press.

Nussbaum, Martha. 1996. *For Love of Country*. Boston: Beacon Press.

Rawls, John. 1993. *Political Liberalism*. New York: Columbia University Press.

Raz, Joseph. 1986. *The Morality of Freedom*. Oxford: Clarendon Press.

Smith, Rogers. 1997. *Civic Ideals: Conflicting Visions of Citizenship in U.S. History*. New Haven: Yale University Press.

Strike, Kenneth. 1996. 'Must Liberal Citizens Be Reasonable?'. *Review of Politics* 58: 41–51.

—. 1998. 'Freedom of Conscience and Illiberal Socialization: The Congruence Argument'. *Journal of Philosophy of Education* 32: 333–60.

Wenar, Leif. 1995. 'Political Liberalism: An Internal Critique'. *Ethics* 106: 32–62.

PART TWO

EQUALITY, JUSTICE, AND GENDER

History, Ethics, and Marxism

G.A. Cohen

1.

When I was a young lecturer at University College London, I taught subjects that were not closely related to my research interests. I was hired, in 1963, to teach moral and political philosophy, but I wrote about Karl Marx's theory of history, for I passionately believed it to be true, and I wanted to defend it against criticism that was widely accepted but which I considered (and consider) to be misjudged. To be sure, I did also have views about issues in moral and political philosophy, but those views did not generate any writing. I had, in particular, strong convictions about justice, and about the injustice of inequality and of capitalist exploitation, but I did not think that I had, or would come to have, anything sufficiently distinctive to say about justice, or about capitalist injustice, to be worth printing.

My conception of moral and political philosophy was, and is, a standardly academic one: they are ahistorical disciplines that use abstract philosophical reflection to study the nature and truth of normative judgments. Historical materialism (which is what Karl Marx's theory of history came to be called) is, by contrast, an empirical theory (comparable in status to, for example, nineteenth century historical geology) about the structure of society and the dynamics of history. It is not entirely without implications for normative philosophy, but it is substantially value-free: one could believe historical materialism but regret that the career of humanity is as it describes, and, more specifically, that, as it predicts, class society will be superseded by a classless one.

Since historical materialism was, at the time in question, the only part of Marxism that I believed[1]—I no longer believed in dialectical materialism, which is a comprehensive philosophy about reality as such—I often said, with the satisfied self-endorsement of youth, that insofar as I was a Marxist I was not a philosopher, and insofar as I was a philosopher I was not a Marxist. In further description of the separation between my philosophical and my Marxist engagements, I shall first explain why my Marxism did not control or affect my moral and political philosophy in a manner that many Marxists and anti-Marxists would have thought that it should, and then why I did not recruit to Marxist or even to socialist service the competence in political philosophy that I was developing through teaching it.

People familiar both with Marxism and with mainstream anglophone normative philosophy might expect the first to challenge the second, since, for the philosophy, normative statements are timelessly true (or false), whereas, according to Marxism, so it is supposed, either there is no such thing as normative truth or it is a truth that changes historically with economic circumstances and requirements. Now, I endorsed—I still do—the stated severely ahistorical view of normative philosophy, but, for two reasons, I was able to reconcile it with my Marxism. For, first, and as I have already indicated, I had shed, by the time I reached University College, my belief in a general Marxist philosophy (dialectical materialism) which is commonly understood to imply skepticism, or, at least, relativism, about value. And, second, I did not believe that historical materialism, in its best interpretation, reduces all values and principles to rationalizations of class interest, but, on the contrary, that it looks to the end of class domination as the beginning of a society governed by 'a really human morality which stands above class antagonisms',[2] a morality that has always had some sort of historical manifestation, within the confinement of class constraint. Accordingly, my particular Marxist convictions did not disturb my view that ultimate normative truth is historically invariant; that, while historical circumstances undoubtedly affect what justice (for example) demands, they do so only because timeless principles of justice have different implications at different times.

Although I thought that Marxism had little to say, in philosophical terms, about justice, I did not think that Marxists could be indifferent to justice. On the contrary: I was certain that every committed Marxist was exercised by the injustice of capitalist exploitation, and that Marxists who affected unconcern about justice, from Karl Marx down, were kidding themselves. I never believed, as many Marxists professed to do, that normative principles were irrelevant to the socialist movement; that, since the movement was of oppressed people fighting for their own liberation, there was no room or need for specifically moral inspiration in it. I thought no such thing partly for the plain reason that I observed enormous selfless dedication among the active communists who surrounded me in my childhood, and partly for the more sophisticated reason that the self-interest of any oppressed producer would tell him to stay at home, rather than to risk his neck in a revolution whose success or failure would be anyhow unaffected by his participation in it. Revolutionary workers and, *a fortiori*, bourgeois fellow-travellers without a particular material interest in socialism, must perforce be morally inspired. But I thought that, while historical materialism threw light on the different historical forms of injustice (such as slavery, serfdom and the condition of being a proletarian), and on how to eliminate injustice, it had nothing to say about what justice (timelessly) is. It therefore did not control my conception of political philosophy.

Nor did I put my Marxism and my philosophy together in an opposite way, by recruiting political philosophy, as I conceived it, to socialist use. For, although I took for granted that socialism was to be preferred to capitalism for reasons of normative principle—and not, as some weirdly suggested, because historical materialism showed its advent to be inevitable—I also thought that socialism was so evidently superior to capitalism from *any* morally decent point of view, with respect to *any* attractive principle (of utility, or equality, or justice, or freedom, or democracy, or self-realization) that there was no necessity to identify the right point(s) of view from which to endorse it, no need to specify what principle(s) should guide the fight for socialism, and, therefore, no call to do normative philosophy for socialism's sake. I did not think that it was incumbent on a socialist philosopher, in his capacity as a socialist, to bother with political philosophy, because the case for socialism seemed to me to be so overwhelming that only sub-intellectual reasons, reflecting class and other prejudice, could persuade a person against it. Animating principles were of course needed by the socialist movement, and they were abundantly present in it. But political philosophy, the systematic search for the right principles, and for the structures (very generally described) that might realize them, was not required by allies, and would be unlikely to make enemies move in a socialist direction, since their resistance to socialism was not a principled one. So I did not engage in moral and political philosophy, in a creative sense. I taught it, but it was not the site of my research work, which was directed towards the clarification and defence of historical materialism.

2.

I had never heard an argument against socialism for which I did not (so I thought) already have an answer in my pocket. Then one day in 1972, in my room at University College, Jerry Dworkin nudged me. He began a process that, in time, roused me from what had been my dogmatic socialist slumber. He did that by hitting me with an outline of the anti-socialist Wilt Chamberlain argument, as it was to appear in Robert Nozick's then forthcoming *Anarchy, State and Utopia*.[3] My reaction to the argument was a mixture of irritation and anxiety. There was a would-be confidence that it depended on sleight of hand, alongside a lurking or looming fear that maybe it did not.

Then Nozick's argument appeared in full force, first in *Philosophy and Public Affairs* in fall 1973, and, finally, in 1974, in *Anarchy* itself, and now I was vigorously engaged by it. It happened that I spent February to May of 1975 in Princeton, in the vicinity of two exceptionally sapient philosophers, namely, Tom Nagel and Tim Scanlon. They were considerably to Nozick's left, but, I was both heartened and puzzled to observe, they were not disconcerted by his arguments. This was perhaps partly for the undeep reason that, unlike me, they had had years of pre-acquaintance with the author and his developing book, and, therefore, the time to form a response to it, long before it appeared; but I am sure that it was at least partly for a certain deeper reason.

That deeper reason relates to the fact that the heart of Nozick's libertarian philosophy is the principle of self-ownership, which assigns to each person full and exclusive rights over the exercise, and the product, of her own powers. For an appeal to self-ownership is latent in the standard Marxist condemnation of capitalist exploitation, according to which the employer steals from the worker what should belong to her, *because* she produced it. It is therefore difficult for Marxists to reject libertarianism without putting a key position of their own into question. And that, I am sure, explains why Marxists like me were vulnerable to Nozick's libertarianism in a way that liberals like Nagel and Scanlon were not. Many friends and colleagues were surprised by how seriously I and some other Marxists took libertarianism. They thought that, since leftish liberals like Scanlon and Nagel could comfortably dismiss Nozick's view, then, *a fortiori*, it should not detain people like me. I believe that the liaison between the concept of exploitation and the principle of self-ownership illuminates the unexpected contrast.

Whether or not people were right to be surprised that I regarded Nozick's challenge as very considerable, I did so regard it, and I resolved, in 1975, that, when I had completed a book that I was then writing on historical materialism, I would devote myself in the main to political philosophy proper, and that is what I have indeed done.

But now let me turn from the somewhat local topic of the demise of my early cavalier attitude to the question of the justification of socialism, to the wider neglect of questions of normative justification in the Marxist tradition. Among other things, I shall explain why some excuses for that neglect that existed in the past are no longer available.

3.

Classical Marxism distinguished itself from what it regarded as the socialism of dreams by declaring a commitment to hard-headed historical and economic analysis: it was proud of what it considered to be the stoutly factual character of its central claims. The title of Frederick Engels's book, *The Development of Socialism from Utopia to Science*,[4] articulates this piece of Marxist self-interpretation. Socialism, once raised aloft by airy ideals, would henceforth rest on a firm foundation of fact.

Marxism's heroic—and possibly incoherent[5]—self-description was in part justified. For its founders and adherents did distinguish themselves from socialist forerunners like Charles Fourier and Robert Owen by forsaking the detailed depiction of imaginary perfect societies, and they did achieve a great leap forward in realistic understanding of how the social order functions. But the favoured classical Marxist self-description, whether incoherent or not, was certainly in part bravado. For values of equality, community, and human self-realization were undoubtedly integral to the Marxist belief structure. All classical Marxists believed in some kind of equality, even if many would have refused to acknowledge that they believed in it and none, perhaps, could have stated precisely what principle of equality he believed in.

Yet Marxists were not preoccupied with, and therefore never examined, principles of equality, or, indeed, any other values or principles. Instead, they devoted their intellectual energy to the hard factual carapace surrounding their values, to bold explanatory theses about history in general and capitalism in particular, the theses that gave Marxism its commanding authority in the field of socialist doctrine, and even, indeed, its moral authority, because its heavy intellectual labour on matters of history and economic theory proved the depth of its political commitment.

And now Marxism has lost much or most of its carapace, its hard shell of supposed fact. Scarcely anybody defends it in the academy, and there are no more *apparatchiki* who believe that they are applying it in Party offices. To the extent that Marxism is still alive, as, for example, one may say that it (sort of) is in the work of scholars like John Roemer and Philippe Van Parijs, it presents itself as a set of values and a set of designs for realizing those values. It is therefore, now, far less different than it could once advertise itself to be from the Utopian socialism with which it so proudly contrasted itself. Its shell is cracked and crumbling, its soft under-belly is exposed.

Let me illustrate Marxism's loss of factual carapace with respect to the value of equality in particular.

Classical Marxists believed that economic equality was both historically inevitable and morally right. They believed the first entirely consciously, and they believed the second more or less consciously, and exhibited more or less evasion when asked whether they believed it. It was partly because they believed that economic equality was historically inevitable that classical Marxists did not spend much time thinking about *why* equality was morally right, about exactly what made it morally binding. Economic equality was coming, it was welcome, and it would be a waste of time to theorize about why it was welcome, rather than about how to make it come as quickly and as painlessly as possible—for the date at which economic equality would be achieved, and the cost of reaching it, were, unlike economic equality itself, not themselves inevitable.

Two supposedly irrepressible historical trends, working together, guaranteed ultimate economic equality. One was the rise of an organized working class, whose social emplacement, at the short end of inequality, directed it in favour of equality. The workers' movement would grow in numbers and in strength, until it had the power to abolish the unequal society that had nurtured its growth. And the other trend helping to ensure an eventual equality was the development of the productive forces, the continual increase in the human power to transform nature for human benefit. That growth would issue in a material abundance so great that anything that anyone needed for a richly fulfilling life could be taken from the common store at no cost to anyone. The guaranteed future abundance served as a source of rebuttal to the suggestion that inequality might re-emerge, in a new form, *after* the revolution—peaceful or bloody, legal or illegal, fast or slow—that the proletariat could and would accomplish. There would be an interim period of limited inequality, along the lines of the lower stage of communism as Marx described that in his *Gotha Programme* critique, but, when 'all the springs of social wealth [came] to flow more freely', even that limited inequality would disappear, because everyone could have everything that they might want to have.[6]

History has shredded the predictions sketched in the foregoing paragraph. The proletariat did, for a while, grow larger and stronger, but it never became 'the immense majority',[7] and it was ultimately reduced and divided by the increasing technological sophistication of the capitalist production process that had been expected to continue to expand its size and augment its power. And the development of the productive forces now runs up against a resource barrier. Technical knowledge has not stopped, and will not stop growing, but productive power, which is the capacity (all things considered) to transform nature into use-value, cannot expand simultaneously and equally with the growth of technical knowledge, because the planet Earth rebels: its resources turn out to be not lavish enough for continuous growth in technical knowledge to generate unceasing expansion of use-value.

It was not only my encounter with Nozick but also my loss of confidence in the two large Marxist factual claims about the prospects for equality that altered the direction of my professional research. Having spent (what I hope will turn out to be only) the first third of my academic career devoting myself to exploring the ground and character of the two predictions described above,[8] I find myself, at the end of the (putative) second third of my career, engaged by philosophical questions about equality that I would earlier have thought do not require investigation, from a socialist point of view. In the past, there seemed to be no need to *argue* for the desirability of an egalitarian socialist society. Now I do little else.

4.

Let us look more closely at the two leading Marxist inevitabilitarian claims that were distinguished above.

The first claim is false because the proletariat is in process of disintegration, in a sense that I shall presently proceed to clarify. The struggle for equality is consequently no longer a reflex movement on the part of an agent strategically placed within the capitalist process itself: socialist values have lost their mooring in capitalist social structure. For, however one chooses to apply the much contested label 'working class', there is now no group in advanced industrial society which unites the four characteristics of (1) being the producers on whom society depends, (2) being exploited, (3) being (with their families) the majority of society, and (4) being in dire need. There certainly still exist key producers, exploited people, and needy people, but these are not, now, as they were in the past, even roughly coincident designations, nor, still less, alternative designations of the great majority of the population. And, as a result, there is no group with both (because of its exploitation, and its neediness) a compelling interest in, and (because of its productiveness, and its numbers) a ready capacity to achieve, a socialist transformation. In confidently expecting the proletariat to become such a group, classical Marxism failed to anticipate what we now know to be the natural course of capitalist social evolution.

It is partly because there is now patently no group that has the four listed features and, therefore, the will to, and capacity for, revolution, that Marxists, or what were Marxists, are impelled into normative political philosophy. The disintegration of the characteristics produces an intellectual need to philosophize which is related to a political need to be clear as never before about values and principles, for the sake of socialist advocacy. You do not have to justify a socialist transformation as a matter of principle to people who are driven to make it by the urgencies of their situation, and in a good position to succeed. And you do not have to decide what principle justifies socialism to recommend it to all people of good will when you think that so many principles justify it that any person of good will would be moved by at least one of them. For, when the group whose plight requires the relief supplied by socialism is conceived as having the four features that I have listed, socialism will then present itself as a demand of democracy, justice, elementary human need, and even of the general happiness.

It is particularly serious, from a political point of view, that the characteristics of being an exploited producer and being in dire need are now much less closely related than they were in the past. The third line of the second verse of the American socialist song 'Solidarity Forever' shows how their coincidence was once taken for granted:

It is we who ploughed the prairies, built the cities where they trade,
Dug the mines and built the workshops, endless
miles of railroad laid;
Now we stand outcast and starving, 'mid the
wonders we have made . . .

This song was sung not only in a revolutionary accent but also by those who were in the forefront of the struggle for the welfare state, which was seen as a struggle for basic minima for *working* people in particular: public provision was regarded as a modest rectification of the wrongs done to labour with respect to the product of its activity. In 'Solidarity Forever', the outcast and starving people who need the welfare state are the very people who created the wealth of society. Compare the famous American lamentation of the nineteen-thirties, 'Buddy, Can you Spare a Dime'. The man says 'Once I built a railroad, made it run . . . once I built a tower, up to the sun . . .' and those creations are supposed to show that he should have at least a dime.

In the lines of those songs, people do not demand relief from starvation on the ground that they cannot produce but on the ground that they have produced and should therefore not be left to starve. Two claims to recompense, *need* and *entitlement through labour*, are fused, in a fashion typical of the communist rhetoric of the time, in the 'Solidarity' verse exhibited above. It was possible to fuse them when the song was written because revolutionaries and progressives saw the set of exploited producers as roughly coterminous with the set of those who needed the welfare state's benefits. Accordingly, they did not sense any conflict between the producer entitlement doctrine implied by the second part of the third line (''mid the wonders we have made') and the egalitarian doctrine suggested in its first part ('Now we stand outcast and starving'), when it is read on its own. For it does not require much argument to show that there is indeed a difference of principle between the appeals in the two parts of the line. Starving people are not necessarily people who have produced what starving people need, and, if what people produce belongs as of right to them, the people who have produced it, then starving people who have not produced it have no claim on it. The old image of the working class, as a set of people who *both* make the wealth *and* do not have it, conceals, in its fusion of those characteristics, the poignant and problematic truth that the two claims to sustenance, namely, 'I made this and I should therefore have it' and 'I need this, I will die or wither if I do not get it', are not only different but potentially contradictory pleas. The libertarian trick is to turn the first plea against the second.

So much on the consequences for the prospects of equality of the fact that the proletariat did not, and will not, gain the unity and power anticipated for it in Marxist belief. Capitalism does not dig its own grave by rearing up an agency of socialist transformation.[9] Socialists have to settle for a less dramatic scenario, and they must engage in more moral advocacy than used to be fashionable. And I now want to discuss, in the spirit of those acknowledgments, an aspect of the present predicament which brings to the fore a basis for demanding equality which is new, relative to traditional Marxist, and also to mainstream liberal, expectations. As we shall see, that new basis is connected with the falsehood of Marxism's abundance prediction, which was the basis, in the past, not for demanding equality, but for believing it to be inevitable.

The new basis of a demand for equality relates to the ecological crisis, which is a crisis for the whole of humanity. The scale of the threat is a matter of controversy among the experts, and so is the shape of the required remedy—if, indeed, it is not too late to speak of remedies. But two propositions seem to me to be true: that our environment is already severely degraded, and that, if there is a way out of the crisis, then it must include much less aggregate material consumption than what now prevails, and, as a result, unwanted changes in lifestyle, for hundreds of millions of people.

Let me distinguish between what is certain and what is conjectural in that uncongenial assessment. It is beyond dispute that Western consumption, *measured in terms of use of fossil fuel energy and natural resources*, must, on average, fall, drastically, and that non-Western consumption, considered in the aggregate, will never reach current Western levels, *so measured*. But the qualification carried by the italicized phrases is important. It is certain that we cannot achieve Western-style goods and services for humanity as a whole, nor even sustain them for as large a minority as has enjoyed them, by drawing on the fuels and materials that we have hitherto used to provide them. It is less certain that the desired consumption satisfactions themselves, the goods and services considered in abstraction from the customary means of supplying them, cannot be secured, by new means, on the desired scale. But I believe that the second claim, about goods and services as such, is also true,[10] and the following remarks proceed under that assumption.

When aggregate wealth is increasing, the condition of those at the bottom of society, and in the world, can improve, even while the distance between them and the better off does not diminish. Where such improvement occurs (and it has occurred, on a substantial scale, for many disadvantaged groups), egalitarian justice does not cease to demand equality, but that demand can seem shrill, and even dangerous, if the worse off are steadily growing better off, even though they are not catching up with those above them. When, however, progress must give way to regress, when average material living standards must fall, then poor people and poor nations can no longer hope to approach the levels of amenity that are now enjoyed by the world's well off. Sharply falling average standards mean that settling for limitless improvement, instead of equality, ceases to be an option, and huge disparities of wealth become correspondingly more intolerable, from a moral point of view.

Notice the strong contrast between the foregoing ecologically grounded case for reduced tolerance of inequality and traditional Marxist belief. The achievement of Marxist equality ('From each according to his abilities, to each according to his needs') is premised on a conviction that industrial progress brings society to a condition of such fluent abundance that it is possible to supply what everyone needs for a richly fulfilling life. There is therefore no longer any occasion for competition for precedence, either across individuals or between groups. A (supposedly) inevitable future plenty was a reason for *predicting* equality. Persisting scarcity is now a reason for *demanding* it.

We can no longer sustain Marx's extravagant, pre-green, materialist optimism. At least for the foreseeable future, we have to abandon the vision of abundance. But, if I am right about the straitened choices posed by the ecological crisis, we also have to abandon, on pain of giving up socialist politics, a severe pessimism about *social* possibility which accompanied Marx's optimism about *material* possibility. For Marx thought that material abundance was not only a sufficient but also a necessary condition of equality. He thought that anything short of an abundance so complete that it removes all major conflicts of interest would guarantee continued social strife, a 'struggle for necessities . . . and all the old filthy business'.[11] *It was because he was so uncompromisingly pessimistic about the social consequences of anything less than limitless abundance that Marx needed to be so optimistic about the possibility of that abundance.*

And that amplifies the explanation of traditional Marxism's failure to bring questions of distributive justice into close focus. Under conditions of scarcity, so traditional Marxism maintains, class society is inescapable, its property structures settle questions of distribution, and discussion of justice is therefore futile, for a political movement whose task must be to overturn class society, rather than to decide which of the many criteria by which it comes out unjust is the right one to use to condemn it. Nor is it necessary to inquire into what, precisely, will be demanded by justice in the future condition of abundance. For communism, in which everyone has what she wants, will then supervene effortlessly, and justice will be achieved, on any conception of it, from utilitarian through egalitarian to libertarian. Devoting energy to the question 'What is the right way to distribute?' is futile with respect to the present and unnecessary with respect to the future.[12]

We can no longer believe the factual premises of those conclusions about the practical (ir)relevance of the study of norms. We cannot share Marx's optimism about material possibility, but we therefore also cannot share his pessimism about social possibility, if we wish to sustain a socialist commitment. We cannot rely on technology to fix things for us: if they can be fixed, then we have to fix them, through hard theoretical and political labour. Marxism thought that equality would be delivered to us, by abundance, but we have to seek equality for a context of scarcity, and we consequently have to be far more clear than we were about what we are seeking, why we are justified in seeking it, and how it can be implemented, institutionally. That recognition must govern the future efforts of socialist economists and philosophers.

NOTES

The present article is a version of parts of the Introduction to my *Self-Ownership, Freedom, and Equality* (Cambridge: Cambridge University Press, 1995). This version was previously published in *Iyyun: The Jerusalem Philosophical Quarterly* 45 (1966), 71–83, whose editors are to be thanked for their kind permission to reprint it.

1. I had once believed the whole thing, as a result of having been raised inside the Canadian communist movement. See *Self-Ownership*, chap. 11, sect. 1.
2. Frederick Engels, *Anti-Dühring* (Moscow, 1954), 133.
3. (New York: Basic, 1974). (The Wilt Chamberlain argument appears on pp. 160–2 of that book.)
4. The book is usually called, in English, *Socialism: Utopian and Scientific*. The version of the title given above translates the more evocative German title: *Die Entwicklung des Sozialismus von der Utopie zur Wissenschaft.*
5. Whether it really was incoherent depends on the exact sense in which socialism was now supposed to *be*, or to *rest* on, science. That matter of interpretation is too complex for me to address here.
6. See *The Critique of the Gotha Programme*, in Karl Marx and Frederick Engels, *Selected Works in One Volume* (Moscow, 1968), 324–5.
7. *The Communist Manifesto*, in Marx and Engels, *Collected Works VI* (London: Lawrence and Wishart, 1976), 495.
8. I did more work on the development of the productive forces than I did on the character and the destiny of the working class, but I had begun a project on class and class conflict, which was set aside when normative questions moved to the centre of my vision.
9. See *The Communist Manifesto*, 496.
10. This means that I believe, among other things, that if a fusion gun is coming, then, relative to how parlous our situation already is, it is not coming soon enough to vitiate the remarks that follow. (It cannot be excluded that Marx's abundance prediction will be vindicated in some distant future. The present remarks perforce reflect my own assessment of likely constraints for a future that is sufficiently extensive to justify extreme concern, whether or not the classical prediction will one day be fulfilled.)
11. *The German Ideology*, in Marx and Engels, *Collected Works V*, 49.
12. What Marx called 'the lower stage of communism' (which, following later Marxist discourse, I shall call 'socialism') provides an objection to that statement, but not a devastating one. The objection is that socialism enforces a rule of distribution ('to each according to his contribution'), which can be represented as an answer that Marxists give to the question of what is the right way to distribute. But this objection to the statement in the text is not devastating, for two reasons. First, socialism is seen as a merely transitional form, and the rule governing it is justified as appropriate to socialism's task of preparing the way for

full communism, rather than as required by abstract justice. Second, Marxism considers the socialist rule to be more or less inescapable, at the given historical stage: it does not regard that rule as a choice requiring normative justification from a substantial menu of policy options.

Egalitarianism Renewed

CHRISTINE SYPNOWICH

How should we formulate a commitment to equality at the beginning of the twenty-first century? The issue of equality was a prominent theme in my 1990 book, *The Concept of Socialist Law*,[1] in which I challenged the common assumption that the socialist commitment to equality is incompatible with legal institutions such as the rule of law and individual rights. Instead of supposing that a society characterized by full equality would be devoid of conflict requiring mediation by law, I contended that such a society would need legal institutions. The issue for socialists was how such institutions should best be understood. Moreover, I suggested that a socialist society would be more supportive of procedural fairness than would less egalitarian societies, pointing to the important connections between principles of equality and procedural justice. I developed this argument in the hospitable climate of the mid-1980s, when questions of justice and equality were at the centre of debates in political philosophy and prominent in the policy platforms of left-wing political parties in capitalist democracies. Furthermore, in the Soviet Union Mikhail Gorbachev was ushering in a new era of perestroika, and it appeared that a genuinely democratic socialism might emerge there. It was a time when the left was reaffirming its ideals and principles in a heady atmosphere of innovation and hope.

How things have changed. Today it is not the rebirth of Soviet socialism but its total collapse that provides the context for reflection on equality. At the same time, we have witnessed the steady decline of the post-war welfare state in most capitalist democracies, sometimes at the hands of putatively progressive governments. The defeat of such 'world-historical' radical projects has engendered a sense of pessimism and loss among the left,[2] as well as an erosion of confidence in the egalitarian institutions of the socialist and liberal traditions of the last century. Moreover, many new dimensions to 'progressive' politics have rushed to fill the void: nationalism, multiculturalism, and issues of identity. It has been said that the century that appeared to be characterized by a conflict between capitalism and communism ended up being dominated by the conflicts of nationality and ethnicity.[3] Such conflicts, bringing with them calls for secession, forced emigration, and war, are pressing indeed, but they invite philosophical resolution that seems unconnected to, if not in tension with, the ideal of equality.

One might think that the obvious lesson of the above is that theory must attend to context, that political philosophy must bear a relation to political events, that political argument should be cognizant of political opinion. Yet political philosophy inevitably has a fraught relation to 'political reality'. Political philosophy consists of abstract, reasoned argument about the ideals of politics. The philosopher must be both engaged with and distant from political events and fellow citizens, neither slavishly following political trends nor oblivious to them.

The difficulty in attending to the reality of politics was brought home to me a couple of years ago when I was on the CBC-Radio program *Ideas*, as a member of a three-philosopher panel on 'The Public Good'.[4] The participants all had a lot to say on the subject and the discussion was lively. But afterwards I was struck by how as philosophers we were incapable, in some fundamental sense, of seriously addressing the idea of the public good. Schooled in the neutralist liberalism that has dominated political philosophy for some decades, we couldn't help considering the idea of seeking a consensus on value to be symptomatic of a dangerous, moralizing conservatism. We thus sidestepped the issue of a truly public good by considering the means by which individuals might pursue their private goods and discussing which of those means—health care, education, or social welfare programs—the public was obligated to provide. Yet our host, Lister Sinclair, not only assumed the cogency of the idea of the public good but took it as the first premise of a discussion of politics. And I realized that for most citizens, and political leaders too, the phrase 'public good' was no embarrassment. They assumed that the task of politics was to support institutions of culture, to enable a degree of civility in citizens' dealings with each other, to provide conditions of self-development and improvement that enriched the public and individual citizens in turn.

But just as political philosophers should be attentive to the political context, it is equally important not to be overwhelmed by, or acquiesce to, political realities. We see instances of the latter, I believe, in some philosophers' enthusiastic responses to the upsurge in nationalism, to the calls for 'recognition' of minority cultures, or to the insistence on the importance of difference among citizens. Of course these challenges needed to be addressed, and a lot of intelligent reflection has rightly taken place. My concern, however, is that we too often simply cater to or accommodate these developments, without assessing them critically. I think that if we marshal the critical tools of political philosophy—particularly the criteria of justice, equality, or autonomy, properly understood—we are led to a much more qualified support.

All this points to the need for a new approach to defend the principle of equality in political theory. I call for both retrieval and innovation. In my view we must retrieve the ideal of equality as a central political principle.[5] As for innovation, I have two proposals. First, we should reject the idea of the neutral state in favour of a view of the state as enabling the betterment of its citizens. Second, we should invoke concepts of mortality, finitude, and restraint in order to ward off utopianism in politics. The upshot is a political philosophy that pursues equality in the light of a plurality of worthwhile ways of living, tempered by a sense of our human limitations and the importance of the proceduralism of the rule of law.

Neutral Liberalism and the Politics of Difference

It is often remarked that political philosophy was in the doldrums for most of the past century. Rebirth came in 1971, with the publication of *A Theory of Justice* by the American political theorist John Rawls.[6] Before Rawls, Anglo-American political philosophy lived in the shadow of the positivist views that had dominated philosophy in the early part of the twentieth century. Logical positivism clearly distinguished between conceptual and empirical enquiry, between matters of fact and matters of value. Matters of value were deemed outside the purview of philosophy. As a branch of political philosophy seeking to direct rather than merely to describe human practices, political theory was therefore cast as a non-subject. Such scientistic ideas lingered in the ordinary language philosophy that succeeded logical positivism, since, by limiting its investigation to the use of existing vocabularies, ordinary language philosophy also rejected normative questions as not truly philosophical ones. But whereas ethics could turn itself into a meta-discipline concerned with the scope and limits of taken-for-granted moral concepts, the intrinsically controversial nature of political prescriptions meant that such a metamorphosis was not available for political theory. Political philosophy could consist only of paltry exercises of ordinary language that interrogated the senses in which speakers use political terms. This was a long way from the ancient Greeks' original, and ambitious, idea of political philosophy as reasoned inquiry into how we ought to live in common.

The diminished role of political philosophy as a normative exercise doubtless reflected not just an empiricist outlook in philosophy but also a smug acceptance of the empirically given; that is, the liberal institutions of capitalist democracies in the post-war period. The dogmatism about politics that came with the Cold War helps explain why political philosophy was in a state of stagnation. Such complacency was jolted, however, by conservative attacks on the welfare state, attacks that prompted the considered response of Rawls.

Rawls's thesis is that inequalities are justified only if they are to the advantage of the worst-off in society. This 'difference principle', as he calls it, is advanced by means of a complex thought experiment in which individuals deliberate about principles of justice in an 'original position' behind a 'veil of ignorance' that prevents knowledge of who they are to be in the society they are designing. According to Rawls, in such a position the parties would opt for basic liberties along with a redistributive scheme; moreover, they would be concerned that society not use political means to endorse one way of living over another. Rawls thus rejuvenates the social contract tradition, founding political prescriptions on claims of a quasi-empirical kind about human reasoning and motivation.

In recent work Rawls has developed this theme of neutrality with the idea of 'political liberalism', in which the state is liberal in a narrowly political sense. The state must eschew any commitment on what Rawls calls 'comprehensive doctrines', that is, substantive philosophical or moral views. Citizens must be reasonable and not ask their fellow citizens to live by others' creeds. They should thus subscribe to the value of neutrality, a value that emerges from practices current in contemporary liberal societies.[7]

Since Rawls's first contributions to political philosophy, the political terrain has shifted from a left–right debate about economic power to controversies about the importance of cultural difference. New critics of Rawls argue that a universal political order is an illusory and self-defeating goal in the face of incommensurable identities and interests. This approach reflects a shift—within feminism, for example—from insisting on equal treatment under the rules to a questioning of the partiality of the rules themselves. Difference theorists insist on the inevitability of a plurality of identities—the diversity of ethnic groups, gender and sexual orientation, race, degrees of physical and mental ability, and so forth—which undermines the possibility of a posture of neutrality as required by Rawls's political liberalism. Neutrality is impossible to achieve, and claims of neutrality are simply a cover for the entrenched positions of the powerful.

The debates about difference present one of the most interesting and formidable challenges to liberal conceptions of justice, a challenge that has prompted some invaluable soul-searching about egalitarian commitments and goals. How should the egalitarian respond? In my view the answer to the difference challenge is not to retreat, as Rawls does, behind the vulnerable fortress of neutrality. Rawls resuscitated political philosophy, but perhaps he did so by keeping it semi-conscious, for in banishing controversy about value from the domain of public debate, his political philosophy looks curiously apolitical.[8] In contrast, I propose we defend the liberal value of self-determination by openly undertaking a commitment on matters of value. Such a commitment would maintain that human beings' dignity depends on their pursuit of the good life—a life of autonomy, self-determination, and freedom from coercion—and that such a life must be available equally to all. These ideals cannot be smuggled into a theory of justice as 'primary goods' that turn out to be the mere instruments for pursuing our particular conceptions of the good, whatever they might be. They are features of the good itself. And, as I will explore further in this essay, the good, the idea of a life autonomously and thus well lived, is central to the pursuit of equality.

CANADA AND THE RECOGNITION OF CULTURE

If context is relevant in understanding and assessing a political theory, one might wonder whether Canada poses a different set of constraints than the American setting that informed Rawls's theory. Although not invulnerable, our welfare state has been more securely rooted in a political tradition of social democracy and community. At the same time, our political culture is somewhat less preoccupied with the sacred right of liberty that underpins Rawls's endorsement of neutrality. Moreover, as Canadians we have been particularly well placed to consider the problem of difference. Canada was constituted by more than one national group, and its federal structure has sought to accommodate this national diversity, albeit with considerable strain. An explicit commitment to 'multiculturalism' has been a feature of the Canadian political and cultural landscape since the 1970s, even though it has sometimes stood in uneasy relation with the ideal of Canada as composed of more than one founding nation. At the same time, Canada's British parliamentary structure has been qualified with a Charter of Rights that both invokes the American Lockean tradition of constitutional rights and revises it in the light of communitarian values regarding legislative supremacy and social goals (e.g., the override clauses of s. 1 and s. 33).

It is thus not surprising that the flourishing of political philosophy after Rawls has been marked by specifically Canadian contributions like Charles Taylor's call for the recognition of distinctive cultural communities such as Quebec and Will Kymlicka's case for a liberal theory of multicultural citizenship.[9] Taylor seeks a place for the ideal of community as a precondition for individual autonomy, but also as something that can transcend the interests of the individual. Kymlicka's work, in contrast, calls for the protection of minority cultures, but with neutral liberal criteria: freedom of choice and equal concern and respect. It is Kymlicka's explicitly liberal position that I consider here.

Kymlicka argues that culture is valuable because it is the context for choice, in the sense both that it provides particular options and that it makes these options meaningful. He insists that citizens have obligations to culture; its survival is 'not guaranteed, and, where it is threatened with debasement or decay, we must act to protect it.'[10] I disagree. The demand to protect culture is essentially a demand to inhibit choice, to encourage affiliation with the values of that culture and discourage affiliation with the values of others. Indeed, the controversy surrounding Bill 101, the Quebec law that set rules about the language of commercial signs, revolved precisely around the tension between choice and culture.

Egalitarian concerns do figure in Kymlicka's argument: minority cultures should be protected to ensure that 'all citizens are treated with genuine equality.' It is not clear, however, that equality can be marshalled in this way. In any society there will inevitably be some cultures with a stronger presence than others.[11] A culture's strength will depend on the number of adherents; their wealth, power, and values; and the extent to which they instill their values in successive generations. But only the weaker status of some cultures has political significance, and only some cultures are unequal in ways that render their members unequal. In Canada, Quebec is an example of the former but not the latter, Aboriginal culture of both, and Polish culture of neither. Further, the aim of cultural equality is anthropologically naïve—trying artificially to preserve culture in the face of a myriad of forces against it. We cannot equalize people's success in their pursuits, be they cultural or otherwise. We can and should, however, try to equalize the life chances of those whose cultural identity renders them unequal to others in politically relevant respects. In the case of Aboriginal people in Canada, for example, we confront a record of poverty and deprivation and lack of self-respect. Remedying their inequality might call for cultural strategies, such as self-government, to restore the sense of self-worth that is essential if Aboriginal people are to participate in their own material betterment. Certainly assimilationist policies of the past have failed to produce economic equality; but whether the new alternatives will succeed is an open question. If they too fail, our reasons for supporting them would have to be other than egalitarian (perhaps the issue becomes one of historical entitlement). Non-Aboriginal Canadians' warranted sense of shame about the plight of Aboriginal people sometimes muddies the issues at stake, but we should realize that the relation between the protection of culture and the promotion of equality is a contingent one.

Culture and the Nation-State

Yet culture is not irrelevant to equality. This becomes evident once we flesh out the non-neutral commitment to individual self-determination with which I countered Rawls. Culture is important for a theory of equality not because it is an arena of choice or an arbitrary marking of the individual that society must recognize in order to show respect. Culture is significant because it contributes to the individual's development. Minority cultures do this, but so, of course, does the majority one. And this obvious fact is one that contemporary political philosophers who portray the public as an empty shell, containing the micro-organisms of individual choices and minority cultures but with no character or aims of its own, seem to find unsavoury. That the larger society has cultural import does not mean it is monolithic or unchanging. Consider how English-speaking Canada's culture has evolved, from distinctly British to what Europeans consider largely American, while its French character has been accentuated and a polyethnic character has emerged. These shifts are not the result of fiat or legislation (the official policy of bilingualism launched in the 1960s is perhaps an exception). Rather, they reflect the inevitable vagaries of historical change—patterns of immigration, the decline of one empire and rise of another, the modernization of Quebec, economic prosperity, political independence, and so forth. The result is a nation that bears the traces of particular nationalities but is not synonymous with them, and that retains an overall national character, however nebulous. The embarrassment I feel in trying to describe this character perhaps reveals the beleaguered state of a pan-Canadian idea. Nevertheless, that idea includes an appreciation for wilderness, an orientation to the seasons, a certain pioneer spirit that has inspired Canadians from early settlers to recent immigrants, tolerance, civility, and openness to cultural diversity. It also includes the less attractive attributes of a colonial society: lack of confidence, inhibitions about the country's role or purpose, and a propensity to defer to the powerful.

Putting aside the precise character of this culture for the moment, I would like to note how crucial the existence of a national character is for equality. This is so, first, because access to such a culture gives one access to other goods. After all, the argument for assimilation—that members of minority groups cannot be equal unless they in some sense integrate into the majority—is not wildly wrong. Integration, it should immediately be noted, is not the same as absorption; it is consistent with individuals' retaining their diverse identities. But all societies have a common currency of success that calls for the pursuit of uniformity among its citizens to some degree. Language is an obvious example, and in Canada it is crucial for the equality of citizens that they learn either English or French (indeed, it is a requirement for the acquisition of citizenship).

A second sense in which a common culture is relevant to equality is that it constitutes the human framework required for the state to provide social benefits such as health insurance and unemployment and welfare payments. The British philosopher David Miller argues that the nation-state embodies a 'common ethos', a public culture that defines the interests and needs of its citizens and how they may be met.[12] This ethos may not be egalitarian in content, but the mere fact of its being common facilitates the pursuit of equality. As well, the idea of a national community points to a set of interconnected people who can enlist in formal structures of reciprocity and mutual aid.[13] This is the reality that underlies the metaphor of the nation as an 'imagined community' of 'deep, horizontal comradeship'. Nationality provides a sense of obligation and trust that can transcend enlightened self-interest, sustaining systems of redistribution from which any one individual may not directly benefit.[14]

For the nation-state to provide the basis for such redistribution, it must cast off its original form as a state that is ethnically homogeneous. 'Nation' cannot pertain to a particular ethnic or racial group; it must be a porous, open-ended association whose qualifications for membership do not depend on ancestry. I noted that Canada is an example of such an association, where 'nation' represents not an exclusive club but in fact a counter to such clubs, to the claims of birth and blood made by minority nationalities.[15] Precisely how nationality can refuse ethnic exclusivity while avoiding another pernicious exclusivity (as in the idea of 'un-American') needs further reflection. Canada is an interesting case where the ethnic basis for nationality has waned, and a political basis has not taken its place. The result is a nation that is inclusive and open, but uncertain about its identity, and that is particularly beset by the centrifugal forces of multiculturalism and sub-nationalisms.

Here an attention to the context in which we do political philosophy has obvious rewards. A concern for the unity of Canada, so prominent in popular debate and likely shared by all contributors to this volume, highlights the untenability of a neutralist view and the importance of something like the 'public good' with which I began. Why care about this arbitrary geopolitical entity, unless one thinks it provides a framework within which the valuable, however diverse and plural, can be pursued? It has been said that Canadians are united by their participation in the 'Canadian conversation'.[16] But this metaphor makes sense only if we conceive of the conversation as meaningful and contentful, seeking a resolution, however provisional, on questions of value.

Autonomy and Equality

This reflection leads to another sense in which culture and equality are intertwined. A common culture is not just a possible means to equality. It is also a measure of equality itself: it is an answer to the question 'equality of what?' often asked by philosophers. Where there is inequality there is an unequal distribution of the material goods that satisfy human needs: food, shelter, and health care. These are not ends but means for pursuing our projects and goals, for leading our lives. Our ultimate purpose is to live autonomously, not just in the sense of being free from coercion, although that is important. We also want to conduct our lives purposefully, making the most of our capacities and opportunities. 'Autonomy' refers to a type of freedom, a moral freedom of self-determination. We do not live autonomously if our lives are purposeless, empty, plagued by ignorance and lethargy, even if we choose such a life. The British philosopher Joseph Raz contends that autonomy involves the 'capacity' not just to choose but to choose well, and there is an obvious sense in which autonomy can be diminished by bad choices. Bad choices are those that close off the possibility of future ones, like the bad choice to forgo an education. A bad choice can in itself stunt our capacities (and ignorance is in some sense a non-autonomous state). Thus William Morris, the Victorian socialist and aesthete, sought the development of human capacities, arguing that conditions of inequality mean the individual's 'skinny and pitiful existence' stunts the ability even to 'frame a desire for any life much better than that which he now endures perforce'.[17]

An important autonomy-enabling social condition is freedom from interference, and it cannot be stressed too much that my call for an interest in the kinds of choices people make—what might be called a 'value of freedom' idea—retains the traditional liberal antipathy to coercion. But non-interference is not sufficient. A second set of social conditions that enable autonomy consists of institutions that assure some minimum level of material well-being, since no egalitarian can conceive of a state of autonomy while hungry or homeless. There are the possibilities provided by culture, in the widest sense of the word. They include such things as literature, art galleries, music, education, physical activity, traditional crafts, and historic architecture. They are various, and my 'value of freedom' theory insists on the plurality of autonomy-conducive choices. They are valuable in part because they enable us to realize our capacities. A society cannot avoid making difficult choices about what to support, but it should aim for an adequate range of choices in the full normative sense, deploying grants, tax relief, or public venues to support enterprises that provide valuable cultural possibilities. In Canada, an egalitarian project of cultural enrichment is manifest in state support for writers and artists; public funds for language teaching for immigrants; and the provision of health insurance, labour legislation, pensions, and social welfare to protect citizens from the vicissitudes of the market.

Cultural diversity provides cultural possibilities that benefit not just the adherents of particular cultures but all of us. The society seeking equality of autonomy thus seeks a supportive environment for a wide range of cultural practices. In turn, cultural possibilities must meet tests of equality and autonomy: they must be widely available, open, and consistent with freedom from interference. It is here that I part company with communitarian arguments for cultural recognition, such as those made by Charles Taylor, which give priority to culture per se. It is not enough that one happens to value one's culture; if the state is to support a cultural practice, then some more general judgment about its value will have to be made.

What I propose is in fact already instantiated to a considerable degree in contemporary liberal practice, which does indeed further some ways of life and not others, subsidizing, for example, ballet over bingo, or parks over drive-in cinemas. I differ, however, on two points: first, regarding our consciousness of, and sense of responsibility for, the cluster of normative judgments that justify decisions about state support for culture; and second, regarding our understanding of culture's relation to equality. The egalitarian must have a concern for culture, since the encultured individual has the capacity to live autonomously, and the egalitarian seeks to ensure that we all have equal access to this capacity for autonomy. Difference will of course thrive: varieties not just of ethnicity or language but of talent and disposition will see to that. However, difference due to unequal access to culture is something the egalitarian society should seek to abolish.

The kind of political theory I have been developing is often dubbed 'perfectionism' to indicate that the task of society is to 'perfect' its citizens.[18] I have certainly called for efforts on the part of the community to facilitate individuals' development; but in framing this within an egalitarian project I cannot help being wary of the potential for tyranny. And I find the term 'perfectionism' unfortunate, for two reasons. First, it suggests a unitary ideal, whereas I have been stressing the plurality of ways in which autonomy can be realized. As Steven Wall puts it in his recent argument for liberal perfectionism, although value-nihilism is ruled out by perfectionism, value-pluralism is not.[19] Second, the term suggests that perfection per se is an achievable goal, whereas there is an obvious sense in which perfection can serve only as a target towards which human beings strive rather than something that is achieved. So 'perfection' is a poor way of designating the very human aspiration of enabling citizens to live equally well. 'The good' is an unfortunate expression for the same reasons: the idea that human ends involve substantive values is tenable only if it avoids such implications of a unitary or Platonic ideal.

Finitude and Utopia

Yet the allure of perfection is hard to resist. Radical political theories and utopian fiction have often centred on the idea of a perfected human being; indeed, in some versions even mortality is to be conquered. The idea of a perfect, immortal person appeared in some of the more fantastic understandings of 'communist man' amongst the Russian Bolsheviks. It had its roots in Marx's Promethean idea of human mastery of nature through labour, and his vision of communism as a solution to the riddle of history, devoid of conflict or tension. It reached its zenith in the preposterous ideas of regeneration that inspired the embalming of Lenin. Such crackpot notions may seem peripheral to a serious inquiry into questions of political philosophy. But notions like these represent the extreme of a more general propensity in our culture. The denial of our finitude is not restricted to radical utopianism but is, in secular form, an underlying conceit of modernity as a whole. Twentieth-century consumerism represents a kind of denial of death in which people seek infinite material gratification, oblivious to the mortification of nature (a creed that has, of course, filled the gap left by the failure of the Bolshevik project in Russia).[20] The recognition of difference, particularly in its postmodern variants, might appear to suggest an acquiescence to human limitation that focuses on the inevitability of diverse, perhaps incommensurable, identities.

But in much of this work there lurks the hope that if we could only hear other voices aright, dialogue would be possible and differences overcome or transcended.

Such ideas sit uneasily with liberal values. A utopianism about human capacities that seemed hospitable to individual diversity in fact ends up conceiving of individuals as universal, abstract possibilities, devoid of frailties and complexities. Real human flourishing is eclipsed and individuality—the myriad of ways in which one person is unlike, and potentially at odds with, another—is repressed. A counter to such perfectionist views need not be a Hobbesian doctrine that finds in us a propensity to war. Rather, it is out of an appreciation for the finitude of individuality that one can best counter utopian perfectionism. Individuals have an inherent capacity for self-ness, for uniqueness, that results in the marvellous complexities of human interaction and renders both politics and political theory necessary.

The realization that our pursuits are constrained by the finitude of our condition should come naturally at the end of a century of warfare and dogmatism pursued for seemingly utopian ends. It does not mean a return to the medieval acceptance of death, which had as its corollary a disregard for the public and political domain of the living.[21] It affirms the utopian, but as an ultimately unsatisfied urge, an impetus for the pursuit of human improvement. Once we acknowledge our finitude, we are prepared to embark on a quest for equality and the public good on behalf of—and in honour of—real-life individual persons.

My emphasis on finitude may appear to undermine perfectionism altogether. But the two ideas can complement each other. There is an epistemological precedent for a reconciliation of finitude with the ideal of human progress in the work of the pragmatist philosopher Charles Peirce. Peirce famously construed true beliefs as those that would have our assent at 'the end of inquiry', a hypothetical state of perfect knowledge in which all the facts were known. A true belief is one that would withstand rational scrutiny come what may; it is a 'regulative ideal' that should guide inquiry, so that we seek to acquire beliefs fit to be held in an epistemically perfect situation. But Peirce equally maintained that we are likely to arrive at such beliefs only if we subject our present conceptions to rigorous scrutiny. We must, therefore, acknowledge our fallibility and the finitude of our perspective, and admit the constant possibility that what we presently take to be true by our best lights is in fact false. Fallibilism and progress go hand in hand. Likewise in politics, we must guide our inquiries by perfectionist ideals—aspiring to achieve a substantive conception of how we should live—while recognizing the limitations of our powers.[22]

Thus our measure in politics is human flourishing. Equality is furthered not by holding the line, excluding questions of value and protecting individuals from each other, as neutralist liberals presuppose. Equality is a central pillar of the public good, a collective ideal that understands social conditions as contributing to a cultural context that shapes the circumstances of individuals' lives. A society's commitment to a culture of human progress enables the realization of its citizens' personal ideals of human progress, and thereby brings us closer to furthering citizens' equality with one another. We therefore have a project that is forward-looking without being utopian, mindful of the neutralist liberal's unease with a paternalistic or moralizing state. It assumes, indeed embraces, human finitude as a source of restraint and caution; it counts on diversity and pluralism; and it is realistic about the political disagreements that will attend the pursuit of human progress. The search for truth, however fallibilist, invites conflict. Such conflict cannot be banished by means of a streamlined, neutralist liberalism, but it is unclear how it can be adequately mediated under current circumstances. Indeed, our existing political institutions—remote channels of representative democracy, frustratingly ineffective systems of local democracy, unaccountable public debate in media held in the grip of modern-day robber barons—seem symptomatic of a liberalism that relegates debate about value to the private domain and invites resigned acceptance of an unjust social order. Yet these institutions—and the injustice they leave untouched—might change if we reconceived the political theories that animate and sustain them.

I have argued against a politics of neutrality, but with the caveat that a more substantive liberalism will be pluralist, acknowledging the variety of ways in which a life might be well lived. Neutrality persists, however, in the important idea of procedural justice that I have defended in my work on socialist law. Procedural justice refers to the principles of generality, predictability, and consistency that underlie the rule of law. It is an essential complement to the pursuit of substantive justice I have outlined here, and a source of that sense of fallibility that Peirce insisted should accompany the august search for truth. The principles of the rule of law are guides towards impartiality—not impartiality about value, but impartiality in adjudication. It is a posture towards which we aim, because we who make and apply law are inevitably partial and situated human beings and because neither full transparency nor full community is possible. The rule of law helps to ensure that we are accorded worth and dignity in the domain of the public, that we are included and counted as citizens. But it also seeks to leave us unimpeded in our particular personal domains, according us respect as private persons. The importance of privacy for us is a reminder that often the civil thing to do is to refrain, rather than to attend.[23] Our efforts at equality, while they cannot avoid substantive commitments to culture and value, must nonetheless express a politics of restraint, which acknowledges the limits of the human condition and, in turn, delineates the limitations of power and authority.

CONCLUSION

In this essay I have outlined an approach to political philosophy that aspires to be mindful of the past century and hopeful for the next. It has four general features. First, it is egalitarian, by which I mean that it affirms the equal worth of human beings and the duty of society to promote that equality by means of economic and social policy. Second, it is committed to the value of autonomy, as a substantive goal of an egalitarian polity and as a form of self-realization that requires cultural possibilities and support. Third, it affirms a nuanced sense of nationality, which tempers the contemporary zest for defending the exclusive demographic characteristics of minorities with the idea of a shared project that includes all citizens within a polity. Fourth, it seeks to temper the ambitions of these ideals with a sense of finitude and the limitations of the human condition, invoking the politics of civility inherent in the rule of law.

This approach is something of a mélange, but not because I harbour a postmodern penchant for eclecticism. I aim rather to include different pushes and pulls in political philosophy because of the insights that they all contain. We have come to realize the inevitable complexity of any adequate political theory because we have witnessed the hopes and disappointments of political projects that have both sought and forsaken the public good. That political philosophy is a matter of critically assessing and harnessing many half-truths may be the single truth that we can glean from a century that has been described as both glorious and barbaric, but whose greatest political legacy is, I think, the idea of equality. And it is in a utopian spirit, if not a confidence in utopia, that I propose to renew egalitarianism.

Notes

I am grateful to David Bakhurst for his assistance in writing this essay, and to the Social Sciences and Humanities Research Council for generously funding my research.

1. *The Concept of Socialist Law* (Oxford: Clarendon Press, 1990).
2. This is well captured by the Canadian political philosopher G.A. Cohen in 'The Future of a Disillusion', *New Left Review* 190 (1992).
3. This is a theme in Eric Hobsbawm, *Age of Extremes* (London: Abacus, 1995).
4. The other members of the panel were Will Kymlicka and Arthur Ripstein, also contributors to this volume.
5. 'Retrieval' comes from the eminent Canadian political theorist C.B. Macpherson, who used the term to defend the liberal tradition's political commitment to autonomy, which, he claimed, was often undermined by liberalism's economic commitment to free enterprise.
6. John Rawls, *A Theory of Justice* (Cambridge, Mass.: Harvard University Press, 1971).
7. Rawls, *Political Liberalism* (New York: Columbia University Press, 1993). I discuss this book in 'Impartiality After Difference', *Review of Constitutional Studies* 3, 2 (1996). See also my 'Justice, Community and the Antinomies of Feminist Theory', *Political Theory* 21, 3 (1993); and 'Some Disquiet about "Difference"', *Praxis International* 13, 2 (1993).
8. This is a theme in the work of Canadian political theorists Bonnie Honig, *Political Theory and the Displacement of Politics* (Ithaca: Cornell University Press, 1993); and Margaret Moore, *Foundations of Liberalism* (Oxford: Clarendon Press, 1993), 198.
9. See Charles Taylor, *Muticulturalism: Examining the Politics of Recognition* (Princeton: Princeton University Press, 1993); and Will Kymlicka, *Multicultural Citizenship* (Oxford: Oxford University Press, 1995).
10. *Multicultural Citizenship*, 83.
11. I develop this argument in 'Equality and Nationality', *Politics and Society* 24, 2 (1996); and in 'Race, Culture and the Egalitarian Conscience', *Canadian Journal of Philosophy* 29, 2 (1999).
12. David Miller, *Nationality* (Oxford: Clarendon Press, 1995), 74.
13. Ibid., 92-3.

14. Benedict Anderson, *Imagined Communities* (London: Verso, 1996), 7, 72.
15. Ernest Gellner argues that nationalism is a peculiarly modern phenomenon, attendant on mass literacy and public education, democratization, social mobility, and the diminution of privilege: *Nations and Nationalism* (Oxford: Blackwell, 1996), chap. 4. A distinction between regressive and progressive nationalisms is made by Hans Kohn with the typology of 'Eastern' and 'Western', the former xenophobic, the latter tolerant (though the typology itself looks xenophobic!): *The Idea of Nationalism* (New York: Collier-Macmillan, 1967). See also Anthony D. Smith, *National Identity* (Reno: University of Nevada Press, 1991), chaps 1 and 4.
16. Jeremy Webber, *Reimagining Canada: Language, Culture, Community and the Canadian Constitution* (Kingston and Montreal: McGill-Queen's University Press, 1994), 9. Will Kymlicka invokes this idea in *Finding Our Way: Rethinking Ethnocultural Relations in Canada* (Toronto: Oxford University Press, 1998), 176.
17. William Morris, 'How I Became a Socialist', in *The Collected Works of William Morris*, intro. May Morris (New York: Russell and Russell, 1966), 23: 281.
18. The Canadian philosopher Thomas Hurka embraces the term 'perfectionism' to capture the idea of a duty to pursue human excellence in *Perfectionism* (Oxford: Oxford University Press, 1993). An interesting case for a link between equality and perfectionism is made by Vinit Haksar, who argues that Rawls's idea that individuals should be treated with equal respect must make reference to human potential and its realization. See his *Equality, Liberty and Perfectionism* (Oxford: Oxford University Press, 1979).
19. *Liberalism, Perfectionism and Restraint* (Cambridge: Cambridge University Press, 1998), 18.
20. See my 'Death in Utopia: Marxism and the Mortal Self', in *The Social Self*, ed. D. Bakhurst and C. Sypnowich (London: Sage Publications, 1995).
21. See Philippe Ariès, *Western Attitudes to Death* (Baltimore: Johns Hopkins University Press, 1974); and my 'Fear of Death: Mortality and Modernity in Political Philosophy', *Queen's Quarterly* 98, 1.
22. See Canadian philosopher Cheryl Misak's *Truth and the End of Inquiry: A Peircean Account of Truth* (Oxford: Clarendon, 1991). A possible problem with drawing on Peirce here is the unitary character of his regulative ideal; in epistemology we aim for a single true theory of the way the world is, whereas the idea of progress in ways of living assumes a diversity of ends. This may be resolved if we consider the latter in terms of a single account of the pursuit of the good, an account that nonetheless understands that the ways in which we might pursue the good are various.
23. I make an argument for such an understanding of privacy in 'The Civility of Law: Between Public and Private', in *Public and Private*, ed. M. Passerin d'Entrèves and U. Vogel (London: Routledge, 2000).

Citizenship and Relational Feminism

JENNIFER NEDELSKY

It is now widely recognized that the great historical proclamations of equality and citizenship actually excluded many.[1] Women's exclusion from the vote, from public office, and from professions such as law continued throughout the nineteenth century in countries proclaiming an Enlightenment commitment to equal rights and citizenship. Of course the dearth of women in public office continues in those countries today, long after the legal extension to women of male rights of citizenship. And we have good reason to believe that this long sustained history of exclusion is not a matter of historical blindspots: the exclusion is built into the very conceptual framework of citizenship and equal rights.[2]

This built-in exclusion has meant that, everywhere in the world, women struggling for equality face a tension in their strategies: to call upon traditional conceptions of citizenship and equal rights to challenge the current subordination and exclusion of women is to call upon a tradition deeply implicated in that very exclusion and subordination; but to fail to do so would be to abandon a tool—both rhetorical and institutional—that has been used throughout the world in emancipatory struggles. The problem has an added complexity when the existing structures of inequalities are among the effects of the colonialism that imposed the nation-state structure—and its accompanying conceptions of citizenship—in the first place.[3] Why should women believe that the language inherited from colonial powers, itself deeply patriarchal in origin, is an appropriate tool against a form of patriarchy itself shaped by that inheritance? Or, to put it more affirmatively: can women reclaim and transform that language so that it can be used to cut against existing patriarchal structures and develop a truly optimal citizenship, without simply imposing an alien (and itself patriarchal) framework?

An affirmative answer is crucial, given the importance of citizenship for both protection and participation in a world defined by membership in states. This essay aims to contribute to the development of a conception of citizenship that can draw on the emancipatory power of the tradition without reinforcing and newly instantiating its exclusionary dimensions. I begin by sketching the dimensions of the tradition of liberal citizenship that I see as limitations to the project of envisioning optimal citizenship. I focus first on the underlying conception of the self and then introduce my alternative conception of a relational self. The relational approach, I argue, invites us to take seriously the contributions of what is often called maternal feminism. Using my reflections on the debate over the usefulness of maternal feminism for understanding citizenship, I explore the issues of the universal versus the particular, the importance of difference in achieving equal citizenship, the importance of caretaking as a source of insight, the conditions of equal respect, and compassion and passion as dimensions of citizenship. Ironically, it is maternal feminism that helps us see that the worldwide split between caretaking and policy-making is unacceptable, not because it is incompatible with equality between men and women, but because it is incompatible with optimal governance and citizenship.

THE LIBERAL CITIZEN-SELF AND ITS LIMITATIONS

Developing an optimal approach to citizenship requires an understanding of the conception of the self that underlies the traditional concept—and ultimately an alternative to that conception. Let me begin with a brief statement of the tradition and its exclusionary qualities, and then turn to the ways the alternative conception of self I have been working on can provide a framework for working through some of the dilemmas of citizenship.

The dominant conception of citizenship is part of a Western liberal tradition that, despite its variations, can be said to rest on a particular vision of the self.[4] That self is an autonomous, rational agent that exercises its capacity for self-determination by choosing its relationships and obligations, especially through the legal vehicles of private property and contract.[5] This picture of the self then generates a set of claims about the rights it must have in order to exercise its capacity for self-determination and rational agency. These rights claims have taken the form of what are seen as 'private' legal rights to contract and to own property, as well as rights of representation or participation in the 'public' realm of politics. Historically, these two sets of rights have been closely linked, in the sense that only those who were capable of exercising their self-determination through contract and property were thought to be suitable participants in the realm of public deliberation.[6]

Of course, it has now been documented in detail, in the realm of both political theory and legal history, how women and other subordinated groups were excluded both from the underlying conception of selfhood and from the corresponding legal rights. The important point here is not just the fact of historical exclusion, but the arguments that such exclusion was built into these paired conceptions of self and rights. If these arguments are persuasive, then it is not possible simply to use these exclusionary concepts to include everyone.[7]

For example, Iris Marion Young's compelling argument about reason is one version of how the exclusion works. She analyzes the conception of impartiality that she sees as central to Western political thought, and shows how it rests on a 'logic of identity'. This image of sameness among citizens is achieved by excluding 'desire, affectivity and the body' from impartial reason, coupled with a corresponding exclusion from the public realm of those people (such as women) identified with the excluded characteristics.

The liberal vision tacitly equates autonomy with independence and has a kind of literal notion of self-determination, which, as I noted, is played out through the choice of relationships and obligations. The intertwining of women's self-interest with that of their children and their families more generally has always made them appear not to be the independent, rational agents that liberal theory presupposed. This same intertwining then implicated them in an affective dimension that not only made them seem ill-suited for the public realm of reasoned deliberation but cast doubt on their capacity for rational agency at all. My point here is that there genuinely is a complex interpenetration of interests and affect for many women. My conclusion, of course, is not that they are therefore ill-suited for the public realm, but that a conception of human autonomy, rational agency, and public deliberation that cannot accommodate the realities of women's lives (or those of men deeply connected to their families) cannot be an adequate conception.

The traditional liberal conception of autonomy is also highly culturally specific. In equating autonomy and independence and focusing on choosing relationships and obligations as key dimensions of self-determination, the traditional conception cannot adequately accommodate cultures where key dimensions of identity and obligation are significantly given by one's place within kin and community networks.[8] The sense of self in those cultures must appear deficient, not fully autonomous, as measured against this liberal vision of the self. As a result, not just the institutions of those cultures but their sense of self needs radical transformation before the liberal model can be used to correct inequalities. This sort of diagnosis should give anyone pause.

THE RELATIONAL SELF

The exclusionary qualities of this conception of self would be enough to condemn it; but I also think that to conceptualize autonomy as independence is to fundamentally misunderstand the nature of autonomy and what really makes it possible: constructive relationships. It is relationships, from child–parent, to student–teacher, to client–state, as well as patterns of relationships among citizens, that make actualization of the human potential for autonomy possible.[9] The self is a fundamentally relational self, which requires constructive relationships for its potential to be fully realized. There is, indeed, a core human capacity for self-creation, a capacity that means we are never fully determined by our relationships or our given material circumstances (including our bodies). We are always in a creative process of interaction, of mutual shaping, with all the dimensions of our existence. But it is misleading to think of this somewhat miraculous (and I think never fully graspable) creative capacity as self-determination and independence.[10]

This alternative, relational conception of the self can help with the problems of an historically exclusionary conception of citizenship in a variety of ways. First, I do not believe it is possible to have a conception of citizenship or of rights that does not have some underlying vision of the self. Some conception of the nature of the human self must ground one's view of the rights to which people are entitled and the ways in which membership in national communities should be conceived and structured. One might suppose, then, that any conception of citizenship will have exclusionary consequences for those with competing visions of the self. But I think my claim that the self is to be understood as essentially relational largely avoids this exclusionary cultural specificity. We need always to inquire into the actual structures of social relationships that shape the 'selves' in any given culture or community. Some of these structures will, in fact, foster a belief in, and an experience of, independent self-determination. These structures and beliefs will matter greatly in understanding both that culture itself and the optimal forms of its transformation. The same approach works equally well in attending to the dynamics and potential for change in a culture where the experience of self is clearly and deeply embedded in kin structure. I also think the claim of creative capacity is widely inclusive. Even cultures with highly determined roles, or spiritual traditions that focus on obeying God's commands or on finding rather than choosing one's path in life, require the capacity for self-creation in order to take on these responsibilities. I think the claim of the creative capacity does not need to translate into the Western tendency to put autonomy (usually understood as independence and self-determination) above other values such as harmony, attentiveness, co-operation, collective responsibility, or social cohesion.

Starting with a conception of the relational self also helps us to appreciate the need for bonds in the development of the autonomy necessary for citizenship. At the same time, it emphasizes the difference between bonds that are constructive and those that are not, providing a standard to which existing relationships can be held. To identify the essentially relational nature of human beings is not to acquiesce in the existing (often oppressive) networks of relationships in which women are embedded.

In sum, focusing on the relationships that bring the potential of the self into actuality also serves to direct attention to the conditions necessary to make equal citizenship a reality. This attention avoids a blind formality that claims to overcome historical exclusion by mere stipulation of inclusion. I will return to this issue in a later section.

Maternal Feminism and Citizenship

The relational approach directs us to a strand of feminist theory, maternal feminism, that grounds itself in particular relations. The appropriateness of maternal feminism for theorizing citizenship has been hotly debated. In my reflections on these debates, I will address the (so far unspoken) question of whether feminist theory, including efforts to articulate and envision equal citizenship for women, can do without some form of the universal claims that have been the foundation of liberal theory and the target of so much useful feminist criticism. These issues are related, since the objections to the application of 'maternal feminism' to the public realm are usually variants of the concern that the intimate relations of mother and child have an inherent particularity (and inequality) that is at odds with the aspiration of generality that all citizens (interchangeably) treat each other as equals and '[differ] in nothing'.[11] Another variant of the criticism is that maternal feminism entails an essentialism that is not only intrinsically wrong-headed but also in opposition to the commonality that should be the core of citizenship.[12]

Despite my agreement with critiques of the universalism characteristic of liberalism,[13] I have come to believe that some form of universal claim of equal moral worth is necessary for the sort of feminist theory and practice I want to foster. At the same time I have been powerfully drawn to maternal feminism and its attempt to do precisely what the critics resist: apply the insights and virtues of the traditionally 'private' realm to the traditionally public, the political. Part of the reason is that I found my own experience of pregnancy, nursing, and infant care to be the source of important insights and transformations that I believe extend beyond my personal relationships.[14] This section offers a series of reflections on how to work through the tensions these issues give rise to and what they reveal about an optimal approach to citizenship.

My view is that feminist theory requires a claim of the equal moral worth of all people; nothing short of that universal claim will be able to ground the liberty and equality claims that virtually all feminists make. Yet I remain uncertain about how the claim of equal moral worth can itself be grounded in our secular age. At one time, the foundation was that all humans have a soul and thus some basic equal moral worth. It may be that in my own view, something like the belief in a human soul is the foundation for my commitment to equal moral worth. But given the powerful, and perhaps appropriate, norms of secular public discourse, it is not at present an acceptable ground for claims of equality. Often the claim is simply asserted, without reference to its justification. The most common alternative is to use the language of human agency or rationality as the foundation. This, however, seems unsatisfactory, since infants, the senile, and the mentally deranged or incompetent have these capacities in such varying degrees—and yet should be seen as equal in moral worth.

In my view the claim of equal moral worth should be a highly formal one. The formal claim tells us almost nothing about what actually flows from it in terms of rights, unless those rights in turn are conceived in highly formal terms. As soon as we want to know anything at all specific about the actual rights people should enjoy, we need to turn to the concrete particulars of their situation. It is here that the feminist insistence on context and particularity instead of abstract universality is crucial. So although the universal claim of equal moral worth is necessary, it is far from sufficient. It does not get us very far at all. What we need to know in each instance is the conditions, the patterns and structures of relations, the institutions and practices that will foster those relations, that together can give effect to the values, such as liberty and autonomy and security, that we think flow from the basic claim of equal moral worth. For example, I have tried to show elsewhere how we should think about autonomy in terms of the relations that foster it.[15]

One of the interesting things about citizenship is that it is regarded as making highly general claims (hence the objections to the relevance of the particularity of mother–child relations) about what all citizens are entitled to by virtue of their citizenship and what should characterize the relations among citizens qua citizens. Yet at the same time, in many cases, citizenship is treated not as a universal claim but as one particular to a given state. It is inclusive with respect to fellow citizens, but explicitly exclusive with respect to non-citizens. Consider Mouffe's rather startling claim that citizens constitute a 'we' in opposition to some 'them'.[16] Equally important, the emphasis that feminists such as Dietz and Mouffe place on participation as the central dimension of citizenship means that citizenship, at least in this respect, cannot simply have a highly formal character. We cannot simply posit the capacity to participate as entailed in equal citizenship, or equal moral worth. There are actual capacities necessary to participate in public discourse, in the shaping of collective decisions. Ultimately we will have to address the question of what those capacities are and how they are to be fostered. The answers to those substantive questions will have to be based on inquiry into concrete particulars. They cannot be generated by deduction from abstract universal principles. So citizenship is an area that requires both a kind of high-level generality (as it is usually conceived) and a considerable degree of concrete specificity. With that in mind, let us turn to the insights available from maternal feminism and my concerns about the positions of its critics.

I think one of the central problems of contemporary democracy is to develop a conception and practice of equality to which difference is central. In the liberal tradition, the equal entitlement to basic rights, the idea of equal citizens or equal human beings, has entailed a denial of difference. There is a sort of self-evident quality to this position. If we are equal in some basic moral or legal sense, it must be that *for those purposes* we are the same. The ways in which we are different are not relevant to our status as citizens or as rights bearers. As I noted earlier, Iris Marion Young has done an especially effective job of analyzing the 'logic of identity' and the relentless exclusion of difference that has characterized an important part of the liberal tradition.[17] I find it striking that, in their opposition to maternal feminism as an approach to citizenship, both Dietz and Mouffe still reflect a version of that logic.

Dietz, for example, affirms Aristotle's view that 'the members of a political association aim by their very nature at being equal and differing in nothing'.[18] My view is that the contemporary challenge is to aim at being equal and different in important ways. To put it another way: we need to understand that our equality as rights bearers, as citizens, should have a meaning that is consistent with our multiple and shifting inequalities and differences. The reality is that we are not equal in strength, intelligence, talents, capacity to communicate verbally, or even capacity for leading our lives in a truly autonomous fashion. We have advantages over one another in some respects, but not others. We relate through multiple differences and inequalities (most of which are contingent constructions), and we cannot achieve whatever it is we are after in asserting equal citizenship without attention to these differences and inequalities. It is for this reason that I think the dismissal of the mother–child[19] relationship as a source of insight for citizenship is misguided.

I would not want to claim that the mother–child relationship should be the model of democratic citizenship. But I object to the dismissal of it as belonging to some completely different realm with no relevance for the public realm. A central task of the mother–child relationship is to develop a relation of mutual respect, one that fosters the autonomy of the child while respecting that of the mother. And this process must take place in the context of great, but shifting, inequalities of power and abilities. Understanding what makes the process successful seems of considerable relevance to the problems of democratic citizenship, of the experience of 'simultaneously ruling and being ruled', and of the shifting role of ruled and ruler. When I first heard Virginia Held deliver her insightful reflections on replacing contract with mothering as the basic metaphor of politics,[20] I heard someone object that she was romanticizing motherhood, assuming it to be always benign. This seems to be a common charge against those trying to draw on the insights of mothering. But the complex task of raising a child is relevant to the problems of democratic citizenship precisely because it is not always benign: we need to learn the dangers of the misuse of power, to learn what makes the task fail as well as what makes it succeed.

There are many instances of attempts to protect, nurture, and help develop abilities and autonomy that inevitably take place in a context of inequality. The student–teacher relationship and the state–client relationship are just two obvious ones. It is hard to conceive of a democracy that would not require some version of both. As citizens we simply do not always stand in a relation of equality to each other, even if we can always claim a formal equality. We need to know how to minimize the many current inequalities that are unnecessary. But we also need to know how to work with the inevitable inequalities that are part of both human difference and complex social structures, such as governments and corporations. Inquiring into what makes a parent–child relationship successful may give us some insights into how the inevitable overlap of equality and inequality can be constructive. And a careful inquiry will also reveal not only the shifting relations of equality and inequality, but the ways in which inequality and equality are always truly a relationship, a set of interactions that affect each other.

Chantal Mouffe has an extremely sophisticated and helpful understanding of identity as shifting and emergent and multiple. But she still wants to insist that citizenship is a 'common political identity': 'The aim is to construct a "we" as radical democratic citizens, a collective political identity articulated through the principle of democratic *equivalence*.'[21] She is careful to insist that 'such a relation of *equivalence* does not eliminate *difference*', but she also tells us that she aims at a 'new conception of citizenship where sexual difference should become effectively nonpertinent'.[22] Both the oppositional construction of the 'we', inevitably opposed to 'them',[23] and the nonpertinence of sexual difference make me nervous. While it seems possible that in some feminist utopia most dimensions of citizenship would be such that sexual difference was irrelevant, I think we must be careful not to move too quickly to that position. In the meantime, I would advocate, as Sara Ruddick does, that we look to the practices of caretaking for insights that attend to difference without essentializing.

Ruddick titles her book *Maternal Thinking*,[24] so she clearly falls into the category of maternal feminists. But, at least to judge by the sections I have focused on, it seems clear that she is not an essentialist. She is conscious of the constructed character of women's traditional roles. What she directs our attention to is not some inherent characteristic of women as mothers, but the practices of caretaking and what we can learn from them.[25] This seems extremely fruitful to me. (I have earlier suggested that in child-raising we find a helpful way of thinking about the practices and patterns of relationships that foster autonomy. This source helps us avoid the classic misunderstanding of autonomy as independence, and helps us see it as a capacity that requires the right kind of sustaining relationships.) For example, Ruddick says (in a way consistent with Mouffe's approach) that standpoint theorists 'have learned from the work of training children [that their task is] to articulate conditions of respect for unpredictable and as yet unimagined difference and variety among and within people.'[26] Among the many things I like about this point is its attention to the *conditions* of respect. Far too many theorists, even feminist theorists, sometimes lapse into discussions about the importance of respect in citizenship without any attention to the conditions that make it possible. What we need is consistent attention to the relations that make it possible to realize values such as autonomy, liberty, and equality. I would call myself, therefore, a relational rather than a maternal feminist. But I believe that attention to the work of caretaking, of which child-bearing and -raising are crucial instances, will be useful in helping us understand the conditions and the patterns of relation necessary to achieve public goals such as optimal citizenship.

When we pay attention to caretaking, we will also pay attention to the ways it is organized around gender, race, and class. Of course, the assignment of some aspects of caretaking to one gender only is not a purely historical construction that can be rearranged. I have in mind pregnancy and nursing. While I am entirely in favour of approaches that foster child care by both men and women, I would be reluctant to assert that the involvement of many (but not all) women in pregnancy and nursing is simply irrelevant to optimal citizenship. At the least, their patterns of participation in public life may be different from men's. There may be periods when their attention is properly focused almost entirely inward, on intimate relations with their families. Thus some of the expectations of ongoing engagement with public discourse may vary depending on the kinds of caretaking that people are involved in, and there will be a strong correlation with gender. To pay attention to these matters does not seem to me to run the risk of essentialism, or a destructively gendered conception of citizenship. But it certainly is not consistent with an a priori aspiration to a citizenship to which gender is not pertinent.

One of the most compelling of Dietz's arguments is that 'a truly democratic defence of citizenship cannot afford to launch its appeal from a position of gender opposition and women's superiority. Such a premise would posit as a starting point precisely what a democratic attitude must deny—that one group of citizens' voices is generally better, more deserving of attention, more worthy of emulation, more moral, than another's'.[27] Connected to her view that mutual respect is central to democratic citizenship, this is an extremely important and complicated point, and it requires a lot more fleshing out than Dietz provides in her articles on citizenship.

Mutual respect may sound like a minimal standard, but I think it is actually a very high one. Among the obvious questions that arise is whether we should treat a fellow citizen who is virulently racist with respect, listening carefully and attentively to his view in our public deliberations. I think the answer is yes, but of course that does not mean we do not think our approach is morally superior. And it will not help enough to simply say that we may judge ideas and approaches as morally superior, but not people or whole categories of people. Again, we need to think in detail about what practices we have in mind as expressing mutual respect, and what conditions would make this possible.[28]

Ruddick also offers some reflections that are helpful in thinking through the problem of the mutual respect required for democratic citizenship. She notes her fear that 'standpoint theorists or their followers will lose sight of the failures and temptations of the caretakers they celebrate.'[29] This fear is echoed by Sarah Hoagland, who draws attention to the common failure of caretakers to ensure that those receiving care help determine the kind of care they get.[30]

Once again, it may be that the family is a fruitful source of insights into what practices of mutual respect look like when they cannot be premised on equal good judgment, knowledge, maturity, or responsibility. For example, although parents must have the ultimate authority in determining the rules that govern the household, those rules can be formulated and imposed in various ways, from authoritarian to consultative. Children can have important insights as well as preferences in the exact terms of those rules and the consequences for their violation. Children relate to rules differently, depending on whether the rules are the result of collective decision-making or imposition by superior power. I am not implying that the proper relationship between those in power and those they govern is that of benign and respectful parents towards their children. In that sense the family is obviously not a model for democratic citizenship. But the recognition that imbalances of power, knowledge, and judgment do not need to preclude genuine participation is relevant to democratic citizenship. Equipped with that knowledge, citizens can resist claims (tacit or explicit) that they have nothing valuable to contribute to policy formation on technically complex issues. And those in power might resist the temptation to deceive or circumvent the public, if they had creatively explored models for providing sufficient information to allow public participation. Similarly women, whose knowledge is important for policy formation but comes from a different source (family responsibilities) and perhaps takes a different form than that now familiar to those in government, need creative forums for effective participation in collective deliberation. In addition, I think the temptation that parents face to replace time-consuming consultation with parental fiat is similar to the temptation that politicians so often give in to. Not only is it probably easier to experiment with participatory forums within the family, but once these skills are developed there, they will provide a base of knowledge to be applied in the 'public' realm.

I think that sometimes the reason people dismiss the family as a source of information about democratic citizenship is that they do not envision a genuinely respectful relationship between parents and children or between spouses. Power differentials seem to preclude anything more than token participation on the part of those not in the superior position. But that view reflects a lack of experience of the genuine exchange of knowledge, insight, and preferences that can contribute to collective decision-making despite the differences that characterize family relations. And, as I said earlier, differences in power, knowledge, and abilities will characterize even optimal democracies. A basic stance of respectful listening is crucial to democratic relations among citizens (with such inevitable differences) and between the governed and those to whom they have entrusted public power. Experiments with optimal family relations and forms of collective decision-making can therefore offer important insights into the challenges posed by democratic citizenship that acknowledges the inevitability of difference, even as it insists on a basic equality.

In sum, those who reject the relevance of family relations and caretaking, much of which has traditionally been carried out by women, not only miss a rich source of insight, but also reinscribe a public–private dichotomy that their own theories usually reject.

The debates over the relevance of maternal feminism also involve the more general debate about universal abstractions versus concrete particulars. One of Dietz's claims is that citizenship must have a general quality, whereas the mother–child relationship is highly particular. She says that while women may be drawn into political engagement by their concerns as mothers, once so engaged their concerns are transformed and they act as citizens rather than mothers. I think it is an open empirical question whether women who engage in public action as mothers generalize *in a different way* because of their frame of reference as mothers. Jean Elshtain has engaged in research on political mothers that may help us answer this question.[31] Of course women who take public action around threats to their children are also acting on behalf of children other than their own. An important form of generalization is taking place. But I would not be at all surprised to find that the nature of the generalization is different. For example, it might well be that the move to abstract principles is different, or absent, or given less weight. It seems likely to me that the particular attachment to actual, specific children keeps their political activity grounded in a way that the activity of those acting from abstract principle often is not. These remain speculations to be explored. What matters is to avoid the mistake of saying that the realm of citizenship is public and general and the realm of mother–child is private and particular, and thus that the latter should not be looked to for insights into the former.

My own experience is that the passionate attachment to my children leads to a sort of openness and responsiveness to the pain of other, unknown mothers, who are unable to comfort, feed, clothe, heal, or enjoy (because of exhaustion, for example) their children. When I had my children, a sense of urgency about the preciousness and vulnerability of all children became a new part of how I saw the world. (This sense is, however, very complicated. In the first seven years after my first child was born and during which my second arrived, I was *less* active politically than I had ever been. But I think that was not a mistake. As they have grown older—even in the few years since I first drafted this argument—I have begun to act on this new sense in ways beyond donating money, as my life starts to shift slowly back into a more public-centred focus. Hence my earlier comments about varying patterns of political participation.) I experience this concern for the children of the world and their mothers as very different from my other longstanding concerns with social justice. I do not think there is only one form of the generalization that moves from personal experience to concern for others, and I do not think those differences are trivial or irrelevant to our understanding of optimal citizenship.[32] I also make different substantive judgments about the importance of the well-being of mothers and children, and the institutions that make that possible, for an optimal society.

Part of what may distinguish the connections to others born of one's attachment to one's own children is compassion. This is another part of what makes the parent–child relation so interesting for politics. There is an important debate about the desirability of compassion as a basic dimension of politics. Some think of it as indispensable to an optimal politics (my view); others are wary of the tendency of compassion to come with condescension. 'Give me my rights and keep your compassion' seems to be the view, which I respect because of the experience of subordination that generates it. This is yet one more version of the question about what kind of respectful stance one wants between citizens, and how that relates to issues of generality and particularity.

A final note on the passions of motherhood and citizenship. I do see a potential tension between the fierce protectiveness of mothers for *their* children and the sort of equal commitment to the rights and well-being of one's fellow citizens that we might wish for. But I would note that once again there is an interesting analogue to the notion of citizenship. Citizenship is itself particular, not universal. Citizens are expected to treat each other as equals, but they are also expected to be willing to fight and die to protect *their* country. And it is routinely assumed that citizens may exclude non-citizens from their country even if they are in dire need (though not if they are in imminent danger from state violence). Citizenship, like the connections to one's children, has built into it the tensions of loyalty, love, and the equal moral worth of all.

Implications for Equal Citizenship

Perhaps the most important lesson from these theoretical reflections is that the knowledge, experience, insight, and emotional connections that women gain from mothering must not be excluded from the public realm. There are too many important substantive areas of public policy for which such knowledge and experience are crucial. Education, food production, protection against violence for all vulnerable people, housing, city and village organization and infrastructure, and family law are just some of the obvious ones. These are areas in which public policy has a defining influence on the 'private realm', and thus cannot be well formulated without intimate knowledge of that impact. But beyond that, I think the ways of knowing that develop from child-rearing (and perhaps more generally from caretaking) are crucial to all public policy formation. Thus if women are responsible for the 'private realm' and are excluded from the public, public policy cannot be adequately formulated. Put the other way around, anyone responsible for public policy must have the education that comes from the experience of child-rearing and material caretaking. Social structures that exclude men from these experiences and then set them up as policy-makers cannot create the proper foundations of citizenship. Optimal citizenship requires appropriate education for those who will hold public office and means for those who have the requisite information about public policy issues to have their voices heard in policy formation.

This issue is, of course, crucial to women and citizenship, but it goes beyond issues of gender. There are other hierarchies formed around the denigration of physical caretaking. In Canada and the United States people of colour are disproportionately employed in caretaking jobs. It is essential that those who do the work of physical caretaking have full, effective (not merely formal) access to the public realm. Until this work is respected, neither children nor the earth will be properly taken care of. The bifurcation of the world into public and private realms, and the relegation of caretaking to the private, creates a disjuncture between those who make policy and those who know what is essential to policy-making. As long as there are social hierarchies, they will map onto the hierarchies of work. The lowest categories of people will do the lowly caretaking. The caretakers will be unprotected and the objects of their care will be ignored because of the policy-makers' ignorance.

It should be clear, then, that if one of the primary ways of enabling women some access to the public realm is to create an exploited class of workers to take over their caretaking responsibilities, this cannot be a good solution to the problem of equal citizenship. At present, nannies and other household workers make it possible for middle-class women around the world to enter the workforce and even the political arena, previously reserved for men. But this cannot solve the problems generated by the bifurcation between caretakers and policy-makers. And it creates a new class of people, almost exclusively women, who are at risk of exploitation and violence. Frequently their vulnerability and their inability to have their voices heard are made worse because they are not citizens of the countries in which they work.

The issue of domestic workers reveals how demanding the challenge is to create the conditions of equal citizenship. It is not sufficient simply to try to include women in existing structures by eliminating formal barriers to their participation in either the workforce or politics. The structures presuppose the bifurcation around caretaking (although working-class women have long had to do the 'double shift' of work outside the home and caretaking inside it). If women are working in the public realm, someone else has to take care of the children. It would take vast structural changes to provide optimal care for children and full access to the public world of work and policy-making for women. And to do so in ways that do not create new exploited classes and recreate the split between caretaking and policy-making is an even more daunting challenge.

The problem of trying to include women in concepts that have exclusions built into them thus has its analogue in the practical, institutional realm. One cannot simply maintain the existing structures and try to include women into them. The structures are premised on the exclusion of those who do caretaking, who are disproportionately women. Just as we need to re-imagine public reason, rational self-interest, and autonomy, we need to restructure the workplace, the family, and the institutions of public decision-making.

This is as true in Canada as it is elsewhere in the world. I think the difference is the degree to which one encounters deep social, ideological, or theological commitments to the ideas that women should be the caretakers of children and the home and that they do not belong in the public realm of politics. I was initially reluctant to define as a precondition of equal citizenship a direct challenge to such commitments. And, indeed, since so many women throughout the world are embedded in caretaking roles, I think it is important to be creative in thinking about ways of ensuring that women have experience in collective decision-making throughout the time when their primary focus is on their own family. I think with the right institutions of small-scale collective decision-making, women's assignment to family care could be rendered compatible with full citizenship participation over their lifetimes.[33] In the end, though, what maternal and relational feminism has shown in the arguments above is that optimal citizenship cannot be based on a structural split between caretaking and policy-making—not because it is incompatible with equality for women, but because it is incompatible with the requirements of citizenship.[34]

I want to close by suggesting that all inquiries into citizenship would be aided by remembering that the purpose of citizenship is not simply to assure equal rights and protection for members of states. It is also to forge sufficient bonds of commonality to enable citizens to work together in defining and implementing the common good. And it is important to remember that exclusion from this dimension of citizenship is at stake in all issues of equal citizenship. Public participation is important not only to ensure equal protection, but to give all members an opportunity to develop the relationships that come from, and in turn facilitate, working for common purposes. Participating in collective decision-making is an important part of human autonomy. And having a role in the ongoing debates that shape and develop the core values of a culture is important, both as an intrinsic part of human autonomy and expression, and in order to ensure that the structures of relationship are such that they foster the autonomy of all. Relational feminism makes it clear that these dimensions of citizenship cannot be achieved by the stipulation of equal rights and respect. The language of equal citizenship can be a useful tool to promote core human values, but only if it directs attention to the concrete specificity (and variety) of the structures of relationship that create the conditions for equal citizenship.

Notes

1. The American Declaration of Independence, 'we hold these truths to be self-evident: that all men are created equal', was treated as consistent not only with the disenfranchisement

of women and the propertyless, but with slavery. The male language of famous phrases such as 'Liberté, Egalité, Fraternité' has been shown to be no simple quirk of historical rhetoric. See, for example, Carole Pateman, *The Sexual Contract* (Stanford: Stanford University Press, 1988), chap. 4.

2. See Pateman, *The Sexual Contract*; Iris Marion Young, *Justice and the Politics of Difference* (Princeton: Princeton University Press, 1990), chap. 4; Ursula Vogel, 'Is Citizenship Gender-Specific?', in *The Frontiers of Citizenship*, ed. Ursula Vogel and M. Moran (London: Macmillan, 1991).
3. For example, First Nations women in Canada, women in South Africa embedded in village culture, and women in Lebanon face the dilemmas of invoking the language of equal citizenship or constitutional rights to transform patriarchal structures that are the 'product of the intersection between the colonial and indigenous domains'. Suad Joseph (referring to Lebanon), interview, *Middle East Report* (July–August 1993), 23.
4. This is particularly true of Anglo-American liberalism.
5. See note 2, and Catherine Keller, *From a Broken Web: Separatism, Sexism, and the Self* (Boston: Beacon Press, 1986). On the historical importance of property and contract, see also Jennifer Nedelsky, *Private Property and the Limits of American Constitutionalism* (Chicago: University of Chicago Press, 1990).
6. See note 2.
7. Vogel has a particularly persuasive argument that women's subordination was 'an integral part of men's citizenship'. 'Is Citizenship Gender-Specific?', 75, n.2.
8. Lebanon is an example. See Suad Joseph, 'Problematizing Gender and Relational Rights: Experiences from Lebanon', *Social Politics* (Fall 1994), 271-85; and 'Gender and Relationality among Arab Families in Lebanon', *Feminist Studies* 19, 3 (Fall 1993), 465-86. See also Samir Khalaf, *Beruit Reclaimed* (Beirut: Dar an-Nahar, 1993) and Safia Antoun Saade, *The Social Structure of Lebanon: Democracy or Servitude* (Beirut: Dar An-Nahar, 1993).

   Strategically, I think there is an interesting link between overcoming the exclusion on the basis of gender and of cultural specificity. In a society such as Lebanon, in which men as well as women experience themselves as embedded in kin and community networks, a conception of the citizen-self that takes account of such embeddedness may then be used to overcome the view that *women's* embeddedness is a barrier to their public participation.
9. I have developed this argument in 'Reconceiving Autonomy', *Yale Journal of Law and Feminism* 1 (1989), 7-36.
10. I have developed this argument further in 'Rights and the Fully Human Self', manuscript.
11. Mary Dietz, quoting Aristotle, 'Citizenship with a Feminist Face: The Problem with Maternal Thinking', *Political Theory* 13, 1 (1985), 19-37, at p. 28.
12. See Dietz, 'Citizenship with a Feminist Face'; and 'Context is All: Feminism and Theories of Citizenship', in *Dimensions of Radical Democracy*, ed. Chantal Mouffe (London: Verso, 1992); and Chantal Mouffe, 'Feminism, Citizenship, and Radical Democratic Politics', in *Feminists Theorize the Political*, ed. Judith Butler and Joan Scott (New York: Routledge, 1992).
13. See, for example, Young, *Justice and the Politics of Difference*; and Seyla Benhabib, *Situating the Self: Gender, Community and Postmodernism in Contemporary Ethics* (New York: Routledge, 1992), chap. 5.

14. I have elaborated some of these insights in 'Dilemmas of Passion, Privilege, and Isolation: Reflections on Mothering in a White, Middle-Class, Nuclear Family', in *Mother Troubles: Rethinking Contemporary Maternal Dilemmas*, ed. Julia Hanigsberg and Sara Ruddick (Boston: Beacon Press, 1999).
15. 'Reconceiving Autonomy'.
16. 'Feminism, Citizenship, and Radical Democratic Politics', 379.
17. *Justice and the Politics of Difference.*
18. 'Citizenship with a Feminist Face'.
19. I am somewhat inconsistent in my usage of the terms 'parent–child' and 'mother–child' (invoked by the critics of maternal feminism as applied to citizenship). Much, but not all, of what is special about the latter relationship can and should be extended to intimate caregivers of both (or all) genders. But much of the source of the insights available to us will come from inquiry into the actual practices of mothers.
20. This argument can be found in 'Non-contractual Society: A Feminist View', in *Science, Morality and Feminist Theory*, ed. Marsha Hanen and Kai Nielson, *Canadian Journal of Philosophy*, supp. vol. 13 (Calgary: University of Calgary Press, 1987).
21. See 'Feminism, Citizenship, and Radical Democratic Politics', 378-9.
22. Ibid., 376.
23. Part of her point, the inevitability of conflict, is one to which I am sympathetic. We should not construct our conception and institutions of citizenship around aspirations to homogeneity and perfect consensus. But the oppositional quality of the construction of the 'we' seems very troubling. I think Catherine Keller's *From a Broken Web* might be of some help in figuring out how some degree of common identification (which sounds better to me than identity) necessary for citizenship is possible without its core being an opposition to 'them'.
24. *Maternal Thinking: Towards a Politics of Peace* (Boston: Beacon Press, 1989).
25. The focus of standpoint theorists, according to Ruddick, 'is not in the first place on gender but on the work itself and the political conditions in which it is undertaken.' They are feminists, 'in virtue of their political ambition to generalize the values of caring labor that are, for reasons of history, inextricably bound up with the lives and values of women. But their aim is not to create a future that is female.' Ibid., 133. See also Joan Tronto, *Moral Boundaries: A Political Argument for an Ethic of Care* (New York: Routledge, 1993) on the importance of learning from the practices of caretaking.
26. Ibid., 134.
27. Dietz, 'Context is All', 78.
28. I have actually seen a version of these practices at work in my law school. There are extremely strong norms of listening patiently and being at least outwardly respectful even to my most longwinded and unreasonable colleagues. There are no rolling eyes or knowing nudges around the table. Ordinarily there is no effort to close off debate so we can just vote and stop listening to these few. I think what sustains this is a commitment (unstated of course) to view all of our colleagues as essentially decent people, who may be wrong (even consistently), but are not wicked, and to believe that everyone is seeking the good of the law school, however much their conceptions of that good may differ. These seem to me to be impossibly high standards of shared commitment for a large democratic polity. It would be dangerous to assume these characteristics of all those who, by accident of birth,

happen to be our fellow citizens. In fact, I think part of what has sustained the mutual respect at the law school is a high degree of homogeneity among the faculty. (And I think part of the resistance of the faculty to diversity is a sense, probably not fully conscious, that the conditions of mutual respect are at risk if we diversify, indeed if we start talking about diversifying. New conditions will have to be developed, which will involve time, effort, and, quite possibly, conflict and anger.)

29. *Maternal Thinking*, 135.

30. Hoagland is the author of *Lesbian Ethics: Toward New Value* (Palo Alto, Calif.: Institute of Lesbian Studies, 1988). Her remarks about caretaking come from a lecture given at the University of Chicago Law School in May 1994.

31. An early piece on political mothers is 'The Mothers of the Disappeared: Passion and Protest in Maternal Action', in *Representations of Motherhood*, ed. Donna Bassin, Margaret Honey, and Meryle Mahrer Kaplan (New Haven: Yale University Press, 1994).

32. I discuss these issues more fully in 'Dilemmas of Passion, Privilege and Isolation'.

33. I offer some elaboration of this idea in the longer version of this essay that will appear in my book, *Law, Autonomy, and the Relational Self: A Feminist Revisioning of the Foundations of Law*.

34. Of course, there is also the age-old principle that it is never prudent to entrust all political power to one group in the hope that they will look after the interests of those excluded. The argument for virtual representation (whether formal or practical) for women is no more persuasive now than when it was raised to oppose women's suffrage in England and the United States.

Birth, Maternity, Citizenship: Some Reflections

INGRID MAKUS

Some worry that the state of world affairs as we enter the next millennium increasingly resembles the chaotic, war-like 'state of nature' so vividly described by the seventeenth-century philosopher Thomas Hobbes. Hobbes's stark portrait forces us to consider this: If we are concerned about the potential breakdown of political order, we have to pay attention not only to such matters as divided sovereignty, relations among states, and the mechanics of warfare. We also have to consider an even more fundamental matter: What constructs are in place to ensure that the helpless infant will be raised and cared for in a way that establishes political continuity?

Concerns about the breakdown of the traditional nation-state, the growth of ethnic nationalism, and the rapid (and increasingly violent) redrawing of territorial boundaries have also made questions surrounding citizenship a high priority. A common way of attributing citizenship to persons in the twentieth century is on the basis of 'birthright'. Given the proliferation of new reproductive technologies, the meaning of citizenship in the new millennium is likely to become tied up with the conditions of 'birth' itself. A well-known twentieth-century thinker, Simone de Beauvoir, has written much about the activities surrounding birth and, in particular, the implications these have for women's place in history. In the first part of this essay I will begin with Beauvoir and then turn to Hobbes. His account, I argue, makes an important distinction between giving birth and giving life, which has significant implications for how we view the state of helpless infancy.

In the second part of the essay I speculate on ways in which my discussion of Beauvoir and Hobbes can illuminate contemporary issues of reproduction, birth, and citizenship, as well as point to areas of inquiry that are, in my view, underdeveloped in contemporary political theorizing.

In the third part of the essay I present some speculations on Jean-Jacques Rousseau, an eighteenth-century thinker who offers some of the most fascinating and complex insights into the conditions we face in advanced civil society. In Rousseau too the helpless infant takes centre stage, in this case conjuring up the image of an all-powerful maternal figure.

1.

In her milestone work *The Second Sex,* Beauvoir draws on an existentialist framework to assess women's condition throughout history and prehistory. She concludes that whereas man has set himself up as human Subject, a maker of history, thought, and deed, woman has consistently been defined as Other, relative to man's needs, and outside human history. As Other, she becomes non-human—either elevated to God-like status or relegated to animal existence. One of the main reasons woman has been defined as Other, according to Beauvoir, is that she has been confined to immanence.

Immanence is expressed in woman's role in reproduction; in giving birth she merely repeats and maintains life. Transcendence, hitherto open only to the male, is expressed in heroism, revolt, the risking of life and the taking of life. Two passages from the *Second Sex* are crucial to illustrate the argument I want to make:

> . . . *giving birth* and suckling are not activities, they are *natural functions* [my emphasis]; no project is involved; and that is why woman found in them no reason for a lofty affirmation of her existence—she submitted passively to her biologic fate.

> The worst curse that was laid upon woman was that she should be excluded from these warlike forays. For it is not in *giving life* but in *risking life* [my emphasis] that man is raised above the animal; that is why superiority has been accorded in humanity not to the sex that *brings forth* but to that which *kills* [my emphasis].[1]

I suggest that Beauvoir fails to make a distinction here between giving birth and giving life. Giving birth may be a 'natural'—in the sense of spontaneous or automatic—outcome of sexual relations and conception. However, giving life is not a 'natural'—i.e., spontaneous—outcome of giving birth if we take into account the exigencies of the human condition. Infants are born helpless, requiring the care of another to provide, at the very least, the nourishment they need to survive. It is the act of providing nourishment or failing to provide nourishment that determines whether the newborn will live or die. And the act of providing nourishment is not 'natural' in the sense that it follows automatically or spontaneously from the act of giving birth. Giving life entails some positive action and, as Hobbes depicts it, rational decision.

I turn to Hobbes's depiction of maternal power and dominion in the state of nature, where the rational element in women's role in reproduction is highlighted and the distinction between giving birth and giving life is sharpened.[2] Two passages are particularly relevant. The first is from *De Cive*:

> . . . it is manifest that he who is newly born, is in the mother's power before any others, insomuch as she may rightly, and at her own will, either breed him up or adventure him to fortune.[3]

The second passage is from *Leviathan*:

> Again, seeing the Infant is first in the power of the Mother, so as she may either nourish, or expose it, if she nourish it, it oweth its life to the Mother; and is therefore obliged to obey her, rather than any other; and by consequence the Dominion over it is hers.[4]

It is important to distinguish between *maternal power* and *maternal dominion* as Hobbes presents them. Maternal *power* rests on the fact that, because it is the woman who gives birth to the infant, she has first access to it, and therefore the first opportunity to exercise the power of life and death over it. Maternal *dominion* is a relationship of authority that is established only if the woman decides to give life to the infant. She can pass away or forgo maternal *dominion*, but not maternal *power*. That is, she can exercise her *power* over the infant so as to forgo *dominion* over it, but she cannot forgo the initial exercise of *power* over it that initial access to the infant gives her.

The exercise of maternal power entails choice. The mother chooses to nourish the infant, thereby giving it life, or she chooses to refuse it nourishment, thereby causing its death. But what would induce her to choose one over the other? It is striking that Hobbes does not appeal to any sort of natural maternal instinct (or paternal instinct) to care for the infant as a way of establishing a connection between giving birth and giving life.

If, as Hobbes suggests, all voluntary acts are undertaken in the hope of achieving some benefit to the perpetrator, then he must show that it is more beneficial to the mother to nourish the infant than to abandon it. He must show that it is in *her* interest to give it life. He does suggest that she may choose to nourish it in the hope of securing a future ally. But this sort of exchange of benefit rests on a *covenant*, because the infant cannot fulfill its part of the bargain—that is, obeying the mother in return for having been saved—until 'hereafter'. However, *covenants* are inoperative in the state of nature.[5]

In effect, then, the Hobbesian state of nature is one in which there is no incentive for the mother or anyone else to save the helpless infant. As such, it is a state where the political community, and even the species, would not be obliged to perpetuate itself. Men and women may have sexual relations; women may give birth; but there is no guarantee that anyone will give life—that is, nourish, care for, and raise the helpless infant.

Hobbes subverts Beauvoir's categories of immanence and transcendence.[6] The activities surrounding birth, in the Hobbesian state of nature, are an engagement in transcendence in Beauvoir's terms. The sex that gives birth is also the sex that has the first opportunity either to give life or to take life. Infanticide is an option consistent with the exercise of maternal power; indeed, it would seem to be the most 'rational' option.

2.

Why should we pay attention to this stark portrait of the Hobbesian state of nature as a corrective to Beauvoir? In this part of the essay I want to suggest a few ways in which

Hobbes's portrait brings into sharper relief what is at stake in some contemporary debates over reproduction; to address some objections to making use of Hobbes in such a fashion; and to note some theoretical directions that Hobbes challenges us to pursue.

It is easy to write off Hobbes's depiction as simply another example of how masculine assumptions pervade Western thought, and of how male thinkers simply get it wrong when they try to account for or describe something that reflects experiences unique to women. Yet I think we should be wary of dismissing Hobbes outright. In many ways he helps us to see more clearly some contradictions surrounding reproduction in contemporary times.

For one, we can already see in his theory what we find in practice today—that granting women the right to govern their own bodies, which is a fundamental right of citizens in liberal democracies, has radical implications when it comes to reproduction. It gives women the potential to exercise the kind of maternal power described in Hobbes's state of nature. Moreover, this appears particularly threatening when it is not associated with any sort of natural maternal instinct to have and care for children, or any sort of natural maternal love. Perhaps we find this particularly troublesome in an era in which one of the most significant achievements for women has been the acquisition of some legal rights to reproductive control (in the form of access to abortion, for example).

One can see in Hobbes the origins of a right of access to abortion as an extension of the right to govern one's own body (the latter being one of the few rights that Hobbes insists subjects must have in civil society). He makes woman the proprietor of her own body, and by extension, the proprietor of any newly conceived 'life' in her own body. As he writes in *The Elements of Law*: 'considering [that] every man by the law of nature, hath right or propriety to his own body, the child ought rather to be the propriety of the mother, of whose body it is a part, till the time of separation, than of the father.'[7] Maternal power extends to the pre-birth stage, one could say, and is connected to the right to govern one's own body.

Hobbes's depiction of the state of nature has been described as exemplifying a particularly masculinist metaphor in which the fantasy of self-generation takes centre stage. The Hobbesian state of nature, it is argued, presents a (false) vision of an autonomous self that denies and subverts the maternal (and the paternal) contribution.[8] This interpretation of Hobbes tends to rely heavily on a passage where he refers to men as springing out of the earth and coming to maturity like mushrooms, 'without all kind of engagement to each other'. But I think this passage shows Hobbes to be very much aware that, given his view of the state of nature, there is no way to account for infants being raised to adulthood (thus the *as if*).[9] And that is precisely his point. In the absence of a natural maternal or paternal instinct, without the inducements that civil society offers, there is no assurance that something which is fundamental to the continuation of the species and the political community will indeed happen—that the helpless infant will be cared for. Only with regulations and laws that provide incentives as well as supports will something that we tend to take for granted occur (for example, Hobbes proposes laws requiring that children be educated and, as an inducement to parents, that children be obligated to honour their parents). If we take the state of nature to be an ever-possible hypothetical condition (as Hobbes indicates) rather than a pre-political or prehistorical one, then we have to pay attention to how the survival of the helpless infant—and hence generational continuity—is ensured.

But do we need *Hobbes* to tell us this? Yes and no. No, in the sense that feminist theorists in particular have already given renewed emphasis to the mother–child relationship. Yes, in the sense that those theorists are increasingly drawing on 'ethic of care' assumptions, assumptions that seem to have become paradigmatic in contemporary discourse.[10] By paradigmatic, I mean that the view of women in general as caring, other-oriented, concerned with maintaining relationships, and more likely to empower than to take power seems to have permeated every domain of social, political, moral, and scientific thought. (For example, some biologists are now arguing that breastfeeding changes the very brain structure of women, making them more other-oriented on the whole; apparently the hormone oxytocin released by the nursing mother affects the wiring of her brain, 'causing an extension of self toward others—that is social behaviour'.[11])

Hobbes's theory is unique in that he accedes to women maternal power without 'maternalism', in contrast to the usual reluctance to let go of the image of woman/mother as caring, connected, other-oriented, and benevolent on the whole. (Indeed, elements of that image are conjured up in fantastical form in Rousseau.) Hobbes gives us a clue as to why the absence of a maternal instinct is more threatening than the absence of a paternal instinct: because women generally have first access to the infant. Men are as likely as women to abandon their infants—but women have more opportunity to do so.

Elisabeth Badinter's historical study of the mother–infant relationship shows that, across various classes, maternal indifference was the norm, and infanticide quite common. She concludes that the seventeenth- and eighteenth-century practice of sending infants out to wet-nurses (where it was expected that most infants would not survive) was 'objectively a disguised form of infanticide'. Interestingly, she finds that twentieth-century historians have been very reluctant to let go of the idea that there is 'a unique feeling, mother love'. Faced with the evidence, they have tended to attribute maternal indifference to high rates of infant mortality. But this view confuses cause with effect, Badinter suggests. It is not so much that mothers were indifferent because so many died; rather, so many died because mothers were indifferent.[12]

How is this image of the Hobbesian, rationally self-interested 'mother' beneficial to women? Invoking it does not lead to the conclusion that we have to suspend women's right to govern their own bodies in order to avoid the chaos of the state of nature. Instead, it leads to reasoning that as a basic condition of liberal society, as a most fundamental right of citizenship, women have the right to govern their own bodies. (It is on this ground that they have acquired a legal right to choose abortion.) However, if they are to exercise the power that this right gives them in the ways required for the perpetuation of the community, then incentives and supports have to be in place to ensure that they do so willingly.

Keeping in mind the Hobbesian distinction between giving birth and giving life is especially useful if we are concerned about communities perpetuating themselves. We can see that communities in which birth rates are going up may in fact be dying. Some Aboriginal communities in Canada, for example, where the traditional social structures and supports for raising children have been all but destroyed without being adequately replaced, are in danger of dying, not because birth rates are declining (in fact the birth rate in many Aboriginal communities is much higher than in non-Aboriginal ones) but because the social and political conditions and supports for ensuring that infants are cared for in appropriate ways are simply not in place. (Reportedly high rates of child abuse and neglect then are not that surprising.)

Distinguishing between giving birth and giving life also provokes some new thinking about the kinds of issues that are salient with respect to citizenship.[13] What seems most straightforward or 'natural'—attributing citizenship by birthright—becomes much more complicated. Preceding the question of how one gets to be a citizen is the question of how one gets to be a member of society in the first place, prompting an examination of the conditions surrounding birth. If we uphold robust versions of citizenship as articulated in Aristotle and Rousseau, it seems imperative that we consider not only to what extent they exclude women and slaves, but also what it means that they recommend (or admire, in Rousseau's case) the practice of exposing 'weak' or 'deformed' infants at birth. And in an age of new reproductive technologies, when the Internet can be used to sell eggs, sperm, and surrogate wombs internationally, establishing citizenship on the basis of parentage becomes more complex. Who are the parents and what is the place of birth of persons 'born' of reproductive material provided by donors from several countries?

Since it is through parent–child relations that physical and political continuity is established, these relations take on political importance. Yet, as Geoffrey Scarre observes, there is little comprehensive discussion of such relations in mainstream contemporary theory. Intergenerational justice, he says, 'has not figured very high on the agenda of most political philosophers'.[14] Feminist theorists take this topic seriously.[15] But there is a general reluctance here to de-sentimentalize parent–child relations. This is evident in the consistent aversion to the contractual exchange model.[16]

Perhaps the problem is not, as is often suggested, that parent–child relations do not fit the presumption of rational self-interested exchange implied in the contract model. Perhaps it is that, in some ways, they fit that model only too well. In liberal society, individuals do make self-interested calculations about the benefits that might accrue from becoming parents. Paradoxically, however, the more 'rational' such deliberation becomes, in the narrow sense of undergoing a thorough cost-benefit analysis, the more irrational it becomes to parent (which does in the end show the need to move beyond such models). Take, for instance, a recent newspaper article where a woman describes how she responds when people ask her why she has decided not to become a parent. Deciding to have children is like deciding to buy a horse, she explains. One can see the benefits (and the costs) involved. But in both cases, she says, the costs simply outweigh the benefits. The continuing decline in what are still called 'fertility rates' (1.5 in Canada in 1997, below the 2.1 level that demographers say is necessary to replace the population) suggest the prevalence of such calculations.

There is another paradox. The more rational the reproductive process becomes—that is, the greater the separation between sex, conception, birth, life—the more we seem to look 'to' or 'for' a standard in 'nature'. At a time when the Internet is providing detailed information on the sale of eggs and sperm,[17] studies that rank hospitals in Canada continue to cite the numbers of 'natural births' as a criterion for the highest ranking.[18] The thinker who perhaps has the most to say about the possibilities of recovering or discovering nature in contemporary times is Rousseau. He also shows us the psychological dangers of putting the spotlight on our shared helplessness at birth—it risks burdening us with an overwhelming image of maternity.

3.

If we want to find the Rousseauian mother writ large, the place to look for her is not in his depiction of the mother who roams the woods with her infant in the original state of nature, nor in his portrait of the Spartan mother who applauds her son's death in victorious war. The place to look is in Rousseau's presentation of the figure of the Governor, whose task it is to form or transform the child Emile, the central character in his philosophical novel, *Emile*, into someone who can live virtuously in corrupt civil society.[19] In the opening pages of that work Rousseau says: 'the sense I give to the name *mother* must be explained: and that is what will be done hereafter.'[20] As he proceeds, it becomes evident that it is the Governor who becomes the 'mother'.

Although Rousseau distinguishes among the tasks that different persons, such as the biological mother, father, nurse, and Governor, might perform in the care of the young Emile, he also implies that this division of labour is undesirable, expressing a preference for, in modern terms, 'one primary care-giver'.[21] In fact the Governor is the primary caregiver, overseeing all details of his charge's care. He prepares for the infant's arrival as a mother might prepare for her newborn child, by overseeing the selection of a wet-nurse. (It is noteworthy that Rousseau assumes here that a wet-nurse will be chosen, since elsewhere he is adamant that women should nurse their own children.) It allows the Governor, who is to live with the wet-nurse and the infant, to establish himself, rather than the biological mother or the wet-nurse (whose activities and diet he also oversees), as the primary 'caretaker' of Emile.

Reminiscent of a primary bond in which the mother and child are inseparable, the Governor and child are never to be parted without one another's consent.[22] Rousseau spells out the way in which the Governor must set up a carefully controlled environment, 'child-proofing' the house so that the child feels free and is not aware that he is being manipulated.

Since Emile must also remain unaware of his complete dependence on the Governor,[23] he is to be taught that he is dependent only on things, not persons. In fact, however, he is indeed dependent on persons, since only persons, such as the Governor, can provide the kind of care that Rousseau advocates for the young pupil—an all-encompassing, self-sacrificing kind of care. The difficulty in finding a suitable Governor, Rousseau says, is finding someone who will be sufficiently attentive to his charge. Such devotion cannot be bought with money, we are told. So that he can devote himself entirely to his charge, the Governor ideally has only one pupil.[24] And he identifies completely with that pupil's accomplishments.[25]

Although it appears at first to be the other way around, woman as mother takes precedence over woman as sexual mate in Rousseau. Rousseau introduces Sophie to facilitate Emile's (second) birth into a sexual being. But Emile needs the Governor as 'mother' before he needs Sophie as sexual mate. One does not die of celibacy, but the helpless infant will die without the care of another. (The Governor relinquishes his hold over Emile only to pass it on to Sophie.[26])

In other words, we find in Rousseau that the infant's dependence on a 'mother' figure is a more fundamental prototype for political and social dependence than man's dependence on woman as sexual mate. The dependent infant has to be transformed into a citizen. And for Rousseau this transformation is complex and difficult—so difficult, it seems, that it can be undertaken only by a 'mother' of the inhuman proportions exemplified by the all-powerful, all-encompassing, self-sacrificing Governor. It is in Rousseau rather than in Hobbes that we find woman as Other, in Beauvoirian terms.

As the network of social and political arrangements that have to be passed on to the next generation becomes more complex, and citizenship more difficult, we should heed Beauvoir's warning: it is only too easy to make woman the Other—that is, to make her bear the costs of the human condition.

Notes

Work on this essay was supported by The President's Fund for the Advancement of Scholarship at Brock University Research Release Time Award.

1. Simone de Beauvoir, *The Second Sex*, trans. H.M. Parshley (New York: Vintage Books, 1974), 71, 72.
2. Here I draw on my examination of Hobbes in *Women, Politics, and Reproduction: The Liberal Legacy* (Toronto: University of Toronto Press, 1996), chap. 1.
3. Thomas Hobbes, *De Cive or The Citizen*, ed. Sterling P. Lamprecht (New York: Appleton-Century-Crofts), pt 2, chap. 9, para. 2, 106.
4. Thomas Hobbes, *Leviathan*, intro. C.B. Macpherson (Middlesex: Penguin Books, 1968), chap. 20, 254.
5. A *covenant*, as Hobbes defines it, entails an exchange of benefits in which one party promises to 'perform hereafter' (*Leviathan*, chap. 14, 193), as opposed to a *contract*, which entails a simultaneous exchange of benefits. In the state of nature, where there are no civil laws to ensure that the third Law of Nature (that individuals perform the covenants they make) is binding, *covenants* are inoperative.

6. And in a much more radical and quite different fashion than commentators such as Virginia Held and Carole Pateman have suggested. Held says that Beauvoir assumes mothering to be natural because she takes on assumptions about reproduction found in such thinkers as Hobbes. See Virginia Held, 'Birth and Death', *Feminism and Political Theory*, ed. Cass R. Sunstein (Chicago: University of Chicago Press, 1990). This is a misreading of Hobbes, I suggest. In fact he makes reproduction 'rational'. Pateman proposes that Beauvoir fails to acknowledge that women risk life in childbirth; I go further and propose that she also fails to acknowledge that the conditions surrounding birth give them the opportunity to take life: see Carole Pateman, 'Equality, Difference, Subordination: the Politics of Motherhood and Women's Citizenship', in *Beyond Equality & Difference*, ed. Gisela Bock and Susan James (New York: Routledge, 1992).
7. Thomas Hobbes, *The English Works of Thomas Hobbes*, vol. 4, ed. Sir William Molesworth (London: Scientia Aalen, 1962), *De Corpore Politico*, pt 2, chap. 4, para. 1, 154.
8. The most elaborate treatment of this theme in Hobbes is Christine di Stefano, 'Masculinity as Ideology in Political Theory: Hobbesian Man Considered', *Women's Studies International Forum* 6 (1983): 633–44; and *Configurations of Masculinity* (Ithaca: Cornell University Press, 1991), chap. 2. See also Seyla Benhabib, 'The Generalized and the Concrete Other', in *Situating the Self* (New York: Routledge, 1992), 153–77.
9. The passage reads: 'Let us return again to the state of nature, and consider men *as if* [my emphasis] but even now sprung out of the earth, and suddenly (like mushrooms) come to full maturity, without all kind of engagement to each other.' *De Cive*, pt 2, chap. 8, para. 1, 100.
10. I develop this theme in 'Feminist Reasoning About Reason', Proceedings of the Ontario Society for the Study of Argumentation, May 1997.
11. Natalie Angier, 'The biology of benevolence', *Globe and Mail*, 14 May 1996.
12. Elisabeth Badinter, 'Maternal Indifference', in *French Feminist Thought: A Reader*, ed. Toril Moi (Oxford: Blackwell, 1987), 151-2.
13. For a cogent summary of contemporary issues surrounding citizenship, see the articles in *Theorizing Citizenship*, ed. Ronald Beiner (Albany: SUNY Press, 1995); and *Immigration & Citizenship in the 21st Century*, ed. Noah Pickus (Lanham: Rowman & Littlefield, 1998).
14. Geoffrey Scarre, 'Justice Between Generations', in *Children, Parents and Politics*, ed. G. Scarre (New York: Cambridge University Press, 1989). See also *Justice Between Age Groups and Generations*, ed. Peter Laslett and James S. Fishkin (New Haven: Yale University Press, 1992) for attempts to fill the gap.
15. For example, see Susan Okin, *Justice, Gender, and the Family* (New York: Basic Books, 1989).
16. For example, see Annette Baier, 'Trust and Antitrust', in *Feminism and Political Theory*; Joyce Trebilcot, ed., *Mothering: Essays in Feminist Theory* (Totowa: Rowman and Allenheld, 1984); and Eva Feder Kittay and Diana T. Meyers, eds., *Women and Moral Theory* (Totowa: Rowman and Littlefield, 1987).
17. A young woman in an interview explains that she has no problem with selling her eggs on the Internet to couples who can use them to create a child she will never see: 'I have a lot of eggs I'll never use. I don't feel that those children would be mine at all. I have no connection to my eggs. None at all.' Peter Cheney, 'Human egg trade lures elite students', *Globe and Mail*, 9 July 1998.
18. Mark Nichols, 'As Nature intended', *Maclean's*, 7 June 1999.

19. I develop this theme more fully in 'The Politics of "Feminine Concealment" and "Masculine Openness" in Jean-Jacques Rousseau', Annual Meeting of the American Political Science Association, San Francisco, 1996.
20. Jean-Jacques Rousseau, *Emile, or On Education*, trans. Allan Bloom (New York: Basic Books, 1979), 38.
21. Ibid., 57.
22. Ibid., 53.
23. Ibid., 120.
24. Ibid., 442.
25. 'Remember that your honor is no longer in you but in your pupil.' Ibid., 246.
26. 'Today I abdicate the authority you confided to me, and Sophie is your governor from now on.' Ibid., 479.

PART THREE

MINORITY RIGHTS, MULTICULTURALISM, AND IDENTITY

The New Debate over Minority Rights

Will Kymlicka

The last ten years have seen a remarkable upsurge in interest among political philosophers in the rights of ethnocultural groups within Western democracies.[1] My aims in this essay are to give a condensed overview of the philosophical debate so far and to suggest some future directions that it might take.

As political philosophers, we are interested in the normative issues raised by such minority rights. What are the moral arguments for or against such rights? In particular, how do they relate to the underlying principles of liberal democracy, such as individual freedom, social equality, and democracy? The philosophical debate on these questions has changed dramatically, both in its scope and in its basic terminology. When I started working on these issues in the mid-1980s, there were very few other political philosophers or political theorists working in the area. Indeed, for most of this century, issues of ethnicity have been seen as marginal by political philosophers. (Much the same can be said about many other academic disciplines, from sociology to geography to history.)

Today, however, after decades of relative neglect, the question of minority rights has moved to the forefront of political theory. There are several reasons for this. Most obviously, the collapse of communism unleashed a wave of ethnic nationalisms in Eastern Europe, which dramatically affected the democratization process. Optimistic assumptions that liberal democracy would rise smoothly from the ashes of communism had to be revised as issues of ethnicity and nationalism emerged. But there were many factors within long-established democracies that also pointed to the salience of ethnicity: the nativist backlash against immigrants and refugees in many Western countries; the resurgence and political mobilization of indigenous peoples, resulting in the draft declaration of the rights of indigenous peoples at the United Nations; and the ongoing, even growing, threat of secession within several Western democracies, from Canada (Quebec) to Britain (Scotland), Belgium (Flanders), and Spain (Catalonia).

All these factors, which came to a head at the beginning of the 1990s, made it clear that Western democracies had not resolved or overcome the tensions raised by ethnocultural diversity. It is not surprising, therefore, that political theorists have increasingly turned their attention to this topic. For example, the last few years have witnessed the first philosophical books in English on the normative issues involved in secession, nationalism, immigration, group representation, multiculturalism, and indigenous rights.[2]

Not only has the debate grown in size, but the very terms in which it is conducted have changed dramatically, and this is what I would like to focus on. I will try to distinguish three distinct stages in the debate.

1. The First Stage: Minority Rights as Communitarianism

The first stage was the pre-1989 debate. Those few theorists who discussed the issue in the 1970s and 1980s assumed that the debate over minority rights was essentially equivalent to the debate between 'liberals' and 'communitarians' (or between 'individualists' and 'collectivists'). Confronted with an unexplored topic, political theorists naturally looked for analogies with other, more familiar topics, and the liberal–communitarian debate seemed the most relevant.

That debate is an old and venerable one within political philosophy, going back several centuries (albeit in different forms), so I won't try to rehearse it in its entirety. Essentially, however, it revolves around the priority of individual freedom. Liberals insist that individuals should be free to decide on their own conception of the good life, and they applaud the liberation of individuals from any ascribed or inherited status. Liberal individualists argue that the individual is morally prior to the community: the community matters only because it contributes to the well-being of the individuals who compose it. If those individuals no longer find it worthwhile to maintain existing cultural practices, then the community has no independent interest in preserving those practices, and no right to prevent individuals from modifying or rejecting them.

Communitarians dispute this conception of the 'autonomous individual'. They view people as 'embedded' in particular social roles and relationships. Such embedded selves do not form and revise their own conception of the good life; rather, they inherit a way of life that defines their good for them. Instead of viewing group practices as the product of individual choices, communitarians view individuals as the product of social practices. Moreover, they often deny that the interests of communities can be reduced to the interests of their individual members. Privileging individual autonomy is therefore seen as destructive of communities. A healthy community maintains a balance between individual choice and protection of the communal way of life, and seeks to limit the extent to which the former can erode the latter.

In the first stage of the debate, the assumption was that one's position on minority rights was dependent on, and derivative of, one's position on the liberal–communitarian debate. If one was a liberal who cherished individual autonomy, then one would oppose minority rights as an unnecessary and dangerous departure from the proper emphasis on the individual. Communitarians, by contrast, viewed minority rights as an appropriate way of protecting communities from the eroding effects of individual autonomy, and of affirming the value of community. Ethnocultural minorities in particular were seen as worthy of such protection, partly because they were most at risk, but also because they still had a communal way of life to be protected. Unlike the majority, ethnocultural minorities had not yet succumbed to liberal individualism, and so had maintained a coherent collective way of life.

This debate over the relative priority and reducibility of individuals and groups dominated the early literature on minority rights.[3] Defenders of minority rights agreed that such rights were inconsistent with liberalism's commitment to moral individualism and individual autonomy, but argued that this just pointed out the flaws inherent in liberalism.

In short, defending minority rights involved endorsing the communitarian critique of liberalism and viewing minority rights as defending cohesive and communally-minded minority groups against the encroachment of liberal individualism.

2. The Second Stage: Minority Rights Within a Liberal Framework

It is increasingly recognized that this is an unhelpful way to conceptualize most minority rights claims in Western democracies. Assumptions about the 'striking parallel between the communitarian attack of philosophical liberalism and the notion of [minority] rights' have been increasingly questioned.[4]

In reality, most ethnocultural groups within Western democracies do not want to be protected from the forces of modernity in liberal societies. On the contrary, they want to be full and equal participants in modern liberal societies. This is true of most immigrant groups, which seek inclusion and full participation in the mainstream of liberal democratic societies, with access to its education, technology, literacy, mass communications, and so forth. It is equally true of most non-immigrant national minorities like the Québécois, Flemish, or Catalans.[5] Some of their members may wish to secede from a liberal democracy, but if they do, it is not to create an illiberal communitarian society, but rather to create their own modern liberal democratic society. For instance, the Québécois wish to create a 'distinct society', but it is a modern liberal society—with an urbanized, secular, pluralistic, industrialized, bureaucratized, consumerist mass culture.

Indeed, according to public opinion polls nationalist minorities—far from opposing liberal principles—often show no statistical differences from national majorities in their adherence to liberal principles. Immigrants also quickly absorb the basic liberal democratic consensus, even when they came from countries with little or no experience of liberal democracy.[6] The commitment to individual autonomy is deep and wide in modern societies, crossing ethnic, linguistic, and religious lines.

There are some important and visible exceptions to this rule. For example, a few ethnoreligious sects voluntarily distance themselves from the larger world—Hutterites, Amish, Hasidic Jews. And some of the more isolated or traditionalist indigenous communities fit the description 'communitarian' groups. The question of how liberal states should respond to such non-liberal groups is an important one, which I have discussed elsewhere.[7]

But the overwhelming majority of debates about minority rights are not debates between a liberal majority and communitarian minorities, but debates among liberals about the meaning of liberalism. They are debates between individuals and groups who endorse the basic liberal democratic consensus but who disagree about the interpretation of these principles in multi-ethnic societies—in particular, they disagree about the proper roles of language, nationality, and ethnic identities within liberal democratic societies and institutions. Groups claiming minority rights insist that at least certain forms of public recognition and support for their language, practices, and identities are not only consistent with basic liberal democratic principles, including the importance of individual autonomy, but may indeed be required by them.

In this second stage of the debate, the question becomes: What is the possible scope for minority rights *within* liberal theory? Framing the debate in this way does not resolve the issues—on the contrary, the place of minority rights within liberal theory remains very controversial. But the terms of the debate have changed. The issue is no longer how to protect communitarian minorities from liberalism, but whether minorities that share basic liberal principles nonetheless need minority rights. If groups are indeed liberal, why do their members want minority rights? Why aren't they satisfied with the traditional common rights of citizenship?

This is the sort of question that Joseph Raz tries to answer in his recent work. Raz insists that the autonomy of individuals—their ability to make good choices among good lives—is intimately tied up with access to their culture, with the prosperity and flourishing of their culture, and with the respect accorded their culture by others. Minority rights help ensure this cultural flourishing and mutual respect.[8] Other liberal writers like David Miller, Yael Tamir, Jeff Spinner, and myself have made similar arguments about the importance of 'cultural membership' or 'national identity' to modern freedom-seeking citizens.[9] The details of the argument vary, but each of us, in our own way, argues that there are compelling interests related to culture and identity that are fully consistent with liberal principles of freedom and equality, and that justify granting special rights to minorities. We can call this the 'liberal culturalist' position.[10]

Critics of liberal culturalism have raised many objections to this entire line of argument. Some deny that we can intelligibly distinguish or individuate 'cultures' or 'cultural groups'; others deny that we can make sense of the claim that individuals are 'members' of cultures; still others say that even if we can make sense of the claim that individuals are members of distinct cultures, we have no reason to assume that the well-being or freedom of the individual is tied in any way to the flourishing of the culture.[11] These are important objections, but I think they can be answered. In any event, they have not yet succeeded in dampening enthusiasm for liberal culturalism, which has quickly developed into the consensus position among liberals working in this field.[12]

However, even those sympathetic to liberal culturalism face an obvious problem. It is clear that some kinds of minority rights would undermine, rather than support, individual autonomy. A crucial task facing liberal defenders of minority rights, therefore, is to distinguish 'bad' minority rights, which involve *restricting* individual rights, from 'good' minority rights, which can be seen as *supplementing* individual rights.

I have proposed distinguishing between two kinds of rights that a minority group might claim. The first involves the right of a group against its own members, designed to protect the group from the destabilizing impact of *internal* dissent (e.g., the decision of individual members not to follow traditional practices or customs). The second kind involves the right of a group against the larger society, designed to protect the group from the impact of *external* pressures (e.g., the economic or political decisions of the larger society). I call the first 'internal restrictions', and the second 'external protections'. Given the commitment to individual autonomy, I argue that liberals should be skeptical of claims to internal restrictions, but should accept external protections, which safeguard the viability of minority cultures.[13] Other liberal culturalists, however, argue that some forms of internal restriction can be accepted, so long as group members have an effective right of exit from the group.[14]

In the second stage of the debate, therefore, the question of minority rights is reformulated as a question within liberal theory, and the aim is to show that some (but not all) minority-rights claims enhance liberal values. In my opinion, this second stage reflects genuine progress. We now have a more accurate description of the claims being made by ethnocultural groups and a more accurate understanding of the normative issues they raise. We have moved beyond the sterile and misleading debate about individualism and collectivism.

Nevertheless, I think this second-stage debate too needs to be challenged. While it reflects a better understanding of the nature of most ethnocultural groups and the demands that they place on the liberal state, it misinterprets the nature of the liberal state and the demands that it, in turn, places on minorities.

3. The Third Stage: Minority Rights as a Response to Nation-Building

Let me explain. The assumption—generally shared by both defenders and critics of minority rights—is that the liberal state, in its normal operation, abides by a principle of ethnocultural neutrality. That is, the state is 'neutral' with respect to the ethnocultural identities of its citizens and indifferent to the ability of ethnocultural groups to reproduce themselves over time. On this view, liberal states treat culture in the same way they do religion—as something that people should be free to pursue in their private life but that is not the concern of the state (so long as they respect the rights of others). Just as liberalism precludes the establishment of an official religion, so too it precludes giving official cultures preferred status over other possible cultural allegiances.

Indeed, some theorists argue that this is precisely what distinguishes liberal 'civic nations' from illiberal 'ethnic nations'.[15] Ethnic nations take the reproduction of a particular ethnonational culture and identity as one of their most important goals. Civic nations, by contrast, are 'neutral' with respect to the ethnocultural identities of their citizens, and define national membership purely in terms of adherence to certain principles of democracy and justice. For minorities to seek special rights, on this view, is a radical departure from the traditional operation of the liberal state. Therefore the burden of proof lies on anyone who would wish to endorse such minority rights.

This is the burden of proof that liberal culturalists try to meet with their account of the role of cultural membership in securing freedom and self-respect. They try to show that minority rights supplement, rather than diminish, individual freedom and equality, and help to meet needs that would otherwise go unmet in a state that clung rigidly to ethnocultural neutrality.

The presumption in the second stage of the debate, therefore, has been that advocates of minority rights must demonstrate compelling reasons to depart from the norm of ethnocultural neutrality. I would argue, however, that this idea that liberal democratic states (or 'civic nations') are ethnoculturally neutral is manifestly false. The religion model is altogether misleading as an account of the relationship between the liberal democratic state and ethnocultural groups.

Consider the actual policies of the United States, which is the prototypically 'neutral' state. Historically, decisions about the boundaries of state governments, and the timing of their admission into the federation, were deliberately made to ensure that anglophones would be a majority within each of the fifty states of the American federation. This practice helped establish the dominance of English throughout the territory of the United States. And the continuing dominance of English is ensured by several ongoing policies. For example, it is a legal requirement for children to learn the English language in schools; it is a legal requirement for immigrants (under the age of 50) to learn English to acquire American citizenship; and it is a de facto requirement for employment in or for government that the applicant speak English.

These decisions are not isolated exceptions to some norm of ethnocultural neutrality. On the contrary, they are tightly interrelated, and together they have shaped the very structure of the American state, and the way the state structures society. (Since governments account for 40 to 50 per cent of GNP in most countries, the language of government is not negligible.)

These policies have all been pursued with the intention of promoting integration into what I call a 'societal culture'. By a societal culture, I mean a territorially concentrated culture, centred on a shared language that is used in a wide range of societal institutions, in both public and private life (schools, media, law, economy, government, etc.). I call it a *societal* culture to emphasize that it involves a common language and social institutions, rather than common religious beliefs, family customs, or personal lifestyles. Societal cultures within a modern liberal democracy are inevitably pluralistic, containing Christians as well as Muslims, Jews, and atheists; heterosexuals as well as gays; urban professionals as well as rural farmers; conservatives as well as socialists. Such diversity is the inevitable result of the rights and freedoms guaranteed to liberal citizens, particularly when combined with an ethnically diverse population. This diversity, however, is balanced and constrained by linguistic and institutional cohesion—cohesion that has not emerged on its own, but is the result of deliberate state policies.

The American government has deliberately created such a societal culture and promoted the integration of citizens into it. The government has encouraged citizens to view their life chances as tied up with participation in common societal institutions that operate in the English language, and has nurtured a national identity defined in part by common membership in a societal culture. The United States is not unique in this respect. Promoting integration into a societal culture is part of a 'nation-building' project that all liberal democracies have adopted.

Obviously, the sense in which English-speaking Americans share a common 'culture' is a very thin one, since it does not preclude differences in religion, personal values, family relationships, or lifestyle choices. Yet it is far from trivial. On the contrary, as I will explain below, attempts to integrate people into such a common societal culture have often met with serious resistance. Although integration in this sense leaves a great deal of room for both public and private expressions of individual and collective differences, some groups have nonetheless vehemently rejected the idea that they should view their life chances as tied up with the societal institutions that operate in the majority's language.

So we need to replace the idea of an 'ethnoculturally neutral' state with a new model of a liberal democratic state—what I call the 'nation-building' model. To say that states are nation-building is not to say that governments can promote only one societal culture. It is possible for government policies to encourage the sustaining of two or more societal cultures within a single country—indeed, as we will see below, this is precisely what characterizes multination states like Canada, Switzerland, Belgium, or Spain.

Historically, however, virtually all liberal democracies have at one point or another attempted to diffuse a single societal culture throughout all of its territory.[16] This should not be seen purely as a matter of cultural imperialism or ethnocentric prejudice. This sort of nation-building serves a number of important goals. For example, standardized public education in a common language has often been seen as essential for all citizens to have equal opportunity to work in this modern economy. Also, participation in a common societal culture has often been seen as essential for generating the sort of solidarity required by a welfare state, since it promotes a sense of common identity and membership. Moreover, a common language has been seen as essential to democracy—how can 'the people' govern together if they cannot understand one another? In short, promoting integration into a common societal culture has been seen as essential to social equality and political cohesion in modern states.[17]

So states have engaged in 'nation-building'—a process of promoting a common language and a sense of common membership in, and equal access to, the social institutions based on that language. Decisions regarding official languages, core curricula in education, and the requirements for acquiring citizenship—all have been made with the intention of diffusing a particular culture throughout society and of promoting a particular national identity based on participation in that societal culture.

If I am right that the nation-building model provides a more accurate account of modern liberal democratic states, how does this affect the issue of minority rights? I believe it gives us a very different perspective on the debate. The question is no longer how to justify departure from a norm of neutrality, but rather whether majority efforts at nation-building create injustices for minorities.

Do minority rights help protect against these injustices? This would be the third stage in the debate, which I am trying to explore in my own recent work. I cannot discuss all of its implications, but let me give two examples of how this new model might affect the debate over minority rights.[18]

4. Two Examples

How does nation-building affect minorities? As Taylor notes, the process of nation-building inescapably privileges members of the majority culture:

> If a modern society has an 'official' language, in the fullest sense of the term, that is, a state-sponsored , -inculcated, and -defined language and culture, in which both economy and state function, then it is obviously an immense advantage to people if this language and culture are theirs. Speakers of other languages are at a distinct disadvantage.[19]

This means that minority cultures face a choice. If all public institutions are being run in another language, minorities face the danger of being marginalized from the major economic, academic, and political institutions of the society. Faced with this dilemma, minorities have (to oversimplify) three basic options:

1. They can accept integration into the majority culture, although perhaps attempt to renegotiate the terms of integration;
2. they can seek the sorts of rights and powers of self-government needed to maintain their own societal culture—create their own economic, political, and educational institutions in their own language. That is, they can engage in their own form of competing nation-building; or
3. they can accept permanent marginalization.

We can find some ethnocultural groups that fit each of these categories (and other groups that are caught between them). For example, some immigrant groups choose permanent marginalization. This would seem to be true, for example, of the Hutterites in Canada, or the Amish in the United States. But the option of accepting marginalization is likely to be attractive only to religious sects whose theology requires them to avoid all contact with the modern world. The Hutterites and Amish are unconcerned about their marginalization from universities or legislatures, since they view such 'worldly' institutions as corrupt.

Virtually all other ethnocultural minorities, however, do seek to participate in the modern world, and therefore must either integrate or seek the self-government needed to create and sustain their own modern institutions. Faced with this choice, ethnocultural groups have responded in different ways.

National minorities

National minorities have typically responded to majority nation-building by engaging in their own competing nation-building. Indeed, they often use the same tools that the majority uses to promote this nation-building—such as control over the language and curriculum of schooling, the language of government employment, the requirements of immigration and naturalization, and the drawing of internal boundaries. We can see this clearly in the case of Québécois nationalism, which has largely been concerned with gaining and exercising these nation-building powers. But it is also increasingly true of the Aboriginal peoples in Canada, who have adopted the language of 'nationhood' and who are engaged in a major campaign of 'nation-building', which requires the exercise of much greater powers of self-government and the building of many new societal institutions.[20]

Intuitively, the adoption of such minority nation-building projects seems fair. If the majority can engage in legitimate nation-building, why not national minorities, particularly those that have been involuntarily incorporated into a larger state? To be sure, liberal principles set limits on *how* national groups go about nation-building. Liberal principles will preclude any attempts at ethnic cleansing, or stripping people of their citizenship, or the violation of human rights. These principles will also insist that any national group engaged in a project of nation-building must respect the right of other nations within its jurisdiction to protect and build their own national institutions. For example, the Québécois are entitled to assert national rights vis-à-vis the rest of Canada, but only if they respect the rights of Aboriginals within Quebec to assert national rights vis-à-vis the rest of Quebec.

These limits are important, but they still leave significant room, I believe, for legitimate forms of minority nationalism. Moreover, these limits are likely to be similar for both majority and minority nations. All else being equal, national minorities should have the same tools of nation-building available to them as the majority nation, subject to the same liberal limitations. What we need, in other words, is a consistent theory of permissible forms of nation-building within liberal democracies. I do not think that political theorists have yet developed such a theory. One of the many unfortunate side effects of the dominance of the 'ethnocultural neutrality' model is that liberal theorists have never explicitly confronted this issue.[21]

My aim here is not to promote any particular theory of permissible nation-building[22] but simply to insist that this is the relevant question we need to address. The question is not 'have national minorities given us a compelling reason to abandon the norm of ethnocultural neutrality?', but rather 'Why should national minorities not have the same powers of nation-building as the majority?' This is the context within which minority nationalism must be evaluated—as a response to majority nation-building, using the same tools of nation-building. And the burden of proof surely rests on those who would deny national minorities the same powers of nation-building as those that the national majority takes for granted.

Immigrants

Historically, nation-building has been neither desirable nor feasible for immigrant groups. Instead, they have traditionally accepted the expectation that they will integrate into the larger societal culture. Few immigrant groups have objected to the requirements that they must learn an official language as a condition of citizenship, or that their children must learn the official language in school. They have accepted the assumption that their life chances, and the life chances of their children, will be bound up with participation in mainstream institutions operating in the majority language.

This is not to say that immigrants may not suffer injustices as a result of nation-building policies. After all, the state is clearly not neutral with respect to the language and culture of immigrants: it imposes a range of de jure and de facto requirements for immigrants to integrate. These requirements are often difficult and costly for immigrants to meet. Since immigrants cannot respond by adopting their own nation-building programs, but must attempt to integrate as best they can, it is only fair that the state minimize the costs involved in the integration it demands.

Put another way, immigrants can demand fairer terms of integration. To my mind, this demand has two basic elements. First, we need to recognize that integration does not occur overnight, but is a difficult and long-term process that operates intergenerationally; this means that special accommodations (e.g., mother-tongue services) are often required for immigrants on a transitional basis. Second, we need to ensure that the common institutions into which immigrants are pressured to integrate provide the same degree of respect, recognition, and accommodation of the identities and practices of immigrants as they have traditionally done with respect to the identities and practices of the majority group. This requires a systematic exploration of our social institutions to see whether their rules and symbols disadvantage immigrants. For example, we need to examine dress codes, public holidays, even height and weight restrictions, to see whether they are biased against certain immigrant groups. We also need to examine the portrayal of minorities in school curricula and the media to see whether they are stereotypical, or fail to recognize the contributions of immigrants to national history or world culture. These measures are needed to ensure that liberal states are offering immigrants fair terms of integration.[23]

Others may disagree with the fairness of some of these policies. The requirements of fairness are not always obvious, particularly in the context of people who have chosen to enter a country, and to date political theorists have done little to illuminate the issue. My aim here is not to defend a particular theory of fair terms of integration, but rather to insist that this is a relevant question that we need to address. The question is not whether immigrants have given us a compelling reason to diverge from the norm of ethnocultural neutrality, but rather how we can ensure that state policies aimed at pressuring immigrants to integrate are fair.

The focus of this third stage of the debate, therefore, is to show how particular minority-rights claims are related to, and a response to, state nation-building policies. And the logical outcome of this stage of the debate will be to develop theories of permissible nation-building and fair terms of immigrant integration.[24]

I believe that we could extend this approach to look at other types of ethnocultural groups that do not fit into the category of national minorities or immigrants, such as African-Americans, the Roma, guest-workers in Germany, or Russian settlers in the Baltics. In each case, I think it is possible—indeed essential—to view their claims to minority rights as a response to perceived injustices that arise out of nation-building policies.[25] Each group's claims can be seen as specifying the injustices that majority nation-building has imposed on them, and as identifying the conditions under which majority nation-building would cease to be unjust.

The most important task facing any liberal theory of minority rights is to better understand and articulate these conditions of ethnocultural justice. I expect that filling in these lacunae will form the main agenda for minority-rights theorists over the next decade.

5. A New Front in the Multiculturalism Wars?

So far I have focused on the significant shifts in the recent minority-rights debate. However, an important assumption underlies all three stages of the debate: namely, that the goal is to assess the *justice* of minority claims. This focus on justice reflects the fact that opposition to minority rights has traditionally been stated in the language of justice. Critics of minority rights had long argued that justice required state institutions to be 'colour-blind'. To ascribe rights on the basis of membership in ascriptive groups was seen as inherently morally arbitrary and discriminatory, necessarily creating first- and second-class citizens.

The first task confronting any defender of minority rights, therefore, was to try to overcome this presumption and to show that deviations from difference-blind rules that are adopted in order to accommodate ethnocultural differences are not inherently unjust. As we've seen, this has been done in two main ways: (1) by identifying the many ways that mainstream institutions are not neutral but are implicitly or explicitly tilted towards the interests and identities of the majority group; and (2) by emphasizing the importance of certain interests that have typically been ignored by liberal theories of justice—such as interests in recognition, identity, language, and cultural membership. If we accept either or both of these points, then we can see minority rights not as unfair privileges or invidious forms of discrimination, but as compensation for unfair disadvantages, and hence consistent with—even required by—justice.

In my view, this debate over justice is drawing to a close. As I noted earlier, much work remains to be done in assessing the justice of particular forms of immigrant multiculturalism or minority nationalism. But in terms of the more general question of whether minority rights are *inherently* unjust, the debate is over, and the defenders of minority rights have won the day. I don't mean that defenders of minority rights have been successful in getting their claims implemented, although there is a clear trend throughout the Western democracies towards greater recognition of minority rights, in the form both of immigrant multiculturalism and of self-government for national minorities.[26] Rather, I mean that defenders of minority rights have successfully redefined the terms of public debate in two profound ways. First, few thoughtful people continue to think that justice can simply be *defined* in terms of difference-blind rules or institutions. Instead, it is now recognized that difference-blind rules can cause disadvantages for particular groups. Whether justice requires common rules for all or differential rules for diverse groups is something to be assessed case-by-case in particular contexts, not assumed in advance. Second, and as a result, the burden of proof has shifted. The burden no longer falls solely on defenders of minority rights to show that their proposed reforms would not create injustices; it also falls on defenders of difference-blind institutions to show that the status quo does not create injustices for minority groups.

So the original justice-based grounds for blanket opposition to minority rights have faded. This has not meant that opposition to minority rights has disappeared. But it now takes a new form: critics have shifted the focus away from justice towards issues of social unity, focusing not on the justice or injustice of particular policies, but rather on the way that the general trend towards minority rights threatens to erode the sorts of civic virtues, identities, and practices that sustain a healthy democracy.

This focus on civic virtue and political stability represents the opening of a second front in the 'multiculturalism wars'. Many critics claim that minority rights are misguided, not because they are unjust in themselves, but because they are corrosive of long-term political unity and social stability. Why are they seen as destabilizing? The underlying worry is that minority rights involve the 'politicization of ethnicity', and that any measures that heighten the salience of ethnicity in public life are divisive. Over time they create a spiral of competition, mistrust, and antagonism between ethnic groups. Policies that increase the salience of ethnic identities are said to act 'like a corrosive on metal, eating away at the ties of connectedness that bind us together as a nation'.[27]

This is a serious concern. There is growing fear that public-spiritedness among citizens of liberal democracies may be in decline, and if group-based claims would further erode the sense of shared civic purpose and solidarity, then that would be a powerful reason not to adopt minority-rights policies. But is it true? Despite much armchair speculation on this question, there has been remarkably little evidence. Reliable evidence is needed here, because one could quite plausibly argue the reverse: namely, that it is the *absence* of minority rights that erodes the bonds of civic solidarity. After all, if we accept the two central claims made by defenders of minority rights—that mainstream institutions are biased in favour of the majority, and that the effect of this bias is to harm important interests related to personal agency and identity—then we might expect minorities to feel excluded from 'difference-blind' mainstream institutions, and to feel alienated from, and distrustful of, the political process. We could predict, then, that recognizing minority rights would actually strengthen solidarity and promote political stability by removing the barriers and exclusions that prevent minorities from wholeheartedly embracing political institutions. This hypothesis is surely at least as plausible as the contrary hypothesis that minority rights erode social unity.

We don't have the sort of systematic evidence needed to confirm or refute decisively these competing hypotheses. There is fragmentary evidence suggesting that minority rights often enhance, rather than erode, social unity. For example, the evidence from Canada and Australia—the two countries that first adopted official multiculturalism policies—strongly disputes the claim that immigrant multiculturalism promotes political apathy or instability, or mutual hostility between ethnic groups. On the contrary, these two countries do a better job integrating immigrants into common civic and political institutions than any other countries in the world. Moreover, both have witnessed dramatic reductions in levels of prejudice and dramatic increases in levels of inter-ethnic friendships and intermarriage. There is no evidence that the pursuit of fairer terms of integration for immigrants has eroded democratic stability.[28]

The situation regarding the self-government claims of national minorities is more complicated, since these claims involve building separate institutions and reinforcing a distinct national identity, hence creating the phenomenon of competing nationalisms within a single state. Learning how to manage this phenomenon is a profoundly difficult task for any state. However, even here there is significant evidence that recognizing self-government for national minorities assists, rather than threatens, political stability. Surveys of ethnic conflict around the world repeatedly confirm that 'early, generous devolution is far more likely to avert than to abet ethnic separatism'.[29] It is the refusal to grant autonomy to national minorities, or (even worse) the decision to retract an already existing autonomy (as in Kosovo), that leads to instability, not the recognizing of their minority rights.[30]

Much more work needs to be done concerning the impact of minority rights on social unity and political stability. This relationship will undoubtedly vary from case to case, and so requires fine-grained empirical investigation. It is not clear that philosophical speculation can contribute much here: we need to wait for more and better evidence.[31] As with concerns about justice, however, it is clear that concerns about citizenship cannot provide any grounds for rejecting minority rights *in general*: there is no reason to assume in advance that there is any inherent contradiction between minority rights and democratic stability.

6. Conclusion

I have tried to outline three stages in the ongoing philosophical debate about minority rights. The first stage viewed minority rights as a communitarian defence against the encroachment of liberalism. This has gradually given way to a more recent debate regarding the role of culture and identity within liberalism itself. In this second stage of the debate, the question is whether people's interests in their culture and identity are sufficient to justify departing from the norm of ethnocultural neutrality by supplementing common individual rights with minority rights.

This second stage represents progress, I think, in that it asks the right question, but it starts from the wrong baseline, since liberal democracies do not in fact abide by any norm of ethnocultural neutrality. And so the next stage of the debate, I propose, is to view minority rights not as a deviation from ethnocultural neutrality, but as a response to majority nation-building. And I have suggested that this will affect the way we think of the demands of both national minorities and immigrant groups. In particular, it raises two important questions: What are permissible forms of nation-building? And what are fair terms of integration for immigrants?

Looking back over the development of this debate, I am inclined to think that genuine progress has been made, although much remains to be done. It is progress not in the sense of having come closer to resolving the disputes, but rather in the sense of getting clearer on the *questions*. The emerging debates about the roles of language, culture, ethnicity, and nationality in liberal democracies are, I think, grappling in a fruitful way with the real issues facing ethnoculturally plural societies today. But getting clearer on the questions is no guarantee of getting clearer on the answers, and I see no reason to expect that a consensus on the answers will emerge any time soon.

Notes

1. I use the term 'rights of ethnocultural minorities' (or, for brevity's sake, 'minority rights'), in a loose way, to refer to a wide range of public policies, legal rights and exemptions, and constitutional provisions—from multiculturalism policies to language rights to constitutional protections of Aboriginal treaties. This is a heterogeneous category, but these measures have two important features in common: (1) they go beyond the familiar set of common civil and political rights of individual citizenship that are protected in all liberal democracies; and (2) they are adopted with the intention of recognizing and accommodating the distinctive identities and needs of ethnocultural groups. For a helpful typology, see Jacob Levy, 'Classifying Cultural Rights', in *Ethnicity and Group Rights*, ed. Ian Shapiro and Will Kymlicka (New York: New York University Press, 1997).
2. Rainer Bauböck, *Transnational Citizenship: Membership and Rights in Transnational Migration* (Aldershot, England: Edward Elgar, 1994); Allen Buchanan, *Secession: The Legitimacy of Political Divorce* (Boulder: Westview Press, 1991); Margaret Canovan, *Nationhood and Political Theory* (Cheltenham, England: Edward Elgar, 1996); Will Kymlicka, *Multicultural Citizenship: A Liberal Theory of Minority Rights* (Oxford: Oxford University Press, 1995); David Miller, *On Nationality* (Oxford: Oxford University Press, 1995); Anne Phillips, *The Politics of Presence: Issues in Democracy and Group Representation* (Oxford: Oxford University Press, 1995); Jeff Spinner, *The Boundaries of Citizenship: Race, Ethnicity and Nationality in the Liberal State* (Baltimore: Johns Hopkins University Press, 1994); Yael Tamir, *Liberal Nationalism* (Princeton: Princeton University Press, 1993); Charles Taylor, 'The Politics of Recognition', in *Multiculturalism and the 'Politics of Recognition'*, ed. Amy Gutmann (Princeton: Princeton University Press, 1992); James Tully, *Strange Multiplicity: Constitutionalism in an Age of Diversity* (Cambridge: Cambridge University Press, 1995); Michael Walzer, *On Toleration* (New Haven: Yale University Press, 1997); Iris Marion Young, *Justice and the Politics of Difference* (Princeton: Princeton University Press, 1990). I am not aware of full-length books written by philosophers in English on any of these topics predating 1990. There have also been many edited collec-

tions of philosophical articles on these issues. For a comprehensive bibliography, see Will Kymlicka and Wayne Norman, eds, *Citizenship in Diverse Societies* (Oxford: Oxford University Press, 2000).

3. For representatives of the 'individualist' camp, see Jan Narveson, 'Collective Rights?', *Canadian Journal of Law and Jurisprudence* 4, 2 (1991), 329-45; Michael Hartney, 'Some Confusions Concerning Collective Rights', ibid., 293-314. For the 'communitarian' camp, see Ronald Garet, 'Communality and Existence: The Rights of Groups', *Southern California Law Review* 56, 5 (1983), 1001-75; Vernon Van Dyke, 'The Individual, the State, and Ethnic Communities in Political Theory', *World Politics* 29, 3 (1977), 343-69; Van Dyke, 'Collective Rights and Moral Rights: Problems in Liberal-Democratic Thought', *Journal of Politics* 44 (1982), 21-40; Adeno Addis, 'Individualism, Communitarianism and the Rights of Ethnic Minorities', *Notre Dame Law Review* 67, 3 (1992), 615-76; Darlene Johnston, 'Native Rights as Collective Rights: A Question of Group Self-Preservation', *Canadian Journal of Law and Jurisprudence* 2, 1 (1989), 19-34; Michael McDonald, 'Should Communities Have Rights? Reflections on Liberal Individualism', ibid., 217-37; McDonald, 'Questions about Collective Rights', in *Language and the State: The Law and Politics of Identity*, ed. D. Schneiderman (Cowansville, Que.: Editions Yvon Blais, 1991); Frances Svensson, 'Liberal Democracy and Group Rights: The Legacy of Individualism and its Impact on American Indian Tribes', *Political Studies* 27, 3 (1979), 421-39; Dimitrios Karmis, 'Cultures autochtones et libéralisme au Canada: les vertus mediatrices du communautarisme libéral de Charles Taylor', *Canadian Journal of Political Science* 26, 1 (1993), 69-96.
4. Marlies Galenkamp, *Individualism and Collectivism: The Concept of Collective Rights* (Rotterdam: Rotterdamse Filosofische Studies, 1993), 20-5. The belief in such a 'striking parallel' is partly the result of a linguistic sleight of hand. Because minority rights are claimed by groups and tend to be group-specific, they are often described as 'collective rights'. The fact that the majority seeks only 'individual' rights while the minority seeks 'collective' rights is then taken as evidence that the minority is somehow more 'collectivist' than the majority. This chain of reasoning contains several non sequiturs. Not all group-specific minority rights are 'collective' rights, and even those that are 'collective' rights in one or another sense of that term are not necessarily evidence of 'collectivism'. See *Multicultural Citizenship*, chap. 3.
5. By 'national minorities' I mean groups that formed complete and functioning societies in their historic homelands prior to being incorporated into a larger state. The incorporation of such national minorities has typically been involuntary, the result of colonization, conquest, or the ceding of territory from one imperial power to another, but it may also arise voluntarily, as a result of federation. The category of national minorities includes both 'stateless nations' (like the Québécois, Puerto Ricans, Catalans, Scots) and 'indigenous peoples' (like the Indians, Inuit, Sami, Maori). For the similarities and differences between these two sorts of national minorities, see my 'Theorizing Indigenous Rights', *University of Toronto Law Journal* 49 (1999), 281-93.
6. On Canadian immigrants, see James Frideres, 'Edging into the Mainstream: Immigrant Adults and their Children', in *Comparative Perspectives on Interethnic Relations and Social Incorporation in Europe and North America*, ed. S. Isajiw (Toronto: Canadian Scholar's Press, 1997), 537-62; on American immigrants, see John Harles, *Politics in the Lifeboat: Immigrants and the American Democratic Order* (Boulder: Westview Press, 1994). On the convergence in political values between anglophones and francophones in Canada, see Stéphane Dion, 'Le Nationalisme dans la Convergence Culturelle', in *L'Engagement*

intellectuel, ed. R. Hudon and R. Pelletier (Sainte-Foy: Presses de l'Université Laval, 1991).

7. See my *Multicultural Citizenship*, chap. 8; and *Finding Our Way: Rethinking Ethnocultural Relations in Canada* (Toronto: Oxford University Press, 1998), chap. 4.
8. Joseph Raz, 'Multiculturalism: A Liberal Perspective', *Dissent* (Winter 1994), 67-79; 'Multiculturalism', *Ratio Juris* 11, 3 (1988), 193-205; and Avishai Margalit and Joseph Raz, 'National Self-Determination', *Journal of Philosophy* 87, 9 (1990), 439-61.
9. Tamir, *Liberal Nationalism*; Miller, *On Nationality*; Spinner, *Boundaries of Citizenship*; Kymlicka, *Liberalism, Community, and Culture* (Oxford: Oxford University Press, 1989).
10. Charles Taylor's account of the 'politics of recognition', which is often described as a 'communitarian' position, can also be seen as a form of 'liberal culturalism', since he too argues that people demand recognition of their differences—not instead of individual freedom, but as a support and precondition for freedom.
11. For a pithy statement of these three objections, see Jeremy Waldron, 'Minority Cultures and the Cosmopolitan Alternative', in *The Rights of Minority Cultures*, ed. Will Kymlicka (Oxford: Oxford University Press, 1995), 93-121.
12. It's an interesting question why this liberal culturalist view—which is a clear departure from the liberal view that was dominant for several decades—has become so popular. I address this in 'Introduction: An Emerging Consensus?', *Ethical Theory and Moral Practice* 1, 2 (1998), 143-57.
13. See *Multicultural Citizenship*, chap. 3. I also argue that most of the minority rights sought by ethnocultural groups within Western democracies fall into the external protection category.
14. This is likely to be the view of those who endorse a 'political' conception of liberalism, rooted in the value of tolerance, rather than a 'comprehensive' conception, rooted in the value of autonomy. See, for example, William Galston, 'Two Concepts of Liberalism', *Ethics* 105, 3 (1995), 516-34; Chandran Kukathas, 'Cultural Toleration', in *Ethnicity and Group Rights*, 69-104. I discuss the differences between these approaches in *Multicultural Citizenship*, chap. 8. For a discussion of the complications in determining what constitutes an 'effective' right of exit, see Susan Okin, 'Mistresses of their own Destiny? Group Rights, Gender, and Realistic Rights of Exit', paper presented at the American Political Science Association annual meeting, September 1998.
15. William Pfaff, *The Wrath of Nations: Civilization and the Furies of Nationalism* (New York: Simon and Schuster, 1993), 162; Michael Ignatieff, *Blood and Belonging: Journeys Into the New Nationalism* (New York: Farrar, Straus and Giroux, 1993).
16. To my knowledge, Switzerland is the only exception: it never made any serious attempt to pressure its French and Italian minorities to integrate into the German-speaking majority. All of the other Western multination states have, at one time or another, made concerted efforts to assimilate their minorities, and only reluctantly gave up this ideal.
17. Of course, this sort of nation-building can also be used to promote illiberal goals. As Margaret Canovan puts it, nationhood is like a 'battery' that makes states run—the existence of a common national identity motivates and mobilizes citizens to act for common political goals—and these goals can be liberal or illiberal (*Nationhood and Political Theory*, 80). Liberal reformers invoke the battery of nationhood to mobilize citizens behind projects of democratization, economic development, and social justice; illiberal authoritarians invoke nationhood to mobilize citizens behind attacks on alleged enemies of the nation, be

they foreign countries or internal dissidents. This is why nation-building is just as common in authoritarian regimes as in democracies (e.g., Spain under Franco, or Latin America under the military dictators). Authoritarian regimes also need a 'battery' to help achieve public objectives in complex modern societies. What distinguishes liberal from illiberal states is not the presence or absence of nation-building, but rather the ends to which nation-building is put, and the means used to achieve them.

18. See the essays collected in my *Politics in the Vernacular: Nationalism, Multiculturalism, and Citizenship* (Oxford: Oxford University Press, forthcoming).

19. Taylor, 'Nationalism and Modernity', in *The Ethics of Nationalism*, ed. J. McMahan and R. McKim (Oxford: Oxford University Press, 1997), 34.

20. On the need for (and justification for) Aboriginal 'nation-building', see *Report of the Royal Commission on Aboriginal Peoples. Volume 2: Restructuring the Relationship* (Ottawa, 1996). Cf. Gerald Alfred, *Heeding the Voices of our Ancestors: Kahnawake Mohawk Politics and the Rise of Native Nationalism* (Toronto: Oxford University Press, 1995).

21. As Wayne Norman notes, these questions about the morality of nation-building have been largely ignored even by philosophers working on nationalism. They tend to ask about the morality of nation-states, not about the morality of *nation-building* states. In other words, philosophers of nationalism typically take the existence of nation-states as a given, and ask whether it is a good thing to have a world of nation-states. They do not explore the processes by which such nation-states are created in the first place (i.e., what methods of nation-building are permissible). See Norman, 'Theorizing Nationalism (Normatively): The First Steps', in *Theorizing Nationalism*, ed. Ronald Beiner (Albany: SUNY Press, 1999), 60.

22. I develop criteria for distinguishing liberal from illiberal forms of nation-building in 'Western Political Theory and Ethnic Relations in Eastern Europe', in *Can Liberal Pluralism Be Exported?*, ed. Will Kymlicka and Magda Opalski (Oxford: Oxford University Press, forthcoming).

23. I believe that the vast majority of what is done under the heading of 'multiculturalism' policy in Canada, not only at the federal level but also at provincial and municipal levels, and indeed within school boards and private companies, can be defended as promoting fairer terms of integration. See *Finding Our Way*, chap. 3.

24. I have discussed minority nationalism and immigrant multiculturalism in isolation from each other, but we also need to consider their interaction. Since both challenge the traditional model of a culturally homogeneous 'nation-state', they are often treated as complementary but separate processes of deconstructing the nation-state. In reality, however, they are often intimately connected, and not always in complementary ways. Consider typical cases of minority nationalism in the West: Catalans, Basques, Puerto Ricans, Scots, Québécois, Flemish. Each of these groups sees itself as a distinct and self-governing nation within a larger state and has mobilized along nationalist lines to demand greater regional self-government and national recognition. However, each of these groups has also had to deal with significant levels of immigration into its region. This has dramatically affected the sort of national identity, and nationalist mobilization, that is feasible and/or desirable for national minorities. Immigration, therefore, is not only a challenge to traditional models of the nation-state; it is also a challenge to the self-conceptions and political aspirations of those groups that see themselves as distinct and self-governing nations within a larger state. This raises a host of interesting questions about whether minority nationalisms themselves must become more 'multicultural'. See

my 'Immigrant Integration and Minority Nationalism', in *Minority Nationalism, Globalization and European Integration*, ed. John McGarry and Michael Keating (Oxford: Oxford University Press, forthcoming).

25. I have made a preliminary attempt to examine the claims of these other types of groups in 'Western Political Theory and Ethnic Relations in Eastern Europe'.

26. There is also a trend towards codifying minority rights at the international level. It is now widely believed in the West that earlier attempts to suppress, coerce, or exclude minority groups were unjust as well as unworkable, and that some minimal set of minority rights is needed to ensure ethnocultural justice. Many scholars and NGOs are therefore trying to institutionalize, at the international level, emerging Western models of minority rights, in the same way that Western liberals after World War II were able to secure a Universal Declaration of Human Rights. Such an international charter of minority rights seems unlikely in the foreseeable future. The trend towards greater recognition of minority rights is strong within Western democracies, but in many parts of Asia and Africa minority rights are still anathema. It is interesting to note that whereas minority rights were opposed in the West on the grounds that they violated Western individualism, in East Asia they are often opposed on the grounds that they violate Asian communitarianism! See Boagang He, 'Can Kymlicka's Liberal Theory of Minority Rights be Applied in East Asia?', in *New Developments in Asian Studies: An Introduction*, ed. Paul van der Velde and Alex McKay (London: Kegan Paul, 1998).

27. Cynthia Ward, 'The Limits of "Liberal Republicanism": Why Group-Based Remedies and Republican Citizenship Don't Mix', *Columbia Law Review* 91, 3 (1991), 598.

28. *Finding Our Way*, chap. 2.

29. Donald Horowitz, *A Democratic South Africa: Constitutional Engineering in a Divided Society* (Berkeley: University of California Press, 1991), 224.

30. Ted Gurr, *Minorities at Risk: A Global View of Ethnopolitical Conflict* (Washington: Institute of Peace Press, 1993); and Ruth Lapidoth, *Autonomy: Flexible Solutions to Ethnic Conflict* (Washington: Institute for Peace Press, 1996).

31. Philosophers' claims about the relationship between minority rights and social unity are often doubly speculative: first we speculate about the sources of social unity (the 'ties that bind'), and then we speculate about how minority rights affect these ties. Neither sort of speculation is grounded in reliable evidence. For example, some political philosophers have suggested (1) that it is shared values that form the bonds of social unity in modern liberal states, and (2) that immigrant multiculturalism and/or multination federalism reduce the level of shared values. No good evidence exists for either of these speculations. I seriously doubt that minority rights have reduced shared values, but I equally doubt that it is shared values that hold societies together. See Wayne Norman, 'The Ideology of Shared Values', in *Is Quebec Nationalism Just?*, ed. Joseph Carens (Montreal and Kingston: McGill-Queen's University Press, 1995). Other philosophers suggest that it is shared experiences, shared identities, shared history, shared projects, or shared conversations that hold countries together. We have little evidence to support such claims about the source of social unity (and even less evidence about how minority rights affect these factors). We simply don't know what are the sources of social unity in multi-ethnic and multination states. To argue against minority rights on the grounds that they erode the bonds of social unity is therefore doubly speculative: we don't know what the real bonds of social unity are, and we don't know how minority rights affect them.

Liberal Nationalism and Multiculturalism

Margaret Moore

Prior to 1989, liberal debate about political and institutional arrangements in the state was confined largely to theories of the just distribution of the goods of social interaction, such as money, power, and status. Some of the central questions of citizenship theory—issues related to group identity, boundaries, and cultural biases in the state—were ignored.[1]

More recently, there has been a shift in debates in liberal democratic theory, and issues connected to pluralism and diversity have increasingly come to the fore. This shift has given rise to new debates in citizenship theory. I will focus here on two of these debates. Both stem from the insight that the state is not, and cannot be, neutral concerning conceptions of the good and ways of life. The first debate suggests that the liberal neutrality defence is problematic, and that those people who care about autonomy and the construction of a free society should actively defend it in terms of those goods. They should be cognizant of the extent to which a free society depends on certain virtues among its citizenry and on bonds of membership and solidarity to undergird liberal justice and democratic governance. The second debate also begins with the insight that the liberal state is not neutral concerning conceptions of the good and ways of life, but is complicit in the reproduction of particular cultures and groups in society. On this view, the liberal state both theoretically and practically (in its policies) privileges certain groups and ways of life. This raises the question of the extent to which the state oppresses and marginalizes groups of citizens, and the kinds of accommodations that are appropriate.

This essay is divided into three parts. In Part 1, I consider the arguments of revisionist liberals and liberal nationalists on the need for a common society, a common public life, to support our obligations as citizens. I call this kind of argument the 'case for unity' because it suggests that a common national identity is necessary to achieving the goods of liberal justice and democratic governance. The second debate, which I consider in Part 2, concerns the extent to which the state should recognize and express the diversity of its citizens. I call this the multiculturalist argument for recognition. On this view, the state is not neutral between groups and ways of life. Some groups have been marginalized by the liberal democratic state, and justice requires the recognition and inclusion of these previously marginalized groups. I argue that these two debates should not take place separately—that those people who argue for the necessity of a common society or a common national identity should consider the arguments of those who are concerned with the denial of particular identities, and the unfair biases of the public structure of society. Conversely, those people who demand special rights to recognize their identity should attend to the liberal nationalist argument that we need to create a common society.

In some sense, the argument that follows—that we should consider both kinds of debates together—is hardly controversial. Indeed, it is becoming a stock criticism of multiculturalist policies that they reify difference, that they lead to division and jeopardize the common and public nature of society. In his book *The Disuniting of America*, Arthur M. Schlesinger, Jr, has argued that multicultural policies have a disintegrative effect on the social fabric of society. 'The cult of ethnicity,' he writes, 'exaggerates difference, intensifies resentments and antagonisms, drives ever deeper the awful wedges between races and nationalities. The endgame is self-pity and self-ghettoization.'[2] Conversely, those who argue for the need to create a common society to forge bonds of unity and solidarity should acknowledge and deal with the increasingly common criticism that these homogenizing policies necessarily marginalize and oppress some groups of people in the society. Each needs to attend to the arguments of the other, because each argument suggests the problems and limitations of the other.

It is also important to consider the two debates together in order to arrive at coherent and intelligent public policy on issues such as educational policies (common schools versus separate schools; curriculum taught), dress codes at work and school, holidays, and state support for various institutions in society.

Relatedly, though on a more theoretical level, it is an important criterion for assessing a *theory* of citizenship that it be able to provide coherent and mutually supporting answers to the various elements in the debate on citizenship. Following Alan Patten, I think we should distinguish between three different components of a theory of citizenship, or three different questions that a theory of citizenship should answer.[3]

A. The first is the *membership* question: Who is to be given the status of citizen? Are all adults residing on the territory of the state to be regarded as citizens, as on the French model? Or is membership granted to those who share similar cultural or national characteristics, as on the German model?

This debate is central to Rogers Brubaker's important study *Citizenship and Nationhood in France and Germany*, in which he considers different conceptions of membership, embodied in the institutional and legal structures of the two states, and relates these conceptions to the rights and obligations of citizens. The answer to the membership question raises issues of nationality and identity, as well as rights and obligations, because different answers presuppose different relations among citizens. Citizens are rarely conceived 'as a mere aggregate of persons who happen legally to belong to a state': indeed, bonds of membership in a national group, and ties of history and shared values, are frequently invoked in response to the question of who should be a member of a state.[4]

B. The second question concerns *entitlement*: To what does the status of citizenship entitle one? What rights do citizens have?

Before 1989, most debates and discussions in liberal and socialist theory centred on this question. T.H. Marshall's famous essay 'Citizenship and Social Class' focused almost exclusively on the entitlement question, arguing that the status of citizenship implied not only civil or political rights, but also social rights. John Rawls's *A Theory of Justice* and *Political Liberalism* were both primarily concerned with the question of entitlement: to explain and justify precisely what citizens of the just liberal political order were entitled to, or what rights they had. But Rawls did not consider the membership question—who is and is not a citizen—at all, and did not directly address the question of citizen obligations either.

C. The third aspect of citizenship theory concerns the *expectations* or requirements that full citizenship involves: What obligations do citizens have? What do we expect of citizens?

The idea that we have a special obligation to participate in public life is usually discussed in terms of various specific obligations: for example, to vote, to take one's turn at jury service, to keep a watchful eye on government. The idea that we have special obligations of this kind is endorsed by many within the republican tradition and by their communitarian allies, who think we should emphasize the duties of citizens rather than just their rights; in addition, there has recently been a flurry of work in the liberal tradition, focusing on the kinds of virtues and obligations that a liberal polity requires.

These, then, are the three central questions of citizenship theory, to which a full theory of citizenship should give coherent and mutually supporting answers. Whereas in recent years the two major debates about citizenship have tended to answer only one or another of these, I argue that we need to consider all three elements of citizenship together. Part 1 below addresses citizen obligations and, specifically, the question of whether some shared identity is necessary to support citizen obligations. Part 2 addresses the issue of entitlements and, specifically, whether people are entitled to have their particular identity recognized or accommodated in the institutions of the state. In the conclusion, I try to suggest the implications of the two debates for arguments about our conception of citizenship and the limits that they suggest for justifiable nation-building and for claims to entitlement.

1. Citizen Virtues and Obligations: The Case for Unity

One prominent line of argument both of liberal nationalists such as Yael Tamir and David Miller and of revisionist liberals such as Stephen Macedo and William Galston is the recognition that a free society can operate only if its citizens accept certain solidarities and liberal virtues.[5] Many liberals, while denying the central claims of the communitarian critique of liberalism, nevertheless have argued that communitarians were right to draw attention to the fact that social justice may require attention to fostering certain kinds of (liberal) virtues and certain kinds of communities. They have tried to focus on the kind of society necessary for liberal citizenship and to address squarely the question of what kind of argument or defence can ground the particular obligations that flow from citizenship in one's own (just) society (rather than any just society).

In his book *Liberal Purposes*, William Galston departs from the neutralist liberal view that citizenship obligations appropriate to a liberal political community will be formed spontaneously through the interplay of the family, civil society, and the political institutions of the state.[6] Instead, Galston focuses on the role of the state in fostering virtue in its various political and social institutions, especially its educational institutions. He also departs from the view endorsed by Rawls in *Political Liberalism* by suggesting that the issue of rational justification (of liberal rights and liberal political institutions) is quite separate from the motivational issue of how to ensure that the relevant rights and duties will be honoured.[7] Galston writes: 'On a practical level, very few individuals will come to embrace the core commitments of liberal societies through a process of rational inquiry. If children are to be brought to accept these commitments as valid and binding, it can only be through a process that is far more rhetorical than rational.'[8]

In Galston's view, liberal citizenship cannot focus only on the justice or fairness of the political principles that are embodied in the state, but must also develop an emotional pride and identification with fellow citizens and with the particular institutions of the society. The sacrifices necessary for the realization of the common good require an emotional identification with the state and with its members. '[C]ivic education,' Galston writes, '. . . requires a more noble, moralizing history: a pantheon of heroes who confer legitimacy on central institutions and constitute worthy objects of emulation. It is unrealistic to believe that more than a few adult citizens of liberal societies will ever move beyond the kind of civic commitment engendered by such a pedagogy.'[9] Although Galston typically terms this emotional identification 'patriotism', it is extensionally equivalent to civic nationalism in requiring both bonds of affection for co-members (co-nationals) and sentiments of affection for the political project (the nation) that unites them.

This argument—that citizenship requires bonds of attachment both to the state and to fellow citizens (or co-nationals)—conceives of national identification as instrumental in achieving the good of liberal citizenship, which in turn is supportive of principles of justice and respect for diversity. Like many other theorists of nationality, Galston assumes that this unity, these bonds of solidarity, will override other, competing forms of identification, or at least provide the glue to bind together people who are diverse in other respects. Nationality is a homogenizing force, emphasizing shared identity, shared culture, history, language, and symbols, and—to the extent that it suggests the nation is an important agency of meaning and justification—concomitantly denies the importance of other (subnational) identity groups. The emphasis on shared ties not only emphasizes the equality and similarity of group members by contrast to neighbouring groups, but also emphasizes the unity of the group and its shared consciousness by contrast to other sources of unity and other forms of collective solidarity.

Another version of this argument focuses on redistribution. In Miller's view, for example, a shared national identity engenders trust among members and in so doing helps to support redistributive practices. Miller's argument is a variation of the communitarian insight that, unless people feel that they share bonds of membership with the recipients of state redistribution, then the individual who is taxed to pay for it will experience that redistribution as coercive and therefore incompatible with individual freedom. He also seems to be making the empirical claim that the political will required to support redistribution will not exist if groups don't share a similar national identity, a feeling that they are engaged in a common political project.

This kind of argument is intuitively plausible, although it is difficult to argue for a straightforward, positive link between shared national identity and liberal justice. The reason, I think, is that the relationship between the two is extraordinarily complex: not only does the self-perception of the national identity affect levels of redistribution, but there is a large bureaucratic and legal structure that intervenes between political sentiments and public policy.[10] In many cases, the state bureaucracy and institutions will continue to fulfill redistributive obligations, regardless of the public's sentiments.

However, I think that Miller is right that, where there is a persistent feeling of non-shared identity, and substantial one-way redistribution (that is, the relationship cannot be defended in reciprocal terms, as mutually beneficial), the long-term continuation of redistributive policies may be in jeopardy. This argument can be made with respect to the position of Northern Ireland within the UK. When the British welfare state was set up, the British sense of national identity seemed to include the Northern Irish as part of the British nation and the territory as part of the United Kingdom. Since that time, particularly since the 'Troubles' of the late 1960s, Britons have come to regard the province as 'a place apart' and the people who live there as unlike them. This suggests that sentiments are not immediately reflected in public policy: at the very least, there is a substantial time-lag between the two, which can be accounted for by the mediating bureaucratic, legal, and political structures of the state.

On the other hand, with poll after poll showing that British taxpayers would like to get out of Northern Ireland, at least one of the two major political parties (Labour) is also advocating withdrawal. Moreover, Northern Ireland is one of the few places in the world that has a recognized right to secession (to join Ireland) should the majority wish it.[11] The desire, on the part of the (mainland) British, to dissociate themselves—legally, juridically, territorially, and in terms of public policy—from the province seems to reflect, at least in part, the asymmetry in national identity between mainland Britons (who think of everyone in Northern Ireland as Irish) and Northern Ireland's Protestants (who think of themselves as 'British'). This suggests that, even though the relationship between social justice and shared national identity is far from direct, Miller's argument about the sentiments that undergird social justice should not be dismissed. It lends support to Miller's argument that, in the absence of reciprocity and shared identity, the political will required to discharge these obligations over the long term may not exist. Shared national identity may not be crucial to the delivery of social justice, but the dispositions associated with shared national identity provide useful support for liberal redistribution; or, to put it conversely, in their absence, and in the absence of mutual benefit, a social justice program may be precarious over the long term.

Another variation of this argument is that a unified body politic, centred on common membership and common allegiance to the political institutions of the state, will help undergird democratic institutions. This is not a new argument. Indeed, in the nineteenth and early twentieth centuries, many writers assumed a close relationship between shared national identity and democracy. The basis of this assumption seems to have been an association between the ideas of national and democratic sovereignty, internal and external self-determination. This is evident in Ernest Renan's definition of the nation as 'un plebiscite de tous les jours',[12] which suggests the consensual and democratic basis of national communities. Apparently supporting this view, many nineteenth- and early twentieth-century nationalists were committed to democratic governance. The potential for divergence between nationalism and democracy was not evident, as nationalists/democrats (often the same people) organized to fight the anti-democratic Russian, Austro-Hungarian, and Ottoman empires.

The intellectual expression of this line of argument is, of course, John Stuart Mill's discussion 'On Nationality' in *Considerations on Representative Government*, in which he argues that democracy can flourish only where 'the boundaries of government coincide in the main with those of nationality'.[13] His argument in support of this contention is based on an analysis of the necessary conditions for a flourishing democracy: 'Among a people without fellow-feeling, especially if they read and speak different languages, the united public opinion necessary to the workings of representative institutions cannot exist.'[14]

Mill's recognition of the need for a common national identity, combined with a nineteenth-century view of historical progress and an ethnocentric view of the merits of different nations, led him to believe that the 'great nations' would enjoy independence and the smaller nationalities would be drawn into their 'orbit'. Today it is no longer plausible to assume that the demise of smaller nationalities is historically inevitable, and it is difficult to justify policies of coercive assimilation in liberal terms. Once we jettison Mill's assumption of the assimilative power of the larger nationalities, it becomes apparent that his argument merely supports the principle that state and national boundaries should coincide.

The idea that there is a mutually supporting relationship between shared national identity and democracy also has contemporary exponents. The strong version of this argument, as put forward by Michael Lind, holds that 'far from being a threat to democracy, nationalism—the correspondence of cultural nation and state—is a necessary, though not sufficient, condition for democracy in most places today.'[15] Lind supports his claim by listing the various linguistically and culturally divided 'multinational' societies in which democracy has not worked well (Cyprus, Lebanon, Sri Lanka, the Soviet Union, Yugoslavia, and Czechoslovakia); and he explores the precarious nature of the three 'successes': Canada, Belgium, and Switzerland.

He does not, however, analyze the various reasons for the breakdown of specific multinational states; nor does he show that it was cultural or national pluralism that threatened democratic institutions. In some cases the states he cites as empirical evidence had weak democratic institutions and/or few democratic traditions. This suggests that his empirical evidence merely supports the view that nationalism is dangerous for the unity of culturally plural states (not necessarily democracies). Indeed, one could interpret the evidence he cites in a quite different way—namely, as indicating that countries with strong democratic traditions (Canada, Belgium, Switzerland) tend to cope better with multinational diversity than do regimes without such traditions (in fact, many of the latter countries have collapsed altogether).

The weaker and more plausible version of this argument claims that multinational and multi-ethnic states can be made to function as democracies—usually by ensuring inclusive power-sharing or consociational arrangements (in the former case) or by forging an overarching political identity (in the latter case)—but that unity is desirable, where it is achievable, because it facilitates trust and deliberation, which are both important to a well-functioning democracy.[16] This weaker version is presented by David Miller in *On Nationality* as one of the reasons why we should ensure that national and state boundaries coincide.

Miller argues that a shared (subjective) sense of membership in a political community and a common commitment to the state are importantly linked to the (deliberative) democratic ideal. Miller recognizes that democracy can function even where there is little shared identity and a weak commitment to the institutions of the state, especially if democracy is understood primarily in terms of procedures of interest aggregation.[17] However, he argues that two important elements of deliberative democracy seem to presuppose that all see themselves as members of a single political community, stretching into the future. These elements are (1) moderation of claims in an attempt to find common ground; and (2) open and uncoerced discussion among all members of the community. The former is more likely in situations where there is a common political identity and a shared commitment to a political project. Concessions are more likely because (1) the person is more confident that he/she will be reciprocated at some later time, and (2) this might be necessary for the common good, to which all are committed. An open and uncoerced discussion is also more likely where all at least share a commitment to the political community and to one another as fellow members. Where there is no such shared identity, there is no need to engage in the discussion. Here Miller's argument points to what is lacking or unexplained in many discussions of 'democratic conversation' as a means to overcome disagreement: in other words, what it is that keeps the interlocutors 'talking'; why, in the face of disagreement, they wouldn't simply stop the dialogue.

It is, however, important to stress that while a unified public sphere, a common sense of shared identity, and a commitment to the political project are functional to a flourishing democracy, this is not, in itself, an argument against group rights or various forms of group representation. In fact, it is compatible with this argument to recognize—though its proponents generally don't—that consociational and other institutional devices for managing conflict are important in deeply divided societies, where trust is lacking and deliberative debate tends to occur *within* groups rather than between them (for example, in Lebanon, Cyprus, and Northern Ireland). In a state made up of two groups with competing and mutually antagonistic national identities, some form of group recognition (consociational democracy or group representation) is essential to achieving a stable political settlement. Group rights are necessary in such cases because the majority-vote rule that confers legitimacy in this context becomes a mechanism of exclusion (since politics tend to follow ethnic or national lines, and who constitutes the majority and who the minority is known in advance).[18]

This type of argument suggests that a shared national identity is important to a well-functioning democracy. It is not absolutely essential, since there are institutional systems designed to facilitate democratic governance in nationally divided societies (Lijphart's famous consociational or power-sharing democracy; and Horowitz's vote-pooling system, designed to encourage interethnic accommodation[19]), but these are difficult to establish and are notoriously unstable. A shared identity as members of a common political community is not absolutely essential to the proper functioning of democratic institutions, but I think it is accurate to say that distrust between groups is destructive to the proper functioning of democracies, and that a shared national identity is helpful to the extent that it reduces the likelihood of distrust. From a conflict-resolution perspective, it is also helpful, because the various institutional arrangements (beyond simplistic majority vote) designed to take into account the divisions in the society are extremely fragile and problematic.[20] All this suggests that the stable functioning of democratic systems is much easier to secure in states where there is agreement on the state and on the state boundaries (i.e., there is a shared national identity). It suggests that relatively homogeneous states enjoy advantages that divided states do not.

2. Multiculturalism and the New Politics of Enlightenment

In this section I will focus on a second important debate that has emerged since 1989, following the demise of the liberal–communitarian debate, and flowing partly from political events. The old politics of entitlement practised by liberals and social democrats was primarily concerned with what rights one had, with liberals focusing on rights protecting individual freedom, and those of more socialist orientation focusing on welfarist rights or social rights in society. In the *new* politics of entitlement, groups are no longer satisfied with equal rights and equal citizenship but also seek the right to recognition of their identity in the public sphere.

One characteristic of this new politics of entitlement is that groups are demanding institutional recognition of their distinct identities. They recognize that the state is not neutral between cultures, not neutral between individuals, but is by its very nature biased towards a particular culture, a particular group identity, usually that of the dominant majority. This is a significant revision to the dominant liberal self-understanding of the state. On the liberal conception, the state should be neutral with respect to individuals, and interfere only when individual actions harm others. Many groups in society now recognize that, in an important way, the state is not neutral. Even so-called civic nations, such as Britain and France, are not neutral with respect to culture. Britain teaches the English language, British history, and English literature in its schools; uses English as the language of parliamentary debate and the bureaucracy, and so on. Similarly in France, the state reproduces Frenchmen by teaching the French language and French history, and conducting its affairs in French. Business customs and public holidays follow the patterns set by the majority religion in Western liberal democracies, Christianity. The layouts of many buildings and the requirements for many jobs presuppose that the basic norm is the able-bodied person. The standards of beauty reflected in advertisements, on television, and in the political sphere reflect typically white faces and bodies. The dominant values and norms are those associated with white males. By questioning these norms, this new politics of entitlement requires that we go beyond questions of distribution to examine the dynamics of decision-making and group power relations, and the biases inherent in the standards (of merit, beauty, and much else) that legitimize inequalities in the society.

Many groups now see the ways in which they are disadvantaged and have demanded specific recognition of their diversity—not merely permission to practise their own customs (etc.) in the private sphere, but alterations in the public sphere to take into account their languages, styles of dress, public holidays, and so on. In her book *Justice and the Politics of Difference*, Iris Marion Young defends radical multicultural policies[21] on the grounds that these are necessary to redress various forms of oppression. She begins her analysis by rejecting the (traditional liberal democratic) view of the state as justified in adjudicating between rival claims on the grounds that it is neutral and impartial. In fact, she argues, liberal theory and the liberal democratic state have been complicit in helping to perpetuate various forms of oppression. She identifies five 'faces' of oppression that various groups may suffer: exploitation, marginalization, powerlessness, cultural imperialism, and violence.[22] She then goes on to suggest three ways of combatting such oppression: through group representation, group vetoes over policies that affect the group directly, and public funding for interest groups to ensure that the 'voices' of oppressed groups are heard.

Young and other proponents of multiculturalism are surely right to draw attention to the fact that, in order to treat people fairly and equally, we must examine the ways in which people legitimately differ from one another. Yet in what follows I will suggest that Young is wrong to think that simply being in a minority, in the way she outlines, constitutes a form of oppression, and that the appropriate remedy is special group rights.

What is missing from Young's analysis is recognition of the need for a common public sphere. Indeed, her blanket description of all forms of minority status as oppressive seems completely unhelpful, and unrealistic, in contemporary circumstances. As revisionist liberals and liberal nationalists have pointed out, there is a need for a common political language and identity, and some common framework in which different people can meet, discuss their commonalities, and recognize each other as fellow citizens.

Once we realize the need for a common public sphere in which to make decisions, it becomes questionable whether Young's proposed solution of group-based policies and group-based representation is indeed appropriate. A vibrant and democratic public life presupposes some common sphere, some political space, in which people can make collective decisions not simply as blacks or women or Jews or Muslims or fundamentalist Protestants but as *citizens* of a common political project, and deliberate over the best (i.e., fairest) ground rules to underpin the basic structure of society.

Indeed, the need for a common political identity, a common sense of one another as citizens, is presupposed in most multiculturalist accounts, but there is little discussion of the conditions that facilitate this recognition of commonality. Near the beginning of her book, Young simply assumes that everyone accepts the fundamental equality of persons.[23] Later, in her positive proposals for a more just society, she puts forward as the model for her solution Jesse Jackson's 'Rainbow Coalition', in which a number of oppressed groups—blacks, women, Hispanics, gays and lesbians, the disabled—join together under an umbrella organization to fight, politically, for an end to oppression.[24] The problem with this model is that it exaggerates the degree of common ground in the political projects of all these groups. The interests of women (considered as a group) in ensuring access to safe abortions may conflict with the interests of the disabled, who have an interest in ensuring that disabilities are not demonized and who want to prevent one manifestation of this, namely the routine aborting of disabled fetuses. The interests of fundamentalist Protestant and Muslim groups may conflict with the interests of lesbian and gay communities. (Interestingly, Young never includes these more conservative groups—Muslims, fundamentalist Protestants—on her list of marginalized groups, even though it is clear that they meet several of the criteria of an oppressed group.[25] Unfortunately, this may not be an oversight; if she had included these types of marginalized groups in her list it would have raised the question of the viability and unity of the Rainbow Coalition model.) It is difficult to imagine how these various injustices can be addressed without some conception that these people are morally equal, first, as human beings, and second, as fellow citizens engaged in a common political project. A politics of difference, in other words, depends on the recognition of underlying unity; yet the proposals that Young puts forward for recognition of difference may in fact make it even more difficult for people to recognize their commonalities.

Many proponents of multiculturalism assume, unproblematically, that multicultural policies of recognition will not entrench differences and will not lead to a more divided, more fragmented society. Will Kymlicka, for example, defines multicultural groups (or immigrants) in contrast to national minorities and argues that immigrants and other cultural minorities are not a problem for the unity and territorial integrity of the state, because they 'typically wish to integrate into the larger society, and to be accepted as full members of it'.[26] Iris Young also has a relatively benign view of the aims and effects of the policies she advocates. In general, she regards multiculturalism as necessary to redress oppression within a society, and she does not consider the question whether such policies, by reifying differences, may have disintegrative consequences. Although at one point she does say that groups are too interrelated and interdependent to allow for their separation and autonomy, even if that would be the best way to protect their identity-related differences,[27] she presents this situation as an empirical fact about modern, pluralist societies, rather than as normatively desirable, or as a limit to the kinds of accommodations that a society should be expected to make.

Kymlicka and Young are right to note that, in many cases, demands by minority cultural or religious groups can be met without jeopardizing the state's public and inclusive character.[28] Often disputes arise in the first place only because of an excessively rigid, and of course false, view of state neutrality on cultural issues. Consider the debate that took place in France over whether Muslim schoolgirls should be allowed to wear headscarves. Such scarves were prohibited on the grounds that religious symbols were disallowed—yet the same schools permitted Christian schoolgirls to wear crucifixes. Moreover, even if crucifixes were prohibited as well, such a rule is not neutral between religious beliefs, because it is possible to be a Christian without any public displays of religious affiliation, whereas modest dress is a positive requirement of Islam; thus forbidding headscarves prevents female Muslim believers from participating fully in the public school system.

Many of the claims put forward by multicultural groups are of precisely this kind. They are demands for increased inclusion, for reduction of barriers. Demands by particular racial or ethnic groups to, say, have their particular history taught in public schools are demands for a more permeable public culture, for a history that acknowledges their diverse contributions. Teaching history in this way would show that the history of Canada or the United States is not just a history of whites, that black people have made important contributions to it. As Spinner-Halev has argued, when this occurs, as it did in the United States with the legacy of Martin Luther King, Jr, the particular contribution that he makes is not as a black, but as an American; and his legacy is not only for blacks, but can be recognized and celebrated by all Americans.[29]

Demands to wear a yarmulke in the military or a turban in the RCMP, like the demand to wear headscarves in schools, are demands not to be discriminated against. They are demands for cultural difference to be permitted and for exceptions to be granted when legislation discriminates against them. These demands not to be discriminated against are not threatening to the *political* identity of the national community. On the contrary, ensuring that all groups are included, that the common identity is constructed in a way that is consistent with such inclusion, may strengthen citizenship by ensuring that no one is left outside it, or marginalized by it, and thereby reducing the risk that excluded groups will develop separate identities that would threaten the political project. It is, therefore, both normatively required, for fair and good public policy, and because it strengthens the national community.

What I am suggesting, then, is that while various identity groups frequently have legitimate claims, there are limits to what can legitimately be demanded, limits that have been suggested both by liberal nationalists and by revisionist liberals. We should not assume that all such demands are divisive, but neither should we assume that all are benign and potentially integrative. Some multicultural groups demand not just increased inclusion but—like national minorities—increased autonomy to ensure that they can protect their cultural differences by erecting structural or institutional barriers between themselves and others.

There are a number of examples of demands for institutional separateness on the part of cultural and identity groups. In Israel, when spouses belong to the same religious group, matters of family law (marriage, divorce, support, custody), which usually fall under the jurisdiction of the state, are treated as falling within the purview of the religious group, to be settled according to the group's particular culture and norms. This means that the various identity groups exercise powers and jurisdiction normally exercised by the state, and that individuals must function, at least in this context, not as Israeli citizens, but as Jews, Muslims, Druze, and Christians. Decisions, of course, vary widely since they are governed by the traditions and texts of the various cultural groups. One problem with this system is that some decisions may be oppressive for group members (e.g., women) who have historically been discriminated against by the group.[30] Another problem is that institutional separateness may lead to the development of competing power bases in the society, bases whose existence depends on reifying or exaggerating the differences between their members and other members of the political community.[31] This in turn may threaten the unity of the society and reduce the capacity of the state to dispense liberal justice and function as a vibrant forum for public dialogue and debate on a wide range of issues.

Demands by multicultural groups for separate schools are also problematic, for these may threaten the common and public nature of the educational system. Consider religious conservatives who object to the secular nature of state-run and state-funded schools and argue for their own schools on the ground (a) that parents have the right to choose and (b) that they constitute a distinctive moral community, with their own particular cultural practices. They seek control over their own schools, which would not only impart the Christian faith to their children, but would also insulate those children from contaminating influences (secular curriculum, children from non-fundamentalist families).[32] Of course, these kinds of demands have been made by other culturally distinct groups as well. Spinner-Halev cites the case of a group in the Jewish Hasidic movement that successfully sought its own school—not just a private yeshiva, but a state-funded school within the New York school board.[33] There have also been calls, particularly in Britain, for state-funded Muslim schools.[34]

Demands of this sort are problematic because they may very well prevent schoolchildren from developing a sense of common political identity (as Canadian, British,

French, etc.) in addition to their particular identities as Jewish or Muslim or Catholic. In some cases, as in Britain and Canada, where there are state-funded Catholic schools, demands by Muslim or Jewish groups for their own state-funded religious schools are demands for fair treatment, and in this context may be justified. But I think that neither in Canada, nor in Britain, are parallel school systems appropriate, and that the best system would be a single, inclusive, and flexible system, which all children attend.

Another important criterion in assessing the legitimacy of any multicultural demand is whether the group is simply seeking permission to do something (without state interference) or is requesting public funds to do it. Public action should be in the public interest, but we should not expect the private actions of groups to meet this criterion. The liberal state is committed to the right to freedom of association, to the value of autonomy, and the importance of choosing one's own life, and tolerance for a number of different ways of life. All this means that there is a presumption in favour of non-intervention (by the state) in private actions, and that groups should be able (in the private sphere) to read and speak their own language, to educate their children according to their own beliefs, to join their own clubs and sports associations and so on, and that these groups and activities should be tolerated even when they are not necessarily in the public interest.

This criterion is important in assessing recent demands by Orthodox Jews in Montreal for their own ambulance service. The argument about preserving the public character of the state suggests that the state should not support, or fund, such a private group-specific service. Indeed, the idea of separate ambulance services for specific groups in society strikes at the very heart of the public character of the state. If ambulance services were group-specific in this way, the service would be duplicated needlessly, and this would lead to lengthy delays, and contribute to the public expense.[35] But, in this case, the Orthodox Jewish community was trying to overcome linguistic barriers (with the largely francophone ambulance staff) and ensure that the medical treatment administered (and the treatment of the body, in the event of death) would be in accordance with the group's religious practices. These requests could—and should—have been accommodated in some way within the public ambulance system. Since they were not, the Orthodox Jewish community was justified in setting up its own voluntary, private service. An important point in assessing this issue is that the Orthodox Jewish community was prepared to pay the costs for this service. This group is voluntarily responding to certain needs within its community. It is voluntary also in the sense that patients (or those coming to their aid) must specifically request this service (by dialling the group's telephone number).[36]

Demands to be included fairly in the institutions of society are demands of justice and should be accommodated; but institutional separateness, funded by the state, should be regarded with suspicion, and countenanced only in deeply divided societies where it is necessary to maintain peace and stability. This is obviously not the case in places like Canada, Britain, or the United States, where the multicultural debate has proceeded furthest. While coercive forms of assimilation are obviously unacceptable, we should also remember that state action should be in the public interest. There is no public interest in preserving diversity: diversity is not an intrinsic good in itself, which should be protected. Indeed, encouraging too much institutional separateness may have the effect of jeopardizing our shared political identity and common political institutions. If liberal nationalists and liberal revisionists are right that the liberal state presupposes certain bonds of unity and solidarity among its citizens, we should protect and nurture these common bonds and ensure that we have a vibrant public space.

3. Conclusion

In this essay I have suggested that there is some merit to the liberal nationalist argument for creating a common society, with a common political identity—not for traditional nationalist reasons, but as a precondition to liberal justice and democratic conversation. At the same time, liberal nationalists should attend to the arguments of multiculturalists, who have pointed to many ways in which public policies have unfairly disadvantaged women and minority groups. In the nineteenth century, nation-building typically involved coercive state policies aimed at assimilating diverse groups in society. This is no longer acceptable or justifiable: nation-building should proceed in ways that are sensitive to the disadvantages some groups suffer as a result of the construction of the public sphere. At the same time, however, in focusing exclusively on issues of identity and non-neutrality, proponents of the new politics of entitlement have not helped us to assess the diverse claims of multicultural groups, or established the extent to which these claims could be justified on some further principle.

This suggests that any attempt to create a common political project will have to proceed by recognizing a variety of identities. The political culture of the state will have to be made, as far as possible, permeable in the sense that a variety of cultural groups will feel included; that they will feel that it is possible to be both Muslim and Canadian; both Aboriginal and Québécois. This involves removing any sort of special discrimination or unfair disadvantages that the group suffers. We have to recognize that demands on the part of identity groups to ensure that their history and cultural practices are included in the larger society are primarily claims to be treated fairly, to be included in democratic debate and decision-making, to ensure that their history is included in the larger history. These demands for fairness, for justice, will help to strengthen citizenship by making the state more inclusive.

We should, however, also consider the insights and arguments of revisionist liberals and liberal nationalists when assessing the new politics of entitlement. If we are to have a common life, we cannot give equal rights to every culture. More than 70 different languages are spoken, as mother tongues, by children in the Toronto District school board area.[37] It is not possible to have a modern state and to give equal recognition to each of these languages. Signs have to be posted in one or two or three languages—I don't know what the upper limit might be—but there is also a need for a common political identity, and some common framework and language, in which different people will be able to meet and discuss their commonalities and recognize each other as fellow citizens.

So far, there hasn't been much debate between the new politics of entitlement and the new liberal nationalism argument. I think that such a debate is necessary, not only to arrive at a coherent theory of citizenship, but in order to develop public policies required to address the cultural issues that press on both debates. I think that both debates raise valid points, and that the range and consequences of the demands of multicultural identity groups have to be assessed using criteria suggested by liberal nationalists; and that liberal nationalist nation-building policies have to be limited by some of the considerations of fairness that multiculturalists have so effectively pressed on. My hope is that this essay will help to spark discussion between participants in these two debates, which, until now, have taken place separately.

NOTES

1. Cultural (and philosophical) diversity was mainly regarded as a background condition that helps justify (thin public) principles of justice. On this view, articulated by Rawls in *Political Liberalism*, the most that we can aspire to in a diverse society, where there is no agreement on a (thick) conception of the good, is agreement on thin public principles of justice and democratic governance. See John Rawls, *Political Liberalism* (New York: Columbia University Press, 1993), xvi–xvii; 145–70.
2. Arthur M. Schlesinger, Jr, *The Disuniting of America: Reflections on a Multicultural Society* (New York: W.W. Norton, 1992), 102.
3. Alan Patten, 'Liberal Citizenship in Multinational Societies', paper delivered at North Hatley, Quebec, Conference on Liberal Justice and Political Stability in Multinational Societies, March 1998.
4. Rogers Brubaker, *Citizenship and Nationhood in France and Germany* (Cambridge, Mass.: Harvard University Press, 1992), 21.
5. Yael Tamir, *Liberal Nationalism* (Princeton: Princeton University Press, 1993); David Miller, *On Nationality* (Oxford: Oxford University Press, 1995); Stephen Macedo, *Liberal Virtues: Citizenship, Virtue, and Community in Liberal Constitutionalism* (Oxford: Clarendon Press, 1990); William Galston, *Liberal Purposes: Goods, Virtues and Diversity in the Liberal State* (New York: Cambridge University Press, 1991).
6. A similar view is taken by Eamonn Callan, in *Creating Citizens: Political Education and Liberal Democracy* (Oxford: Oxford University Press, 1997), 103–15. Like Galston, Callan accepts that a positive attitude of attachment to co-nationals and to the political community is a prerequisite for liberal citizenship, although he disagrees with Galston about the fundamental value of liberalism (for Galston it is diversity; for Callan it is autonomy) and also about the extent to which the abridgment of reason is a necessary part of citizenship education.
7. Rawls's proposed remedy to what he calls the 'stability' problem is, first, the requirement that there be an overlapping consensus on a political conception, and, second, an account of the reasonable person, to whom his theory is addressed. This solution explains why reasonable people should endorse and abide by fair or just political principles, but it doesn't explain the special obligations that the individual has for the state s/he lives in, or why the

individual should accept special burdens to redistribute wealth to co-members, rather than to the most needy people in the world.

8. Galston, *Liberal Purposes*, 243.
9. Ibid., 244.
10. See Daniel Weinstock, 'Is There a Moral Case for Nationalism?', *Journal of Applied Philosophy* 13, 1 (1996), 87–100.
11. This is Article 1(a) and (c) of the Anglo-Irish Agreement. The full Agreement is reprinted in *The Future of Northern Ireland*, ed. John McGarry and Brendan O'Leary (Oxford: Clarendon Press, 1990), appendix one.
12. Ernest Renan, 'Discours et conférences' (1887). Quoted in Alfred Cobban, *National Self-Determination* (Oxford: Oxford University Press, 1945), 64.
13. John Stuart Mill, 'Considerations on Representative Government', in *Utilitarianism, On Liberty and Considerations on Representative Government* (London: Everyman, 1993), 394.
14. Ibid., 392.
15. Michael Lind, 'In Defense of Liberal Nationalism', *Foreign Affairs* 73, 3: 87–99 at 94.
16. Even Lijphart says that there should be an 'overarching consensus' in the society. See Arend Lijphart, *Democracy in Plural Societies: A Comparative Exploration* (New Haven: Yale University Press, 1977). This seems to suggest that consociationalism is inappropriate for nationally divided societies (where there is no overarching consensus—the political community itself is the subject of dispute) but is possible in racially divided societies (like South Africa) and ethnically divided societies (like Lebanon).
17. Miller, *On Nationality*, 97.
18. This problem has been well documented in Northern Ireland from 1921 to 1972, which was governed democratically on a Westminster first-past-the-post majoritarian system. See Brendan O'Leary and John McGarry, *The Politics of Antagonism: Understanding Northern Ireland* (London: Athlone Press, 1996), 107–52.
19. See Lijphart, *Democracy in Plural Societies* and Donald Horowitz, *Ethnic Groups in Conflict* (Berkeley: University of California Press, 1985).
20. Notable failures include Northern Ireland in 1974 and Cyprus (1960–3). In the case of Lebanon, on the other hand, the power-sharing regime did last for 32 years. That could be considered a success.
21. I use the term 'multiculturalism' here not as a descriptive term, to describe a society with many diverse cultures, but as a normative term, to describe a political program of recognition by the state of these diverse cultures.
22. One problem with this account is that it lumps together economic and cultural factors. Nancy Fraser has argued that this is problematic because these different forms of oppression may be handled in different ways. Economic disadvantages may be remedied by standard liberal anti-discrimination laws, rigorously applied, or institutional transformation of the capitalist market in a socialist direction, whereas oppression based on cultural differences may require a group-based remedy. See Nancy Fraser, 'Recognition Or Redistribution? A Critical Reading of Iris Young's *Justice and the Politics of Difference*', *Journal of Political Philosophy* 3, 2 (1995), 168–70. This point is also made, with reference to the Fraser review, in Jeff Spinner-Halev, 'Land, Culture and Justice: A Framework for Collective Recognition', manuscript, 6.
23. Iris Marion Young, *Justice and the Politics of Difference* (Princeton: Princeton University Press, 1990), 37.

24. Ibid., 188–9.

25. This was pointed out by Tariq Modood, in response to questions at the Conference on Citizenship in Diverse Societies: Theory and Practice, Toronto, Ontario, 5–6 October 1997.

26. Will Kymlicka, *Multicultural Citizenship: A Liberal Theory of Minority Rights* (Oxford: Oxford University Press, 1995), 10–11.

27. Young, *Justice and the Politics of Difference*, 260.

28. In his book *Finding Our Way: Rethinking Ethnocultural Relations in Canada* (Toronto: Oxford University Press, 1998), Will Kymlicka offers empirical evidence to support the view that the official policy of multiculturalism in Canada has had integrative effects. In his book, however, 'multiculturalism' refers primarily to the official policy of the Canadian government since 1971, whereas in this paper I am referring to the academic debate around multiculturalism, which is more radical (it includes group representation, group vetoes, support for Afrocentric education, and so on), and which is defended mainly in terms of identity politics. I think it is confusion between the academic discourse and the official Canadian policy of multiculturalism that accounts for the confusion and ignorance that Kymlicka notes, with some puzzlement, in *Finding Our Way*, 22.

29. Jeff Spinner-Halev, 'Cultural Pluralism and Partial Citizenship', in *Multicultural Questions*, ed. Steven Lukes and Christian Joppke (Oxford: Oxford University Press, forthcoming).

30. This is one of the main points that Ayelet Shachar convincingly makes in her article 'Group Identity and Women's Rights in Family Law: The Perils of Multicultural Accommodation', *Journal of Political Philosophy* 6, 3 (1998), 285–305 at 291.

31. Shachar, 288, notes that in deeply divided societies such as India and Israel, the motivation for granting cultural groups some political autonomy is to maintain social and political peace. My argument does not apply to multicultural policies defended in these terms, but only to those justified in terms advanced by Iris Young, and applicable to societies like Canada, the United States, Australia, and, increasingly, Western Europe.

32. Callan, *Creating Citizens*, 157–61, discusses this issue in the context of *Mozert v. Hawkins Board of Education*. He argues that a liberal state cannot tolerate education that is designed to instill 'ethical servility' in its students.

33. Jeff Spinner-Halev, 'The Religious Challenge to Diversity and Equality', paper delivered to the Annual Meeting of the American Political Science Association, San Francisco, September 1996, 21–3. He also cites *Board of Education of Kiryas Joel v. Grunet 114 U.S. 2490 (1994)*.

34. Spinner-Halev, 'Cultural Pluralism and Partial Citizenship', manuscript, 30.

35. Duplication of service was the main objection made against Hatzolah, the Jewish medical emergency group, by Urgences-Santé, Montreal's ambulance service. See Monique Beaudin, 'Firefighters want emergency group closed', *Montreal Gazette*, 7 March 1997.

36. Indeed, one wonders whether the public ambulance service objected so vigorously because they disliked the competition. The Hatzolah volunteers had more medical training than the firefighters and tended to arrive on the scene more quickly, even without the benefit of sirens. See Susan Schwartz, 'A call to action', *Montreal Gazette*, 14 Dec. 1998.

37. Virginia Galt, 'Schools fear for immigrant students', *Globe and Mail*, 3 March 1998.

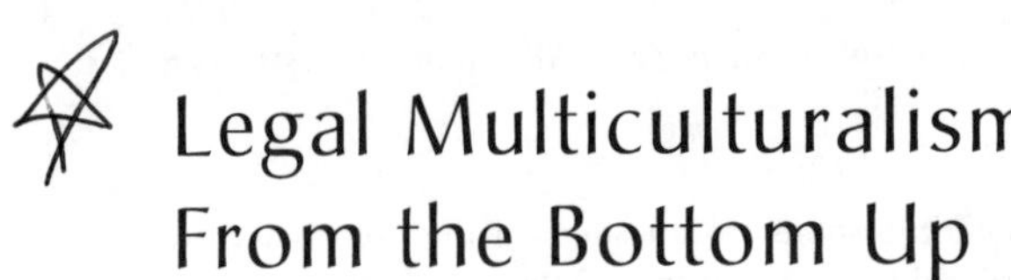

Legal Multiculturalism From the Bottom Up

DENISE G. RÉAUME

The challenge of multiculturalism is that of negotiating the relationship between two or more normative systems within a political unit. Religious communities will each have their own set of rules about how members should conduct themselves vis-à-vis each other and outsiders; Aboriginal communities may be committed to a particular use of natural resources as a means of providing a livelihood for members; linguistic communities will want formal provision for the use of their language in important social and political contexts; some groups will be able to organize matters internally, while others will need the co-operation or assistance of the state. The legal system is also a normative system—a complex set of rules guiding behaviour and facilitating human activity. The diverse concerns and ways of life of multiple, overlapping communities will produce a complicated web of rules and practices, injunctions and prohibitions, permissions and entitlements. These various normative systems will often be able to coexist peaceably; but at other times—in particular, when a cultural norm system conflicts with the legal system—they will be in conflict with each other.

The law conceives of itself as the ultimate arbiter and authority in a society. Law may regulate anything. Its prohibitions are clearly a form of regulation, but even when behaviour is permitted, it is by grace of the law. Given the omnipresence of law and the coexistence of groups of people committed to a variety of normative systems, issues raising the question of accommodation are everywhere and always potentially present in a modern state. Any body of legal doctrine—whether constitutional, statutory, or common law—can become the site for a cultural contest. The question arising in all these contexts is: To what extent and under what circumstances should the law take cognizance of, or even defer to, the norms of cultural minorities within the

state so as to foster or facilitate cultural autonomy—that is, the ability of cultural communities to live in accordance with their own norms? This is not a question that lends itself to clear, precise, and easy answers. The ultimate question—legal or moral—is always one of how much autonomy to foster. The enjoyment of autonomy is always a matter of degree.

Because of the interplay of these features—the range of legal contexts in which conflict may arise, and the need to decide how much autonomy is desirable—no exhaustive list of discrete cultural rights or group-differentiated rights, no comprehensive blueprint dictating where and when and how special treatment of cultural minorities is appropriate, is likely to capture multiculturalism as a legal phenomenon. Efforts to produce lists and blueprints can be illuminating; ultimately, though, legal experience cannot be so confined.[1] The only rule that could hope to capture how the law should respond to conflict arising out of cultural difference across the many contexts in which the issue may arise would be too abstract to be much help. Figuring out whether and how to accommodate cultural difference will require attention to the nuances of the legal context as well as the community's internal understanding of its practices.

The search for a blueprint for cultural accommodation shares with the legislative form of rule-making a 'top-down' approach: both seek to determine at the outset which groups will be protected to what extent in which contexts, and to lay down the appropriate framework. Most ambitiously, such efforts may involve the recognition of legal power within some communities to govern (some of) their own affairs; alternatively, one may envision a single law-making authority for all groups, but one charged with enacting different rules for different groups as appropriate. This approach works well when clear lines can be drawn between the communities or subject areas to be regulated. But problems can also be solved and law made from the bottom up. A 'bottom-up' approach deals with issues as they arise in the ordinary course of interaction. It is the form of law-making suitable to the courts. When disputes arise under statute or the common law, the courts may be asked to incorporate difference into laws of general application simply by interpreting them in a manner appropriate to the cultural context. It will likely never be possible to anticipate all the circumstances in which conflict may arise out of cultural difference, so as to be able to provide for it in advance. Some conflicts will arise interstitially and must be resolved interstitially. It may also be, as it is in the development of legal norms generally, that there is something to be gained from not trying to deal with all issues in a top-down fashion. Sometimes the handling of moral questions can benefit from close analysis of concrete contexts, on the basis of which a more general principle may eventually be formulated. In other words, good theory can sometimes benefit from a bottom-up approach to problems.

All these legal regulatory methods will be needed to deal with the full range of possible conflicts between law and culture; indeed, they may have to be combined in order to accommodate the demands of any given group. Different legal mechanisms may be better suited to different issues. In addition, the scope of the differences that separate minority norms and practices from those of the rest of society may be relevant to the resolution of a particular dispute. One minority community may adhere to a way of life that is comprehensively incompatible with the lifestyle of others; another may differ only in relatively contained spheres. The scope of difference and the legal options will influence one another. Pervasive and substantial differences will pull in the direction of (comprehensive or partial) self-government, giving the minority the institutional capacity to make and enforce its own laws. Where a group

differs from the majority in only a small number of localized features, however, full-scale self-government would be overkill; either discrete laws or adjudicative sensitivity may be adequate to meet its needs. In considering these options, the size of the community—which will affect its ability to sustain a relatively separate existence—should be taken into account. A choice must also be made between territorial and other ways of demarcating the group to be accommodated; territorial solutions are neat, but often not feasible when members of a minority group are interspersed throughout the larger population.

Finally, each claim must be assessed as to whether and how much it deviates from legal notions of acceptability. In one case, a community's rules may impose on its members (or on outsiders) treatment that can only be described as a violation of fundamental human rights. In another, the rules may deviate from those normally countenanced by the legal system, but not so as to implicate human rights. Even if the legal authorities think that, on balance, their preferred way of doing things is more generous or more sensible than that followed by a minority community we need not judge the latter's way to be morally reprehensible. Again, even when the rules of two groups differ significantly, each set of rules may be so well adapted to the circumstances of the group that there is no unfairness in either.[2]

In this essay I explore one angle on culture/law conflict: judicial pronouncements on the legal validity of a certain kind of effort to enforce community norms. The judgment that certain behaviour is required or prohibited can permeate a cultural community's normative system at a variety of levels. The cases examined here involve not the direct attempt to punish, but the use by cultural communities of facilitative legal instruments to support their internal normative structure. Arising interstitially through litigation, these disputes illustrate both the variety of legal contexts in which such issues may arise and the importance of attention to legal context. They provide an opportunity to examine how legal doctrine has conceptualized the question of how much autonomy to afford cultural communities through a bottom-up method of reasoning about concrete cases. One benefit of paying attention to the variety of legal contexts in which disputes over cultural accommodations may arise is that it makes apparent the variety of legal techniques available for constructing the scope of autonomy appropriate to various groups. Self-government need not be thought of as comprehensive law-making authority, for which only some communities may be eligible.[3] In the final section, I illustrate how a variety of legal techniques can be used to craft the autonomy regime appropriate in scope to each community seeking protection for its own practices.

USING PRIVATE LAW TO ENFORCE CULTURE: THE LEGAL CONSTRUCTION OF CULTURAL AUTONOMY

A culture, whether all-encompassing or localized, is a normative order and as such has features that parallel those of the legal system. Some of its rules form, in effect, its constitution: these may include procedural rules about the formulation of other rules, but they are unlikely to be confined to the procedural. Culture consists of a way of life.

As such its fundamental rules include mandatory injunctions about how to behave—what conduct is right or wrong.[4] In many groups, some of these rules have, in effect, entrenched status: they cannot be changed at will, although they may change incrementally as a result of organic development and reinterpretation. Understanding the normative posture of the cultural rules or practices in question sets the scene for analyzing conflict. From this perspective, Kymlicka's approach—presumptively validating rules directed at outsiders for the protection of the group while exhibiting suspicion about rules imposing restrictions on insiders—is puzzling.[5] At its core, a culture is a set of rules and practices, some mandatory, directed at insiders—it does, after all, constitute their way of life. All such rules and practices restrict in some measure. Only contingently, in cases of certain kinds of interaction between cultural communities, is there a need for rules directed at outsiders. When external protections are sought, it is in order to allow the community to live according to its different internal normative structure. To forbid a cultural community to impose internal restrictions, or to overzealously control its ability to do so, is to reduce its mandatory norms to mere exhortations. Assessment of a group's rules should hinge not on whether they impose internal restrictions, but on the nature of those restrictions.[6]

A discrepancy between the mandatory norms of a minority culture and those of the legal system will obviously generate conflict; but conflict may also arise when culture makes mandatory that which is legally optional. For the law has a monopoly on coercive force: cultural communities can use force to enforce their mandatory norms only with the permission of the law. There are many good reasons to deny cultural groups the power to use force to punish; for present purposes I will assume without arguing that this is the right decision. Nevertheless, there are other ways in which a cultural community may manifest its belief in the mandatory nature of its norms, and the law will sometimes be called upon to pass judgment on the acceptability of these responses to the violation of community norms. It does not follow from the fact that a group should not be able to take punishment into its own hands that the law should refuse to enforce any adverse consequences of a member's deviation from internal norms. A community may, for example, practice informal sanctioning such as shunning. Insofar as this behaviour falls within the realm of the legally permissible—no one has a right to the good offices of others—there is no conflict. Indeed, to forbid shunning would be to compel people to associate with particular others against their wishes—a violation of principles of freedom of association. The law may not approve of the reasons for the shunning; nevertheless, legal principles protect such behaviour, and in so doing protect a community's ability to enforce its norms though such means, even though the psychological effects may be quite severe. The same analysis will apply to expulsion if it merely amounts to permanent refusal to associate with the former member.

More controversial is signalling the mandatory nature of fundamental norms by tying tangible benefits of participation in the community to adherence to them. Cultural and legal status become intertwined when groups make use of the facilitative mechanisms of the law in order to carry on their normative enterprise.[7] Churches own property for the purposes of conducting religious worship; utopian societies withdraw from the materialism of the world by acquiring their own property in order to organize the means of production according to different principles; religious groups seeking to educate their children in a climate consistent with their beliefs run schools and employ teachers; communities may also operate hospital staff in an effort to provide health care according to their own principles. In some cases membership is defined by reference to adherence to group norms, and is, in turn, tied to economic or other benefits. Disobedience can result in expulsion, which results in withdrawal of benefits. In other cases, community agents may enter into other legally recognized roles, such as that of employer, as they conduct enterprises integral to the community's ends, and may seek adaptations of the normal employment relationship to facilitate those ends.

That is not to say that the law must automatically lend its tools to these purposes; the law itself provides means of drawing lines between the acceptable and the unacceptable. Common law rules and many statutory dictates are formulated in vague, indeterminate language, giving the courts considerable leeway in determining lawfulness. In addition, many rules have a general built-in exception; often the question of how much autonomy to afford arises through the interpretation of the applicability of such exceptions. The indeterminacy embedded in the rules and their exception clauses allows the courts to exercise cultural sensitivity to the extent appropriate, but also to invalidate communal schemes that go too far. These doctrinal caveats and limits amount to a judge-made equivalent of the general British statutory rule, imposed in many African colonies, that certain subject matters must be decided in accordance with indigenous customary law unless that law was repugnant to 'morality or natural justice'.[8] As a general *rule*, this may be all one can say; all the work remains to be done at the level of determining whether a particular norm is repugnant. Although there are undoubtedly cases in which a 'repugnancy proviso' must be invoked in order to prevent serious injustice, the courts would do well to exercise this power with caution. If the norms of minority group life are invalidated every time they have a consequence that is at variance with expectations within the wider society, the result is to protect these practices only to the extent that they operate entirely in the private realm—those areas the law chooses not to regulate—or to make them subject to the veto of each member of the community, putting the community at the mercy of opportunistic defections. In the final analysis, that would amount to little more than toleration of cultural difference, not accommodation.

The use of legal institutions to make rights in private law hinge on membership in a cultural community is the first form of intertwining of cultural and legal status to explore. Under these circumstances, membership in a community may have its privileges, but loss of membership also has consequences. Sometimes the only means a group has to express the mandatory nature of its rules is to deprive those who disobey them of membership status. Few would argue that the state should interfere with a group's ability to determine its own membership. However, to distinguish sharply between community control over the criteria of membership and over the distribution of tangible assets and opportunities, protecting the former but not the latter,[9] is to miss the crucial normative connection that can exist between these matters from the inside of a given culture. Again, such an approach risks depriving membership of significant meaning by reducing it to the realm of the purely private or symbolic.

When churches, for example, hold their property in trust for the use of their members, the logical connection between cultural status and legal rights is tightest: one who ceases to be a member ceases to hold any beneficial interest in the property and can therefore be excluded from its use. The legal institution of property is indifferent as between a wide variety of uses to which property may be put. As a fairly content-neutral vessel, the law of property adopts an owner's purposes in fashioning legal rights and obligations. When those purposes are bound up with creating a way of life, therefore, the law itself mandates taking cognizance of these communal purposes.

Most dramatically in cases of schism, disputes over property ownership must be resolved in accordance with the fundamental constitutional commitments of the community, whatever they may be.[10] If property is held in trust for the members of a church, a dispute over who the real members are is a dispute over who the proper owners are, and vice versa. A dispute resulting in schism often hinges on which beliefs are central to the group, adherence being required by the group's foundational norms. Those norms may also incorporate an internal decision-making authority charged with regulating belief, and hence membership. Whatever the community's internal structure, decisions about ownership will turn on the proper interpretation of its internal norms. To do other than try to decide in accordance with the group's own understanding of itself is to redefine the community.[11] If, for example, property is held for the benefit of the Free Church, which, it is found, believes in the establishment of religion, a court cannot award the property to a faction that favours relinquishing that principle—even if it constitutes a majority of churchgoers—without thereby changing the belief structure of the Free Church from a church founded on the establishment principle into one based on majority rule. That the establishment principle is a tenet of the Free Church imposes constraints on Free Church members—and those who cease to hold this belief, whatever their numbers, lose the right to the use of the church's property. Even if there are good reasons for preferring democratic decision-making over other forms of social organization, it would clearly be improper for the legal system to interfere.

A similar dynamic is in play when individual non-conformity disrupts a community in which belief is combined with everyday practices concerning work and social life. The *Hofer* case from the Hutterite community demonstrates, in another form, the internal connection between conformity and membership.[12] The Hutterites use the institution of property to form agricultural colonies within which all assets are shared communally. All members of the colony work for the good of the whole; all are taken care of by the colony. There is no individual ownership of any property, however small. This form of ownership is reinforced through contract, adult male members agreeing to the colony's articles of association, which stipulate that all property is communal. This way of structuring everyday life flows from their religious beliefs.

Membership in a Hutterite colony is tied to membership in the church: a colony member who ceases to accept the tenets of the Hutterite faith loses his membership in the colony through losing his membership in the church. With this loss comes the tangible loss of entitlement to share in the assets of the community. This rule clearly imposes constraints on members. Again, to the extent that the institutions of property and contract allow individuals and groups to further their own purposes, these purposes are adopted by the law: the determination of legal entitlements must refer to the internal rules of membership.

The general limit on the law's willingness to adopt the purposes of private actors is phrased in terms of the indeterminate notion of 'public policy': it is always open to the courts to find that a contract or restriction on title is unenforceable because it is contrary to public policy. The question in *Hofer*, then, was whether the Hutterites' communal property regime was contrary to public policy. Hofer acknowledged his loss of membership—indeed, he relinquished it—but sought to sever that fact from the question of his economic entitlements by claiming a share in the community's assets based on his contribution to them. But public policy is not a weapon to be invoked lightly. While the economic consequences for Hofer of being excluded from the community's assets are obviously severe, both the normative and the (potentially) economic consequences of his challenge for the rest of the community are equally stark. Hofer's claim would have converted a communal property system into one of deferred individual ownership—a very different regime. A finding in his favour would change the basis on which the remaining members of the community are bound to each other,[13] for a permanent commitment to communal ownership would no longer be possible. Under these circumstances, the invocation of public policy would amount to a finding that this communal property regime was one that no reasonable person could have agreed to and would thereby stigmatize as irrational the rest of the community. This seems too harsh a judgment to make about the Hutterian way of life, and the Supreme Court was not willing to make it. In other words, tying one's future this closely to others' may not be to everyone's liking and may impose some hardship, but it is not repugnant to morality.

There is, in principle, a third alternative, which illuminates the fairness concerns in such cases. Had the Hutterites had a practice of making a nominal payment to departing members—not based on any calculation of the value of their contribution to the assets, but merely to prevent destitution[14]—Hofer's claim could have been partially met without undermining the communal property regime for the rest of the community. However, such a resolution is not available to the courts. Litigation frequently has a winner-take-all quality: either the communal property regime is valid, in which case Hofer takes nothing, or it is invalid, in which case he is entitled to a full valuation of his contribution. The courts often cannot 'split the difference' between litigants. In this respect, legislative intervention requiring some provision for departing members might seem an attractive solution. But is it? In the modern welfare state, it is not true that someone in Hofer's position is left destitute—the state has various income support programs that could have been made available to him. These pro-

grams are paid for out of general tax revenues, to which the Hutterites contribute just as any other productive members of society do. In other words, one might argue that the Hutterites could fairly consider the welfare schemes that their taxes support to be adequate contribution to the relief of Hofer's urgent need in the aftermath of his expulsion. Given that the Hutterites are not heavy users of publicly funded state services in general, their tax dollars may be considered to cover their responsibility to departing members.

A second use of facilitative legal instruments occurs in the employment context. Disputes arising out of the dismissal of teachers from religious schools for failure to conform to religious standards illustrate the connection between conformity with substantive internal norms and access to employment benefits.[15] Operating a denominational school involves providing an atmosphere for students that is consistent with the fundamental convictions of the religious community. A teacher who openly defies important norms cannot contribute to the ethos the school is trying to create. To take account of this cultural context, the courts have decided that, at common law, the open-ended concept of 'just cause for dismissal' includes dismissal for denominational cause, thus giving religious schools a power that public schools lack to police the conformity of teachers with important aspects of religious practice. The courts have, in effect, made conformity to important religious teachings an implied term of the contract of employment.[16] From the internal point of view, agreement to such a term is the price of participation in this community endeavour. To hold otherwise is effectively to deny to the school the ability to control the educational environment and therefore to impair the ability to ensure socialization into the dominant conception of the community's values. If a teacher cannot be dismissed for violating religious precepts, a case might be made that the school cannot impose employment conditions that amount to constructive dismissal. Such a finding might, in turn, impair the extent to which the school can even publicly register its disapproval of the teacher's behaviour, if to do so would undermine the teacher's authority in the classroom and make it difficult for her to carry on in the job. As in the expulsion cases, a teacher's success in keeping her job on her terms would change the basis on which other members of the community can associate with each other. It would change the environment of the school from one in which certain behaviour is openly disapproved to one in which it is tolerated.

This is not to deny the severity of the consequences for the teacher who is dismissed, but it can hardly be argued that the teacher's reasonable expectations have been violated if she has been schooled in the requirements of her own religion and alerted to the requirements of the job. The teacher may ardently wish for a change of religious policy on a particular issue; may even sincerely believe that the church and school misunderstand the religion's own traditions. Nevertheless, the law cannot be used as a means of forcing such a change in understanding without implying that the effort to provide a particular educational environment is morally repugnant. In determining the limits of just cause for dismissal, the question ought to be whether it is unreasonable to seek and agree to religious conformity as a term of employment,

given the nature of the denominational school enterprise. This is not to say that there are no conditions of employment that would fail this test, but its limits have not yet been tested very far. Cases so far have mostly involved teacher violation of religious rules about marriage; the courts have not been willing to declare the desire to teach—by word and by deed—lifelong monogamy as the only sanctioned family form to be contrary to morality and natural justice.

The Scope of Cultural Autonomy: A Legal Tool Kit

These examples also show that cultural autonomy can vary in scope, its realm defined for each group by the variety of legal mechanisms that construct it. Alternatively put, self-government can be constructed in various degrees and through other means than the formal delegation of full legislative authority—either through a federal structure or through the recognition of a relatively comprehensive third order of government, as with Aboriginal self-government initiatives. Less comprehensive means include decision-making structures with limited jurisdiction as well as adaptations to statutory regimes and common law rights. This may be the form of self-government best suited to groups who hold a world view that differs from that of the majority in a significant but relatively narrow manner. The Hutterites, for example, have achieved a form of self-government through a particular form of property ownership. As long as their adherence to the principle of communal property is respected, they can live according to their own lights in most important (to them) respects. This depiction of communal property as a form of self-government should sound familiar, since individual property ownership has long been understood as a means of autonomously ordering an individual's life.

Sometimes, however, a claim will be made to complementary accommodations in other spheres of law. Take, for example, the membership dispute in *Lakeside Colony of Hutterian Brethren v. Hofer et al.*[17] Here, instead of contesting the consequences of loss of membership, an expelled person challenged the validity of his expulsion. The case turned not on the substantive criteria used to determine membership, but on the court's assessment of the colony's procedures. Generally, a voluntary association may adopt any procedures it sees fit, subject to the requirements of natural justice. In *Lakeside Colony*, a member named Hofer (a different Hofer) was expelled for disobedience. At a meeting called to discuss his disobedience, Hofer behaved disruptively and was asked to leave. In his absence, the others decided to impose a punishment of mild shunning, requiring him to eat and worship apart from the others for a period. When called back to the meeting, Hofer refused to accept punishment; he was then told that such defiance constituted self-expulsion. A month later, when Hofer had not left the colony or turned over the assets he controlled, the colony sought an order requiring him to vacate and relinquish these assets. In response, Hofer argued that his expulsion was invalid because he had not been given proper notice of the penalty to be imposed and an opportunity to defend himself.

From the colony's point of view, the social structure of Hutterite colonies is grounded on a very strict code of conduct that requires a high degree of obedience to the decisions of the officials of the colony. Given the small size of these communities and the close interaction of all members with each other and with officials, Hofer must have understood the consequences of his disobedience. Lacking the means to enforce punishment through the use of force, the colony could only expel the recalcitrant member and seek his ejection from the colony's land through the courts. The colony was in effect seeking to have natural justice interpreted in accordance with Hutterian social circumstances. Standard notice provisions may make sense in communities without the intimacy of Hutterite colonies, but in a close-knit society they impose an unnecessary formality on the community. The Supreme Court refused this accommodation in a decision that might be argued to foster a kind of 'creeping legalism'[18] at odds with the way of life of the Hutterites. In this case, the cost to the community may not seem particularly high (the colony did ultimately expel Hofer, this time following the court's suggestions). But it does not seem unreasonable for the Hutterites to seek recognition for their internal procedures that complements legal recognition of their right to expel the determinedly disobedient.

In order to provide the freedom to live according to distinctive norms, it will often be necessary to piece together accommodations in a number of areas of law. For example, Roman Catholics, while not seeking the degree of separation from the rest of society pursued by the Hutterites, nevertheless have sought various accommodations in the realm of education. Some denominational school rights have been part of the Canadian constitutional framework since 1867.[19] In Ontario, they guarantee the right to a Catholic school system at public expense. It has become established that this right includes the right to a separate administrative structure, so that decisions about a wide variety of issues can be made by members of the community. Until recently, separate school boards also levied taxes on the supporters of the system to fund these schools.[20] Such institutional autonomy is feasible in part because of the size of the Catholic population, which makes it relatively easy to gather sufficient numbers of families together regionally to form school districts. This structure constitutes a limited form of self-government for Catholics—limited because they have not been given authority to make law with respect to every aspect of life within their community. Nor have they sought such power. For the most part they are content to intermix with the rest of the population and to be governed by rules of general application. Those norms and practices in which Catholics do differ from others fall mainly within the private realm and therefore into the category of behaviour that the state does not seek, and may not be constitutionally allowed, to regulate. To protect these differences, they do not need comprehensive independent formal law-making authority. But they do value being able to run their own school system so that their children are thoroughly socialized in Catholic values. Effective control requires a somewhat independent governance structure for denominational schools.

The issue of employee discipline in denominational schools fits into this picture as a further aspect of the recognition of communal educational autonomy. In dealing with constitutionally protected schools, the courts have recognized that constitutional status must carry with it a right to fire or discipline teachers for serious departures from denominational standards. As we have seen, they have created the concept of 'denominational cause' as a variant on the common-law concept of 'just cause' for dismissal. The later enactment of anti-discrimination laws threatened to reduce the autonomy that denominational schools had achieved through adaptation of the common law by introducing new statutory restrictions on freedom of contract. The common law provided no protection against discrimination by an employer. Employers were free to hire whomever they chose and to dismiss employees for any reason, subject to notice requirements. Human rights codes now generally prohibit discriminatory hiring and firing. But even this recalibration of the rights and duties of employers and employees has recognized the autonomy needs of religious schools. The Ontario code includes an explicit exemption from the prohibition on certain forms of discrimination for various organizations, including schools serving a particular religious community, provided that the criterion relied on is a '*bona fide* qualification because of the nature of the employment'.[21] The legislature has thus recognized that the integrity of a separate school system may require the freedom to make employment decisions that would be discriminatory were they made in another context.

The autonomy accorded to religious groups[22] in the education context, then, is achieved through mechanisms that range from independent, education-specific governance structures, to interpretation of common law rights to adapt them to the normative structure of the group, to exemptions from legislative initiatives regulating the employment relationship. Some such package of legal accommodations will need to be crafted for each cultural community seeking to protect its practices from the preferred ways instantiated in statute or the common law. The package will look different for each community, since each differs in the ways in which its practices vary from the mainstream and the scope of those differences.

CONCLUSION

This brief excursion into some common law and statutory debates about the accommodation of cultural difference has been designed to illustrate the fluid and multifaceted nature of the legal construction of cultural autonomy. Since almost any area of law could either contribute to or detract from cultural autonomy, legal actors must be constantly ready to consider whether, in a given dispute, the law should take cognizance of or even defer to the competing norm of a minority community. The only legal test that can be formulated is that cultural autonomy should be respected unless its exercise in a particular case is repugnant to justice. Judges ought not to regard this as a licence to invalidate every practice that does not conform to majority standards; to do so would be to confine culture to the wholly informal realm of conscience and gentlemen's agreements. Instead, the repugnancy proviso should be regarded as setting a seriousness threshold: only if a practice is sufficiently unjust to cross this threshold should the law intervene. The threshold cannot be described with any precision. It will have to be defined over time in the course of considering concrete disputes. Nevertheless, conceiving of the rule as involving this sort of threshold should encourage judges to take seriously the normative life of the cultural community in question, and to temper the tendency to fall back on mainstream perspectives.

Notes

I am grateful to the Wright Foundation, University of Toronto, for research funding that enabled me to begin thinking about these issues, and to David Halporn for valuable research assistance.

1. See, for example, the excellent taxonomy of Jacob Levy, 'Classifying Cultural Rights', in *Ethnicity and Group Rights*, ed. Will Kymlicka and Ian Shapiro (New York: New York University Press, 1997). Although Levy worries that his list may be too long, I would argue that it is better to err on this side rather than to foreclose developments in our thinking by deploying rigid categories to describe the sorts of things that count as cultural rights.
2. Denise G. Réaume, 'Justice Between Cultures: Autonomy and the Protection of Cultural Affiliation', *University of British Columbia Law Review* 29, 1 (1995), 131–2.
3. See Kymlicka's analysis of the self-government rights of national minorities, by contrast with which other subnational groups can claim only polyethnic rights. Will Kymlicka, *Multicultural Citizenship* (Oxford: Clarendon Press, 1994), 27–31.
4. In religious communities these rules will include articles of faith—propositions the truth of which must be accepted.
5. Kymlicka, *Multicultural Citizenship*, 35–44.
6. Kymlicka sometimes seems to acknowledge this in identifying as his concern internal restrictions that violate 'basic political and civil liberties'; ibid., 36. If this is meant to limit the class of internal restrictions that is impermissible, we need a clearer account of the dividing line between basic rights violations and the mere imposition of adverse consequences. Kymlicka's division is not very helpful, since as examples of the unacceptable he often offers very serious rights violations, while his examples of minority practices that should be accommodated rely on practices that are utterly inoffensive (such a wearing turbans). Missing is any detailed discussion of the in-between category. 
7. Denise G. Réaume, 'Legal Enforcement of the Norms of Social Groups: Techniques and Principles', in *Citizenship, Diversity and Pluralism: Canadian and Comparative Perspectives*, ed. Alan Cairns, John Courtney, David Smith, Peter Mackinnon, and Hans Michelman (Montreal and Kingston: McGill-Queen's Univesity Press, 1999).
8. J.N. Matson, 'The Common Law Abroad: English and Indigenous Law in the British Commonwealth', *International Comparative Law Quarterly* 42 (1993), 753.
9. Ayelet Shachar, 'Group Identity and Women's Rights in Family Law: The Perils of Multicultural Accommodation', *Journal of Political Philosophy* 6 (1998), 285.
10. Denise G. Réaume, 'Common Law Constructions of Group Autonomy: A Case Study', in *Ethnicity and Group Rights*, ed. Will Kymlicka and Ian Shapiro (New York: New York University Press, 1997).
11. Lon L. Fuller, 'Two Principles of Human Association', *The Principles of Social Order: Selected Essays of Lon L. Fuller*, ed. Kenneth I. Winston (Durham, NC: Duke University Press, 1981), 85.
12. *Hofer v. Hofer* (1970), 13 D.L.R. (3d) 1 (S.C.C.).
13. Ryan Rempel, 'Anabaptist Relations with the State: Forms for the Coexistence of

Sovereignties', LL.M. dissertation, University of Toronto, 1998, 53–4; Carol Weisbrod, *The Boundaries of Utopia* (New York: Pantheon Books, 1980).

14. According to Weisbrod, this was a fairly common, although discretionary, practice in nineteenth-century utopian societies.
15. *Re Essex County Roman Catholic School Board and Porter* (1978), 89 D.L.R. (3d) 445 (Ont. C.A.); *Caldwell v. Stuart* (1984), 15 D.L.R. (4th) 1 (S.C.C.); *Re Daly et al. and Attorney General of Ontario* (1997), 38 O.R. (3d) 37 (Ont. Ct. Gen.Div.) This issue has arisen both in disputes at common law, constructed exclusively in contract, and more recently in disputes under human rights codes.
16. *Daly*, ibid.
17. (1992), 97 D.L.R. (4th) 17 (S.C.C.) The following description is a simplified version of a very complex fact situation. In simplifying, I have tried not to distort the legal and moral issues. For a more extensive discussion of the case see Réaume, 'Legal Enforcement of the Norms of Social Groups: Techniques and Principles'.
18. Fuller, 'Two Principles', 79.
19. *Constitution Act, 1867*, s. 93.
20. This right to levy taxes was recently removed by the Ontario government in its centralization of the education system. *Education Quality Improvement Act*, S.O. 1997, c. 31, s. 257.106. This removal has been challenged, unsuccessfully so far, as a violation of s. 93 of the Constitution Act, 1867: *Ontario English Catholic Teachers' Association v. Ontario (Attorney General)* [1999] O.J. No. 1358 (Ont. C.A.) (Q.L.).
21. *Ontario Human Rights Code*, R.S.O. 1990, c. H.19, s. 24(a).
22. Although only Catholic schools enjoy the widest measure of autonomy, including separate governance structures funded publicly (and only in some provinces), any religious school can take advantage of the concept of denominational cause or the exemption from the prohibition on discrimination; *Garrod v. Rhema Christian School* (1992), 15 C.H.R.R.D./477 C.H.R.R.D.; *Parks v. Christian Horizons* (1992), 16 C.H.R.R.D./40.

What Not to Do About Hate Speech: An Argument Against Censorship

Stephen L. Newman

One problem I have with legislation on hate propaganda is that it treats hatred as an anomalous phenomenon—as though it were some vile, unexpected thing that crawled out from under a rock—when in fact virtually all political communities are rife with hatreds, large and small. To paraphrase Henry Adams, politics often reveals itself to consist of nothing more substantial than the systematic organization of hatreds.[1] In a mature democracy like Canada, however, these dislikes, no matter how strongly felt, are normally expressed within the rules of the political game. Rhetorically, political antagonists may pledge a battle to the death; but they, their followers, and the general public understand that the terms of engagement will be limited to verbal jousts. Rarely will their animosities carry even the most hardened political enemies beyond the realm of personal vituperation. It helps matters, of course, that politics in the mature democracies tends to be organized largely around economic rather than social or religious issues. Compromise seems easier, even with one's enemies, when it comes to dividing the pie (especially when the pie is always growing).[2] Still, old hatreds grounded in, say, regional, ethnic, or linguistic differences may emerge from the shadows quickly enough should economic issues be seen as having a high symbolic content. The political parties that inspired Adams's comment about the systematic organization of hatreds warred chiefly over the federal tariff, but continually waved 'the bloody shirt of rebellion' in the face of the American electorate for nearly half a century as a means of channelling deep-seated regional animosities going back to the Civil War. Hatred persists in democratic politics because a common citizenship cannot magically turn enemies into friends and because political elites often benefit from the manipulation of hostile emotions.

It goes without saying that hatred is dangerous. We rightly fear that it may break out of the constraints imposed by the normal rules of politics. That is why in most democratic states norms of civility are strictly enforced on the floor of the legislature, even if they do not prevail in the wider public discourse. Legislation targeting hate propaganda does not seek to do away with all incivility. Rather, it singles out speech intended to promote hatred of an identifiable ethnic, racial, or religious group. In effect, it attempts to segregate particular forms of hatred and make public expression of these hatreds (but these only) impermissible. One rationale for this proscription tends to focus on the special vulnerability of the groups against whom hate speech is directed. A second rationale addresses the fragility of multi-ethnic, multicultural societies. I think it makes sense to treat these as prudential rather than moral arguments. *If* it is the case that minority ethnic, racial, or religious groups are in serious threat of harm, and/or *if* the stability of society is seriously jeopardized by inter-group animosities, *then* it seems to me to make good sense to ban hate speech calculated to bring about pogroms or civil war. But if the threat to minority groups is remote and the society is stable, I would question the need for laws proscribing hate speech. We may prefer that citizens always regard one another with warm feelings of solidarity; nonetheless, Canadian as well as American history teaches that a healthy democracy can survive considerable discord so long as most everyone agrees to abide by the rule of law.

To say that all multi-ethnic, multicultural societies will be better off for having muzzled hate propaganda strikes me as an over-broad generalization. It seems more likely that some will be better off while others will receive no tangible benefit *and might incur some real harms*. The more factionalized the society and the higher the levels of inter-group hostility, the more reasonable it will be to censor hate speech in an effort to dampen conflict. But where tolerance, even a grudging tolerance, is the norm, and the likelihood of inter-group violence is low, it seems to me that the introduction of a ban on hate speech is as likely to present an occasion for conflict as it is to preserve the calm of society. My assumption here is that genuine dislike and distrust of at least some other groups within the society, if not full-blown hatred of them, will commonly be found in multi-ethnic, multicultural societies as an inescapable feature of each group's identity.[3] By proscribing expressions of this dislike, the state risks politicizing ethnocultural identity and creating a divisive political issue where none existed before.[4] Moreover, there is always a danger inherent in expanding the power of the state to regulate speech that the legislation will go too far, interfering with the robust exchange of views that we want and expect of democratic debate.[5] Where the risk of instability is low, therefore, our legitimate concern to preserve freedom of expression ought to override our desire to limit the harm (real or potential) to society represented by hate speech.

The special vulnerability of minority groups presents a more difficult problem, in my view. I think a case could be made that, as a matter of political morality, hate speech targeting minority ethnic, racial, or religious groups should be proscribed. At the core of the argument would lie the familiar (liberal) claim that all citizens are entitled to equal concern and respect. It would only need to be shown that the members of vulnerable minority groups are deprived of their equality rights by the creation of an atmosphere of hostility fostered by hate speech. That the threat of physical harm is remote—the haters may be known to be few in number and not powerful—is irrelevant to this argument. The fact that the targeted groups are perceived to be vulnerable, both by themselves and by others, creates a presumption of significant harm in the mere fact of hate propaganda. Who is to say that hateful words will not spark hateful deeds, if not today then perhaps tomorrow or the day after that? Our concern with equality would appear to dictate that it is fundamentally unjust to make the members of minority groups live with this sword hanging over them.[6]

My difficulty with this line of reasoning is that the distinction it insists upon making between minority victims of hate speech and majority victims is ultimately untenable. Hate speech, by its very nature, is threatening, and *all* victims of hate speech have reason to fear the potential for violence that it represents. Given that the historical record in many places is one in which social prejudice has been linked with overt acts of discrimination and political oppression, it is understandable that minority groups would display a particularly strong aversion to ethnic or racial slurs and other expressions of hatred directed towards the group. Building on this point, some legal scholars in the United States, notably those associated with critical race theory, argue that hate speech places a special burden on minority groups because it forms part of a nexus of institutionalized racism and sexism. On their understanding, hate speech is itself a form of violence against which the targeted minorities are entitled to protection by the state.[7] Mari Matsuda, for one, attempts to make the case for this position by recounting incidents of racist speech, presenting her narratives of the victims' pain as evidence of the real harm done by 'assaultive words'.[8] At most, however, her stories serve only to explain the heightened sensitivity of historically oppressed groups to continuing expressions of prejudice; though profoundly disturbing, her narratives do not establish an equivalence between the psychological effects of hate speech and acts of violence. Moreover, her concern with institutionalized racism causes her to neglect or minimize the significance of hate speech for the rest of the population when the force of her own narratives suggests that living in the presence of hatred is cause for insecurity whatever the status of the societal group to which one belongs.[9]

If we grant that the effects of hate speech are indiscriminate, as I believe they are, then hateful utterances against persons from majority groups will seem no less of an affront to equality rights than hate speech directed towards minorities. As always, the context in which the offensive words are spoken will make a huge difference in terms of their impact upon the victim; feelings of personal vulnerability will increase or decrease with the circumstances, as will the victim's assessment of the harm presented. In some cases, majority status may be enough to immunize the victim against the effects of hate speech.[10] But there is no reason to assume that this will always be so for all members of the 'majority', especially given that what passes for the majority in most analyses undertaken for these purposes typically comprises multiple group identities, each with its own sense of vulnerability. In short, the moral argument from equality favouring legislation against hate propaganda leads us back to the notion of banning *all* instances of hate speech. But this, as I have already argued, is impractical; given the dynamics of group identity, you cannot legislate perfect civility and complete tolerance in a multi-ethnic, multicultural society. Absent a high probability of violence, I conclude that our concern for equality offers no more of a justification for banning hate speech than does our interest in social stability.[11]

The prospect of violence changes the equation, however. No society can rationally value free speech above its own survival; nor can a legitimate concern with preserving free expression for the purposes of democratic debate justify overlooking a real and present danger to the lives and property of one's fellow citizens. There are places in the world today, notably in the fledgling democracies of Eastern Europe, Asia, and Africa, where ethnic, racial, and religious divisions are so severe as to put into question their very coherence as unified political entities. Unless and until their democracies mature, there seems little possibility that local hatreds can be systematically organized through the normal channels of electoral politics. Under these circumstances, a ban on hate speech makes eminent good sense from the prudential point of view. So too, I would argue, did the ban on Nazi hate propaganda in Germany after the Second World War; seen in historical context, it was probably necessary to the successful democratization of the country. But I find myself wondering if the ban is still necessary today, given Germany's considerable experience as a free and democratic nation.[12] As for the situation in Canada, I see no reason why hate propaganda deserves to be viewed as presenting the level of threat that would justify censorship. Yet, as Joseph Magnet reports, 'Canada has more hate propaganda legislation than any other country in the world'; and, according to one recent study, fully 74 per cent of Canadians favour laws prohibiting speech and writing that promotes hatred towards a particular group.[13]

In a recent article Samuel LaSelva argues that Canadian attitudes reflect the facts of Canadian pluralism, and that the nature of pluralism in Canada may provide a coherent rationale for the censorship of hate speech. In brief, LaSelva argues that societal endorsement of multiculturalism brings into existence distinctive categories of harm and offensiveness that do not exist in a society that conceives of itself as a 'melting pot', like the United States. Thus, because Canada regards itself as a multicultural society of a certain sort, it assumes a moral obligation to protect the dignity of identifiable ethnic, racial, religious, and linguistic groups. LaSelva's perspective incorporates the 'communitarian' notion that group membership is (or under certain circumstances can be) a fundamental political good, providing individuals with both a core sense of personal identity and a cultural matrix defining the parameters of a worthwhile way of life. From this it follows that affirming the dignity of group membership is part and parcel of affirming the equality of all citizens and perhaps even a necessary component of social justice.[14] Recognizing that strong group identities will also engender inter-group antipathies, LaSelva entertains a justification of censorship rooted in Canada's peculiar form of pluralism; hate speech may justly be censored insofar as it affronts the value all Canadians assign to group membership and, at the same time, threatens to disturb the comity among groups required to make Canadian pluralism succeed.[15]

It seems to me that this line of argument, although useful in distinguishing between the Canadian and American cases, makes no deep inroads on the anti-censorship position I have laid out here. As before, the argument for censorship remains contingent and circumstantial: surely, some threshold must be passed before the level or intensity of hate propaganda poses a serious threat to the dignity or the security of discrete social groups. Likewise, unless one assumes that mutual tolerance on the part of groups is wholly superficial, the comity of a large, pluralistic society is not likely to be disturbed by the ravings of a relatively small number of hate-mongers. The majority of persons may find hate speech distasteful (one hopes that they do); but this hardly justifies employing the coercive power of the state to enforce public morality. In a pluralistic society where the accommodation of difference has long been a settled principle of political life, as in Canada, hate propaganda seems to me less of an alarming political evil than an instance of appallingly bad manners.[16] The promotion of multicultural values within civil society, by both public and private entities, would seem a far more effective response without encroaching on the right of free expression. In short, I hold that in a mature democracy like Canada, the appropriate answer to hate propaganda is more speech, not less.

I have argued that we are not likely to rid our society of hatred; but that does not mean we should be indifferent toward it. Democracy is founded on trust: trust that our elected leaders will not abuse their powers of office; trust that our fellow citizens will observe the rules of the political game, even when we find ourselves divided over issues of fundamental importance. Deep and abiding hatred makes trust impossible. So too, however, does fear of those who hate. What makes democracy workable in spite of our differences is tolerance, not acceptance. Pluralism succeeds because we have learned to put up with those who disagree with us over the most important things; we have learned to live side by side with those who are not like us, whose skin is another colour, who worship different gods, speak different languages, and so on. We do not always respect these others and sometimes—perhaps more often than we let on—we do not like them; nor do they necessarily like and respect us. But we all respect each other's political rights, and that is the slender commonality on which democratic trust is built in a pluralistic society. It is the means by which we are able to move beyond Henry Adams's sardonic conception of politics as the systematic organization of hatreds to embrace a larger conception of the nation as a community of interests. In a multi-ethnic, multicultural 'settler' society like Canada, politics is the bridge that groups cross to find a common identity capable of binding the whole together. While it is not entirely unreasonable to fear that hate speech might find a receptive audience (even a healthy democracy can be corrupted), the battle for hearts and minds will not be won through censorship. Those who would combat the spread of hatred by silencing hate speech betray their own distrust of democracy. By treating hate like a contagion, they slight the moral and intellectual capacities of others. We should not allow our fear of those who hate to endanger our trust in democracy by subverting our faith in the practical intelligence and the good will of our fellow citizens.[17]

Some proponents of censorship have argued that hate speech does not deserve legal protection because it fails to make any positive contribution to democratic debate.[18] Indeed, because it is more like a verbal slap in the face than an honest attempt to impart information or articulate a political position, hate speech is characterized by these critics as an impediment to fruitful dialogue. Moreover, in a final irony, because the victims of hate speech may be intimidated or even silenced by their fear of the hate-mongers, tolerating hate speech is said to abridge rather than to protect the right of free speech.[19] On this account, a true democratic conversation requires that hate speech be suppressed.

Again, the case for censorship is not without merit: even in stable societies where the potential for violence is low, the psychological harm suffered by victims of hate speech is real and their discomfort deserves the consideration of their fellow citizens. Nonetheless, I would distinguish between the dispositional consequences of hurtful words and silencing brought about by physical intimidation or legal restraints. While our interest in liberty requires protection against the latter, I do not see how the law can protect persons against the former without sacrificing freedom of expression. That words have consequences is simply an inescapable cost that all who cherish free speech must bear.[20] I further submit that hate-mongers can end up playing a salutary role in the democratic conversation in spite of themselves, by inspiring the rest of us to speak out against hatred. The idea is not so much to get the haters to see the error of their ways as to expose them for what they are so that others will not be misled.[21] To those who would censor hate speech in the name of democracy I say we should meet hate propaganda with truth, not censorship, education, not legal penalties, and show the courage of our democratic convictions.

Notes

I thank Margaret Moore and Ian Greene for their comments and suggestions.

1. Henry Adams, *The Education of Henry Adams* (New York: Modern Library, 1931), 7.
2. Cf. Robert Dahl, *On Democracy* (New Haven and London: Yale University Press, 1998), 166-9.
3. Joseph Raz writes that 'One of the difficulties in making multiculturalism politically acceptable stems from the enmity between members of different cultural groups.' See Raz, *Ethics in the Public Domain* (Oxford: Clarendon Press, 1994): 163, quoted in Samuel LaSelva, 'Pluralism and Hate: Freedom, Censorship, and the Canadian Identity', in *Interpreting Censorship in Canada*, ed. Klaus Petersen and Allan Hutchinson (Toronto: University of Toronto Press, 1999), 51. LaSelva goes on to observe that 'Such enmity is not simply due to ignorance *but is endemic to multiculturalism and other forms of value pluralism*' [emphasis added].
4. Timothy C. Shiell argues that something like this happened on American college and university campuses as a result of the introduction of campus speech codes. See *Campus Hate Speech on Trial* (Lawrence: University of Kansas Press, 1998).
5. LaSelva, in 'Pluralism and Hate: Freedom, Censorship and the Canadian Identity', argues that it is wrong to assume that state regulation of hate speech puts us on a slippery slope leading inevitably toward a broader censorship. He treats censorship as one more form of state regulation, no different in principle from the power to tax, noting that 'even if it is granted that over-regulation is more likely and more detrimental in the area of speech than in other areas, it does not follow that the solution is to prohibit regulation altogether'

(p. 50). While I find LaSelva's argument persuasive for some forms of speech (e.g., libel or commercial speech) where the dangers of over-regulation seem tolerable, I think he errs in extending his argument to political speech. If the state over-regulates commercial speech, say, we can still seek redress by exercising our freedom of political expression. But if the state over-regulates political speech, we might very well lose the capacity to express our opposition to its policies.

6. I attribute reasoning along these lines to at least one strand of Catherine MacKinnon's argument against pornography, treating it as a form of hate speech that induces acts of violence against women. See *Only Words* (Cambridge, Mass.: Harvard University Press, 1993). Similarly, Mari J. Matsuda argues that the targets of racist hate speech correctly perceive the threat of violence in racist slurs. See her 'Public Response to Racist Speech: Considering the Victim's Story', in Mari J. Matsuda, Charles R. Lawrence III, Richard Delgado, and Kimberle Williams Crenshaw, *Words That Wound: Critical Race Theory, Assaultive Speech and the First Amendment* (Boulder, Col.: Westview Press, 1993). In the Canadian context, similar fears of violence and overt acts of discrimination linked to hate speech are expressed by L.W. Sumner, 'Hate Propaganda and Charter Rights', in *Free Expression: Essays in Law and Philosophy*, ed. W.J. Waluchow (Oxford: Clarendon Press, 1994), 170–1.

7. On the genesis of critical race theory and an overview of its approach to free expression, see the introduction to *Words that Wound*. For a similar treatment of hate speech as a form of violence contributing to the subordination of women and racial minorities, see MacKinnon, *Only Words*. Samuel Walker places the arguments advanced by the critical race theorists and feminists like MacKinnon in historical context in *Hate Speech: The History of an American Controversy* (Lincoln: University of Nebraska Press, 1994), 136–43.

8. Matsuda, 'Public Response to Hate Speech', 17–22.

9. Matsuda's concern with institutionalized racism leads her to define hate speech in an exceptionally broad way. She treats 'gutter racism' (explicit racial epithets), 'covert' or 'sanitized' racist comments, and even complaints of 'reverse discrimination' as virtual equivalents. 'From the victim's perspective, all of these implements inflict wounds, wounds that are neither random nor isolated'; Matsuda, 'Public Response to Racist Speech', 23–4. Clearly her conceptualization of racist speech opens the way to the censorship of considerably more than just hate propaganda, though Matsuda's specific proposals are narrowly tailored to accommodate (as much as possible) First Amendment jurisprudence. Her treatment of racist speech within the context of institutionalized racism also serves to reveal the degree to which, at least in some quarters, the campaign against hate speech fronts for a much broader political agenda. On this point, see Walker, *Hate Speech*, chap. 7.

10. Matsuda, 'Public Response to Racist Speech', 39.

11. It may be objected that I over-emphasize the effects of hate speech on the psychic well-being of individuals and underplay its significance as a form of oppression directed against persons as members of targeted groups. The critical race theorists I have cited here attempt to establish just such a connection between hate speech and the suffering of historically oppressed racial minorities. In their account, what merits censorship are solely expressions of hatred that target the oppressed. But as Matsuda's desperate attempt to parse the phrase 'Zionism is racism' makes clear, distinguishing the oppressors from the oppressed is not quite so easily done. (See her 'Public Response to Racist Speech', p. 40.) It seems to me that one of the inescapable facts of life in virtually any imaginable multi-ethnic, multicultural society will be an abundance of historical grievances remembering past instances of oppression and nursing a sense of injustice over their legacy in the present. I do not see how

the state can justly sort out these rival claims, much less police the speech of 'oppressors' while tolerating the same sort of offensive (and hurtful) speech on the part of the 'oppressed'.

12. Cf. Ronald Dworkin, *Freedom's Law: The Moral Reading of the American Constitution* (Cambridge, Mass.: Harvard University Press, 1996), 223–6.
13. Joseph Magnet, 'Hate Propaganda in Canada', in *Free Expression,* ed. W.J. Waluchow (Oxford: Clarendon Press, 1994), 229; Paul Sniderman, Joseph F. Fletcher, Peter H. Russell, and Philip E. Tetlock, *The Clash of Rights* (New Haven: Yale University Press, 1996), 64. Curiously, there have been relatively few prosecutions of hate speech under Canadian law. This suggests that the real importance of the laws proscribing hate propaganda is their symbolic affirmation of Canadian multiculturalism.
14. Cf. Iris Marion Young, *Justice and the Politics of Difference* (Princeton: Princeton University Press, 1990). Young, like the critical race theorists, focuses almost exclusively on the importance of affirming the dignity of marginalized or exploited groups as a means of counteracting centuries-old forms of oppression. And yet, if we are to take seriously the view that group identities are important to people, the logic of her position would suggest that *all* instances of hate speech deserve to be censored.
15. Samuel V. LaSelva, 'Pluralism and Hate: Freedom, Censorship, and the Canadian Identity'.
16. This comment is not intended to trivialize the effects of hate speech on its victims; I only mean to put in perspective the level of threat posed by such speech to the stability and vitality of a healthy democracy.
17. To be clear, I am suggesting that democratic politics has an educative effect; through political co-operation rival and perhaps antagonistic groups learn to trust one another and may discover that they have interests and even values (if only political values) in common.
18. See, for example, Cass R. Sunstein, *Democracy and the Problem of Free Speech* (New York: Free Press, 1993), 154; also Charles R. Lawrence, 'If He Holler Let Him Go: Regulating Racist Speech on Campus', in *Words that Wound*, 74; and (from a Canadian perspective) Allan C. Hutchinson, *Waiting for Coraf: A Critique of Law and Rights* (Toronto: University of Toronto Press, 1995): 202–6.
19. Owen Fiss, *The Irony of Free Speech* (Cambridge, Mass.: Harvard University Press, 1996), 16-18.
20. Cf. Ronald Dworkin, *Freedom's Law*, 221–2.
21. In this vein, the distinguished French historian Pierre Vidal-Naquet argues that the appropriate response to those who deny the reality of the Holocaust is not to ban their works but to refute their claims. 'In doing so,' he writes, 'we are not placing ourselves on the same ground as our enemy. We do not "debate" him; we demonstrate the mechanisms of his lies and falsifications, which may be methodologically useful for the younger generations.' See *Assassins of Memory: Essays on the Denial of the Holocaust* (New York: Columbia University Press, 1992), 76. But see also David A.J. Richards, *Toleration and the Constitution* (New York and Oxford: Oxford University Press, 1986). Richards justifies tolerance of hate speech as a way of expressing both our commitment to equality and our belief in 'the civilizing community of humane discourse'. He argues that 'we most undercut, as a democratic community of equal respect, substantive ideologies of racial and other inequalities when our principles extend to exponents of such views the dignifying equal respect for their moral

powers as persons. Our practice thus embraces them in the vital, moralizing experience of a community of equal respect that most piercingly displays the nature of its moral community when it respects the conscience of advocates of ideologies at war with equal respect' (p. 192).

Toleration, Canadian-Style: Reflections of a Yankee-Canadian

Melissa S. Williams

If to be Canadian means to be 'not American', as we so often hear in laments over the lack of a distinctive Canadian identity, then what is it to be an American immigrant to Canada? One must be an oxymoron, a hyphenated 'American-not-American'. Perhaps the cognitive dissonance intrinsic in such an identity partially explains why the naturalization rates for immigrants to Canada from the United States are among the lowest for all immigrant groups, and why US immigrants to Canada take longer than any other group to adopt Canadian citizenship. For me, as an American political theorist who spends many of her waking hours thinking about democratic citizenship, taking up permanent residence in Canada logically entailed adopting Canadian citizenship at the earliest possible moment. From that point of view, my integration into the Canadian political community was straightforward. Developing an appreciation for the differences between liberal democratic political culture in the US and in Canada, however, has been a more circuitous process, one that remains incomplete.

The starkest moment of my American incomprehension of Canadian political thought and practice was my first encounter with the so-called 'notwithstanding clause' of the Canadian Charter of Rights and Freedoms.[1] Having no sense at all of the parochialism of my position, I viewed constitutions as providing firm boundaries to the political, defining the fences and hedges between which the hurly-burly of politics may play itself out. Not that constitutional principles are separable from politics, either in their origin or in their application; certainly they should be kept open to revision through political processes. But that, I believed, was the business of extraordinary processes of constitutional amendment, not of ordinary legislatures exercising their ordinary powers. All the more so, I would have thought, in a parliamentary democracy, sadly lacking the protection of trusty checks and balances between legislative and executive powers that secure the American constitutional order from political excesses. Principles are fundamental; political choices can be contingent and based on pragmatic considerations—in short, unprincipled.[2] Americans since Jefferson have been wont to view the truths they perceive as self-evident. It was certainly self-evident to me that the notwithstanding clause, by providing an escape hatch from the requirements of the Constitution, invited an unprincipled political order. Self-evidently, it courted illegitimacy.

The tension between a secure order of fundamental rights, on the one hand, and democratic self-rule, on the other hand, has not yet been resolved on the level of theoretical principle by leading constitutional thinkers. At best, those scholars (among whom Bruce Ackerman stands out as the most influential) articulate the recursive relationship between fundamental rights and democratic sovereignty: constitutional law yields to deep shifts in democratic will during rare but transformative moments in the political culture.[3] During times of 'normal' politics, constitutional fundamentals are supremely untroubled by democratic doubt, and function very well to bind political choices. The difficulty of constitutional amendment means that transformations in fundamental law respond to changes in democratic will only when those changes are profound and persistent, and only after considerable political deliberation. But this American solution, most of the time, effectively resolves the dilemma in favour of fundamental principles (as interpreted by the unelected judiciary) and gives limited scope for democratic revision. Moreover, in the popular American mind, it is the sense of the permanence of the fundamental law that dominates; the tension between this and the doctrine of popular sovereignty is not apparent, and the authority of the Bill of Rights rests implicitly on a residue of faith in natural right.

Constitutional scholars have characterized the notwithstanding clause as Canada's most distinctive contribution to constitutionalism.[4] What makes it distinctive, and Canadian, is that it resolves a deep problem in constitutional theory not by stating a principle, but by instituting a practice. Because a legislative override of the Charter must be renewed every five years, the notwithstanding clause makes an ongoing practice of political deliberation necessary within both the judicial and the legislative branches of government. The Canadian solution thus resolves the problem in practice by refusing to dissolve the tension between fundamental law and democratic rule in theory. Nor does it settle for the *appearance* that it has resolved this tension, as in the American case. In declining to give judges the last word on fundamental rights, it also makes the exercise of democratic power accountable to principle, and persistently so, by requiring the periodic review of legislation that conflicts with Charter rights. In this manner the notwithstanding clause imposes an obligation of deep deliberation over political choices that may conflict with Charter rights.[5] It makes the tension between democratic will and fundamental rights more accessible to citizens, and in doing so, one hopes, may make them more judicious guardians of those rights, conscious of both the risks and the responsibilities of self-government. In the US, by contrast, the revisability of fundamental rights sounds like a heresy to all but elite ears, despite its place in the constitutional system. The notwithstanding clause both expresses and (again, we hope) reinforces the comparative ease with which Canadians live with moral ambiguity and a plurality of values.

Early in my time in Canada, I understood that this is a Burkean society, in which practices unfold through time whose rationality and coherence is only implicit. What guides these practices is not, first and foremost, a concern to respect abstract and universal principles. Rather, at their best, they are driven by a combination of a spirit of humanity and a preoccupation with social stability. As commentators often note, it is the trinity of 'peace, order and good government', not 'life, liberty, and the pursuit of happiness', that fuels the engine of Canadian political practice—for better and for worse, but more often for better, I think. Canadians miss out on the drama and elation of a politics of high principle, but they gain a peaceful, humane, and surprisingly innovative political culture. In such a culture civility takes precedence over moral righteousness; getting along takes precedence over getting it right. The notwithstanding clause is an institution infused with this spirit. It expresses a confidence in Canadians' ability to work out in practice, and through long deliberation, solutions to political problems that can be squared with our commitment to basic individual rights. It conveys a respect for the complexity of political challenges, an acknowledgment that when we seek to reconcile social needs, political wishes, and fundamental principles, we cannot always perceive the solution in advance but must sometimes stumble upon it in the process of debate and institutional experimentation. The notwithstanding clause institutionalizes a practice of muddling through while keeping a steady eye on the principled commitments at stake, and this is what makes it distinctively Canadian. I see a similar propensity for muddling through at work in the Canadian approach to toleration. Making some sense of it theoretically is my project in the remainder of this essay.

My adopted country has a reputation for being a very tolerant society, willing to respond to injustices that have their roots in cultural difference more readily than its neighbour to the south.[6] To take one recent example, American feminists and human rights activists rightly celebrated as a moral milestone the recent American decision to grant asylum to a woman who feared that she would be subjected to ritual female circumcision if she returned to her native Togo.[7] Yet Americans may not be aware that Canada was first to grant asylum on these grounds, two years before the American decision.[8] Indeed, Canadians sometimes seem to invite ridicule or caricature for the extent of their generosity to the marginal in Canadian society. A fugitive from the American criminal justice system, who was wanted for writing a threatening letter to a judge, recently fled to Canada. Before long, the strain of being a fugitive outweighed his fear of prosecution, and he tried to turn himself in to Canadian authorities. They refused to arrest him, and instead offered to help him apply for asylum and for welfare.[9] Somehow it is difficult to imagine that a fugitive from Mexican justice who had found his way into Texas would have been so graciously received by the authorities there.[10]

But occasionally even Canadians draw the line and decide that some practices and activities are intolerable. If we explore the boundaries of Canadian toleration in practice, what we find is that the Canadian approach to toleration, like the Canadian approach to the constitutionalization of rights, leads us to understand Canadian liberalism as being as much a matter of practice as it is one of principle.[11]

Consider three issues that have recently invited Canadian actions or proposals to suppress the practices or activities of ethnic or religious minorities:

Female genital mutilation. Beyond displaying a willingness to grant asylum to women or girls who fear that they will be forced to undergo ritual female circumcision if they are returned to their native countries, both federal and provincial authorities in Canada have taken measures to prevent the practice among immigrants to Canada. Despite some arguments that official action to suppress female circumcision is a form of cultural imperialism, there have been several official declarations of the illegality of the practice, as well as calls for the active prosecution of those who perform it.[12]

Hijab. In recent years several Quebec public authorities have invited controversy by prohibiting girls or women from wearing *hijab* in public institutions.[13] A *hijab* is a headscarf worn by many Muslim women who regard it as an obligatory prescription of Islam. In one widely noted case, a municipal judge in Montreal, apparently relying on rules of practice that prohibit headgear of any kind in the courtroom, expelled a woman from a courtroom for wearing *hijab*.[14] A year later, a 13-year-old student was suspended from her school for wearing *hijab* and told not to return until she conformed with a dress code prohibiting clothing that 'marginalizes' students. The school's principal declared that 'Distinctive clothing like a *hijab* or neo-Nazi regalia could polarize aggression among young people.' Quebec's deputy premier commented: 'Religious freedom, like all others, has its limits. . . . Our role is not simply to allow the exercise of these freedoms but also to establish limits.' An editorial declared, without any apparent sense of irony, that *hijab* 'is a rallying symbol for Muslims in their struggle against the Western satan', and that accepting this symbol contributes 'to our own destruction and that of our values, values of equality and tolerance.' Lorraine Pagé, who heads Quebec's largest federation of teachers' unions, stated that *hijab* expresses 'a well-defined place for women, women whose lives do not completely conform to the perspective of equality that we're looking for.'[15]

Militant Islamic groups. In the spring of 1997 Hani Abdul Rahim al-Sayegh, a Saudi man, was arrested by Canadian authorities. He was later deported to the United States for his alleged involvement in the 1996 terrorist attack in Dhahran, Saudi Arabia, that killed 19 US airmen and injured hundreds of others. A Canadian Security Intelligence Service (CSIS) report alleged that Sayegh was a member of the Saudi branch of the Iranian-funded Hezbollah, an extremist Shiite Muslim movement dedicated to the violent resistance of non-Islamic influences in the Middle East and to the overthrow of Israel. The report further asserted that 'Hezbollah has established an infrastructure in Canada that can assist and support terrorists seeking a safe haven in North America' and that 'Hezbollah members in Canada receive and comply with direction from the Hezbollah leadership hierarchy in Lebanon.'[16] The Sayegh case brought renewed attention to concerns about the activities of Islamic terrorist groups in Canada.[17]

Of course, the deportation of an accused murderer who acknowledges his membership in a terrorist organization is not, in itself, an example of an official decision not to tolerate a cultural minority's beliefs or practices. Yet the Sayegh case does raise questions of toleration because of the links that various commentators have made between Canada's liberal policies of immigration and multiculturalism and the presence of militant groups within Canadian borders. A news article on the presence of Hezbollah organizations in Canada declared, 'While the United States, France and other countries with big ethnic populations also have trouble pursuing suspected terrorists without stereotyping minority groups, Canadians are particularly sensitive about offending immigrants.'[18] In an April 1997 report, CSIS stated that 'Many of the world's terrorist groups have a presence in Canada,' and that 'militant groups use Canada for fund raising, safe haven, and recruiting Canadian citizens in ethnic communities.' It also raised concern that these organizations might be planning terrorist attacks within Canada as well as in other countries.[19] In response to the Sayegh case, the Canadian Jewish Congress requested that the federal immigration minister 'tighten regulations on refugee claims from Iran, Syria and other nations believed to sponsor terrorism.'[20] David Harris, former chief of strategic planning at CSIS, made a direct connection between Canadian multiculturalism and the activities of militant groups. 'The situation in Canada is somewhat confused by the multicultural aspect of Canada,' he said. But he commented further: 'The very fact that you've got a group of people here with the track record for violence that Hezbollah has should be of grave concern to Canadians.'[21]

The fear that an excess of toleration fosters groups that would, if they could, weaken the moral and political order that sustains toleration is a recurrent theme in liberal democracies, and one that often runs just beneath the surface of discussions of Islam in the West. Occasionally one hears the thesis stated very starkly; as the American journalist Steven Emerson put it in a recent speech to the Canadian Club of Toronto:

> [T]oday, the reach of militant Islam is a lot closer than the perceived safety of your television sets. . . . [T]he West is facing a proliferating extremist movement, deliberately hiding under mainstream religious protection in its own backyard. It is an extremist ideological movement that is increasingly anchored in the heart of the West, yet whose values and goals are totally antithetical to Western values of pluralism, separation of church and state, and the unacceptability of terrorism and violence to achieve political goals.[22]

Although Emerson is careful to distinguish the majority of moderate Muslims from the extremists he wishes the news media to expose, he blames a culture of improvident tolerance for extremists' ease of movement in the West: 'It is this blindness, this naiveté, political correctness—call it what you will—that is at the core of a great deception now taking place.'[23] '[T]he incontrovertible evidence shows that these groups have championed the politics of international terrorist leaders and movements while simultaneously pressing the "hate crime" button in American society to intimidate critics of militant Islamic fundamentalism.'[24] Together, these worries suggest the conclusion that Western democracies should take care to avoid policies that enable groups to form enclaves within which they may engage in subversive activities. Canada's generous immigration and multiculturalism policies are often viewed in this light.

If we explore the argumentation that underlies these practical judgments about what Canadians should not tolerate, we find that they blend three conceptually distinct discourses of toleration, each of which has historically had an important place in the theory and practice of liberal toleration: *autonomy*, *equality*, and *peace*. Each provides strong foundations for tolerating and accommodating religious and cultural minorities; each also provides strong reasons for drawing limits to what we are prepared to tolerate, and these limits come to the fore in the cases sketched here.

The debates over whether we should outlaw and criminalize female circumcision take place mostly on the terrain of a discourse of autonomy. Some critics of the practice focus on the fact that it is most often performed on young girls. Not only do these girls often protest vehemently against the act of circumcision, but they are in any case too young to give their informed consent. Either way, they cannot be seen as agents whose autonomy is respected within these rituals. Others argue that even if the practice were available only to women who have passed the legal age of consent, circumcision is so harmful that no rational person could actually consent to it. That some women do consent, in such cases, simply reflects their lack of genuine autonomous agency. To give their consent must reflect their internalization of oppressive norms concerning women's subordination to men and the need to secure their future husbands' exclusive sexual access to them by suppressing their own sexuality.[25]

If autonomy arguments provide strong grounds for refusing to tolerate female circumcision, they also provide some reasons in favour of accommodating it. Some reject as 'false consciousness' arguments the claims that adult women are not exercising autonomy when they make a conscious choice to undergo the practice. This response is certainly a component of the complaint that critiques of the practice constitute a form of cultural imperialism.[26] Will Kymlicka's defence of special recognition for cultural minorities is directly grounded in the principle of autonomy. Kymlicka argues that because we can meaningfully exercise our capacity for free choice only within the context of a secure system of social meanings—that is, a culture—a concern for the principle of autonomy should lead us to protect minority cultures that are under threat. Although Kymlicka does not extend this argument to immigrant cultures, he has been criticized for his unwillingness to do so.[27] Thus his autonomy-based argument for accommodation might be available to women who wish to preserve their cultural identity by participating in the rituals of female circumcision.

As for whether to tolerate *hijab* in public institutions, we find that most of the arguments are articulated in terms of the principle of equality. A principle of difference-blind equality requires that, where reasonable dress codes exist in public institutions, they be applied equally to all. From this perspective, granting exceptions to one group or another is an unjustifiable preference. Others justify restrictions on *hijab* in the name of equality for women: *hijab*, they take it, is an emblem of women's subordination to men and of their exclusion from full participation in the public sphere. Refusing to accommodate *hijab* is therefore equivalent, in the eyes of such critics, to refusing to accommodate women's subordination.

On the other hand, some of the strongest arguments in favour of accommodating *hijab* also arise from a concern for equality. Certainly it is a requirement of public policy in any democratic society that no law should single out a group for discriminatory treatment. Yet even policies that are *prima facie* neutral may sometimes impose disproportionate burdens on some religious or cultural groups. In these cases, a purely negative conception of toleration—a policy of benign neglect, or *laissez faire*—will not be sufficient to secure equality before the law. Where no overriding public purpose can justify the disproportionate impact of public policy on a particular group, an egalitarian defence of toleration requires that we go beyond passive acceptance of a group and take positive action to accommodate its practices. Treating individuals as equals may require giving direct recognition to the groups to which they belong, for to apply a universal standard is sometimes to impose the norms and practices of the dominant groups upon oppressed groups and simply require the latter to conform to the ways of the former.[28] *Hijab* is clearly among the practices that can claim accommodation on these grounds. Current codes of dress, which were defined from the perspective of majority religions, impose a burden on Muslims' participation in public life that other citizens don't have to bear: others don't have to sacrifice their adherence to the requirements of their faith in order to enter a courtroom or a schoolyard.

Charles Taylor's famous essay on the politics of recognition draws another strong connection between equality and group recognition or accommodation.[29] If respect for the equality of persons requires recognition of their authentic cultural identities as well as the protection of their rights as individuals, then there are good reasons for believing that refusal to accommodate a minority's religiously mandated modes of dress constitutes a form of non-recognition or misrecognition that denies them equal standing in the political community.

A concern for peace and social order clearly predominates in discussions of the third issue I sketched above—the possible link between permissive multicultural and immigration policies and the presence of violent insurgent groups in Canada. Toleration is all well and good, up to the point where it renders us vulnerable to attack from groups that do not recognize others' right to toleration. Once these groups become strong enough to threaten others' rights, we have not just a right but an obligation to suppress them. As Hobbes taught us, peace is the precondition of all other human goods, and any regime that tolerates threats to peace is not fulfilling its most basic obligation to the people it governs.

Yet a concern for peace has also provided some of the strongest reasons for toleration and accommodation. Indeed, the received wisdom about the historical origins of liberal toleration locates the practice of toleration neither in autonomy nor in equality but in a desire for peace. Following the Reformation, the story goes, control of the state apparatus passed back and forth between Protestants and Catholics as each group sought to secure its own power through violent suppression of the other. They paid the costs of such intolerance over and over, until finally they happened upon toleration as an alternative. As Michael Walzer sums it up, the form of toleration that emerges out of the religious wars of the sixteenth and seventeenth centuries 'is simply a resigned acceptance of difference for the sake of peace. People kill one another for years and years, and then, mercifully, exhaustion sets in, and we call this toleration.'[30]

In this form, toleration is primarily a negative practice, the product of a decision not to attempt to suppress another group. But a concern for peace can also sustain a more generous account of toleration, one that gives more emphasis to even-handedness than to non-interference. In this respect it resembles the egalitarian defence of toleration and accommodation that acknowledges the ways in which public requirements may contain implicit biases. The peace-based version of this argument is that when a group feels itself to be unjustly burdened, it is much more likely to attempt to subvert the peace. We are all familiar with the slogan 'No justice, no peace!' What is surprising is how long a history this idea has enjoyed in liberal theory. In one passage in the first *Letter Concerning Toleration*, Locke even goes so far as to suggest that the magistrate's failure to treat religious groups even-handedly is the *sole cause* of conspiracies against the state by religious minorities:

> [T]here is *only one thing* which gathers people into seditious commotions, and that is oppression. . . .
>
> Take away the partiality that is used toward them in matters of common right, change the laws, take away the penalties unto which they are subjected, and all things will immediately become safe and peaceable; nay, those that are averse to the religion of the magistrate will think themselves so much the more bound to maintain the peace of the commonwealth as their condition is better in that place than elsewhere; and *all the several separate congregations, like so many guardians of the public peace*, will watch one another, that nothing may be innovated or changed in the form of the government, because they can hope for nothing better than what they already enjoy—that is, an equal condition with their fellow subjects under a just and moderate government.[31]

Against this background, it seems reasonable to expect that members of religious or cultural minorities that are labelled as disloyal, subversive, and terrorist by the state, and are singled out for special scrutiny by police agencies, will be less inclined than others to recognize the legitimacy of the state, and more vulnerable to recruitment into genuinely subversive organizations.

Autonomy, equality, and peace are our strongest reasons for tolerating those with whom we strongly disagree, and they also provide excellent justifications for drawing firm limits to toleration. But these powerful reasons often pull against one another in particular cases. Autonomy might lead us to accommodate a minority culture, but if that culture entrenches a strong internal hierarchy—most often a gendered one—then equality gives us very good reasons to refuse toleration. Peace may be best served by making space for a group's claims; if we deny them, they may feel they have been treated unjustly, and this may encourage them to disrupt social order. Yet accommodation may not square with either autonomy or equality. Perhaps the group does not respect or protect the autonomy of its own members. Perhaps there are other groups with similar claims, whom we have no interest in accommodating because it would be costly to us without serving our interest in peace. In the latter case, a concern for peace stands in tension with one principle of equality: that like cases should be treated alike.

Liberal philosophy does offer us a principle by which to order these three reasons for toleration: it stands them in a hierarchical relationship to one another. Autonomy is clearly the loftiest of the three. Indeed, as Joseph Raz points out, autonomy 'is sometimes thought to be the specifically liberal argument for toleration: the one argument which is not shared by non-liberals'.[32] Autonomy does stand in close proximity to equality, the second pillar of liberal justice, and as such also a moral ground of toleration. In Will Kymlicka's argument for group accommodation, autonomy and equality are particularly close allies. Although it is the principle of autonomy that provides the strongest substantive reasons for protecting the stability of cultures, it is the principle of equality that does the work of justifying *special* protections for national minorities: the accident of being born into a minority culture is not a justifiable reason for being more vulnerable than others to losing the conditions of one's autonomy. But still there is a hierarchy here, and some critics argue that Kymlicka should simply drop the arguments from equality and rest exclusively on the autonomy argument.[33]

However autonomy and equality stand in relation to one another, they stand together as the justice-based arguments for toleration, and as such rise above peace. Philosophers tend to grace the justice-based reasons for toleration with the status of *moral* reasons while peering down their noses at peace, which they present as a *merely prudential* reason for toleration.[34] The claims of justice clearly have ethical priority over peace, even if, in exigent circumstances, we must sometimes sacrifice justice to order for the sake of preserving the very possibility of just institutions.

As a guide to moral reasoning and to practice, the consequence of this philosophic hierarchy of reasons is clear. We begin with the two pillars of liberal justice, autonomy and equality, and reason from them about whether a particular minority practice is consonant with them. If it is, then we ought to permit it; if not, we should feel justified in discouraging or, in appropriate circumstances, suppressing it. As Chandran Kukathas nicely sums it up: 'We establish the limits of tolerance in principle and then whether or not particular practices are consistent with them, and thus determine whether or not to intervene in traditional societies or minority groups by providing state subsidies, disincentives, or penalties for particular practices.'[35] The difficult work, this approach supposes, consists in knowing what we ought to do as a matter of justice. If the claims of justice must be tempered by pragmatic concerns about social stability, this is something that must be dealt with in context and is not susceptible to philosophical analysis.

All of this appears well and good until we recognize that, *in practice*, we do not so neatly separate considerations of justice from those of peace. Consider again the three cases we have examined. The debates over *hijab* do focus on justice issues, but these concerns blend wantonly with others, such as the threat of Islamic fundamentalism, and loyalty to Canadian values. The arguments concerning Hezbollah 'cells' in Canada focus almost exclusively on questions of security and do not consider any of the justice-based reasons in favour of generous immigration and multicultural policies. Even the debates over female circumcision, which superficially appear to be concerned exclusively with justice issues, are often pervaded by implicit linkages between that practice and Islam, which is viewed as threatening. Although academic commentators are increasingly careful to note that female circumcision is not an Islamic practice *per se*, the connection is still strong in the popular mind and comes to the surface in news articles with titles like the one that appeared in the *Reader's Digest* a few years ago: 'Women Are Being Abused, Even Mutilated . . . All in the Name of Islam.'[36]

If we review the history of toleration in liberal societies, we find that the claims of peace often interpenetrate the claims of justice in our practical reasoning about what to tolerate and what to suppress. In practice, we do not observe a strict hierarchy of arguments; indeed, we often side with peace over justice even in the absence of a 'clear and present danger' to social order (to invoke a parochial Americanism). Sometimes we accommodate what justice would teach us to suppress because we fear that failure to do so would lead to a gradual weakening of the foundations of social order, even if not to an immediate calamity. Sometimes we accommodate despite the dictates of justice not because we feel threatened but because the minority in question is so non-threatening as to make us feel that we can afford to be generous. This tendency is most apparent in the treatment of insular, apolitical, and pacifist Anabaptist sects such as Hutterites and Amish, whose restrictions on the autonomy of their own members run counter to justice-based arguments for toleration but whom we tend to accommodate nonetheless because peace is not threatened by our doing so.[37] If in these cases a concern for peace leads us to accommodate more than justice alone would allow, it is more common that a concern for peace leads us to refuse toleration even where justice would require it. Probably the starkest case in the twentieth century, in both Canada and the United States, was the internment of all citizens of Japanese origin on the basis of slim evidence that a few people of Japanese ethnicity were involved in espionage against the state.

In practice, then, our judgments about toleration reflect both a concern for justice and a concern for peace or order, but—contrary to the philosophic hierarchy of values—the latter very often overrides the former. From this we might simply conclude that we are hypocritical or morally weak, that we fail to live up to our own moral principles. But I think there is a more interesting conclusion to draw: namely, that we should take the claims of peace more seriously as ethical concerns. In particular, in a democratic society, the effort to seek peaceful co-operation among groups, to find practices that both sides can live with, is sometimes necessary as a precondition for a sense of shared membership in a political community. Toleration and accommodation are sometimes motivated by a desire not to alienate those with whom we will share a future. This motivation is substantively similar to the one that lay behind Locke's plea for even-handedness, discussed above, and as such falls within the broad category of peace-based arguments for toleration. Certainly it is possible to think of circumstances when these concerns lead to unconscionable compromises with autonomy and equality. We should be careful not to celebrate it as a good in itself. But surely it embodies a political value that we should—and in fact do—weigh alongside autonomy and equality in reaching judgments about what to tolerate in particular cases.

The impulse to accommodate for the sake of building the social trust that is the precondition for shared political community appears all the more justifiable when we compare the minority practices we would suppress with the mainstream practices we accept out of habit. As we saw, the principled liberal approach to toleration begins by analyzing whether a particular practice is consonant with the requirements of justice, and either accepting or rejecting it on the basis of that analysis (assuming that civil order is not immediately at risk one way or the other). But this model of moral reasoning leaves aside the question of how we came to focus on *this* practice, belonging to *this* group; nor does it require us to compare our judgments in one case with our acceptance or rejection of other practices. Critical self-scrutiny, however, will reveal that sometimes a latent fear of a particular group, or a strong distaste for a particular practice, will shape what social scientists call case selection. By this route we may consider whether Muslim women may wear *hijab* in the courtroom, but not whether nuns may wear habits; whether female circumcision should be banned, but not whether male circumcision, or breast implants, should be banned; whether Islam prescribes women's subordination to men, but not whether Christianity does. In the process, we run the risk of applying a much stricter scrutiny to the practices of religious and cultural minorities than we apply to mainstream or majority groups. And to the extent that we devise such double standards—or appear to do so, in the eyes of the minorities in question—we impede the construction of social trust that is, as Locke told us, a desideratum of all stable and legitimate polities.

As Bernard Williams has recently written, 'The case of toleration is, unsurprisingly, a central one for distinguishing between a strongly moralized conception of liberalism as based on ideals of individual autonomy, and a more sceptical, historically alert, politically direct conception of it as the best hope for humanly acceptable legitimate government under modern conditions.' Williams notes that the moralistic variety of liberalism 'has been dominant in American political philosophy in the last twenty-five years.'[38] American-style liberalism is a highly principled affair. It follows the lessons of the moral philosophers and gives strong ethical priority to the claims of autonomy and equality. It reaches judgments about minority practices by reasoning directly from these premises to conclusions about what should be tolerated and what suppressed. The danger in this approach is that unconscious or undisclosed prejudices about the threat a particular group poses to liberal institutions can shape moral reasoning in unjustifiable ways, and lead liberals to impose more demanding criteria on minority religious and cultural practices than they impose on those of the mainstream.

Perhaps even more important, by postulating a strict hierarchy of values and a clear structure of moral reasoning, from fundamental principles to particular cases, American-style liberalism closes off avenues of inquiry that might, in the end, yield more creative solutions to intergroup conflicts. This approach takes both minority and majority practices as fixed, static, and internally undifferentiated; it does not recognize that within each culture there may be a multiplicity of meanings that attach to a practice, and that some of these meanings may be quite consonant with liberal commitments while others are less so. For some women, indeed, *hijab* is oppressive; but for others it offers liberation from sexual objectification, and so carries an empowering and feminist significance.[39]

Canadian-style liberalism tends to ask first what would be necessary to accommodate a group—particularly if the group in question is sizeable and therefore a potentially formidable adversary. Historically, the impulse to accommodation arises from the coexistence of the anglophone majority and the francophone minority, and much of the practice of accommodation has been focused (albeit imperfectly and often inadequately) on the latter. But the habit of accommodation as a conflict-avoiding strategy appears deeply embedded in Canadian political culture, and has increasingly become a habit of generosity from which other cultural minorities benefit. The danger of this approach is that it may sometimes lead to accommodations or group privileges that cannot be easily reconciled with basic principles of justice. For example, there are good reasons to believe that Ontario's system of publicly funded separate schools for Catholics (but not for other religious groups) is unjustifiable, however understandable it may be as a historic accommodation.

In recent years, however, particularly since the Charter, Canadian liberalism has very constructively combined the historic impulse to accommodate with conscientious attention to the claims of autonomy and equality. Although the claims of justice may now, in the Canadian model of liberalism as in the American model, have *ethical* priority over the claims of peace and stability, the difference remains that in Canada the claims of peace often enjoy *deliberative* priority. By this I mean that practical judgments about minority practices increasingly *begin* with the question of what changes to both majority and minority practices would be required in order to find an arrangement that both groups could live with. With this question in the foreground, participants in the discussions can consider a wide variety of practical options. Some of these may be variations on the current majority practice; some may be variations on the minority practice; others may be altogether new. Each of these options is weighed simultaneously against a standard of peace—what each side would accept without a threat of coercion—and the standards of justice.

Giving peace its due in our moral deliberations about toleration can lead us to a much more inventive form of liberalism. It allows us to hear the multiplicity of voices within minority communities explaining the meanings of their practices, and to give our support to the emancipatory meanings that are available within each culture's traditions. It can lead us to see that the principles of autonomy and equality are often more capacious than we assume, and can permit us to advance aspirations to freedom and equality in many different, context-dependent ways.[40] In contrast, the rigid application of liberal standards to reified practices forces members of minorities to choose between their religious or cultural identity and their identity as equal participants in a shared political project.

We might do well to look to Canada as a model of the alternative. A distinctly Canadian approach to toleration is gradually emerging in the efforts to accommodate Aboriginal claims for rights of self-government and for other special rights; in multicultural policies that provide symbolic recognition to immigrant cultures and assistance for their integration into key social, economic, and political processes; and in special exemptions from laws that are especially burdensome for religious minorities. Despite the very important differences among these different forms of group recognition, and among the different groups they seek to accommodate, they have all arisen within practices of political deliberation and ethical judgment that incorporate both the good of justice and the good of peace, sacrificing neither to the other. Like the notwithstanding clause, the Canadian variety of toleration is theoretically messier than the American alternative, but on the whole it makes for a less doctrinaire, more creative and dynamic, and more humane liberalism.

Notes

I wish to acknowledge Edward Andrew, Rupert Gordon, Genevieve Johnson, Annabelle Lever, Laurence McFalls, Cheryl Misak, Daniel Weinstock, David Welch, Linda White, and participants in the York University political theory colloquium for their thoughtful and helpful comments on earlier drafts of this essay. Undoubtedly I have failed adequately to address the points they raised, and they should not be held responsible for my errors and oversights. I also wish to thank Nancy Rosenblum, whose invitation to participate in a conference on Law and Religion at Brown University in the spring of 1997 first set me to thinking about the relationship between autonomy, equality, and peace in the liberal theory and practice of toleration.

1. The Canadian Charter of Rights and Freedoms consists of sections 1–34 of the Constitution Act of 1982. Sections 2–15 articulate fundamental freedoms, democratic rights, mobility rights, legal rights, and equality rights. Section 33, known as the 'notwithstanding clause', provides in part: 'Parliament or the legislature of a province may expressly declare in an Act of Parliament or of the legislature, as the case may be, that the Act or a provision thereof shall operate notwithstanding a provision included in section 2 or sections 7 to 15 of this Charter.' In other words, the same constitutional document both guarantees certain enumerated rights and permits legislatures to override some of those rights. Under section 33(3), a legislative override of the Charter expires after five years and must be renewed to remain in effect.
2. Cf. Ronald Dworkin, *Taking Rights Seriously* (Cambridge, Mass.: Harvard University Press, 1977), 22.
3. Bruce Ackerman, *We, The People* (Cambridge, Mass.: Harvard University Press, 1991).
4. See Robert C. Vipond, *Liberty and Community: Canadian Federalism and the Failure of the Constitution* (Albany: State University of New York Press, 1991), 192.

5. This interpretation of the notwithstanding clause is indebted to Peter H. Russell, 'Standing Up for Notwithstanding', *Alberta Law Review* 29, 2 (1991), 293–309. Admittedly, I have presented here the rosiest possible view of s. 33, without the caveats Professor Russell so judiciously provides. Skeptical readers of earlier versions of this essay have rightly pointed out that the notwithstanding clause has not always been employed so as to improve political deliberation, but has sometimes had the contrary effect. After the Constitution was patriated without Quebec's consent, the Parti Québécois passed a blanket application of s. 33 to all its legislation as a form of constitutional protest, rendering the override clause impotent as a deliberation-enhancing device for Quebec legislation that might stand in tension with the Charter. Later, in December 1988, the Quebec National Assembly invoked s. 33 to override the Supreme Court's decision that Bill 101 (Quebec's legislation mandating French-only signs outside commercial establishments) was a Charter violation. This use of the notwithstanding clause enraged many English-speaking Canadians outside Quebec, and was a key factor in the failure of the Meech Lake Accord, which would have granted constitutional recognition to Quebec as a 'distinct society' within Canada. If we agree with supporters of the 'distinct society' clause that it would have enabled constructive constitutional and political dialogue between francophones and anglophones within Canada, then the notwithstanding clause functioned again, in this case, to obstruct rather than encourage deep deliberation. Finally, critics of s. 33 often point out that it was adopted in the middle of the 'night of the long knives' (2–3 Nov. 1981) as a last-ditch political expedient to overcome various provincial leaders' opposition to the Charter in order to achieve the Constitution's patriation. It is paradoxical, at the least, that a constitutional device aimed at enhancing deliberation was itself adopted in so non-deliberative a manner (though one might make a Machiavellian point that all great constitutions were founded in crime).

   In defence of my interpretation of the deliberative potential and purpose of s. 33, I appeal to the arguments of its most prominent defenders, Paul Weiler and Peter Russell. Russell makes clear that the override clause can deliver its beneficial effects for deliberation only when it is properly used, i.e., 'when it is invoked only after a reasoned debate in the legislature' ('Standing Up', 298–9). For this reason, he is strongly critical of the Supreme Court's decision to uphold Quebec's blanket use of the override, mentioned above, in *Ford v. A.G. Quebec* (1988) 2 S.C.R. 712. Both Russell and Weiler support an amendment to s. 33 that would protect against its misuse by requiring that legislatures pass override legislation twice, once before and once after an election. The purpose of this 'sober second thought' provision would be precisely to prevent the rash exercise of s. 33 and to encourage more extensive public discussion of the issues at hand; Russell, 301–2; Paul C. Weiler, 'Rights and Judges in a Democracy: A New Canadian Version', *University of Michigan Journal of Law Reform* 18, 1 (1984), 90–1, n. 116. A full-blown defence of the notwithstanding clause would have to examine closely the various cases in which it was used, as well as those in which it was considered but not used, to see whether, on balance, it has had the effect of enhancing political deliberation. Worthy as that project is, it goes beyond my purposes in the present essay.

6. Certainly Canadians pride themselves on being more tolerant than their American neighbours. In a 1989 survey, Canadians selected 'tolerant' as the word that best described the 'ideal Canadian'; Americans favoured 'independent-minded' as their ideal trait. Cited in James W. St. G. Walker, *'Race,' Rights and the Law in the Supreme Court of Canada: Historical Case Studies* (Waterloo, Ont.: Wilfrid Laurier University Press, 1997). This is not to say, of course, that Canadians always manage to live up to their self-image.

7. 'Woman Fearing Ritual Can Stay in U.S.', *Globe and Mail*, 15 June 1996, A20. For a description of the various practices that fall under the heading of female circumcision or female genital mutilation, see Joseph H. Carens and Melissa S. Williams, 'Muslim Minorities in Liberal Democracies: The Politics of Misrecognition', in *The Challenge of Diversity: Integration and Pluralism in Societies of Immigration*, ed. Rainer Bauböck, Agnes Heller, and Aristide R. Zolberg (London: Avebury Press, 1996).
8. 'Finding New Grounds for Refuge,' *Maclean's*, 8 Aug. 1994, 14–15.
9. 'Fugitive Can't Get Arrested, Wrote Threatening Letter', *Globe and Mail*, 7 Aug. 1997, A8.
10. Though, as Cheryl Misak has reminded me, one must wonder what sort of reception a Mexican fugitive would have received in Canada.
11. Cf. Ronald Dworkin, *A Matter of Principle* (Cambridge, Mass.: Harvard University Press, 1985).
12. 'Genital Mutilation Declared a Violation', *Globe and Mail*, 22 May 1996, A4 (statement by Ontario Human Rights Commission that the practice violates Ontario law); 'Controversial Bill Studied', *Globe and Mail*, 3 Oct. 1995, A17 (federal bill introduced to impose a sentence of up to five years on any person who performs a female circumcision); 'Taking Steps to Stop Female Genital Mutilation: Quebec's Human Rights Commission Vows to Prosecute Physicians and Parents', *The Medical Post*, 11 April 1995, 60; 'Mutilating Girls Already Illegal, Says Rock', *Calgary Herald*, 12 April 1994, A8.
13. Cases concerning Islamic covering continue to arise outside Quebec as well. In Toronto, for example, a bus driver for the public transit system recently insisted that a pass holder remove her veil before he would allow her on the bus (this despite the fact that she was veiled in the photo on her pass). See Michael Valpy, 'Veil of Tears: Muslim Woman Back on Bus', *Globe and Mail*, 1 Sept. 1999, A1, A7.
14. 'Muslim Woman Expelled by Judge for Wearing Head Scarf in Court', *Montreal Gazette*, 2 Dec. 1993, A1–A2.
15. Reported in 'Veiled Threats in Quebec', *Maclean's*, 28 Nov. 1994, 47.
16. 'Terrorist Group Active in Canada: Spy Agency', *Toronto Star*, 29 March 1997, A11. See also 'Hezbollah Has Arm in Canada: CSIS "Evidence" Says Would-Be Refugee Helped Kill 19 Americans in Saudi Arabia', *Globe and Mail*, 29 March 1997, A1, A7; 'Saudi Man Admits He Once Belonged to Hezbollah Group', *Toronto Star*, 5 April 1997, A3; 'Judge Says Canada Can Deport Suspect in Lethal Saudi Bombing', *New York Times*, 6 May 1997, A7.
17. The existence of such organizations has been reported by the media since at least 1993. See, e.g., 'Terrorist "Cell" Set Up in Canada', *Calgary Herald*, 18 March 1993, A2.
18. Anthony DePalma, 'Saudi Case Casting a Light on How Militants Infiltrate and Exploit Canada: Open Borders and Generous Refugee Policies Help Suspects Get In', *New York Times*, 4 May 1997, 8.
19. Quoted in DePalma, 'Saudi Case Casting a Light'.
20. 'CIC Seeks Meet with Axworthy Over Hezbollah', *Canadian Jewish News*, 17 April 1997, 5.
21. Quoted in DePalma, 'Saudi Case Casting a Light'.
22. Steven Emerson, 'Why the Media Doesn't Warn About the Threat, Lies and Hatred of Islamic Terrorists', *Canadian Speeches: Issues of the Day*, January–February 1997, 4.
23. Ibid., 8.
24. Ibid., 9.

25. See, e.g., Susan Okin, 'Reply', in Susan Okin et al., *Is Multiculturalism Bad for Women?* (Princeton: Princeton University Press, 1999), 125–6.

26. L. Amede Obiora's essay 'Bridges and Barricades: Rethinking Polemics and Intransigence in the Campaign Against Female Circumcision', *Case Western Reserve Law Review* 47: 275–378 (1997), is an impressively thorough and well-argued response to Western feminist critiques of female circumcision from an African feminist perspective. She discusses the issue of 'false consciousness' at pp. 313-18. Obiora's essay is the finest account of female circumcision and the theoretical issues it raises that I have yet encountered.

27. See Joseph Carens, 'Liberalism and Culture', *Constellations* 4, 1 (1997), 35–47.

28. For examples of the equality-based argument for group accommodation, see, e.g., Kymlicka, *Multicultural Citizenship*, 108-15; Iris M. Young, *Justice and the Politics of Difference* (Princeton: Princeton University Press, 1990); Melissa Williams, 'Justice Toward Groups: Political Not Juridical', *Political Theory* 23, 1 (1995), 67–91.

29. Charles Taylor, 'The Politics of Recognition', in *Multiculturalism and 'The Politics of Recognition'*, ed. Amy Gutmann (Princeton: Princeton University Press, 1992), 25–73.

30. Michael Walzer, *On Toleration*, (New Haven: Yale University Press, 1997), 10.

31. John Locke, *A Letter Concerning Toleration*, ed. Patrick Romanell (Indianapolis: Bobbs-Merrill, 1995 [1689]), 54–5 (emphasis added).

32. 'Autonomy, Toleration, and the Harm Principle', in *Justifying Toleration*, ed. Susan Mendus and David Edwards (Cambridge: Cambridge University Press, 1988), 155.

33. Geoffrey Brahm Levey, 'Equality, Autonomy, and Cultural Rights', *Political Theory* 25, 2 (1997), 215–48.

34. See, e.g., Susan Mendus, 'Introduction', in *On Toleration*, ed. Mendus and David Edwards (Oxford: Clarendon Press, 1987), 1–16, where she distinguishes 'rational', 'moral', and 'prudential' grounds for toleration. As she notes (11), 'The argument from prudence justifies toleration by reference to considerations of public order, and thereby suggests that where tolerance will not foster good order in society, it should be abandoned.'

35. Chandran Kukathas, 'Cultural Toleration', in *NOMOS 39: Ethnicity and Group Rights*, ed. Ian Shapiro and Will Kymlicka (New York: New York University Press, 1997), 71. Kukathas goes on to argue for a regime of toleration that gives much less scope to the principles of autonomy and equality than I would defend.

36. Ann Louise Bardach, 'Women Are Being Abused, Even Mutilated . . . All in the Name of Islam', *Reader's Digest*, January 1994, 78–82.

37. See Jeff Spinner, *The Boundaries of Citizenship: Race, Ethnicity, and Nationality in the Liberal State* (Baltimore: Johns Hopkins University Press, 1994), 95–108. Spinner's discussion is highly nuanced, and I do it an injustice by drawing out only one of its themes.

38. Bernard Williams, 'Toleration, a Political or Moral Question?', *Diogenes* 44, 176 (1996), 35–48.

39. Katherine Bullock, 'The Politics of the Veil', Ph.D. thesis, University of Toronto, 1999.

40. Joseph Carens demonstrates this in rich detail in his book *Culture, Citizenship and Community: A Contextual Explanation of Justice as Even-Handedness* (Oxford: Oxford University Press, 2000).

Charles Taylor's Pedagogy of Recognition

CLIFFORD ORWIN

On a recent visit to Toronto,[1] the American sociologist Nathan Glazer remarked that, with one exception, the books on multiculturalism most widely read in the United States today are attacks on multiculturalism: this, he thought, did not refute but confirmed the current ascendancy of that doctrine. The exception, he noted, was a book constructed around an essay by a Canadian, Charles Taylor's 'The Politics of Recognition'.[2]

It seems, then, that in the United States, at least, Taylor's essay enjoys hegemonic status among discussions favourable to multiculturalism. While it could owe this status to Taylor's obtrusive white maleness, somehow I doubt it: few groups have been so effectively marginalized in American life as Vice-Presidents for Life of the New Democratic Party. Let us then give our neighbours the benefit of the doubt and ascribe their interest in Taylor's essay to their appreciation of the richness and subtlety of its argument. The essay is of particular interest to those of us who labour in universities, whether north or south of the border, for it concludes with a discussion of the implications of the 'politics of recognition' for universities. More precisely, it attempts to sketch a response to the demand for recognition that would be worthy of a university. It is this response that I examine in the present essay.[3] My conclusion is that Taylor's program, while a noble effort, represents an attempt to square a circle: that it fails as it is bound to fail.

1.

As a formulation of that to which individuals and groups in liberal society deem themselves to be entitled today, 'recognition' is the latest in a series of watchwords of which the original was 'toleration'. Because toleration remains fully intelligible today and because it affords a stark contrast with recognition, I will briefly discuss it as a way of clarifying the significance of the demand for recognition.

One classic formulation of liberal toleration is ascribed to Voltaire: 'I disagree with what you say, but I will defend to the death your right to say it.' (Whether Voltaire ever actually said this is not our concern.) This position, however worthy of a free man (the original meaning of 'liberal') it may have been deemed in the eighteenth century, would strike many on campus today as grudging or stunted. For by disagreeing with what you say, I am treating you with disrespect and insensitivity, and your self-esteem is bound to suffer. If I say that I doubt the worth of your 'culture'—these days every group with a grievance constitutes a 'culture'—but as a liberal I defend your right to practise it, you're far more likely to resent my contempt than to appreciate my tolerance.

This isn't the way it was supposed to be. At the beginning of the liberal era, disagreement was presumed (certainly in religious matters), as was the natural tendency of disagreement to breed intolerance and worse. It was assumed, therefore, that admiration and gratitude were due those who tolerated in spite of disapproving. (Indeed, in the absence of disapproval, tolerance would lose all meaning). Just as I (the Voltairean) was to show myself strong enough to refrain from punishing you for my disapproval, so you were to show yourself strong enough to bear the latter. The very success of liberalism has spoiled us in North America: taking tolerance for granted, we insist on respect or even love.[4]

George Washington was surely no radical relativist, but he anticipated in his wisdom the problem that now dogs the question of 'diversity'. In writing to the Jewish community of Newport, Rhode Island, he contrasted the situation prevailing in monarchic Britain, where the established church tolerated other churches, with that in America, where there was (on the federal level, anyway) no established church:

> The citizens of the United States of America have a right to applaud themselves for having given mankind examples of an enlarged and liberal policy: a policy worthy of imitation. All possess alike liberty of conscience and immunities of citizenship. It is now no more that toleration is spoken of, as if it was by the indulgence of one class of people, that another enjoyed the exercise of their inherent natural rights. For happily the government of the United States, which gives to bigotry no sanction, to persecution no assistance, requires only that they who live under its protection should demean themselves as good citizens . . . (letter of 18 August 1790).

In the American republic there could be neither a tolerating nor a tolerated class of citizens; rather, all—being equally citizens and equally endowed with a natural right to worship as they saw fit—faced one another as equals. Liberalism did not so much guarantee toleration as abolish its possibility by abrogating those privileges and disabilities that toleration had mitigated but at the same time perpetuated.

Washington's position here is substantially the same as that of John Locke in his *Letter on Toleration* of a century earlier. In effect, Washington exposes the title of that work as a misnomer, for toleration, to the limited extent that it had been practised prior to Locke, had in fact presupposed an established church to do the tolerating and dissenting churches to be tolerated. Locke, however, had argued that the very notion of an established church implied a confusion of the proper realms of church and state: he had argued for what came to be known as 'separation' of church and state. Locke was glad to live with the misnomer of his title, aware as he was that new wine goes down most easily when marketed in old bottles. But the more clearly we grasp what he and early liberalism were about, the more clearly we can grasp the problem posed for liberalism by the contemporary version of toleration, the so-called 'politics of difference'.

Liberalism à la Locke and Washington tolerated difference but did not celebrate it. More precisely, it tolerated (some) differences without exalting difference as such. Differences were tolerable to the extent that they were secondary—to the extent that they deferred to the primacy of sameness, that is, to the universality of liberal rights. What the United States required of its citizens, as Washington's letter clearly indicates, was that everyone deport himself as a good liberal, in the broad generic sense of a lawful and loyal citizen of liberal democracy. Insofar as all were alike in this fundamental respect, then all differences that did not tend to subvert this alikeness were admissible. 'Pluralism' was neither here nor there, neither an asset to the regime nor a detriment to it. If it was valued, it was as Washington values it in his letter, as a salient confirmation of the crucial point that united the citizens: their universal acceptance of the fundamental liberal right to lead one's life as one wished, bounded of course by respect for the equal rights of every other to do the same. The point was not that the Jews were different and claimed a right to be valued as such, but that as law-abiding citizens they were the same and were to be valued as such. One cannot say that, publicly speaking, they were valued despite being Jews (for under the new regime every tolerant religion was deemed as good as any other). Neither, however, were they valued because of it.

This, then, was the original version of pluralism. To speak more precisely, a certain skepticism concerning the existence of a definitive or comprehensive good, combined with quasi-universal agreement as to what was, practically speaking, definitively bad (i.e., endless fruitless quarrels over such a good) to support a non-relativistic confidence in what was right: the practices of liberalism itself. One settled, then, for what Locke, Voltaire, and Washington offered: agreement on liberal essentials, disagreement but toleration in all other realms. One made one's peace with toleration recognizing that the alternative was intolerance.

2.

As I've already suggested, however, no one in the university today seems satisfied with mere toleration of the sort that Voltaire is supposed to have endorsed. The spirit of contemporary campus life is better captured by something that Thomas Hobbes indubitably said: 'To disagree with someone, is to dishonor him.' If to disagree with someone is indeed to dishonour him, then disagreement is an offence that is quite naturally resented as such. One will require not merely toleration of one's position but agreement with it, or more precisely and in contemporary lingo, 'affirmation' or 'recognition' of its 'worth' or 'validity' as a position. 'Affirmation' isn't quite agreement, and 'validity' isn't quite truth, for on the presumption of relativism 'value'-laden positions cannot be either true or false. Affirmation does confer full acceptance, however—and thus honour rather than dishonour. Similarly, today it is not so much a matter of affirming the validity of arguments as of 'cultures' or 'lifestyles', which are deemed more fundamental than arguments.

It is at such affirmation that the politics of difference aims. Its partisans demand that we honour them by affirming or recognizing the differences they bring to the liberal table. They demand recognition *as* women, *as* blacks, *as* gays, *as* Chicanos. They reject the liberal politics of universality for a post-liberal one of identity. They thus promote what is ambiguously an expansion of liberalism (which is how they present it to alumni, state legislatures, and other outsiders) and a repudiation of it. Relativism, too long embraced by too many liberals as the core of liberalism, now figures as simultaneously its apex and its negation. In the end, liberalism too is but one way of life, one set of values, which as such cannot deny equal recognition to other ways of life, other sets of values. Liberalism is passé; long live liberalism.

One important expression of the politics of recognition on campus today is 'multiculturalism'. Multiculturalism is often touted for broadening the minds of mainstream students by compelling them to come to grips with cultures other than their own. It seems to be largely on the basis of this presumption that most people outside the university approve of it. This is no accident, since these are the terms in which proponents of multiculturalism sell it to a wider public. From what I have heard and seen, however, not much of this broadening of minds actually happens.

For sure, students today could use some expanding of their cultural horizons. Have these ever been narrower? I can't answer that question, but it makes sense to pose it. The decline of reading, an indifference to high culture even among young people from educated families, and the growing vocationalization of education at even the elite universities have fostered a generation whose ignorance can be stunning. If they are computer-literate, that is often the extent of their literacy. I doubt that any generation of university students has ever known less about other times, and I am not persuaded that they know much about other places.

Multiculturalism to the rescue? Not likely. As it is practised, its effect is not so much to rescue students from immersion in the here and now as to apply firm downward pressure upon whatever heads happen to bob above the surface. Far from combatting parochialism, so-called multiculturalism reinforces it.

Multiculturalism represents not a genuine opening to the foreign but the crowning expression of the ideology of this place, this time. As Charles Taylor has put it,

> the reason for [the proposed multiculturalization of the university curriculum] is not, or not mainly, that all students may be missing something important through the exclusion of a certain gender or certain races or cultures, but rather that women and students from the excluded groups are given, either directly or by omission, a demeaning picture of themselves, as though all creativity and worth inhered in males of European provenance. . . . Enlarging and changing the curriculum is therefore essential not so much in the name of a broader culture for everyone as in order to give due recognition to the hitherto excluded. . . . The struggle for freedom and equality must pass through a revision of . . . images (65–6).

Insofar, then, as a pedagogy of recognition 'broadens' that majority of students who do not demand recognition for themselves but are summoned to accord it to others, it is not primarily by informing them of the ways of other cultures. It is by calling them to perform a duty incumbent on them as members of our own.

There is another reason why openness to foreign cultures does not loom particularly large in multiculturalism as actually practised. Not only is the issue as it typically presents itself not one of openness but of affirmation or recognition, but what we are most urgently called upon to recognize is not 'foreign cultures' at all. Rather, it is the formerly or presently 'marginalized' groups within North American society; not foreign 'cultures' but domestic 'subcultures'. These range from Native Americans and Hispanics to groups defined not by a culture in the usual sense of the term but by race, gender, or sexuality.

True, the 'recognition' demanded by these groups includes some considerable rewriting of history to atone for the mainstream culture's past neglect or oppression of their ancestors. Hence at many colleges 'diversity requirements' require students to take a course in either a non-Western culture or a marginalized Western subculture. Still, it is impossible to grasp the demands for intellectual diversity that are heard in the universities today except as expressions of the moral imperative of the politics of recognition. And this inevitably affects both the nature of such requirements and the substance of the courses taught.

3.

Enter Taylor and 'The Politics of Recognition'. Taylor traces the rise of this politics through the generations of modern thought from the Enlightenment to the present, showing how the demand for recognition has emerged from the womb of modern thought (44–51), and articulating its political ramifications with special attention to the problem of racial, ethnic, and linguistic minorities within the bosom of liberal democracy (51–73). A full consideration of his arguments and the issues they raise is beyond the scope of my present effort, although it would be well worth undertaking for anyone seeking to clarify his or her own position on these questions. Today I will consider only the final section of Taylor's argument, which concerns itself specifically with the politics of recognition as practised on college campuses.

Professor Taylor is sympathetic to the demands for recognition of groups that have previously been denied it. At the same time he is aware of the problematic character of what we may call recognition on demand. As he sees it, 'the logic behind some of these demands [for recognition] seems to depend upon a premise that we owe equal respect to all cultures.' There is an alternative premise, 'a more radical, neo-Nietzschean standpoint, which questions the very status of judgments of worth as such, but short of this extreme step (whose coherence I doubt), the presumption seems to be of equal worth' (66). Taylor offers a marvellous critique of the 'neo-Nietzschean' standpoint, indeed one that could hardly be improved upon (66, 69–70).

Professor Taylor is willing to honour the presumption of equal worth on the grounds that 'all human cultures that have animated whole societies over some considerable stretch of time have something important to say to all human beings' (66). But by a presumption he means only 'a starting hypothesis with which we ought to approach the study of any other culture'. 'The validity of the claim has to be demonstrated concretely in the actual study of the culture.' And even the presumption as he states it does not, strictly speaking, imply the *equality* of cultures, for the fact that all have something important to teach us need not mean that all have something equally important to teach us, or even that any lesson or lessons taught by one might not be better taught by some other. 'It makes sense to demand as a matter of right that we approach the study of certain cultures with a presumption of their value. . . . But it can't make sense as a matter of right that we come up with a final concluding judgment that their value is great, or equal to others' (68–9). All equally deserve a hearing, but the outcome can't be preordained. 'On examination, either we will find something of great value in culture C, or we will not. But it makes no more sense to demand that we do so than it does to demand that we find the earth round or flat, the temperature of the air hot or cold' (69). There can be no moral stipulations as to the outcome of a rational or scientific inquiry, and Taylor's welcome claim is that investigations of the ultimate worth of cultural practices are examples of rational inquiry. His analogies with geography and meteorology imply the prospect that discoveries of moral truths are as possible as discoveries of physical ones.

On the other hand, Professor Taylor is aware that moral inquiry lags far behind the physical sciences in the solidity of its accomplishments to date. While his essay contains no recommendations for the reform of inquiry in the physical sciences, he does offer some for the reform of moral studies. He suggests that while the ultimate aim is a definitive evaluation of the respective superiorities and inferiorities of the various cultures, we are still very far from such an evaluation. First of all, we lack the requisite understanding of these cultures. Second, we lack the necessary universally applicable criteria of evaluation. At present we possess only the criteria peculiar to Western culture. Not only would it be presumptuous to force all other cultures to pass before the bar of our tribunal; it would be to contradict the very presumption of equal worth that we are supposed to have extended to them. Adequate criteria of judgment must themselves emerge only in the fullness of time through the dialogic interplay of the cultures. Taylor, borrowing a term from Hans-Georg Gadamer, describes this process as the 'fusion of horizons'. It seems pretty certain that in Professor Taylor's view we are generations, even centuries, away from the requisite combination of knowledge of the different cultures, on the one hand, and a fused super-horizon, on the other.

Thus does Professor Taylor navigate between the Scylla of relativism and the Charybdis of insensitivity. His compromise calls upon activists to be satisfied with provisional recognition of their respective 'cultures' as worthy of further scrutiny on terms equal to those granted any other 'culture'. Foot-draggers in extending such recognition are urged to reflect that they are not, after all, succumbing to relativism and the incoherent demand for full vindication of every self-described 'culture' that presents itself.

Speaking as a foot-dragger, I find much to endorse in Professor Taylor's scheme. I for one have never championed 'Western culture' or 'the canon'. (Canons are for churches, not universities.) I would even argue that among the defining characteristics of 'Western culture' worth preserving today is its openness to the non-Western. This openness has been and remains a necessary condition of its vitality. In this sense, Taylor's challenge to his colleagues to transcend their Westernness through confrontation with the non-Western appeals at the same time to what has always been best in (and unique to) the West itself.

Even Professor Taylor's suggestion that the criteria of judgment should themselves be regarded as provisional, subject to constant revision as a result of the dialogue itself, does no more than make explicit what was actual already in Socratic dialogue. Indeed, what he intends could be understood as an expansion of that dialogue, the possibility and necessity of which was always implicit in it. Even before Socrates, Herodotus devoted himself to the confrontation of Greek and non-Greek civilizations with the intention of achieving a synthesis of the wisdom inherent in each, and Thucydides saw no possibility in the Greeks that was not equally present in the barbarians, out of whom the Greeks had arisen and to whom they would return. Aristotle contended that of all the regimes known in his day, the best was a barbarian one hostile to the Greeks. For the West to cultivate the greatest possible openness to non-Western principles and practices, to suspend any notions of its own superiority except (paradoxically) inasmuch as it is manifest in this very suspension, would be a thoroughly Western thing to do. *Nihil humanum alienum puto* is a principle as Western as apple pie. By all means bring on the Buddha; you'll get no argument from a notorious Philhellene like myself.

So far, then, am I in agreement with Professor Taylor. But I also want to suggest some possible reservations about his approach. The more one examines his proposal, the more it seems to rest on certain premises concerning the human truth that are both uniquely Western and highly debatable. I offer this objection not so much in my name as in his own, as it seems to be his own view that such cogency as his project possesses must rest on its neutrality as between Western and other cultures. Consider, for instance, the crucial presumption that the 'dialogic interplay of cultures' will yield a 'fusion of horizons'. This phrase, as I have already noted, is borrowed from the German philosopher Gadamer; the term 'horizon' entered philosophic currency through Nietzsche. It expresses a historicist view peculiar to the latest stage of Western philosophy. However desirable it may be to canvass all the human alternatives—which I do not for a moment deny—it is quite possible that this 'fusion of horizons' will prove both impossible and superfluous.

First, it may well be that the crucial human alternatives are exclusive of one another and admit of no fusion. Professor Taylor seems to presume that some blend of Plato and the Buddha exists somewhere over the horizon that subsumes and improves upon both of them, but of this we have every right to be skeptical. It may well be that in the course of time all the fundamental human alternatives have already been articulated, and that what defines the human situation is not ultimate synthesis but only hard choices. (As you may have guessed, I'm not Hegel.) I have in mind such recalcitrant issues as the primacy of freedom versus that of virtue, of reason versus revelation, of life and its terrors versus *nirvana*—oppositions that resist being stirred into the same syncretic soup. My bet is that as the twenty-third century dawns (if it does) Socrates and the Buddha and Confucius and Jesus and Kant will still stand in proud apartness from each other, and that every attempt to mix and match them will prove as futile and ephemeral as they have proved to be up to now. My point here is not that no new human possibility is likely to appear, but rather that if it does it is unlikely to succeed in superseding the earlier ones. And this means that serious seekers of the life most worth living will eschew the fusion of horizons in favour of vetting the claims of the most compelling unfused horizons.

In defence of Professor Taylor's apparent presumption of an evolving 'fusion of horizons' and consequent consensus concerning the human good, one might point to the much greater homogeneity that exists in the world today in comparison with even a generation ago. And who can deny that 'fusion' has occurred? Just look at the menus of the restaurants in California that feature a cuisine by that name; the chocolate sushi wasabe roll is *de rigueur.* Yet whatever has happened on menus, what has happened in the world is Westernization. The massive influence of the West on the way of life of the rest of the planet has been countered by the minor influence of the rest of the planet on the way of life of the West (acupuncture, martial arts, 'Eastern religion', and so on). Some regions or countries have resisted Westernization (as in the Islamic world) and some have proved too wretched to benefit from it (as in Africa). But the countries that have prospered have done so by going Western, and the Western way of life, with all its warts, gains ever accelerating prestige as the unique life of choice in the world today. Increasingly, 'non-Western' cultures are failed cultures, obscurantist and fanatical cultures, or Westernizing cultures. No one really expects Korea to remain Confucian in the long run (some of my Korean interlocutors give even an attenuated Confucianism only one more generation) and there is already some confusion as to what remains Chinese about the new Chinese technical elites or Indian about the Indian ones.

Nor can one really claim that non-Western immigrants to Western countries have succeeded in initiating a conversation with the host culture, or shown much interest in doing so. The children of these immigrants are aggressively Western; I speak as someone who has taught hundreds of them. The harsh truth must be told: the 'politics of recognition' is fundamentally a politics of integration, which does not increase but decreases diversity or pluralism or whatever you would call it.[5] The rights claimed, as I have already argued, are Western rights; 'multiculturalism' and 'recognition' are Western concepts. Under these conditions, where not much 'dialogic interchange of cultures' takes place even within the universities, it seems doubtful that much will take place outside them. (Let no one mistake my position for one of Western triumphalism; I would be the first to admit that in all too many respects the Western culture that has triumphed is a debased version of itself.)

Lastly, I am puzzled by the apparent interchangeability for Professor Taylor of 'horizon' and 'culture'. The notion that the super-horizon will emerge from the 'dialogic interchange of cultures' seems to presume that the relevant unit for moral inquiry is the culture. It seems that in his view every aspect of a culture is to be interrogated first and last as an aspect of that culture, with an eye to rendering a positive or negative verdict on that culture. So many points for Socrates is so many points for Greek culture; so many points for the Buddha, so many points for Indian culture. There seems to be a presumption here alike of cultural determinism and of the unity of cultures, each of which I find highly rebuttable. To cast Socrates as the spokesman for a supposed Hellenic culture, Confucius as the spokesman for 'Chinese culture', Buddha as a spokesman for 'Indian culture' would be to fail to do justice both to these individuals and to the complexity and vitality of their respective 'cultures'. Not even Socrates can speak for Hellas; not even Confucius for China. Why Socrates, and not Homer or Sophocles or Thucydides or Epicurus? Why Confucius rather than Lao Tzu, or even that vast exercise in anti-Confucian thought Ch'an (Zen) Buddhism? (I won't even mention such other possible paladins of Chineseness as Mao Zedong.) The harder we look at precisely the most impressive cultures, the less it looks as if there is a 'Hellenic' or 'Chinese' or 'Indian' answer to any important human question. And it is the answers to the important human questions that we are seeking here. Although a primitive society may come to light that is unanimous on certain issues, what typifies rich and complex cultures is their tensions.

Furthermore, to interpret major figures from any 'culture' as merely or primarily spokesmen for that 'culture' is to cast them in terms they themselves would reject as reductionist and misleading. Not only did Socrates not present himself as an authoritative spokesman for Hellas, he never presented himself as a spokesman for Hellas at all. He offered himself, not very modestly, as a spokesman for truth—and therefore, if need be, against Hellas. To treat him as a representative of Hellenic 'culture' (i.e., of a supposed uniform Hellenic world view) is to make of him something both more and less than he claimed to be. So too for the Buddha, who preached the Four Noble Truths, not the Four Indian Truths. Socrates and the Buddha taught Hellenes and Indians only incidentally: they addressed human beings as such. The differences between them are not primarily differences between Hellas and India, just as the differences between the Buddhist scriptures and the Hindu ones quite transcend everything Indian. Professor Taylor's implicit historicism, like his presumption of the equal worth of cultures, is itself a merely Western conception (and a post-Hegelian one, at that). Inasmuch as these underlie his entire scheme, one wonders whether they will be subjected to the challenge implicit in the 'fusion of horizons' between the West and other cultures neither egalitarian nor historicist (to say nothing of the challenge implicit in those earlier stages in the thought of the West itself that were neither egalitarian nor historicist).

One of the defects of Professor Taylor's essay, it seems to me, is that because he begins from the politics of recognition and offers his plan of study as a response to it, he couches this plan in terms of 'culture' that are in fact inappropriate to it. To sum up: any proposed dialogue among 'cultures' supposes a reified notion of 'culture' to which no actual way of life responds. And this means that even if we approve of an expanded human dialogue such as Taylor proposes, we can't conceive of it as a dialogue among cultures. This alone suffices to disqualify it as an answer to contemporary demands for recognition of cultures as cultures. Professor Taylor proposes an intellectual project in response to a political demand, and there is no real fit between the two.

Be this as it may, suppose that we accept Professor Taylor's proposal to scrutinize without fear or favour every opinion of the human good and every well-entrenched cultural practice that presents itself to us, the most exotic no less than the most familiar. Such an inquiry would necessarily plunge us into just the intense controversy that most academics prefer to avoid, for it is impossible that critical scrutiny will not be experienced (and resented) as such. The opinions and practices most dangerous to scrutinize, today as in the time of Socrates, are familiar rather than exotic. Indeed, they are precisely those opinions that support multiculturalism and the politics of recognition.

4.

We have arrived, then, at the question of the practical or political bearing of Professor Taylor's proposal. Could he or any other collaborator in such a project expect a friendly reception from the partisans of the politics of recognition? I have my doubts. The 'recognition' these groups demand does not consist in having their opinions taken seriously, if that means scrutiny of their adequacy as guides to life. They are not likely to acquiesce in being required to justify themselves before the highest (though still evolving) principles of humanity. Whoever so acquiesces must acknowledge the possibility that the elements of his way of life that will be discarded may exceed those that will be retained; that, at the end of the day, very little may be left of it.

The 'fusion of horizons' is high-sounding, but such a project can really proceed only by the locking of horns. Whatever Professor Taylor's favoured methodology, if he raises fundamental questions he will give fundamental offence. This is a realm in which even provisional answers sting. All of Socrates' answers were provisional—indeed, he did not answer but asked—yet that did not render him any less offensive to his interlocutors. Precisely because his understanding of a given problem was only the best he could do at the time, he was determined to test it to the utmost, and there was no way to do that but to press it vigorously in the face of determined opposition. The question, then, is not whether we should be complacent about our present convictions—Socrates would agree with Professor Taylor that we should not—but how we should go about improving them. If the answer is that we must confront (and submit ourselves to confrontation by) those who disagree with them, then, the stakes being high, passions will run high as well. It doesn't matter whether we conduct this confrontation in person or in the pages of scholarly journals. To question is to challenge, to challenge is to provoke, and to provoke is to offend.

Those who claim recognition today seek validation, not challenge. One example will suffice. Recently, in conjunction with its annual orientation programs for new students, my own university held a 'Bisexuality Awareness Week', sponsored by the student government and the Association of Gay, Lesbian, and Bisexual Students. Its premise, as one of the organizers earnestly explained in the student newspaper, was that 'prejudice depends on ignorance'. Obviously what this young woman seeks for bisexuals is not the ruthless critical scrutiny to which Socrates exposed his interlocutors. She yearns not for *elenchos* (refutation) but for acceptance, and is not about to accept the former as a token of the latter. From her point of view, to understand bisexuality is to accept it; to challenge it is to misunderstand it. And misunderstanding, where based on wilful prejudice that defies enlightenment, is not merely a defect but an offence.

Professor Taylor is correct that, by any reasonable standard, validation offered on demand is spurious, and no less so for presenting itself as whole-hearted and unconditional. Even less is it genuine if compelled, although Professor Taylor—oddly, for someone with so much experience of university life—omits all mention of compulsion or its threat as a motive for extending recognition. In fact, groups are rarely shy about bringing pressure to bear to obtain the recognition they seek. Perhaps they are confused enough to mistake coerced for spontaneous deference. Perhaps, on the other hand, they know exactly what they're doing. Suspecting that the 'recognition' extended to them by the 'hegemonic' culture is grudging, they interpret it as attesting not to our respect for their ways but to our acknowledgment of their power. This too can do wonders for a group's self-esteem. Yet no doubt there is something unsatisfying about coerced recognition, which explains why groups that were surly before obtaining recognition can remain just as surly afterwards.

In any case, one can hardly expect groups with a grievance, whose complaint is that they have been undervalued or even oppressed, to submit to scrutiny as willingly as a more secure and self-confident group might do. Inasmuch as they experience their status as 'marginal' and that of their critics as 'hegemonic', they are likely to experience even the barest suggestion of criticism as a slight. The activists among them, hardened veterans of the 'politics of recognition' whose interest it is to maintain a constituency, will certainly interpret any criticism of their position as an attempt to perpetuate their subservience. For a transitional period, at least—and it may prove a long one—it will be necessary to treat all such groups with the utmost delicacy. Precisely this, however, would preclude any serious attempt to determine what is and is not of value in their 'cultures'.

Or, perhaps more to the point, it will be forbidden to attempt to assess the worth to *our* culture of what are in fact 'subcultures' of it. Here the exigencies of campus politics will serve to neutralize a further qualification of Professor Taylor's presumption of the equality of cultures, namely that '[he] has worded his principle [of the presumption of equal worth due all cultures] to exclude partial milieux within a society, as well as short phases of a major culture . . . [since] there is no reason to believe that, for instance, the different art forms of a given culture should be all of equal, or even of considerable, value; and every culture can go through phases of decadence' (66). This qualification is of the greatest importance. According to Professor Taylor himself, not even that provisional presumption of equality owed to any culture, taken as a whole, is also owed to its parts: no particular aspect of a culture can benefit from a presumption that its worth is equal to that of other aspects of that culture or to the corresponding aspect of other cultures. It is then distinctly possible, for example, that no art yet produced by the Zulus will rank with the novels of Tolstoy (cf. 42, 71–2). Professor Taylor's concession that every culture can go through phases of decadence cannot but remind us of certain remarks of Nietzsche: for instance, 'three infallible signs of the decadence of a society [are] vegetarianism, international law, and the emancipation of women.' That no one on campus today would dare endorse Nietzsche's position will confirm the extent to which any discourse about decadence today (and so about the relative worth of cultures themselves and given aspects of cultures) is constrained by the politics of recognition.

The example of bisexuals may seem atypical and therefore tendentious, but again I insist that the real impetus behind multiculturalism on campus comes not from Koreans and Czechs but from blacks, women, gays, Hispanics; and just as they do not represent distinct cultures (at most, they represent subcultures), so their concerns are not cultural but ideological. The personal *is* the political, as feminists are always reminding us, and within the context of so-called multiculturalism, the cultural is the political, too. Granting recognition to the various groups pressing for it would be as much a political act as was the recognition of Communist China, and must be accompanied by protocols every bit as constraining.

But perhaps the nub of the problem, and the clearest way of underlining the unsatisfying ambiguity of Professor Taylor's proposal, is precisely the question of the presumption of equality owed to each culture. He is certainly correct in stating that 'the logic behind some of these demands [for recognition] seems to depend upon a premise that we owe equal respect to all cultures.' As we have seen, he acquiesces in this logic. In his hands, however, this 'premise' becomes a 'presumption', and a presumption is something provisional. But this premise is anything but provisional for its adherents in the university today, whether those clamouring for recognition or those hastening to extend it. On the contrary, it is moral bedrock, the dogmatic truth on which all else depends and to which all else must be adjusted. Hence the attractiveness to these groups of what Professor Taylor dubs 'a more radical, neo-Nietzschean standpoint, which questions the very status of judgments of worth as such'. While we may agree with Professor Taylor in 'doubt[ing] the coherence [of this standpoint]', he will have to agree with us in recognizing its amazing power and attractiveness in an age of radical egalitarianism, and the consequent disinclination of its partisans to doubt its coherence.

From the dogmatic premise of the equality of cultures, however defended (if indeed it is defended at all) the imperative of equal recognition is held to follow. As with the premise, so with the consequence: there is nothing provisional about the recognition thus demanded. My culture is equal to yours, and that's that, no ifs or buts: this is what I'm insisting that you recognize.

Two sorts of cultures would submit to the vetting of their worth that Professor Taylor proposes: on the one hand, healthy, vibrant, self-confident ones, cultures that are accustomed to scrutiny, don't much care what professors say about them, and are too busy to keep up with it anyway; safely dead ones, on the other. Socrates and Buddha will pass tamely under his knife, as will major living cultures whose place in the world is secure. If these are the cultures Professor Taylor aims to probe, all success to him. But inasmuch as his project would require him to scrutinize even or precisely those parties and 'cultures' to whom he has extended equal recognition—which again proved to rest on a merely provisional presumption—he would have hell to pay.

Whatever the worth of Professor Taylor's scheme otherwise, it will not serve to propitiate the deities that reign on campus today. If he has not resolved the crucial dilemma besetting liberal education, he has certainly posed it. To probe the claims of any of the parties seeking recognition, whether or not they present themselves as 'cultures', is to offend them and so the prevailing ethos as well. It is to display what is bound to be taken not for an open mind but for a closed one. Professor Taylor writes as if the compromise that he proposes will lay to rest the political disputes over recognition within the university, permitting us to get on with the transpolitical business of elaborating transcultural standards of worth. In fact these disputes will continue to rage, and any attempt to interrogate cultures is bound to remain hostage to them.

In theory Professor Taylor's challenge to dogmatic relativism is unequivocal. In practice it would likely prove ambiguous. It lends itself to two interpretations, the one bold and the other craven. The brave Taylorite will forge ahead in his scrutiny of cultures, refraining from gratuitous offence but recognizing that offence cannot be avoided. He will suffer all that one suffers on campus today for having given offence. His less daring colleagues, on the other hand, will see in Professor Taylor's project an excuse for endless temporizing. They too will congratulate themselves on having avoided slipping into relativism. Granting every 'culture' the recognition it demands, they will concede that this recognition is merely provisional. At the same time, stressing how very far we still are from being able to specify the relevant standards, they will scrupulously refrain from offending anybody. They will dither, avoiding the unpleasantness that would have resulted not only from having specified such standards here and now, but from an aggressive effort to make progress towards determining them. In particular they would take forever to decide whether Zulu culture has produced any work comparable in worth to that of Tolstoy. Profuse in their etiquettes of recognition and sparing in their criticisms, they will drag their feet until the Last Judgment, on which day our puny verdicts will no longer matter. This I fear would prove the effectual truth of Professor Taylor's proposal. In time everyone will see (although few will care) that the supposed 'provisionality' of the recognition bestowed on demand is the merest fig leaf, that the rejection of relativism in theory cloaks its acceptance in practice, and that no one really aspires to much save avoidance of rocking the boat.

By acceptance of relativism in practice I mean acceptance of the pseudo-relativism characteristic of the Western university. It is false precisely because it serves a dogmatism, that of freedom and equality. The pedagogy of recognition, like the politics of recognition, is an aspect of 'the struggle for freedom and equality' (66). The potential supineness of Professor Taylor's project betrays its fundamental contradiction. It sets out to transcend Western parochialism, but it does so in the service of Western parochialism. What defines the current version of that parochialism is precisely the politics of recognition. It is the orthodoxy on campus today, and as such is as intellectually liberating as any other orthodoxy. Professor Taylor wants to have it both ways, avoiding offence to those who are easily offended, whom he is too sensitive to wish to offend and who cannot be offended with impunity, while preserving his freedom to assess the relative worth of all the various human alternatives. But hasn't he already declared his fealty to one alternative, by accepting as his point of embarkation the politics of recognition? It is striking that in his references to assessing the worth of foreign cultures, all the examples are aesthetic, as if it were primarily as art critics that we approached these cultures. That there is not so much as a mention of non-Western (or pre-Western, or earlier Western) political alternatives suggests how completely the primary questions are settled for Taylor, and settled on the terms of the contemporary West.

Notes

A variant of this essay was delivered at Arrábida, Portugal on 6 October 1999 under the auspices of the Graduate Program in Political Theory and Political Science of the Catholic University of Portugal and the Institute of Social Sciences of the University of Lisbon. A Portuguese translation of that text is forthcoming in *Analise Social* (Lisbon). The author is grateful to these institutions and to Dr João Carlos Espada for permission to publish this English version in the present volume.

1. 22-23 September 1999.
2. Charles Taylor, 'The Politics of Recognition', in Taylor et al., *Multiculturalism: Examining the Politics of Recognition*, ed. Amy Gutmann (Princeton: Princeton University Press, 1994), 65–6. All in-text page references in the present essay are to this edition.
3. I have previously expressed my views on the current North American university scene in 'All Quiet on the (post-)Western Front? Multiculturalism and the North American University', *The Public Interest* (Spring 1996), 3–21 (reprinted in *Multiculturalism*, ed. Robert Emmet Long [Bronx, NY: H.W. Wilson Company, 1997], 43–56); and in 'Multiculturalism to a Point', *Academic Questions* (Fall 1998), 31–7. A few sentences of the present essay are lifted from the second of these articles, with the kind permission of the publisher.
4. My treatment of the distinction between the older discourse of toleration and the newer one of recognition owes much to the excellent discussion by Adam Wolfson, 'What Remains of Toleration?', *The Public Interest* (Winter 1999), 37–51.
5. I have elaborated this claim in the second of my articles listed above in Note 3.

PART FOUR

NATIONALISM AND SELF-DETERMINATION

Lifeboat

Dominique Leydet

The image of nations as lifeboats conveys one aspect of their complex nature. One finds oneself tossed on the high seas in the company of individuals who are largely strangers, not of one's choosing. And yet the survival of all depends on the ability to co-operate successfully. What is attractive about this image is that it highlights the contingency of nations. Unlike voluntary associations, nations are not chosen by their members on the basis of shared principles. Most of us are simply born into a particular national community and try to deal as best we can with what that membership entails. Furthermore, nations have no particular telos. Although it is possible to reconstruct and try to explain the circumstances that have led to the fact that nation X is said to exist, the process through which it developed remains contingent and has no predetermined end. Thus, the nationalist project of having states' borders match the limits of distinct pre-political communities has no obvious necessity, and existing nation-states themselves must be seen as the contingent products of contingent histories.

But there is also a sense in which this picture is misleading. As David Miller has remarked, in a national community 'people are held together not merely by physical necessity, but by a dense web of customs, practices, implicit understandings, and so forth.'[1] Moreover, the image of the lifeboat can hardly account for the fact that a nation is a community that stretches back into the past. As Miller argues, the obligations that fellow countrymen have to one another 'do not arise simply from the present fact of their cooperation; they can appeal to their historic identity, to sacrifices made in the past by one section of the community on behalf of others, to back up the claims they make on one another now.'[2] Perhaps the greatest danger in a nation's cutting itself off from its past is that it loses any way of conceiving the legitimacy of inherited obligations. It is only by thinking of a nation as implying a common inheritance that Canadians can make sense of their specific obligations towards Aboriginal peoples, even though present-day Canadians are not the ones who 'stole' Aboriginal lands.

Pace Miller, these two reactions are not necessarily in contradiction; yet the metaphor does bring out the problematic character of the relationship between nations and their past. In this essay I propose to clarify how we should think about that relationship by discussing two important dimensions of it: the contingency of a nation's past and how that past can be made to contribute to a political community's self-understanding. In the first part, I defend what I find attractive in the liberal-contractarian view of political community (which inspired the image of the lifeboat) against a criticism formulated by Bernard Yack[3] with specific reference to Jürgen Habermas's constitutional patriotism. Yack argues that in starting from the coexistence of individuals (to quote Rawls) 'at the same time on a definite geographical territory',[4] the contractarian tradition fails to recognize the importance of pre-political communities. I will therefore start by discussing Habermas's writings, in the hope of demonstrating that this aspect of the liberal-contractarian view, far from representing a fatal flaw, is the product of a right-minded appreciation of the contingency of both nations and states.

In the second part I will explore the consequences of this acknowledgment of contingency on the role we allow history in strengthening a sense of collective identity. Specifically, I will look at the notion of 'national history' as it appears both in David Miller's book *On Nationality* and in more recent writings by Gérard Bouchard. My aim here is to show why even such versions of national history are misguided when applied to societies characterized, and often divided, by cultural and ethnic diversity. If history is to help a political community reinforce its ethical bonds, it must be understood in an essentially critical way, divorced from any nation-building mandate. Through this discussion, I hope to clarify the extent to which Miller's criticism of the lifeboat picture is correct, while arguing that the consequences he draws from it are not ultimately compelling.

1.

In 'The Myth of the Civic Nation', Bernard Yack shows how both ethnic and civic nationalisms ignore the contingent character of nations. On the one hand, ethnic nationalists try to gloss over this problem 'by picking out one source of identity in our ever-changing communal heritage and turning it into a norm against which we should measure our political communities'.[5] To this end they first project a largely artificial continuity between our current cultural identities and some discrete ethnic communities in the past and then assume that these communities maintain their character through time, even in periods where there is little evidence of ethnic consciousness. On the other hand, civic nationalists like Michael Ignatieff also deny the contingency of national communities by portraying them as 'created by the choice of individuals to honor a particular political creed',[6] thus 'turning national belonging [into] a form of rational attachment'.[7] If ethnic nationalists obscure the contingency of nations by redescribing them as 'always having been there', civic nationalists do the same by portraying them as the product of conscious choice, as a kind of voluntary association based upon the rational acceptance of certain political principles.

As for social contract theories themselves, they avoid any discussion of pre-political communities; instead, they give an atemporal account of individuals coexisting on a given territory and present arguments intended to elaborate and justify the rules of co-operation to which such individuals would likely agree. Yack's point is that these arguments must always start from a 'predefined group of individuals',[8] a pre-political community whose existence is simply assumed, not characterized or explained. Ultimately there is nothing in these theories that can justify in normative terms why this particular group of individuals rather than another, or even humanity as a whole, should form the political community. This all-important assumption made by social contractarians becomes apparent only when the boundaries of the pre-political community are themselves in question; otherwise the myth that political associations rest on individual consent is maintained.

Yack illustrates this point by showing that although Habermas's constitutional patriotism says all kinds of interesting things about *what* should be the basis of a new democratic Germany, it cannot explain *why* the issue of German reunification itself ever arose. Such an explanation would have to include an explicit reference to the pre-political German community of shared memory and experience. In fact, if constitutional patriotism is to make sense at all it must be as 'a way of situating universalistic principles in the "horizon of the history of a nation"'.[9] Habermas tacitly admits as much, but the problem is that, like contractualists in general, he cannot explicitly acknowledge this assumption, since this would mean recognizing that nations are not simply created by choice.

In the following, I do not want to judge the extent to which Yack's analysis of constitutional patriotism is correct, nor to explicitly defend Habermas's view. Rather, I want to take up Yack's criticism of the conceptual gap in the liberal-contractarian account of political associations. My starting point will be Habermas's confrontation of this issue in his more recent writings. Through him, I will attempt to defend the liberal view, which I understand as drawing the correct conclusions from its acknowledgment of the contingency of political communities.

In his recent work, Habermas has recognized that the liberal tradition and, in particular, its Kantian offshoot do not offer much in the way of a normative justification for the boundaries of an association of free and equal citizens:

> Kant ascribes to every human being as such the right to have rights and to regulate his life in common with others in such a way that everyone can enjoy equal liberties in accordance with public, coercive laws. But this does not settle who may actually make use of this right with whom and when; nor does it settle who may unite into a self-determining commonwealth on the basis of a social contract.[10]

It is only retroactively, once a democratic constitution has been successfully instituted, that it becomes possible to describe the participants in its foundation as the sovereign people. This presupposes that borders themselves are not disputed. Although this was the case for the United States (where the act of foundation took the form of a severing of ties with the colonial metropolis), and in France (where it involved an internal change of regime), in general nation-states do not emerge as the seamless creation of a distinct people living in isolation. Here, then, it seems that liberal theory can't help us much.

So what should we do? According to Habermas, we should simply accept that there does not seem to be any normative solution to this problem and recognize the essentially contingent character of borders. What we should not do is follow the nationalist position that the principle of self-determination of nations can offer such a solution. The idea of a collective right to self-determination must presuppose something like a homogeneous nation concentrated in a particular territory. Yet such homogeneity is more often than not an illusion that camouflages cultural/ethnic diversity. In most cases, therefore, secession can only create new disgruntled minorities, and thus reproduce the problem that precipitated the implosion of the state, with similar tensions reemerging in different clothes—unless, of course, one is ready to see suppressive policies enacted from above to enforce a fictive vision of national homogeneity.

Now, many defenders of self-determination would argue that in fact they do not presuppose such homogenity. Certainly Habermas seems to set up a false dichotomy. For him there seems to be no alternative between ethnic nationalism, on the one hand, and republicanism, on the other. Many nationalists today defend an inclusive conception of the nation that does not require internal homogeneity but relies on the integration of minorities.[11] Yet I do not think that this weakens the thrust of Habermas's argument, which questions the supposed unproblematic character of the collective subject assumed by the principle of self-determination: if minorities remain opposed to the nationalist project and do not see themselves as part of the nation on behalf of which self-determination is to be exercised, then the inclusive character of the nation supported by the nationalists, although reassuring, does nothing to answer the problem he has highlighted. To the extent that the existing constitutional state does respect the fundamental rights of individuals who are members of national or ethnic minorities, including cultural rights, it is not clear how secession represents an improvement over the status quo. Of course, this remark implies a commitment to a consequentialist position. Whether nationalists embrace such a perspective, asking themselves whether or not the success of their movement would indeed increase overall utility, remains an open question.

Does this essentially negative argument do anything to answer Yack's criticism? It is precisely because the existence of 'a' prepolitical community with clear boundaries is rarely unproblematic that the liberal view cannot use it as its starting point. It simply acknowledges the existence of particular state borders and shows how the individuals who live inside them are called upon to share equal rights and obligations. The liberal position does not give us a normative answer to where those borders should fall, unless the question is raised in a context where individual rights are being violated (e.g., colonial domination, foreign occupation, or oppression). Otherwise, liberals will tend to be cautious about using the language of self-determination to effect a change of borders.

In this sense, the liberal assumption that Yack criticizes is not really an assumption at all. Rather, it should be seen as an attempt to deal with the contingent character of nations and the pluralism of political communities. The liberal view is that since neither the utopia of a universal state nor the dream (or nightmare) of a perfect fit between nations and states is a real possibility, what we have to do is work out, within existing borders, which political principles and institutions are just and inclusive enough to give us the means to settle our differences and establish compromises.

This does not mean that we should not acknowledge the problems often faced by national and ethnic minorities. Habermas himself recognizes that even in states where the political culture would satisfy the requirements of constitutional patriotism, collective decisions about ethical-political issues, based on the majority principle, would still closely reflect the relative numerical strength of communities and often run against the wishes and needs of minorities. As Habermas writes:

> Legal orders as wholes are also 'ethically imbued' in that they interpret the universalistic content of the same constitutional principles in different ways, namely, against the background of the experiences that make up a national history and in light of a historically prevailing tradition, culture and form of life. Often the regulation of culturally sensitive matters . . . is merely a reflection of the ethical–political self-understanding of a majority culture that has achieved dominance for contingent, historical reasons.[12]

Constitutional patriotism cannot and, in fact, does not pretend to be the whole answer to the problems faced by minorities. It would be absurd to think that the centripetal tensions provoked by the presence of minorities in a state can be weakened through the top-down development of an overarching collective identity. Conceptions of national identity cannot be the answer to such problems. In fact, there is no substitute for recognizing the demands of minorities and addressing them in the only adequate way: via institutional reforms. In the case of democratic constitutional states, several routes are open, from federalism to different forms of decentralization. What such institutional means must achieve is the effective guarantee of cultural autonomy, group specific rights, and so on.[13] As Will Kymlicka writes: 'What matter are not symbols, but the facts on the ground—whether a national minority has sufficient control over decisions regarding language, education, immigration, and economic development to ensure its long-term viability.'[14] To say this is not to commit ourselves to acknowledge the nationalist thesis about nations and the right to self-determination. As Kymlicka has shown convincingly,[15] one needs only to recognize culture as a primary good to individuals to justify the importance of minority rights. Put another way, we do not need to recognize groups or 'nations' as part of our moral ontology to achieve this end.

2.

So if we accept that political communities are like lifeboats in the sense that they are mainly the product of a 'historically accidental coexistence on the same (arbitrarily demarcated) piece of land',[16] must we embrace the view that the obligations that fellow countrymen have towards one another stem simply 'from the present fact of their cooperation'?[17] As I mentioned at the beginning of this essay, I oppose this atemporal vision, which might be conveniently invoked to argue, for instance, that the past oppression of blacks in the US is irrelevant today since slavery has long been consigned to the dustbin of history, or that the official status of the French language outside Québec must be rescinded since it does not merit a special status with respect to other minority languages. To understand why French 'enjoys' such a status, one has to refer to a common past that ties Canadians together today, no matter when they or their forebears arrived on this land. The question is to clarify how we should think of this bond. In other words, how do we reconcile the contingency of nations with our need to think of them as ethical communities that inherit obligations from the past? This might look like a difficult task, since the second requirement supposes a continuity from past to present that the first one seems to deny.

One possible response would be to draw a veil over this contingency through the concoction of a national history that can make sense of, and give meaning to, the various circumstances and events from which the present community emerged. As Renan famously noted, this may require that we get our history wrong,[18] in the sense that we learn to forget some 'episodes' and rewrite others so they may fit in the narrative we are trying to create. In the grand style, this produces something like Michelet's *Histoire du XIXe siècle*. Today, supporters of liberal nationalism like David Miller still consider such an exercise to be both legitimate and important, if done the right way.

According to Miller,[19] national histories respond to the feeling of discomfort often provoked by an awareness of the forced character of our nation's genesis. National histories typically project certain characteristics, now seen as constitutive of the national identity, backwards onto past populations, who may well have been oblivious to any such feelings of national awareness. Miller recognizes, in short, that writing national history requires that, in part at least, the past be mythologized.

Such mythologizing seems to run against our contemporary conceptions of history, which share an essentially critical understanding of its task. Yet he believes we should not simply dismiss the project: 'it may not be rational to discard beliefs, even if they are, strictly speaking, false, when they can be shown to contribute significantly to the support of valuable social relations'.[20] Miller sees historical myths as serving two important functions in the creation of a national identity. First, they strengthen the belief that the nation, as it exists today, is solidly anchored in the past and 'embodies a real continuity between generations.'[21] Second, they play a 'moralizing role' in providing models of the various virtues that we should seek to emulate. In short, such myths can be justified by the fact that they strengthen the nation as an ethical community.

Of course, Miller does not claim that the outright falsification of the past can be condoned as such. A distinction must be made between unsubstantiated reinterpretations of the past and outright fabrication or obliteration of facts.[22] The relevant distinction, he writes, is not 'between the truth of "real" history and the falsehood of "national" history, but between national identities that emerge through open processes of debate and discussion . . . and identities that are authoritatively imposed by repression and indoctrination'.[23]

Still, his argument avoids the crucial problem raised by the project of writing a national history. Indeed, it is difficult to see how such a history, by its very nature, could be reconciled with the formation of a national identity through 'open debate and discussion'. After all, myths can rarely withstand open debate and discussion. Moreover, attempts at writing national history are usually made in the larger context of nation-building projects and are seldom intended simply to provide a subject of discussion for a cultivated public: rather, their aim is explicitly to influence school curricula. When a version of national history takes the form of a textbook studied by schoolchildren in the context of the classroom, it won't do simply to rely on the general climate of freedom that characterizes a given society to calm our doubts about what are, 'strictly speaking', falsehoods. In such a context, the distinction between what Miller ironically calls 'real' and 'false' history remains relevant.

As Benedict Anderson brilliantly showed, the construction of national genealogies is never gratuitous. Quoting Renan's famous remark that 'Tout citoyen français doit avoir oublié la Saint-Barthélemy, les massacres du Midi au XIIIe siècle',[24] Anderson correctly suggests that Renan presupposed, first, that his contemporaries must have been reminded of those forgotten events; and, second, that the reminder must have taken a particular form, emphasizing that in both cases the victims and the perpetrators alike were fellow Frenchman—when in fact that was not true. Thus one becomes aware of 'a systematic historiographical campaign, deployed by the state mainly through the state's school system, to "remind" every young Frenchwoman and Frenchman of a series of antique slaughters which are now inscribed as "family history"';[25] the purpose being to strengthen a sense of national belonging.

The question here is whether something like Renan's conception of a national history and its role in creating a national identity is still possible today, now that democratic constitutional states have discovered their multinational and polyethnic makeup. After all, Renan's contemporaries were not reminded of the fact that most of the Albigensians massacred in the thirteenth century did not speak French at all, but Provençal or Catalan. This fact simply did not fit in the narrative that was being constructed and taught in the schools of the République. What is being 'remembered/forgotten' is thus always the product of a political choice. The political commitments that led to such obfuscation in nineteenth-century France would be unacceptable today, given the development of liberal sensitivities and the evolution of history as an academic discipline. Nor is it clear that such an exercise would lead to a strengthened sense of shared identity. Instead, it might simply engender resentment, especially in culturally diverse societies, such as Canada, which are often divided along cultural/ethnic lines. Even if Miller's version of this exercise would leave 'open the possibility of differing interpretations',[26] he would still want to have his story start from the premise of a single British nation: a concept that not all British subjects—for instance, those Scots who see themselves as constituting a nation—would welcome.[27]

In short, the very idea of writing a national history raises three issues that Miller does not seriously confront: first, its standing towards history as an academic discipline; second, its relation to the state; third, the problem of internal pluralism. In recent writings, Gérard Bouchard has made a more serious attempt to consider these issues. In *La Nation québécoise au futur et au passé*,[28] he defends a revised conception of national history and tries to show that it can be reconciled with both the canons of scientific history and the reality of an ethnically and ideologically diverse society. Bouchard highlights two main elements of any project of writing a national history: first, it is necessarily written from the perspective of a 'we' to whom it also addresses itself. Second, it is bound to have an 'official character' and be closely associated with the state, which is in fact its main sponsor.[29] As Bouchard is well aware, and as we saw briefly above, the main criticism of national history is that it presupposes the unproblematic existence of a 'we' that is retroactively projected, thereby linking present and past by virtue of continuities that are largely fictitious.

Confronted by this problem, Bouchard answers, first, that any history contains such back-projections, and that putting the past into a linear form is, in fact, one of the main epistemological conventions of history, if not its primary function in Western civilization.[30] Second, he tries to differentiate between acceptable and unacceptable forms of such projections. What the historian should avoid at all costs is to project his 'we' as a given and make any teleological assumptions about what should be the 'end' towards which that 'we' is headed. To do this, the historian must describe the 'we' as it really was, in all its uncertainties and successive transformations, at each stage of its development.[31] Thus Bouchard appears to aim at a form of national history that would not involve drawing a veil over the contingency of nations and their beginnings, but would, on the contrary, acknowledge them.

As to the second danger, that a national history can easily become the ideological servant of the state, Bouchard argues that today it should be possible for historians to avoid being railroaded: together the methodology of social history and a comparative perspective should help them maintain objectivity and distance from their subject matter. Moreover, in the context of an open society, where unanimity has been replaced by internal diversity, it simply would not be possible to subsume the whole nation under the rubric of a single party, class, or ethnic group and write the history of the nation strictly from that perspective.

The first test for Bouchard's conception is whether he himself avoids these pitfalls in his own programmatic description of what a national history of Québec should look like. In fact, I will argue that he fails this test, since his view is developed on the basis of certain teleological assumptions. The choices that predicate his conception are themselves debatable and point to the necessarily contentious nature of any national history written in the context of a complex society, where there is no uncontestable pre-political community that could stand as its subject.

Bouchard's troubles begin as soon as he tries to define the nation which is to be the subject of his history. He defines the Québec nation as a 'francophonie de type Nord-américain' characterized by a high degree of diversity, since it includes ethnic minorities such as Anglo-Quebecers and cultural communities. Its common denominator is the capacity to communicate in French.[32] Thus Bouchard tries to strike a balance between a purely civic conception of the nation, which he criticizes as too thin, and an ethnic conception, which he repudiates. What he proposes is an inclusive, cultural conception. It is this 'we' that is to be projected back on to the past, it is this 'we' whose development and successive transformations we are invited to follow. The problem is that this 'we' is a very recent construct, which is not recognized by many of those it purports to include. It is not accepted by the particular wing of the nationalist movement towards which much of Bouchard's argument is directed. Nor, more importantly, is it accepted either by most Anglo-Quebecers, who consider themselves Canadians first and foremost, or by most Aboriginal people, who, *pace* Bouchard, refuse to see themselves as the first Quebecers.[33]

This objection is cogently stated by Bouchard himself: 's'il est vrai que la science historique tire ses prémisses de l'actuel, comment peut-elle projeter dans le passé une cohésion collective qui ne se trouve pas dans le présent?'[34] In other words, if the 'we' that is projected onto the past does not exist in the present, since so many individuals do not recognize themselves or others as part of it, how can the national historian use it as a reference point? Bouchard responds by claiming that this is the wager a historian can choose to make both as an intellectual and a citizen. He adds:

> ces paris qu'elle fait sur le présent et les démonstrations qu'elle en tire, c'est la manière dont la science historique, réactualisée, peut agir en quelque sorte sur le présent et ainsi contribuer à la culture qui se fait. Ce faisant, elle exerce une responsabilité éminente dans la mesure où elle contribue à mettre en place les fondements d'un consensus et à imprimer à la société une direction nouvelle.[35]

However, if it is the case that the national historian's starting point is not a presently existing 'we' but rather one that he wants to help create on the basis of his own political choices, then it is difficult to avoid the accusation that he is indeed making some teleological assumptions. What guides his view of the community's past is a certain conception of what its end should be. I do not think that this is a problem specific to writing a national history of Québec, although it is certainly more acute in the case of a society whose political future is the subject of an intense debate. My claim is rather that this is a problem characteristic of national history per se. Such history is usually part and parcel of a project of nation-building and thus contains, implicitly or explicitly, a vision of the direction favoured by the author and his supporters for their political community. This telos acts as a unifying perspective that allows the historian to present an often fragmented and divided past as constituting the national history of a single nation.

It is interesting to note here the road that Bouchard briefly considers, but decides not to follow. In his opening remarks he writes that, as a consequence of the recognition of our society's cultural and ideological diversity, we may have to abandon the project of constructing a 'mémoire intégrée', and resign ourselves to describing a 'mémoire multiple, éclatée' or a 'mémoire des mémoires'.[36] In the end, though, he chooses to pursue the first alternative, which leads him to fashion his integrated concept of a 'nation québécoise'.[37] Again, I think the temptation to which he succumbs is inherent in the very idea of a national history. You want one history, not histories; one memory, not memories—and the question must be whether this goal is desirable or even possible in the context of pluralistic and divided societies like Québec and Canada. In foreclosing on the question of whether there is or can be, in fact, such an integrated memory, Bouchard is presupposing the kind of continuity that he should want to distance himself from, if he truly wishes to remain on the right side of his own distinction between acceptable and unacceptable backward-projections. By starting from the premise of 'one nation', with 'one memory', he must in the end—his own best intentions notwithstanding—fall back into denial of the contingency of nations.

I do not think that we need to subscribe to a positivist view of history to see that national history appears, then, as belonging to a different species of historical writing than what is understood today as academic history. Although it is true that any history will, to some extent, show the imprint of its author's political convictions, one should distinguish between a historian who tries as far as possible to avoid mixing her own opinions with what she is doing as a historian (even though we know that she can never be entirely successful in this) and someone who engages in this activity from a militant point of view, with the goal of 'working on the present' and 'help[ing] to establish the basis for consensus', indeed of 'steer[ing] the society in a new direction'.

Does this criticism of the very idea of a national history, particularly in the context of today's liberal and pluralist democracies, mean that I believe we should avoid history altogether? Certainly not. I do think that countries (such as Canada) that are trying, with varying degrees of enthusiasm, to come to terms with their multinational and polyethnic make-up need more history rather than less. The question is the kind of history we require. My claim is that national history, even in the form defended by authors like Miller and Bouchard, is precisely what we need to avoid. What we should look for is an essentially critical history that can help us come to terms with the situation of Aboriginal peoples, the state of the French language outside Québec, relations between Québec and the rest of Canada, and so on. The same, obviously, should be true for Québec. Instead of writing a national history from the fictitious perspective of a reconciled society, sharing a basic consensus on what it is and where it should go, it would be more interesting and more helpful to write from the perspective of its actual divisions, in the hope of achieving a better understanding.

As Habermas has argued,[38] if history cannot play its traditional role of giving meaning and form to a national tradition, it can make us aware of the need to take a reflexive and critical attitude towards national continuities. Every tradition possesses its dark underside, and the task of historiography is not to gloss over it in order to fabricate a unified version of the community's past and nourish its collective identity.[39] Its role is rather to build a critical consciousness of history, which can be developed only through conflicting interpretations of the past.

But if we do question continuities, and insist on the fragmented nature of our political community's past, do we not run the risk of weakening the ties that bind fellow countrymen together and thus making them more reluctant to accept the obligations they owe one another, including those contracted in the past? This is David Miller's position, which ultimately strikes me as unconvincing. It is premised on the idea that we can recognize that past injustices have implications for us only if we can picture, for instance, the first white settlers in New France as our forefathers in an emotionally resonant way. Or, for a different kind of example, if only today's very diverse Canadian population could see itself as still somehow subsumed under the two founding nations, then it could accept the idea of Canada's duality. But I do not accept this as true. We need only see ourselves as members of a political community inscribed in time in order to recognize a minimal kind of continuity. This continuity does not commit us to thinking of the *habitants* or the First Nations as our common ancestors; however, it does require that we recognize the past injustices perpetrated by the state against portions of the population as having consequences that cannot be disallowed today. It also implies that myths such as that of the 'two founding nations' say something about the past that cannot simply be dismissed, since it still echoes into the present. Myths should not be treated as sacred cows, but neither should they be rejected out of hand; rather, they should be discussed, in a historically informed way, in order to deepen our understanding of both the past and the present, even if this means facing unpleasant facts.[40]

Of course, Miller's point is not so much to deny all this as to say that this conception of the ties that bind a community to its past will not prove as effective as the one he favours. Hence the idea of a national history as a kind of 'noble lie'. In a sense he may be right, although it is difficult to know to what extent this empirical claim is true or not.[41] Still, this hypothetical advantage should be balanced against the risks we would run in following such a route, as discussed above. On the one hand, it is not clear that such a project is even possible today, given the evolution of history as a discipline. On the other hand, national histories, in their efforts to present a unified and ultimately reconciled version of the past, tend to soften the harsher contours of the conflicts that have divided the populations inhabiting a given territory over time. This may make contemporaries less aware of past injustices and, consequently, more reluctant to recognize their collective obligations today. It may also spark new resentments on the part of those who would feel shortchanged by a bowdlerized version of their past. In short, the potential losses far outweigh the gains.

It is time to make one last visit to our lifeboat. This image highlights the contingency of any nation in a way that should make us wary of any attempt to see it as constituting the pre-existing subject underpinning a political community. It also underlines the contingency of any political association. In this sense, there are no 'real' countries as opposed to artificial ones. There are only political communities in which fellow citizens have obligations towards one another in virtue of their common membership in a community inscribed in time and thus endowed with a past that it can neither rewrite nor dismiss. If you should ever find yourself in a lifeboat in the company of strangers, you might do well to ask yourself how you all ended up there.

Notes

1. David Miller, *On Nationality* (Oxford: Clarendon Press, 1995), 41.
2. Ibid., 42.
3. Bernard Yack, 'The Myth of the Civic Nation', in *Theorizing Nationalism*, ed. Ronald Beiner (Albany: State University of New York Press, 1999), 103–19.
4. John Rawls, *A Theory of Justice* (Oxford: Oxford University Press, 1971), 126.
5. Yack, 'The Myth of the Civic Nation', 110.
6. Ibid., 104.
7. Michael Ignatieff, cited by Yack, ibid.
8. Yack, 'The Myth of the Civic Nation', 108.
9. Ibid.
10. Jürgen Habermas, 'On the Relation between The Nation, the Rule of Law, and Democracy', in *The Inclusion of the Other. Studies in Political Theory*, ed. Ciarian Cronin and Pablo De Greiff (Cambridge, Mass.: MIT Press, 1998), 140.
11. See, for instance, Kai Nielsen, 'Cultural Nationalism, Neither Ethnic nor Civic', in *Theorizing Nationalism*, ed. Ronald Beiner, 119–31; Michel Seymour, with Jocelyne Couture and Kai Nielsen, 'Introduction: Questioning the Ethnic/Civic Dichotomy', in *Rethinking Nationalism*, ed. Jocelyne Couture, Kai Nielsen, and Michel Seymour, *Canadian Journal of Philosophy*, supplementary vol. 22 (Calgary: University of Calgary Press), 1–65.
12. Habermas, 'On the Relation', 144–5.
13. Ibid., 145. See also Habermas, 'Struggles for Recognition in Constitutional States', *European Journal of Philosophy* 1, 2 (1993), 137–40.
14. Will Kymlicka, 'Misunderstanding Nationalism', in *Theorizing Nationalism*, ed. Ronald Beiner, 140.
15. Will Kymlicka, *Liberalism, Community and Culture* (Oxford: Clarendon Press, 1989).
16. Stephen Holmes, 'Liberalism for a World of Ethnic Passions and Decaying States', *Social Research* 61, 3 (1994), 606.
17. Miller, *On Nationality*, 42.
18. Ernest Renan, 'Qu'est-ce qu'une nation?', *Qu'est-ce qu'une nation? et autres essais politiques*, ed. Joël Roman (Paris: Presses pocket, 1992), 41.
19. Miller, *On Nationality*, 34.
20. Ibid., 36.
21. Ibid.
22. Ibid., 38–9. Miller cites as an example of obliteration the fact that Trotsky was erased from the historical record of the 1917 revolution by Stalin and his successors.
23. Ibid., 39.
24. 'Every French citizen must have forgotten the St Bartholomew's Day slaughter, and the massacres of the Albigensians in the thirteenth century.' Renan, 'Qu'est-ce qu'une nation?', 42.

25. Benedict Anderson, *Imagined Communities* (London, New York: Verso, 1991), 201. Contrast Anderson's reading of Renan to Miller's in *On Nationality*. According to the latter, what Renan is saying here is that 'no Frenchman could recognize as his forebears those who had carried out the massacres. It is not denied that the events occurred, but they do not form part of the story that the nation tells itself' (*On Nationality*, 38).
26. Miller, *On Nationality*, 180.
27. It is worth noting that Miller does not recognize the Scots as a nation, since they share with the rest of Britain a specific British national identity (ibid., 173–4). Miller understands the latter as excluding the former, and refuses to see Great Britain as a multinational state.
28. Gérard Bouchard, *La Nation québécoise au futur et au passé* (Montréal: vlb éditeur, 1999), 83–143.
29. Ibid., 86–90.
30. Ibid., 96.
31. Ibid., 97.
32. Ibid., 125. Whether Aboriginal people are part of this nation is not entirely clear. If we follow Bouchard's definition of the nation, only those who can communicate in French are. But it is clear that Bouchard favours their progressive inclusion, presumably through their learning French. See his discussion of how, in Mexico and in Australia, a relation of direct filiation is traced between the white population and Aboriginal people. He adds the following: 'L'idée que des Blancs puissent s'inscrire symboliquement dans une filiation autochtone ancienne peut laisser sceptique; c'est qu'on n'arrive pas à se détacher d'une conception biologique des origines *collectives*' (ibid., 149, n. 45). What is interesting is that he does not consider whether Aboriginal people themselves would accept such a filiation; whether they, in fact, see themselves as part of that collectivity whose genesis is to be reconstructed.
33. Ibid., 117.
34. '[I]f it is true that the science of history draws its premises from the present day, how can it project into the past a collective cohesion that does not exist in that present?' Ibid., 140.
35. '[W]agering on the present and drawing illustrations from it is the way a reinvented history can work on the present and thus contribute to the culture that is being created. In so doing, it plays a very important role, for it helps to establish the basis for consensus and to steer the society in a new direction.' Ibid.
36. 'integrated memory', 'multiple, fragmented one', or a 'memory of memories'. Ibid., 89.
37. Ibid., 125.
38. Jürgen Habermas, *Écrits politiques*, trans. Christian Bouchindhomme and Rainer Rochlitz (Paris: Cerf, 1990), 235. See also Habermas, 'Grenzen des Neohistorismus', *Die Nachholende Revolution* (Frankfurt a. M.: Suhrkamp, 1990), 155.
39. This is dramatically true in the case of Germany, of course. But it would be a mistake to think that what Habermas has to say is relevant to the German case only. All traditions do have their dark underside, although some are obviously darker than others.
40. On the idea of the two founding nations, see A.I. Silver, *The French-Canadian Idea of Confederation 1864–1900*, 2nd ed. (Toronto, Buffalo, London: University of Toronto Press, 1997).
41. For a cogent criticism of the thesis (defended by Miller, among others) that a strong

national identity is linked to a greater degree of social cohesion and solidarity, see Wayne Norman, 'Les points faibles du modèle nationaliste libéral', in *Libéralismes et nationalismes: Philosophie et politique* (Ste-Foy: Presses de l'Université Laval, 1995), 83–6.

Communities of Memory

W. James Booth

This essay discusses one dimension of a long-standing political philosophical problem: (collective) memory and identity. It is a philosophical essay, and insofar as it treats of current politics at all, it does so only in using France and Germany as case studies illustrating the weight of the past in constitutional-patriotic democracies. Yet its origins and inspiration are Canadian. While in France for a conference, I took my six-year-old daughter Madeleine to the Verrières Ridge area in Normandy, south of Caen, where members of the Montreal-based Black Watch regiment, among them her grandfather, had fought a particularly bloody battle in July 1944. There, in that *lieu de mémoire*, the memory of one moment in Canada's and her family's past was passed on to her. But the same region is the locale of more than one memory. This was made plain to us by the large billboards on the road announcing a Quebec/Caen festival inspired by the origins there of one of Canada's 'founding peoples'. My first reaction, driving past these signs, was to wonder, half-seriously, whether the Quebec government had sponsored similar festivals in the countries of origin of other Quebecers—in the Côte d'Ivoire, for instance, or Haiti, or Vietnam, or Ireland. Then it occurred to me that I had also intended to take my daughter to the town in Normandy from which her grandmother's family had emigrated in the 1700s. I wanted this tie to be part of my child's memory-identity, in much the same way that her name is—for her grandmother too was named Madeleine. This small corner of Calvados, then, is the site of many memories: of Canada at war, of a nationalist provincial government and the roots of francophone Quebec, of individuals and their families whose lives have been bound up with Normandy and its past. These memories seem at once objectively *there*, given, and evoked or created; solid anchors of our overlapping identities and yet malleable; collective and individual; the cement of solidarity, but also contested and exclusionary. They are, in short, emblematic of the politics of memory.

This essay looks at one aspect of those politics: the relationship between memory, political identity, and moral accountability. Now, while identity statements often appear as propositions about current time-slice sets of values, institutions, and so on, I will treat them here as something more than present-tense descriptions of our culture or political life. I will also treat their moral-political content as extending beyond demands for recognition. Identity claims, when pushed, characteristically seek something else: to establish the sameness, the continuity of a person or community across time and in the face of apparent change. Central for the discussion here is that these claims typically also have a moral-temporal dimension: they ground ideas of attribution and responsibility, for deeds past and for the future. What I want to discuss, then, are the ways in which we think of a political community as existing continuously over time, and as therefore being the subject of attribution, accountable for the past which belongs to it, and responsible for a future which is also its own.

Let me begin with a story that illustrates some of the principal features of the controversies I shall be addressing. In 1992, François Mitterrand, then President of the French Republic, was asked to lend his voice, on behalf of France, to the commemoration of the July 1942 roundup of Jews at the Vélodrome d'Hiver (commonly abbreviated to Vél' d'Hiv) in Paris and their subsequent deportation to Nazi concentration camps. Specifically, he was asked to have the Republic acknowledge the role of France in the persecution of Jews and others during the dark years of occupation. The Republic, then, was called upon, in an act of atoning remembrance, to inscribe in its public memory the complicity of France in these crimes. Mitterrand at first resisted: 'The Republic, across all its history, has constantly adopted a totally open attitude [with regard to the rights of all its citizens]. Thus, do not demand an accounting of this Republic' (Conan and Rousso 1996, 60–1). At the core of this refusal of responsibility and of public remembrance was the claim that France was identical with free, republican, France. Thus, the Vichy regime was a parenthesis in the continuous history of the Republic, 'a new regime, different and temporary', as Mitterrand described it (*Le Monde*, 15–16 Nov. 1992, 6). The France that is the Republic is not, on this view, the proper locus of responsibility for these crimes, nor the community burdened by the duty of remembering them. In the end, a commemorative plaque was installed at the site of the Vél' d'Hiv, though the Republic's homage to the victims of these crimes grudgingly referred to Vichy as the 'de facto authority called "the Government of the French State"' (Conan and Rousso 1996, 91; in 1995, Jacques Chirac did accept responsibility on behalf of France).

Here we can see the intertwining of one (constitutional-republican) conception of political identity, responsibility, and remembrance. The sameness of the country across time is grounded in its institutional and constitutional-normative continuity. Regime forms that break with that continuity also thereby cease to be 'ours'. They are not part of what 'we' were and so not the objects of public remembrance, of our collective memory of ourselves as we were. We are not the inheritors of a past that belongs to someone else—Nazi Germany, or the Vichy collaborators. Most fundamentally, because we are not one with the perpetrators, because we do not share with them a political identity, we are not accountable for their injustices. The issues raised in the Vél' d'Hiv remembrance incident are at the heart of one of the most enduring perplexities in political thought: the question of what constitutes the identity of a political community and what obligations flow from that shared something called identity.

Early Western political reflection picked out some of the essential strands of these questions. How, Aristotle asked, are we to determine whether 'a city [is] the same city as it was before, or not the same but a different city?' (*Politics* 1276a, 18–20). It is easy to answer this, he suggests, when people and place are separated and two cities emerge where once there was one. But is the city the same across time simply by virtue of being inhabited by people of one race (*genos*)? Or because they live in the same bounded space? Are ethnicity and territory, jointly or separately, the foundations of political identity? The physical markers of identity, shared geography and ethnicity, are insufficient, Aristotle argues, for the sort of commonality that we count as political. (Presumably, though, a common space is a necessary condition and 'common origins or race' [*homophulon*] helpful in preserving unity. See Aristotle, *Politics* 1303a, 25–30 and for commentary Loraux 1996, 82–3.) Political commonality, then, seems rather to consist in a partnership in political institutions and practices, and a sharing in a certain perception of justice. In short, what is common, politically speaking, is something akin to a constitution. The identity of a regime, Aristotle concludes, is the continuity of its constitutional form. Or, more accurately, this is what he *seems* to conclude. For as Nicole Loraux (1997, 267) observes, Aristotle's apparent commitment to constitutional identity is made questionable by the very phrasing that he uses to express it: 'when *the* city passes to another constitution'. The definite article (*the* city, *hē polis)* suggests that there is some entity, 'the city', that while remaining one and the same, nevertheless moves from one constitutional form to the other. Aristotle's hesitation here is not merely of philological interest. Rather, it serves to highlight the double-sided ambiguity of his formulation of political identity: on the one hand, the absence of a political commonality in the ethnicity/territorial definition seems unsatisfactory and, on the other, the claim of the possibility of a radical rupture in identity in the constitutional thesis appears overstated, as if one community ceased to exist and another came into being with the installing of a new constitutional order.

Putting aside for the moment such revealing paradoxes, allow me to draw two observations from Aristotle's formulation of this matter. First, the issue of identity is one that explicitly involves a temporal dimension: the question of the sameness of a person/community that undergoes change over time. Second, the question of what it means to speak of that sameness through time is at its core normative in character. This is so because it is this sameness or identity that makes possible the recognition of a community as a single subject of attribution through time, an agent or author capable of being held to account. (See Ricoeur 1992, 294–5.) Indeed, for Aristotle what gives rise to the conundrum in the first place is the issue of whether, after a revolution, the newly founded political community is liable for the past, for the debts, fiscal and others, of its predecessor. Of the three candidates for the ground of identity that Aristotle discusses, territory, race or ethnicity, and constitutional form, the first two together tend to create strong identities through time while the third invites us to consider new regimes as separate selves, foreign to earlier states (even though occupying the same space and populated by the same people). If the new regime shares in an identity with the old, then the scope of accountability would not be hard to discern: there would be a single subject of imputation. But if we view the community as radically new, and thus a different and separate entity from earlier regimes, then there would be no single (diachronic), accountable subject compelled to assume the debts of governments past, and so it would no more be held to account for their deeds than one individual would be for the actions of another.

Since the focus here will be on the issues invoked by the presence of the past in political identity and the ethical burdens that it brings with it, let me begin by laying out a cluster of prominent theories of political identity, sketching for each the moral weight of the past that it allows.

(1) Nationalism and its variants, in which identity is rooted in some (usually non-political) notion of shared traits (ethnicity, culture, language) and territory. Such an identity easily absorbs the long duration of a community's existence, and sees sameness even in the midst of the most radical changes, political or other, induced by the passage of time. Memory of a certain kind, the ingathering and making present of that sameness through time, is a central motif of nationalist politics. It also erects very high barriers to admission, and is typically exclusionary in its conception and practice of belonging. If humans are in 'the grip of particular and distinguishing memories and of particular and distinguishing local passions' (Hampshire 1983, 135; Beiner 1992, 121), and their political identity includes a common history and memory—a 'community of recollections', as John Stuart Mill ([1861] 1962, 307) called it—a union with the dead and the yet-to-be born, then immersion in such a community and its mores cannot 'be shared, exchanged or acquired—and that is precisely why [it has been made into] the locus of national identity' (Finkielkraut 1987, 126–7. See also Todorov 1989, 256, and Burke [1790] 1955, 38–9, 110). Identity of this deep type is an almost natural barrier to outsiders, and citizenship serves only to express and protect the political locale of that identity.

(2) At the other pole, a hyper-liberal belonging in which the only morally relevant form of sharing is a roster of rights, universal in scope and thus available at least in principle to every human *qua* human. Accordingly, neither our particular space in the world (our country), nor our interests, nor lastly our past or future together, our common time, can confer legitimate privileges on us. For if indeed humans are all similarly situated as rights-bearers, then particularity of historical time, place, religion, ethnicity, and so on, and the self-preference that flows from these strong, non-rights type, markers, are extraordinarily difficult to justify. The only past relevant for identity and belonging would be the succession of rights-governed events and transactions. History of the 'blood and soil' type would clearly be meaningless, if not repugnant. But even a more benign cultural history would be publicly irrelevant, being at most a heuristic vantage point on the impartial and universal code of rights. (See Ripstein 1997, 220–3.) This view is, in principle, suspicious of thick notions of membership, that is, notions in which are embedded identity markers other than those derived from a table of rights. Or better, it is suspicious of granting such notions any regulative status over our ideas and practices of citizenship. Since all human beings are rights-bearers, and because that is the dominant and publicly relevant def-

inition of membership, the world should, in this account, resemble a collection of rights-holders for whom a shared past would be only of folkloric interest. Memory and the long duration of that sameness, things particular to us as members of this political locale, are irrelevant here. In Tzvetan Todorov's words: 'Memory is dethroned, not in the interests of forgetting, of course, but of certain universal principles and the "general will"' (1995, 18-19). Put more polemically, such a hyper-liberal world, carried to the extreme, would be a neighbourhood of the rootless and memory-less rather than a high-barrier, closed (bounded by their 'thick' identities) community of citizens. (The analogy to neighbourhoods is Walzer's [1983, 36–7].)

(3) Occupying something like a middle position is a constitutional patriotism that seeks a reconciliation between the universalist demands of liberal principle and the need for a robust political identity, including a shared history, that is required for a flourishing democratic life. French republicanism is the canonical illustration of this middle path, but its contours can also be discerned in elements of the Canadian, Quebec, and American political experiences. Constitutional patriotism, centred around universal democratic principles, aims to unite the universalist aspirations of liberalism (broadly construed), and its emphasis on willed or voluntary membership, with the republican idea of a political life in common, an identity-conferring *patria*. To be citizens of such a regime is to subscribe to a set of locally instituted but nevertheless universal principles. When I say 'locally instituted' here I mean rooted not only in space but also in time, that is, having a deep sense of historical continuity of a political/constitutional type. Of course, closure and the distribution of membership remain features of this regime, though the barriers are themselves now understood to be deduced from (and constrained by) the universal-democratic principles that are the constitutional core of this society. Civic competence, politically defined, is the main entry requirement, not ethnic belonging, religion or other ascriptive or non-political attributes. In sum, we could say that citizenship of the constitutional-patriotic sort stands midway between (for example) national membership of the kind in which the boundary markers are defined according to some cluster of exclusionary, non-political attributes, and the nomadic world of itinerants and their neighbourhoods. The horizon of membership is traced using only those properties that would be counted as legitimate by the members of that society while, at the same moment, that limited horizon itself and a strong sense of membership within it are seen as preconditions of any healthy form of democratic political life.

Now as I remarked above, political identity is not just a temporal proposition, but a moral-temporal one: the continuous self is what allows us to hold individuals and political communities to account for their past; and it also lays out a claim of duty towards the future continuation of this same self. So we would expect that in our three classes of identity theory sketched above (nationalist, hyper-liberal, constitutional-patriotic) are also embedded sets of propositions about identity and its relationship to liability for the past (and responsibility for the future). Plainly, these propositions about responsibility would mirror the duration and denseness of the relevant past in their foundational accounts of identity: with nationalism, at least in principle, making us one with our past and thus fully accountable for it; liberalism picking out only a narrow band of continuity, with a corresponding thinness of responsibility for that past; and finally, constitutional patriotism, in which identity, shared memories, and responsibility are dense but strictly within the limits of the past of the constitutional order and its practices of freedom. (See Viroli 1995, 9, 13–14, 174.) How these understandings of the temporal-moral dimension of identity, of the presence of the past, accountability and memory, shape their respective positions on matters of identity, difference and citizenship will be a subtheme of the pages that follow.

Let me now return to the Mitterrand/Vél' d'Hiv incident and venture that there is something unsettling in his exculpatory claim. That the Vichy years belong to France and are part of its history and identity seems a natural, almost a compelling, intuition. We may grant that the sense of being ours and a source of enduring responsibility is heightened where the current regime stands in an uninterrupted relation to its predecessors (in the way that the centuries of slavery belong to the United States, though slavery and its principles have long since been decisively rejected). But does a rupture in regime form alone absolve a political community of the deeds that were done during this constitutional hiatus or prior to the act of constitution-making? Do the deeds of the *ancien régime* or of an interloper government cease to belong to that community? The affirmative answer appears unsatisfactory, for just the reasons suggested in (Loraux's reading of) Aristotle's discussion of continuity: Periclean Athens and Athens under the Thirty seem, in one important sense, one and the same city—though it is also true to say of them that the democratic character of the former and oligarchical nature of the latter are profoundly different variations of this common self. Yet if we attempt (in any other than nationalist discourse) to construct a theory of identity which would make this (constitutionally discontinuous) past ours, see the present 'we' as the subject of attribution for past deeds, and burden us with the remembrance of this past and the duty of atonement, we are brought up short. If not in the regime form, then where are we to find that sameness across time that renders this past ours and not someone else's? The 'blood and soil' response provides one sort of account, though dubious empirically and at odds with the normative underpinnings of a liberal democratic society. By the same token, the republican thesis (implied in Mitterrand's response to the proposed public commemoration of Vél' d'Hiv) that this 'was not ours, but another community's past', a thesis that rests on the idea of a radically new political and moral birth, seems in its own way untenable and morally repugnant since it holds out before us an easy path to the forgetting of injustice and to a facile self-absolution.

These issues are still more salient in Germany's post-Second World War history. On the one hand, the moral burden of the past weighs heavily there, and with it the ideas of identity, continuity, and memory. On the other hand, Germany is moving towards a greater openness to immigration and a diversification of its population, and is part of the general European movement towards the creation of a supra-national European identity. The friction between the community of memory, drawn to the particularity of the past and its burdens, and the emerging openness of membership in a new kind of constitutional political community (domestic and Europe-wide), is perhaps most apparent there. And thus I turn to Germany and to Habermas (as one if its character readers) to illustrate these tensions, which are by no means a German problem alone, but seem rather to be just part of our condition as moderns.

Here I shall only sketch the outlines of Habermas's work on these topics. Their core consists of the demands of openness and diversity on the one side and the ethics of remembrance and responsibility on the other. The first set of imperatives is placed on the agenda by increasing immigration, both from Eastern Europe and from the developing world; German reunification; and the move towards a European political community. These have combined to sharpen the tension between the exclusionary nation-state (bounded by ethnicity, language, a community of fate, and so forth) and the universalist underpinnings of liberal democracy (Habermas 1996, 492). They lead us to ask how a liberal state, committed to a type of indifference to any particularist markers, can justify the criteria by which it excludes immigrants; to ask how, in a liberal society, German reunification can be viewed as the bringing together of a pre-political ethnic group. Lastly, we are asked to reflect on what is to become of the nation-state and its practices of citizenship in a Europe moving towards a supranational political life.

While these first questions clearly require distinct responses, there is nevertheless a common thread running through Habermas's treatment of them. And that is the guiding thought that citizenship and national consciousness, united in the first republican experiments of early European modernity, can (and need to) be separated (Habermas 1996, 495). The liberal democratic political community and membership in it are shaped by principles that abstract from any non-political markers. Not only does it abstract from these varied non-political properties, but it also assumes the character of a voluntary, elective community, a 'community of will' (*Willensgemeinschaft*) as Habermas terms it (1996, 494, 496-7; see also 1990a, 159; 1990b, 208). Nations survive, under this new dispensation, as cultures or cultural identities, as traditions to be appropriated critically, and as heuristic vantage points from which the universal principles of the public sphere are interpreted (1996, 500, 507; 1990b, 220, 223). But the publicly relevant sense of identity and belonging is constitutional (universal-democratic) in character, and so in principle open to outsiders; it understands German reunification as the extension of democracy and not as the ingathering of ethnic Germans under one political authority; and at least in principle, it is available for political life at the European rather than the traditional nation-state level. In short, for Habermas the possibilities that Germany will become (a) a multicultural society and (b) part of a European political community depend precisely on the adherence to a constitutional patriotic pattern of identity and belonging (1990b, 217).

If that were the end of it, then Habermas's interventions in these matters would amount to the claim that identity and its expression in citizenship are constitutional (normative and institutional) in character, that they are strictly a matter of adhesion to a set of publicly recognized political values of an abstract (universal) democratic type. But in fact, as was remarked above, there is a second set of issues here, those centred around the past, and including an ethics of remembrance and responsibility. The past and its relation to (German) identity haunt Habermas's work: on the political level, the reunification of Germany has, in his view, reawakened the nationalist temptations of the past, and nationalism in the German (unlike the French) context has historically not been a friend of democracy (Habermas 1990a, 158–9). And not only has the nationalist construction of identity not been amenable to the flourishing of political liberty, but in the near-to-impermeable closedness of the *Volksgemeinschaft* (ethnic community), it is fundamentally hostile to the diversity of a modern democratic society. Along one dimension, then, the past matters because in its surviving traces it can threaten the universal-democratic present. Its temptations are to be revealed as poisonous and expunged from our midst. Yet along a second dimension Habermas sees a need not to jettison the past in the name of a secure post-national political identity, but on the contrary to embrace it, to keep the memory of the past alive in the face of the amnesiac seductions of the 'normalizers' of German history; to underscore that it is ours, something for which we—and no one else—are responsible. One central aspect of the identity problem is evident here: the tension between the vision of a 'rational identity' centred around universal norms of (roughly) a liberal democratic type and setting the ideal of a post-1949 German political identity, and an identity, laden with responsibility and remembrance, that is the legacy of the unmasterable past. To follow Habermas as he wrestles with this tension is to understand the depth of the conflict between the liberal/constitutional patriotic construction of identity (and likely that of modernity more generally) and the role of (collective) memory and responsibility for the past.

Now Habermas himself, in his interventions in the 'historians' debate', and in his praise of Daniel Goldhagen's *Hitler's Willing Executioners* (1996) in the midst of controversies over its assertion of a distinctive (annihilationist), long-enduring, and culturally embedded form of German anti-Semitism, directs us to the normative core of the idea of the presence of the past, one that lies beyond a merely genealogical relation to it, and that ends (I will suggest) by calling into question the possibility of attaining that level of abstractness or political impersonality needed for constitutional patriotism or, *a fortiori*, for a supranational political life. In the following pages, I will use Habermas's engagements in the *Historikerstreit* to suggest that propositions such as the one that the universal has particular roots do not do full justice to the weight of the past in our political lives. The identity question, in its temporal/normative dimensions, suggests that for all their abstractness and impersonality, the constitutional project and its related citizenship practices are deeply embedded in a community of memory and in the sort of identity that such intergenerational communities have at their core. Specifically, they are embedded in the moral claims of remembrance and responsibility that a sameness, an identity, across time bequeaths to members of a political community.

The original impetus for the historians' debate was the issue of the 'normalization' of recent German history through both a recovery of the long horizon of that country's pre-1933 past and via a comparative study of the National Socialist period, seeing it not as unique but as a part of the twentieth century's experience of totalitarianism in the Soviet Union and elsewhere. 'Normalization' here meant the possibility of treating German history in a detached and scientific fashion. To this Habermas answered, agreeing on the character of the *historian's* craft. But the heart of this dispute, he contended, lay elsewhere. What was at stake was not so much the question of the historian's scholarly detachment as the issue of memory, identity, and politics. For Habermas's opponents, a German identity grounded in a sense of the past obsessed with the National Socialist years, with the Holocaust at their core, would make a life in common next to impossible (Stürmer 1987, 36, 38). Normalizing German history was no abstract pursuit, but on the contrary was essential to the making of a healthy political identity. Habermas too recognized the essentially public character (moral/political identity) of this debate and he responded, insisting on the burden of the past and the imprescriptible nature of the Holocaust within it. It was a debt-producing, incorrigible legacy to the community's collective memory and identity, and one to be sheltered from the erosion of time, forgetting, and normalization. Academic normalization was, from this latter vantage point, a way of relieving the moral burden of the past, of de-centring Auschwitz in the collective memory of this past (Habermas 1997).

What, then, is the nature of this past of debt and remembrance? We might begin with Habermas's observation that 'We cannot simply pick and choose our own traditions . . .', though it is ours to decide what future to fashion out of them (Ferry 1988, 438–9). We cannot choose, from among our stock of memories, those memories bound up with our belonging to this specific community. We are given the totality of our past, whether as individuals or as members of a community, and though our attitudes towards its varied parts may differ, sometimes applauding, other times repudiating, it is intertwined with our identity in its entirety. A German memory with Goethe, but without the National Socialist years, would be unthinkable. (See Améry 1977, 122.) It is something given to us, into which we are 'thrown'. That this is our past is a fact at once non-elective and unalterable; it is something very much like a fate and as Charles Péguy wrote 'It is not given to man to make for himself another cradle' (quoted in Finkielkraut 1991, 88). We are, at least in that sense, members of a 'community of fate'. One (though not the only) way in which this fated past is present among us is in the traditions, the forms of life, in the fabric woven of past and present, that are core parts of what it means to share in an identity (Habermas 1989b, 233–4, 236). The past, then, is present in our traditions, and again in what is often a non-elective manner: in, Bergson observed ([1939] 1993, 84–5), the quasi-memory of habit, in the modes of thought and so forth that are part of that legacy. And of course it is also present in those chosen moments when, by deliberate decision, we put the past into words, monuments, days of remembrance. In brief, it is present in our identity as a (collective) actor across generations.

Here we might still well be on the terrain of an archaeology of political identity, giving an account of its origins and transmission. But Habermas suggests that this presence of the past involves something more than an account of our origins, of our *berceau* (cradle) in Péguy's image. And he intimates (with the uncertainties to be discussed below) that it is not simply present in the fashion just sketched, as the remnants of a cultural tradition. It is rather the wellspring of accountability: burdening us, giving us pride or shame, making us accountable. We think back to that past, commemorate it in public, atone for it and, occasionally, try to forget it. And we do this because, in an important sense, it is *ours*: not somebody else's past, memories, or debts, but ours. Remembrance (and forgetting) depends on the fact that the past can be prefaced by the possessive pronoun 'our'. However much we may have changed as a political body over time, those changes are scalar in relation to our past self: they modify us, but do not constitute us as a new (political) self (Williams 1976, 202–5). Not only, then, are we bequeathed traditions, but we also inherit responsibility, a liability for the past and for those deeds that were produced from the core of 'our life together' ('aus der Mitte unseres Lebenszusammenhanges') (Habermas 1997; 1989a, 251; 1989b, 236). The presence of the past is here moral, and not genealogical or traditional. Because it is ours, it is with us always, even through the changes we undergo in the passing of the years. The past and the dead (like those yet to be born) make claims on the living, long after they and the events around them have entered the historical past (Ferry 1988, 438; Habermas 1994, 514–15). And, we might add, long after those traditions that are our inheritance have been transformed beyond all recognition.

In fact, Habermas's arguments are ambivalent. On the one hand, his account is of the ethics of the debt to the past. The National Socialist period polluted Germany and left even those born after the war with a responsibility for the past, a responsibility that cannot be expiated, and whose call is answered, in the first instance, with atoning remembrance (Ferry 1988, 438; Habermas 1994, 514-15; 1989b, 236). It is almost as if what is at work here is the idea of collective shame. Yet Habermas, while seeming to invoke just that idea, nevertheless calls it an 'archaic' sentiment, suggesting that he is ill at ease with it (1989a, 252). And so Habermas, in these discussions, sometimes adopts another vocabulary, a language of responsibility rather more assimilable to the idea of constitutional patriotic identity than the notion of shame: as when he speaks of 'life forms' and the 'web of cultural threads' when giving an account of the mark left on the community by the past (1989a, 251; 1989b, 233, 236; 1997). Christian Meier has remarked that this language allows for a way of addressing the presence of the past that invokes tradition not as a stained character, not as an irreversible source of shame and an object of remembrance, but as a cultural artifact; as if, were these life forms to be sufficiently transformed in the course of a long-term, successful experiment in democracy, then the burden of the past would be lifted too (Meier 1987a, 272–3). Why, Meier asks, does Habermas, in discussing the responsibility of the present generation for the deeds of their predecessors, not say simply that they 'live in a state called Germany . . . our responsibility comes to us from being German'? (Meier

1987a, 273; for commentary see Maier 1997, 55–6, 59–60). Or, in the words of the then Speaker of the Bundestag, Philipp Jenninger, on the occasion of the fiftieth anniversary of *Kristallnacht*: 'the past is part of our identity' and (quoting an Auschwitz survivor), 'Young Germans must accept that they are Germans, they cannot stand apart from this fate . . .' (Jenninger 1988; Jenninger resigned in the wake of a controversy over this speech).

The response to Meier's question is surely not just that it is the archaic quality of the idea of shame that leads Habermas to seek out another way to express the presence of the past. Yet an answer as to why he finds such language difficult to accept is by no means straightforward. And all the more so since it seems a dominant concern of his to foreclose a therapeutic but immoral forgetting of the past. Atonement and remembrance are duties; forgetting is an evil. His interventions both in the historians' debate and in urging a positive reception of Goldhagen's book in Germany have had as one of their central motifs an adamantine resistance to any effort to lighten, modify, or relativize the burden of the past. How to understand this? A partial explanation is that Meier's language of Germans and Germany as a collective extending across generations asserts, from Habermas's standpoint, just the wrong (*Volk*-like) sort of continuity. Something further in the way of a response can be drawn from Habermas's reflections on constitutional patriotism and national identity. Modern identity, he writes, has no fixed content given in advance; it is revisable and flexible and involves a critical appropriation through the open discursive life of a community (Habermas 1976). The openness of identity to critical revision, coupled with the separation in late modernity of national identity and political membership rooted in universal-democratic principles, rests uneasily with the idea of the past as a present, imprescriptible burden. The latter, seen from the vantage point of identity as culture and culture as imagined, willed, and revisable, appears to be almost a form of Sophoclean *miasma*, of collective pollution. And in its denseness and impermeability, in its strengthening of the possessive and particularist pronoun 'our', it ill serves the desiderata of universality and openness.

Let us unfold this idea of revisable identities one step further. Consider this influential current of thought: collective identities are seen as constructed, things made, manipulatively by mobilizing elites or in open democratic discourse. So likewise the collective memory that is part of these identities is constructed and contestable. (See Tamir 1993; Anderson 1991; Miller 1995; some recent applied examples include Zerubavel 1995 and Karakasidou 1997.) The emphasis on the present weaving of the past, memory, and political identity is clearly a commodious one for modernity and liberalism, which have difficulty accepting ideas of shame, burden, and fate, and the obligations they claim to impose. The idea of the nation as, in Renan's phrase, 'a daily plebiscite' has an attractive ring for those who find the idea of the burden of the past in the present to be deeply inconsistent with an underlying commitment to autonomy. For it suggests the possibility of a *Willensgemeinschaft* (willed or voluntary community) as an (in principle) liberal form of belonging, no longer grounded in archaic (i.e., involuntary, exclusionary, often violent, and false, if not irrational) notions of a community of fate, blood, and soil. The imagined, and always revisable, identities/memories of this post-traditional view have yet another advantage: being malleable, they are also porous, allowing for change, for exit, and for pluralism in admission. The barriers that surround communities thus understood would be sufficiently flexible, because so little rooted in a community of memory and fate, of necessary identity, that change within, and admission to, them would hardly be troubling. Not surprisingly, those who search for political legitimacy in the past and a community's memory of it find these arguments repugnant, witness some of the hostile Greek nationalist responses to Anastasia Karakasidou's assertion (1997, 228–37) of the recent origins (as opposed to eternalness), and constructed character (rather than nature-like quality), of the Greekness of Macedonia. For this translation of the weight of the past into a construct, an invention and a quasi-ideology, would immediately strip that past of its mobilizing and legitimizing functions.

While objections of the sort just sketched show us the implausibility of an extreme form of the view that the past is just something given to us, our nature (or our nature-given *telos* or end), it is important to see how partial and incomplete are *both* the ideas of the past as simply given and the memory of it as a strict 'construction'. Here let me venture a provisional, and by no means exhaustive, bit of clarification. On one compelling account, offered by Walter Benjamin, we always see the past from the vantage point of the present, and of its needs and conflicts ([1940] 1968, 255, 261). The contours of our appropriation of the past change, then, according to what presses in the present. Related to this is a second claim, equally plausible, namely that the past, at least in its public and political form, must be called into existence, put into words or commemorated in stone; provided a vocabulary that will allow it to emerge. Indeed, among its original significations, the classical Greek word for remembering, *mnaomai*, meant to mention something or someone (Benveniste 1954, 13). The past needed a maker of words, a poet or historian, Homer or Herodotus, to save its deeds from the oblivion of silence. The constructivist reading, then, is surely right in this sense: that all of these actions contain at least in principle an element of will, of artifice, in the present. It is not the case, then, that we are, strictly speaking, bequeathed our past, or thrown into it. We appropriate it, with all that that entails about the mechanisms, the power, and the passions that fuel both forgetting and remembering, and determine what pieces of the past will be hallowed and which consigned to obscurity (Foucault 1972, 128–31). The debates over Vichy in contemporary France and over Germany and the Holocaust make clear the weight of the present in shaping a community of memory.

But the view that our past is something given—a fate or a datum, and not a piece of artifice—also captures an important dimension of our relationship to it. Notice in those same examples that we give voice to the past, dispute it, forget it as something not made by us but that rather calls us, seeks to impose a duty on us. In invoking it, and giving it voice and remembrance, we answer its call. We do not make, or construct, this past. It is there, remembered or submerged, here and present or awaiting a triggering event to bring it back: a witness's voice, a bearer of memory, as in Claude

Lanzmann's *Shoah*. And even when nothing else remains of the past, the taste of a madeleine dipped into a cup of tea can recall 'the immense edifice of memory' of youth, home, towns and persons (Proust [1913] 1987, 46–7). Observe again that the past matters so much because it is ours, indeed it is us; malleable, to be sure, but nevertheless something, and something that matters. (See Lowenthal 1985.) We therefore know why, for instance, the 'revisionist' approach to the Holocaust is fundamentally flawed: not only because it seeks to advance evil in the here and now, because its construction of the past is hurtful in the present, but because it does a grievous wrong to the past, a past that, in one sense, lies within its grasp, available for distortion or suppression, but that, in another sense (moral and ontological), lies beyond its powers of artifice and reinterpretation. We understand, in short, why the historian Pierre Vidal-Naquet (1995) calls the practitioners of this art 'the assassins of memory'. (See also Bédarida 1993, 21–2.) To rob us of our memory is to destroy something that is a part of us, something essential to who we are, something arguably as crucial to our identity as our physical person.

Consider, then, what it would mean to adopt the proposition, in its full-blooded form, that political identity could be fashioned in one fell constitutional swoop. We would then have to say that we have freed the 'who we are' of identity from its long roots in the past. A public space constructed in the image of a constitutional patriotism, with universal-democratic principles at its centre, almost seems to invite a shedding of the past of the sort that was proposed in the controversy over the Vél' d'Hiv commemoration (Schlink 1988, 59–60, 67–8). And we might be tempted to see this as emancipatory, freeing us from the 'syndrome', as Henry Rousso calls it, of the past. Yet as the Mitterrand incident suggests, there is a profound moral uncertainty at the centre of this emancipation, for in shedding the past, in styling ourselves new model citizens, we also thereby relieve ourselves of responsibility for it; if we are, politically speaking, a new 'self', we can then treat the deeds and debts of the regimes in power before this rupture as those of another 'self'. But the conjunction of the postnational or constitutional identity and the ethics of remembrance debates invites us to consider how difficult—or impossible—it is to escape our embeddedness in the community extended through time, the community of remembrance (and anticipation) that is the basic temporal/narrative fabric of a common life and shared identity. For that reason, among others, there are limits to the level of abstraction from particularity that can be achieved. It would be to understate those limits to describe them as a cultural matrix with heuristic implications through which an overarching set of universal principles may be filtered and interpreted. They are rather limits that claim an obligation to past and future, a duty to remember and to correct. They also lay claim to the centre of our identity: absent this memory, we would not be what we are. They are, then, *our* collective memories, and so not substitutable; *our* obligations, past and future: these give the past and our memory of it their characteristic particularity. That too must come at the expense of their universality.

'We in the land of the perpetrators' ('*wir, im Lande der Täter . . .*'): Habermas's (1997) phrase points to a community in which the past is a living moral presence. It acknowledges that the public space of any community more enduring than a neighbourhood of passersby is saturated by the past and the memory of it. It is saturated not in some incidental manner but essentially, because to be a political community, a people, a family, religious community, or a profession involves a tie between past, present, and future. These are not embedded simply in the sense of having a temporal-spatial nexus, a genealogical tie of some kind. Rather they are rooted in a narrative that can be prefaced by the pronoun 'our', a narrative that voices both an appropriation, a memory, of the past and an anticipation of the future. (See Le Goff 1990, 8; Le Goff 1992, 111; on nation and history see Miller 1995, 23ff, 41–2.) That 'our' also constitutes its members as a subject of attribution, not in the full-blooded sense of author and action, but as bearing responsibility. Yet the historical burden that Habermas says Germans share in even today, the duty to remember that flows from it, and the centrality of both of these to their common identity: these together weigh heavily against the constructivism of the post-traditional, 'imagined communities' reading. And it weighs heavily not just against this post-traditional idea of identity. For if a community, its past, and the interweaving of that past and the memory of it with its enduring identity, must be prefaced by the possessive pronoun 'our', if what we are as a community is our past living in the present, then revision, exit, and entrance all seem much more difficult than the liberal universalist might imagine. (On the possessiveness of collective memory, see Ricoeur 1997, 437.) Fated, ours, not porous—thus three liberal desiderata are contravened: not chosen, hence heteronomous; ours, hence particular and essentially local in character; not porous, hence exclusionary (Loraux 1996, 109; Todorov 1989, 254ff). Something like this would seem to be one cost of the debt to the past.

Allow me now to turn the tables on the claim that is implicit in what I have thus far discussed: that the temporal-moral nature of political identity yields a single type of moral imperative: 'Remember!' Perhaps there is an ethics of forgetting, as well; one that may on occasion trump the duty to remember. We have been told that forgetting is as necessary to existence as memory is, perhaps more so, and that a surfeit of memory, or an obsessive absorption in the past, can be destructive of life (Nietzsche [1874] 1957, 6–7; Renan [1882] 1992, 41). In *L'Écriture ou la vie*, Jorge Semprun, reflecting on the years after his liberation from Buchenwald concentration camp, writes, 'I chose forgetting, I put in place, without too much concern for the good of my own identity, founded essentially on the horror, and no doubt the courage too, of the experience of the camp . . . the strategy of voluntary amnesia, cruelly systematic' (1994, 292). There are times when, for individuals and communities both, life and the future require that we forget, let the past go: the command to remember must be weighed against the imperative to let the dead bury their dead. And just perhaps, though we cannot choose our *berceau* or cradle, we *can* will to forget it and its legacy to us.

Since, as Nicole Loraux suggests, the political is the final authority over collective memory, we may find there the agent who will disencumber us of this past (Loraux 1986, 3; see also Ricoeur 1997, 449–53). Amnesties and acts of legal prescription are some of the ways in which societies from ancient Athens to our own have elected to forget for the sake of a future in common. On other occasions, collective memories have been crafted, leaving out the source of the pollution. This the former German Democratic Republic leadership did when it fashioned the new Germany as born out of the internal communist resistance to Hitler, thereby absolving the infant state of its father's sins. And in post-Second World War France, De Gaulle managed to put a stop to the threat of a divisive settling of accounts among Frenchmen by essentially bracketing Vichy and collaboration as a parenthesis in the ongoing history of the Republic. The now defunct communist regimes of the Soviet Union and its allies massively rewrote their pasts to serve the needs of the present. (Loraux 1988, 9–23, discusses amnesty ancient and modern. On Germany, see Combe 1990. For France, see Rousso 1990. On the Soviet Union and Eastern Europe see Brossat 1990.) Forgetting and memory, then, both seem vital to our common life; and it is equally possible that we might have too much of either. An excess of forgetting would turn us into leaves, to be scattered by the winds; mere neighbours passing one another by in little more than a community of interests. Too much memory would be lead in our wings, denying us a future, and closing off the possibility of openness to others not a part of our community of memory. So in the end, it might be best to forget, or at least to allow the workings of time their naturally corrosive effects on the actuality of the past. For its opposite, the labours of a remembering identity, must inevitably draw us away from the openness of the yet-to-be-constructed universal-democratic future, and into our burden, our fate; into the 'sleeplessness' ('Schlaflosigkeit'), as Nietzsche called it, of those who cannot forget.

Yet, needless to say, there is something odd in the idea of a willed forgetting. And something unstable, as the failures of virtually all the national exercises in amnesia mentioned above have shown: the struggle throughout the former Communist bloc to recover the past from its Soviet-era distortions; Vichy, 'a past which will not pass' ('un passé qui ne passe pas'); Bitburg, the *Historikerstreit*, the fiftieth anniversary of the end of the war in Europe, the Goldhagen book, and outbreaks of xenophobic violence show that the past has a way of breaking through the happy forgetfulness of our present contentment. The mercy of amnesia is hard to hold on to, it seems; the promised lightness of our being difficult to redeem. Listen again to Jorge Semprun: 'Despite the detours, the deliberate or involuntary censoring, the strategy of forgetting . . . despite all the pages written to exorcize this experience . . . despite all this, the past preserved the shattering power of the smoke and snow [of Buchenwald], just as on the first day' (1994, 297). But it is not merely that forgetting or refashioning is an unstable foundation upon which to build a constitutional-patriotic identity, since the past has a habit of returning involuntarily, in an almost Proustian fashion. More than that, forgetting, especially if it is forgetting of our past injustices and our responsibility for them (or of our past benefactors and our debt of grateful remembrance to them), savours of a wrong, of the violation of a duty, or, as Habermas writes, of the debt of atoning remembrance. Time and human volition cannot erase the fact of what has been done, and since we are our past as well as our futures, they cannot erase the presence of the past, though they can of course repress recognition of it. Nor can they absolve us of the moral burdens that we, individually and collectively, assume for our past, though again the recognition of that moral imperative can be denied. Denying it, then, does not free us from its reality and, though nothing within or among us may call us back to that past, there are likely others who will awaken us from the sleep of forgetting and seek to force us to do the work of remembrance. Yet even if perchance these voices of the past, these Furies calling on us, were to fall silent, we would still say of a community of forgetting, such as the one of the lotus-eaters that Homer describes in the *Odyssey*, and of Odysseus's companions who eat there and forget their way home, that theirs would be a world without a common life and shared identity, and a place missing a crucial ethical dimension.

Memory and politics is a theme that (somewhat surprisingly) has emerged out of the backwaters of a Burkean evocation of tradition to become a vital and disputed area of reflection on identity, and a matter of not inconsiderable political importance. Perhaps its becoming an object of analysis and debate is evidence both of the imperative to remember and of the slipping away of memory as a living presence at the heart of communities and their identities: the withering of what Françoise Zonabend (1980) called the '*mémoire longue*', the long, unifying memory of a community. (See also Lowenthal 1985, 376ff.) If that withering portends a weakening of political identity, it remains to be seen whether alternatives constructed on a post-traditional foundation will do the same work. Indeed, whether the same work still needs to be done is an unsettled issue. For on one account (approximately that sketched as the liberal one at the outset of this paper), what is acceptable in the work of thick identities (i.e., the cultural residue left after the xenophobic and exclusionary elements are washed out) becomes in modernity essentially folkloric, having been supplanted by the cement of rights and democratic freedoms. That latter issue has not been my principal concern here. Rather, I have wanted to draw attention to the moral importance of memory in political identity. Here the threatened loss is of the community as a subject of moral imputation across time, the idea that we are not only creatures of the moment, but the bearers of our past and holders of a responsibility to our future as a community. Whether the loss of the long duration of our accountability as a community is counterbalanced by the openness that the dissolution of memory-identity brings, and by the liberation from the 'insomnia' of too much remembering, is something worth considering.

Note

This essay is a substantially revised version of an article that originally appeared in the *American Political Science Review* 93 (1999), 249-63; copyright APSA. The author is grateful to Joshua Dienstag, Erwin Hargrove, Herbert Kitschelt, Chris Manfredi, James Murphy, Anne Sa'adah, George Tsebelis, Kurt Weyland, and the *American Political Science Review*'s referees for comments on the arguments of this paper.

Bibliography

Améry, Jean. 1977. *Jenseits von Schuld und Sühne. Bewältigungsversuche eines Überwältigen.* Stuttgart: Klett-Cota.

Anderson, Benedict. 1991. *Imagined Communities*. London: Verso.

Aristotle. *The Politics*. 1932. Translated by H. Rackham. London: William Heinemann.

Bédarida, François. 1993. 'Comment est-il possible que le "revisionnisme" existe?' Reims: Noria (Cahier 4).

Beiner, Ronald. 1992. *What's the Matter with Liberalism?* Berkeley: University of California Press.

Benjamin, Walter. [1940] 1968. 'Theses on the Philosophy of History'. In Walter Benjamin, *Illuminations*. Edited by Hannah Arendt. Translated by Harry Zohn. New York: Schocken.

Benveniste, Émile. 1954. 'Formes et sens de mnaomai'. In *Sprachgeschichte und Wortbedeutung. Festschrift Albert Debrunner*. Bern: Francke.

Bergson, Henri. [1939] 1993. *Matière et mémoire*. Paris: Presses Universitaires de France.

Brossat, Alain, ed. 1990. *À l'est, la mémoire retrouvée*. Paris: La Decouverte.

Burke, Edmund. [1790] 1955. *Reflections on the Revolution in France*. Indianapolis: Library of Liberal Arts.

Carens, Joseph H. 1987. 'Who Belongs? Theoretical and Legal Questions about Birthright Citizenship in the United States'. *University of Toronto Law Journal* 37 (Fall): 413-43.

Combe, Sonia. 1990. 'RDA: Des commémorations pour surmonter le passé nazi'. In Brossat, ed. (1990).

Conan, Éric, and Henry Rousso. 1996. *Vichy, un passé qui ne passe pas*. Paris: Gallimard.

Devant l'histoire: Les documents de la controverse sur la singularité de l'extermination des Juifs par le régime nazi. 1988. Paris: Cerf.

Dienstag, Joshua F. 1997. *Dancing in Chains: Narrative and Memory in Political Theory*. Stanford: Stanford University Press.

Ferry, Jean-Marc. 1988. 'Interview with Jürgen Habermas'. Translated by Stephen K. White. *Philosophy & Social Criticism* 14, 3/4: 433-9.

Finkielkraut, Alain. 1987. *La Défaite de la pensée*. Paris: Gallimard.

—. 1991. *Le Mécontemporain: Péguy, lecteur du monde moderne*. Paris: Gallimard.

Foucault, Michel. 1972. *The Archaeology of Knowledge*. Translated by A. M. Sheridan Smith. New York: Pantheon.

—. 1977. 'Nietzsche, Genealogy, History'. In *Language, Counter-Memory, Practice: Selected Essays and Interviews / Michel Foucault*. Edited by Donald F. Bouchard. Translated by Donald F. Bouchard and Sherry Simon. Ithaca: Cornell University Press.

Goldhagen, Daniel J. 1996. *Hitler's Willing Executioners: Ordinary Germans and the Holocaust*. New York: Vintage.

Habermas, Jürgen. 1976. 'Können komplexe Gesellschaften eine vernünftige Identität ausbilden?' In *Zur Rekonstruktion des Historischen Materialismus*. Frankfurt am Main: Suhrkamp.

—. 1987. *Eine Art Schadensabwicklung. Kleine Politische Schriften. VI*. Frankfurt am Main: Suhrkamp.

—. 1989. 'Apologetic Tendencies'. In *The New Conservatism*. Translated by Shierry Weber Nicholsen. Cambridge: MIT Press.

—. 1989a. 'Historical Consciousness and Post-Traditional Identity'. In Habermas (1989).

—. 1989b. 'On the Public Use of History'. In Habermas (1989).

—. 1990a. 'Die Stunde der nationalen Empfindung: Republikanische Gesinnung oder

Nationalbewußtsein?' In *Die nachholende Revolution. Kleine Politische Schriften. VII.* Frankfurt am Main: Suhrkamp.

—. 1990b. 'Nochmals: Zur Identität der Deutschen'. In *Die nachholende Revolution. Kleine Politische Schriften. VII.*

—. 1994. 'Burdens of the Double Past'. Translated by Sidney Rosenfeld and Stella P. Rosenfeld. *Dissent* (Fall): 513-17.

—. 1996. *Between Facts and Norms.* Translated by William Rehg. Cambridge: MIT Press.

—. 1997. 'Warum ein "Demokratiepreis" für Daniel J. Goldhagen? Eine Laudatio'. *Die Zeit*, 14 March 1997.

Hampshire, Stuart. 1983. *Morality and Conflict.* Oxford: Basil Blackwell.

Historikerstreit: Die Dokumentation der Kontroverse um die Eigenartigkeit der nationalsozialistischen Judenvernichtung. 1987. Munich: Piper.

Jenninger, Philipp. 1988. 'Gedankveranstaltung aus Anlaß der Pogrom des nationalsozialistischen Regimes gegen die jüdische Bevölkerung vor 50 Jahren'. (Speech to the Bundestag on the fiftieth anniversary of the National Socialist regime's pogrom against the Jewish population.)

Karakasidou, Anastasia N. 1997. *Fields of Wheat, Hills of Blood: Passages to Nationhood in Greek Macedonia 1870-1990.* Chicago: University of Chicago Press.

Kriegel, Blandine. 1995a. 'Vichy, la République et la France'. *Le Monde*, 8 Sept. 1995: 14.

—. 1995b. 'Pardon et crime d'état'. *L'Histoire* (November): 78.

Le Goff, Jacques. 1990. 'Preface'. In Brossat, ed. (1990).

—. 1992. *History and Memory.* Translated by Steven Rendall and Elizabeth Claman. New York: Columbia University Press.

Loraux, Nicole. 1986. *The Invention of Athens.* Translated by Alan Sheridan. Cambridge, Mass.: Harvard University Press.

—. 1988. 'Pour quel consensus?' *Le Genre humain* 18: 9-23.

—. 1996. *Né de la terre: Mythe et politique à Athènes.* Paris: Seuil.

—. 1997. *La Cité divisée.* Paris: Payot & Rivages.

Lowenthal, David. 1985. *The Past Is a Foreign Country.* Cambridge: Cambridge University Press.

—. 1996. *Possessed by the Past: The Heritage Crusade and the Spoils of History.* New York: Free Press.

Maier, Charles S. 1997. *The Unmasterable Past: History, Holocaust, and German National Identity.* Cambridge, Mass.: Harvard University Press.

Meier, Christian. 1987a. 'Kein Schlußwort. Zum Streit über die NS-Vergangenheit'. In *Historikerstreit: Die Dokumentation der Kontroverse um die Eigenartigkeit der nationalsozialistischen Judenvernichtung.* Munich: Piper.

—. 1987b. 'Eröffnungsrede zur 36. Versammlung deutscher Historiker in Trier, 8. Oktober 1986'. In *Historikerstreit.*

Mill, John Stuart. [1861] 1962. *Considerations on Representative Government.* South Bend, Ind.: Gateway.

Miller, David. 1995. *On Nationality.* Oxford: Clarendon Press.

Nietzsche, Friedrich. [1874] 1957. *The Use and Abuse of History.* Translated by Adrian Collins. Indianapolis: Library of Liberal Arts.

Nora, Pierre. 1984. 'Entre mémoire et histoire'. In Pierre Nora, ed. *Les Lieux de mémoire: La République*. Vol. I. Paris: Gallimard.

—. 1992. 'L'Ère de la commémoration'. In Pierre Nora, ed. *Les Lieux de mémoire: Les France*. Vol. III. *De l'Archive à l'emblème*. Paris: Gallimard.

Nozick, Robert. 1974. *Anarchy, State and Utopia*. New York: Basic Books.

Parfit, Derek. 1984. *Reasons and Persons*. Oxford: Oxford University Press.

Proust, Marcel. [1913] 1987. *À la recherche du temps perdu*. Vol. I. *Du côté de chez Swann*. Edited by Jean-Yves Tadié. Paris: Gallimard. Bibliothèque de la Pléiade.

Renan, Ernest. [1882]1992. *Qu'est-ce qu'une nation?* Paris: Agora.

Ricoeur, Paul. 1988. *Time and Narrative*. Vol. III. Translated by Kathleen Blamey and David Pellauer. Chicago: University of Chicago Press.

—. 1992. *Oneself as Another*. Translated by Kathleen Blamey. Chicago: University of Chicago Press.

—. 1997. 'Gedächtnis-Vergessen-Geschichte'. In *Historische Sinnbildung: Problemstellungen, Zeitkonzepte, Wahrnehmungshorizonte, Darstellungsstrategien*. Edited by Klaus E. Müller and Jörn Rüsen. Hamburg: Rowohlt.

Ripstein, Arthur. 1997. 'Context, Continuity, and Fairness'. In *The Morality of Nationalism*. Edited by Robert McKim and Jeff McMahan. Oxford: Oxford University Press.

Rousso, Henry. 1990. *Le Syndrome de Vichy de 1944 à nos jours*. Paris: Seuil.

Schlink, Bernhard. 1988. 'Recht-Schuld-Zukunft'. In *Geschichte-Schuld-Zukunft (Loccumer Protokolle 66. 1987)*. Edited by Jörg Calließ. Rehburg: Evangelische Akademie Loccum.

Semprun, Jorge. 1994. *L'Écriture ou la vie*. Paris: Gallimard.

Stürmer, Michael. 1987. 'Geschichte in geschichtslosem Land'. In *Historikerstreit: Die Dokumentation der Kontroverse um die Eigenartigkeit der nationalsozialistischen Judenvernichtung*. Munich: Piper.

Tamir, Yael. 1993. *Liberal Nationalism*. Princeton: Princeton University Press.

Todorov, Tzvetan. 1989. *Nous et les autres*. Paris: Seuil.

—. 1995. *Les Abus de la mémoire*. Paris: Arléa.

Vidal-Naquet, Pierre. 1995. *Les Assassins de la mémoire*. Paris: Seuil.

Viroli, Maurizio. 1995. *For Love of Country: An Essay on Patriotism and Nationalism*. Oxford: Oxford University Press.

Walzer, Michael. 1983. *Spheres of Justice*. New York: Basic Books.

Williams, Bernard, 1976. 'Persons, Character and Morality'. In *The Identities of Persons*. Edited by Amélie Oksenberg Rorty. Berkeley: University of California Press.

Zerubavel, Yael. 1995. *Recovered Roots: Collective Memory and the Making of Israeli National Tradition*. Chicago: University of Chicago Press.

Zonabend, Françoise. 1980. *La Mémoire longue: Temps et histoires au village*. Paris: Presses Universitaires de France.

Civic and Ethnic Nationalism: Lessons from the Canadian Case

PHILIP RESNICK

INTRODUCTION

The problem of citizenship and civic identity takes on a special character within multinational federations or states, that is, states in which there is more than one important linguistic or cultural community with legitimate claims to think of itself as a nation or nationality. The problem of multiple or diverse identities within multinational states is compounded by the desire to attribute positive or negative connotations to different forms of nationalism. Not surprisingly, the adherents of majority-group nationalism may look down at the adherents of minority-group nationalism, and vice versa. They may also resort to normative terms to distinguish between the ostensibly legitimate form taken by their own version of national identity, in contrast to the less legitimate form taken by their counterparts' versions.

One very powerful rubric for delineating forms of nationalism in contemporary debates is that of civic and ethnic nationalism. What this essay will argue is that such a distinction is not particularly helpful in sorting out the problems that multinational states face. On the contrary, we would gain much from recognizing that what is at stake in such situations, more often than not, are contending forms of civic nationalism—much as there may be rival views as to what particular group constitutes the *demos*, in other words the relevant citizenry, in more unitary-type states. What follows is an attempt to illuminate the nature of the civic–ethnic debate and to bring home certain lessons drawn from the Canadian case that may have wider import for the politics of citizenship and diversity.

CIVIC AND ETHNIC NATIONALISM

In recent years there has been a growing tendency to distinguish between two types of nationalism: civic and ethnic. Though definitions vary, 'civic nationalism' usually refers to a form of national identity based on shared citizenship within a state irrespective of the ancestry, race, ethnic origin, or religion of its inhabitants. Examples from our own day might include the United States, the United Kingdom, France, and the majority of Western countries.

'Ethnic nationalism', by contrast, refers to certain shared ascriptive affinities that members of a particular national grouping are said to have. These may be rooted in common ancestry, religion, language, cultural values, and the like. A key distinction between ethnic and civic nationalism is the primordial character of the former. One is born into a particular ethnic nation and cannot simply slough this identity off for another. Nor can outsiders, defined as persons not born into this primary ethnic group, become members of it in the way that outsiders can become citizens of a state into which they were not born. Many of the nationalities of Eastern Europe, both in the nineteenth and in much of the twentieth century, were of the ethnic genre; and one can find examples enough today in the Balkans, various parts of the Middle East, Central Asia, and beyond.

Well-known writers on nationalism have used the civic–ethnic divide to illuminate their work. Anthony Smith has contrasted the 'civic–territorial' type of nationalism of the West, based upon a common civic culture, with the 'ethnic–genealogical' type of nationalism of the East, where common descent and a shared ancestral culture loom large.[1] Liah Greenfeld characterizes civic nationalism as open and voluntaristic, in contrast to the exclusiveness of ethnic nationalism.[2] Michael Ignatieff, in his account of six contemporary forms of nationalism, stresses the role of ethnic nationalism in the disintegration of nation-states and sees the main battle of our time between the adherents of civic nationalism 'who still believe that a nation should be a home to all, and race, color, religion, and creed should be no bar to belonging', and the adherents of ethnic nationalism 'who want their nation to be home only to their own'.[3]

At one level, such distinctions seem to capture an important characteristic of the contemporary experience. The Bosnian conflict, for example, with its mass displacements, killings, and so-called ethnic cleansing, seemed to reflect an atavistic return of hatreds based upon religion and ethnic origins in a part of the world that had already experienced bitter ethnic conflict in earlier periods. For a time, Sarajevo became the symbol of the eclipse of civilized behaviour and human decency on the southern fringes of Europe, in the aftermath of the meltdown of Yugoslavia. In similar fashion, the slaughter of Tutsi by Hutu in Rwanda in the mid-1990s recalled the Nazi genocides of the Second World War, or that visited upon the Armenians in 1915. Surely, here were examples of ethnic nationalism at its worst.

And so they were. But we need to be careful about too facile a differentiation between civic nationalism—the sage, anesthetized version we think we are heirs to in the West, and ethnic nationalism—the primitive, bloodthirsty version enacted by our benighted counterparts in the Balkans or the lake region of Central Africa. We need but recall the ability of supposedly civilized Western states to engage in murderous warfare, as was the case for the belligerents during the First World War, in the name of a nationalism that was more civic than ethnic in character. Or evoke various civil wars of the past century and a half—the American one of 1861–5 or the Russian of 1918–21, to name only two—where ethnicity had little to do with the conflict and deep differences over politics and civic culture a great deal more. Civic nationalism, in itself, is no guarantee of comity.

On closer examination it turns out that the civic–ethnic divide is merely the latest in a series of binary terms that has been invoked at various times by writers on nationalism and national identity. Friedrich Meinecke made much of the distinction between *Kulturnation* and *Staatsnation*, cultural nation/nationalism and political nation/nationalism, at the beginning of this century.[4] The first taps into some of the same cultural, historical, ascriptive sources that ethnic nationalism speaks to; the second, with its more state-based, citizen-oriented notion of national identity, more clearly reflects the sorts of values embodied in civic nationalism. The distinction that Hans Kohn made between the West, where 'the rise of nationalism was a predominantly political occurrence, preceded by the formation of the future national state', and the East, where nationalists sought 'to redraw the political boundaries in conformity with ethnographic demands', was similar in character.[5]

Other writers have tried to differentiate between nationalism and patriotism. The roots of both words go back to the Latin, and the two have been part of Western political discourse, both as positive terms of self-identification and as negative terms of opprobrium, for many centuries.[6] Confining the discussion to the twentieth century, one can point to authors who have tried to defend patriotism as a potential good against nationalism, its evil sibling. Carlo Rosselli, the Italian anti-fascist writer, is a good example, distinguishing between patriotism, which he identified with claims for liberty based on respect for the rights of other peoples, and nationalism, which he associated with the politics of aggrandizement practised by reactionary regimes.[7] In the run-up to German unification in the 1989–90 period, Jürgen Habermas, the German critical theorist and philosopher, was prepared to defend *Verfassungspatriotismus*—patriotism of the constitution—based upon loyalty to universalistic political principles of liberty and democracy, as opposed to nationalism, with its dark historical resonances.[8] Maurizio Viroli, in a powerfully written essay, has defended the values of civic solidarity as against those of ethnocultural unity, what he calls a patriotism of liberty against the closed-minded rhetoric of nationalism.[9]

Here again there is much overlap with the civic–ethnic divide. The defenders of patriotism—republican patriotism in the case of Viroli—extol the virtues of common citizenship in contradistinction to any blood-bond or ethnic calling. They want to preserve the valid aspects of shared political community that national identity can speak to, without evoking the intolerance and the appeal to the primordial that nationalism too easily fosters. The language of patriotism seemingly provides a way to do this.

Other binary distinctions also colour discussions of nationalism. Yael Tamir, in a recent study, defends liberal nationalism against its illiberal counterparts on the one hand, but also against anti-nationalist liberals on the other.[10] Her liberal nationalism, with its opening to civic education and cultural realities, is ultimately closer to the spirit of the civic, rather than the ethnic, variety. Then there are authors who draw distinctions between the nationalism of large states and that of small ones. The supporters of large-state nationalisms, from Friedrich Engels in the mid-nineteenth century[11] to twentieth-century liberal writers like Pierre Elliott Trudeau,[12] have tended to associate it with more universal and encompassing forms, akin in spirit to civic nationalism, and to identify small-state nationalisms with more particularistic and retrograde forms, closer in spirit to ethnic nationalism. The supporters of small-state nationalisms, on the other, have often felt the need to be more defensive in their arguments.[13]

When one canvasses this broad literature and bears in mind how normative the subject of nationalism in all its guises is, one needs to ask a number of questions. How clearly demarcated are the lines between civic and ethnic forms of nationalism in the first place? Between patriotism and nationalism? Between large-state nationalism and small? Is there not a danger that writers will use such divisions to extol their own particular version of nationalism as the good form (i.e., civic), and castigate that of their opponents as evil (i.e., ethnic)? Or that proponents of intolerant forms of nationalism, attuned to changing intellectual currents in our day, will seek to dress their own brand up as civic? Is there not also the possibility that ethnic forms of identity may acquire a whole new lease on life within the very contours of what pass for civically constructed societies? These are some of the issues I wish to explore in the remainder of this paper, with reflections drawn primarily from the Canadian case.

The boundary question lies at the heart of any discussion of different typologies of nationalism. Authors like Anthony Smith or John Armstrong would underline the ethnic origins of all nations.[14] It is not necessary to endorse this position in order to recognize ethnic or religious underpinnings to forms of nationalism that we think of today as civic. Liah Greenfeld has done a nice job of illuminating the Protestant roots of English nationalism in the sixteenth century, on which first British nationalism, and then the British Empire were built.[15] Michael Lind, in a recent analysis of American national identity, has referred to its Anglo-Protestant character during the first long phase that saw the promulgation of the Constitution and consolidation of the United States, and to the nativist antipathy to different immigrant groups, not to speak of Blacks, in subsequent periods. It is only in recent decades that multiculturalism and multiracialism have become more important features of American political culture.[16] The Catholic and royalist underpinnings of France played a significant role in the subsequent evolution of that country, even after the French Revolution had proclaimed universalistic principles of citizenship in documents such as the Declaration of the Rights of Man and the Citizen. There was much backsliding from these universalistic principles during the Dreyfus affair at the end of the nineteenth century, and by the Vichy regime during the Second World War; the anti-immigrant pronouncements of Jean-Marie Le Pen's National Front are pointed reminders of similar tendencies in our own day.

Germany's plunge from the overtly liberal constitutionalism open-to-all of the Weimar Republic into the blood-and-soil racism of the Nazi period is the most extreme twentieth-century example of how fragile constructs of national identity based upon civic nationalism can be. In the contemporary world, religious fundamentalism—in India, in the Muslim world, in Israel, in the Orthodox countries of Eastern Europe, and elsewhere—represents an ongoing challenge to secular state structures, based upon putatively civic foundations. Even if the dangers of fundamentalism are sometimes exaggerated, it remains the case that topics such as 'What is a Jew?' and 'What is a Hindu?' can trigger sharp debates in countries like Israel and India precisely because they speak to question of underlying national identity.

Nationalism and Citizenship within Multinational States

Let me turn from these general considerations to the more specific problems that the division between civic and ethnic nationalism poses for multinational states. In countries like Belgium, Switzerland, Spain, Canada, and the United Kingdom, competing visions of nation, state, and citizenship may be found. The roots of statehood may themselves be contentious, as Belgian history would suggest.[17] French-speaking Swiss and their German-speaking counterparts may share a country, but not necessarily a single form of identity.[18] There are both Catalan and Basque versions of history to compete with the Spanish one.[19] Scottish nationalists do not see the history of Scotland in the same fashion as their English 'countrymen'.[20]

What is at stake is how one defines the subject of democratic citizenship in multinational states. What is the *demos*? The whole of the population of a particular country (i.e., Belgians, Spaniards, Britons, or Canadians), or the inhabitants of that particular territory populated by Flemish-speakers, or Catalans, or Scots, or Québécois? Large-state nationalists, if one may call them that, clearly identify with the larger state ensemble. They are with Johann Gottfried Herder when he argues that 'the most natural state is *one* nationality with one character.'[21]

Small-state nationalists, on the other hand, whether they are hard-line political secessionists or softer sociological/cultural nationalists, define the *demos* with reference to a smaller territory than the existing Belgian, Spanish, British, or Canadian state. They are with Herder when, in the same passage cited above, he goes on to argue: 'Nothing appears so indirectly opposite to the end of government as the unnatural enlargement of states, the wild mixing of all kinds of people and nationalities under one scepter.' For traditional small-state nationalists, their sense of identity may have a lot to do with ethnic background. For their more modernizing and pluralistic confrères, ethnicity is a good deal less attractive as a construct—even if language, culture, and a sense of shared history have ongoing importance. There may thus exist quite different versions of small-state nationalism, with *ethnos* and *demos* playing distinctive roles in each.[22]

The crucial dividing line, therefore, may lie less between civic and ethnic nationalism than between traditional and modernizing versions of nationalism. The adherents of small-state nationalism today, whether in Catalonia, Scotland, or Quebec, are likely to be open to accepting new immigrants into their respective societies; to be supporters of democratic methods in the pursuit of their aims; and to be broadly respectful of human rights. In this regard, they are not very different from the adherents of large-state nationalisms.

Small-scale nationalist movements can certainly prove themselves intolerant; but they are not alone in this regard, as the treatment of national minorities by majorities in various of the unitary states of Western Europe or in the United States would suggest. Political theorists and outside observers must apply universal standards of criticism, and must not simply assume that greater moral legitimacy resides with large-scale versions of citizenship or identity than with small ones.

THE CANADIAN CASE

Critics of secessionist-type nationalist movements usually tend to see them as ethnically driven. Confining myself to the Quebec situation, let me cite a number of examples along these lines. For Pierre Trudeau, 'Nationalists—even those of the left—are politically reactionary because, in attaching such importance to the idea of nation, they are surely led to a definition of the common good as a function of an ethnic group, rather than of all the people, regardless of characteristics.'[23] For Ramsay Cook, 'As René Lévesque made plain in 1968, nationalism is an idea that demands not special status or asymmetry, but equal state sovereignty, and, all too often, "ethnic cleansing", though not necessarily of the brutal Serbian variety.'[24] For Michael Ignatieff, 'In every modern nation, the nationalist myth that nations have a self-contained, "pure" ethnic identity comes up against the recalcitrant desire of ordinary people to breed across ethnic lines. . . . Does the Québécois nation comprise all those who live there, or only those who were born French-speaking?'[25]

Some might also be tempted to identify patriotism with love of the larger ensemble and nationalism with the ethos of smaller societies. Thus the English-language version of the Canadian national anthem uses the expression 'true patriot love' with reference to Canada; the concept of patriotism was a powerful motivating force in English Canada during both World Wars.[26] By contrast, it could be argued that French Canadians were more given to thinking of themselves as 'la nation canadienne française', and little given to using the language of *patrie*.[27]

Now it is true that the very term 'French Canadian', which dominated discussions of the national question in Canada until the 1960s, was itself ethnic-racial-religious in character. This was the way that traditional exponents of French Canadian nationalism defined their society. One important French-Canadian historian, Lionel Groulx, entitled a book published in 1922 *L'Appel de la race*. Another, J.-M.-R. Villeneuve, talked about the establishment of a French and Catholic state in the St Lawrence valley, where the French race would be able to 'fulfil its supernatural vocation'.[28] As two Quebec sociologists note, 'One can only understand the term French-Canadian and Catholic race in relationship to the ethnic underpinnings that structured identity between 1867–1930; these terms were used in contradistinction to what was taken to be its opposite—the Anglo-Saxon and Protestant race.'[29]

If we scratch the roots of the larger Canadian identity, we quickly come up against ethnic roots on the English-speaking side as well. The language of incipient English-Canadian nationalism in the nineteenth century was imperially oriented and British in character. Except for federalism, the political institutions of the Dominion of Canada were British in inspiration; and much early Canadian nationalist writing harped on the country's northern/British characteristics. Until the post-1945 period, it can be argued, the political culture of non-French Canadians was British-derived.[30]

This tendency contributed to anti-immigrant prejudice in the first part of the twentieth century, during a period of massive immigration from Southern and Eastern Europe;[31] on the positive side, it helped give shape to those parts of Canada's political tradition that were held to give the country its unique character. Peace, order, and good government, for example, were often contrasted with republicanism in the republic to the south. Canadian political culture was built out of a combination of Tory traditionalism and Whig reformism, with a small additional infusion of British-derived labourism. A less ruggedly individualistic version of the good society than the American one, more hierarchical on the one hand, more statist on the other, tended to prevail. There was relatively less commonality between this British-derived vision of Canadian society and the traditionalist French-Canadian one than a jejune reading of Canadian history would suppose. Indeed, one can say that part of the fragility of Canada as a country down to today flows from the very different cultural points of departure of the two 'founding peoples'. As the French political scientist André Siegfried noted in 1906: 'After a hundred and fifty years of life in common . . . under the same laws and the same flag [the French and English] remain foreigners, and in most cases adversaries. The two races have no more love for each other now than they had at the beginning.'[32] As Alexander Potter, writing in 1923, noted: 'There is neither common racial origin, nor common language; neither common customs, nor common aspirations.'[33]

It does not follow that a Canadian civic nationalism could not be built on these earlier foundations, or that the vision of Canadian identity that has come to dominate in the post-1945 period on the English-speaking side has not largely freed itself from its British moorings. The history of post-war Canada is one of evolution in this direction: the Canada Citizenship Act 1947; the ending of appeals to Judicial Committee of the Privy Council in 1949; first Canadian-born Governor-General in 1952; the waning use of the term 'Dominion' by Canadian governments from the 1950s on; the adoption of the maple leaf flag in 1965, replacing the British-derived ensign; multiculturalism as official government policy from the 1970s on; patriation of the Canadian Constitution in 1982, along with its made-in-Canada Charter of Rights and Freedoms.

But why might Quebec nationalism not travel the same road, starting at a later point in time? The Quiet Revolution of the 1960s symbolized the transition from a more traditional, defensive type of French-Canadian nationalism, in which religion and the past played a crucial role, to a more modernizing, liberal form of nationalism. With it came the waning in power of the Catholic Church, the new salience of the government of Quebec, modernization of the education and health systems, and heightened emphasis on the French language as the all-important constitutive element in the majority Quebec identity.[34]

Contemporary Quebec nationalists claim to speak the language of civic, not ethnic, nationalism. Louis Balthazar writes: 'If nationalism can be defined as an intemperate manifestation of chauvinism, this is less and less true of contemporary Quebec nationalism. [T]he passage from a French-Canadian traditional national consciousness to the new idea of a Quebec allegiance has meant a gradual redefinition of Quebeckers' identity and a move from ethnic to territorial nationalism.'[35] Greg Neilsen observes: '[B]y the 1960s the development of the Quebec sovereignty argument had shifted from the old ethnic nationalism of the Duplessis era to a modern civic nationalism founded on territory and language rather than religion and race.'[36] The Parti Québécois drapes itself in such language in most of its pronouncements. When former PQ Premier Jacques Parizeau slipped up, on the night of the October 1995 referendum, and blamed 'money and the ethnic vote' for the defeat of the YES side, members of his own camp were livid.[37]

One might argue, in fact, that the most overtly ethnic form of nationalism in Canada today is Aboriginal nationalism. Aboriginal peoples' claims to land ownership and self-government rests on the argument that they were Canada's first peoples. Despite an enormous amount of intermarriage and mingling with European settlers over time, there is much emphasis on blood and ancestry in contemporary First Nations discourse. As Gerald Alfred, a Mohawk political scientist, writes: 'Kahnawake has demonstrated the saliency of race as a feature of national political identity, even in the context of racial-biological ambiguity which would seem to indicate a reliance upon other factors such as language or residency.'[38] This emphasis on racial characteristics, along with the huge political and economic costs that would be entailed in any wholesale move towards territorially entrenched Aboriginal sovereignty in Canada or an Aboriginal-based legal system, has made many reluctant to accept proposals of the sort contained in the recent massive report of the Royal Commission on Aboriginal Peoples.[39]

There is another sense in which ethnicity has returned to Canadian debates about national identity, even outside Quebec. This has to do with the importance that the federal government has come to place on multiculturalism in its reformulated definition of Canada's national identity. Canadian census forms, in recent years, have introduced ever-greater refinements into the categories used to identify ethnic and racial origin. (It is interesting that 765,000 respondents to the 1991 census identified themselves as Canadian by origin, even though this category did not figure on the list; they refused to be pigeonholed into the ethnic categories that were provided.) Employment equity legislation has helped give wide currency to the term 'visible minority' and has made such minorities (along with women, disabled people, and Aboriginal people) the targets of affirmative action programs in the public sector. There is a new politics of multiculturalism in the air that critics like Neil Bissoondath fear may itself be undermining the basis for a more universalistic sense of identity.[40] Is Canadian multiculturalism little more than the masochistic celebration of Canadian nothingness, as Gad Horowitz has stated?[41] Does the very insecurity of its ethnic antecedent contribute to the lack of an English-Canadian sense of rootedness in our own day?[42]

Multiculturalism certainly makes the task of promoting a purely civic Canadian identity more difficult. The politics of difference, which has come to be inscribed in the Canadian Charter of Rights and Freedoms, can in itself be corrosive of any kind of shared national values. Jean Bethke Elshtain has observed with reference to the United States: 'For those pushing a strong version of identity politics, any politics that doesn't revolve around their identities is of no interest to them. There is no broad identification with a common good beyond that of the group of which one is a member.'[43] David Miller writes: 'Radical multiculturalism wrongly celebrates sexual, ethnic, and other such identities at the expense of national identities.'[44]

Identity politics takes on an added dimension in a multinational state such as Canada. It makes it more difficult to distinguish between the multinational dimensions of the Canada–Quebec relationship, for example, and the multi-ethnic strands within Quebec and English-speaking Canada.[45] For certain critics, the whole purpose of the federal multiculturalism policy was 'to short-circuit Quebec nationalism by making the French Canadian nation but one component of the multiethnic dimension that is Canada'.[46] Even if one does not buy this argument, the fact remains that multiculturalism has further complicated Canada's political debates. It has made the forging of constitutional agreement so much the more difficult, as perspicacious observers like Alan Cairns have pointed out.[47] It may well have contributed to the ultimate demise of the Charlottetown Accord of 1992—the last wholesale attempt at constitutional reform in Canada.

So there can be non-civic forms of nationalism (e.g., Aboriginal) within a society that is overtly civic in its orientations; and there may be a new fostering of ethnic identities by the very agencies of government that most would look to as incarnations of civic identity.

THE CHALLENGES FACING MULTINATIONAL STATES

A number of dangers face multinational states such as Canada.

(1) One is the danger of great-nation chauvinism, denigrating the national identities of smaller sub-state nationalisms, like Quebec's, as particularistic and narrowing. Eric Harris made the following confession in 1927: 'We British Canadians possess a sense of racial superiority which seems to be innate in us, and which we do not acknowledge even to ourselves.'[48] This can all too easily lead to a holier-than-thou mentality, to the invocation of the virtuous character of pan-Canadian nationalism, its inherently civic nature, against the ethnic and intolerant character of Quebec nationalism. As an example, let me cite a passage written by the late Toronto historian Kenneth McNaught. '[One of the] most striking facts about the English-speaking view of Canada is that it rejects racial nationalism. . . . The English-speaking view has always anticipated a Canadian nationality in which the significance of racial origin will diminish rather than increase. . . . English-speaking Canadians have a . . . reluctance to contend directly with the ever more extreme racial nationalism of Quebec.'[49] This doesn't really help the debate. As Jean-Pierre Derriennic, himself a committed opponent of Quebec sovereignty, astutely observes: 'For a resident of Quebec, there are two possible forms of civic nationalism: a Quebec civic nationalism and a Canadian civic nationalism.'[50] It is about time that Canadians outside Quebec woke up to this fact.

(2) The arrogance of hard-core indépendantistes can also pose problems. For them, the only road to national self-realization lies through political independence. Anyone who deviates from the straight and narrow path is misled, indoctrinated, or the dupe of blocking ethnic minorities. This reinforces internal divisions in Quebec by heightening the concerns of linguistic and cultural minorities.[51] It also makes more moderate partisans of Quebec sovereignty uncomfortable. Lise Bissonnette, the former editor of *Le Devoir*, states: 'For me sovereignty has always been a conclusion rather than a religion. . . . Extremist discourse has always frightened me and I hate when people have recourse to it.'[52] Jean Larose argues: 'I have often defined myself as an anti-nationalist sovereigntist. . . . Nationalism by its very nature tends to be ethnic. In becoming independent, Quebec may perhaps be able to finally escape from its logic.'[53] The point of all this is to underline the danger of forgetting, as Jacques Parizeau has so clearly done in his recently published *Pour un Québec souverain*, that a broad coalition is required to carry any democratically conducted referendum in favour of Quebec sovereignty. Hard-line nationalism is counterproductive to the more open discourse that civic nationalism, especially in a linguistically and ethnically divided society like Quebec, requires.

(3) Once the spiral of break-up has been set in motion, the result may be one that a majority in neither camp really welcomes, but that competing visions of national identity seem to render inevitable. Intransigence, demagoguery, a one-sided recitation of slights and grievances, become the order of the day. Hard-line nationalist spokesmen drown out more accommodating points of view. There is insufficient emphasis on the ties that bind, and a logic that demands ever-greater devolution of powers to one's own national grouping. Something of this logic was at work in the events that led to the break-up of Czechoslovakia.[54] A similar process can be observed in the enhanced powers that the regions and language communities have acquired in Belgium in recent years.[55] How far can such processes go without triggering a total melt-down? In such an event, is it certain that the use of force can be avoided, especially if significant elements within the seceding territory are calling for its partition and for their own continued attachment to the larger, pre-secession state?[56] We need to take such threats seriously, however peaceful the history of Canada has been until now.

In the end, I reject the view that the Canadian debate is a civic versus ethnic debate. Whatever the ethnic foundations on both sides of the Canada–Quebec divide may once have been, what is ultimately in contention today is a civic versus civic version of what the overarching state structure ought to be. It is as logical for a sovereigntist-minded Québécois to wish that Quebec were a fully independent nation-state as it is for a non-sovereigntist-minded Québécois to wish it to remain a constituent part of Canada. The language used by the former can be just as much the language of civic republicanism as that used by the latter. Guy Bouthillier, a prominent Quebec nationalist, writes: 'The sovereigntist movement must constantly remember that it stands for equality between peoples regardless of their size, for the republican idea of founding a country of citizens and not of ethnic groups, for a country freed from any ethnic obsession.'[57] The language of this version of Quebec nationalism is certainly very different from the invocation of race that dominated nationalist discourse in the first part of the twentieth century. This much one needs to acknowledge, whether one is ultimately convinced by Bouthillier's protestations of good faith or not.

I also think we need to revisit the discourse of patriotism and nationalism that was referred to at the beginning of this paper. In recent years, the words 'nation' and 'national' have been used by many English Canadians to describe Canada or Canada-wide institutions as a whole. Expressions such as 'national government', 'national organizations', and 'national newspaper' are common with reference to institutions that are, or claim to be, Canada-wide in character. There were concerns in the 1960s about developing a strong sense of Canadian nationalism (e.g., vis-à-vis the United States).[58] The language of the opponents of the Canada–United States Free Trade Agreement in 1988 was very much that of state sovereignty and cultural nationalism. For some time in Canada, 'patriotism' has been perceived to have something of a retrograde ring, and the only time it has been widely encountered in recent Canadian political debate was with reference to the patriation (or repatriation) of the Canadian Constitution in 1982. But that could be seen as severing one of the few remaining 'colonial' ties binding Canada to the United Kingdom.

For some representative figures in Quebec, 'patrie' and 'patriotism' had other implications. For example, Jean Chrétien, Prime Minister of Canada and leader of the Liberal Party of Canada, made a rather telling observation at the time of the October 1995 referendum. Quoting Jean Lesage, who had been Premier of Quebec at the time of the Quiet Revolution in the early 1960s, he stated that he viewed Quebec as his 'patrie' (homeland) and Canada as his 'pays' (country).[59] Here 'patrie' speaks the language of the heart rather than the head, much as it does for the contemporary adherents of republican patriotism. But the 'patrie', where Chrétien and many other Quebec federalists are concerned, is not a sovereign state; rather, it is a sub-state unit with claims to sociological, if not fully political, nationhood.

An example such as this makes it difficult for me to accept Walker Connor's argument that 'Nationalism and patriotism are vitally different phenomena and should not be confused through the careless use of language.'[60] I happen to think that these two terms are interchangeable. The inhabitants of small-scale nations lacking in sovereignty can speak the language of patriotism just as easily as can those of large nations; the inhabitants of large-scale nations, no less than small, can speak the language of nationalism. Theorists of ethnonationalism on the one hand, and of patriotism on the other, can devise whatever dichotomies they like; by themselves these cannot help resolve the more intractable problems that conflicting national sentiments (or shall we call them conflicting visions of *patria*?) bring to the surface.

The prospect of break-up—of the transition from the civic nationalism of the larger ensemble to that of its components—haunts countries like Canada and Belgium at the end of the twentieth century. It is precisely the actual moment of transition, should it arise, that could prove the most dangerous. In the Canadian case there has been talk of partition by linguistic minorities; the clearly expressed intention on the part of Aboriginal peoples to refuse to be part of any sovereign Quebec;[61] the likelihood of serious bickering between Quebec and Canada over such questions as the division of the federal debt; in short, the prospect of a divorce that, unlike Czechoslovakia's, would be less-than-velvet.[62] I tend to agree with Jean-Pierre Derriennic when he writes: 'The difficulty is not for Quebec to be independent; it lies in Quebec becoming independent.'[63] Undoing the glue that binds may turn out to be a much greater problem than the proponents of Quebec sovereignty are willing to recognize.

The challenge for multinational federations is to find a way to acknowledge multiple national identities within ongoing state structures, retaining those things that need to be kept together—external relations, defence, economic ties, citizenship—even while accepting deep diversity in others.[64] This may require asymmetrical federal arrangements or an out-and-out confederal arrangement—issues that merit further exploration in the years to come.[65]

At the beginning of the twenty-first century, in societies where liberal democratic values are strongly entrenched—something as true for Quebec as it is for Canada as a whole—we gain nothing by labelling one form of identity (i.e., the pan-Canadian) civic and the other (i.e., the Quebec) ethnic. Evoking the Bosnian or Rwandan or Chechnyan situations may be good for scoring debating points; I doubt it can help us get to the bottom of our own predicament, which is primarily about competing versions of civic identity.[66]

What is ultimately at stake in the Canadian debate (and, I suspect, in the Belgian and Spanish and, eventually, British) is whether it is possible to have more than one version of civic identity within a single state. I am convinced that the answer is YES, though I am by no means certain that my compatriots, either in Quebec or in Canada outside Quebec, see things in the same way I do. For hard-line Quebec nationalists, a Quebec identity overlapping with a Canadian identity is unacceptable; nothing less than a sovereign Quebec state, with its own flag flying at the United Nations, will do. For many English-speaking Canadians outside Quebec, all provinces are equal; there can be no special status for Quebec and no acknowledgment that more than one nation can exist within the boundaries of an internationally recognized state.

The challenge of national identity in multinational states is ongoing, and far more acute than the one that faces states with a more coherent sense of identity. Keeping such states together requires a willingness on the part of the members of both majority and minority nationalities to make concessions to other points of view. It means refraining from dismissing alternative versions of identity as ethnic, and playing up, by comparison, the civic virtues of one's own position. And it means recognizing that multiple national identities make impossible a single overarching sense of what it is to be a Canadian, a Belgian, or a Spaniard. The concrete experiences of such states in facing these challenges may have more to teach us, today, than abstract ruminations about civic versus ethnic forms of nationalism.

NOTES

1. Anthony Smith, *National Identity* (Harmondsworth: Penguin, 1991), chap. 1.
2. Liah Greenfeld, *Nationalism: Five Roads to Modernity* (Cambridge, Mass.: Harvard University Press, 1992), 11.
3. Michael Ignatieff, *Blood and Belonging: Journeys into the New Nationalism* (New York: Farrar, Straus, & Giroux, 1993), 249.
4. Friedrich Meinecke, *Cosmopolitanism and the National State* (Princeton: Princeton University Press, 1970); first published in German in 1907. Cf. the discussion in Peter Alter, *Nationalism,* (London: Edward Arnold, 1989), 8–9.
5. Hans Kohn, *The Idea of Nationalism* (New York: Macmillan, 1945), 329–31.
6. For an interesting discussion of the use of the term *patria* by Machiavelli, see Nicholas Xenos, 'Civic Nationalism: Oxymoron?', *Critical Review* 10, 2 (Spring 1996), 213–31.
7. Carlo Rosselli, *Scritti dell' esilio,* cited in Maurizio Viroli, *For Love of Country: An Essay on Patriotism and Nationalism* (Oxford: Clarendon Press, 1995), 162.
8. Jürgen Habermas, *Die Nachholende Revolution,* (Frankfurt: 1990). Cf. the discussion in Viroli, 169–72.
9. Viroli, *For Love of Country,* Epilogue.
10. Yael Tamir, *Liberal Nationalism* (Princeton: Princeton University Press, 1993).
11. Cf., for example, Friedrich Engels' critical comments on the Swiss: 'The struggle of the early Swiss against Austria, the heroic shot of Tell, the immortal victory at Mortgarten—all of this represented the struggle of restless shepherds against the thrust of historical development, a struggle of hidebound, conservative, local interests against the interests of the entire nation. They won their victory over the civilization of that period, but as punishment they were cut off from the whole later progress of civilization.' Cited in Rosa Luxemburg, *The National Question: Selected Writings,* ed. Horace B. Davis (New York: Monthly Review Press, 1976), 119.
12. Cf. Pierre Elliott Trudeau, *Federalism and the French Canadians* (Toronto: Macmillan, 1968), 193, where he writes: 'One way of offsetting the appeal of separatism is by investing tremendous amounts of time, energy, and money in nationalism, *at the federal level.*'
13. Cf., for example, the very title of the noted Hungarian theorist Istvan Bibo's essay 'The Distress of the East European Small States', in *Democracy, Revolution, and Self-Determination: Selected Writings,* ed. Karoly Nagy (Boulder, Col.: Atlantic Research Publications, 1991), 12–86.
14. Anthony Smith, *The Ethnic Origins of Nations* (Oxford: Blackwell, 1986); John Armstrong, *Nations before Nationalism* (Chapel Hill: University of North Carolina Press, 1982).
15. Greenfeld, *Nationalism,* chap. 1, 'God's Firstborn: England'.
16. Michael Lind, *The Next American Nation: The New Nationalism and the Fourth American Revolution,* New York: Free Press, 1995. Lind, however, is a critic of multiculturalism, because he sees it as obfuscating more substantive class differences in contemporary American society.
17. For a good illustration, compare the classically French-centred, unitary approach to Belgian history of the nineteenth-century historian Henri Pirenne, *Histoire de la Belgique des origines à nos jours* (Bruxelles: La Renaissance du livre, 1972) with the documents that have been collected in the anthology edited by Theo Hermans, *The Flemish Movement: A Documentary History 1780–1990* (London: Athlone Press, 1992).

18. Cf., for example, Uli Windisch, *Les Relations quotidiennes entre Romands et Suisses Allemands* (Lausanne: Payot, 1992).
19. Cf. J. Marias, *Consideracion de Cataluña* (Barcelona: Acervo, 1996); Michael Keating, *Nations against States: The New Politics of Nationalism in Quebec, Catalonia and Scotland* (London: Macmillan, 1996), chap. 5; J.L. Sullivan, *ETA and Basque Nationalism: The Fight for Euskadi: 1890–1986* (London: 1988).
20. Cf. D. McCrone, *Understanding Scotland: The Sociology of a Stateless Nation* (London: Routledge, 1992); and Tom Nairn, *The Breakup of Britain: Crisis and Neo-Nationalism* (London: Verso, 1977).
21. J. G. Herder, *Idee zur Philosophie*, cited in Viroli, 123.
22. Reinhardt Lepsius, 'Ethnos und Demos,' *Kölner Zeitschrift für Soziologie* 38, 4 (1986): 751–9.
23. Trudeau, *Federalism*, 169
24. Ramsay Cook, *Canada, Quebec, and the Uses of Nationalism*, 2nd ed. (Toronto: McClelland and Stewart, 1995), 245.
25. Ignatieff, *Blood and Belonging*, 172.
26. For an example of wartime patriotic discourse, compare the following statement by Rev. D.C. Chown, head of the Methodist Church of Canada, at the time of the December 1917 federal election, when conscription for service overseas was the key issue. 'The elector who votes for the anti-conscription policy degrades the term Canadian. . . . If I voted against the Union government leadership, I would feel that I was opposing the most patriotic movement ever known in the Dominion of Canada.' Cited in Kenneth McNaught, *The Penguin History of Canada* (Harmondsworth: Penguin, 1969), 218.
27. In this regard, see the entries in Ramsay Cook, ed., *French-Canadian Nationalism* (Toronto: Macmillan, 1968).
28. J.-M.-R. Villeneuve, 'And Our Dispersed Brethren?' in Cook, ed., *French-Canadian Nationalism*, 202.
29. Gilles Bourque and Jules Duchastel, *L'Identité fragmentée* (Montreal: Fides, 1996, 200); my translation.
30. Cf., among others, Carl Berger, *The Sense of Power: Studies in the Ideas of Canadian Imperialism 1867–1914* (Toronto: University of Toronto Press, 1970); Peter Russell, ed., *Nationalism in Canada* (Toronto: McGraw-Hill, 1966).
31. J.S. Woodsworth, *Strangers within Our Gates or Coming Canadians* ([1909] Toronto: University of Toronto Press, 1972); Donald Avery, *'Dangerous Foreigners': European Immigrant Workers and Labour Radicalism in Canada, 1896–1932* (Toronto: McClelland and Stewart, 1979).
32. André Siegfried, *The Race Question in Canada* (Toronto: Carleton Library, 1966), 85.
33. Alexander O. Potter, *Canada as a Political Entity* (Toronto: Longmans, 1923), 9.
34. For a good discussion of this period in Quebec history, see Kenneth McRoberts, *Quebec: Social Change and Political Crisis*, 3rd ed. (Toronto: McClelland and Stewart, 1988), chaps 5–6.
35. Louis Balthazar, 'The Faces of Quebec Nationalism', in *Quebec: State and Society*, 2nd ed., ed. Alain Gagnon (Toronto: Nelson, 1993), 17.
36. Greg Neilsen, 'Culture and the Politics of Being Québécois,' in *Quebec Society: Critical Issues*, ed. Marcel Fournier et al. (Toronto: Prentice-Hall, 1997), 91.

37. 'Senior members of the Parti Quebecois and its government winced when Mr Parizeau articulated his sense of ethnic rage—confirming the worst fears and bleakest perceptions of the nationalist movement.' Graham Fraser, 'Making raw appeal to francophones pained supporters', *Globe and Mail*, 1 Nov. 1995. The same article cites Alain Noël, a Quebec political scientist and supporter of the YES side: '[Parizeau] looked out of control . . . at a unique and critical moment in Quebec history, when the whole world was watching and wondering about the nature of the sovereignty movement. . . . The sovereignty movement has never been so strong, and in a few words he wiped out that progress. Now many people are ill at ease for having voted Yes.'
38. Gerald R. Alfred, *Heeding the Voices of our Ancestors: Kahnawake Mohawk Politics and the Rise of Native Nationalism* (Toronto: Oxford University Press, 1995), 190. Kahnawake is a Mohawk Indian reserve on the south shore of the St Lawrence River near Montreal.
39. Cf. John Gray, 'Absent aboriginals: not a word about natives', *Globe and Mail*, 24 May 1997, D9, which documents the lack of support among mainstream Canadians for the recommendations of the Royal Commission on Aboriginal Peoples.
40. Neil Bissoondath, *Selling Illusions: The Cult of Multiculturalism in Canada* (Toronto: Penguin, 1994).
41. Cited in Gina Mallet, 'Has Diversity Gone Too Far?', *Globe and Mail*, 15 March 1997, D2.
42. Eric Kaufmann, 'Condemned to Rootedness: The Loyalist Origins of Canada's Identity Crisis', unpublished ms., 32.
43. Jean Bethke Elshtain, *Democracy on Trial* (Concord, Ont.: Anansi, 1993), 57.
44. David Miller, *On Nationality* (Oxford: Clarendon Press, 1995), 135.
45. Cf. Will Kymlicka, *Multicultural Citizenship: A Liberal Theory of Minority Rights* (Oxford: Clarendon Press, 195), 187–91.
46. Marcel Adam, 'Le multiculturalisme nuit à la cohésion sociale en cultivant les différences', *La Presse*, 26 Nov. 1994, cited in Guy Bouthillier, *L'Obsession ethnique* (Montreal: Lanctot, 1997), 56; my translation.
47. Alan Cairns, 'Political Science, Ethnicity, and the Canadian Constitution', in *Disruptions: Constitutional Struggles from the Charter to Meech Lake* (Toronto: McClelland and Stewart, 1991); Alan Cairns, 'Dreams Versus Reality in "Our" Constitutional Future: How Many Communities?', in *Reconfigurations: Canadian Citizenship and Constitutional Change* (Toronto: McClelland and Stewart, 1995).
48. W. Eric Harris, *Stand to Your Work: A Summons to Canadians Everywhere* (Toronto: Musson Book Co., 1927), cited in Ray Conlogue, *Impossible Nation: The Longing for Homeland in Canada and Quebec* (Stratford, Ont.: Mercury Press, 1996), 27.
49. Kenneth McNaught, 'The National Outlook of English-Speaking Canadians', in *Nationalism in Canada*, ed. Peter Russell (Toronto: McGraw-Hill, 1966), 61–71.
50. Jean-Pierre Derriennic, *Nationalisme et démocratie: Réflexions sur les illusions des indépendantistes québécois* (Montreal: Boréal, 1995), 29; my translation.
51. Cf. Jane Jensen, 'Quebec: Which Minority?', *Dissent* (Summer, 1996), 43–6.
52. Marcos Ancelovici and Francis Dupuis-Déri, eds, *L'Archipel identitaire* (Montreal: Boréal, 1997) 120–1; my translation.
53. Ibid., 72–3; my translation.
54. Cf. Petr Pithart, 'Czechoslovakia: The Loss of the Old Partnership', in *Seeking a New*

Canadian Partnership, ed. Leslie Seidle (Montreal: Institute for Research on Public Policy, 1994), 163–9; Frédéric Wehrlé, *Le Divorce Tchéco-Slovaque* (Paris: L'Harmattan, 1994).

55. Cf. Bernard Remiche, 'Divorce à la belge', *Le Monde diplomatique*, February 1997, 11.
56. Two public opinion polls conducted by Southam/Compas showed strong support in English Canada both for partition of Quebec and for the use of military force to help bring it about, in the event of a YES vote for Quebec sovereignty in a future referendum. *Vancouver Sun*, 15–16 May 1997.
57. Bouthillier, *L'Obsession ethnique*, 207–8; my translation.
58. Cf. Abraham Rotstein and Gary Lax, eds, *Getting It Back: A Program for Canadian Independence* (Toronto: Clarke, Irwin, 1974); Philip Resnick, *The Land of Cain* (Vancouver: New Star Books, 1977), chap. 5.
59. Jean Chrétien made this statement during a televised address to the people of Canada on 25 Oct. 1995, five days before the Quebec referendum resulted in a narrow victory for the opponents of Quebec sovereignty.
60. Walker Connor, *Ethnonationalism* (Princeton: Princeton University Press, 1991), 196.
61. Cf. Grand Council of the Crees of Quebec, *Sovereign Injustice: Forcible Inclusion of the James Bay Crees and Cree Territory into a Sovereign Quebec* (Nemaska, Qué.: 1995).
62. Daniel Drache and Roberto Perin, eds, *Negotiating with a Sovereign Quebec* (Toronto: Lorimer, 1992); Robert Young, *The Secession of Quebec and the Future of Canada* (Montreal and Kingston: McGill-Queen's University Press, 1995).
63. Derriennic, *Nationalisme et démocratie*, 25.
64. Cf. Charles Taylor, *Reconciling the Solitudes: Essays on Canadian Federalism and Nationalism* (Montreal and Kingston: McGill-Queen's University Press, 1993), chap. 8.
65. Cf., for example, Philip Resnick, *Toward a Canada-Quebec Union* (Montreal and Kingston: McGill-Queen's University Press, 1991); Jeremy Webber, *Reimagining Canada* (Montreal and Kingston: McGill-Queen's University Press, 1994), chap. 7; Kenneth McRoberts, *Misconceiving Canada: The Struggle for National Unity* (Toronto: Oxford University Press, 1997), chap. 10.
66. Given its ethnic underpinnings, Aboriginal nationalism poses a potentially different challenge in countries such as Canada. But it is a much less significant threat to Canada's survival as a state than is Quebec nationalism.

The True Nature of Sovereignty: Reply to my Critics Concerning *Trudeau and the End of a Canadian Dream*

Guy Laforest

Sovereignty, for an academic, a scholar, or an intellectual, is first and foremost freedom of the mind. This mental sovereignty ought to include the capacity to reflect critically on the strengths—and the weaknesses—of one's own arguments. A free mind should be able to reconsider, to revise and refine one's ideas. I will undertake such an endeavour in this chapter, re-evaluating my first major book, *Trudeau and the End of a Canadian Dream*, in the light of the arguments and judgments of those who have assessed it critically.

Trudeau and the End of a Canadian Dream was published in French in 1992, about one month prior to the referendum on the Charlottetown Accord, then translated and published in English a few months before the October 1995 Québec referendum on sovereignty-partnership. The book is thus inseparable from both the constitutional travails of the Canadian state and the political restlessness of Québec in the last quarter of the twentieth century. The following anecdote tells the whole story.

My publisher in French, Denis Vaugeois from Septentrion, suggested the following title : 'Trudeau and the End of THE Canadian Dream'. My publisher in English, Philip Cercone at McGill-Queen's, had his own preference: 'Trudeau and THE Canadian Dream'. He wanted no end at all. I stuck to my idea. In the choice of a title, an author ought to be truthful to his or her readers. Much has changed in Canadian politics since the late 1980s, when I started to work on the book. I shall begin with some considerations on the political context then and now, as well as some personal notes about political theory in Canada.

1. Canadian Politics, Then and Now

In the late 1980s Europe was in turmoil. The Berlin Wall was about to fall. A few years later, Germany would be reunited and the imperial Soviet Union would collapse. In Canada there was also a lot of excitement in the air. The Meech Lake Constitutional Accord, recognizing Québec as a distinct society within Canada and renovating central institutions of the federation, such as the Supreme Court and the Senate, was awaiting its fate. In late June 1990, it would have to be either ratified or rejected. Thereafter Québec would, at long last, be either a willing partner in the federation or, in case of failure, anxiously contemplating its future and its options. Either way, an important element of the Zeitgeist was the idea that the political landscape of the country was about to be dramatically altered. Between 1988 and 1992, one could believe that our situation of political deadlock would soon be overcome. I certainly thought so. In 2000 it is next to impossible to harbour such convictions. The Meech Lake Accord is long gone and forgotten. The Charlottetown Accord was voted down in referendums throughout the country. The Québec government's proposal of sovereignty-partnership was rejected by its own people, with the slimmest of margins, in late October 1995. The last years of the twentieth century witnessed an erosion of civility all right, but no major constitutional change.

In 1954, one of my predecessors at Université Laval's Faculté des sciences sociales, Maurice Lamontagne, published an important book entitled *Le Fédéralisme canadien: Évolution et problèmes*. He concluded that, in the early 1950s, Québec's position in the Canadian federation was ambiguous, hybrid, and that it could not last. According to Lamontagne, Québec could not, for its own sake, remain half in and half out, deprived of both the full benefits of participation in Canada and the advantages of sovereignty.[1] Lamontagne was profoundly wrong. As the new century begins, Québec remains half-in and half-out. Its position is ambiguous, hybrid, and has remained so for at least fifty years. I shall come back to this point in my own conclusion.

In the late 1980s, I felt I was writing in an era of impending change. A decade later, I feel I am surrounded by institutional stalemate. There is no political need to hurry with one's writing.

I am a member of the Meech Lake generation. This means that I belong to a group of social scientists and philosophers who wrote their first major works after 1987, on topics and issues related in some way, theoretically or politically, to the Meech Lake Accord. To borrow an expression from a US economist, W.W. Rostow, debating—directly or obliquely—the merits of the Meech Lake Accord has had the significance of an intellectual take-off for members of this group, which includes Wayne Norman, Sam LaSelva, Will Kymlicka, Jeremy Webber, Margaret Moore, Alain Noël, Christian Dufour, Janet Ajzenstat, Linda Cardinal, Diane Lamoureux, François Rocher, Daniel Salée, Daniel Jacques, and Guy Lachapelle. Other scholars such as Ronald Beiner, Stéphane Dion, and Alain-G. Gagnon, although they are of roughly the same age as the Meech Lake generation and have also been involved in the Meech Lake debate, had autonomous and specific intellectual identities before the first signing of the Accord in April 1987.

Integration versus fragmentation; federalism versus secession; liberal justice versus the politics of difference, identity, and recognition. These are some of the conceptual clashes stimulated by the Canadian debate over the merits of the Meech Lake Accord. For Canadian theorists, deciding in their own minds whether or not Québec ought to be recognized as a distinct society in the Constitution proved to be much more than a parochial concern. It gave them a privileged perspective and key insights as their 'home issues' gained prominence in world politics, as well as in the social sciences and philosophy, during the 1990s. These remarks are aimed at the work of the members of the Meech Lake generation; they also apply to the thought of Charles Taylor, the most prominent contemporary Canadian philosopher. His seminal essay of the 1990s, *Multiculturalism and 'The Politics of Recognition'*, was preceded, a decade earlier, by an interpretation of the Canada–Québec imbroglio based on the Herderian categories of identity and recognition.[2]

I studied at McGill with Taylor and James Tully. Their influence on my thinking is easily recognizable in *Trudeau and the End of a Canadian Dream*. Taylor's teaching, and his own example, showed me the value of bringing together the intellectual histories of Québec and English-speaking Canada. Tully made me see better the task of understanding actions and intentions in the history of ideas; moreover, his work in early modern political theory taught me much about Locke's language of trust, loyalty, consent, and resistance. I also studied at Laval, and it was there that I ended up working throughout the 1990s.

Laval enjoys a rich tradition in the social sciences. I am keenly aware of my debts to many predecessors who have enriched the Canada–Québec debate over the years: Gérard Bergeron, Léon Dion, Fernand Dumont, Jean-Charles Falardeau, and Maurice Lamontagne, among others. One way to look at my book is to see it as a moment in my conversation with the late Léon Dion. For I had reached the conclusion that the Canadian dream that had just passed away with the rejection of the Meech Lake Accord was in an important sense his own project. I will now turn to the book, its arguments, and its context.

2. *Trudeau and the End of a Canadian Dream* in Context

In January 1991 I made a presentation in the Salon Rouge of Québec's Assemblée Nationale, to the members of the Bélanger-Campeau Parliamentary Commission on the future of Québec. The Commission had been put together by the province's Premier, Robert Bourassa, with the support of the Leader of the Opposition, Jacques Parizeau, in the months following the death of the Meech Lake Accord. The Commission was bipartisan in spirit, joining together long-time independentists in the Parti Québécois and federalists immensely disappointed by the failure of Meech Lake. *Trudeau and the End of a Canadian Dream* took a similarly bipartisan approach, offering a generous interpretation of federalist doctrine in twentieth-century Québec. I argued that the dominant interpretation of Canadian federalism in the political and intellectual traditions of Québec—two founding peoples, two distinct societies—had great nobility. It was a legitimate political project, a valid Canadian dream. I also argued that this dream had been dealt crushing blows by both the process and the substance of Canada's constitutional evolution between 1980 and 1982. The book examined the first Québec referendum campaign of 1980, and analyzed the promises made at the time by the Prime Minister of Canada, Pierre Elliott Trudeau. It then proceeded to interpret the significance, for Québec, of the constitutional revisions of 1982 in the light of John Locke's theory of political trust and legislative sovereignty. In short, the book argued that those revisions reduced Québec's legislative powers without the province's consent. This was the message that I tried to convey as forcefully as

I could to the members of the Bélanger–Campeau Commission. Much of the book is devoted to twentieth-century intellectual history. The following excerpt from the introduction explains this choice :

> Intellectuals can be seen as microcosms, as ideal-types of the Canadian-Québécois experience in its totality—the experience of two solitudes brought together by rational voluntarism but holding together uneasily, perpetually tempted to yield to incomprehension. I shall especially emphasize the paradigmatic figures of Léon Dion, André Laurendeau, Ramsay Cook, F.R. Scott and, of course, Pierre Elliott Trudeau.[3]

I argued in the book that the 1982 transformation of the Constitution was incompatible with the federalist, binationalist Canadian patriotism of Québec intellectuals such as Laurendeau and Léon Dion. After emphasizing the crucial role played by Pierre Trudeau in the derailment of the Meech Lake Accord, I addressed myself, in a serious, if somewhat naïve way, to federalist politicians in Quebec City and Ottawa, such as Claude Ryan, Gérald Beaudoin, and Arthur Tremblay. I argued that their Canadian patriotism had become politically impossible within the apparently unmovable constitutional parameters of 1982. In conclusion, I tried to imagine what conditions would permit a genuine partnership between Canada and Québec. I listed the following elements: establishment of two distinct judicial systems and charters of rights, recognition of the fact that Québec represents a people, a distinct national society; a revised division of powers between the central government and its partners; and finally, giving a new name, 'Canada–Québec', to the restructured political community.

In 1967 Canada celebrated the centennial of Confederation. A new Québec had emerged with the Quiet Revolution, and it sought substantial modifications to the institutions of Canadian federalism, so as to better preserve and promote the distinct character of its society in the Americas. In 1992, when my book went to press a couple of months before the referendum on the Charlottetown Accord, I saw no desire in Canada to make these accommodations. There was no need to rejoice, but also no time to lose. I now turn to the arguments of my critics.

3. The Critics and their Arguments

I share with Marcel Adam, a retired political analyst from the newspaper *La Presse* in Montréal, a deep commitment to understand as thoroughly as possible the essential role played by Pierre Elliott Trudeau in Canadian politics. In the context of 1979-80, Adam agrees with me that Trudeau was, at the very least, consciously ambiguous in his referendum promises, aimed at securing the votes of undecided citizens. It was this ambiguity that led me to apply to the episode the methods of the history of ideas concerning contexts and intentions. Adam also supports my reply to those who, like Michael Behiels, believe that, from the 1950s to the 1970s, Trudeau's record on constitutional matters was clear: no need for institutional decentralization, no desire to appease Québec nationalists, no place for the dualistic vision (two peoples, nations, or distinct societies) in a restructured federation. Quoting from Trudeau's most important book of the 1960s, *Federalism and the French Canadians*, Adam shows that Trudeau frequently referred to the 1867 Constitution as a compromise, a pact, a quasi-treaty, between two federating parts—a document moreover that should not be modified unilaterally.[4] On these matters Pierre Trudeau was not as categorical, as crystal-clear, as Behiels (along with most ardent Trudeauites, such as Michael Bliss, Ramsay Cook, and my colleague Max Nemni) contends.

Nevertheless, Marcel Adam argues that, in my book, I was ready to accept the traditional Péquiste interpretation of the events of 1981 and 1982.[5] On 16 April 1981, barely three days after having won the provincial election, René Lévesque entered in a common front with seven other provinces in order to block Mr Trudeau's constitutional offensive. He accepted a kind of provincial equality in the common approach with regard to an amending formula. Thus he and the PQ are partly responsible for the political and juridical demise of the theory that Québec had its own constitutional veto. I agree with Adam on this point; Lévesque did indeed undermine the foundations of a veto right for Québec. Moreover, during the constitutional negotiations of November 1981, Lévesque was the first to abandon his allies when he accepted Trudeau's initial proposal to call a referendum. When the latter, a few hours later, outlined his idea in greater detail, Lévesque changed his mind and rejected the proposal. But the damage was done. I agree with Adam on this point as well, and I have written about it elsewhere.[6] In addition, Adam suggests that the Québec government, under Lévesque, did not dare to call a referendum of its own to delegitimize the 1982 Constitution in the only province where it was not approved in the legislature. The fact of the matter is that neither Lévesque nor Trudeau dared to consult the citizenry on this key issue. Since 1982, no government of Québec, or of Canada, has asked its people either to accept or to reject the Canadian Constitution.

I have a lot of admiration for P.A. Dutil, a historian of ideas with a sophisticated understanding of the place of liberalism in the evolution of Québec. In the early 1990s, Dutil did great work establishing the *Literary Review of Canada* as a new meeting place for ideas. (It is now in the able hands of David Berlin, Helen Walsh, and Anthony Westell.) Reviewing my book, among others, after the demise of the Charlottetown Accord, Dutil suggested first that I had simplified the relationship between intellecutal history and contemporary political debates. F.R. Scott, portrayed in my book as a champion of liberal individual rights and a harbinger of the Trudeau vision of Canada, was also, as Dutil rightly points out, a dedicated socialist. André Laurendeau, viewed as the champion of distinct society status for the Québec political community in a federal but asymmetrical union, was also, as Dutil again correctly notes, a cultured and refined individualist. Upon reflection, it is obvious that my narrative removed some of the complexity of key intellectual figures. I thus grant the point that I glossed 'too easily over difficult inconsistencies'.[7] In more recent work, I have tried to provide a more comprehensive analysis of Trudeau's writings from the 1950s onwards.[8] On the relationship between the thoughts of Trudeau and Laurendeau in the context of Canada's recent constitutional transformations, I maintain my position. The Meech Lake Accord, which would have supplemented rather than replaced the 1982 Constitution in our fundamental law, offered a legitimate way to reconcile the visions of both men. Dutil suggests that I ignore the fact that two of Mr Trudeau's most ardent disciples, Ramsay Cook and Michael Behiels, are also great admirers of Laurendeau. I recognize the impeccable scholarship of Behiels and Cook in their studies of the latter. However, on constitutional matters they espoused Trudeau's approach and rejected the distinct society model, without distancing themselves explicitly from Laurendeau.[9]

However critical one may be of the process that led to the 1982 constitutional package, many critics, including Dutil, suggest that it is now time to move on. What really matters is the content, the substance of this new element in our fundamental law. The package must be judged on its merits. What has it done to the Canadian political system? How has it affected the culture and institutions of Québec? I am quite willing to present arguments on these questions.

My first point is to refuse any clear-cut dichotomy between process and substance. In constitutional matters, process becomes a part of substance. The way in which a federal political community has made major changes becomes a fixture in the landscape of its political culture. Having done something once creates a strong temptation to repeat the same pattern of behaviour, if circumstances require it. The 1982 revisions demonstrate that radical constitutional changes can be made without the consent of Québec. If it has been done once, it can be done again. A decade ago, while the fate of the Meech Lake Accord was still up in the air, James MacPherson and Peter Hogg had this to say on this issue :

> The accord is entirely consistent with the fundamental assumptions on which this country was founded in 1867 and on which it has operated ever since.
>
> What is unnatural, and unfaithful to 122 years of constitutional development, is a situation in which Quebec is estranged from the constitution. Never before have constitutional changes as important as those adopted in 1982 come without Quebec's consent.[10]

The 1982 changes obtained the force of law across the land in part because of very doubtful judiciary interpretations of the nature and content of our constitutional conventions at the time. To his last day, Donald Smiley maintained that the Supreme Court of Canada ignored a convention according to which unanimity would be required for such radical changes. On the issue of Québec's right of veto, the words of Peter Russell haunt us still: 'I think the Supreme Court of Canada, when that issue was put to it after patriation, couldn't give an intellectually honest answer.'[11]

I remain convinced that Mr Trudeau's government violated the rule of law in the early 1980s when it invited the Queen to promulgate the new Constitution while Québec's Court of Appeal was still hearing a Reference by the province concerning its right of veto. It would have been more consistent with our traditions and practices to wait until the end of the judiciary process. In the matter at hand, the executive intimidated the judiciary. In the recent past, the federal government of Canada has argued, with the support of the Supreme Court, that a unilateral declaration of independence by Québec would violate the rule of law. Considering what happened in 1982, this invocation rings somewhat hollow. I would reformulate Ottawa's position in the following manner: the rule of law if necessary, but not necessarily the rule of law. This doctrine was candidly expounded by Thomas Flanagan, addressing his peers in the Royal Society of Canada:

> In practice . . . the Canadian constitutional amendment process is so gridlocked that, in the event of a crisis, it may be necessary to act quickly and fix up the legal niceties afterwards. Insisting on the rule of law strengthens Canada's hand because it precommits the government to protecting the national interest, but a government faced with a genuine secession crisis cannot let itself be tied up in knots by constitutional lawyers.[12]

In *Trudeau and the End of a Canadian Dream*, I used Locke's stark, radical terminology to characterize the 1982 revision as a breach of trust. I agree with Jean-Guy Prévost that, with regard to legitimacy, our context called for (and still does) a somewhat less Manichean vocabulary; more about that in my fuller discussion of Prévost's analysis. However, about the fact that 1982 represented a breach in the trust, the loyalty, that many Quebecers felt towards the Canadian federation, I remain adamant. To quote Peter Russell:

> Proceeding with new constitutional arrangements that were opposed by the province of Quebec and the Canadian majority broke a fundamental understanding at the foundation of this country. Ever since then, we Canadians have been living dangerously, sharing a constitution whose legitimacy is questioned by a constituent element of the political community.[13]

Process, then, is part of substance. If our political tradition is subverted with respect to process, then the substance of that tradition is also subverted. In the Canadian experience, this means much more than the constitutional obsession of a few bespectacled Québec intellectuals. Again, however, I agree with P.A. Dutil that other arguments about substance ought to be presented. Is it true, as he suggests with regard to the content of the 1982 revision, 'that there isn't much there to dispute'?[14] I beg to differ with him, and I offer the following reasons.

A. In its first article, the Canadian Charter of Rights and Freedoms states that there are indeed reasonable limits to the exercise of rights in a 'free and democratic society'. In this key provision, judges are not instructed to take into consideration the federal nature of Canada. Article one is too universalistic in scope. I do not think that reasonable limits should be exactly the same in a monolingual unitary state and in a bilingual, multicultural federal state such as Canada. Thus, in my judgment, the 'reasonable limits' provision is a defederalizing device.

B. The key architect of the current Canadian government in constitutional matters, Mr Stéphane Dion, argues that the genius of Canada resides in its promotion of 'plural identities'. One should be proud to be a Quebecer and a Canadian. If all national groups in the world were to seek and obtain an independent state, the consequences would be chaos and mayhem. In the words of Charles Taylor, the transition from multinational empires to democratic multinational states must be completed.

The 1982 revisions and the Charter failed to recognize Quebecers as a people, a nation, or a distinct society. The latter expression, devoid of any ethnic connotations, was crafted by André Laurendeau during his time with the Royal Commission on Bilingualism and Biculturalism in the 1960s. In 1982, Canada moved towards accepting its multinational identity. The Charter openly referred (in section 25) to the rights of Aboriginal peoples. But such recognition of 'plural identities' did not extend to Québec. I shall leave the last words on the matter to Alan Cairns:

> . . . the charter was a nationalizing, Canadianizing constitutional instrument intended to shape the psyches and identities of Canadians. The Charter, accordingly, was a constitutional weapon analogous to disallowance, with its objective of constraining the diversities that federalism both reflects and sustains.[15]

According to a young scholar from Québec, Marc Chevrier, even judges sitting on the benches of the Supreme Court have been Canadianized in this fashion. Reviewing the Vriend case, which concerned the rights of homosexuals in Alberta, the Court insisted that in 1982, through their representatives, the Canadian people had chosen, in the context of a redefinition of Canadian democracy, to adopt the Charter.[16] This is the kind of myth-making and revisionism that becomes possible only after political psyches and identities have been thoroughly refashioned. In truth, 'the Canadian people' had little choice in 1981–2.

C. The Charter of Rights grants symmetrical language rights to persons belonging to the English and French majorities, and to their corresponding minorities in Québec and elsewhere in Canada. It does not take into account the asymmetrical situation of the two languages in North America. Language and culture are excluded from the list of legitimate grounds for affirmative action in the section concerning equality rights (15.2). Moreover, in the Charter, language rights, being fundamentally the property of individuals, are disconnected from the communities that could provide them institutional support. This has led to neglect of the historical rights of minority language communities outside Québec, and to contestable jurisprudence on the relationship between freedom of expression and language issues in Québec.[17]

D. The 1982 revisions shifted the balance of powers between the executive, legislative, and judicial branches of government in favour of the last. In Canada, all top judicial appointments, including the selection of the members of the Supreme Court, are made by the prime minister of Canada. The Charter should not have been enshrined before a thorough federalization of the judicial system.

E. The section concerning multiculturalism (27) does not specify that in Canada cultural diversity should blossom in harmony with a public sphere operating predominantly in French in Québec and in English elsewhere. Such a provision would have enhanced Québec's ability to integrate immigrants.

F. At the constitutional conference of February 1968, the federal government of Lester Pearson indicated its four priorities for a comprehensive constitutional reform:

1. repatriation of the amending formula and enshrinement of a Charter of Rights
2. rebalancing of the division of powers between the central government and the provinces
3. reform of central institutions such as the Senate and the Supreme Court
4. elimination of quasi-imperial devices, such as the power to disallow provincial legislation, the role of lieutenant-governors, and the declaratory power.

The 1982 package implemented the first priority but rendered significant action on all other fronts tremendously difficult. Movement is not impossible, but there has been none since 1982. I conclude that the balance between the federal government and the provinces has been altered, to the advantage of the former. According to Kymlicka, 'English-speaking Canadians have adopted a form of pan-Canadian nationalism that emphasizes the role of the federal government as the embodiment and defender of their national identity.'[18] The 1982 revision strengthened this aspect of Canadian political culture. Again according to Kymlicka, the result has been to 'undermine the provincial autonomy that has made it possible for Quebeckers to express their national identity'.[19]

In matters of process as well as substance, I was strongly opposed a decade ago to the constitutional reforms promoted by Pierre Trudeau. I remain steadfast in this opposition.

Robin Mathews, Gary Caldwell, and Stephen Clarkson have expressed critical views on my book while still finding substantially objectionable Trudeau's constitutional and political efforts. Instead of looking for the common ground between federalists and sovereigntists in Québec, I should have persevered in the search for an alliance with Canadian federal patriots. As Caldwell put it, I chose to abandon the Canadian 'higher ground'.[20]

In Locke's theory, there comes a moment when successive breaches of trust lead to the dissolution of government. I thought indeed that the events of the 1980s, culminating with the failure of the Meech Lake Accord, had moved Québec beyond that threshold. I believed that irreparable damage had been done to the federal regime, that Quebecers no longer had any obligation to obey and respect Ottawa's authority. Robin Mathews is right to suggest that the logic of the book leads to this radical conclusion, although it remains veiled in most of my arguments.[21] Ten years later, it is obvious that Quebecers continue to obey and respect the federal government. They vote in elections, pay their taxes, respect the laws. There is much less 'gravitas' in the air. My book hints that a rebellion would have been justified. I have always claimed that political theory holds no monopoly on historical truth and practical judgment.[22] I have the utmost respect for the behaviour of the Québec citizenry in the 1990s. The purpose of the present essay is to acknowledge that my post-Meech-Lake conclusions may have been hasty and ill-advised. The following excerpt is taken from Mathews' review:

> Many non-Québécois, however, doubt that seriously wounding Quebec can further a pan-Canadian nationalist trend. Many non-Québécois, moreover, doubt that Trudeau ever seriously wanted even a pan-nationalist Canada. He wanted a modern, liberal, capitalist democracy. He wanted a levelled liberal culture.[23]

I take it that Mathews, like George Grant, dissociates the liberal civic nationalism of Trudeau from any meaningful respect for the historic particularities of Canada. In the end, according to Mathews, I can only reproduce for Québec the categories of Trudeau's liberal logic. The contours of my proposal for a sovereign Québec associated with Canada are as disrespectful of Québec's internal complexity as Trudeau's vision was of Canada's internal complexity. With regard to *Trudeau and the End of a Canadian Dream*, I plead guilty to this charge. In the debates leading to the 1995 Québec referendum, and in its quite acrimonious aftermath, I have done my share to take into greater consideration Québec's minorities and 'plural identities'.[24]

Gary Caldwell, like Mathews, regrets the neo-liberal turn that Canada took with the 1982 Constitution. He shares my analysis of the evolution of Canadian political culture. In his mind, the real separatists are those who, like Trudeau, abandoned the federal compromises of 1867. I should have argued that Trudeau's Canada had been disloyal to Québec; anchored in Québec's loyalty to the principles of Confederation, I would have stood on stronger ground to imagine future options for Québec and Canada. This is a valid point. My own intellectual journey in the literature on federalism and secession has led me to conclude that Québec, whatever the odds, has a duty to exhaust all ordinary juridical and political means within the Canadian regime before bifurcating towards another sovereignty referendum. In one of my contributions to the *Beyond the Impasse* project, I discuss at length two directions that should be taken:[25]

1. A referendum in Québec on the legitimacy—or illegitimacy—of the 1982 revision.
2. A reference to Québec's Court of Appeal, and ultimately to the Supreme Court, asking some of the questions that were not properly framed by our government in the early 1980s concerning Québec's right of veto in the 1867 Constitution.

In my judgment, these two gestures would be acts of loyalty towards the ideals of the Canadian political experiment, ideals cherished by people like Mathews and Caldwell. These two critics, along with Stephen Clarkson, are in the end not too optimistic about the prospects for either Québec or Canada to retain their distinctive character in a homogenized and globalized political environment.[26] Speaking about

Québec alone, I can only try to console them in the following way: the odds are better than they were in 1763 and 1840.

In 'Locke, Laforest et le problème constitutionnel canadien', Jean-Guy Prévost launches the strongest and most comprehensive rebuttal of the arguments of my book:

> Such is the binding either/or logic at work in the mind of Laforest. Either a constitutional law has received the approval of the people, preferably through a referendum, and then it becomes fully legitimate; or this ratification was not sought, rendering crystal-clear the illegitimacy of the law and therefore dissolving the authority of the government. It has to be one way or the other: there is no middle ground.[27]

Prévost argues that my book offers unequivocal support and a clear conscience to the partisans of secession. It deprives the federal regime of any moral foundation in Québec. With regard to *Trudeau and the End of a Canadian Dream*, Prévost is essentially right. In *De la prudence*, *De l'urgence*, and *Beyond the Impasse*, I have tried to assess in a more ecumenical way the historical actions and current obligations of federalists and sovereigntists alike.[28] In his own interpretation of Locke, Prévost suggests that I have neglected the fact that the English thinker's concepts were forged in extraordinarily dramatic circumstances. Locke's worst nightmare had two parts: not only the loss of liberty, but also the damnation of his soul through the imposition of Catholicism; hence his low threshold of toleration vis-à-vis arbitrary and abusive manifestations of power. Prévost is right to note that the circumstances of contemporary Canada and Québec are not so dramatic. Employing the language of Locke, in our context, is exaggerated. We should relinquish absolute moral imperatives for the vocabulary of compromise. There was an element of inflammatory, revolutionary rhetoric in *Trudeau and the End of a Canadian Dream*. I agree that my prose should have been more moderate, more prudent.

4. Conclusion

Political theorists in Canada and Québec have made significant contributions in the last decades to the debates concerning the nature of federalism, democracy, liberalism, and nationalism. The quality of their own sustained dialogue in their own scholarly communities, while the ship of their political regime navigated on troubled waters, remains edifying in comparative perspective. It also remains true, however, that our political system does not measure up to our country's reputation abroad. In both symbolic and substantial matters, Québec's distinctiveness is not adequately acknowledged. In its institutions, Canada has not completed the transition from one part of a multinational empire to a multinational democratic state. In Ottawa as well as in the provinces, political executives are all too powerful. Maybe Canadian political theorists have spent too much time talking about identity, diversity, and recognition, neglecting some of the forms that despotic rule can still take in contemporary political regimes. Critical vigilance is also required, therefore, with respect to the practice of political theory. In this essay I have tried to apply this requirement to my own work in *Trudeau and the End of a Canadian Dream*.

NOTES

1. Maurice Lamontagne, *Le Fédéralisme canadien : Évolution et problèmes* (Québec: Presses de l'Université Laval, 1954), 284, 286.
2. Compare Charles Taylor, *Multiculturalism and 'The Politics of Recognition'* (Princeton: Princeton University Press, 1992), 52 ff., with Charles Taylor, *Reconciling the Solitudes: Essays on Canadian Federalism and Nationalism* (Montreal and Kingston: McGill-Queen's University Press, 1993), 100 ff.
3. Guy Laforest, *Trudeau and the End of a Canadian Dream* (Montreal and Kingston: McGill-Queen's University Press, 1995), 9.
4. Marcel Adam, 'La Théorie du pacte trouve en Trudeau le pourfendeur qu'il n'a pas toujours été', *La Presse*, 18 April 1991, B–2.
5. Marcel Adam, 'La Loi constitutionnelle de 1982 est-elle entachée d'illégitimité?', *La Presse*, 12 March 1993, B–2.
6. Guy Laforest, *De la prudence* (Montreal: Boréal, 1993), 52–3.
7. P.A. Dutil, 'Elite Dreams', *The Literary Review of Canada* (November 1992), 12–15.
8. Laforest, *De la prudence*, 59–84. Guy Laforest, *De l'urgence* (Montreal: Boréal, 1995), 39–50. Other Québec scholars have also attempted to make sense of Trudeau in this light. See Léon Dion, *Québec 1945–2000*, vol. 2, *Les Intellectuels et le temps de Duplessis* (Sainte-Foy: Presses de l'Université Laval, 1993), 195–9, 271–312. See also Daniel Jacques, *Les Humanités passagères: Considérations philosophiques sur la culture politique québécoise* (Montreal: Boréal, 1991), 49–52, 134–9, 245–6. Finally, see Claude Couture, *Paddling with the Current: Pierre Elliott Trudeau, Etienne Parent, liberalism and nationalism in Canada* (Edmonton: University of Alberta Press, 1998), 25–50.
9. For an analysis of Ramsay Cook's own inconsistencies, see Laforest, *De la prudence*, 75–6. For a sharply polemical defence of Trudeau, describing the supporters of Meech Lake as promoters of 'a very narrow ethnic construction of the concept of duality', see Michael Behiels, 'Trudeau as Nation Breaker', *Literary Review of Canada* IV (July–August, 1995), 8–11.
10. James C. MacPherson and Peter W. Hogg, 'A precious opportunity: Why Meech Lake should be ratified', *Globe and Mail*, 16 Nov. 1989, A–7.
11. Quoted by Robert Bothwell, *Canada and Quebec: One Country, Two Histories* (Vancouver: University of British Columbia Press, 1995), 179.
12. Thomas Flanagan, 'Canada and Quebec: Where are We Now?', in David M. Hayne, *Can Canada Survive? Under what Terms and Conditions?* Transactions of the Royal Society of Canada, series VI, vol. VII, 1996 (Toronto: University of Toronto Press, 1997), 23.
13. Peter Russell, 'Can Quebeckers be a Sovereign People?', *Canada Watch* IV, 2 (1995), 38.
14. Dutil, 'Elite Dreams', 14.
15. Alan Cairns, 'Reflections on the Political Purposes of the Charter: The First Decade' in *Reconfigurations: Canadian Citizenship and Constitutional Change*, ed. Douglas E. Williams (Toronto: McClelland and Stewart, 1995), 197.
16. Marc Chevrier, 'Le Papisme légal', *Argument* 1, 2 (1999), 82.

17. See André Burelle, *Le Mal canadien* (Montreal: Fides, 1995), 67–74, and Will Kymlicka, *Finding Our Way: Rethinking Ethnocultural Relations in Canada* (Toronto: Oxford University Press, 1998), 157–8.
18. Kymlicka, *Finding Our Way*, 166.
19. Ibid.
20. Gary Caldwell, 'Social Change in Contemporary Québec', *Journal of Canadian Studies* XXI, 4 (Winter 1995), 160.
21. Robin Mathews, 'Separating the Siamese Twins', *Canadian Forum* (October 1995), 54.
22. Laforest, *De la prudence*, 172.
23. Mathews, 'Separating', 54.
24. See Laforest, *De l'urgence*, 98–103, and Guy Laforest, 'Standing in the Shoes of the Other Partners in the Canadian Union', in *Beyond the Impasse: Toward Reconciliation*, ed. Roger Gibbins and Guy Laforest (Montreal: IRPP, 1998), 51–82.
25. Guy Laforest, 'The Need for Dialogue and How to Achieve It', in *Beyond the Impasse*, 413–28.
26. See Stephen Clarkson's review in *Canadian Journal of Political Science* XXVI, 2 (June 1993), 384–6. Clarkson, like the other critics, says some nice things about my book. I have chosen to emphasize the 'imputed defects' rather than the 'lauded qualities' in this assessment.
27. Jean-Guy Prévost, 'Locke, Laforest et le problème constitutionnel canadien', *Bulletin d'histoire politique* IV, 3 (1996), 56.
28. Laforest, *De la prudence*, 166–72; *De l'urgence*, 148–51; Laforest, 'The Need for Dialogue and how to Achieve It', in Gibbins and Laforest, eds, *Beyond the Impasse*, 413–28.

The Supreme Court's Reference on Unilateral Secession: A Turning Point in Canadian History

Stéphane Dion

The opinion rendered by the Supreme Court of Canada on unilateral secession, on 20 August 1998, is a turning point in the history of the Canadian federation. It confirms that a unilateral secession would have no basis in law.

The Court indicated that, by law, secession requires a constitutional amendment, which has to be negotiated. It added that only clear support for secession can give rise to an obligation to undertake such constitutional negotiations.

The consequence of the opinion from the Supreme Court of Canada is the confirmation of a right enjoyed by Quebecers: the right never to have their full belonging to Canada jeopardized unless they have clearly expressed their desire to renounce it.

This right also benefits all other Canadians, who have the pleasure of having Quebec as a part of their country. Canadians outside Quebec have the right never to lose Quebec unless Quebecers have clearly renounced Canada. And like their fellow citizens in Quebec, they have the right, in the event of any attempt at secession, to have that secession duly negotiated, in the sincere desire to achieve justice for all.

The Government of Canada believes that it has the moral duty to refuse to negotiate the loss of Canada for Quebecers unless they have clearly supported secession. The opinion by the Supreme Court confirmed that there is a clear legal basis for such a refusal to negotiate in an atmosphere of ambiguity. In the case of a unilateral declaration of independence by a provincial government, the Government of Canada is legally justified in continuing to honour peacefully its constitutional responsibilities towards the population of that province.

The Government of Quebec, for its part, claimed that international law would prevail over Canadian law in the event of a unilateral declaration of independence, thus stripping the Canadian government of its ability to conduct its own evaluation of Quebecers' preferences. Only the Supreme Court could confirm that the Government of Quebec would not be legally justified in attempting to effect secession unilaterally. On 20 August 1998, the Court did just that.

So that we can appreciate just how much of a turning point this opinion of the Court was, I will first set out the way in which the secessionist parties in Quebec contemplated effecting a secession. We will see that their understanding of things was based on a legal myth, an erroneous theory of a right to secession. Second, I will show that this legal myth disappeared because of the clarifications set out in the Supreme Court's opinion.

1. The Myth of an Automatic Right to Secession

Quebec's separatist parties, from the Rassemblement pour Indépendance Nationale to the Bloc Québécois, imagined that they had the right to effect Quebec's independence on the basis of a simple electoral victory. They maintained that, under international law, a party that wins the majority of seats in the National Assembly and thus forms the government would have the right to proclaim itself to be the government of an independent country.

Over time, these parties acknowledged that holding a referendum would be a necessary step to confirm Quebecers' will to effect independence. Ever since then, they have claimed that a referendum question drafted by the Government of Quebec, provided it had a majority in the National Assembly, could lead to a declaration of independence from the moment that an absolute majority of the votes cast (50 per cent plus one) indicated a favourable response to that question. The unilateral declaration would be valid for the entire territory of Quebec, regardless of the opinions of voters in the various regions of the province, because the territorial integrity of Quebec, though not that of Canada, would be protected by law.

If the separatist parties agreed that the unilateral declaration of independence might be preceded by negotiations with Canada, this was, once again, not because they felt they were legally obliged to undertake such negotiations. If they offered to negotiate, it was to facilitate the transition and to conclude what they called an 'economic association'—what they now call a 'political and economic partnership'—with Canada.

Through the procedure set out in Bill 1 in 1995, An Act Respecting the Future of Quebec, the Government of Quebec had maintained that, at any time during those negotiations, it could unilaterally proclaim itself to be the government of an independent state. It was planning a year-long period of negotiations following a referendum victory, 'unless the National Assembly decides otherwise'. Following that unilateral declaration, all citizens, in Quebec and in Canada as a whole, as well as all governments, in Canada and abroad, would be legally bound to consider the Government of Quebec to effectively be the government of an independent state. The negotiations could continue, but between two independent states.

This entire process is based on a legal theory that confuses self-determination with the right to secession. It takes for granted that once it has been elected, and especially once it has won a referendum, the Government of Quebec can declare Quebec's independence under international law, on the basis of the right of peoples to self-determination. The Attorney General of Quebec argued in Quebec Superior Court in April 1996, in *Bertrand vs. Bégin*, that the process of accession to independence 'was sanctioned by international law and that the Superior Court had no jurisdiction in that regard'.

Many people sincerely believed that this theory was founded in law. That belief influenced their choice in the 1995 referendum. Secession is a radical change that is already sufficiently grave without the complication of undertaking it on the basis of an erroneous legal theory. For these assertions would inevitably have been challenged in the courts in the event that a government attempted to effect independence unilaterally. Can we imagine that not a single Quebecer would have launched a court challenge to a unilateral process to strip Quebecers of their rights as Canadians? It was worth the effort to clarify these matters in advance, in an atmosphere of calm, rather than in the upheaval of an eventual attempt at secession.

This essential clarification was provided by the Supreme Court of Canada on 20 August 1998.

2. The Obligation of Clarity

The Supreme Court refuted the myth of an automatic right to secession based on a referendum or an election. It found the argument that a majority vote would make it possible to effect secession by circumventing the Constitution to be 'unsound'. It stated that this argument 'misunderstands the meaning of popular sovereignty and the essence of a constitutional democracy' (par. 75). In fact, 'the secession of a province from Canada must be considered, in legal terms, to require an amendment to the Constitution' (par. 84).

Nor does the right of peoples to self-determination confer a right to effect secession unilaterally, except in situations of former colonies, oppressed peoples, military occupation, or possibly the denial of the right to internal self-determination. 'Such exceptional circumstances are manifestly inapplicable to Quebec. [. . .] Accordingly, neither the population of the province of Quebec, even if characterized in terms of "people" or "peoples", nor its representative institutions, the National Assembly, the legislature or government of Quebec, possess a right, under international law, to secede unilaterally from Canada' (par. 138).

The Court did not rule out the possibility that the Government of Quebec might attempt to effect secession unilaterally. But the scenario it depicted had little to do with the one contemplated by the Parizeau government in 1995. Such an attempt would not be made 'under colour of a legal right' (par. 144) and would be made within a context in which Canada would be entitled 'to the protection under international law of its territorial integrity' (par. 130).

The secession of a province requires an amendment to the Constitution, 'which perforce requires negotiation' (par. 84) 'within the existing constitutional framework' (par. 149). This means that the Government of Quebec would be negotiating as a provincial government within the framework of the Canadian Constitution, from which it derives its powers. At no point in those negotiations would it have the right to proclaim itself unilaterally to be the government of an independent state.

The Court did not address the complex mechanics of eventual negotiations, much less the difficult process of determining the various parties to such negotiations. It did specify, however, that the negotiation process would require the reconciliation of various rights and obligations 'by the representatives of two legitimate majorities, namely, the clear majority of the population of Quebec, and the clear majority of Canada as a whole, whatever that may be' (par. 93). The words 'Canada as a whole', rather than 'the rest of Canada', indicate that the Government of Quebec would find itself dealing with a party whose very broad responsibilities would also extend to those Quebecers who wished to remain Canadian.

Such negotiations would inevitably address 'many issues of great complexity and difficulty'. The Court referred to, among other things, economic issues, the debt, minority rights, Aboriginal peoples, and territorial boundaries. 'Nobody seriously suggests that our national existence, seamless in so many aspects, could be effortlessly separated along what are now the provincial boundaries of Quebec' (par. 96). The success of such negotiations could well hinge on an agreement to modify boundaries. The Government of Quebec cannot rule out in advance such a possibility.

All the parties to the negotiations on secession would be governed by four constitutional principles identified by the Court: 'federalism, democracy, constitutionalism and the rule of law, and the protection of minorities' (par. 90). The practical consequence of this is that the Government of Quebec could not determine on its own what would or would not be negotiable. It 'could not purport to invoke a right of self-determination such as to dictate the terms of a proposed secession to the other parties' (par. 91). Instead, it would have to negotiate so as to address the interests of 'the federal government, of Quebec and the other provinces, and other participants, as well as the rights of all Canadians both within and outside Quebec' (par. 92), and of Aboriginal people (par. 139), on every issue, from division of the debt to the question of boundaries.

The four constitutional principles identified by the Court would not only govern any negotiation on secession, but would also make such negotiations obligatory if the population of Quebec clearly expressed its will to secede (par. 90). 'The clear repudiation of the existing constitutional order and the clear expression of the desire to pursue secession by the population of a province would give rise to a reciprocal obligation on all parties to Confederation to negotiate constitutional changes to respond to that desire' (par. 88).

The Attorney General at the time, the Honourable Allan Rock, addressed the moral aspect of this obligation to negotiate in a speech to the House of Commons on 26 September 1996, setting out the reasons for the reference to the Supreme Court: 'The leading political figures of all our provinces and the Canadian public have long agreed that the country will not be held together against the clear will of Quebecers.' Similarly, Prime Minister Jean Chrétien said on 8 December 1997 that 'in such a situation, there will undoubtedly be negotiations with the federal government' (*Le Soleil*, 8 Dec. 1997; translation). I myself have stressed this principle many times in my speeches and public letters, starting with my first statement as a minister, in which I indicated that 'in the unfortunate eventuality that a strong majority in Quebec were to vote on a clear question in favour of secession, I believe that the rest of Canada would have a moral obligation to discuss the division of the territory' (*Le Soleil*, 27 Jan. 1996; translation).

In itself, the obligation to negotiate does not change much in terms of political reality. As the constitutional expert Peter Hogg has noted, 'Even without the court's ruling, the political reality is that the federal government would have to negotiate with Quebec after a majority of Quebec voters had clearly voted in favour of secession. It is safe to say that there would be little political support for a policy of attempted resistance to the wish of the Quebec voters' (*Canada Watch*, vol. 7, 34–5). The significant element lies elsewhere: in the solid and irrefutable causal link that the Court establishes between this obligation to negotiate secession and the *clarity* of support for secession.

The obligation to negotiate can stem only from 'a decision of a clear majority of the population of Quebec on a clear question to pursue secession' (par. 93). There is no such obligation if the expression of democratic will 'is itself fraught with ambiguities. Only the political actors,' the Court tells us, 'would have the information and expertise to make the appropriate judgment as to the point at which, and the circumstances in which, those ambiguities are resolved one way or the other' (par. 100).

So the Government of Quebec is certainly free to use its parliamentary majority to have the National Assembly adopt a referendum question drafted by the Government, and then to put that question to Quebec voters. But the Government of Canada, as a 'political actor' and a 'participant in Confederation', also has the duty to make its own evaluation of the clarity of the question and the size of the majority in question, before concluding that it is bound to negotiate the break-up of Canada.

In this context, the Government of Canada notes that the Court has defined secession as an act 'to withdraw [. . .] from the political and constitutional authority' of a state, with a view to 'achieving statehood for a new territorial unit on the international plane' (par. 83). The Government of Canada thus believes that, for a question to be clear, it would have to address that issue alone, without referring to a possible partnership. Quebecers would have to express clearly 'that they no longer wish to remain in Canada' (par. 92) in order to make Quebec an independent country.

As for the majority required, the Government of Canada sees the numerous references made by the Court to a 'clear majority' as confirmation that a majority of 50 per cent plus one is insufficient. In addition, the Court's reference to a 'clear majority as a qualitative evaluation' (par. 87) indicates that it is more than a question of numbers. The proper conduct of the referendum process as a whole would also have to be taken into account for the referendum result to be deemed free of ambiguity both in terms of the question asked and in terms of the support it achieved.

The Court thus established a right to negotiate secession on the basis of clear support, in accordance with constitutional principles. But the Court did not establish a right to secession as such. The negotiations may fail: 'It is foreseeable that even negotiations carried out in conformity with the underlying constitutional principles could reach an impasse' (par. 97). And what would we do then? 'We need not speculate here as to what would then transpire. Under the Constitution, secession requires that an amendment be negotiated' (par. 97).

That refusal to speculate is wise and realistic, given that the negotiation of a possible secession raises difficult questions and wrenching choices. Therein lies the 'black hole' that the Leader of the Opposition in Quebec's National Assembly Mr Jean Charest, has always warned us of, and rightly so. The only thing that can be said is that governments should take pains to act, under all circumstances, within the constitutional framework, in accordance with the democratic values and constitutional principles set out by the Court. A government that chose to act outside the established law would run a great risk of being unable to maintain the obedience of its citizens.

Could the Government of Quebec then try to obtain international recognition? The Court weighed the probabilities in that respect very prudently and realistically. 'A Quebec that had negotiated in conformity with constitutional principles and values in the face of unreasonable intransigence on the part of other participants at the federal or provincial level would be more likely to be recognized than a Quebec which did not itself act according to constitutional principles in the negotiation process' (par. 103). Moreover, the Court made it clear that Quebec's governing institutions 'do not enjoy a right at international law to effect the secession of Quebec from Canada unilaterally' (par. 154).

We can understand the Court's prudence on this point in light of the international community's extreme reluctance to recognize unilateral secession. There are, unfortunately, many populations in the world who desire their independence to an almost unanimous degree, who are victims of unimaginable exactions by the states to which they belong, and yet do not succeed in obtaining international recognition as independent states.

And so we Quebecers should not opt to secede in the expectation that international support will be forthcoming against the will of the Canadian state. Instead, we should count on the honesty of other Canadians. We should rely on the values of tolerance that we all share in Canada, and which would be essential to the conduct of those painful and difficult negotiations. And therein lies the contradiction of the secessionist project: since other Canadians are good and reasonable people, why should we want to separate from them?

CONCLUSION

It has now been more than a year since the Supreme Court of Canada rendered its opinion on unilateral secession. The Quebec government has had all that time to gauge the chasm that separates the unilateral approach to secession it contemplated in 1995 from an approach that would comply with the principles of legality and clarity set out by Canada's highest court.

In moral terms, Quebecers have the right not to have their belonging to Canada threatened unless they have clearly renounced it. That right belongs to Quebecers, not to governments. The Government of Canada has made a commitment to respect that right fully, and it is incumbent upon the Quebec government to do the same.

A referendum question along the lines of those asked in 1980 and 1995 could not lead to Quebec independence, because it would be too ambiguous to make the negotiation of secession obligatory. Effecting secession would require a shared conviction that it is what Quebecers clearly want. Advocates of Quebec independence and of Canadian unity alike must be able to interpret the question and the results of the consultation in the same way. Otherwise, negotiation of secession would be impossible.

Again, the Government of Canada cannot infringe upon the prerogatives of the National Assembly, and it has never sought to do so. The National Assembly has the power to ask Quebecers any referendum question it sees fit. But only 'a clear majority of the population of Quebec on a clear question to pursue secession' (par. 93) can provide the Government of Canada with the assurance that Quebecers want it to negotiate the end of its constitutional responsibilities toward them and, more broadly, the end of their belonging to Canada.

With clear support for secession, there would be an obligation to undertake negotiations, but they would still be fraught with uncertainty, and no one can predict in advance the results of those negotiations, including the question of borders.

I am convinced that if one were to put a clear question to Quebecers, they would vote against secession. They want to stay in Canada; they are attached to this country that they have built with their fellow Canadians.

And yet this whole debate could be avoided. All the Quebec government has to do is announce tomorrow morning that it will never hold a referendum unless, one day, it becomes evident that a consensus exists in Quebec in favour of its ceasing to be a part of Canada and becoming an independent country. If the Government of Quebec were to issue such a statement, the referendum uncertainty would disappear, together with all the costs and waste of energy it entails. We would all do better to work together to improve our quality of life and to solve the social problems that demand all our attention, and all our unity.

Vision: Towards an Understanding of Aboriginal Sovereignty

DALE TURNER

> The geese migrate because they have responsibilities to fulfil at different times and in different places. Before they fly they gather together and store up energy. I believe strongly that our people are gathering now, just like the geese getting ready to fly. I am tremendously optimistic that we will soon take on the responsibility we were meant to carry in the world at large.
>
> Jim Bourque[1]

INTRODUCTION

As Canadians head into the new millennium, understanding the meaning of Aboriginal sovereignty, in both theory and practice, will be one of our most serious moral and political challenges.[2] In this chapter I will outline a vision of what I take to be Aboriginal peoples' role in asserting and protecting their sovereignty within a Canadian constitutional democracy. The contemporary legal and political relationship between Aboriginal governments and the Canadian state is characterized as 'trust-like' or 'fiduciary' in nature. In the following discussion, I claim that if Aboriginal peoples want to be recognized as self-determining sovereign political entities, then the trust relationship must be driven by legal and political practices that include Aboriginal practitioners in more substantive ways. The purpose of this chapter, and of my work in general, is to explain what it would mean for Aboriginal peoples to be 'included' in Canadian legal and political practices.[3]

My discussion has three parts. I begin by examining the final report of the Royal Commission on Aboriginal Peoples and show that the Commission's work, while an extensive, expensive quasi-listening exercise, was, at least in one regard, doomed to failure.[4] For many Aboriginal peoples, the Commission did not reconcile the 'wisdom of the elders', expressed in the Commission's public hearings and research program, with the contemporary legal and political discourse of Aboriginal rights and sovereignty in Canada. The reason is that the discourse of the elders and the discourse of contemporary Aboriginal rights are often at odds with respect to defining Aboriginal peoples' place in Canadian society.

I shall examine the final report's 'vision chapter' and show that the guiding principles of a renewed relationship (mutual recognition, mutual respect, sharing, and mutual responsibility) are nothing more than a wish list without concomitant changes in public attitudes about Aboriginal peoples and the way their philosophies are included in contemporary Aboriginal legal and political practices. Finding ways of accommodating Aboriginal peoples in Western European intellectual traditions has given rise to several competing schools of thought—most of which do not seriously engage Aboriginal ways of thinking about the world.[5]

The second part explores a way of renewing the relationship that is more Aboriginal-inclusive. In this paper I am not so much concerned with what kinds of political and legal strategies Aboriginal peoples ought to adopt in order to assert and protect their sovereignty; rather, I shall address the more fundamental issue of *who* should formulate these strategies and why. I shall use James Tully's notion of a 'mediator' and recast it from an Aboriginal perspective. In *Strange Multiplicity*, Tully outlines a sophisticated way of looking at the evolution of Western European constitutional theory, and in the process of laying out his investigation he shows that it is possible for the Western tradition to accommodate Aboriginal voices on their own merit.[6] It is a matter of seeing our constitutional practices in a different way. The virtue of Tully's political vision is that it is firmly embedded in the Western philosophical tradition, yet allows Aboriginal voices to speak for themselves.

In the final section I explore the claim that it is Aboriginal mediators—'word warriors'—who should largely be responsible for asserting and protecting Aboriginal sovereignty within Canadian legal and political practices. In so doing, however, they must leave Aboriginal philosophies intact; that is, the legitimacy of Aboriginal ways of thinking about the world are not up for negotiation. Aboriginal philosophies—the wisdom of the elders—guide the strategies that word warriors use to engage Western intellectual discourses. I believe that Aboriginal intellectuals must pay closer attention to these kinds of intellectual discourses; indeed, our survival depends on engaging them.[7] Aboriginal law and politics in Canada are very quickly evolving into a highly sophisticated overlapping set of practices. Gaining expertise in these practices necessarily involves learning complex legal, political, historical, and philosophical discourses. Word warriors have a responsibility to critically engage these discourses and to do so in accordance with the wisdom of the elders. Further, by making their way into these agonistic intellectual communities—driven by non-Aboriginal institutions, interests, and methodologies—word warriors will be able to create stronger, more vibrant, Aboriginal intellectual communities. Hopefully, in time, these people will create the legal and political spaces necessary for traditional forms of government to thrive within a more inclusive Canadian democratic state.

The RCAP and its Discontents

One important reason the issue of Aboriginal sovereignty is political is what I call 'Kymlicka's constraint':

> For better or worse, it is predominantly non-aboriginal judges and politicians who have the ultimate power to protect and enforce aboriginal rights, and so it is important to find a justification of them that such people can recognise and understand.[8]

Over the past few hundred years, Aboriginal peoples have come to understand only too well the meaning of this imposed imperative. The Royal Commission on Aboriginal Peoples, an instrument of the federal government, was created to seriously consider the content and meaning of Aboriginal rights in Canada. One important source of conflict was the issue of Aboriginal 'incorporation'.[9] For many, Aboriginal incorporation is synonymous with extinguishment of rights and sovereignty; yet for Aboriginal peoples, incorporation implies that Aboriginal peoples entered into treaty relationships only on the understanding that their sovereignty was never to be surrendered.

I believe that Aboriginal incorporation was the central legal and political dilemma the Commission had to consider, and it was one of the main reasons the Commission delayed its final report for over a year.[10] However, the impasse was at least partly created by the organization and structure of the Commission itself. The Commission's mandate evolved through two phases. The first phase was a massive listening and information-gathering exercise consisting of four rounds of public hearings, in the course of which the Commission was responsible for drafting and implementing a comprehensive research plan. The second phase of the Commission's life was supposed to consolidate the material (evidence) from the hearings and research phase and produce a comprehensive final report to be tabled in Parliament.[11]

There is no doubt that the public hearings generated an overwhelming amount of information. In this sense, the Commission can be said to have listened to Aboriginal peoples. The Commissioners, especially the non-Aboriginal Commissioners, were profoundly affected by the testimony in the public hearings. The research program itself was ambitious, extensive, and supposedly cutting-edge. To be sure, the Commissioners had more than enough information to produce a useful final report. The problems for the Commissioners began in phase two, when they attempted to consolidate the material from the hearings and research with the existing legal and political practices of Aboriginal public policy in Canada.

The Aboriginal Commissioners knew all too well what life was like in Aboriginal communities, but they were not by any stretch of the imagination legal and political experts on the same level as the non-Aboriginal Commissioners.[12] In phase two, the Commission's focus shifted from engaging Aboriginal voices to engaging the language of public policy. As the Commission's mandate unfolded, Aboriginal voices seemed, at least from the perspective of the Aboriginal Commissioners and employees of the Commission, to disappear. Nevertheless, the Commissioners persisted and produced a report that argues for a particular vision of Canada, one that returns Aboriginal peoples to their rightful place in the Canadian social and political landscape.

The last chapter of the final report's first volume, entitled 'The Principles of a Renewed Relationship', reflects the historical re-evaluation of the relationship. In it the Commission argues that no new relationship can be negotiated without renewing our understanding of the historical relationship. This chapter, originally called 'the vision chapter', lays out four principles that ought to guide the renewed relationship: mutual recognition, mutual respect, sharing, and mutual responsibility.

Mutual recognition 'calls on non-Aboriginal Canadians to recognize that Aboriginal people are the original inhabitants and caretakers of this land and have distinctive rights and responsibilities that flow from that status'.[13] The Commissioners go on to add: 'Mutual recognition, thus, has three major facets: equality, co-existence and self-government.'[14] The principle of mutual respect focuses on one aspect of the concept of respect: 'the quality of courtesy, consideration and esteem extended to people whose languages, cultures, and ways differ from our own but who are valued fellow-members of the larger communities to which we all belong'.[15] The third principle is sharing: 'the giving and receiving of benefits'.[16] The fourth principle, mutual responsibility, is described as involving 'the transformation of the colonial relationship of guardian and ward into one of true partnership'.[17]

The justification for these principles is articulated in both Aboriginal and non-Aboriginal ways of thinking. In effect, the vision chapter is a kind of summary of the hearings, in which Aboriginal peoples stated over and over the need for Canadians to change their attitudes about Aboriginal peoples and their cultures. It expresses the Commission's plea to change the deeply embedded attitudes of the dominant culture, especially the attitudes that shape Aboriginal policy-making in Canada. This is an enormous task, given some of the practical consequences of adopting the four principles. For example, consider two points made in the context of the principle of sharing:

> . . . Third, as a long overdue act of justice, Aboriginal people should regain access to a fair proportion of the ancestral lands that were taken from them.
>
> Fourth, if sharing is to be a valued part of the renewed relationship, both parties need to be in a position to engage in exchanges on an equal basis. Meaningful sharing is not possible under conditions of poverty and dependence, so strong and effective measures need to be taken to address the often appalling inequalities that separate Aboriginal and non-Aboriginal Canadians in such sectors as health, housing, income and overall living conditions.[18]

History has shown that when it comes to sharing the resources of Aboriginal communities, 'trust-like' principles fade: the relationship becomes brutally driven by non-Aboriginal needs and interests. The guidelines quoted above imply enormous changes to Canada's current social, economic, and political landscape. The vision chapter calls for two improbable (if not impossible) events to occur. First, *as a matter of justice*, Canadian governments are to recognize the sovereignty of Aboriginal peoples and return portions of their lands to them. And second, *as a matter of justice*, Canadian governments are to facilitate the process of empowering Aboriginal communities so they become more economically and politically self-sufficient. In the current relationship, Aboriginal peoples go through bureaucratic channels to obtain virtually every resource their communities require for their physical survival, channels in which they face uncompromising resistance. Justice may demand a certain course of action, but history has shown Aboriginal peoples time and time again that it by no means guarantees that action.

The Commission claims that the four principles of the vision chapter set the stage for their recommendations on Aboriginal governance, suggesting how the historical injustices articulated throughout Volume One might be redressed by developing the just political relationship and governmental structures outlined in Volume Two. The vision chapter contains an imperative for all Canadians: if we want a relationship of peaceful co-existence with Aboriginal peoples, then we must change our attitudes about them and their cultures. How to move this imperative into the public space, especially into our legal and political practices, is a serious challenge in Canada, one with both philosophical and practical dimensions. The final report is a serious attempt to meet this challenge, but it did not effectively embed the wisdom of the elders into its critiques of contemporary Aboriginal legal and political practices in Canada. This task, I contend, is one that Aboriginal peoples must embrace themselves. A Royal Commission, after all, ultimately serves the interests of the federal government. In the next section, I will refer briefly to the recent work of James Tully and show how we can reshape our understandings of a cross-cultural legal and political relationship, one that includes Aboriginal voices speaking for themselves.

Mediators

In his 1995 book *Strange Multiplicity*, James Tully examines the 'politics of cultural recognition' in the context of the evolution of constitutionalism in Western political thought.[19] In his philosophical investigation, Tully embraces a political vision in the form of Haida artist Bill Reid's sculpture 'The Spirit of Haida Gwaii'. It is worth quoting Tully's description in full:

> The sculpture is a black bronze canoe, over nineteen feet in length, eleven feet wide, and twelve feet high, containing thirteen passengers, *sghaana* (spirits or myth creatures) from Haida mythology. *Xuuwaji*, the bear mother, who is part human, and bear father sit facing each other at the bow with their two cubs between them. *Ttsaang*, the beaver, is paddling menacingly amidships, *qqaaxhadajaat*, the mysterious, intercultural dogfish woman, paddles just behind him and *Qaganjaat*, the shy but beautiful mouse woman is tucked in the stern. *Ghuuts*, the ferociously playful wolf, sinks his fangs in the eagle's wing and *ghuut*, the eagle seems to be attacking the bear's paw in retaliation. *Hlkkyaan qqusttaan*, the frog, who symbolizes the ability to cross boundaries (*xhaaidla*) between worlds is, appropriately enough, partially in and out of the boat. Further down in the canoe, the ancient reluctant conscript, brought on board from Carl Sandburg's poem, 'Old Timers', paddles stoically (up to a point). *Xuuya*, the legendary raven—the master of tricks, transformations and multiple identities—steers the canoe as her or his whim dictates. Finally in the cen-

tre of this motley crew, holding the speaker's staff in his right hand, stands the *Kitslaani*, the chief or exemplar, whose identity, due to his kinship to the raven (often called *Nangkilstlas*, the One who gives orders), is uncertain. *Bill Reid asks of the chief, 'Who is he? That's the big question.' So the chief has come to be called 'Who is he?' or 'Who is he going to be?'*[20]

Through the course of his book, Tully lays out the complex intellectual landscape from which contemporary debates in constitutional theory have evolved. He cites three conventions found in common constitutionalism: mutual recognition, continuity, and consent. In the context of Aboriginal peoples, mutual recognition means recognition and accommodation of the fact that Aboriginal peoples are equal self-governing nations. This relationship was first manifested in the early treaties. The second convention, continuity, means that Aboriginal nations did not relinquish their sovereignty when they entered into treaty relationships with the Crown. The convention of continuity has been superseded by the unilaterally imposed practice of discontinuity or extinguishment. The third convention, consent, is intimately related to the two other conventions. It demands that any change in the political relationship that affects the nature of the relationship requires the consent of the concerned parties. This is embedded in the oldest fundamental convention of democratic political thought, 'quod omnes tangit ab omnibus comprobetur': 'what touches all should be agreed to by all'.[21]

Tully argues, as the Commission did in the vision chapter, that these fundamental conventions, already embedded in constitutional practice, must be renewed in contemporary constitutional practices if we are to embrace diversity in its richest form. Peaceful coexistence among conflicting parties is possible, but only from within a dialogical relationship:

> . . . a mediated peace is a just peace: just because it is a constitutional settlement in accord with the three conventions of justice and peaceful because the constitution is accommodated to the diverse needs of those who agree to it. If this view of constitutionalism came to be accepted, the allegedly irreconcilable conflicts of the present would not have to be the tragic history of our future.[22]

According to Tully, a just constitutional relationship is one negotiated between parties that have embraced the three conventions.

Contested political relationships, like the one characterized in the 'Spirit of Haida Gwaii', are negotiated where 'the passengers vie and negotiate for recognition and power.' The leader, the chief, has a specific role within this kind of political relationship. Tully's last two sentences in *Strange Multiplicity* are prophetic:

> Of equal importance to their pacific way of life, they also never fail to heed what is said by the chief whose identity has remained a mystery until this moment. She or he is the mediator.[23]

The mediator, for Tully, is able to embrace the three conventions of constitutionalism—the four principles defended in the vision chapter—and put them into practice. Another important quality of the mediator is that she or he is able to show others how to act appropriately within this complex politics of cultural recognition.

Tully offers his book primarily as a way for non-Aboriginal people to understand a constitutional relationship among a variety of politically recognized participants. A non-Aboriginal mediator must recognize the legitimacy of Aboriginal ways of thinking and living, and weave them into her own philosophical attitudes. Mediators, then, enter into legal and political discussions of sovereignty guided by rich, inclusive sets of assumptions about Aboriginal peoples, political sovereignty, and especially political recognition. One virtue of Tully's approach is that the meaning of Aboriginal incorporation becomes embedded in the discourse and practices of the negotiated relationship itself. Aboriginal explanations of incorporation are central to the evolving legal and political discourses of Aboriginal rights and sovereignty *because* the meaning of sovereignty, and its consequences in practice, is contested between the negotiating parties.

The most important and complex convention is that of mutual recognition. Aboriginal peoples, and especially their philosophies, are not recognized by most non-Aboriginal legal and political practitioners as equal in value to the philosophical traditions of Western European cultures. As long as Kymlicka's constraint remains in effect—that is, as long as Aboriginal people must rely on non-Aboriginal judges and politicians to defend their rights—Aboriginal philosophies will never be recognized as genuinely equal in value to Western philosophical traditions. If Aboriginal peoples take this aspect of the relationship seriously, and I certainly do, then Aboriginal intellectuals must re-evaluate the ways in which Aboriginal ways of thinking about the world are brought to negotiation tables, Supreme Court factums, and university classrooms. As Aboriginal people we have offered our philosophies up for Western European scrutiny for far too long, especially in the context of asserting our rights in the Canadian legal and political communities.

Tully shows that Canadians should hold on to their most valued political conventions, but that at the same time they must renew them in the political reality of twenty-first-century Canadian politics. Tully uses an Aboriginal example to drive home the point that any just political relationship is by nature one that is always contested, and therefore requires people to negotiate in accordance with the three time-tested conventions of the Western European constitutional tradition. But Tully's vision, while deeply respectful of Aboriginal political thinking, is necessarily incomplete. Mediators come from many different communities; my question is, 'Who will be an Aboriginal mediator?' In the next section I will explore an Aboriginal example and turn to the Anishnabai tradition of a vision quest.

Vision

Traditionally, for an Anishnabai boy to become a man he must have a vision. That is, he must know what his purpose is in life. Developing such a vision involves a long process of learning the physical and spiritual landscapes that he has inherited from his ancestors. It also requires one to develop a keen sense of hearing—the ability to listen to the world. The survival of the community depends on individuals accepting their responsibilities, but they cannot do so unless they have learned the necessary skills. Surviving in a sometimes hostile world requires not only finely developed practical skills, but knowledge. Various competent practitioners taught children the skills necessary for survival, while tribal elders passed on knowledge, along with the stories that made sense of their world: creation tales, Anishnabai moral and political philosophy, and Anishnabai cosmology. This was the Anishnabai way, and it worked well for countless generations.[24]

What kind of vision does an Anishnabai require as we head into the next millennium? Seeking a vision means seeking understanding of the landscapes in which one is inextricably embedded. The brutal reality is that these landscapes have changed drastically since the arrival of Europeans. What has not changed for the Anishnabai is the need to survive in a sometimes hostile world. Some of the landscapes in which we live were familiar to our Anishnabai ancestors, but the tools required for survival have changed. The responsibility that one must embrace in order for the community to survive still calls for special skills and knowledge. Much of the knowledge required for survival has traditionally been passed on to the youth by wisdom-keepers and other learned people in the community.

Unfortunately, among the most devastating landscapes that have been forced upon Aboriginal peoples are the Western European discourses of rights and sovereignty. These intellectual traditions have created discourses on property, ethics, political sovereignty, and justice that have subjugated, distorted, and marginalized Aboriginal ways of thinking. The result has been an Aboriginal intellectual landscape that is shaped by Eurocentric discourses, some of which were purposely designed to exclude Aboriginal ways of thinking.

The knowledge and skills required to participate in the legal and political discourse of Aboriginal rights in Canada have become, for better or worse, a significant part of the Aboriginal intellectual landscape. The discourse on Aboriginal rights has evolved without a significant contribution by Aboriginal intellectuals, yet its effects on Aboriginal communities have been devastating. Consequently, Aboriginal peoples have viewed these Eurocentric legal and political discourses with skepticism, and efforts to embrace them have often been seen as a sign of assimilation. There is an element of truth to this view, but I claim that if Aboriginal peoples want to survive as distinct political communities, then Aboriginal people must turn their energies to these intellectually imposed landscapes.

Robert Allen Warrior, an Osage English professor, writes:

> If our struggle is anything, it is a way of life. That way of life is not a matter of defining a political ideology or having a detached discussion about the unifying structures and essences of American Indian traditions. It is a decision—a decision we make in our minds, in our hearts, and in our bodies—to be sovereign and to find out what that means in the process.[25]

Warrior is claiming that Aboriginal peoples can assert their intellectual sovereignty in imaginative ways without embracing Western ways of understanding the world. He argues that American Indian intellectuals have

> by and large [been] caught in a death dance of dependence between, on the one hand, abandoning ourselves to the intellectual strategies and categories of white, European thought and, on the other hand, declaring that we need nothing outside ourselves and our cultures in order to understand the world and our place in it.[26]

He optimistically adds:

> When we remove ourselves from this dichotomy, much becomes possible. We see first that the struggle for sovereignty is not a struggle to be free from the influence of anything outside ourselves, but a process of asserting the power we possess as communities and individuals to make decisions that affect our lives.[27]

This last comment is worthy of closer examination, especially in the context of the legal and political discourse of Aboriginal rights.

Warrior seems to be suggesting that our struggle to exercise our intellectual sovereignty simply requires us to assert a power we already possess. In one sense he is right; that is, in the end it is up to us to assert our philosophies, and we have to decide as a community to do so. But there is another aspect to this unilateral assertion of intellectual sovereignty, especially when we consider the legal and political discourse of Aboriginal rights. This is the fact that the non-Aboriginal legal and political intellectual community, by and large, does not recognize our intellectual traditions as being valuable sources of knowledge (never mind wisdom). Our 'tribal secrets' are of anthropological or historical interest only—the majority of non-Aboriginal academics are still most interested in generating a discourse *about* Aboriginal people. Aboriginal understandings of political sovereignty are given little attention, if any at all, in the contemporary academic theoretical discourse of sovereignty.

Of course, this lack of attention does not lower the value of Aboriginal philosophical traditions. But it is not enough for Aboriginal intellectuals simply to assert their intellectual sovereignty in the already vigorous mainstream intellectual community. *As a matter of survival*, Aboriginal intellectuals must engage the non-Aboriginal intellectual landscape from which their rights and sovereignty are articulated and understood. Unlike Aboriginal intellectuals carving out their own communities and asserting their intellectual sovereignty within them, I am suggesting that Aboriginal intellectuals must develop a community of practitioners within the existing dominant legal and political intellectual communities.

For example, since the Calder decision in 1972, Aboriginal legal theory in Canada has moved in new directions. Douglas Sanders, Brian Slattery, Russel Barsh, Bruce Clark, Patrick Macklem, and Kent McNeil, among others—all non-Aboriginal legal scholars—have, over the past thirty years, established 'Native Law' as a sophisticated subject of specialization within the broader field of law.[28] Over the past ten years, though, Aboriginal legal scholars such as Mary Ellen Turpel, Sakej Henderson, Patricia Montour, Darlene Johnstone, Mark Dockstator, and John Borrows have created a stronger Aboriginal presence in the conservative field of law. These Aboriginal intellectuals are engaging the discourse of Aboriginal rights in creative, sophisticated ways while remaining connected to their communities. Slowly, as more and more Aboriginal people become experts in Aboriginal legal studies, they will become publicly recognized as the intellectual authorities on Aboriginal law in Canada.[29]

Bruce Trigger makes a similar plea in the context of professional historians and anthropologists:

> While Native people have played the major political role in challenging the image that other North Americans have of them, non-aboriginal historians and anthropologists have been working to dispel myths that their predecessors helped to create. . . . It is essential that more Native people who are interested in studying their past should become professional historians and anthropologists, so that their special insights and perspectives can contribute to the study of Native history . . . so the distinction between professional anthropologists and historians on the one hand and Native people on the other should give way to disciplines in which Native people play an increasingly important role. Such collegiality will mark the beginning of a new phase in the study of Native history.[30]

Of course, these are long-term goals for Aboriginal peoples. A major problem with increasing the Aboriginal presence in the academic community is that, for most Aboriginal students, the university remains a hostile environment. Many Aboriginal students still face residential-school attitudes, even in universities, and therefore most do not finish their degrees. Trigger is talking about developing a community of Ph.D.s, when the truth is that most Aboriginal students do not graduate from high school. Nonetheless, his point is well taken, and I believe it is *one* important way of empowering Aboriginal peoples. The problem, then, is *how* to establish a thriving, diverse Aboriginal intellectual community. This will be especially difficult in fields such as philosophy, economics, and political science.

From an Aboriginal perspective, the necessity for the kind of intellectual community I am calling for is a brutal consequence of the Aboriginal–European-newcomer relationship. For far too long, Aboriginal peoples have had to use Western European discourses of rights and sovereignty to explain their place in the world. To renew the relationship by returning Aboriginal voices to their rightful place will take some time. We have to rebuild our ship while we are at sea. Word warriors can assist the renewal process by assembling reminders for the dominant culture. For word warriors to do so effectively, they must know how non-Aboriginal intellectual traditions have affected Aboriginal intellectual landscapes. This is an enormously difficult task, but our survival depends on word warriors engaging Aboriginal and non-Aboriginal intellectual traditions seriously and in ways that assert and protect our sovereignty. Through this process non-Aboriginal people can come to understand better what Aboriginal people mean when they claim they are sovereign people.

The other factor that will be essential for renewing the relationship is Aboriginal leadership. Leaders must stop relying solely on Western discourses to explain the content of their rights and focus their energies on their own people. It is not only policy-makers who need to listen to the wisdom of the elders. If Aboriginal sovereignty, however it is explained, is to become an integral part of the Canadian social and political landscapes, then intellectuals and leaders must work together. Taiaiake Alfred describes the dilemma of contemporary Native leadership as one of deciding 'whether to seek internal peace by meeting the needs of the community and restoring it to strength and health, or to promote stability in relations with others by satisfying the demands and expectations of mainstream society'.[31] Word warriors can help with the second part of the dilemma. Historically, our leaders have had to be historians, lawyers, anthropologists, philosophers, and politicians in order to be heard by the dominant society. A community of word warriors, representing many nations, needs to focus outwards and find their way into the dominant intellectual, legal, and political communities in Canada.

This is where Tully's notion of a mediator is helpful. He has offered a way for philosophers, especially political philosophers, to see their own field of study in a way that includes, even demands, Aboriginal participation. But Tully's mediator must negotiate with an Aboriginal mediator. An Aboriginal mediator is a person who engages the imposed legal and political discourses of Aboriginal rights and sovereignty guided by the belief that the knowledge and skills to be gained from that effort are necessary for the survival of all Aboriginal peoples. This is why I envision Aboriginal mediators as 'word warriors'.

Chief Dan George writes:

> We have discarded our broken arrows and our empty quivers, for we know what served us in the past can never serve us again.... It is only with tongue and speech that I can fight my people's war.[32]

Now is the time to take this change in Aboriginal people's reality seriously. Aboriginal people cannot realize this vision alone, but non-Aboriginal people must not think for us. Aboriginal people can listen to reason, engage in philosophical inquiry, and construct coherent and convincing arguments and explanations that will, we hope, be put to good use. But we will always tell our own stories in our own ways.

Notes

1. This remark begins the Royal Commission on Aboriginal Peoples' final report. Jim Bourque was an important Métis leader whose influence at the Commission was profound, even if it was only for a brief time. Sadly, Jim passed away before the final report was released, which makes the spirit of his words all the more important for those he left behind to gather strength.

2. I am using the concept of Aboriginal, or tribal, sovereignty in this chapter to capture, albeit crudely, the unique relationship that Aboriginal peoples have to their territories. More important, the explanations of Aboriginal sovereignty I am concerned with are ones articulated by Aboriginal people themselves. For example, the Eeyouch of Eeyou Astchee (Cree of Northern Quebec) state that for countless generations we have carefully looked after the land and all the creatures that inhabit it. Central to our values has always been the idea of sharing. As an elderly Cree told his nephew when handing down to him custody of the family land, 'You will look after this land, take care of it as a white man would his garden. It is up to you to protect, preserve, make rules where necessary and enforce good hunting practices. You will look after it as I have shown you in the past. You will also look after your people and share what you have on the land'; from Grand Council of the Crees [Eeyou Astchee], *Never Without Consent: Stand Against Forcible Inclusion into an Independent Quebec* (Toronto: ECW Press, 1998), 17.
3. I want to make it clear from the beginning that I am concerned with only one dimension of the Aboriginal–European-newcomer relationship; that is, the legal and political practices that largely determine the content of Aboriginal rights discourse in Canada. I am thinking of professors, judges, policy-makers, policy analysts, and to some extent Aboriginal leaders.
4. See Office of the Prime Minister, press release, 27 Aug. 1991: *The Mandate: Royal Commission on Aboriginal Peoples, Background Documents*. I will refer to the Royal Commission on Aboriginal Peoples as 'the Commission' or 'RCAP'.
5. A good example is the literature on the liberal-communitarian debate. The debate has evolved over the past twenty years or so with virtually no input from Aboriginal peoples. This is because Aboriginal rights are accommodated within a minority-rights model of rights, which can then be subsumed within a broader theory of political rights. For a sophisticated account that genuinely attempts to accommodate Aboriginal people within contemporary liberal political thought see Will Kymlicka, *Multicultural Citizenship: A Liberal Theory of Minority Rights* (Oxford: Oxford University Press, 1996).
6. James Tully, *Strange Multiplicity: Constitutionalism in an Age of Diversity* (Cambridge: Cambridge University Press, 1995).
7. This statement demands a brief comment on what I mean by 'survival'. As an example, consider the philosophy of John Locke. One can engage Locke as a political philosopher, an epistemologist, or, to a lesser extent, a metaphysician. That is, Locke can be studied as a central figure in the Western European philosophical tradition. Aboriginal intellectuals should study Locke in this context, too, but should also read him as an esteemed thinker whose theory of property and views on political sovereignty were explicitly used to justify the dispossession of indigenous lands in the New World. This second kind of investigation is useful for Aboriginal peoples because it helps explain why Aboriginal understandings of tribal sovereignty have been marginalized from the earliest times. Of course, it is another issue whether these kinds of investigations yield results in, say, the form of favourable land-claim negotiations and Supreme Court decisions. Since the outcomes of these legal and political practices have potentially brutal consequences for the survival of Aboriginal communities, I'm suggesting that we must pay closer attention to the way we assemble our reminders, and how we use them in these more serious and meaningful contexts.
8. Will Kymlicka, *Liberalism, Community and Culture* (Oxford: Clarendon Press, 1989), 154.
9. See Will Kymlicka, *Multicultural Citizenship*.
10. The final report was tabled in parliament on 21 November 1996.

11. The final report consists of five volumes and is over 3,200 pages long.
12. Of the four Aboriginal Commissioners—George Erasmus, Paul Chartrand, Viola Robinson, and Mary Sillett—only Paul Chartrand had a legal background, and then as a practising lawyer. Of the three non-Aboriginal Commissioners, Bertha Wilson was a former Supreme Court judge, Peter Meekison was a law professor, and René Dussault was a Quebec Superior Court judge.
13. RCAP, *Report of the Royal Commission on Aboriginal Peoples*, vol. 1, *Looking Forward, Looking Back* (Ottawa: Canada Communication Group, 1996), 678.
14. Ibid.
15. Ibid., 682.
16. Ibid., 685.
17. Ibid., 689.
18. Ibid., 688.
19. Tully, 1.
20. Ibid., 17–18, emphasis added.
21. Ibid., 74 and 122.
22. Ibid., 211.
23. Ibid., 212.
24. See Ruth Landes, *Ojibwa Religion and the Midewiwin* (Madison: University of Wisconsin Press, 1968); Christopher Vecsey, *Traditional Ojibwa Religion and its Historical Changes* (Philadelphia: American Philosophical Society, 1983); Basil Johnston, *Ojibway Heritage* (Toronto: McClelland and Stewart, 1976).
25. Robert Allan Warrior, *Tribal Secrets: Recovering American Indian Intellectual Traditions* (Minneapolis: University of Minnesota Press, 1995), 97–8.
26. Ibid., 123.
27. Ibid., 124.
28. See Brian Slattery, 'First Nations and the Constitution: A Matter of Trust', *Canadian Bar Review* 71 (1992), 261–93; Brian Slattery, *Ancestral Lands, Alien Laws: Judicial Perspectives on Aboriginal Title* (Saskatoon: Native Law Centre, University of Saskatchewan, 1983); Bruce Clark, *Native Liberty, Crown Sovereignty: The Existing Aboriginal Right of Self-Government in Canada* (Montreal: McGill-Queen's University Press, 1990); Patrick Macklem, 'Distributing Sovereignty: Indian Nations and the Equality of Peoples', *Stanford Law Review* 45, 5 (1993), 1312–67; Kent McNeil, 'The Constitutional Rights of Aboriginal Peoples in Canada', *Supreme Court Law Review* 255 (1982).
29. See John Borrows: 'Frozen Rights in Canada: Constitutional Interpretation and the Trickster', *American Indian Law Review* 22 (1997), 37; 'With or Without You: First Nations Law in Canada', *McGill Law Journal* 41 (1996), 629; 'Constitutional Law From a First Nation Perspective: Self-Government and the Royal Proclamation', *University of British Columbia Law Review* 28 (1994), 1; 'Contemporary Traditional Equality: The Effect of the Charter on First Nation Politics', *University of New Brunswick Law Journal* 43 (1994), 19; Negotiating Treaties and Land Claims: The Impact of Diversity Within First Nations Property Interests', *The Windsor Yearbook of Access to Justice* 12 (1992), 179; 'A Genealogy of Law: Inherent Sovereignty and First Nations Self-Government', *Osgoode Hall Law Journal* 30 (1992), 291; 'The Trickster: Integral to a Distinctive Culture', *Constitutional Forum* 8, 2 (Winter 1997).

See also J.Y. Henderson and Russell Barsh, 'Aboriginal Rights, Treaty Rights and Human Rights: Tribes and Constitutional Renewal', *Journal of Canadian Studies* 17 (1982), 55; D.M. Johnston, *The Taking of Indian Lands in Canada: Consent or Coercion* (Saskatoon: University of Saskatchewan Native Law Centre, 1989); Mary Ellen Turpel, 'Patriarchy and Paternalism: The Legacy of the Canadian State for First Nations Women', *Canadian Journal of Women and the Law* 6 (1993), 174; Mary Ellen Turpel-Lafond, *First Nations' Resistance: Post-Colonial Law* (Toronto: University of Toronto Press, forthcoming).

30. Bruce Trigger, *The Cambridge History of the Native Peoples of the Americas, vol. 1, North America Part 2*, ed. Bruce Trigger and Wilcomb E. Washburn (Cambridge: Cambridge University Press, 1996), xvii.
31. Taiaiake Alfred, *Peace, Power, Righteousness: An Indigenous Manifesto* (Oxford: Oxford University Press, 1999), 97.
32. Chief Dan George, *My Heart Soars* (Surrey, BC: Hancock House Publishers, 1989), 91.

PART FIVE

IN DIALOGUE WITH THE HISTORY OF POLITICAL PHILOSOPHY

The Platonic Challenge to the Modern Idea of the Public Intellectual

Thomas L. Pangle

Political theorists in contemporary Canada, as in the West generally, play the role of public intellectuals. As such we contribute to a, or the, 'public philosophy'—either by clarifying and enriching the 'public philosophy' that already, if only implicitly, exists, or by seeking, through more or less revolutionary efforts, to elaborate a new 'public philosophy'.[1] But in playing this role, are we conscious enough of, restive enough about, the script that has been written for us? Are we theoretically critical about the very idea of the public intellectual, and the related notion of a 'public philosophy'? Have we been attentive to how peculiar, how recent, how contestable this idea is, in all its versions? I do not mean to suggest that we should, even if we could—in our modern world—altogether eschew the role of public intellectual. But we might play the role more skeptically and more circumspectly than we have hitherto. We might practise our 'profession' with an openness to, and some actual embrace of (within the constraints of the modern predicament), the *original* meaning of 'political philosophy'. My own work may be characterized as in large part preoccupied with promoting this kind of reform in our conception of our vocation, above all by shedding some light on the Platonic alternative to our reigning idea of the public intellectual.

For there is no idea of the public intellectual in Plato, and no place for any such idea. It is my impression that there is no place for the idea of the public intellectual in any text written prior to the Enlightenment. The idea of the public intellectual is an idea born in, and inseparable from, the Enlightenment. But as soon as we confront this fact, we recognize how important it is to begin any comprehensive reflection on the meaning of the public intellectual by considering precisely the *absence* of that idea from pre-modern thought, and especially from Plato. For only thus will we begin to grasp the most important earlier conception of the political responsibilities and social consequences of the life of the mind—the conception *against* which the idea of the public intellectual rose up in antagonism, or as a replacement.

If we ask what takes the place, in Plato, of the idea of the public intellectual, we notice immediately that at the centre of the Platonic stage is the idea, or rather the figure, of the *citizen-philosopher*, personified in Socrates. More precisely, Socrates, as immortalized in both Xenophon and Plato, is generally acknowledged to have been the first *political* philosopher, the founder of political philosophy.[2] As such, Socrates is distinguished from his fellow citizens, from the poets, and, above all, from the so-called 'pre-Socratic' philosophers—along with the sophists, who followed eventually in the wake of these last. But what substantively distinguishes the Socratic from the pre-Socratic? What is a 'philosopher', in the strict Platonic sense, and why, according to the Platonic dialogues, were the philosophers and sophists prior to Socrates *not* civic philosophers? What was it that Socrates initiated, as the first '*political* philosopher'?

We learn from the Platonic dialogues that philosophy in the strict sense emerged with the quest to uncover the nature of the universe through unassisted reasoning, on the basis of evidence available to man as man. The philosophers sought the lasting causes of all things, and, in particular, of humanity and its doings. The philosophers meant to establish the true human good, by clarifying those authentic needs whose genuine satisfaction constitutes human thriving. Yet even though some of the great pre-Socratics and their sophist students may have played, from time to time, an active role as citizens and even as leaders in various cities, they were *not* citizen-philosophers. They were not political philosophers. Why not, or in what sense not?

To begin with, we can express the Platonic answer in a nutshell as follows: the philosophic inquiry into nature as a whole, and into human nature as a part of the whole, convinced the pre-Socratics that the most fundamental beliefs upon which any and all civic life must rest are in fact artificial illusions, without basis in, contradicted by, and indeed having the function of hiding, reality. In the words of Plato's Athenian Stranger: 'And indeed they declare that some small portion of the political art is in partnership with nature, but most is artificial, and thus the whole of legislation, whose establishments are *not* true, is not by nature, but artificial' (*Laws* 889d–e).

Now this perspective is, as the Athenian Stranger and his statesman-interlocuter Kleinias stress, manifestly subversive of obedience to law. This outlook inevitably subjects its proponents—insofar as they and their doctrines become known—to the danger of understandable ostracism or worse, on the grounds that they are corrupters of the city and of the family. It is therefore not surprising that, as the first great sophist, Protagoras, stresses, in the Platonic dialogue of that name, all his predecessors 'used covering wings', 'made concealments', and 'hid' their wisdom 'behind veils' (*Protagoras* 316d6, e5)—and 'I myself,' he adds, 'have taken other precautions' (317b6–7). As the dialogue proceeds, Protagoras conveys his critique of political life only by way of a richly allegorical 'myth'. Yet Protagoras proudly indicates that in this myth, and otherwise, he is much more open than were his great predecessors. And for his daring Protagoras paid heavily. He apparently ended his life fleeing an Athenian court conviction for impiety, and the Athenian democracy proceeded to make his book on the gods the object of the first public book-burning recorded in history.[3] No writing of Protagoras survives, and what we know of him and his teachings comes almost entirely from the vivid memory preserved with care in the writings of Plato. A similar fate attends the writings of the other sophists.[4]

Yet we can find a full and frank presentation of some of the chief features of the anti-civic arguments of the pre-Socratics in some very special texts: on the one hand, in Platonic passages where, in private conversations with Socrates, certain sophists are so provoked by Socrates that they momentarily 'spill the beans'; on the other hand, and perhaps more fully revealing, in Platonic passages where certain young citizens report arguments they have heard from the sophists—arguments that these youths find deeply troubling or powerfully attractive, or both.

Thus we find Plato's brother Glaucon, at the commencement of the second book of the *Republic*, elaborating a fuller version of the arguments introduced by the sophist Thrasymachus in the first book. The critique of civic justice that Glaucon reports is centred on the contention that the laws and mores that define civil society's notions of right and wrong do *not* express what humans are *naturally* inclined towards, and are far from opening avenues to the natural flourishing or true fulfillment of those who live by the rules. The true nature of civic justice is merely that of a social contract. In other words, civil society's moral rules are nothing more than artificial conventions, constructed over time by and for the mass of men who seek through these rules to limit (though it would be impossible to end) one another's natural, mutually exploitative, pursuit of fulfilling selfish goods. The rules are meant especially to prevent the very few truly strong and gifted from exercising their natural capacity to flourish by dominating or using the rest, who are their natural inferiors in capacity for happiness. Justice, or the restraint of the pursuit of one's own true welfare in order to avoid injuring the welfare of others, is not *intrinsically* good for anyone, and in fact blocks access to complete happiness for *everyone*; such behaviour becomes *qualifiedly* good for the *defective* majority because it is a kind of mean between doing what is truly best—procuring happiness for oneself and one's loved ones at the expense, or through the neglect, of others—and suffering what is worst: that is, exploitative injury by others who are better able to obtain happiness for themselves and their loved ones.

The massive evidence offered for the truth of this insight is the fact that human beings everywhere reliably obey the laws *only* when the laws have *sanctions*. Strip a man of the *conventional* and *extrinsic rewards* for justice (of the security of his property and loved ones, of his standing in the community, and of his *reputation* for justice, including his fame for having made what are called 'sacrifices' for a just cause); leave a man with *nothing but* his having acted justly, his having subordinated self-concern to concern for others or for something beyond self; and—Glaucon asks, in the name of those whose position he is explaining—how could anyone *honestly* deny that justice, justice in and by itself, is bad for the simply just person?

Furthermore, as Thrasymachus earlier insisted, those who make and enforce the laws always do so with a strong bias in their own favour, partly avowed and partly hidden—often even from themselves. When appeal is made to '*the* city', or to '*the* community', or to 'the rule of law' as to something that *transcends* particular interest—when the country is held up as something for the sake of which each citizen ought to be ready to sacrifice himself and his personal interests—what is *obscured* is the fact (implicit in the very concept of sacrifice) that the city is *not* a natural, let alone an organic, unity. Human society is surely *not* like an ant colony or a beehive. Every *human* society is most decisively divided between *rulers* and *ruled*, law-makers and law-obeyers, whose respective conventional positions are *not* designated or justified by any natural difference or natural bond. The ruling group—be it the majority, as in a democracy, or a minority, as in other regimes—acts as a constructed alliance or coalition of predominantly self-concerned beings, standing over and *against* the ruled. The laws or rules may *apply* to all, and of course *claim* to be in the interest of all, or of the so-called 'public'; but the laws are made and enforced with a view to the interest of the majoritarian or minoritarian *ruling class* or group(s).

Glaucon's eloquent and powerful restatement of the sophistic position is supplemented and deepened by his brother Adeimantus, who stresses the moral incoherence of the typical arguments given by fathers in *praise* of justice. Adeimantus complains especially about the appeal fathers make to the providential gods. For that appeal shows that even or precisely those who preach justice do so *not* on the grounds that justice is *intrinsically* good, but only on the grounds that it is backed up by great extrinsic rewards and punishments.

Indeed, civil society's overwhelming dependence on religious belief, and the city's preoccupation with worshipping, placating, and beseeching providential deities, is, according to the pre-Socratics, the most massive sign of the illusory character of civic consciousness (see *Laws* 889eff.). For natural science reveals no evidence whatsoever for such providential gods. On the contrary: natural science reveals a world governed by unchanging and will-less necessities (ibid. 966e–967d).

Who or what are the thinkers who traffic in such anti-civic teachings? What defines, what motivates, the so-called *sophists*—those itinerant professional teachers of 'rhetoric' and 'virtue' who are in Plato the most obtrusive, politically speaking, of the pre-Socratic thinkers? The first man to apply to himself the term 'sophist', in the sense that subsequently became famous, seems to have been Protagoras. In Plato's presentation, Protagoras boasts that by thus naming and proclaiming himself, he is declaring openly the project that has been the covert agenda of a long series of deviously subversive wise men among the Greeks, starting with Homer and Hesiod and continuing notably with the great lyric poet Simonides. While pretending, on the surface, to be reverent respecters and conveyors of the pious tradition, these poets and their intellectual heirs have embedded in their writings a hidden teaching that seeks to woo the best young men of Greece *away* from allegiance to the ruling elites, to become instead the admirers and disciples of the poets themselves, as the avatars of wisdom (*Protagoras* 316c–317c).

This amazingly bold declaration is muted considerably in response to Socrates' rather demagogic questioning. In the first place, Protagoras distinguishes himself from other sophists, who, he says, 'corrupt the young' by teaching them science: Protagoras claims that he, by contrast, teaches a student only what the student comes to learn, namely 'good counsel in household affairs, so that he might best manage his own household; and also good counsel about civic affairs, so that he might gain the greatest power' (318d–e). When Protagoras accedes to Socrates' apparently benign reformulation of this to mean a claim to teach 'the political art' and 'to make men good citizens', (319a), Socrates springs his trap—laying down a challenge to Protagoras in the name of the basic principles of Athenian democracy (that is, of the city in which Protagoras is at the moment trying to drum up respectable business). For in democracy every citizen is *already* presupposed to be a good citizen, and to know sufficiently the political art; elitist, not to say oligarchic, claims to teach *special* political wisdom, for large sums of money, are highly suspicious.

Protagoras seeks to elude this Socratic net by retreating into the beautiful haze of his great allegorical myth, which Protagoras then interprets to mean that *all* he does is teach the sons of the rich a small, tiny supplement to what they have already learned from their parents and school teachers—but, Protagoras must remind his clientele in the audience, this innocuous little supplement is of course well worth the *enormous* sums of money Protagoras charges. In other words, the sly young quasi-plebeian Socrates very quickly, and very easily, gets the great, old, but insufficiently cautious Protagoras on the ropes of incoherence. (Or at least that is the *story* Socrates rushes to tell outsiders immediately after the private indoor confrontation with the great sophist. For we learn of Socrates' encounter with Protagoras only through overhearing a narration by Socrates to several nameless, idle, rich, and gossipy associates.) This and the rest of the conversation between the pesky young Socrates and the evasive and increasingly irritated old Protagoras allow us to discern clearly enough Protagoras's true agenda, an agenda that can be said to be more or less typical of the most prominent sophists. Protagoras takes over the personally liberating theoretical insights of his poetic and philosophic predecessors, and on this basis establishes a *practical* teaching that guides the exploitative or at any rate self-aggrandizing careers of active political men. In the process, Protagoras wins for himself a comfortable fortune, and a vast fame—as the thinker who has had the manly daring to be the first to speak out as a 'sophist', or teacher of 'virtue' and 'the political art'.

As the dialogue proceeds, however, we see that Socrates leads us to raise this searching question about Protagoras: does not his passionate pride, in his fame as a man of courage, as a *Promethean* spirit, indicate that his concern to be manly, and to be known as courageous, is *not* strictly controlled by his prudent wisdom about his own true good? In other words, does not Protagoras slip back into—or has he perhaps never fully escaped—the belief in a virtue that transcends prudent self-concern? But is such a virtue intelligible on the basis of the critique of civic virtue that Protagoras has taken over from the pre-Socratic philosophers? Does devotion to such virtue not entail an unfounded hope that the devotion will have favourable extrinsic consequences for the devotee? More generally, we may legitimately ask if Protagoras's attachment to *money* is not excessive: that is, if it does not betray an exaggerated expectation of his own prosperity, of his security or immunity from disaster—an exaggerated conception of his own *importance*, in the great scheme of things.

These questions are prompted not only by Socrates' stunning proof of Protagoras's self-contradiction on the issue of the unity of virtue, and especially on the separability of courage from wisdom or prudence; the questions are also prompted by the juxtaposition Socrates creates between the career of Protagoras as a sophist and the career of what one is tempted to call the Socratic sophist—Simonides. For in the latter part of the dialogue, Socrates celebrates the sophistic wisdom of the poet Simonides. Socrates agrees with Protagoras's characterization of the wise Simonides as a poet with a complex hidden message. But Socrates suggests that Protagoras is far from having taken the measure of the wisdom and the greatness of Simonides, as expressed in this esoteric poetry. Simonides was at least as free and cosmopolitan a spirit as Protagoras, and as successful at obtaining fame and fortune. But Simonides—at least as Socrates presents him—put no serious stock in these external goods. The wise Simonides valued wealth and glory only as means, as tools, for obtaining a situation in life that would allow him the greatest possible independence and the fullest access to the most promising young of his own and future generations. For the sake of those young, and for his own satisfaction, Simonides wrote subtle poetry, which Socrates declares he himself has 'studied thoroughly'. The hidden teaching of that poetry, as interpreted by Socrates, adumbrates an account of the fundamental, permanent—and permanently beautiful, if permanently austere—constituents of the human situation. It is this wisdom *alone* that the Socratic Simonides teaches to be the core of such happiness as is available to man as man: 'for,' as Socrates says, summarizing the teaching he attributes to the poetry of Simonides, 'this alone is faring badly—to be deprived of scientific knowledge' (345b5). And to secure for himself and other kindred spirits the richly pleasing experience and display and contemplation of this thinking and knowing, Simonides was prepared to perform, when necessary, such unmanly deeds as flattery of tyrants—without shrinking from the instructive, public, poetic, confession of his own lack of conventional manliness.

Socrates' evocation of Simonidean wisdom allows us to glimpse the decisive difference between the sophistic movement, initiated by Protagoras, and the previous philosophic and poetic wisdom upon which this sophistry is parasitic. The sophists would appear to have vulgarized and, worse, rendered confused, the earlier wisdom—by diluting, if not abandoning, the pure passion for knowledge, and by making knowledge into a tool or weapon for the securing of fame and fortune.

Yet this is *not* Plato's last word on the thought of Protagoras. In the *Theaetetus* and the *Cratylus* we are shown Socrates many years later, in the last days of his life, wrestling with the radically relativist and subjectivist teaching that is summed up in the most famous Protagorean remark: 'man [meaning to say, each different, individual, human] is the measure of all things—of the things that are, that [or how] they are, and of the things that are not, that [or how] they are not.' What is strange about the entire presentation is this: Socrates succeeds in so thoroughly discrediting this radical Protagorean relativism—by indicating its inner incoherence, by showing how it contradicts all the evidence of common sense, and by showing how it renders Protagoras's own life as a teacher absurd—that the reader is compelled to wonder why Socrates ever took the teaching seriously, and, what is more, how so intelligent a man as Protagoras could ever have proposed it seriously.

In seeking an answer at least to the former question, we sooner or later are led to consider the dramatic setting Plato gives to his dialogue *Theaetetus*. At the end of the *Theaetetus*, Socrates says he must now go off to appear at his arraignment to answer Meletus's accusation of him on the charge of impiety. In the dialogue entitled *Euthyphro*, we learn that, a few minutes later, while waiting his turn at the Stoa of the King, Socrates met Euthyphro, and carried on with Euthyphro the famous conversation on piety. In that conversation, Socrates heard from Euthyphro that to the latter it had been revealed, through repeated and unmistakable prophetic inspirations, that the gods, as the supreme powers in the universe, are at war over justice and injustice, and that only he who hears the truth from them can know what is pious and impious, what is right and what is wrong, in the most important respect (*Euthyphro* 5d–6b). Socrates repeatedly attempts to shake Euthyphro's confidence in these claims by demonstrating his, or their, incoherence; but the Socratic dialectic proves an almost complete failure, in the face of the deeply moving and impressive experiences Euthyphro is convinced that he has undergone. In the *Cratylus*, whose dramatic date is not made precise, but that—since the chief interlocuter is Hermogenes—evidently takes place near the time of Socrates' trial, Socrates reconsiders the Protagorean doctrine. *This* time, however, he characterizes that doctrine in an astonishing way. Socrates identifies the Protagorean thesis, and the entire philosophic tradition associated with it—which may mean all the philosophers with the exception of Parmenides, all the philosophers who hold that the universe exists only in motion or as becoming—as a version of what Socrates says he has heard from Euthyphro.

What this means becomes clearer when we attend to another crucial hint given in the *Theaetetus*. There (162c–e) Socrates indicates that the famous 'man is the measure' statement must be understood, and qualified, in the light of a second, almost equally famous—or infamous—Protagorean pronouncement: 'I exclude from my speech and my writing the question of whether the gods exist or do not exist.' Protagoras would repeat this statement, according to Socrates, in order to reject the imputation to him of the thought that 'the Protagorean "measure" is spoken as applying to gods no less than to humans.' If we put this evidence together with several other important clues we find in the *Theaetetus* (see esp. 157e–158b, 170a–e, 172b, 178a–179a), I believe we are led to entertain the following possibility: that Protagoras sought, through his deliberately exaggerated subjectivist formulation, to signal the impasse to which rationalism prior to Socrates had been brought by its incapacity to dispose of the challenge of revelation as represented most vividly by a man like Euthyphro. We may surmise that perhaps no one prior to Protagoras had faced so clearly how doubtful the purely theoretical life and the purely theoretical or scientific enterprise must become, in the face of philosophy's inability to exclude the possibility that the universe has no nature in the strict sense, but is instead the mysterious product of elusive, conflicting, and willful providential deities, who reveal themselves, for unfathomable reasons, to some humans and not to others.

This suggestion makes more intelligible what is perhaps the most important and unforgettable passage in the *Theaetetus* (172cff.): the long 'digression' in which

Socrates interrupts his examination of the Protagorean thesis in order to present his *own* conception of the character, and the reasons for the superiority, of the philosophic life. This account of Socratic *political* philosophy makes clearer than any other in Plato, I believe, that the *chief* purpose of the Socratic 'turn' is the successful vindication of the theoretical life, or the re-establishment, on a firm basis, of the enterprise of Socrates' wise predecessors. The vindication of the theoretical-philosophic life is at the same time the critique of the political life. But the *Socratic* critique of the city and the civic is a very different kind of critique from the one we have in the doctrines of the sophists. Socrates does *not* base his critique on a theory or account of human nature—an account whose basic premises, after all, are always contestable by a man like Euthyphro, or surely by more thoughtful defenders of the city and its gods. By the same token, Socrates does *not* base his critique solely or chiefly on the evidence afforded by empirical observation of the *behaviour* of cities and citizens, of lawgivers and rulers; in particular, he does not rest his refutation of the civic opinions on the observation that those *opinions* are contradicted by the civic *deeds*. Socrates does not scorn such scientific evidence; but he does not find it to be conclusive. What then *is* the character of the distinctively Socratic critique of the political life?

The Socratic critique proceeds by way of 'dialectics', of what Socrates calls the 'midwifing art' that expresses his 'terrible erotic passion for refuting'. Socrates refutes in conversation the articulate young who *begin* by being firmly rooted in, and guided by, and able to express and argue clearly for, the fundamental civic opinions about justice and nobility. The Socratic refutation—for example, of Polemarchus—proceeds *on the basis of* those civic opinions, and on the premises underlying those civic opinions. The Socratic refutation succeeds by bringing to light grave contradictions in those opinions and premises. The Socratic critique is an *immanent* critique, and those who are refuted *cannot* question the premises of the refutation, because those premises are *their own*. What is most important, however, is *not* the refutation itself, but rather the consequence for the young person who is so refuted. The young who have the intelligence and the strength of soul truly to follow and grasp and drink in the meaning of the refutation undergo a profound change in spirit. The refutation of their opinions about justice and nobility entails or carries in its wake a refutation of their experiences (see especially *Theaetetus* 161e4–8): that is, they come to doubt the most important apparent experiences they previously believed themselves to have had. They undergo a new and undeniable experience: they discover that the insight into the contradictory character of the city's conceptions of justice and nobility renders all the inspiring beliefs associated with those conceptions no longer credible, at least in their original interpretations. The young who truly recognize that they have been refuted alter, fundamentally, their conception of the human situation. They become converted to philosophy, or to the conviction that the philosophic way of life, and the philosophic vision of the world, or of nature, and of divinity, and of justice, and of nobility is true. In bringing about and witnessing this conversion, Socrates reproduces, and thus confirms, the conversion that he himself must originally have undergone. And Plato, by preserving in his writings a record of the Socratic process of verification, conveys to future generations of potential philosophers indications of both the path of conversion and the reproducibility of that path.

To be sure, in his account of his own doings in the *Theaetetus*, Socrates makes it clear that only a very few of the young have the capacity to undergo a true or full conversion. Even among the elite with whom Socrates can converse at any length, the vast majority wind up refusing to listen—in one way or another. The conclusive confirming evidence that Socrates gathers is thus not copious; and this would seem to explain the fact that even at the very end of his life, Socrates speaks as if his gathering of confirming evidence is not simply a thing of the past. For Socrates, the theological question is never entirely closed, it would seem. This feature of the account in the *Theaetetus* also prompts us to wonder whether Socrates does not feel the need to gather supplementary evidence from truncated refutations of the unpromising—even, perhaps, refutations of some of the old, who can be assumed to be so settled in their convictions that it would be utterly unreasonable to expect them to undergo the conversion to philosophy. In the *Laws*, and especially in the opening pages of that long dialogue, we do indeed witness a remarkable theological outcome of a Socratic refutation of two shrewd old statesmen, born and raised in the most traditional and orthodox of all Greek cities. Those statesmen are not, as a consequence of the refutation, converted to philosophy; but they do react by spontaneously abandoning the cardinal theological tenet of their civic creeds.

In reward for this wrenching sacrifice, the old statesmen are shown a legal order far more reasonable and noble than any previously known to them, and are allowed a vision of law-inspiring divinity far purer and more in accord with nature than any of which they have previously heard. And this brings us to what we may call the politically *constructive* aspect of the Socratic critique of politics. This aspect is of course much more visible in the great political dialogues—the *Republic*, and the *Laws*, and to a lesser extent the *Gorgias*. The theme of these dialogues is the 'best regime by nature', or that 'true political art' of which, Socrates boasts, he is 'one of the very few, not to say the only, practitioner in Athens'. In elaborating the 'best regime' of the *Republic*, or even the 'second or third best regime' of the *Laws*, the Socratic philosopher brings out the diamonds hidden in the rough of actual politics. The Socratic critique of civic opinion, unlike the pre-Socratic critique, does not lead to the conclusion that the entire realm of civic opinion ought to be simply left behind, as hopelessly deluded. The Socratic critique leads to an immanent self-transcendence of the civic, rather than to an abandonment of the civic. Or to put it another way: precisely by criticizing civic opinion for being contradictory, Socrates insists that we must try to decide which of the two contradictory premises in each crucial case can and must be maintained, and which abandoned. The ordinary civic opinions prove to be not simply false, but, so to speak, half-false—and therefore half-true.

This means, of course, that Socrates does not reveal the purer and more consistent notions of justice and nobility and divinity that are embedded in ordinary moral opinion without simultaneously laying bare the tawdriness and incoherence of ordinary moral opinion. Socrates cannot demonstrate why virtue and moral responsibility must be understood as centred on knowledge of the most important things, and vice on ignorance of them—without casting severe doubts on the intelligibility of human and divine retributive punishment. Socrates cannot show that we mean by true virtue an inner spiritual excellence choice-worthy strictly for its own sake—without forcing us to confront the extent to which virtue is ordinarily motivated by a sense of shame, and of desert, and of corresponding hope. We cannot be brought to recognize that our being is given its intensity by an erotic love of the beautiful that seeks from the start what is everlasting—without feeling some contempt for the mundane objects of mortal, corporeal need that constitute the main preoccupation of ordinary civic life and action. We cannot appreciate the austere divinities of the *Republic* without smiling at the childishness of our initial expectations or demands from divinity.

Yet none of this adds up to a program of civic reform. The chief practical implication of Platonic political philosophy is a kind of moderating, or indeed even a chastening, of political zeal, or of the angry passions and ambitious hopes that animate and often inflame civic life. Even this lesson is not one that is welcome, or that can expect to meet with great success. The same reasons that make most of even the best young people turn away from the Socratic refutations ensure that the vast majority of citizens and statesmen will be unable and hence unwilling to follow very far the Platonic critique of civic life. No doubt the *Laws*, and to a lesser extent the *Republic*, contain important useful general lessons in constitutionalism: for instance, the third and sixth books of the *Laws* provide the classic justification for, and institutional elaboration of, the mixed regime; the second and seventh books of the *Laws*, and to some extent the third book of the *Republic*, outline the classic principles of civic education, and reveal in particular the central role of music, or the fine arts, in such education; to take a final example, the ninth and tenth books of the *Laws* present a teaching on the principles of penal law that, in accord with the Socratic doctrine which traces virtue to knowledge and vice to ignorance, exemplifies and thereby promotes a tempering of punitive indignation. And everywhere in Plato we find a profound, if profoundly qualified, respect for political life: the Platonic dialogues promote a respect for politics that is centred on, and justified by, the hidden directedness of law and lawfulness towards that which transcends law. According to Plato, the call of citizenship draws men up and out of their narrow concerns for material, personal, and familial security and contentment; the experience of civic life awakens in the best men a longing for greatness, for excellence—for a responsibility and hence a fulfillment and a salvation that will give life meaning and dignity otherwise unknown. Politics centred on the quest for justice and nobility gives life seriousness. That is why the political vocation has the potential to provoke in those who hearken to it an intense concern for the *truth* about the principles and hopes and dreams that inspire and are inspired by political action. But this rich potential, if it is to be fully realized, must encounter the bracing challenge of the philosophic or theoretical life. Only then does the political man begin to discover the cave-like character of civic life, and thus the life beyond the cave toward which civic life unknowingly gropes, and that gives to civic life its ultimate high justification—and, at the same time, its sense of limits. For the ambition to rule does not find a good reason for stopping short of noble but ultimately self-corrupting imperialism unless that ambition is checked by some awareness, however dim or veiled, of the higher dignity and richer satisfaction of the leisured theoretical life. One of the most important ways in which the Socratic–Platonic philosophers have, down through the centuries, sought to inculcate this awareness is through their attempts to influence and modify the theology, and especially the conception of the divine, of their respective communities.

Now in the preceding, very sketchy, suggestions as to the nature of that Socratic idea of political philosophy which takes the place, as it were, of the modern idea of the public intellectual, I have selected especially those features that allow one to appreciate the enormous difference between the Socratic conception of the civic role and responsibility of the life of the mind, and the competing modern idea of the public intellectual. Let me close by attempting to characterize briefly the concern that is the defining heart of the modern departure.

Socratic political philosophy, I have contended, has as its chief *raison d'être* the vindication of the rational theoretical life, and of the conception of divinity discovered by strict reasoning, in the face of the challenge posed by purported experiences of supra-rational and indeed contra-rational divine revelations and laws. Modern political philosophy, I would like to suggest, has something akin as its fundamental animating goal. But modern political philosophy is born out of a grave obfuscation: out of a loss of understanding or awareness of this theological import of Socratic dialectics.

If we follow the precious lead given us by Nietzsche, in aphorisms 95 ('*The Historical Refutation as the Decisive Refutation*') and 96 ('*In hoc signo vinces*') of *Daybreak: Thoughts on the Moral Prejudices*, and apply Nietzsche's indications, in a properly modified form, to the great thinkers of the Enlightenment such as Montesquieu, we may succinctly formulate the theologico-political heart of the Enlightenment enterprise. The moderns begin from the following grand historical hypothesis: that the prevalence in the world of belief in supra-rational revelations of contra-rational divine laws is caused not by the existence of the deities believed to reveal themselves in and through those laws, but instead by pathological political and social and economic conditions. For human beings are by nature beings who are largely satisfied by mundane prosperity. Humans have turned to imaginary deities who demand the transcendence and even the sacrifice of worldly prosperity, only because worldly prosperity is so uncertain. If their lives were made secure, and invested with a modicum of worldly dignity, humans might well continue to imagine and worship supernatural deities who would help them assuage the fear of death, but one would find that those supposed deities and their purported commandments would cease to contradict in any significant way and would instead simply support the rules and practices and institutions that reason showed were necessary for worldly prosperity. Religions and gods and commandments that stood in the way of this 'progress' would either disappear or would be reinterpreted by their believers so as to become practically unrecognizable shells of their former selves. As the transformation of the conditions of social existence proceeded, as the mass of mankind was blessed with greater and greater satisfaction of its true natural needs, the empirical proof of the hypothesis, and thus the resolution of the most fundamental theoretical as well as existential problem, should become plainer and plainer.

The moderns proceeded to elaborate competing and complementary versions of a vast political project that would vindicate this hypothesis. Philosophy or science, they proposed, can and must be reconceived as politically and socially active in such a way as to direct this revolution in the conditions of human existence. Philosophy must replace the cave with the Enlightenment. Political philosophy must become actual lawgiving, in the most comprehensive sense. It would appear that modern rationalism was compelled to blind itself to the fact that the theoretical or contemplative life is the fullest answer to the deepest spiritual needs of human nature. For the basic modern hypothesis which has just been stated is obviously incompatible with a conception of human nature as erotic in the Platonic sense. Certainly this much is true: the moderns (with the possible exception of Spinoza) are defined by their conviction that the life of free reasoning and thinking can be vindicated only at the cost of ceasing to advance the claim that this life and this life alone truly fulfills human nature.

But from the outset a massive practical difficulty had to be surmounted: genuine philosophy and philosophers (even in the new sense) were—and remain—very, very rare, and very deeply misunderstood. Philosophy was therefore required to recruit a kind of cosmopolitan spiritual army of subordinates. Philosophy had to debase its own name, lending that name to the officers of the new army—the '*philosophes*'. The new rationalism had to inspire cultural cadres, composed of lesser lights who would obediently carry forward—not altogether self-consciously—the theological-political struggle of secularizing social transformation and humanistic cultural revolution. This is the deepest significance, the truly world-historical significance, of the idea of the public intellectual. And this insight we acquire if, and only if, we approach the idea of the public intellectual from a Platonic perspective. For there is no more telling sign of the decisive flaw in the Enlightenment and its idea of the public intellectual than that the deepest purpose of that idea has been lost sight of by all its proponents[5]—and that it is only those enlightened by the rediscovery of the undiminished intrinsic power of the theoretical challenge posed by its enemy who can still appreciate the grandeur of theological-political ambition of the modern project.

That project has achieved, and we may hope will continue to achieve, unprecedented liberation of the mass of mankind from oppression and material want. But the study of Socrates reveals at what enormous cost—and thus spotlights the human need now most desperately requiring our triage. Modernity from its outset, at first deliberately and then ever more unconsciously, denied or eclipsed what Plato's Socrates teaches us is the deepest, the defining, erotic longing of the human soul. Our civilization is consequently slipping into an ever darker ignorance of what is most truly human, and at the same time trans-human, in man. To realize our being as human requires rootedness in dedication to non-utilitarian moral excellence; from such roots grows a destiny that becomes fully actualized in the leisured but intensely active life of the mind: an electrified awakeness to unriddling the truth about the permanent, if problematic, contours of the whole, and of the human situation within the whole. The struggle to roll back the obscuration of this destiny is the most urgent public vocation of political philosophy in our epoch.

NOTES

1. See, e.g., Michael Sandel, *Democracy's Discontent* (Cambridge, Mass.: Harvard University Press, 1996).
2. Cicero, *Tusculan Disputations* 5.4; *Academics* 1.4; *Brutus* 8; see also Xenophon, *Memorabilia* 1.1.11–16, 4.7.1–8.
3. The sources are gathered and discussed in chapter 2, 'Le Procès de Protagoras', of Eudore Derenne, *Les Procès d'impiété intentés aux philosophes à Athènes au Vme et au IVme siècles avant J.-C.* (Liège: Vaillant-Carmanne, Bibliothèque de la Faculté de philosophie et lettres de l'Université de Liège, 1930). Guthrie's discussion is quite inadequate (he seems to be unaware of Derenne's important book), not least because he is unalive to the philosophic implications of the reports of this and other trials for impiety: *The Sophists* (Cambridge: Cambridge University Press, 1971), 263; see also 235n.2. For the best synoptic study of the relevant historical context, see Peter J. Ahrensdorf, 'The Question of Historical Context and the Study of Plato', *Polity* 27 (1994), 113–35.
4. See H. Diels and W. Kranz, *Die Fragmente der Vorsokratiker*, 2 vols (Zurich: Weidmann, 1985); there are just five undisputed and four doubtful brief fragments preserved from the writings of Protagoras, in quotations from various ancient authors: 2.262–8.
5. A particularly striking and impressive example is John Stuart Mill. The opening of his essay, 'Theism' (in *Essays on Politics and Culture*, ed. Gertrude Himmelfarb [Garden City, NY: Anchor-Doubleday, 1963]) comes to the brink of the recognition that the foundation of modern rationalism and science is to be laid in an evolving historical experience that is logically prior to or that does not presuppose the truth of scientific method; but Mill veers away from this insight into the foundations of modern science, bedazzled as he is by the apparently unquestionable authority of that science and its method (385–7). Though Mill repeatedly decries arguments about the existence of God that commit the fallacy of *petitio principii* (392, 398), Mill's own arguments are vitiated by just this fallacy. For Mill proceeds on the merely 'granted' and unargued premise that 'the legitimate conclusions of science are entitled to prevail over all opinions, however widely held, which conflict with them' (387; see similarly 405, 429–30, 439–40); the only support he brings to this premise is the observation that 'a man would be laughed at who set it down as one of the alternative suppositions that there is no other cause for [something] than the will of God' (440). Laughter is not a substitute for argument, especially on the part of one who claims to take logic and science as the canon of existence—and who is capable, as the rest of the essay indicates, of refutation and argumentation on a high and penetrating level. But because Mill for some reason fails to face his lack of foundation, he pays the heavy price of failing to grasp the foundational problem that was seen so clearly by his superior predecessors, who as a consequence

launched (and who therefore could not, like Mill, presuppose) the Enlightenment. See Leo Strauss, *Philosophie und Gesetz*, in *Gesammelte Schriften*, 2 vols thus far, ed. Heinrich Meier (Stuttgart: J. B. Metzler, 1996–) 2.20–1.

Coercion and Disagreement

ARTHUR RIPSTEIN

Liberalism arose as a doctrine about how to deal with disagreement. The classical tradition in liberal thought—from Hobbes and Locke through Kant and Hegel—supposed that political institutions provide solutions to problems about disagreement that arise in their absence. And, at least since Locke, liberals have argued that the state need take no interest in other sorts of disagreement.

My aim in this paper is to look at contemporary debates about disagreement through the lens of the earlier liberals' conception of it. For the classical liberals, the first question of political philosophy concerned the terms on which people interact with each other, and problems of disagreement arose in relation to those terms. Focusing on Kant's formulation of the problem, I will lay out the distinctive idea of reciprocity and mutual respect that makes up his solution to the problems of disagreement that he sees. After illustrating and elaborating that idea in the juridical home in which Kant saw it, I will say something about the conception of normative justification that underlies it. I will conclude with some brief and tentative suggestions about what light that conception of justification might shed on certain recent debates about liberalism and disagreement.

1. The First Question of Political Philosophy

From Hobbes and Locke through Kant and Hegel, discussions of private law and punishment were essential elements of any work of political philosophy. Those thinkers took it for granted that the primary justification of a coercive central authority is its role in protecting people from each other. Although the thinkers in this tradition differ greatly, both in their conception of the need for protection and in their description of the problem, all of them suppose that the terms on which people interact with each other have a certain sort of primacy over relations between the state and its citizens.[1]

The political world in which we live differs in important ways from that in which the classical liberals wrote. Questions about the relations between the state and its citizens have acquired a new importance with the rise of the modern state, whose legitimate functions go beyond that of protecting people from each other. Health, education, equality of opportunity, and (though now unfashionable) distributive justice are no less essential roles of the state. These legitimate functions do not show that the role of the state is different in kind, but rather that there is more to justice than some seventeenth- and eighteenth-century thinkers might have thought. But they still have important lessons to teach us, especially about disagreement and the justification of coercion.

2. Disagreement between Private Parties

I propose to begin by thinking through the problem of disagreement as it arose for the classical liberals. The problems, and their solutions, are illuminating, because the classical liberals saw the state, and the justification of coercion, in terms of a problem about disagreement. While the subject matter of those disagreements may have changed, the structural problem they pose has not. I'll take Locke and Kant as my exemplars—though considerations of space will make my treatment of them regrettably schematic.

Locke and Kant focused respectively on two distinct types of disagreement, and saw the state as remedying the problems arising from intractable disagreement in the state of nature. For Locke, the state of nature is merely 'inconvenient': although persons have rights, and know what those rights are, disputes arise because they often disagree about facts. Lockean rights are rights in property, so a property-based example will illustrate: you and I may use incompatible marking systems to stake out land that we have improved. As a result, we may stake out the same piece of land, or overlapping portions of the other's land, and disagree—entirely in good faith—about who owns what. The minimal solution to this sort of disagreement is Locke's solution: we appoint a neutral arbiter and empower him both to decide questions of fact and to enforce those determinations, rather than allow either of us to impose his will on the other through force. By giving up our enforcement power to the arbiter, we give his decisions a degree of finality that is otherwise impossible.

For Kant, the fundamental type of disagreement is different, and deeper: the problem is that we don't have any rights at all until we know how to apply them to concrete cases. Another example: suppose that you, in a moment of Darwinian inspiration, scatter tomato seeds, hoping to harvest those hardy ones that survive on their own without further tending. I, meanwhile, focusing on the relation between agriculture and culture, come upon what seems to me a wild tomato plant, and tend and water it until it bears fruit. Just as I am picking the tomatoes, you come along and point out that they are of your seed. Who gets to keep the tomatoes?[2] Here there is no factual disagreement: we both agree about what happened. We also subscribe to a common principle, which each of us invokes in support of our own claim to the tomatoes: people are entitled to the fruits of their efforts. What we disagree about is how that principle applies to the case at hand. Yet if Kant's diagnosis of the situation is gloomier than Locke's—no mere inconvenience, but the outright absence of rights—his solution is not dissimilar on its face. In order for us to have rights, we need an impartial arbiter to determine which rights we have and to enforce those determinations. In another way, of course, Kant's analysis goes much deeper, because he sees that the problem does not arise out of the fact of disagreement. Instead, it arises out of a fundamental problem of human interaction: if persons with separate ends are to live together on terms of mutual respect, *none* can be allowed to set the terms of their interaction unilaterally. Instead, an impartial arbiter is needed. But the arbiter is not just a fact-finder and enforcer; the arbiter must pronounce about the rights that we have. No arbiter, no rights. In order for the parties to have rights, they must not only make claims against each other, but they must recognize that in particular cases those rights transcend their own understanding of their application.

This point needs some filling out. Kant's key insight is that people have rights with respect to each other rather than with respect to things. Locke's concern about unilateral enforcement is a partial indication of this point. If I suppose that my rights are fixed by what I take them to be, I also suppose that your rights are so fixed, in which case I have in an important sense failed to grasp what is crucial about the concept of a right. For Kant, rights are reciprocal limits on freedom; as such, they cannot be determined unilaterally by one of the parties to a dispute. Instead, all are free insofar as all respect the rights of others. To have a right to something is to have others recognize that right; in this, Kant follows Rousseau. But—and this is crucial—Kant sees that the relevant sort of recognition is not simply a matter of fact. As a matter of fact, one person may not recognize another person's right in a particular case. But those who reject the claims of right do not thereby exempt themselves from them. This conclusion follows directly from Kant's idea that one person cannot set the terms of his or her interactions with others unilaterally. Reciprocity is definitive of the concept of a right.

Kant's understanding of the justification of political institutions is thus fundamentally different from Locke's. For Locke, the justification comes from the fact that all consent to a mutually advantageous scheme. For Kant, the justification of political institutions is that they make freedom possible. As a result, Kant supposes that force can be used to bring others into legal relations. The use of force is legitimate because only by having everyone under legal relations can anyone be free.

3. Two Conceptions of Respect

Kant's point about the reciprocal structure of rights can be brought into focus by thinking about a contrast between two ways in which institutions might be said to be organized around ideas of respect for persons. Both of these ideas are familiar, and though sometimes mutually supporting, they are also sometimes in tension. Thinking through the tension enables us to see why reciprocity is so central to Kant's political philosophy,[3] and also to liberalism itself.

The idea that justice requires respect for persons admits of two very different interpretations. Both are radically individualistic, because both suppose that to respect a person is in some measure to exempt him or her from conscription into common projects. But they are very different, and sometimes even incompatible.

The first idea of respect demands that nobody be forced to do anything except on terms that he or she accepts. On this view, to respect a person is to defer to him, to grant him or her a veto of sorts regarding the ways in which he will be treated. This conception of respect has had a long and distinguished history in, or perhaps underneath, the social-contract tradition in political philosophy. If we can show that someone has—or (failing that) would have, or (failing that) should have—accepted certain standards of conduct, we have no hesitation about holding him or her to those standards. But if someone does not consent to some standard of conduct, we are more hesitant about holding him or her to it. A related conception of respect figures in arguments about informed consent in the medical context. A person can be used in an experiment or subjected to a dangerous treatment only if she agrees to it. Consent ensures that others are not simply using her for purposes of their own, since it ensures that she shares those purposes, at least to some extent. I will call this conception 'respect as deference to subjectivity', or simply 'respect as deference'.

The other, very different idea supposes that the idea of respect gets its importance in relation to an idea of *equal* respect. On this second understanding, then, the demands of respect are always relational: respecting one person must be compatible with equal respect for others. Some may find this second idea of respect slippery, or even elusive. This second idea of respect can be summed up in Kant's idea that between two private persons, neither may set the terms of their interactions unilaterally. That is, the limits of one person's freedom or security cannot be set unilaterally by another; instead, persons must moderate their behaviour in the same ways.

Let me illustrate with several examples. All are drawn from non-malicious interactions between persons pursuing their separate ends. Legal systems, ancient and modern, have been pretty much of one mind on the question of how to handle such accidental injuries. They have said that if your injury was the result of my carelessness, I must make up your losses, that the loss is my misfortune rather than yours. The point can be put in terms of Kant's idea of reciprocity: each of us is entitled to an equal level of liberty to go about our affairs, and each of us is entitled to a like level of security against the results of the carelessness of others. Provided that all exercise appropriate care for the safety of others, any losses that result must lie where they fall, for to shift such losses would put too great a burden on liberty. Conversely, those whose injuries are the result of another person's failure to exercise appropriate care for their safety are entitled to be compensated by their injurers, for to allow injurers to leave those costs where they lie would be to put too great a burden on security.

This idea of equal restraint is at odds with the idea of respect as deference because it requires that the standards of conduct be *objective* in at least three distinct ways, corresponding to three ways in which persons might ask that others defer to their subjectivity. First, some might be willing to be moderate their behaviour up to the point at which they would want others to moderate theirs. For example, I might gladly put up with your high-speed driving on residential streets, provided that you would put up with mine. But you might prefer safer streets and gladly do without the thrills of high-speed driving. However exactly our disagreements are resolved, one thing is clear: the idea of reciprocity precludes each of us from setting the standard that will govern only him- or herself: any standard that governs my driving *also* governs your security, and vice versa. So we cannot simply proceed in disagreement.

Second, I might agree that I must moderate my behaviour, but insist that I can only be asked to do my best, and so refuse to take responsibility if I injure you because I was careless or perhaps distracted by a sad song on the radio. The idea of reciprocity precludes this, because your security cannot be made to depend on my abilities.

Third, I might ask for special consideration for my vulnerabilities. We fail to interact on terms of respect if your freedom is limited by my vulnerability—if you must desist from what you are doing because I disapprove of your activities, or even if I am made ill by them. In each of these cases, we fail to interact on terms of reciprocity insofar as your right to either liberty or security depends exclusively on facts about me.

None of these three claims—that I would have put up with the same from you, that I meant no harm, or that my vulnerability merits special protection—appears to be a claim about the rights of others. Instead, they are claims about me, and me alone. But thatat's just the point: the claim that I was doing my best, or meant no harm, or require special assistance from you, amounts to the claim that the question of what I owe to others, or can demand of them, should depend on facts about me alone. It analyzes an interaction between persons by looking at only one of them, and so substitutes respect as deference for equal respect.

Each of the aspects in which the standard of care is objective is at odds with the idea of respect as deference because each specifies a way in which people cannot 'opt out' of equal protection. In cases in which someone is genuinely incapable of moderating his behaviour in light of the interests of others, special accommodations may need to be made. But far from showing a greater respect for that person, any such accommodations treat him as less than an equal. Children are so accommodated precisely because they are *not* full participants in civil society.

The common law has long articulated this idea of reciprocity through the idea of the reasonable person. The reasonable person is not the rational person who pursues his ends effectively. Nor is she the typical or average person. Instead, reasonable persons are, as John Rawls puts the point in a related context, '[moved by a desire for] a social world in which they, as free and equal, can cooperate with others on terms all can accept. They insist that reciprocity should hold within that world so that each benefits along with others.'[4] On this understanding, whether or not a person is behaving reasonably depends upon whether her behaviour is compatible with interacting with others on grounds of reciprocity. The reasonable person serves as a representative person, who has interests in both liberty and security. In deploying the device of the reasonable person, the law has no choice but to make substantive assumptions about the importance of particular interests in liberty and security. For example, how safely may one drive? Since people can be presumed to have both a liberty interest in going about their affairs quickly and a security interest in being free from injury by others, some balance between these must be struck. Where it will be struck will inevitably depend upon substantive judgments about the relative importance of the interests in question. Although most interests in both liberty and security are relatively uncontroversial, their relative weight may not be. I will say something more below about how disagreements about such matters might be resolved in a way that is consistent with reciprocity. For now, the important point is that the distinctive feature of the reasonable-person test is that the balance between those interests is not struck by looking at their weight in a particular case, but rather at their more general importance to a person's ability to live a self-directing life. Thus the fact that I stand to gain a great deal by driving dangerously on some occasion, or that your losses would be comparatively small, does not enter into the assessment of the reasonableness of my behaviour. Conversely, to impose burdens on me for the sake of your advantage is also not considered. To allow the strength of my desire, or even need, on some occasion to set the limits of your security would amount to allowing me to set the terms of our interaction unilaterally. The idea of the reasonable person is a way of making this idea of reciprocity concrete.

It is perhaps worth noting that in most cases the two models of respect do not conflict, because in most cases considering one person's views and making sure that he accepts the terms on which he is being treated does not compromise respect for others. Moreover, institutions organized around the idea of equal respect will certainly require private citizens, in their dealings with one another, to defer to each other's subjective demands. So I may not make demands of you without your actual consent: I can't dump garbage on your lawn, assuming that you wouldn't mind, or wash your windows in your absence and then demand payment for my services.

But the two conceptions of respect certainly can (and do) conflict when it comes to making rules about the terms on which people may interact with each other. In order to treat people with *equal* respect, it may be necessary for institutions to hold particular people to standards that they do not fully accept, because reciprocity requires that they be held to common standards. If one person is free to veto any standard he does not like, he is effectively able to set the terms of his interaction with others, terms which *they* may not like either. To treat both parties with respect, we need to hold them to a common standard, one that protects them equally from each other.[5]

4. Respect and Justification

The idea of mutual respect underwrites a particular conception of justification. Although that conception of justification is clear, I think, in Kant's political thought, it is also in tension with a favourite device of liberal political philosophers, namely the social contract. The social-contract theorist at least appears to be arguing that his preferred institutions and principles of justice are acceptable to all. As a result, he may appear to take on a massive burden of justification, committing himself to justifying his principles to all on terms they already accept. That is, the social-contract approach seems committed to respect as deference. I'm not sure that is the most helpful way to read social-contract arguments, but rather than get bogged down in such matters I will simply sidestep questions about the contract device, and focus instead on the problem that it is supposed to solve, a problem of enabling people to live together on grounds of reciprocity. Talk about unforced agreement is just a way of making this idea of reciprocity vivid; the terms of social interaction must be acceptable to all, not because of some idea that any dissenters are entitled to exercise a veto, but because mutual respect requires that persons interact on terms that are acceptable to persons who respect *each other*.

Rather than talk about ideal agreement, we do better to look at why the justification of coercion is important. Although the social-contract tradition appears to argue that coercion can be justified only on grounds of consent, the most pressing questions about the use of force arise when people are *unwilling* to accept the claims of others against them. If one person injures another and is unwilling to pay damages, the question is not whether the injurer really is (somehow or other) willing to pay after all, but under what conditions it is legitimate to require payment. Again, the fundamental question of punishment is not whether the criminal already accepts the punishment, but whether it is justified when the criminal does not accept it. In the same way, the general question of justification is not whether everyone against whom coercion is exercised is somehow committed to acknowledging its legitimacy. Whether or not such a question makes sense as part of a more general account of morality, it is out of place in political philosophy. Political philosophy must ask whether there is some way to justify the use of coercion in cases in which it is unwelcome. To suppose that coercion is illegitimate unless the wrongdoer accepts the standard by which he or she is judged is to give up on the idea of fair terms of interaction, for it is to allow wrongdoers to set the terms of their interactions with others unilaterally. If one person is free to exempt himself from norms applying to others, he is thereby allowed to set the boundaries of his own behaviour—in which case he is also allowed to set the boundaries of another person's security.

Consider the case of the recalcitrant wrongdoer who denies liability or refuses punishment on the grounds that he has done no wrong. Here the problem of justifying a coercive response is not one of justifying damages or punishment on terms the wrongdoer already accepts, but rather of justifying them even if he does not accept those terms. To use force in such circumstances might seem, well, coercive. But that's just what's at issue. The world would be a nicer place if coercion were never necessary—if nobody ever did anything wrong, or if wrongdoers were always repentant and eager to make restitution. The knot of questions about the justification of tort liability and punishment are not questions of that sort. Instead, they are questions about the legitimate use of coercion when people do wrong. For example, if I wrongfully injure you, I must pay you damages—with the word 'must' meaning something like 'on pain of having my property seized or my wages garnished'. If you get an injunction stopping me from raising livestock in my backyard, and I do not clean up my act quickly, I can be held (and literally—that is, locked up) in contempt of court.

5. PRIVATE LAW AND PUBLIC REASON

Examples of private matters between individuals may seem to be beside the point for contemporary debates about pluralism and disagreement. Although the disagreements on which Locke and Kant focus can lead to conflict (even severe conflict), any conflict they lead to is in another sense shallow: both parties to a disagreement can readily recognize shared premises, and can agree that an impartial arbiter will render their rights secure, if only they can find one acceptable to both.

A third type of disagreement, deeper than those on which Locke and Kant focus, is also possible. Both Locke and Kant took it for granted that the abstract principles governing human interaction were pretty obvious. Yet—as many people have pointed out—those things are also subject to much disagreement. In particular, where questions arise about things other than who owns what—for example, about whether women ought to participate fully in society, whether offensive material ought to be tolerated, or what role religion should play in public life—disagreements run deep, and seemingly cannot be resolved through the creation of appropriate bodies charged with applying principles to particulars. Those sorts of problems are the stuff of much contemporary political debate.

Such disagreements about the terms on which people should interact are practical: people cannot simply agree to disagree when their disagreement concerns the terms on which they interact. When such disagreements arise, two types of problems are possible. The first concerns the *likelihood* of their resolution in a way that is satisfactory to members of both camps. We might call this the empirical problem of stability. It arises whenever people disagree about the basic terms on which they interact, or about matters they consider so fundamental as to undermine their willingness to interact with those with whom they interact. (Recall Rousseau's suggestion that people cannot live in peace with those they regard as damned.) In the limiting case, the problem can arise when a single person does not agree about the expectations that are placed upon him or her. I call it an empirical problem, rather than a moral one, because it arises out of the fact of disagreement itself, rather than from the content of moral principles. When people disagree about fundamental matters, only force will decide between them. Philosophers are notoriously lacking in expertise on such matters, so I will say nothing about what the solution to the empirical problem of disagreement might be, or even about how to go about finding it. I merely flag it here to contrast it with another, quite different problem.

The second problem is not an empirical problem but a moral one. It arises only when one of the parties to a disagreement is committed to some conception of equal concern and respect. This problem concerns the *justification* of the use of force in the face of disagreement about the justification of the use of force. It is one thing to coerce someone on grounds that he or she does not accept; it is also easy enough to coerce someone whom one does not regard as an equal. The new, and harder, question concerns how we might justify coercing someone in a way that is compatible with thinking of him or her as an equal, and worthy of respect. One familiar way to treat persons with respect is to treat them only in ways to which they have somehow—freely, knowingly, or perhaps even implicitly—given their consent. But where someone does not consent to being treated in a particular fashion, what could justify so treating him anyway?

Let me illustrate this point by returning to my earlier example of the recalcitrant wrongdoer who does not believe that he has done wrong. Examples of such wrongdoers are depressingly easy to think of: the racist who does not understand why he should not hurt members of a despised group, the rapist who believes that 'no' means 'yes', the gang member who believes that he should have no loyalty to people outside his gang, and the drunk (or reckless) driver who would gladly put up with dangerous drivers on the road, if only he could drive while drunk (or reckless). Indeed, Alan Norrie has asserted that most criminals fall into this category and are opposed to the oppressive laws—including those protecting persons and property—for the violation of which they are coerced.[6] I put aside any worries about the sincerity of those who claim to reject prevalent standards of the criminal law. If they are insincere, the problem does not arise. So let us suppose they do not merely reject the authority of the state to punish them but, further, believe their behaviour to be acceptable.

What do we do in the face of the wrongdoer who denies he has done anything wrong? One possibility is to decline to punish, on the grounds that we must respect his opinion. Some may find this approach acceptable, but it appears to face two distinct kinds of problems, parallel to the two problems of stability I've mentioned. First, it may raise worries about safety. Some of these worries might result from a concern about providing people with incentives to pretend to reject the moral principles the law seeks to enforce. But the same concerns might arise even if we supposed that we could somehow control that part of the problem. As my examples were meant to suggest, there are a significant number of people who reject the law's claims, at least on particular topics.

Here too we find a parallel second problem. Again, the second problem is a specifically *moral* one. It arises only subject to an understanding of justice in terms of reciprocity and equal concern and respect. This second problem arises because failing to address the wrongdoer's wrong—treating his opinion as just as good as our commitment to reciprocity and equal respect—would allow him to set the terms of his interactions with others unilaterally. To do so would not merely conflict with an opinion we happen to hold dear; it would also undermine our very reason for worrying about the wrongdoer's attitude toward his deed. It is only if we care about interacting with him on terms of respect that his opinion counts for anything. But that claim must not be confused with the superficially similar claim that we can treat him with respect only if we defer to his opinion.

It is easy to run these two problems together. Indeed, I suspect that some of its harshest critics suppose that liberalism makes solving the empirical problem of stability a precondition of any solution to the moral problem, so that those who reject liberal premises are necessarily outside its legitimate purview. In our century, liberal states have been more stable than illiberal ones. Be that as it may, liberalism is a doctrine about the *justification* of coercion; as such it cannot claim that coercion is legitimate only when it is unnecessary.

Yet anti-liberals insist on depicting liberalism in just this way. Consider, for example, the view notoriously put forward by Carl Schmitt. The Schmittian says: 'We eliminate those with whom we disagree; the criminal is our enemy, as we are his; neither of us is better than the other in any way, but we happen to have the guns just now.'[7] Yet there is no reason to suppose that we owe the Schmittian an answer on his own terms. To meet his demand would be to allow him to unilaterally dictate the terms of political life. Insofar as a liberal tries to reason with him, it is because of a commitment to interacting with him on terms of respect. If he insists that he should get to make the rules, there will be no answer that he will accept, but the liberal has grounds for refusing to accede to his demand. So we may well feel that we owe it to him to try to convince him. It is always possible that he will reject such efforts. But there is no argument that can be made—on any topic—that makes it impossible to give such a response; no argument that can convince all on their own terms, whatever those terms may be. He is rejecting the fundamental principle in light of which the liberal supposes that political institutions must be justified to those who resist their claim. In order to create and sustain fair terms of interaction, we may finally have no choice but to use force to achieve justice. In so doing, though, the liberal is not simply doing what the Schmittian would do if he had the force or the numbers to coerce us unilaterally. For we are trying to treat him as our equal.

Now the Schmittian might come along and say: 'This is just an impasse; your view is on all fours with mine. Each of us is arguing from premises that the other rejects; I am just more clear-headed about what I am doing.' The Schmittian is right if he is claiming that the liberal and anti-liberal are alike in making arguments that rest on premises which the other party might reject without self-contradiction. But the liberal's argument in favour of justice is not an epistemological argument that liberalism is somehow without premises, or even without controversial premises. It is a moral argument that rests on moral premises. The fact that there are other possible premises, moral or otherwise, which are incompatible with the liberal's premises, only goes to show that the liberal is putting forward a normative argument. Given that the liberal *conclusions* are not compatible with everything someone might do or think, it is hardly surprising that his premises would also be incompatible with certain other possible premises. And it is no more surprising that those who reject the conclusions might have doubts about any premises that entail them. But that is an abstract (and trivial) feature of arguments in general: if all the premises of an argument are compatible with everything, the conclusions of the argument will also be compatible. The possibility of arguments that deny the moral premises does not show that the liberal is wrong. Competing views may be on all fours when it comes to the ability to persuade a determined opponent. But that cannot be the test of any view, for all views fare equally on it.

6. Pluralism and Political Disagreement

I now want to turn, too briefly, to the question of political disagreement. I'll frame the problem of disagreement by looking at some of the debate surrounding John Rawls's recent claim that liberalism must be understood as a political doctrine rather than a moral one, and his related claim that liberalism is a way of coming to terms with what he calls 'the fact of reasonable pluralism'. For Rawls, the fact of reasonable pluralism provides an explanation of the limits to the use of force. It also provides an account of the sense in which liberalism can be said to be 'neutral' on questions about the good life.

Many have found Rawls's arguments wanting. For example, Michael Sandel has accused Rawls of political quietism, of simply laying out what (some) Americans happen to think.[8] Stanley Fish has suggested that liberals cannot 'give reasons to the devout'.[9] Jeremy Waldron has charged that the empirical fact of pluralism extends beyond Rawls's concern with 'reasonable' pluralism, since people frequently disagree at least as much about justice as they do about questions of the good.[10] Others have disregarded Rawls's insistence that pluralism must be reasonable, and have pointed out that a wide variety of regimes inconsistent with liberalism might be set up so as to contain the disruptive effects of pluralism.[11] All these critics have been distracted by the word 'pluralism'; as a result, all have missed out on liberalism's characteristic focus on equal respect as the central issue in understanding the justification of coercion. All of these challenges are meant to show that Rawls has no principled way of responding to those who are illiberal. All presume that this is a serious problem for Rawls, because as a liberal he owes an answer to those who are illiberal, and that answer must be given in terms that his illiberal challengers are willing to accept. Otherwise, so the criticism goes, liberalism is just another sectarian doctrine, different only from illiberal doctrines in the fact that it happens to be ascendant in certain countries.

Despite their clear differences, I deliberately lump these arguments together because they are representative of a certain way of setting up the problem of coercion. All of them see the problem of coercion as most acute in the case of those who are illiberal. And all of them appear to suppose that Rawls's unwillingness to engage the grand questions of metaphysics reflects either a naïve belief that people are more likely, as a matter of fact, to agree about the right than the good, or an indifference to the claims of those who do not already share his liberal values.

The difficulty with these arguments should now be clear. All suppose that liberalism (or at least its Rawlsian version) is committed to respect as deference. But it cannot be so committed, because any such commitment would be at odds with liberalism's core commitment to reciprocity, that is, to the idea that one person may not set the terms of interaction with others unilaterally.

This is not to say that broad agreement to reciprocity will eliminate all other disagreement. Disagreement will survive. Where demands are not for differential treatment but for different interpretations of equal respect, disagreement is real, and reasonable. It is reasonable in the proprietary sense: that is, it is not incompatible with interaction on terms of reciprocity. But disagreement about what reciprocity requires may be inevitable. Democracy and deliberation provide the only credible solutions here, not because they are alternatives to reasonableness, but because they are ways of finding solutions to reasonable disagreement that are compatible with equal respect. Where all are committed to equal respect, deliberation provides a way of resolving disagreements about just what equal respect requires, because it makes it possible for all to have their say, and for those who do not prevail to accept the legitimacy of the process.[12] Deliberative processes are legitimate only if all really do have a chance to participate; but, here too, having a chance to participate cannot mean having a veto if debate is not structured on the terms one would most prefer. Indeed, the need for reciprocity is probably greater in deliberative contexts than it is elsewhere. Those who reject ideas of reciprocity cannot make their rejection the measure of the political rights of others any more than they can make them the measure of their private rights.

7. Conclusion

I have tried to sketch a distinctive conception of reciprocity as mutual respect. Not everyone finds those ideas attractive; I have tried to explain why liberalism can be comfortable in appealing to them even in dealing with those who reject it. The point is not that the anti-liberal has somehow contradicted himself by demanding respect while refusing to extend it to others. Instead, the point is that the anti-liberal is wrong to assert that the liberal has contradicted *himself* by refusing to yield to the anti-liberal's demands. The anti-liberal is taking up a certain sort of rhetorical posture, claiming to unmask the liberals' pretense of respecting all persons. The anti-liberal's argument attempts to show that the liberal position contradicts *itself* by judging where it claims not to judge.

There is an interesting irony here. A decade ago, critics of liberalism accused it of subjectivism about the good. More recent critics—or sometimes the same critics—now suggest that liberalism is unable to accommodate subjectivism about the right. But the liberal is not committed to respecting all views on their own terms, or to withholding judgment. Instead, the liberal is committed to equal respect, and must come up with a way of defending the use of force that is consistent with a commitment to equal respect—not with a way of justifying it that is consistent with a *rejection* of equal respect. Once we distinguish between competing conceptions of respect, we see that this challenge can be met.

Notes

I am grateful to Cheryl Misak for a series of conversations that provoked me to write this paper.

1. Libertarians have focused on private interaction, but have done so to the exclusion of other, equally important questions.
2. This example is a variant on one offered by Christine Korsgaard in 'Taking the Law into Our Own Hands: Kant on the Right of Revolution', in *Rethinking the History of Ethics: Essays in Honor of John Rawls*, ed. Christine Korsgaard, Barbara Herman, and Andrews Reath (Cambridge: Cambridge University Press, 1996).
3. Kant's moral philosophy, by contrast, appears to make deference to subjectivity central. In the *Groundwork*, Kant makes the idea of giving a law to oneself crucial to freedom. Depending on exactly how one understands that complex idea, Kant might be thought to be rejecting the possibility of any sort of legitimate authority. For an elaboration of this

idea, see Robert Paul Wolff, *In Defence of Anarchism* (New York: Harper and Row, 1970) where it is argued that a law can bind a person only if he or she consents to it as matter of fact. For a more nuanced reading of Kant, according to which moral legislation is not to be understood entirely in terms of facts about the lawgiver, see Christine M. Korsgaard, 'Creating the Kingdom of Ends', in her *Creating the Kingdom of Ends* (Cambridge: Cambridge University Press, 1996).

4. John Rawls, *Political Liberalism* (New York: Columbia University Press, 1993), 50.

5. I put aside many prominent attempts—from Rousseau through Habermas—to square the circle by showing that initial appearances are deceiving, because everyone has committed themselves to our principles of justice. In holding a person to those principles, we are simply holding him to his own commitments, and so, in Rousseau's famous words, forcing him to be free.

   The difficulty with the Rousseauian arguments comes in spelling out those commitments in a way that is not either vacuous or false. Not surprisingly, the difficulty is most evident in involving people who *deny* the claims of others against them. Consider the example of a committed criminal or gang member who supposes that his greatest commitment is to his crime family. The claim that he is mistaken, or somehow at odds with his own deepest commitments, can be construed in either of two ways, neither of which seems very promising. The first of these construes it as some kind of claim of fact. The difficulty comes in making the factual claim seem anything but fantastic. Whether or not the criminal has the last word on what he is committed to, his actions and words taken together may well disclose no concern for the interests of others. The second way of understanding the claim construes it as some sort of metaphysical claim about what is implicit in the criminal's ability to speak and act at all. On this construal, whatever the criminal does or says, he is revealing his underlying commitment to respecting the rights of others. This interpretation of the claim gets into trouble in avoiding emptiness. If any such commitment really is implicit in all action, it would seem that the gangster can manage to live up to his commitment by doing whatever it is that he does. Put slightly differently, the problem is that if such a commitment is presupposed by all action, it will also be compatible with all action. But if it is compatible with all action, it will not provide the resources needed for criticizing the criminal, let alone coercing him. For the criminal will have honoured his deepest commitments after all. It will just turn out that the commitment to respecting the rights of others can be honoured in a variety of quite surprising ways, such as killing people on the instructions of one's crime family or gang.

6. Alan Norrie, '"Simulacra of Morality"? Beyond the Ideal/Actual Antinomies of Criminal Justice', in *Philosophy and the Criminal Law: Principle and Critique*, ed. Antony Duff (Cambridge: Cambridge University Press, 1998).

7. Carl Schmitt, *The Concept of the Political*, trans. George Schwab (New Brunswick, NJ: Rutgers University Press, 1976). See also David Dyzenhaus, *Legality and Legitimacy* (Oxford: Oxford University Press, 1997).

8. Michael Sandel, *Democracy's Discontent* (Cambridge, Mass.: Harvard University Press, 1996) and also 'Review of *Political Liberalism*', *Harvard Law Review* 107 (May, 1994), 1765.

9. Stanley Fish, 'Mission Impossible: Settling the Just Bounds Between Church and State', 97 *Columbia Law Review* 2255 (1997).

10. Jeremy Waldron, 'Justice Revisited', *Times Literary Supplement*, 18 June 1993, 5.
11. Will Kymlicka, 'Two Models of Pluralism and Tolerance', in *Multicultural Citizenship* (Oxford: Oxford University Press, 1995).
12. The same point applies to the distinction between the public realm of reciprocity and the private realm of happiness. In one way, this distinction is constitutive of liberalism. But—and this is crucial—the boundary between public and private is neither empirical nor *a priori*. Instead it is substantive, and frequently contested. The liberal claim to neutrality is not a claim about a particular way of drawing the line between public and private, but rather a claim about the constitutive place of the distinction between public and private—between those questions about which we owe a justification to strangers with whom we interact, and those about which we may seek to justify ourselves to others, but that are not fundamental features of the terms on which we interact with them. The precise line cannot be drawn except in relation to substantive views about which of the ways in which persons are vulnerable to others matter, and the fundamental interests that people have with respect to their treatment by others.

Liberalism and Moral Subjectivism

Edward Andrew

In the last decade or more, my work has concentrated on the moral vocabulary of liberalism. Spurred by the Canadian Charter of Rights and Freedoms, I wrote *Shylock's Rights: A Grammar of Lockian Claims* to explore the meaning of the rights-based liberalism we adopted from the American political practice of judicial review of entrenched rights and the political theories justifying that practice. Following the passage of the North American Free Trade Agreement, I wrote *The Genealogy of Values: The Aesthetic Economy of Nietzsche and Proust* to examine the meaning of the language of trade and trade-offs. It was in the wake of the decline of socialism or collapse of moral barriers to capitalist expansion (and perhaps in a senile and self-indulgent effort to understand my Presbyterian roots) that I have just written *Conscience and its Critics: Protestant Conscience, Enlightenment Reason and Modern Subjectivity*.

Rights, values, and conscience are the holy trinity of liberalism, of a polity conceived as a marketplace of moral and consumer choices. Rights protect choices; they do not direct us to what is choice-worthy—that is the job of values and conscience. Values are what are chosen. Although often conceived as the principles governing choice, these principles—if conceived as values—are themselves chosen; one stands on principle but one renegotiates one's values. As Charles Fried put it, 'The trade-offs between life and other ends expresses [*sic*] exactly what is the value of life.'[1] That is, there are no values without evaluation, without relativistic estimation of the better and the worse, without choice. Conscience is what sanctifies choice. While Marx and Engels, in *The Communist Manifesto*, defined conscience as free competition and consumer sovereignty in the religion business, conscience is fundamental to our moral self-understanding. John Rawls and Will Kymlicka tell us that freedom of conscience is our most fundamental human right—although they do not analyze the phenomenon of conscience, as Michael Walzer and George Kateb do.[2]

An enduring characteristic of liberalism, since the time of Locke, has been the deconstruction of conscience (as the contingent product of our upbringing, education, social circumstances, experience, and associations) and the championship of freedom of conscience as the most fundamental of human rights. Indeed, if individuals do not have the capacity or the entitlement to judge right and wrong, good and evil, then, as Edmund Burke and Jeremy Bentham argued, there are no human rights—just civil rights, rights that are the offspring of law, decided by civil authorities.[3] Perhaps an even stronger reason why conscience is integral to the justification of liberal democracy pertains to our claims for equality. While we are not equal with respect to our capacity to reason (or to calculate consequences), we are equal with respect to what matters most, namely, our moral choices. Hobbes deserves respect for providing an argument for human equality, distinguishing himself both from those liberals who simply stipulate the equality of human beings and from those who implicitly predicate it on equal susceptibility to pleasure and pain. However, the Hobbesian equal vulnerability to violent death lacks the moral purchase of equality in terms of our moral choices.

Thus rights, values, and conscience enjoy a central place in the moral vocabulary of liberalism. They function to articulate what liberals conceive to be demands of a good life. While philosophers have traditionally opposed the Right (whether Platonic justice or Kantian moral law) to the Good (whether conceived as happiness, virtue, or excellence), the distinction has not yet hit the streets. Most citizens of liberal democracies conceive of rights as good things, and think that the more rights there are, the better off the citizenry is. A proposition correlating the number of lawyers to the welfare of the citizenry would appear less intuitively obvious to most individuals—whereas in reality it is the same proposition as 'the more rights the better'. If there is one right as sacred as the right to freedom of conscience, it is the right to the best lawyer that money can buy.

Shylock's Rights championed right (both Platonic justice and Kantian moral law), while subjecting rights to critical analysis. Rights are the right (impersonal justice) personalized and privatized, made one's own—*my* rights, *your* rights, *her* rights, *our* rights, *their* rights. Whereas justice is not owned by anyone, rights are properties of individuals or groups. Justice exists between individuals; rights exist as personal possessions. Whereas the antithesis of right is wrong or injustice, the antitheses of rights are obligations. I have a right to do something that I am not obliged to do, and I have no right to do something that I am obliged to do. To have a right does not imply a worthy use of that right; the right to vote or to resist injustice does not entail a duty to do so. The right of national self-determination is independent of the prudent exercise of that right; rights entail the right to do wrong. If I have a right to my five-dollar bill, I have a right to burn it in front of a street person who has asked me for it, however morally unattractive it would be for me to do so.

I make these remarks not because I think rights are bad things, but to clarify the grammar or structured usage of rights-discourse. In fact, I think the entrenchment of rights in Canada is part curse and part blessing; what Charles Taylor calls 'comity' between Québécois and anglophone Canadians has become severely strained with the clamour of claims, the stridency of assertion of rights, while James Walker has made a strong case for the necessity of human-rights legislation for religious and ethnic minorities in Canada.[4] What I wish to establish here is that rights function to maximize choice; one can exercise or waive one's rights, one can use or abuse one's rights, one can exercise one's rights in morally attractive or unattractive ways.

Peter Singer thinks that human rights should be extended to animals because there is no proof that humans have immortal souls and animals do not.[5] Even without that proof, one might say that humans should have human rights and animals have animal rights. But if animals have rights, they cannot choose either to exercise or to waive them; in extending rights to animals, therefore, we lose one of the distinctive characteristics of rights-discourse.[6] To be sure, some defend fetal rights even though fetuses cannot claim or waive their rights, and others defend the merciful termination of life even when the sufferer cannot give her informed consent to death. But most liberals would be uncomfortable with a euthanasia policy that was not based on the informed consent of the dying person. Whereas the vocabulary of sanctity of life suggests an emphasis on preservation of life at all costs, a language of rights suggests choice, consent, will. Those who extend rights to animals, fetuses, and others incapable of consent risk eroding what is distinctive about the grammar of rights. Alternative moral vocabularies, such as those of obligation, care, love, need, interest, and so forth, could supplement the language of rights without eroding its distinctive structure. Little is to be gained by making rights to be an all-encompassing and self-sufficient moral vocabulary.

The reigning moral vocabulary, which competes and peacefully coexists with rights, is the language of values. If rights are the right personalized and privatized, values are the good conceived as personal or group possesssions—*my* values, *your* values, *her* values, *our* values, *their* values. To be sure, people talk of universal values or common values when they mean universal principles or common goods. Or they sometimes strain language in referring to objective values or intrinsic values—values without valuation. To be sure, Kant referred to human dignity (*Wuerde*) as *innern Wert* to distinguish it from *Preis*, or the *relativen Wert* of things.[7] But Kant thought the language of dignity or worthiness (*Wuerde*, *Wuerdigkeit*) limited the language of values (*Werte*). Nietzsche eliminated the Kantian limit of human dignity in his values-discourse; men and women, just like things, have more or less value, more or less power at their command, relative to others.

One of the unique features of values-discourse is that it has no ready converse. One speaks of virtue and vice, good and evil, true and false, beautiful and ugly, sacred and profane, right and wrong, rights and obligations, but one cannot speak of unvalues or disvalues. Values are always somehow good, or perhaps their goodness is a function of their being ours. Just as the idea of conscience stresses not so much that one's judgment is right as that it is one's own (not custom-built or fashionable or imitated from others), so one's values are one's own good, not some common good. As Nietzsche said, 'whatever can be common always has little value.'[8] For Locke, what is common is waste. Can we say that waste is the converse of value? But waste is valuelessness, not negative value. In ordinary usage, value is limited by valuelessness on the one hand and the invaluable on the other. For reasons we shall return to, the priceless is not the valueless but the invaluable. Perhaps the best antithesis to values is costs. For Locke, the value of consumable commodities is purchased by the pains or costs of labour. Since moral philosophy has parted company with economics and paired up with aesthetics, we have no cost side of the ledger sheet.

Thus there is no handy converse or antithesis to values. Aristotle's *Nicomachean Ethics* began with the proposition that all men aim at an apparent good. He did not seem to entertain the possibility of human beings' deliberately choosing evil. I cannot here go into what Aristotle meant by deliberate choice or weakness of will; I merely wish to suggest that talk about values and about conscience lies in the shadow of Aristotle's teleology. Our values and our consciences, while free, are somehow yoked to the apparent good. Perhaps what we mean by values is what Aristotle meant by apparent goods.

Aristotle did not make it clear whether human aims and apparent goods are related by definition or by fact. Are all human aims by definition apparent goods or values? Does the goodness of the object attract the human aim, or does the aim constitute the goodness of the pursuit? Whatever the answers to these questions, it is at least clear that, for Aristotle, there is a difference between an apparent good and a real one. Are values apparent goods, without the conceptual antithesis of real goods? For Plato, moral philosophy begins with conflicting opinions about what is good and culminates in unifying knowledge of what is good. Could we say that values are opinions about the good, divorced from Plato's and Aristotle's understanding that knowledge of the good is a real possibility?

If values are neither apparent goods (as opposed to real ones) nor real goods (as opposed to apparent ones), then they are neither opinions nor knowledge about what is good. How can we specify the form of values-discourse, other than by saying that it is limited by the idea of the valueless and the invaluable? In *The Genealogy of Values*, I argued that values-discourse is a form of anti-Platonic idealism. Nietzsche and Proust were presented as paradigmatic evaluators in that the former thought nothing was inherently good, and the latter, that no one was inherently lovable. Both considered morality a matter of taste and aesthetics, and both thought that the values of things and persons depended on subjective estimation. Whereas political philosophers from Plato and Aristotle to Mill and Marx thought economics to be an integral aspect of moral philosophy but did not refer to principles, virtues, loves, loyalties, or purposes as values, Nietzsche knew nothing about economics but converted the languages of moral purposes, virtues, and principles into the language of values. The signs of the flight from economics to aesthetics are manifest in common usage of values, which means anything but economic maximization. Nietzsche's Zarathustra says: 'Whatever has a price has little value.'

Anti-materialism inheres in values-discourse. Just as a person with taste lacks crude sensual tastes, a person with values seems to lack sensual desires. If we were to conduct a survey on the good things in life, we would probably get responses of rare roast beef, a vivid sunset, an exciting sporting event, or perhaps Margaret Atwood's ideal of multiple orgasms with a spouse who washes the dishes. But these good things never appear in survey research on human values. If any of the good things above were mentioned in a survey of human values, the surveyor would think the respondent had 'no values' or was too stupid to understand the question. No one responds 'constant sex' to a question about her values.

Talk about values seems to preclude talk about material needs. If one were to say 'I value food, you value health, she values housing', one would expect that I am not in extreme want of food but that I like good food and am able to pay for it from a fairly expansive budget, that you are not longing to recover from a severe illness but that you spend a lot of time jogging or doing aerobics and a lot of money on vitamins and health clubs, and that she is not homeless but houseproud, willing and able to devote a large share of an elastic demand curve on feathering her nest. Values speak of choices, not of needs; they comprise a language of the options of the marketplace, not of the mandatory and universal provision of a welfare state.

If we were to overhear the sentence, 'I value you very highly', we would be inclined to think 'Oh, oh! She's telling him to get lost. She neither needs him nor loves him. She might esteem various qualities of his body, mind, and character and may not even be irritated by these estimable qualities, but they are not indispensable to her being. She is looking elsewhere.' Values are relational and exchangeable goods; they represent the language of the marketplace, of trade and trade-offs, not of deep loves or strong loyalties. As Heidegger said: 'No one dies for mere values.'[9]

Values-discourse idealizes both the good and the necessary things of life, or idealizes them in harmony with the demands of the market. Values are luxury goods in the marketplace of moral options. If values-discourse constitutes an idealization of life experience, it also falsifies life experience or converts the way we live into the way we want to be seen to live. For example, survey research on Canadian and American values indicates that Canadians value racial tolerance above all else, and Americans, independent-mindedness. May I limit myself to saying that there is as much truth in the one self-image as the other.

What then is the cost side of the language of values? It has colonized other moral languages very rapidly; we forget that for the first two decades of this century, Harvard-trained social scientists spoke about 'walues', suggesting either the alien nature of this new term or the Germanic origins of the professors who introduced the lingo that is now as American as apple pie. It has converted the language of virtues into values, but not the converse—vices. All values are positive, not negative; the converse of good is evil, of beautiful is ugly, of true is false, of holy is unholy, but we have no converse of moral, aesthetic, cognitive, and religious values. The new lingo has converted loves and needs into values, but, whereas 'loves' has a converse of hates and 'needs', superfluities, 'values' has no known antithesis. Values-discourse flattens the moral landscape. Constitutive attachments and optional embellishments are conceived as the products of choice, will, evaluation; everything is subjected to relativistic estimation at the marketplace. The civic realm of universal principles and the personal realm of strong ties and unshakeable loyalties are subjected to the imperial sway of market evaluation. Social democratic principles of universal provision (of health care, day care, public broadcasting, etc.) are undermined when it becomes widely accepted that each person has her own values.

Aside from the hasty and unreflective translation of other moral languages into the language of imperial commerce, what are the other costs of values-discourse? Values, unlike opinions, are not openly provisional, but exhibit a subjective certainty, a point of view that likes where it is. 'These are my values' is not an invitation to discussion but a declaration of cultivation, a display for purposes of impressing others. 'These are my opinions about health care' is an invitation to discussion, opening oneself to differences of opinion and the possibility of resolving them through reasoned debate. Values-discourse resists the educative experience of political dialogue or philosophic conversation. Values, as Richard Rorty says, are 'final vocabularies', not in the sense that we take our stand on values—one trades in values as one stands on principle—but in the sense that there is nothing more to be said, that philosophic or civic dialogue about the meaning of the good life is pointless.

The language of conscience shares some common family features with the language of values, although, like rights, it is an older and healthier sister than the language of values. But not so old. Hitler was wrong to say: 'Conscience is a Jewish invention. It is a blemish like circumcision.'[10] He was wrong because the word 'conscience' first appears in the New Testament. The Old Testament equivalent of the New Testament *syneidesis* was *leb* (heart). There are no Sanskrit, Chinese, or Japanese equivalents to *syneidesis*, *conscientia*, the old English *inwit*, or the German *Gewissen*. The first article of the Universal Declaration of Human Rights declares: 'All human beings are born free and equal in dignity and rights. They are endowed with reason and conscience and should act towards one another in a spirit of brotherhood.' If many languages do not have a word answering to the concept of conscience, one might think the Universal Declaration to be a form of Western and liberal imperialism. The Chinese translate conscience as *liang xing* and the Japanese as *ryo shin* (both literally mean good heart).

The heart is internal or hidden, as conscience connotes interiority. The old English *inwit*, which James Joyce attempted to revive in *Ulysses*, brings out this innermost aspect of humanity. The heart may have its reasons but does not usually provide them. While reason and speech belong together (*logos* means both reason and speech), conscience is 'dumb'; as Martin Heidegger said, 'Only in keeping silent does the conscience call.'[11] Conscience, unlike reason, is not communicative. If the call of conscience is heard more clearly away from the crowd, it addresses oneself, not others. Its reasons—'I could not live with myself if I did that' or 'I should not want to become the kind of person who participates in that'—are not communicable; if stated publicly, they are self-promotion.

If conscience, like the heart, is *alogos* (speechless), it does not bear the heart's connotation of love, compassion, or benevolence. Jean Calvin wrote: 'He who trusts only his conscience and neglects reputation is cruel.'[12] Most thinkers of the eighteenth-century Enlightenment rejected the dictates of conscience for this reason and replaced the inner-directed moral individualist of the seventeenth century with the sociable man, sympathetic and benevolent to others, governed by public opinion or moved by desire for social esteem and fear of social censure. The good-heartedness of eighteenth-century moralists constituted a rejection of seventeenth-century individualism, whether Hobbesian egoism, Miltonian conscience, or the Lockean incoherent mixture of the two. The reintroduction of conscience into moral philosophy by Rousseau, Kant, and later John Mill constituted a repudiation of the other-oriented character of Enlightenment social psychology, its view that conduct is regulated by public opinion, by social approval or disapproval. Conscientious duty seemed heartless to the moral sentimentalism of Shaftesbury, Hume, and Diderot, as it may seem to contemporary sentimentalists.

The reason and conscience with which, according to the Universal Declaration of Human Rights, we are all endowed cannot then be identified with head and heart. Enlightenment reason elevated the heart (in the sense of the social affections) while deprecating conscience (the divine within humans) as anarchic egalitarianism. Conscience is tied in relations of attraction and repulsion to reason; often they are identified and then they split apart as conscienceless reason (bourgeois prudence or scientific technique) and irrational conscience (godly psychopathy or revolutionary romanticism).

While reason and speech belong together, conscience is 'dumb', *alogos*. If one's values or the dictates of conscience are proclaimed, they become self-advertising, which is the essence of values-discourse but denatures the call of conscience or turns it into its opposite. Let us examine the unthought relationship of reason and conscience with respect to conscientious objection to warfare, a central, if contested, aspect of the liberal tradition, and John Rawls's position on the subject. We may well agree with Rawls that 'a conscript army is less likely to be an instrument of unjustified foreign adventures' than a professional army.[13] Inverting the practice of some liberal democracies, Rawls maintained that conscientious objection must be based on political, not religious, principles.[14] Our horizontal obligations to our fellow citizens have political primacy over our vertical obligation to God. Individuals have no right to conscientious objection in just wars or when the defence of liberty is at stake. Those who refuse to be conscripted into military service must demonstrate that war aims are unjust. However, Rawls recommended that liberal states accept limited conscientious refusal and civil disobedience to encourage opponents to express their opposition publicly and to appeal to publicly accepted principles. Rawls replaces the silent call of conscience with public debate eschewing religious principles for the overlapping consensus of liberal democracies.

The difficulty with Rawls's proposal is that some individuals cannot put into words the grounds of their refusal to participate in the military, even if they have mastered the difference between just and unjust wars. For some individuals, life would not be worth living if they had to kill others in a cause they found questionable. An alternative to Rawls's proposal would be for liberal democracies to provide some dangerous alternatives to military service (in hospitals, jails, mines, fire departments, rescue services) to differentiate those unwilling to kill from those unwilling to die, or to distinguish genuine conscientious objection from Hobbesian rights of cowardice. For Hobbesians unwilling to die for their country, the loss of citizenship might be the appropriate response: as Hobbes said, banishment is not punishment but just a change of air. That is, the institutionalized encouragement of dumb conscience, as well as fostering communicative competence or enlightened intersubjectivity, would be no danger to, and might be a worthy goal of, liberal democracies.

An enduring feature of liberal theory is the deconstruction of conscience and the celebration of freedom of conscience. When Richard Rorty praised Freud for demonstrating the contingency of our moral standards,[15] he did not indicate that the deconstruction of conscience appears to inhere in liberalism. Locke's *Essay Concerning Human Understanding* (I.iii.8) insisted that conscience is not an innate practical principle but is a received opinion, contingent upon one's upbringing, education, and social circumstances. To be sure, conscience played an important role in Locke's *Letters concerning Toleration* and *Two Treatises of Government* in determining the legitimacy and illegitimacy of governments and of their violent overthrow. John Mill deprecated Bentham (and implicitly his father, as well as many thinkers of *les philosophes*) for ignoring the motive of conscience.[16] Mill thought conscience was not innate but acquired, developed through the natural desire to be at one with with one's fellow human beings.[17] Although Mill distinguished between the internal sanction of conscience and the external sanction of social censure, Mill scholars cannot decide whether the inner sanction of conscience is ultimately reducible to social approbation or disapprobation. David Lyons writes:

> Mill clearly associates external and internal sanctions very closely, thinking of them all as means of social control and distinguishable from other devices, such as taxation, by an element of condemnation. But I think we do no favor to Mill if we emphasize his assimilation of internal to external standards.[18]

However, Mill certainly needs favours if we are to make a coherent position from his apparently opposing views that men of conscience stand up to public opinion and that conscience is ultimately derivative of public opinion. The Canadian liberal journalist Michael Ignatieff carries on the grand tradition of holding conscience to be a socially constructed myth, while waving this mythic weapon at those less caring than he.[19]

Conscience and Its Critics shows that Enlightenment thinkers tended to oppose freedom for conscience (its irrational, egalitarian, and anarchic character if expressed in political practice) but to favour freedom of conscience (insofar as it was limited to thought, not action). Kant, so untypical of the Enlightenment in his critique of empiricism, sensualism, utilitarianism, and social sensibilities, joined up with Bentham in enunciating the Enlightenment's creed of good citizenship: to criticize freely while obeying punctually.[20]

Freedom of conscience has been construed by radicals such as Milton, Paine, and Blake, as well as contemporary liberals such as Kymlicka and Rawls, to mean the separation of church and state. However, Hume, Voltaire, and Diderot followed Hobbes in favouring a policy of skeptical tolerance; such a policy would be most effectively advanced, and religious enthusiasm diminished, by an established church that ceded to the state ultimate authority in ecclesiastical policy. John Mill sounded a Humean note when he suggested that putting the odious Irish Catholic clergy on the government payroll would diminish their zeal or motivation to proselytize; Mill thought establishing an Irish Catholic church would turn its priesthood into pampered and sluggish civil servants, as harmless as Anglicans.[21] The United States has pursued the policy of separating church and state, while Britain and Canada have followed a policy of combining toleration and church establishment. One wonders whether Rawls and Kymlicka support the religious zeal that seems to accompany the separation of church and state.

Freedom of conscience means freedom of religion, or, more specifically, freedom for those non-ceremonial religions or faiths that do not take up public space or attempt to bind (*re-ligare*) citizens together in a public communion or community. Freedom of conscience fosters private, interior religions and challenges public communion; it takes the *ligio* from religion. Freedom of conscience also means freedom of thought and of speech. Mill's celebrated *On Liberty* provides us with an unsurpassed defence of freedom of speech but tells us nothing about conscientious objection to war, civil dissent, rights of parliamentarians to break caucus discipline, rights of defendants and jurors, and so forth. Is the last word of the liberal Enlightenment to speak freely and obey punctually? Diderot wrote: 'We must speak out against senseless laws until they're reformed and, in the meanwhile, abide by them. Anyone who on the strength of his own personal authority violates a bad law thereby authorizes everyone else to violate the good.'[22]

Conscience is the language of moral subjectivity about which liberals are most ambivalent. Whereas reason searches for truth, conscience searches for one's own truth. Whereas individuals are unequal with respect to their reason in the opinion of Plato, Aristotle, St Thomas, Voltaire, Hume, Diderot, and Condorcet, individuals are equal with respect to their conscience in the opinion of Luther, Lilburne, Rousseau, Kant, Blake, Wollstonecraft, and Godwin. The question is: if rationalism, classical or modern, has no place for irrational conscience, what becomes of democratic claims to equality?

If conscience is banished from a liberal moral vocabulary, except in formulaic invocations of freedom of conscience, what becomes of the language of rights and values? Diderot, in his article 'Natural Right' for *L'Encyclopédie*, had the skeptical penetration to see that natural rights and conscience stood or fell together.[23] The Universal Declaration of Human Rights clearly asserts that human rights and conscience stand together. But if the right of individual judgment of right and wrong is dismissed as uncivilized—and Diderot, Bentham, and Burke were by no means alone in the eighteenth century in thinking so—then we are left with civil rights, rights that are the offspring of laws imposed by civil authorities steeped in tradition or utilitarian doctrine. But, in addition to civil rights, we shall all have our own values to supplement our moral vocabulary. And values, as I hope to have shown, do not have the cloudy, spectral, and metaphysical quality Enlightenment thinkers attributed to conscience. Stripped of the metaphysics of conscience, values are consumer choices.

NOTES

1. Charles Fried, *An Anatomy of Values: Problems of Personal and Social Choice* (Cambridge, Mass.: Harvard University Press, 1970), 209.
2. John Rawls, *Political Liberalism* (New York: Columbia University Press, 1993), 58–61, 310-15, 335, and Will Kymlicka, *Multicultural Citizenship* (Oxford: Oxford University Press, 1995), 26, 158, assert that freedom of conscience is the most fundamental human right but do not provide any analysis of the concept of conscience, as do Michael Walzer, *Thick and Thin: Moral Argument at Home and Abroad* (Notre Dame: University of Notre Dame Press, 1994), 97–104 and George Kateb, 'Socratic Integrity', in *Integrity and Conscience: Nomos XL*, ed. Ian Shapiro and Robert Adams (New York: New York University Press, 1998), 77–112. To be sure, contemporary political philosophers talk a lot about *autonomy*, or Kantian autonomy de-transcendentalized or Kant without God, freedom, and immortality. However much *conscience* and *autonomy* overlap, they are in crucial respects distinct. Whether in the stronger Kantian or weaker contemporary formulations, autonomy is tied more closely to law than conscience, which traditionally stands in non-conforming or dissenting opposition to law. Second, while Kantian practical reason prescribes for all moral agents, conscience is normally thought to prescribe only for oneself; my conscience does not prescribe what you should do. Thus autonomy is more universalist or bureaucratic than conscience, which is more anarchic or antinomian than autonomy.
3. See Jeremy Waldron, *Nonsense upon Stilts: Bentham, Burke and Marx on the Rights of Man* (London: Methuen, 1987).
4. James W. St. G. Walker, *'Race', Rights and the Law in the Supreme Court of Canada* (Toronto: Wilfrid Laurier Press, 1997).
5. Peter Singer, 'Why I believe great apes should have human rights', *The Times Educational Supplement* 1372 (19 Feb. 1999), 22.
6. To be sure, I think human beings have moral obligations to animals and I would favour a complete ban on the use of animals in psychological experiments. As a teenager, I worked for the National Research Council at the University of British Columbia, purportedly doing mathematics but actually cleaning up after animals and destroying them after experiments were complete. The thousands of hairless mice I destroyed, after their use in experiments for skin cancer, gave me dreams for years afterwards about facing a rodent in a judge's wig with the excuse that I was just obeying orders. However, I did not find it as unconscionable as our experiments on monkeys in which electrodes were placed in the monkeys' brains to measure their reactions to psychologists sneaking up behind them and shouting 'boo'. Indeed, we proved that the closer to the monkey and the louder the shout, the greater the measurable reaction. The monkeys that did not die in the course of the experimentation were mercifully destroyed. In short, I strongly believe that we have a moral obligation not to inflict unnecessary suffering on animals, but I do not think they have a correlative right not to be used for human welfare—because they can neither claim nor waive that right. My position should only be troubling to those who think rights-discourse constitutes a free-standing and self-sufficient moral system.

7. Immanuel Kant, *Fundamental Principles of the Metaphysics of Ethics*, trans. Thomas K. Abbott (London: Longmans Green, 1919), 63.
8. Friedrich Nietzsche, *Beyond Good and Evil*, trans. Walter Kaufmann (New York: Vintage, 1966), 53.
9. Martin Heidegger, 'The Age of the World Picture', in *The Question of Technology and Other Essays*, trans. William Lovitt (New York: Harper and Row, 1977), 142.
10. Herman Rauschning, *Hitler Speaks* (London: Thornton Butterworth, 1939), 220.
11. Martin Heidegger, *Being and Time*, trans. J. Macquarrie and E. Robinson (New York: Harper and Row, 1962), 343.
12. Jean Calvin, *Seneca's de Clementia*, cited in David Lee Foxgrover, *John Calvin's Understanding of Conscience* (Ph.D. dissertation, Claremont Graduate School, 1978), 244–5.
13. John Rawls, *A Theory of Justice* (Cambridge, Mass.: Harvard University Press), 380.
14. Ibid., 365, 377.
15. Richard Rorty, *Contingency, Irony, and Solidarity* (Cambridge: Cambridge University Press, 1989), 30.
16. John Stuart Mill, *Collected Works*, ed. John M. Robson (Toronto: University of Toronto Press, 1969), vol. 10, 15, 95.
17. Ibid., 231; also, vol. 15, 649–50.
18. David Lyons, *Rights, Welfare, and Mill's Moral Theory* (New York: Oxford University Press, 1994), 129.
19. Michael Ignatieff, *The Warrior's Honor: Ethnic War and the Modern Conscience* (Toronto: Viking, 1998), 12.
20. Jeremy Bentham, *A Fragment on Government*, ed. J.H. Burns and H.L.A. Hart (Cambridge: Cambridge University Press, 1988), 10; Immanuel Kant, *Foundation of the Metaphysics of Morals and What is Enlightenment?*, trans. Lewis W. Beck (Chicago: University of Chicago Press, 1950), 287, 291.
21. Mill, *Collected Works*, vol. 6, 85–7.
22. Denis Diderot, *Political Writings*, trans. John Hope Mason and Robert Wokler (Cambridge: Cambridge University Press, 1992), 74.
23. Ibid., 17.

Weaving a Work

Barry Cooper

When the editors asked me for a 'sketch' of the 'basic thrust' of my 'work', I was—like many of the individuals whose essays are collected here—flattered, of course, but I was even more perplexed. What 'work'? I have published things, but was it all coherent enough to be worthy of the name 'work'? On reflection two things came to me. The first was the image of weaving, to which I shall return at the end of this essay. The second was a remark that Marshall McLuhan once made. Canada, he once said, is like the DEW line—a chain of radar stations across the arctic intended to provide a distant early warning of incoming Soviet munitions from across the pole. In some respects the west, especially Alberta and BC, is central Canada's DEW line. It is a part of the country where social, political, and intellectual experiments have taken place in an atmosphere of friendly antagonism to the rest of the country. We westerners enjoy what McLuhan called 'freedom of comment, a kind of playful awareness of issues' unknown in Toronto, Ottawa, or Montreal. 'They take themselves too damn seriously; they have no choice.'[1] McLuhan was talking about Washington, London, and Paris rather than the great metropoles of central Canada, but for a westerner the point is clear.

Like other human beings, people who become political scientists are formed by their experiences. A Texan educated at Hotchkiss, Yale, and Harvard who takes a position at the University of Manitoba, with a scholarly concern for the evolution of liberalism, will bring a different complex of experience to bear on the question than will a Nova Scotian educated at Moncton's Beaverbrook High, Dalhousie, and Cambridge who ends up at Waterloo. This general observation, it seems to me, applies with particular force for westerners, whether they live in Edmonton or Montreal.

As a matter of biographical fact, I was born in Vancouver and educated at a BC boarding school, UBC, and Duke. I taught at Bishop's University, McGill, and York before coming to Calgary in 1981. During the summers of my youth I spent time on the ranches of my uncles in the foothills west of Nanton, Alberta, on fishing boats off the west coast, in logging camps, and on a pipeline crew. My first political recollection was of my two grandfathers discussing the victory of W.A.C. Bennett in 1952. My maternal grandfather, born in Newfoundland, and at one time a member of the IWW, asked: 'Social credit? What does it mean? It's not socialism; I know that.' My paternal grandfather, a lifelong Tory who had served as the first mayor of Nanton, knew about the Social Credit of Premiers Aberhart and Manning but confessed that Bennett's politics looked rather different.

Several years later I was enrolled in Alan Cairns's seminar on Canadian politics and I had occasion to recollect the discussion of my two grandfathers. In an offhand comment, Professor Cairns said he considered it rather odd that, in a province that had known Social Credit and the NDP for the better part of a generation, they were still called minor third parties. 'They're not "minor" here,' he said. My grandfathers' struggle to make sense of political reality using a vocabulary developed from another place and Professor Cairns's obvious and commonsensical resistance to a kind of alien conceptualization were two modes of regional self-understanding that, I now see, were mutually reinforcing.

I wrote my honours essay on the politics of the United Fisherman and Allied Workers' Union under the direction of Ed Black. Guided by Homer Stevens, a devout Communist, the UFAWU had a lively political presence among my shipmates. The editorials of George North in *The Fisherman* were a rich source of pro-Soviet opinion, much of which was reproduced and discussed in my honours essay. I also employed Roberto Michels's notion of an 'iron law of oligarchy', which I had read about in a course on political parties.

Walter Young, who was a strong supporter of the NDP as well as an analyst of their fortunes, considered my appropriation of Michels dubious and my analysis of the ideological commitments of the leadership of the UFAWU misguided. He asked me a number of probing questions on Michels. Did I, for example, think his treatment of the SDP in his book *Political Parties* was fair? I said I had no idea if it was fair since I had only read Part Six, which deals with the 'iron law'. Professor Young was not pleased with this answer, but I was excused—perhaps 'saved' would be a better word—by Don Smiley, who was the chairman of my examination committee. 'Oh c'mon, Walter,' he said in his unmistakable voice, 'nobody reads anything in Michels except the iron law stuff.' Professor Smiley's remarks prompted my first realization that distinguished scholars such as Professor Young might also hold political views about pragmatic political affairs.

When I left for graduate school I had been to England once, to play rugby; to California and Hawaii a dozen times for family vacations; and once to Ottawa for a public-speaking contest. I was not quite a clever, ambitious provincial like Julian Sorel, but I was very aware of how much I didn't know. I knew something about Canadian politics and history, thanks to the presence of so many outstanding Canadian scholars at UBC. But I had taken more courses in classics than in political philosophy,[2] and upon graduation was far more interested in spending the summer in Europe with Charles Pentland (currently teaching international relations at Queen's) than in starting more serious study in Durham, North Carolina.

I stopped at Duke for a couple of days on the way to Europe. Fred Fletcher, now teaching at York, met me and showed me around. Ed Black had directed both Fletcher and me and a few other UBC graduates to Duke; I was attracted by the Commonwealth Studies Center and the generous support provided for students interested in the Commonwealth and from the Commonwealth. It had been established in the mid-1950s, chiefly through the efforts of Taylor Cole. The Secretary of the Commonwealth Center, for the first year I was at Duke, was Peter Meekison, who also was a former UBC undergraduate (in engineering). Meekison soon left for the University of Alberta for a career of great distinction, most notably contributing to the fashioning of s.33 of the 1982 Constitution Act.

There were, in other words, a number of outstanding Canadian students at Duke, so that I felt thoroughly comfortable pursuing the study of Canadian politics in the piedmont of North Carolina.[3] Professor Black had told me before I left UBC that I should be sure to take the political philosophy courses of John Hallowell, but I felt no particular attraction to political theory. Indeed, I had grave reservations about the whole question of going to graduate school. Perhaps I should have become a lawyer after all.

When I returned from what had been an eye-opening European tour with Pentland, I was prepared to do some studying. Durham was a long drive from Washington and an even longer one from Atlanta, and the Duke Library was enormous. In addition, a new faculty member, Allan Kornberg, had joined the Department. Kornberg was from Winnipeg's North End; he had played for the Blue Bombers and supported his family through graduate school at Michigan by wrestling professionally. He was superbly trained in quantitative analysis and a strong believer in the 'behavioural persuasion' that I had been introduced to by a more skeptical Kal Holsti in the honours seminar at UBC. Kornberg's enthusiasm was contagious and I set about mastering the intricacies of parametric and non-parametric statistics. For two summers I sweltered in Ann Arbor at the Institute for Behavioral Research, learning all I could about causal modelling, factor analysis, and matrix algebra. I wrote my master's thesis on the changing methodologies of the voting studies. At one point Tom Flanagan, now a colleague in Calgary, and I wrote a 'purist' non-parametric analysis of V.O. Key's classic study of southern politics. It was not, however, accepted for publication, which puzzled us a great deal.

Flanagan had gone to Notre Dame and was already familiar with much of the material that Professor Hallowell was introducing to me. In particular, he had taken several courses from Eric Voegelin, who lectured regularly at Notre Dame. Flanagan wrote his M.A. thesis on Spinoza; we finished our comps together in record time and he left for Berlin to begin work on his Ph.D. thesis on Robert Musil. I stayed in Durham, taught American government to Duke undergraduates, and decided I was not prepared to do a lot of data analysis for my dissertation. Having figured out how to perform some fairly complex mathematical and statistical procedures—long before the advent of SPSS and personal computers—I seemed to have lost interest in quantitative analysis, and decided to write my Ph.D. on something else.

Professor Kornberg[4] understood my position, and John Hallowell was willing to supervise my Ph.D. work. But what would I write on? Edward Tiryakian in sociology and William Poteat in the Divinity School had both taught courses that required me to read *The Phenomenology of Perception* by Maurice Merleau-Ponty. At the time I hardly understood a word of what Merleau-Ponty was writing about, but a footnote, on Marxism, suggested that he might have some political writings as well as the opaque philosophy I had read. Besides, Professor Tiryakian found Merleau-Ponty important for his own 'existential-phenomenological-sociological' work, so I was confident I could find something somewhere that pertained to political science.

I asked Professor Hallowell if I could write on Merleau-Ponty and he had but one question: 'Is he dead? You see, Mr Cooper,' he went on, 'if he's not dead he may have something more to say.' When he learned that Merleau-Ponty had, indeed, fallen silent, he agreed that I should go to Paris to do the necessary research.[5]

I arrived in Paris in time for the last of the *événements* of May 1968. The demonstrations and the ferocity of the CRS, the riot police, were impressive, but I had the feeling that voter registration in Durham was politically more significant, and certainly more useful. When Raymond Aron published *La Révolution introuvable* in the fall of 1968 I found I agreed with his analysis, though with regret.[6] By then I knew that Aron had known Merleau-Ponty, Sartre, and the rest of the *Temps modernes* people and that he had broken ranks with them shortly after the Liberation. I sought him out, bearing a letter of introduction from Professor Hallowell. Aron was generous with his time and pleased to answer my naive questions. Most important, he told me of Alexandre Kojève. 'Kojève,' he said, 'is the colossus behind Merleau.' He added, 'I do not believe in that "theory of recognition" business.' I hardly knew what he was talking about, though Merleau-Ponty's *Humanisme et terreur* is fully infused with a Kojèvian *problématique*.[7]

I filed away the name of this Kojève fellow for future reference, and continued the *explication de texte* for my dissertation.

I returned to Durham for an oral examination on my thesis, passed, and was quickly hired to teach at Bishop's University in Lennoxville. The students were pleasant but no more intellectually engaging than the faculty. After Christmas I also taught a course on Marx at McGill. I had been recruited to replace a popular but untenured teacher who was, moreover, a practising Marxist. His practice evidently led him afoul of the administration and he was summarily deprived of his position. I inherited a large and committed collection of students. We spent the introductory class disputing the reading list and the significance of the Paris 'events'. One of the people present disagreed strongly with the Aronian perspective I had adopted and ended his polemic oration with the words: 'I know; I was there!' He was astonished and deflated when I replied, 'So was I.' There were many fewer students present the following week. I am still unsure whether that was because I was not an appropriate sympathizer or because I insisted we read nothing but the texts of Marx: no Marcuse, no Althusser, no Adorno.

Charles Taylor and John Shingler provided plenty of intellectual stimulation and I would have been honoured to remain at McGill. Through a series of administrative inefficiencies, however, no offer was forthcoming and I moved to York for the 1970s.

Toronto, like Montreal, had plenty of intellectual life. At York, one could profitably disagree with Neal and Ellen Wood; at the University of Toronto, C.B. Macpherson presided over a devoted coterie of students and Allan Bloom soon arrived to present a worthy counterpoint. At York I taught courses on classical political thought (which turned my attention again to Voegelin's work on Plato and Aristotle), politics and literature, and Canadian political thought.

York and the Canada Council were both generous then, and had modest funds available for junior faculty to undertake unproven projects. About 1973, I organized a conference on Canadian political thought. Some of my colleagues and a few of the participants queried whether there was such a thing. I was confident that it existed, but I was motivated even more by the experiences I had had discussing public affairs with my Toronto friends as well as with Toronto political scientists. I was puzzled not so much by the fact that so many of them had found a spiritual home in the NDP as by the fact that we seemed to be operating within quite distinct visions of the country.

For example, C.B. Macpherson's famous study *Democracy in Alberta* was hailed almost universally as a classic, a superb penetration of the problems, and a template for what was then just beginning to be called 'western alienation'.[8] But at UBC I had already learned that Macpherson's study, while interesting, was limited by what Allan Cairns had called its 'quasi-Marxist' approach. On presenting the book to classes, I was struck by how deeply it was at variance with my own experience of Alberta and the recollections of my family. The York conference, particularly the work presented by younger colleagues, including Rainer Knopff and David Bercuson, now also colleagues at Calgary, helped clarify, at least in my own mind, what had merely puzzled (or occasionally exasperated) me before.[9]

In the meantime I was pursuing the hint about the importance of Kojève that Aron had given me. With the aid of Canada Council and later SSHRCC research grants, and a bilateral exchange program between Canada and France, I was able to spend a considerable amount of time in France, chiefly in Paris but also at the Hegel and Marx Research Center in Poitiers. I undertook some translations, but mostly I immersed myself in French political and philosophical texts.[10] Ten years after I had defended my thesis on Merleau-Ponty, I published an extensively revised version.[11] In 1984 I published a big book on Kojève and Hegel, as well as a study of Foucault that, although it was written later, appeared prior to the Hegel book.[12] A few years later Frank Fukuyama gained international notoriety with his exposition of Kojève, and Foucault has become a major intellectual industry.[13] So far as I was concerned, by 1980 I thought I had an adequate contextual understanding of post-war French political thinking and how it related to the traumatic political events that country has endured.

I had also been studying Voegelin, not least because, to my mind, he provided a more comprehensive and intelligible context than the French philosophers, one that made it easier for me critically to understand their reflections. One of the fundamental interpretative assumptions of Voegelinian political science was set forth in the early pages of his most famous book, *The New Science of Politics*:

> Human society is not merely a fact, or an event, in the external world to be studied by an observer like a natural phenomenon. Though it has externality as one of its important components, it is as a whole a little world, a cosmion, illuminated with meaning from within by the human beings who continuously create and bear it as the mode and condition of their self-realization. It is illuminated through an elaborate symbolism . . . and this symbolism illuminates it with meaning in so far as the symbols make the internal structure of such a cosmion, the relations between its members and groups of members, as well as its existence as a whole, transparent for the mystery of human existence. The self-illumination of society through symbols is an integral part of social reality, and . . . inversely, the symbols express the experience that man is fully man by virtue of his participation in a whole which transcends his particular existence, by virtue of his participation in the *xynon*, the common, as Heraclitus called it, the first Western thinker who differentiated this concept. As a consequence, every human society has an understanding of itself through a variety of symbols, sometimes highly differentiated language symbols, independent of political science; . . . hence, when political science begins, it does not begin with a *tabula rasa* on which it can inscribe its concepts; it will inevitably start from the rich body of self-interpretation of a society and proceed by critical clarification of socially pre-existent symbols.[14]

Voegelin's work on the history of political philosophy, as well as his own political science, is sufficiently complex to engage lesser minds for a very long time. Before I began serious study of his work, on its own terms, I *used* the insight expressed in the above quotation to clarify the perplexities I had experienced with respect to Canadian politics and political thought.

Specifically, if the symbolism by which central Canadians expressed their understanding of the country—as found, for example, in the initial terms of reference of the 1963 Royal Commission on Bilingualism and Biculturalism—were opaque to westerners and standing in need of a more or less elaborate interpretation, then this symbolic disjunction corresponded to, and expressed, a social and political reality. Moreover, since it is the purpose of political science to provide a conceptually clear account of political reality—as Voegelin also taught—then any political scientist interested in the reality of Canadian politics had better pay attention to the symbolisms by which Canadians gave meaning to their varied existences as Canadians.

Stating such a methodological position is easier than carrying it out in practice. In the event, I undertook an extensive survey of the *Canadian Historical Review* and associated publications, *The Canadian Journal of Economics and Political Science* and its successor journals, *Canadian Literature*, and several smaller publications such as the *Journal of Canadian Studies*. In addition, following what I had learned from Foucault, I looked at such famous series as the 'Frontiers of Settlement', the 'Makers of Canada' and, of course, the SSRC series on Social Credit which included the famous Macpherson contribution already mentioned. The Voegelinian analysis brought into focus the symbolism by which Canadians have expressed their variegated experiences; the Foucauldean analysis examined the study of western politics from a base in central Canada as the deployment of 'power-knowledge'. For example, Pierre Berton wrote a very popular book on the Canadian Pacific Railway called *The National Dream*, but I can recall my grandfather discussing the CPR as if it were a vivid nightmare both for him and his neighbours. What did this conflict in interpretations, symbolism, and experience mean?

In my course on Canadian political thought I occasionally assigned poetry and fiction as well as more explicitly political texts such as Lord Durham's great *Report* or the *Confederation Debates*. The problems that arose in interpreting the conflicting symbols in the literature of Upper Canada (Susanna Moodie, for example) and of the prairies (Wallace Stegner, for example), recapitulated the problems I was discovering in the writing of Canadian history (Donald Creighton versus W.L. Morton, for example) or the deployment of massive and well-funded research operations based at Toronto or Queen's to provide an authorized account of western politics and society.

Eventually, I encountered a suitable formula in the 'practical criticism' of Northrop Frye. History, said Frye, is a story of what happens; myth is a story of what happens all the time. Myth, in other words, provides the interpretative context for history. On Frye's argument, the privileged vehicle for the articulation of myth is imaginative literature; the reality it expresses, he has argued at great length, and in several places, is the experience of identity, which is local and regional, not national.[15] The most important and controversial conclusion I drew from Frye's literary studies (along with the work of other literary critics such as Dennis Duffy)[16] is that the political unit Canada has no identity. It has several identities expressed in several regional and literary mythologies. What is particularly significant, at least for a westerner, is that the parochial myth of southern Ontario that gives genuine expression to a regional identity is expressed in the misleading language of a pan-Canadian 'identity'.

On occasion there have been some comic political consequences. On 25 March 1983, Joe Clark, of High River, Alberta, described William Davis, of Brampton, Ontario, as a regional candidate for the leadership of the federal Progressive Conservative Party, which leadership Clark eventually won. On 7 June, four days before the convention voted to select a new leader, Premier Davis hosted a dinner at an exclusive Toronto club for 150 people who had helped in his bid for the leadership. In his remarks to his supporters that night he commented on Clark's statement, which had been made some ten weeks earlier—a very long time in politics. 'I am not a regional candidate,' he said, 'I believe in Canada, not a community of communities,' a term that Clark had borrowed from Frye by way of Montesquieu, and had used to describe what the historian J.M.S. Careless had called Canadians' limited identities.[17] As one observer noted, 'Davis's eyes filled with tears as he spoke of his commitment and his audience was visibly moved.'[18] The image of an Ontario premier weeping while the hearts of his otherwise hard-nosed political supporters swelled with patriotic pride was, to a westerner, ridiculous and laughable. That is, westerners were tempted to write off the whole embarrassing scene as evidence of the regrettable inability of Ontario, and especially that part of it centred on Toronto, to deal with a genuine challenge to its own self-understanding and self-satisfaction. No westerner, not even the accommodating Mr Clark, would have taken Premier Davis's words at face value.

What William Davis *meant* in his criticism of Joe Clark was that his myth of Canada, of the old colony of Canada, of Upper and Lower Canada, of Canada East and Canada West, of Ontario and Quebec, reflects the real Canada. In homage to three great mythographers of an earlier day, Harold Innis, Donald Creighton, and Arthur Lower, we may call it the myth of Laurentian Canada. Combining the arguments of Foucault, Voegelin, and Frye, along with other literary critics, I have written a number of scholarly essays on this subject, as well as a good deal of journalism.[19]

Turning back to political philosophy, the conclusion to which I was drawn in *The End of History* was not that 'history' was 'ended', which is an imaginary ideological conceit, but that (as Fukuyama argued, at least in part) it forms the ideological horizon for modern self-understanding. In Hegelian (and Marxian) symbolism, this kind of self-consciousness was based upon a particular configuration of what Kojève called 'given-being', his translation of Hegel's *Sein*, and more or less what has conventionally been understood by external or material nature. More specifically, I argued that technological transformations of the natural world and the production of the technological society—the *technique* of Jacques Ellul—was the 'material presupposition' for an understanding of politics as posthistorical.[20] However, since the whole Hegelian symbolic complex was, in Voegelin's words, a 'second reality'—that is, a magical construction of Hegel's consciousness—it would be necessary to examine technology on its own terms.

Now, George Grant had followed the Kojève and Ellul path some distance, and his work was a useful starting point.[21] In addition, however, I found it necessary to rely on Hannah Arendt, particularly her concept of action, which was most extensively developed in *The Human Condition*, though some of the presuppositions were treated as well in *The Origins of Totalitarianism*.[22] In 1989 I was asked to deliver the Covey Lectures in Political Theory at Loyola University of Chicago and used the occasion to discuss the political significance of technology using both Arendt and Voegelin to provide a theoretical approach to the phenomena.[23] One of the conclusions I drew from the study of 'posthistorical' life in the technological society was that entertainment and the media, especially TV, were central agencies of control. Of course, Grant had made the point in his own way on this issue as well, though he did not consider the particular importance that must be given to television, and especially TV news.[24] In a study of TV news on CBC I showed how the product reinforced a particular 'posthistorical' view of reality.[25]

Eric Voegelin died in 1985. Shortly thereafter one of his former students, Ellis Sandoz, along with several other scholars, made plans to organize his papers and to bring out an edition of his collected works. Voegelin's papers are on deposit at the archives of the Hoover Institution, Stanford, where he ended his career as Henry Salvatori Distinguished Scholar and Senior Research Fellow.

I had first met Voegelin in graduate school when Professor Hallowell asked me to meet him at the airport and deliver him to his hotel. At the time he was in his late 60s, a solid, hefty man, with thinning red hair covered with a beret. I drove slowly from the airport to Durham and enjoyed a private seminar with the great man: I would ask questions and he would respond. Over the next few years he would lecture occasionally within commuting distance from Toronto, or at York, or at the American Political Science Association meetings. In 1981, I visited him in Stanford for a few days. Over the years I had written a number of articles and reviews of his work, and I had a general idea of the development of his thought.[26] I had no idea, however, of the extent of his *Nachlass*.

With the aid of a grant from the Earhart Foundation, and later from SSHRCC, I was able to consult this extensive collection of drafts, manuscripts prepared for publication, notes, lecture outlines, and, of particular interest to me, about fifty boxes of correspondence with some of the finest scholars of the century, as well as with lesser minds. One of the most interesting exchanges, with Leo Strauss, took place over the course of thirty years. Most of it was in German and, at least on the Strauss side, was written in a hand that even Voegelin on occasion could not read. Peter Emberley and I worked for over a year to bring together a more or less adequate translation (in fact, Emberley did the lion's share of the transcribing and translating, enlisting several of his colleagues in the German Department at Carleton and even prevailing upon Strauss' daughter, Jennifer Strauss-Clay, for help deciphering her father's more unintelligible scrawls). We sent the exchange between these two great political scientists to several scholars acquainted with their work for their comments, and collected the results under the title *Faith and Political Philosophy*.[27]

The discovery of the collection at the Hoover led me to a consideration of Voegelin's years in Germany during the 1950s. I had met Peter Opitz, now the director of the Geschwister-Scholl Institute for Political Science at the University of Munich, which Institute Voegelin had established during the 1950s, many years earlier, and when I received a Konrad Adenauer Award from the Humboldt Foundation in 1991, I was able to examine the German materials as well. Opitz was in the midst of organizing a Voegelin Archive in Munich and the nearby University of Erlangen housed Voegelin's entire personal research library. Opitz asked me to teach a course on Canadian politics at Munich and Jürgen Gebhardt asked me to repeat it at Erlangen, which I did. Most of my time, however, was spent examining Voegelin's literary remains and other material they had accumulated.

As a result of this work during the 1990s, I edited or co-edited two volumes of Voegelin's *Collected Works*,[28] and completed a major study of Voegelin's work of the 1940s.[29] In addition, I have, along with a former student, Jodi Cockerill, collected a large number of interviews of people who knew Voegelin, which we plan to publish under the title *Voegelin Recollected*, and I plan a second study of Voegelin's work as it developed during the 1950s and 1960s. In Canadian politics, I am completing a second edition of a book on the government of Ralph Klein[30] and, with Lydia Miljan, a study of Canadian journalists.

I promised at the beginning of this paper to return to the notion of weaving. This image is more ambiguous than McLuhan's DEW line. What is warp and what is woof?[31] Perhaps it would be better to speak of braiding, since braids more easily come undone. In any event, my work has combined analysis of the major questions in the history of political thought, especially classical political philosophy, with the immediate questions of the day. In the first enterprise I have been guided chiefly by Voegelin, but also by Arendt and Strauss. In the second, which is concerned chiefly with the place of the west in the nation, it has been more of a team effort.

NOTES

1. *Maclean's*, 'The Table Talk of Marshall McLuhan', arranged by Peter C. Newman, June 1971.
2. I took Professor W.J. Stankiewicz's survey on the history of western political theory as a matter of course. In fact, however, I did not read very much of his work until much later, particularly his ground-breaking analysis of ideology. See 'W.J. Stankiewicz' Search for a Philosophy of Ideology', in *Holding One's Time in Thought: The Political Philosophy of W.J. Stankiewicz*, ed. Bogdan Czaykowski and Samuel LaSelva (Vancouver: Ronsdale Press, 1997), 237–50.
3. Among Duke graduates are Keith Archer, Ed Black, George Breckenridge, Colin Campbell, Rod Church, Harold Clarke, John Courtney, Tom Flanagan, Fred Fletcher, Bill Hull, Ken Kernaghan, Peter Meekison, Neil Nevitte, Jene Porter, Ken Reshaur, and David Smith. The vast majority of these people have been Canadianists.
4. Indeed, my first publication was co-authored with him: 'Procedural Changes in the Canadian House of Commons: Some Reflections', *Journal of Constitutional and Parliamentary Studies*, 2 (1968), 1–18. We later edited, along with Bill Mishler, *The Resurgence of Conservatism in Anglo-American Democracies* (Durham: Duke University Press, 1988).
5. Flanagan returned from Berlin to Durham a week or so before I left for Paris. 'You're from Canada,' he said. 'Do you know where Calgary is?' I confessed I even had some personal knowledge of the place. 'Do you think I would like it there?' he asked. I assured him it was just the sort of place he was looking for and that he was bound to find endless happiness. It turned out to be sound advice, since he has been at the University of Calgary ever since.
6. Aron, *La Révolution introuvable: Réflexions sur les événements de mai* (Paris: Fayard, 1968).
7. Merleau-Ponty, *Humanisme et terreur: Essai sur le probleme communiste* (Paris: Gallimard, 1947).
8. C.B. Macpherson, *Democracy in Alberta: Social Credit and the Party System*, 2nd ed. (Toronto: University of Toronto Press, 1962).
9. It is, perhaps, worth recalling that 'alienation' is a central Marxist category, along with 'false consciousness' with which it is closely associated. It is a straightforward interpretative move to understand 'western alienation' as a product of the 'false consciousness' from which westerners regrettably—and, from the privileged perspectives of central Canada, unfortunately—suffer.
10. I translated Aron's Gifford Lectures, *History and the Dialectic of Violence: An Analysis of Sartre's Critique de la Raison Dialectique* (Oxford: Blackwell, 1975), and two books by Aron's pupil Jean Baechler, *The Origins of Capitalism* (Oxford: Blackwell, 1975), and *Suicides* (New York: Basic Books, 1979).
11. *Merleau-Ponty and Marxism: From Terror to Reform* (Toronto: University of Toronto Press, 1979). About the same time I published a couple of articles on the Hegelian (or Kojèvian)

context of Merleau-Ponty's philosophical views: 'Hegelian Elements in Merleau-Ponty's *La Structure du comportement*', *International Philosophical Quarterly* 15 (1975), 411–25; 'Hegel and the Genesis of Merleau-Ponty's Atheism', *Studies in Religion* 6 (1977), 665–71.

12. *The End of History: An Essay on Modern Hegelianism* (Toronto: University of Toronto Press, 1984); *Michel Foucault: An Introduction to the Study of His Thought* (Toronto: Mellen, 1984).
13. On Fukuyama, see my 'The End of History: Déjà-vu all over again', *History of European Ideas* 19 (1994), 377–83.
14. Eric Voegelin, *The New Science of Politics: An Introduction* (Chicago: University of Chicago Press, 1952), 27–8.
15. The two most important sources are *The British Garden: Essays on the Canadian Imagination* (Toronto: Anansi, 1971) and *Divisions on a Ground: Essays on Canadian Culture*, ed. James Polk (Toronto: Anansi, 1982). Properly speaking, both 'Imagination' and 'Culture' in the subtitles ought to be plural. This aspect of Canadian literary production was brought out particularly well by Dennis Duffy, *Gardens, Covenants, Exiles: Loyalism in the Literature of Upper Canada/Ontario* (Toronto: University of Toronto Press, 1982).
16. Notably Arthur MacMechan, *Headwaters of Canadian Literature* (Toronto: McClelland and Stewart [1924] 1974); Janice Kulyk Keefer, *Under Eastern Eyes: A Critical Reading of Maritime Fiction* (Toronto: University of Toronto Press, 1987); Laurence Ricou, *Vertical Man/Horizontal World: Man and Landscape in Prairie Fiction* (Vancouver: University of British Columbia Press, 1973).
17. Careless, 'Limited Identities in Canada', *Canadian Historical Review* 50 (1969), 1–11.
18. The story is recounted in P. Martin, A. Gregg and G. Perlin, *Contenders: The Tory Quest for Power* (Toronto: Prentice-Hall, 1983), 53.
19. On the scholarly side, see 'Western Political Consciousness', in *Political Thought in Canada*, ed. Stephen Brooks (Toronto: Clarke Irwin, 1984), 213–38; 'The West: A Political Minority', in *Minorities and the Canadian State*, ed. N. Nevitte and A. Kornberg (Toronto: Mosaic, 1985), 203–20; 'Looking Eastward, Looking Backward: A Western Reading of the Never-Ending Story', in *Constitutional Predicament: Canada After the Referendum of 1992*, ed. Curtis Cook (Montreal and Kingston: McGill-Queen's University Press, 1994), 89–108; 'Theoretical Perspectives on Constitutional Reform in Canada', in *Rethinking the Constitution*, ed. Tony Peacock (Toronto: Oxford University Press, 1996), 217–32; 'Political Science in Canada: 1970–1995', *Political Science Reviewer* 25 (1996), 100–26. Most of the journalism has been written with David Bercuson for the Sun chain, for the Southam chain, or for 'The West' column in the *Globe and Mail* (1997–8). Finally, I wrote a biography, *Alexander Kennedy Isbister: A Respectable Critic of the Honourable Company* (Ottawa: Carleton University Press, 1988), that showed in great detail how the history of what is now western Canada is a far cry from the history of the interests of the old colony of Canada—Upper and Lower Canada—in what is now the west. Bercuson and I have also combined to write a couple of popular books on Canadian politics: *Deconfederation: Canada Without Quebec* (Toronto: Key Porter, 1991), and *Derailed: The Betrayal of the National Dream* (Toronto: Key Porter, 1994). We have also completed a manuscript on the west today, but our Toronto publisher has not yet been persuaded of its merits.
20. 'The Meaning of Technology at the End of History', University of Minnesota, Center for Humanistic Studies, *Occasional Papers* no. 7 (1986).
21. See 'Ab Imperio usque ad Imperium: The Politics of George Grant', in *George Grant in Process: Essays and Conversations*, ed. Larry Schmidt (Toronto: Anansi, 1978), 22–39;

'Ideology, Technology and Truth', in *The Ethical Dimension of Political Life: Essays in Honor of John H. Hallowell*, ed. F. Canavan (Durham: Duke University Press, 1983), 138–55; 'Hegelian Imperialism', in *Sojourns in the New World: Reflections on Technology*, ed. Tom Darby (Ottawa: Carleton University Press, 1986), 25–67.

22. See 'Action into Nature: Hannah Arendt's Reflections on Technology', in *Democratic Theory and Technological Society*, ed. Richard B. Day, Ronald Beiner, and Joe Masciulli (London: Sharpe, 1988), 316–35; 'Nihilism in Technology', in *Nietzsche and the Rhetoric of Nihilism*, ed. Tom Darby et al. (Ottawa: Carleton University Press, 1989), 165–81.
23. See *Action Into Nature: An Essay on the Meaning of Technology* (Notre Dame: Notre Dame University Press, 1991).
24. See 'How to Watch TV News', *The Idler* 28 (May 1990), 17–22 and 'Plato and the Media', in *Public Policy and the Public Good*, ed. Ethan Fishman (New York: Greenwood, 1991), 15–28.
25. See *Sins of Omission: Shaping the News at CBC TV* (Toronto: University of Toronto Press, 1994). Although this material was not included in the book, coverage of western Canada, including the 1988 winter Olympics held in Calgary, tended to reproduce the imagery of 'western alienation'.
26. See 'A Fragment of Voegelin's History of Western Political Thought', *Political Science Reviewer* 7 (1977), 23–52; 'Voegelin's Concept of Historiogenesis', *Historical Reflections* 4 (1978), 232–51; 'Reason and Interpretation in Contemporary Political Theory', *Polity* 11 (1979), 387–99; 'An Introduction to Voegelin's Account of Western Civil Theologies', in *Voegelin the Theologian*, ed. John Kirby and William M. Thompson (Toronto: Mellen, 1983), 213–38; 'Eric Voegelin's Early Career', in Morton A. Kaplan, ed., *The World and I* 2, 1 (Feb. 1986), 696–703; 'A Key to Voegelin', *Review of Politics*, 52 (1990), 648–50.
27. *Faith and Political Philosophy: The Correspondence Between Leo Strauss and Eric Voegelin*, ed. and trans. Peter Emberley and Barry Cooper (University Park: Penn State University Press, 1993).
28. The first, Voegelin's *The Form of the American Mind*, was co-edited with Jürgen Gebhardt, as vol. I, *The Collected Works of Eric Voegelin* (Baton Rouge: Louisiana State University Press, 1995); the second was Voegelin, *Revolution and the New Science*, vol. VI, *The History of Political Ideas*, Voegelin's *Collected Works*, vol. XXIV (Columbia: University of Missouri Press, 1998).
29. *Eric Voegelin and the Foundations of Political Science* (Columbia: University of Missouri Press, 1999).
30. *The Klein Achievement* (Toronto: University of Toronto Press, 1996).
31. These are significant questions, at least for political philosophy. See R.B. Onians, *The Origins of European Thought About the Body, the Mind, the Soul, the World, Time and Fate* (Cambridge: Cambridge University Press, 1951), 349ff.

The Immanent Counter-Enlightenment

Charles Taylor

1.

Enlightenment and counter-Enlightenment: two very difficult terms to define. Every attempted description is perhaps tendentious. And mine doesn't claim to be an exception. What I want to do is bring out what I think is a striking fact of our modern culture, that is, Enlightenment-influenced culture. (I might have said 'post-Enlightenment', in the sense of 'in the wake of the Enlightenment', but refrain in order to avoid the other, tendentious implication: that the Enlightenment is somehow over, behind us.)

The Enlightenment awakened a reaction from defenders of the 'traditional' forms of life and society it criticized. This is what we usually call the counter-Enlightenment, the reaction from outside. But it also has provoked over time an immanent reaction, an attack on its most cherished ideals 'from within'. Of course, an important interpretive leap is being made with the use of these two words in inverted commas. In what way can the attack on Enlightenment values in our day by someone like Foucault or Derrida, or a century ago by Nietzsche, be called an attack from within? Because these writers share something important with a dominant strand of Enlightenment thought, something that we might call, for short, the denial of transcendence. Seen in this perspective, the reaction I'm discussing here can be said to be an immanent revolt; and that in two senses: both a revolt from within, and a rebellion against the limits of immanence itself.

2.

I've introduced an immanence/transcendence distinction here: two notoriously difficult and slippery terms. I'm going to try first to reduce some of the potential slippage by saying a bit more about what I mean by them; and then try to show that in this sense the dominant trend of Enlightenment thought—and, indeed, post-Enlightenment culture—has been towards the denial of transcendence.

Denying transcendence here means denying that human life finds any point beyond itself. The strong sense—which has continually arisen in human history—that there is something more, that human life aims beyond itself, is stamped as an illusion; and judged to be a dangerous illusion, one that always threatens to breed disastrous, anti-human consequences. The denial gives rise to what we might call an exclusive humanism, one based exclusively on a notion of human flourishing, which recognizes no valid aim beyond that.

The crucial feature of the transcendent in this sense is that it relates to a point of life that is 'beyond life'. Transcendence may also have other dimensions (e.g., the belief in something that transcends nature and the world). These very often come into play as well. But what I am focusing on here as the crucial issue raised by the Enlightenment is the active, practical question turning on the point of life.

In so doing, I am trying to get at something that is essential not only in Christianity but in a number of other faiths, such as Buddhism. Although it enters different faiths in very different forms, the fundamental idea that they share might be grasped in the claim that life isn't the whole story.

One *could* take this expression to mean something like: life goes on after death, there is a continuation, our life doesn't totally end in our deaths. I don't mean to deny what is affirmed on this reading, but I want to take the expression here in a somewhat different (though undoubtedly related) sense.

What I mean is something more like: the point of things isn't exhausted by life, the fullness of life, even the goodness of life. This is not meant to be just a repudiation of egoism, the idea that the fullness of my life (and perhaps the lives of people I love) should be my concern. Let us agree with John Stuart Mill that a full life must involve striving for the benefit of humankind. Then acknowledging the transcendent means seeing a point beyond that.

One example is the insight that we can find in suffering and death not merely negation, the undoing of fullness and life, but also a place to affirm something that matters beyond life, on which life itself originally draws. The last clause seems to bring us back into the focus on life. It may be readily understandable, even within the purview of an exclusive humanism, how one could accept suffering and death in order to give life to others. On a certain view, that too has been part of the fullness of life. Acknowledging the transcendent involves something more. What matters beyond life doesn't matter just because it sustains life; otherwise it wouldn't be 'beyond life' in the meaning of the act. (For Christians, God wills human flourishing, but 'thy will be done' doesn't reduce to 'let human beings flourish'.)

This is the way of putting it that goes most against the grain of contemporary Western civilization. But there are other ways of framing it. One that goes back to the very beginning of Christianity is a redefinition of the term 'life' to incorporate what I'm calling 'beyond life': for instance, the New Testament evocations of 'eternal life', and the famous line in the Gospel of John 10.10: 'I am come that they might have life, and that they might have it more abundantly.'

Or we could put it in a third way: acknowledging the transcendent means being called to a change of identity. Buddhism gives us an obvious reason to talk this way. The change here is quite radical, from self to 'no-self' (*anatta*). But Christian faith can be seen in the same terms: as calling for a radical decentring of the self, in relation with God. ('Thy will be done.') In the language of Abbé Henri Bremond, in his magnificent study of French seventeenth-century spiritualities,[1] we can speak of 'theocentrism'. This way of putting it brings out a similar point to my first way, since most conceptions of a flourishing life assume a stable identity, a self for whom flourishing can be defined.

So acknowledging the transcendent means aiming beyond life, or opening yourself to a change in identity. But if you do this, where do you stand with respect to human flourishing? There is much division, confusion, uncertainty about this. Historic religions have in fact combined concern for flourishing and transcendence in their normal practice. It has been the rule that the supreme achievements of those who went beyond life have served to nourish the fullness of life of those who remain on this side of the barrier. Thus prayers at the tombs of martyrs brought long life, health, and a whole host of good things for the Christian faithful; and something of the same is true for the tombs of certain saints in the Muslim lands; while in Theravada Buddhism, for example, the dedication of monks is turned (through blessings, amulets, etc.) to all the ordinary purposes of flourishing among the laity.

Over against this, there have recurrently been 'reformers' in all religions who have considered this symbiotic, complementary relation between renunciation and flourishing to be a travesty. They insist on returning religion to its 'purity', and posit the goals of renunciation on their own, as goals for everyone, and disintricated from the pursuit of flourishing. Some are even moved to denigrate the latter pursuit altogether, to declare it unimportant, or an obstacle to sanctity.

But this extreme stance runs athwart a very central thrust in some religions. Christianity and Buddhism will be my examples here. Renouncing, aiming beyond life, not only takes you away, but also brings you back to flourishing. In Christian terms, if renunciation decentres you in relation with God, God's will is that humans flourish, and so you are taken back to an affirmation of this flourishing, which is biblically called *agape*. In Buddhist terms, Enlightenment doesn't just turn you from the world, but also opens the flood-gates of *metta* (loving kindness) and *karuna* (compassion). There is the Theravada concept of the Paccekabuddha, concerned only for his own salvation, but he is ranked below the highest Buddha, who acts for the liberation of all beings.

Thus apart from the stance that accepts the complementary symbiosis of renunciation and flourishing, and beyond the stance of purity, there is a third one, which I could call the stance of *agape/karuna*.

3.

Enough has been said to bring out the conflict between modern culture, in the wake of the Enlightenment, and the transcendent. In fact, a powerful constitutive strand of modern Western spirituality involves an affirmation of life. It is perhaps evident in the contemporary concern to preserve life, to bring prosperity, to reduce suffering, worldwide, which I believe is without precedent in history.

This concern arises historically out of what I have called elsewhere[2] 'the affirmation of ordinary life'. What I was trying to gesture at with this term is the cultural revolution of the early modern period, which dethroned the supposedly higher activities of contemplation and the citizen life, and put the centre of gravity of goodness in ordinary living, production, and the family. It belongs to this spiritual outlook that our first concern ought to be to increase life, relieve suffering, foster prosperity. Concern above all for the 'good life' smacked of pride, of self-absorption. And beyond that, it was inherently inegalitarian, since the alleged 'higher' activities could be carried out only by an elite minority, whereas leading rightly one's ordinary life was open to everyone. For people of this moral temper, it seems obvious that our major concern must be our dealings with others, in justice and benevolence; and these dealings must be on a level of equality.

This affirmation, which constitutes a major component of our modern ethical outlook, was originally inspired by a mode of Christian piety. It exalted practical *agape*, and was polemically directed against the pride, elitism, one might say, self-absorption of those who believed in 'higher' activities or spiritualities.

Consider the sixteenth-century Reformers' attack on the supposedly 'higher' vocations of the monastic life—for them, the vocations that were meant to mark out elite paths of superior dedication were in fact deviations into pride and self-delusion. The really holy life for the Christian was within ordinary life itself, living in work and household in a Christian and worshipful manner.

This earthly, one might say, earthy critique of the allegedly 'higher' was later transposed and used as a secular critique of Christianity and, indeed, religion in general. Something of the same rhetorical stance adopted by Reformers against monks and nuns was taken up by secularists and unbelievers against Christian faith itself, a faith that in their view scorns the real, sensual, earthly human good for some purely imaginary higher end, the pursuit of which can only lead to the frustration of the real, earthly good, to suffering, mortification, repression, and so forth. The motivations of those who espouse this 'higher' path are thus, indeed, suspect. Pride, elitism, and the desire to dominate all play a part in this story too, along with fear and timidity (also present in the earlier Reformers' story, but less prominently).

In this critique, of course, religion is identified with the second, purist stance above; or else with a combination of that stance and the first 'symbiotic' (usually labelled 'superstitious') stance. The third, the stance of *agape/karuna*, becomes invisible. The reason is that a transformed variant of it has in fact been assumed by the secularist critic.

4.

In the last paragraphs I have been talking about modern culture, and secularism. But can these be laid at the door of the Enlightenment? For many people, this question expresses a minor quibble. It is simply obvious to them that it is the Enlightenment which has produced modern secular culture. In fact, things are much more complicated. The Enlightenment was, and is, a many-stranded affair.

Central to the Enlightenment, I would argue, are two related *idées forces*. The first is that we can and should take our own fate, history, society in hand, as we have never done before (overcoming our condition as minors, as Kant put it in 'Was ist Aufklärung?'[3]); and the second is that we are enabled to do so because we see our condition in a new, clearer light, and possess or are capable of acquiring knowledge about it that we never have had before. These two ideas come together in the slogan Kant takes up in his 'Aufklärung' essay: 'Sapere aude', dare to know. The move from minor status to self-responsibility requires that we be ready to acquire the knowledge and to accept the truths that we need to run our lives. It demands the courage to break with all the forces of sloth, blind habit, fear of the unknown, and misplaced trust in authority that kept us from knowledge before. Daring and knowledge are thus inseparably linked.

A concept that is inescapable in this complex of ideas—that is indeed complementary to it—is that of the motivated illusion. We didn't dare to know before, because we were held back by all those forces of ignorance and fear. We were under an illusion about our own condition. But this wasn't just a neutral factual error. It was held in place by powerful emotions: fear, sloth, loyalty, awe. Hence it took and takes courage to make the break.

Something like this, I think, is essential to the narrative self-understanding of Enlightenment. What can vary, of course, is what exactly ends up being defined as the motivated illusion. It is just too simple to say that it is always identified as religion, as it undoubtedly is in the militantly secularist version. But although it is not identified with religion as such, my sense is that the major drift of the Enlightenment narrative, as it has come down to us, takes the transcendent as I am defining it here—namely, as the positing of a point to life beyond life—and locates that notion of transcendence in the very centre of the zone of illusion.

Thus, in general, modern Enlightenment-influenced culture is not anti-religious as such. There is hostility to religion, but this outlook is far from universal (particularly in the US, with its high rates of religious belief and practice). And yet I believe that a denial of transcendence has penetrated far beyond the ranks of card-carrying, village-atheist-style secularists: that it also shapes the outlook of many people who see themselves as believers.

This is a difficult area in which to make clear, well-attested affirmations. I'm talking not (necessarily) about what people explicitly believe, but about a climate of thought, a horizon of assumptions. We might better speak of an eclipse of the transcendent, rather than the spread of a new doctrine negating it. For many of our contemporaries, particularly the younger ones, it is as though the transcendent, in the sense I'm using the term here, were off their maps altogether. There is a widespread spiritual hunger, but it is often met by turning to forms that lie within the reach of an exclusive humanism, as with many variants of the human potential movement; or else in ways that thoroughly blur the boundary between immanent and transcendent; as if this whole issue, so central to all the great religious traditions, were no longer visible to many people.

This eclipse, in the form many people live it today, is relatively recent, a matter of the last half-century. It has accompanied a heightened sense of self, an ethical turn that I have tried to describe as an ethic of 'authenticity'.[4] This massive change in modern culture is something I believe we still very inadequately understand. It is clear that it has roots going back to the Enlightenment, that in some ways an earlier polemical denial of transcendence has helped to bring about what I'm calling its eclipse today. But it is also true that this latter has undercut the militant denial as well. With the blurring of the distinction, both parties to the old battles of secularists against clericals can begin to appear strange, as coming from another age. The shift is perhaps particularly visible in France, just because of the virulence of the earlier conflict there.[5]

5.

Now, just because I am dealing here with an eclipse rather an explicit denial of transcendence, with a climate of opinion rather than a doctrine, there will always be some distortion involved in the attempt to lay this climate out in a set of propositions. But I'm going to do that anyway, because I believe that this climate encapsulates a certain understanding of our predicament, and I don't know any other way of articulating it.

Spelled out in propositions, then, this understanding would read something like: (a) that for us life, flourishing, driving back the frontiers of death and suffering, is of supreme value; (b) that this wasn't always so; it wasn't so for our ancestors, or for people in other earlier civilizations; (c) that one of the things that prevented it from being so in the past was precisely a sense, inculcated by religion, that there were 'higher' goals; (d) that we have arrived at position (a) through a critique and overcoming of (this kind of) religion.

We live in something analogous to a post-revolutionary climate. Revolutions generate the sense that they have won a great victory, and identify the adversary in the previous régime. A post-revolutionary climate will be extremely sensitive to anything that smacks of the ancien régime, and will see backsliding even in relatively innocent concessions to generalized human preferences: thus Puritans who saw the return of popery in any ritual, or the Bolsheviks who compulsively addressed people as 'Comrade', proscribing the ordinary appellation 'Mister'.

I would argue that a milder version of this kind of climate is pervasive in our culture. To speak of aiming beyond life is to appear to undermine the supreme concern with life that characterizes our humanitarian, 'civilized' world. It is to try to reverse the revolution and bring back the bad old order of priorities, in which life and happiness could be sacrificed on the altars of renunciation. Hence even believers are often induced to redefine their faith in such a way as not to challenge the primacy of life.

My claim is that this climate, often unaccompanied by any formulated awareness of the underlying reasons, pervades our culture. It emerges, for instance, in the widespread inability to give any human meaning to suffering and death, other than as dangers and enemies to be avoided or combated. This inability is not just the failing of certain individuals; it is entrenched in many of our institutions and practices—for instance, the practice of medicine, which has great trouble understanding its own limits, or conceiving some natural term to human life.[6]

What gets lost, as always, in this post-revolutionary climate is the crucial nuance. Challenging the primacy of life can mean two things. It can mean trying to displace the saving of life and the avoidance of suffering from their rank as central concerns of policy. Or it can also mean making the claim, or at least opening the way for the insight, that more than life matters. These two interpretations are evidently not the same. It is not even true, as people might plausibly believe, that they are causally linked, in the sense that making the second challenge 'softens us up' and makes the first challenge easier. Indeed, I want to claim (and did in the concluding chapter of *Sources of the Self*) that the reverse is the case: that clinging to the primacy of life in the second (let's call this the 'metaphysical') sense is making it harder for us to affirm it wholeheartedly in the first (or practical) sense.

But I don't want to pursue this claim right now. The thesis I'm presenting here is that it is in virtue of its 'post-revolutionary climate' that Western modernity is inhospitable to the transcendent. This claim, of course, runs contrary to the mainline Enlightenment story, according to which religion has become less credible because of the advance of science. There is, of course, something in this, but it isn't in my view the main story. Indeed, to the extent that it is true—that people interpret science and religion as being at loggerheads—it is often because of an already felt incompatibility at the moral level. It is this deeper level that I have been trying to explore here.

In other words, to oversimplify again, the obstacles to belief in Western modernity are primarily moral and spiritual, rather than epistemic. I am talking about the driving force here, rather than what is said in justification of unbelief in arguments.

6.

But I am in danger of wandering from the main line of my argument. I have been painting a portrait of our age in order to be able to suggest that exclusive humanism has provoked, as it were, a revolt from within. The revolt has been against what one could call a secular religion of life, which is one of the most striking features of the modern world.

We live in an extraordinary moral culture, measured against the norm of human history, in which suffering and death, through famine, flood, earthquake, pestilence, or war, can awaken worldwide movements of sympathy and practical solidarity. The fact that these movement are made possible by modern media and modes of transportation, not to speak of surpluses, shouldn't blind us to the importance of the cultural-moral change. The same media and means of transport don't awaken the same response everywhere; it is disproportionately strong in ex-Latin Christendom.

Let us grant also the distortions produced by media hype and the media-gazer's short attention span; the way dramatic pictures produce the strongest response, often relegating even more needy cases to a zone of neglect from which only the cameras of CNN can rescue them. Nevertheless, the phenomenon is remarkable. The age of Hiroshima and Auschwitz has also produced Amnesty International and Médicins Sans Frontières.

Of course, the Christian roots of this aspect of our moral culture run deep. First, there is the extraordinary missionary effort of the Counter-Reformation Church, taken up later by the Protestant denominations. Then there were the mass-mobilization campaigns of the early nineteenth century—the anti-slavery movement in England, largely inspired and led by Evangelicals; the parallel abolitionist movement in the United States, also largely Christian-inspired. Then this habit of mobilizing for the redress of injustice and the relief of suffering worldwide becomes part of our political culture. Somewhere along the road, this culture ceases to be simply Christian-inspired—although people of deep Christian faith continue to be important in today's movements. Moreover, this breach with the culture of Christendom was probably required for the impulse of solidarity to transcend the frontier of Christendom itself.

This is the complex legacy of the Enlightenment that I am trying to describe here. It incorporates a powerful humanism, affirming the importance of preserving and enhancing life, of avoiding death and suffering, an eclipse/denial of transcendence that tends to make this humanism an exclusive one, and a dim historical sense that the first of these came about through and depends on the second.

From its beginning two and a half centuries ago, this developing ethos encountered resistance. In its very influential Utilitarian variant, it was seen as a kind of flattening of human life, rendering it 'one-dimensional', to use an expression that gained wide currency later. Life in the 'Crystal Palace', to quote Dostoyevsky's protagonist in *Notes from Underground*, was felt as stifling, as diminishing, as deadening, or as levelling. There were clearly at least two important sources of this reaction, though they could sometimes be (uneasily) combined.

One was the continuing spiritual concern with the transcendent, which could never accept the idea that flourishing human life is all there is, and bridled at the reduction. The other sprang from the older aristocratic ethos, and protested against the levelling effects of the culture of equality and benevolence. It apprehended a loss of the heroic dimension of human life, and a consequent levelling down of human beings to the bourgeois, utilitarian mean. That this concern went well beyond reactionary circles we can see from the case of Tocqueville, who was very worried by the kind of reduction of humanity that threatens us in a democratic age. He feared a world in which people would end up being occupied exclusively with their 'petits et vulgaires plaisirs', and would lose the love of freedom.[7]

7.

Now, these resistances against the primacy of life were nourished by long-standing traditions, those of the transcendent on one hand, and certain long-existing standards of honour and excellence on the other. What I am calling the immanent revolt is a resistance that does not spring from either of these traditional sources. It is neither grounded in transcendence, nor based on the historically received understandings of social hierarchy—though it may be inspired by earlier versions of the warrior ethic, as we see with Nietzsche.

This revolt from within unbelief, as it were, against the primacy of life reflects less a belief in the existence of something beyond than a sense of being confined, diminished, by the acknowledgment of this primacy.

So as well as an external counter-Enlightenment, nourished by the traditions that the Enlightenment relegated to the zone of illusion, there has grown an immanent counter-Enlightenment that shares in, even sometimes intensifies, this rejection of the past. But just as the secular Enlightenment humanism grew out of the earlier Christian, *agape*-inspired affirmation of ordinary life, so the immanent counter-Enlightenment grew out of its external predecessor.

Where this primarily happened was in the literary and artistic domains that grew out of Romanticism and its successors. The Romantic movement was one of the important loci of the counter-Enlightenment, even if it was also always much more than this. Protest against a world that had been flattened, denuded of meaning, was a recurring theme of Romantic writers and artists, and this attitude blended easily with counter-Enlightenment commitments, although it didn't have to. At least such a stance made it impossible to align oneself with the crasser variants of Enlightenment secularism, such as Utilitarianism.

The immanent counter-Enlightenment comes to existence within this domain of Western culture. From the beginning, it has been linked with a primacy of the aesthetic. Even where it rejects the category and speaks of an 'aesthetic illusion' (as with Paul de Man), it remains centrally concerned with art, and especially modern, post-Romantic art. Its big battalions within the modern academy are found in literature departments.

Paradigmatic of this aestheticized counter-Enlightenment is Mallarmé. Like his Parnassian predecessors, he identifies the search for the Ideal, for Beauty, with a turning away from life:

Ainsi, pris du dégoût de l'homme à l'âme dure
Vautré dans le bonheur, où ses seuls appétits
Mangent . . . .
Je fuis et je m'accroche à toutes les croisées
D'où l'on tourne l'épaule à la vie, et, béni,
Dans leur verre, lavé d'éternelles rosées,
Que dore le matin chaste de l'Infini

Je me mire et me vois ange! et je meurs, et j'aime
—Que la vitre soit l'art, soit la mysticité—
À renaître, portant mon rêve en diadème,
Au ciel antérieur où fleurit la Beauté!
(*Les Fenêtres*, 21–32)[8]

In this early poem you can still see the earlier religious sources of dissatisfaction with bare life. The image of the window, invoked repeatedly in different forms, divides the universe into a lower portion and a higher. The lower is likened to a hospital, life to a kind of putrefaction; but above and beyond is the river, the sky; and these images are still saturated with the resonances of the religious tradition: 'Infini', 'ange', 'mysticité'.

Later, after his spiritual crisis of 1866–67, Mallarmé emerges with something like a materialist view of the universe. Underneath everything we see is 'le Rien', 'le Néant': nothingness. But the poet's vocation is nonetheless imperious and he will even speak of it in terms that borrow from the Romantic tradition of an original perfect language: for example, he writes that poetry is concerned with 'l'explication orphique de la Terre'.[9]

In terms of belief, Mallarmé has joined the Enlightenment—even a rather extreme, materialist version of it. But in terms of the point of human existence, he couldn't be farther removed from it. The primacy of life is decisively rejected, treated with revulsion. What emerges is something like a counter-primacy of death.

It is clear that for Mallarmé the realization of the poetic vocation, achieving the purified language, essentially involves something like the death of the poet—certainly the overcoming of all particularity; but this process, it seems, is consummated only in actual death: 'Tel qu'en Lui-même enfin l'éternité le change.'[10]

> Tout ce que, par contre coup, mon être a souffert, pendant cette longue agonie, est inénarrable, mais heureusement je suis parfaitement mort, et la région la plus impure où mon Esprit puisse s'aventurer est l'éternité, mon esprit, ce Solitaire habituel de sa propre Pureté, que n'obscurcit plus même le reflet du Temps.[11]

Mallarmé becomes the first great modern poet of absence ('aboli bibelot d'inanité sonore'[12]), to be followed by others including Eliot and Celan. What is absent, clearly, is the object ('Sur les crédences, au salon vide: nul ptyx'[13]); but this absence is something that can be attained only via the absence, in a sense the death, of the subject ('[Car le Maître est allé puiser des pleurs au Styx / Avec ce seul objet dont le Néant s'honore]'[14]). A strange parallel is set up with the earlier religious tradition, but within the framework of denied transcendence.

Death and the moment of death have an ineradicable place in the religious traditions: death as the giving up of everything, of one's very self, in Christianity; the hour of death as a crucial moment, therefore ('pray for us now and at the hour of our death'); a status it has in most Buddhist traditions as well. In Christian terms: the locus of death, as the place where one has given everything, is the place of maximum union with God; and therefore, paradoxically, the source of most abundant life.

In this new post-Mallarmé perspective, the locus of death takes on a new paradigm status. The Christian paradox drops away: death is no longer the source of life. But there is a new paradox: there seems to be a renewed affirmation of transcendence, in the sense I'm using the term here, that is, of a point to life beyond life. But at the same time that point is denied, in the sense that it has absolutely no anchorage in the nature of reality. To search for this point in reality is to encounter only 'le Néant'.

This paradoxical idea, which we would call immanent transcendence, is one of the principal themes of the immanent counter-Enlightenment. Death offers in some sense the privileged perspective, the paradigm gathering-point for life. This idea recurs again and again in our culture, and not necessarily by way of Mallarmé. Heidegger's 'Sein-zum-Tode' is a famous example, but the theme is taken up in rather different forms in Sartre, Camus, and Foucault, was echoed in the 'death of man' fad propagated by the latter, and so on. And in the variant that spoke of the 'death of the subject', the paradoxical affinities with certain religious outlooks—perhaps most obviously Buddhism—were patent.

8.

Alongside that intellectual movement, and interwoven with it, is another kind of revolt against the primacy of life, inspired mainly by the other source of resistance in the external counter-Enlightenment, the resistance against levelling, in the name of the great, the exceptional, the heroic.

The most influential proponent of this kind of view has undoubtedly been Nietzsche. And it is significant that the most important anti-humanist thinkers of our time, including Foucault, Derrida, and, behind them, Bataille, all draw heavily on Nietzsche.

Nietzsche, of course, rebelled against the idea that our highest goal is to preserve and increase life, to prevent suffering. He rejects this idea both metaphysically and practically. He rejects the egalitarianism underlying this whole affirmation of ordinary life. But his rebellion is in a sense also internal. Life enforces inequality in its moments of most exuberant affirmation.

So this Nietzschean conception remains within the modern affirmation of life in a sense. There is nothing higher than the movement of life itself (the Will to Power). But it chafes at the benevolence, the universalism, the harmony, the order. It wants to rehabilitate destruction and chaos, the infliction of suffering and exploitation, as part of the life to be affirmed. Life properly understood also affirms death and destruction. To pretend otherwise is to try to restrict it, tame it, hem it in, deprive it of its highest manifestations, of what makes it something you can say 'yes' to.

A religion of life that would proscribe death-dealing, the infliction of suffering, is confining and demeaning. Nietzsche thinks of himself as having taken up some of the legacy of pre-Platonic and pre-Christian warrior ethics, their exaltation of courage, greatness, elite excellence. And, central to that, death has always been accorded a paradigm significance. The willingness to face death, the ability to set life lower than honour and reputation, has always been the mark of the warrior, his claim to superiority.[15] Modern life-affirming humanism breeds pusillanimity. This accusation frequently recurs in the culture of counter-Enlightenment.

Of course, one of the fruits of this counter-culture was Fascism—to which Nietzsche's influence was not entirely foreign, however true and valid is Walter Kaufmann's refutation of the simple myth of Nietzsche as a proto-Nazi. But notwithstanding Kaufmann's rebuttal of the cruder view of Nietzsche, the fascination with death and violence recurs, for example in the interest in Bataille shared by Derrida and Foucault. James Miller's book on Foucault shows the depths of this rebellion against 'humanism', as a stifling, confining space one has to break out of.[16]

My point here is not to score off neo-Nietzscheanism, as some kind of antechamber to Fascism. (As though any of the main spiritual tendencies of our civilization was totally free of responsibility for Fascism.) The point is to allow us to recognize that there is an anti-humanism which rebels precisely against the unrelenting concern with life, the proscription of violence, the imposition of equality.

The Nietzschean understanding of enhanced life, which can fully affirm itself, also in a sense takes us beyond life; and in this it is analogous with other, religious notions of enhanced life (like the New Testament's 'eternal life'). But it takes us beyond by incorporating a fascination with the negation of life, with death and suffering. It doesn't acknowledge some supreme good beyond life, and in that sense sees itself rightly as utterly antithetical to religion. The 'transcendence' is, once again in an important sense and paradoxically, immanent.

9.

What I have been calling the immanent counter-Enlightenment thus involves a new valorization of, even fascination with, death and sometimes violence. It rebels against the exclusive humanism that dominates modern culture. But it also rejects all previous, ontically-grounded understandings of transcendence. If we took account of Nietzschean versions of the immanent counter-Enlightenment, we might perhaps change our picture of modern culture. Instead of seeing it as the scene of a two-sided battle, between 'tradition', especially religious tradition, and secular humanism, we might rather see it as a kind of free-for-all, the scene of a three-cornered—perhaps ultimately a four-cornered—battle.

There are secular humanists, there are neo-Nietzscheans, and there are those who acknowledge some good beyond life. Any pair can gang up against the third on some important issue. Neo-Nietzscheans and secular humanists together condemn religion and reject any good beyond life. But neo-Nietzscheans and acknowledgers of transcendence are together in their lack of surprise at the continued disappointments of secular humanism; together also in the sense that the secular humanist vision of life lacks a dimension. In a third line-up, secular humanists and believers come together in defending an idea of the human good, against the anti-humanism of Nietzsche's heirs.

A fourth party can be introduced to this field if we take account of the fact that the acknowledgers of transcendence are divided. Some think that the whole move to secular humanism was just a mistake, which needs to be undone, and that we need to return to an earlier view of things. Others, among whom I place myself, think that the practical primacy of life has been a great gain for humankind, and that there is some truth in the 'revolutionary' story: this gain was in fact unlikely to come about without some breach with established religion. (We might even be tempted to say that modern unbelief is providential, but that might be too provocative a way of putting it.) Yet we nevertheless think that the metaphysical primacy of life is wrong, and stifling, and that its continued dominance puts in danger the practical primacy of life.

I have rather complicated the scene in the last paragraph. Nevertheless, the simple lines of the 'revolutionary' story sketched earlier still stand out; that is, we have been liberated from the illusion of a good beyond life, and thus enabled to affirm ourselves. This liberation may take the form of an Enlightenment endorsement of benevolence and justice; or it may be the charter for the full affirmation of the will to power—or the 'free play of the signifier', or the aesthetics of the self, or whatever the current version is. But it remains within the same post-revolutionary climate. For those fully within this climate, transcendence becomes all but invisible.

Of course, we might want to set aside this three-cornered picture, on the grounds that contemporary anti-humanism isn't significant enough as a movement. Indeed, if one focuses one's attention only on certain fashionable professors of comparative literature, this argument might seem plausible. But my sense is that the impact of this third stream in our culture and contemporary history has been very powerful, particularly if we take account of Fascism, as well as of the fascination with violence that has come to infect even Enlightenment-inspired movements, such as Bolshevism (which is far from being the only such case). And can we exempt the gory history of even 'progressive', democratic nationalism?

10.

If we do adopt the three-cornered picture, however, some interesting questions arise. Explaining each of the three corners from the standpoint of the other two is somewhat of a challenge. In particular, anti-humanism is not easy to explain from the Enlightenment perspective. Why this throwback, on the part of people who are 'liberated' from religion and tradition?

From the religious perspective, the problem is the opposite. There is a too quick and too slick explanation right to hand: the denial of transcendence is bound to lead to the crumbling and eventual breakdown of all moral standards. First secular humanism and then eventually its pieties and values come under challenge. And in the end we are left with nihilism.

I am not saying that there is no insight at all in this account. But it leaves too much unexplained. Anti-humanism is not just a black hole, an absence of values, but also a new valorization of death, and sometimes violence. And some of the fascination with death and violence that it re-articulates reminds us forcefully of many of the phenomena of traditional religion. It is clear that this fascination extends well beyond the borders of anti-humanism. As I just mentioned, we can see it also in the heirs of the Enlightenment; but it recurs repeatedly and unmistakably in the religious tradition as well. The Gulag and the Inquisition are testimony to its perennial force.

But this sharp rebuttal to a too self-indulgent religious explanation renews the problem posed to an exclusive humanism. If there is something perennial, recurring, here, whence comes it? We don't lack for immanent theories of a human propensity to evil, all the way from sociobiology to Freudian speculations on a death principle.

But these have their own counter-Enlightenment thrust: they put a severe limit on any hopes for improvement. They tend to cast doubt on the central Enlightenment idea that we are in charge of our fate.

At the same time, from the perspective of transcendence, some considerations seem obvious. Exclusive humanism closes the transcendent window, as though there were nothing beyond—and more, as though it weren't an irrepressible need of the human heart to open that window, and first look, then go beyond. As though feeling this need were the result of a mistake, an erroneous world-view, bad conditioning, or worse, some pathology. Two radically different perspectives on the human condition. Who is right?

Well, who can make more sense of the life all of us are living? Seen from this angle, the very existence of modern anti-humanism seems to tell against exclusive humanism. If the transcendental view is right, then human beings have an ineradicable bent to respond to something beyond life. Denying this is stifling. But then, even for those who accept the metaphysical primacy of life, this outlook can itself come to seem imprisoning. It is in this sense, rather than in the rather smug, self-satisfied view that unbelief must destroy itself, that the religious outlook finds anti-humanism unsurprising.

From within this outlook, we might be tempted to speculate further, and to suggest that the perennial human susceptibility to be fascinated by death and violence is at base a manifestation of our nature as *homo religiosus*. From the point of view of someone who acknowledges transcendence, this fascination is one of the places where the aspiration to something beyond most easily goes when it fails to take us there. This doesn't mean that religion and violence are simply alternatives. On the contrary, it has meant that most historical religion has been deeply intricated with violence, from human sacrifice down to inter-communal massacres. Because most historical religion remains only very imperfectly oriented to the beyond. The religious affinities of the cult of violence in its different forms are indeed palpable.

What it might mean, however, is that the only way fully to escape the attraction towards violence lies somewhere in the turn to transcendence, that is, through the full-hearted love of some good beyond life. A thesis of this kind has been put forward by René Girard, for whose work I have a great deal of sympathy, although I don't agree on the centrality he gives to the scapegoat phenomenon.[17]

But whatever explanatory view we adopt, I hope I have said something to accredit the notion that no serious attempt to understand the Enlightenment today can do without a deeper study of the immanent counter-Enlightenment. The classical scenarios of the two-sided struggle keep in the shade everything we can learn about these two major protagonists through their differences from and affinities to this third contestant that they have somehow conjured in their midst.

Notes

1. Henri Bremond, *Histoire littéraire du sentiment religieux en France depuis la fin des guerres de religion jusqu'à nos jours* (Paris: A. Colin, 1967–68).

2. See *Sources of the Self* (Cambridge, Mass.: Harvard University Press, 1989), chapt. 13.
3. In *Kants Werke*, vol. VIII (Akademie Textausgabe, Berlin: Walter Gruyter, 1968), 33–42.
4. See *The Malaise of Modernity* (Toronto: Anansi Press, 1991).
5. See the interesting discussion in Émile Poulat, *L'ère postchrétienne* (Paris: Flammarion, 1994).
6. Cf. Daniel Callahan, *What Kind of Life: The Limits of Medical Progress* (New York: Simon and Schuster, 1990).
7. Alexis de Tocqueville, *De la Démocratie en Amérique*, vol. 2 (Paris: Garnier-Flammarion, 1981), 385.
8. 'Thus, seized with disgust at the hard-souled man who wallows in the pleasures on which his appetite feeds.... I flee and cling to all the windows from which one can turn one's back on life; and blessed in their glass, bathed in eternal dews, in the chaste morning of the Infinite, I look at myself and see an angel! and I die, and I long—whether the window be art or mysticism—to be reborn, wearing my dream as a diadem, in the anterior sky where Beauty flowers!'
9. 'the Orphic explanation of the Earth'.
10. 'As into Himself, at last, Eternity changes him.'
11. 'Everything that, as a result, my being suffered during that slow death was hilarious, but happily I am perfectly dead, and the most impure region where my Spirit can venture is eternity, my spirit, that habitual Recluse of its own Purity, which even the reflection of Time no longer obscures'; letter of March 1866 to Henri Cazalis, reproduced in *Propos sur la poésie* (Monaco: Editions du Rocher, 1946), 66.
12. 'abolished knick-knack of sonorous inanity'; *Plusieurs sonnets*, IV, 6.
13. 'On the credenzas in the empty sitting rooms: no ptyx'; ibid., 5.
14. '(For the Master has gone to draw tears from the Styx / With this object, the only one in which Nothingness takes pride)'; ibid., 7–8.
15. Hegel makes this feature of the traditional honour ethics central to his dialectic of the master and the slave. In the original struggle for recognition between warriors, each shows that he is worthy of such recognition precisely by setting his life at hazard. The key to dignity is this 'Daransetzen'. *Phänomenologie des Geistes*, chapt. 4.
16. James Miller, *The Passion of Michel Foucault* (New York: Simon and Schuster, 1993).
17. See René Girard, *La Violence et le sacré* (Paris: Grasset, 1972); and *Le Bouc émissaire* (Paris: Grasset, 1982).

Notes on Contributors

EDWARD ANDREW was born in Toronto and raised in Vancouver. He obtained his B.A. from the University of British Columbia and his Ph.D. from the London School of Economics. He worked as a logger and a social worker before becoming an academic, and has taught political science at the University of Toronto since 1969. Andrew has written *Closing the Iron Cage: The Scientific Management of Leisure* (1981; reprinted 1999); *Shylock's Rights: A Grammar of Lockian Claims* (1988); *The Genealogy of Values: The Aesthetic Economy of Nietzsche and Proust* (1995); and *Conscience and Its Critics: Protestant Conscience, Enlightenment Reason and Modern Subjectivity* (2000).

RONALD BEINER was born in Montreal in 1953. He was educated at McGill University (B.A. 1975) and at Balliol College, Oxford (D.Phil. 1980), studying with Charles Taylor both at McGill and at Oxford. After teaching in England for five years (University of Southampton, 1978–83), he taught for one year at Queen's University (Kingston, Ontario), and in 1984 moved to the University of Toronto, where he is now Professor of Political Science. He has also held a visiting professorship at the Hebrew University of Jerusalem. His books include Hannah Arendt's *Lectures on Kant's Political Philosophy* (edited, 1982); *Political Judgment* (1983); *Democratic Theory and Technological Society* (co-edited, 1988); *What's the Matter with Liberalism?* (1992; winner of the Canadian Political Science Association's 1994 Macpherson Prize); *Kant and Political Philosophy: The Contemporary Legacy* (co-edited with W. James Booth, 1993); *Theorizing Citizenship* (edited, 1995); *Philosophy in a Time of Lost Spirit: Essays on Contemporary Theory* (1997); and *Theorizing Nationalism* (edited, 1999).

W. JAMES BOOTH is Professor of Political Science at Vanderbilt University. He received his B.A. and M.A. from McGill University and his Ph.D. from Harvard. He has taught at Duke University, McGill, and most recently at Vanderbilt. Booth is the author of *Households: On the Moral Architecture of the Economy* (Cornell University Press), *Interpreting the World: A Study of Kant's Philosophy of History and Politics* (University of Toronto Press) and co-editor of *Rationality and Politics* (with Patrick James and Hudson Meadwell, Cambridge University Press), and

Kant and Political Philosophy: The Contemporary Legacy (with Ronald Beiner, Yale University Press). He is also the author of many scholarly articles, which have appeared in academic journals in the US, Britain, France, and Germany. Booth is a Canadian, raised in Montreal, where his parents still live. From 1982 to 1985 he worked for the Canadian Department of External Affairs, primarily in the Soviet/East European Bureau.

EAMONN CALLAN is a citizen of Canada and the Republic of Ireland. He was born in Dublin in 1953 and educated at University College, Dublin, where he studied English, Greek and Roman Civilization, and Education. He came to Canada in 1978 to study for a doctorate in the Philosophy of Education at the University of Alberta. After completing his doctorate, he joined the Faculty of Education at the University of Alberta. In 1999 he left Canada to become a Professor of Education at the Stanford University School of Education. His research investigates questions of civic identity and justice in educational policy. The author of *Autonomy and Schooling* (1987) and *Creating Citizens* (1997), he is currently working on a book about multicultural education and nation-building.

JOSEPH H. CARENS was born in Shelby, Ohio, and grew up near Boston. He did his undergraduate degree in philosophy at the College of the Holy Cross and his graduate work at Yale University, where he received an M.Phil. in religious studies and an M.Phil and Ph.D. in political science. His first academic job involved teaching political theory and public administration to probation and parole officers in North Carolina. He then spent four years at Lake Forest College, a year at Wesleyan University, a year in the US Office of Personnel Management, and four years at Princeton University before moving to the University of Toronto, where he has been happily settled since 1985. His latest book, *Culture, Citizenship, and Community: A Contextual Exploration of Justice as Evenhandedness* (2000) is deeply shaped by the experience of living in Canada.

SIMONE CHAMBERS was born in Montreal and received her B.A. from McGill University before attending Columbia University for her Ph.D. studies. She is Associate Professor of Political Science at the University of Colorado, at Boulder. Professor Chambers has published articles in *Journal of Political Philosophy* and *Politics and Society*. Her book *Reasonable Democracy: Jürgen Habermas and the Politics of Discourse* won the American Political Science Association's 1997 Prize for Best First Book in Political Theory. She is currently writing a book on the role of popular deliberation and democratic participation in constitutional change.

G.A. COHEN was educated at McGill and Oxford universities, where he obtained, respectively, a B.A. in Philosophy and Politics and a B.Phil. in Philosophy in 1963. For twenty-two years he was a Lecturer and then a Reader in Philosophy at University College, London. In 1985 he became Chichele Professor of Social and Political Theory and a Fellow of All Souls, Oxford. Professor Cohen is the author of *Karl Marx's Theory of History: A Defence* (1978), *History, Labour, and Freedom* (1988), *Self-Ownership, Freedom, and Equality* (1995), and *If You're an Egalitarian,*

How Come You're So Rich? (2000). Cohen has given lectures all over the world, including the Tanner Lectures at Stanford University in 1991 and the Gifford Lectures at Edinburgh University in 1996. He was made a Fellow of the British Academy in 1985.

BARRY COOPER, a fourth-generation Albertan, was educated at Shawnigan Lake School, the University of British Columbia and Duke University, where he received his doctorate in 1969. He taught at Bishop's, McGill, and York universities before going to the University of Calgary in 1981. For the past twenty-five years he has studied Western political philosophy, both classical and contemporary. Although much of his teaching has focused on Greek political philosophy, his publications have been chiefly in the area of contemporary French and German political philosophy, and over the years he has spent considerable time in Europe, teaching and doing research. Cooper's other area of continuing interest has been Canadian politics and public policy, where he has brought the insights of political philosophers to bear on contemporary issues, from the place of technology and the media in Canada to the ongoing debate over the constitutional status of Quebec. He has written, edited, or translated over twenty books, most recently *Eric Voegelin and the Foundations of Modern Political Science* (1999) and *Governing in Post-Deficit Times: Alberta during the Klein Years* (2000). He is a fellow of the Royal Society of Canada.

STÉPHANE DION was born in 1955. He obtained bachelor's and master's degrees in political science from Université Laval in 1977 and 1979 respectively, and a doctorate in sociology from the Institut d'Études Politiques in Paris. He taught political science at the Université de Moncton in 1984 and the Université de Montréal from 1984 until January 1996, when he accepted an invitation to join the federal government as President of the Queen's Privy Council for Canada and Minister of Intergovernmental Affairs. During his academic career he was a visiting professor at the Laboratoire d'économie publique in Paris, senior research fellow at the Brookings Institution in Washington, DC, co-editor of the *Canadian Journal of Political Science*, and research fellow with the Canadian Centre for Management Development. The author of numerous scholarly articles, Professor Dion co-wrote (with André Blais and Donald E. Blake) *Governments, Parties & Public Sector Employees: Canada, United States, Britain & France* (1997). Many of his speeches as a minister of the Crown have been collected in his *Straight Talk: Speeches and Writings on Canadian Unity* (1999).

WILL KYMLICKA was raised in London, Ontario, and received his B.A. in philosophy and politics from Queen's University in 1984, and his D.Phil. in philosophy from Oxford University in 1987. He is the author of *Liberalism, Community, and Culture* (1989), *Contemporary Political Philosophy* (1990), *Multicultural Citizenship* (1995), *Finding Our Way: Rethinking Ethnocultural Relations in Canada* (1998), and *Politics in the Vernacular: Nationalism, Multiculturalism and Citizenship* (2000), and the editor of *The Rights of Minority Cultures* (1995),

Ethnicity and Group Rights (co-edited with Ian Shapiro; 1997), and *Citizenship in Diverse Societies* (co-edited with Wayne Norman; 2000). He has been a visiting professor at several universities in Canada and abroad, including Toronto, Ottawa, Carleton, Princeton, and the European University Institute. He is currently a Queen's National Scholar at Queen's University, and a recurrent visiting professor in the Nationalism Studies program at the Central European University in Budapest.

GUY LAFOREST was born in Quebec City in 1955. He took his university training at Ottawa, Laval, and McGill, where he received a Ph.D. in Political Science in 1986. He started teaching at Université Laval in 1988, after two years as a lecturer and post-doctoral fellow at the University of Calgary. A full Professor since 1996, he served as Book Review Editor and Co-Editor for the *Canadian Journal of Political Science* between 1990 and 1996. He was also a Research Fellow for the Centre d'Études et de Recherches Internationales (Paris) from 1993 to 1996, and for the Institute for Research on Public Policy from 1996 to 1998. His publications include *Trudeau et la fin d'un rêve canadien* (1992, English translation, 1995), *De la prudence* (1993), *De l'urgence* (1995), *Beyond the Impasse: Toward Reconciliation* (co-edited with Roger Gibbins; 1998, in English and in French). Guy Laforest was the Head of the Department of Political Science at Laval between 1997 and 2000.

DOMINIQUE LEYDET was born and raised in Montreal. She studied political science at McGill University and completed her Master's degree in philosophy at Université Paris IV (Paris-Sorbonne). She did her doctoral studies in Paris and Berlin, completing her Ph.D. at the École des Hautes Études en Sciences Sociales (Paris). After four years of teaching at the University of Ottawa, she moved to the department of philosophy at Université du Québec à Montréal. Her main areas of interest in political philosophy are the theory of democracy and contemporary German political thought. She is currently writing a book on compromise and deliberation in deep political conflicts.

INGRID MAKUS is Associate Professor of Politics at Brock University in St Catharines, Ontario. She obtained her B.A. at the University of Winnipeg, and her M.A. and Ph.D. at the University of Toronto. She is currently working on a book that draws on both contemporary (communitarian, postmodern, feminist) and traditional (Platonic, Aristotelian, Rousseauian) accounts of political life to explore contemporary debates over identity politics and rights discourse in liberal societies such as Canada. A key theme in the book is the need to ensure political continuity through the education of citizens and the establishment of justice between generations. She is the author of *Women, Politics and Reproduction: The Liberal Legacy* (1996).

MARGARET MOORE was born in Sudbury, Ontario, and educated at the University of Western Ontario and the London School of Economics and Political Science. Upon returning to Canada, she taught in the departments of Political Science at York University (Toronto) and the University of Waterloo. She is the author of

Foundations of Liberalism (1993) and *Ethics of Nationalism* (forthcoming). She is the editor of *National Self-Determination and Secession* (1998) and has written articles for a number of journals, including *The Monist, Political Studies*, and *Review of Politics*.

JENNIFER NEDELSKY received her Ph.D. from the Committee on Social Thought at the University of Chicago. Professor of Law, Political Science, and Women's Studies at the University of Toronto, she is the author of *Private Property and the Limits of American Constitutionalism* (1990) and various articles on the nature of rights and constitutionalism. Her primary research interest is feminist theory, and she is currently writing a two-volume work tentatively entitled *Law, Autonomy and the Relational Self: A Feminist Revisioning of the Foundations of Law.* She is also engaged in a research project on the nature of judgment.

STEPHEN L. NEWMAN is Associate Professor and Chair of the Department of Political Science of York University. Born and raised in the United States, Newman received his B.A. from the University of Rochester and earned his M.A. and Ph.D. from Cornell University. Prior to his appointment at York in 1985, he taught for five years at Ripon College in Wisconsin. He is the author of *Liberalism at Wits' End: The Libertarian Revolt Against the Modern State* (1984), as well as a number of shorter pieces defending liberalism against its critics, left and right. The inspiration for the present essay was provided by an encounter with a student in an introductory political theory course at York who objected to being assigned Marx's 'On the Jewish Question' because it employs anti-Semitic stereotypes and was thus, in the student's view, a form of hate speech deserving censorship.

WAYNE NORMAN lived the first year of his life and the first year of his professional career in London, Ontario. With a B.A. from Trent University in Peterborough, Ontario, and a Commonwealth Scholarship, he completed a Ph.D. in political philosophy at the London School of Economics in 1988. After a short stint at the University of Western Ontario, and a longish one at the University of Ottawa, he moved to the University of British Columbia as the first holder of the Chair in Business Ethics in 1997. He now divides his research time between ethical issues in business, on the one hand, and problems of citizenship and nationalism, on the other. His first book was *Taking Freedom Too Seriously?* (1991). More recently he has co-edited, with Will Kymlicka, *Citizenship in Diverse Societies* (2000), and completed a forthcoming book, tentatively titled *Thinking Through Nationalism*. He has held visiting positions in four countries, published in six languages, and been invited to contribute articles on numerous subjects to international reference works, including the *Routledge Encyclopedia of Philosophy, Philosophy of Law: An Encyclopedia*, the *Oxford Handbook in Practical Ethics*, and the *Blackwell Companion to Applied Ethics*.

CLIFFORD ORWIN was born and raised in Chicago and studied at Cornell (primarily with Allan Bloom) and Harvard (primarily with Harvey Mansfield). He has taught at the University of Toronto since 1973, and has held visiting appointments at Harvard, Chicago, the École des Hautes Études en Sciences Sociales (Paris), and the Hebrew University. In recent years he has paid frequent visits to Jerusalem, Lisbon, and Seoul, and participates in an annual dialogue recently initiated between North American and Hungarian political theorists. His most important work to date is *The Humanity of Thucydides* (2nd ed., 1997). His current projects include a book on compassion, a series of articles on Rousseau, and a study of the political thought of Flavius Josephus.

THOMAS L. PANGLE was born in 1944 in Gouverneur, New York. He graduated from Cornell University (B.A., 1966) and the University of Chicago (Ph.D. in Political Science, 1972), and has been a Professor in the Department of Political Science, University of Toronto since 1979. He has taught at Yale, Dartmouth, the University of Chicago, and the École des Hautes Études en Sciences Sociales (Paris). A Feaver MacMinn Visiting Scholar at the University of Oklahoma, recipient of Guggenheim, Siemens, Connaught, and three National Endowment for the Humanities fellowships, and a Fellow of the Royal Society of Canada, he has also been awarded The Benton Bowl, Yale University (for contribution to education in politics) and the Robert Foster Cherry Great Teacher of the World Prize, Baylor University. He was Senior Advisory Editor, *Books in Canada* 1995–8, and General Editor, *The Agora Editions* (Cornell University Press), 1997–present. His publications include *Montesquieu's Philosophy of Liberalism* (1973); *The Laws of Plato* (translated with notes and a book-length interpretive study; 1980); *The Spirit of Modern Republicanism: The Moral Vision of the American Founders and the Philosophy of Locke* (1988); *The Ennobling of Democracy: The Challenge of the Postmodern Age* (1992); *The Learning of Liberty: The Educational Ideas of the American Founders* (co-authored with wife Lorraine; 1993); and *Justice Among Nations: On the Moral Basis of Power and Peace* (co-authored with Peter J. Ahrensdorf ; 1999; named an 'Outstanding Academic Title' of 1999 by *Choice Magazine*).

DENISE RÉAUME was born and raised in Windsor, Ontario, a largely overlooked outpost of 'la francophonie' in Canada, but one that has survived since the earliest days of European exploration of North America. The experience of growing up a member of a deeply rooted ethnic and linguistic minority in an area transformed by post-war immigration and bombarded with American media has created an enduring interest in cultural interaction. She was educated at Queen's University, where she studied history and philosophy followed by law, and undertook graduate studies in law at Oxford University. Since 1982 she has taught in the Faculty of Law, University of Toronto. She has written extensively on Canadian language rights issues, and has also begun to explore the extent to which the values of multicultural pluralism have been recognized in law.

PHILIP RESNICK was born in Montreal and received his university education there, at McGill; in Toronto; and in Paris. He has been a professor in the Department of Political Science at the University of British Columbia since 1971. He has been actively involved, both as an academic and as a media commentator, in the ongoing debates about Canadian unity. His major publications include *Letters to a Québécois Friend* (with Daniel Latouche, 1990); *The Masks of Proteus: Canadian Reflections on the State* (1990); *Thinking English Canada* (1994); *Twenty-First Century Democracy* (1997); and most recently, *The Politics of Resentment: British Columbia Regionalism and Canadian Unity* (2000).

ARTHUR RIPSTEIN was born in Winnipeg. He graduated from the University of Manitoba in 1981 and earned his Ph.D. in Philosophy from the University of Pittsburgh in 1986, and his M.S.L. from Yale Law School in 1994. He joined the Department of Philosophy at the University of Toronto in 1987, was promoted to Professor in 1996, and was appointed to the Faculty of Law in 1999. Laurance Rockefeller Visiting Fellow at Princeton in 1995–6, he held a Connaught fellowship in spring term 2000. His research and teaching interests include torts, criminal law, legal theory, and political philosophy. He is the author of *Equality, Responsibility and the Law* (1999), as well as numerous articles in legal theory and political philosophy, and co-editor of *Law and Morality* (1996). He is an associate editor of *Ethics*, and serves on the editorial board of *Legal Theory*. His popular work has appeared in the *Globe and Mail* and on CBC Radio's *Ideas*.

CHRISTINE SYPNOWICH is Professor of Philosophy at Queen's University, Kingston. Born in London, England, in 1960, she grew up in Canada and completed her B.A. and M.A. in Political Science at the University of Toronto, where she edited *The Varsity* as an undergraduate. In 1983 she took up a Commonwealth Scholarship to write a D.Phil. in political theory at Balliol College, Oxford. While in Europe she taught in Oxford, Leeds, and Leiden, returning to North America to take up positions at York, the University of California at San Diego, and Queen's. She is the author of numerous essays and a book, *The Concept of Socialist Law* (1990), and is editor, with her husband, David Bakhurst, of *The Social Self* (1995). She has two children.

CHARLES TAYLOR was born in Montreal in 1931. He received his first B.A. in History at McGill University in 1952, and then moved to Oxford, where he completed a second B.A. (in Politics, Philosophy, and Economics), and his D.Phil. (1961). He has taught at McGill (where he is currently Professor Emeritus in the Department of Philosophy), Université de Montréal, Princeton University, the University of California at Berkeley, and Oxford, where he was the Chichele Professor of Social and Political Theory and a Fellow of All Souls College (1976–81). Taylor was the former Vice President of the federal NDP and President of the Quebec NDP. His recent books include *Sources of the Self* (1989), *The Malaise of Modernity* (1991; based on the Massey Lectures for the CBC), *Multiculturalism and the Politics of Recognition* (1992), *Multiculturalisme: Différence et démocratie* (1994), and *Philosophical Arguments* (1995). Taylor's current research concerns the political culture of modernity.

JAMES TULLY, FRSC, grew up on Vancouver Island and was educated at the

University of British Columbia and the University of Cambridge. He taught in the departments of Political Science and Philosophy at McGill University for 19 years before returning to the west coast in 1996 as the Chair of Political Science at the University of Victoria. He teaches and writes on contemporary political philosophy and its history. Recent works include *Philosophy in an Age of Pluralism: The Philosophy of Charles Taylor in Question* (1994); and *Strange Multiplicity: Constitutionalism in an Age of Diversity* (1995). He has also edited, with Alain-G. Gagnon, *Struggles for Recognition in Multinational Societies* (forthcoming).

DALE TURNER is a Teme-Augama Anishnabai from Lake Temagami, Ontario. He has degrees from Concordia University (B.A. 1992) and McGill University (Ph.D. Philosophy 1998). In 1993–4 he was the research associate to the two co-directors of research at the Royal Commission on Aboriginal Peoples in Ottawa. An Assistant Professor in Government and Native American Studies at Dartmouth College in Hanover, New Hampshire, he is currently editing his thesis, 'This is Not a Peace Pipe: Towards an Understanding of Aboriginal Rights', for publication. His recent work has focused on the area of indigenous rights and sovereignty.

DANIEL WEINSTOCK was born in Montreal in 1963, and received both his B.A. (1983) and his M.A. (1986) from McGill, where he studied with James Tully and Charles Taylor. He did his D.Phil. at Oxford, and spent time at Harvard and Columbia before returning to his hometown to take up a position in the Department of Philosophy of the Université de Montréal. In 1998–9 he was a Laurance S. Rockefeller Fellow at the Center for Human Values, Princeton University. He has published in many areas of moral and political philosophy, mostly on issues to do with justice and stability in multinational societies. He has also taken an active part in policy debates. Most recently, he was a member of the task force struck by Quebec's Minister of Education looking into the place of religion in Quebec's public schools.

MELISSA S. WILLIAMS is Associate Professor of Political Science at the University of Toronto, where she has been teaching political philosophy since 1992. In the 2000–1 academic year she is the Laurance S. Rockefeller Visiting Professor at Princeton University's Center for Human Values. She arrived at the University of Toronto after completing her Ph.D. at Harvard University. Williams is author of *Voice, Trust, and Memory: Marginalized Groups and the Failings of Liberal Representation* (1998) and co-editor of *Identity, Rights and Constitutional Transformation* (2000). She has also published articles in various journals (*Political Theory*, *Canadian Journal of Political Science*, *Citizenship Studies*) and in edited volumes on contemporary democratic theory. Her current research focuses on the concepts of toleration and impartiality.